The Illustrated
Hockey
Encyclopedia

Mutual Street Arena, Toronto

The Illustrated
Hockey
Encyclopedia

by Gary Ronberg

Special Photography by Melchior DiGiacomo

Edited by Robert A. Styer

A Balsam Press / Rutledge Book

New York

Copyright © 1984 by Balsam
Press, Inc.

All rights reserved. No part of this
work may be reproduced or trans-
mitted in any form or by any means
without written permission from the
publisher.

Designed by Allan Mogel

Manufactured in the United States
of America

Distributed by
Kampmann & Company
9 East 40th Street
New York, New York 10016

Library of Congress Cataloging in Publication Data

Ronberg, Gary
   The illustrated hockey encyclopedia.

   Rev. ed. of: The hockey encyclopedia. 1974.
   1. Hockey—North America—History. 2. National
Hockey League—History. 3. World Hockey Association—
History. I. Styer, Robert A. II. Ronberg, Gary. Hockey
encyclopedia. III. Title.
GV848.4.N7R66   1984   796.96′2′0321   84-11169
ISBN 0-917439-03-1

Contents

Introduction

Until the late sixties, professional hockey progressed with almost agonizing sluggishness, but since then, no sport has seen greater change. For decades after its turbulent beginnings, the National Hockey League remained a closed association of six teams, though by the early sixties, the league was drawing crowds that averaged well over 90 percent of capacity. Then, prompted by the threat of competition and the lure of lucrative national television exposure, the NHL expanded. It doubled its size in 1966–67, added four more teams in the next five years, absorbed the more successful franchises of the World Hockey Association, and became a flourishing nationwide league of 21 teams in both the United States and Canada.

THE HOCKEY ENCYCLOPEDIA is a reference book that attempts to put into perspective the burgeoning growth of pro hockey by recounting the sport's already substantial story, from frozen ponds to palatial arenas, from financial thin ice to gushing profits. First published in 1974, this new edition has been completely revised and updated, both textually and pictorially. It is our intent that this "new" book keep pace with the "new" look of the National Hockey League.

—The Editors

Mike Liut holds the fort against Ranger forechecking.

Frank Calder, President, NHL, 1917-43

Mervyn ("Red") Dutton, President, NHL, 1943-46

Clarence S. Campbell, President, NHL, 1946–1977

John Augustus Ziegler, President, NHL, 1977–

Presidents

Frank Calder

Frank Calder, a Scotsman, was a schoolteacher in England until 1900 when he arrived in Canada to become a sports writer and then sports editor of the Montreal *Witness* In 1907, he succeeded William J. MacBeth as sports editor of the Montreal *Herald,* and later became that paper's financial editor.

Calder was serving as secretary of the National Hockey Association when it went out of existence in 1917 and was replaced by the National Hockey League. He became the president and league's first president and secretary-treasurer. On January 25, 1943, during an NHL Governor's meeting in Toronto, Calder suffered a heart attack and was rushed to St. Michael's Hospital. Later he was taken to Montreal, where he died in Western Hospital on February 4.

Mervyn ("Red") Dutton

After recovering from wounds suffered at Vimy Ridge in World War I, Mervyn Alexander "Red" Dutton began his professional hockey career in the 1921-22 season with the Calgary Tigers of the Western Canada Hockey League. This league folded at the end of the 1925-26 season, and Dutton joined the Montreal Maroons of the National Hockey League. After the 1929-30 season he was traded to the New York Americans for Lionel Conacher, and on April 24, 1935, was named manager of the Americans. Although financial problems caused the National Hockey League to take control of the Americans on October 19, 1936, Dutton remained manager through their final season (1941-42).

When Frank Calder suffered a heart attack on January 25, 1943, the National Hockey League Governors named Dutton managing director, and an executive committee composed of Edward W. Bickle of Toronto and Lester Patrick of New York was chosen to aid him. He remained managing director until September 8, 1944, when he was elected presi-dent. He served in this capacity for two seasons, 1944-45 and 1945-46. (Note: the NHL had no president from January 25, 1943, to September 8, 1944.)

Clarence Sutherland Campbell

Clarence Sutherland Campbell studied law at the University of Alberta where he earned a Rhodes scholarship to Oxford University. During the Great Depression he refereed in the National Hockey League for three seasons (1936-37, 1937-38, and 1938-39). He was commissioned in the Canadian Army in World War II, and later was with the Canadian War Crimes Unit at Nuremberg during the war crimes trials. On June 18, 1946, he was appointed executive assistant to Red Dutton, and on September 4, 1946, was elected president of the National Hockey League, a position he held for 31 years until August 25, 1977.

John Augustus Ziegler

On June 22, 1977, John Augustus Ziegler was elected president of the National Hockey League; he took office on August 26. Ziegler had attended the University of Michigan from which he had graduated in 1957 with a law degree. He was vice-president and general counsel for the Detroit Red Wings from 1970 to 1977.

When the National Hockey League took control of the California Golden Seals from Febraury 15, 1974, to July 27, 1975, Ziegler along with James D. Cullen of St. Louis and Arthur Morse of Chicago directed the club on the league's behalf. In June, 1976, he was named chairman of the NHL Board of Governors, an office he held for two seasons (1976-77 and 1977-78).

The Montreal A.A.A., circa 189

Where and when did hockey begin? Who invented it and how? Why? These are good questions, the answers to which nobody knows for certain. Probably no one ever will know. Hockey has its roots in a number of games, which were popular in countries other than Canada, the country generally credited as hockey's birthplace. Ancient carvings show the Greeks, for example, playing their version of hockey as early as 500 B.C. In the seventeenth century an ice game known as *kolven* was popular in Holland.

Even the source of the term "hockey" is a mystery. French explorers visiting the St. Lawrence River Valley in 1740 reported coming upon a band of Iroquois Indians whacking with sticks at a hard ball and reacting to certain misdirected blows by shouting, "Ho-gee!" which meant "It hurts!" A more scholarly explanation for the origin of the name "hockey" is that it derives from the French word *hoquet,* meaning shepherd's crook, or bent stick, both of which resemble a hockey stick.

AN UNCIVILIZED PASTIME

An article in a London newspaper in 1862 confirms the fact that a form of ice hockey was played in England as early as the mid-ninteenth century.

Hockey . . .ought to be sternly forbidden, as it is not only annoying [to leisurely skaters on a pond] but dangerous. In its right place, hockey is a noble game, and deserving of every encouragement; but on the ice it is in its wrong place and should be prohibited. Any weak spot on the ice is sure to give way if the ball [puck] should happen to pass near it or over it; for the concourse of fifty or a hundred personals all converging on the same point is a test which no ice, save the strongest, is able to bear.

The writer may have had a Victorian's priggish disapproval of the game, but perhaps that helped him to describe its nature better.

When a mass of human beings precipitates itself recklessly in any direction accidents are certain to follow. . . .The game is by no means what it ought to be, as it is impossible to enforce the rules in such a miscellaneous assembly. . . .

And finally, a parting condemnation.
It is more than annoying to have the graceful evolutions of a charming quadrille broken up by the interruptions of a disorderly mob, armed with sticks and charging through the circle of skaters and spectators to the imminent danger of all. I should be truly glad to see the police interfere whenever hockey is commenced.

Because field hockey had been a popular sport in England for centuries, it is logical to assume that youths simply transferred a crude version of that game to frozen ponds during the winter (much to the consternation of casual skaters on those ponds). The object of the game was simple enough—using a stick or a sticklike instrument to propel a small object into a designated area. Other games of the time had similar objectives: Irish hurling, the Canadian-Indian game of baggataway (or lacrosse), and shinny, a game played in the Northeastern United States in the late 1800s. Shinny was probably the most basic version of the game we know today as hockey. Players attempted to control a ball or piece of wood with the ends of their sticks and then to evade defenders and shoot the object between stones set four or five feet apart. Walter Prichard Eaton, recalling his days as a boy, described his shinny games in the December, 1913, issue of *Outing* magazine.

I can hear the roar of the runners yet, and see the white powder fly as the leader doubled and the whole pack ground their skate blades into the ice and reversed in pursuit. I can still feel the sting of the cold December evening on my hot cheeks as I went for my coat when the game was over, and see the solemn green sunset up the pond to the west. The boys are at it yet, though they all have "store sticks" now, and call the game hockey.

CANADA CLAIMS THE GAME

While the U.S. and other countries merely dabbled with various primitive forms of hockey, Canada adopted the sport and eventually refined it to a game of strategy, organization, and somewhat less mayhem. For this contribution Canada has claimed the right to call itself the birthplace of the game. Henry Roxborough spoke for countless Canadians in 1964 when he wrote of the Canadian claim on the game.

Today, with ice hockey a truly international game, fans are developing a world-wide interest in its origins. It is conjectured that the real ancestors of hockey might have been either Greeks, Hollanders, Englishmen, Scandinavians or early Americans. Therefore, while records are available, Canadians should stake their claim to be the founding fathers of the world's fastest game. Unless we do, our priority might be challenged by foreign pretenders. . . .

Let us frankly recognize that the tools of hockey—the sticks, the skates, the ball-type puck and certainly ice itself—didn't originate in Canada. However, there is ample justification for our boast that hockey on ice, as it is now generally played, is an original Canadian creation.

In Canada hockey's development was as natural as the changing of the seasons. In the spring, summer, and fall, there were other games to play, but when the long, cold, hard winters came, young boys by the thousands took to frozen ponds. For pucks they used pieces of wood, tin cans, or horse apples. They erected boards around the ponds to keep the puck from getting lost in the snow. They bored poles into the ice to designate the goals. Goaltenders wrapped their legs with newspapers and magazines, and when shooters began lifting their shots higher, the goalies strapped on baseball chest protectors. Until a company in Montreal began manufacturing ice hockey sticks in the late 1880s, hockey players either used field hockey sticks or made their own. Before skates were produced, early players fastened or clamped steel

"Shinnie" in Scotland

blades to their street shoes. (The sites of such games eventually became known as "a rink," which means "course" in Scotch.)

Recalling his shinny stick in a spirit similar to that of a Canadian, Mr. Eaton wrote, "A good, natural stick was a treasured possession, and one never went skating without it. You hung your skates from it on your way to the pond. You used it to hammer over the lever when you put your skates on. It was a club to test the strength of new ice, or to make a hole over a brook when you were thirsty."

Hockey took Canada by storm in the latter part of the nineteenth century; everyone wanted to play and usually did. As a result the early games were wildly disorganized and confusing, with as many as 30 players on a side. Home teams had the option to change referees at will, and during one particular contest, no fewer than eight referees were employed until the home team—and crowd—were satisfied. Goal judges never dreamed of being enclosed in a glass booth, as they are today, secluded and secure from the action and emotions churning about them. In the early days the goal judge stood directly behind the goalposts, nimbly dodging shots that flew goalward and players who fought for the puck around him. The crowd, ringing the ice and

guzzling liquor to ward off the cold, more than influenced the goal judge's calls; it dictated them. To signify a goal, the goal judge pulled a white handkerchief from his breast pocket and waved it in the biting cold. Not until a man named Francis Nelson had the idea of fastening a fishing net between the goalposts could one be reasonably sure whether a shot had found its mark.

As they do today, referees originally used whistles to order stoppages in play. But steel whistles stick to wet lips in subzero cold, so a referee named Fred C. Waghorne got cowbells approved as standard equipment until the game was finally moved indoors. It was Waghorne, the top referee of his day, who also invented the faceoff. For years referees had been beginning play by placing the puck on the ice, taking in hand the stick blade of each contesting player, and placing them against the puck. The players were supposed to begin their battle for the puck after the referee moved aside and yelled, "Play!" Players being players, however, they often jumped the gun, much to the discomfort of the referees. During one particularly painful night in Paris, Ontario, Fred C. Waghorne ordered both players to place their sticks on the ice, 18 inches apart. Waghorne then backed off a bit, tensed for his getaway, and tossed the puck between the sticks.

Such faceoffs have been standard since.

A SEMBLANCE OF ORDER

With hockey growing as fast as it was, there was an obvious need for organization and a uniform set of rules. In 1885, some hockey fans in Montreal, calling themselves the Amateur Hockey Association of Canada, started by limiting the number of players on a team to seven. At the same time in Kingston, Ontario, hockey's first league was being formed, comprised of the Royal Military College, the Kingston Athletics, the Kingston Hockey Club, and Queen's University, which won the league's first championship. Soon more leagues had sprouted throughout Ontario and Quebec, and by the 1890s, hockey had spanned Canada's great prairies and reached her Western shores. By 1895, there were more than 100 hockey teams in Montreal alone.

In 1892, Lord Stanley of Preston, Canada's governor general at the time, had an idea. "There does not appear to be any outward sign or visible sign of

Referee's outdoor "whistle"

the championship at present," he said, "and considering the interest that hockey matches now elicit, and the importance of having the games fairly played under generally recognized rules, I am willing to give a cup that shall annually be held by the winning club." Stanley's gift, which cost $48.50

at the time, would become the game's most treasured possession, the Stanley Cup.

In 1893 the Cup was awarded to the Montreal Amateur Athletic Association club for winning the Amateur Hockey Association title. In the spring of 1894, when the Montreal AAA battled the Ottawa Capitals for the Cup, one newspaper reported, "The hockey championship was decided here tonight, and never before in the history of the game was there such a crowd present at a match or such enthusiasm evinced. There were fully five thousand persons at the match, and tin horns, strong lungs and a general rabble predominated. The ice was fairly good. The referee forgot to see many things. The match resulted in favor of Montreal by a score of 3 goals to 1."

Also in 1893, organized hockey was first played in the United States. To this day both Yale University and Johns Hopkins University claim to have been the hosts. The first American hockey league was a four-team conference established in New York City in 1896. In the league's first game, played on December 15 of that year, the St. Nicholas Skating Club defeated the Brooklyn Skating Club 15-0. The other two members of the league were the New York Athletic Club and the Crescent Athletic Club of Brooklyn. The following year the Baltimore Hockey League was formed, and by 1898, teams were playing in Pittsburgh, Philadelphia, Chicago, and Washington, D.C. By 1902, there were three leagues with at least some representation in New York City, including a collegiate league of Harvard, Yale, Brown, Princeton, and Columbia. The game had also spread to Boston and Cleveland.

North of the border, hockey was challenging lacrosse as Canada's national game. It was a challenge soon sustained. In 1911, when a riot at a lacrosse game in Toronto left many hospitalized, thousands of lacrosse fans turned their attention to hockey. Hockey players became heroes in the eyes of the worshiping, though unruly, crowds.

The seventh player, or "rover," as he was called, was especially popular, though his work was less than glorious. He would cruise in and pop the puck into the net after his teammates had done the dirty work of working it into position for him. The hockey term "hat trick" originated in those early days, as the result of fans passing a hat for players who performed unusual scoring feats.

"Throughout this early period Canadians were regarded as the undisputed experts in the game," wrote hockey historian George Sullivan. "This was due in no small part to the differing attitudes of Americans and Canadians. In this country [the United States] it was often the case that a boy played hockey in order to skate. But in Canada a boy skated in order to play hockey."

"Canadians," said Edward Bigelow, who coached some fine Harvard hockey teams in the late twenties, "may be said to be born and raised with skates on their feet and hockey sticks in their hands. With constant playing they learn the things instinctively that all hockey players in this country try so hard to acquire. . . .".

The Amateur Hockey Association flourished in the 1890s, but just before the turn of the century, disagreement between the AHA and the Capitals, a club desiring to join the league, resulted in wholesale withdrawals and then disbandment of the AHA. A new league took over, the Canadian Amateur Hockey League, made up of the Capitals and former AHA members Quebec, Victoria, Ottawa, and the Toronto Shamrocks.

THE BEGINNINGS OF A PRO GAME

After the 1986-97 season the Berlin (Kitchener) club had been expelled by the Ontario Hockey Association for paying some of its players. Playing on this club had been a dentist, Dr. John L. "Doc" Gibson, who later migrated to Houghton, Michigan to practice his dentistry. He formed a hockey club called the Portage Lake Hockey club

and began paying Canadian players to come and play there. By 1904, other entrepreneurs in the area were doing the same thing, and hockey's first professional league, the International Pro Hockey League, was founded. Playing for pay was denounced in Canada until a team in Sault Ste. Marie, Ontario, joined the IPHL. By now stars such as Fred ("Cyclone") Taylor and Hod Stuart were commuting to the United States for $500 a game, and that sum soared to an exorbitant $1,000 per game when other stars followed: Newsy Lalonde, Art Ross, Sprague Cleghorn, and Spunk Sparrow. Limited, however, by the seating capacity of their rinks, owners simply couldn't meet the salary demands of their star players. In 1907, the IPHL went out of business.

Undaunted by the 'Americans' failure, the Ontario Professional Hockey League began in 1908. Two years later another pro league followed, the National Hockey Association, which included a team known as the Montreal Canadiens. When the bidding war between the two leagues threatened to destroy both of them, they merged, keeping the name National Hockey Association. There were NHA teams in Renfrew, Cobalt, Haileybury, and Ottawa, and three in Montreal—the Shamrocks, Wanderers, and Canadiens.

Then Frank Patrick, an adventurous sort, his brother Lester, a player for the Wanderers, and their father, Joseph, bolted to the West Coast to organize their own league, the Pacific Coast Hockey Association. Predictably, they began waving money in the faces of Eastern stars and soon relieved the NHA of such established players as Taylor, Lalonde, and Frank Nighbor. Before long the PCHA was playing the NHA for the Stanley Cup.

Innovators from the outset, the Patricks did more to streamline hockey than anyone else at the time. They put numbers on their players' uniforms. They ignored the NHA's restrictions on goaltenders. (The NHA had stubbornly refused to allow a goaltender to assume anything but an upright position and

Victoria Senators of 1912

permitted him to field shots with only his stick or glove. To do otherwise meant an automatic two-dollar fine.) The Patricks divided the ice into three parts with blue lines, introduced playoffs, and began to keep records of assists as well as goals. In 1910, the leagues on both coasts agreed to play their games in periods of 20 minutes each instead of the two 30-minute periods that had been standard until then.

In 1914, World War I shook the world, and Canadians went off to battle with everyone else. The few hockey players who remained at home were not permitted to play professionally. By 1917, the NHA had shrunk to six teams, one of which was the Northern Fusiliers, who represented the 228th Battalion of

the Canadian Army. When the 228th was ordered overseas, the NHA was left with only five teams and some gaping holes in its schedule. It was decided that the Toronto team, owned by unpopular Eddie Livingstone, would be dropped and its players redistributed among the other four clubs. Livingstone rebelled, of course, so on November 22, 1917, NHA owners met in Montreal and decided to exclude Livingstone from a new league rather than throw him out of the old one.

THE NHL IS BORN; A TEMPESTUOUS CHILDHOOD

The new league, which Livingstone was not invited to join, had four teams: one in Ottawa, one in Toronto, and two

Cyclone Taylor

in Montreal—the Wanderers and Canadiens. The new association called itself the National Hockey League, named Frank Calder its president, and announced a 22-game schedule running from mid-December through early March. (Following the Patricks, the owners also agreed to allow goaltenders to block shots with their bodies.)

Although the NHL was clearly on the brink of prosperity, the next few years were not easy ones. The furious Eddie Livingstone was constantly threatening to establish his own league. On New Year's Day, 1918, Montreal's Westmount Arena burned down, leaving

Foster Hewitt recreates first broadcast.

the Wanderers with no place to play. Eventually, the team was disbanded. In 1920, Quebec dropped out of the NHL, and the next year the Montreal Canadiens were sold for $11,000.

These problems were minor compared to those on the West Coast, where the new Western Canada Hockey League had suddenly appeared and was competing with the Patricks. With player salaries already exceeding gross income, the Patricks were in serious financial trouble. Unlike the old International League, whose rinks were too small, the Patricks had built arenas that were too large to survive on hockey alone. Before the 1923-24 season, Seattle dropped out of the Patricks' league, and Vancouver and Victoria joined the rival WCHL. (Also at this time the West Coast abandoned the rover and adopted six-man hockey, which the East had been playing for years.)

In March, 1923, the NHL took a giant step forward when a young man

named Foster Hewitt sat down before an upright telephone and "broadcast" hockey for the first time, direct from the Mutual Street Arena in Toronto. In 1924, Dr. David Hart, father of the Canadiens' manager-coach, Cecil Hart, donated a trophy to be awarded annually to the most valuable player in the NHL. The Hart Trophy was first won by Frank Nighbor (who had left the West for Ottawa) by a single vote over defenseman Sprague Cleghorn of the Canadiens. The following year Nighbor would also be the first to win the Lady Byng Trophy, an award for gentlemanly conduct as well as for superior play.

In 1925, the delayed penalty rule was approved, mandating that no team would play with fewer than four players on the ice at any time. A player who incurred a penalty while his team was already playing two men short, would leave the ice but would be replaced until one of his penalized teammates returned.

PROSPERITY AND THE FIRST EXPANSION

By now the NHL was doing so well that it was considering franchise applications from the United States. New York, Boston, Philadelphia, and Pittsburgh all wanted hockey. In 1924, Boston became the first American team to enter the NHL, and a second club, the Maroons, was awarded to Montreal. The following year teams were granted to New York and Pittsburgh for $15,000 each.

Just before the 1926-27 season, the Patricks, realizing that their venture in Western hockey was doomed, sold their league to the NHL for $250,000. With the players from the Patricks' league, the NHL was now able to stock new clubs in New York, Chicago, and Detroit. Stars such as Frank Boucher and the Cook brothers, Bill and Bun, wound up with the Rangers, and Eddie Shore joined the Boston Bruins.

The NHL now consisted of two divisions and a total of 10 teams. The Canadian division included the Ottawa Senators, the Toronto Maple Leafs (formerly the St. Patricks, whom Conn

Smythe had purchased), the New York Americans (purchased from Hamilton for $75,000), the Montreal Canadiens, and the Montreal Maroons. In the American Division were the New York Rangers, the Boston Bruins, the Pittsburgh Pirates, the Detroit Cougars, and the Chicago Black Hawks. The year 1926 was also the first in which the Stanley Cup became the exclusive property of the NHL, and the schedule was increased to 44 games.

In 1927, forward passes were allowed in the center and defending zones, goaltenders' pads were limited to 10 inches instead of 12 in. width, and sticks were restricted to 53 inches in length. The following year, forward passes were allowed in defensive and neutral zones and from the neutral zone into the attacking zone if the receiver was in the neutral zone when the pass was made. No forward passes, however, were permitted inside the attacking zone. By 1930, forward passing was permitted in all three zones, but an offensive player could not precede the puck into the attacking zone—still the basic off-sides rule in hockey today.

Professional hockey had evolved a basic structure that it would retain for the next 40 years despite attrition and occasional changes in team names. In 1930, Detroit became known as the Falcons instead of the Cougars, and three years later the Red Wings instead of the Falcons. Philadelphia disappeared from the NHL in 1930, not to return until 1967. In 1934, the Ottawa franchise was transferred to St. Louis, where it folded in 1935, leaving the league with eight teams. In 1938, the Montreal Maroons disbanded. When the Brooklyn (formerly New York) Americans dispersed four years later, the NHL was left with the six franchises that would achieve pro hockey's greatest financial success: Boston, Chicago, New York, Detroit, Montreal, and Toronto.

For the 1942-43 season the schedule was increased to 50 games, and in the Stanley Cup playoffs that spring, the first- and third-place teams met in one semi-final, the second- and fourth-place

TONIGHT 8 30
Boston Bruins at Maple Leafs

AMERICAN SECTION PLAYOFF

THE THIRD HOLE

Can he make it? — or will the Leafs crush him underfoot tonight?

Toronto Stanley Cup poster

clubs in the other. The schedule would expand to 60 games in 1946, when player bonuses and playoff guarantees were introduced, and reach 70 games in 1949. The first of the annual All-Star games was played in Toronto's Maple Leaf Gardens in 1947.

HALLOWED TALES

It had now been more than two decades since the NHL had expanded to the United States, and during this era some of the game's finest traditions and legends were established. In 1928, for instance, the Chicago Black Hawks were shackled with the famed "Curse of Muldoon." It is said to have happened this way. In 1926, Pete Muldoon had been named as the Hawks' first coach, but even though his club won almost half its games and led the league in scoring, Muldoon was fired just before the 1927-28 season. Seething with anger, Muldoon reportedly told owner Fred McLaughlin that the Hawks would never win the NHL championship, and

for the next 40 years, they didn't.

Also in 1927-28, Lester Patrick, then coach of the New York Rangers, left his post behind the bench to play goal for his team in the Stanley Cup finals. Trailing the Montreal Maroons one game to none, the Rangers had suffered further misfortune when their only available goalie, Lorne Chabot, was struck in the eye by a shot and was unable to continue. After Eddie Gerard, the Maroons manager, refused to allow New York to use either Montreal's spare goaltender or a minor league goalie who had been watching the game from the stands, Patrick retreated to the Rangers' dressing room with his team and donned the pads himself.

The Rangers then trooped back for perhaps the finest hour in their history. Fiercely guarding Patrick, they defeated Montreal in overtime. They lost the next game, but took the next two—and the Cup.

On December 22, 1928, Arthur Dupont broadcast the first game in

Montreal history. "The hockey people of that era looked upon radio with a great deal of suspicion," Dupont recalled years later. "They feared that if stories of the games came into the home without cost, it would ruin attendance. As a result we were limited to a brief description of the third period and a summary. . . ."

INNOVATIONS AND INITIATIVES

By now hockey had developed a number of stars: Lalonde, Taylor, Nighbor, Joe Malone, Clint Benedict, Reg Noble, Joe Hall, Babe Dye, Aurel Joliat, Cy Denneny, Howie Morenz, Nels Stewart, Bill and Bun Cook, Frank Boucher, George Hainsworth, and Ace Bailey. While the players sold the product through their efforts on the ice, executives such as Lester Patrick, Frank Calder, and Conn Smythe pondered how to improve it. Patrick, for example, argued that the game was still too cozy, too defensive-minded. "I believe we must open it up," he said. "Our follow-

19

ers are entitled to action, not for a few brief moments but for three full twenty-minute periods. This open style demands better stickhandling and faster skating."

Meanwhile, Smythe was building a new arena in Toronto. It was the height of the Depression, but Smythe was irrepressible. "How can there be a Depression?" he said. "They're printing new money all the time, aren't they? There's more money around today than there was yesterday, isn't there?" Capitalizing on construction workers who needed the work and rewarding them with stock in the new building, Smythe had his new hockey arena within a year. He called it Maple Leaf Gardens.

No problem seemed too large to Smythe, who was determined to put a first-class team in his first-class building. He felt the Leafs needed a young hotshot then with Ottawa, King Clancy. Informed that the price was steep—several players plus $35,000 in cash—Smythe talked some of his friends into contributing. Still short, he bet on a horse (his own) and won. Clancy became one of the finest and most popular players the Maple Leafs have ever had. He is now a vice-president with the club.

In 1930-31, the NHL picked its first All-Star team. At center was the brilliant Howie Morenz, on the wings, Aurel Joliat and Bill Cook. On defense were Eddie Shore of Boston and King Clancy of Toronto. Chicago's great George Gardiner was in the nets.

Shore was known as much for his blood-curdling escapades as for his ability. Once against Toronto, Shore was on the ice with the Bruins enjoying a two-man advantage but trailing 1-0. Trying to kill the penalty, Ace Bailey of the Leafs won the faceoff and ragged the puck for a full minute before firing it into the Boston end. Shore raced back, picked up the puck, and started up ice only to be flattened by Clancy. Frustrated, Shore spotted Bailey, weary now from his earlier heroics, and decked him from behind. The Toronto player fell to the ice and lay motionless.

He was carried off on a stretcher and lay between life and death for days with serious head injuries. Eventually, Bailey recovered, but he never played hockey again.

Only three years later another of the game's finest stars was dead. Howie Morenz was enjoying one of his best seasons in 1937, when he caught his skate in a rut and broke a leg while chasing a puck into the corner. What seemed to be a routine injury became a tragedy two months later when Morenz died of an embolism. More than 20,000 people filled the Montreal Forum to pay their final respects to Morenz.

THE DAWN OF THE MODERN ERA

The thirties drew to a close with more stars and colorful players wearing NHL uniforms, among them the famed

Aurele Joliat

"Kraut Line" in Boston, comprised of center Milt Schmidt and wings Bobby Bauer and Woody Dumart. In New York, Rangers coach Lester Patrick brought up his son, Muzz, to play on the same club with brother Lynn. The New Yorkers also boasted another budding star in Bryan Hextall, whose two sons would follow him to the NHL three decades later.

Also, the game had been altered by more significant rule changes. A penalty shot had been instituted in 1934, and in 1938, it became an even more dramatic play when the puck carrier was permitted to skate right to the goalmouth. A rule prohibiting "icing the puck" was also introduced in 1938, and two years later the home team was required to resurface the ice between periods. In 1943, when the center red line was introduced to speed up the game, professional hockey took its last major step to the modern game. By 1945, the officiating staff for a game had been standardized at one referee and two linesmen, and by the fifties, the referee was using hand signals to inform fans of rule infractions. In 1949, it was ruled that clubs could dress no more than 17 players, exclusive of goaltenders, for a game.

With the beginning of World War II, some familiar names were suddenly missing from the line scores as hockey players, like other Canadians, went off to war. (On November 21, 1942, the NHL eliminated overtime periods because of tightened travel schedules.)

In January of 1943, NHL President Frank Calder was on his way to a league meeting in Toronto when he collapsed of a heart attack. Two weeks later he was dead. The NHL selected Red Dutton to succeed him, with the understanding that Calder's personal choice, Clarence Campbell, would eventually take over.

The forties began with the Boston Bruins winning the NHL championship and ended with the Detroit Red Wings in the midst of a seven-year grip on the title. Their dynasty wouldn't be broken until 1956. Between the dominance of the Bruins and the Wings, New York won the title in 1941-42 (it hasn't done it

Maple Leafs goalie, Turk Broda

since), and the Montreal Canadiens began a winning tradition that has never paled.

DYNSTIES IN MONTREAL AND DETROIT

The beginning of Montreal's rise came in 1942-43, when the Canadiens introduced a bull-strong right wing, Maurice Richard, who scored five goals in 16 games before being sidelined with a broken ankle. The following year coach Dick Irvin put Elmer Lach at center, Toe Blake on left wing, and Richard on the right. Soon labeled "the Punch Line," the three led the Canadiens to the top. With a dynasty clearly in the making, Montreal lost only 5 of 50 games in 1943-44 and ran away with the NHL championship They capped the season with their first Stanley Cup since 1931. Richard potted a record five goals in one semi-final game against Toronto.

The Rocket was just revving up; the next year was to be the finest of his career. Averaging a goal a game, he became the first NHL player to score 50 goals in a single season, and during one stretch, he scored 15 in nine games. As the Canadiens again ran away with the title, the Punch Line finished 1-2-3 in scoring and no less than five Canadiens made the All-Star

team. (Detroit's Flash Hollet was the only outsider.) Montreal lost only fourteen games (one in the 1943 playoffs) in two seasons.

Toronto gave its already blazing rivalry with Montreal another splash of fuel in the spring of '45 by eliminating the Habs in the playoff semi-finals. The Maple Leafs then won the Cup against Detroit on Babe Pratt's goal in the seventh and deciding game.

With the war drawing to a close, players were returning sporadically during the 1945-46 season and left league rosters in a constant state of disarray. It didn't affect the Canadiens, however, who swept both the league title and the Stanley Cup.

The following year Clarence Campbell became the NHL's new president, Frank Selke began as general manager of Montreal, and Gordie Howe, a young right wing, started with Detroit. The Canadiens won their fourth championship in a row, but they would have to savor it for eight seasons before claiming another. With Howe, Detroit was about to put together the longest chain of titles in league history.

Early in the 1947-48 season, Toronto's Maple Leaf Gardens was the scene of the league's first All-Star game. More than 14,000 saw the All-Stars defeat Conn Smythe's Stanley Cup champions 4-3. After Smythe fashioned a five-for-

two swap with Chicago to obtain Max Bentley, who had won two scoring titles in a row, the Leafs charged to their first championship in a decade. They celebrated with their second Cup in a row.

Then the Red Wings soared. Under general manager Jack Adams and coach Tommy Ivan, Detroit had assembled what would become known as "the Production Line": Sid Abel at center and Ted Lindsay and Gordie Howe on the wings. Detroit raced to the league title, fell to Toronto's third straight Stanley Cup team that spring, then won seven more titles and four Cups in eight years. Never before or since has the league been so dominated by one team.

Hockey charged into the fifties with players like Howe, Richard, Lindsay, and Abel leading the way. The NHL had a wealth of stars, including Red Kelly and Terry Sawchuk of Detroit, Doug Harvey of Montreal, Milt Schmidt of Boston, and Chuck Rayner of New York. Only the Chicago Black Hawks, who consistently finished out of the playoffs, lacked a bona fide star. (Their time would come, however.)

The fifties saw only one major rule change. In 1956, it was decided that a penalized player on a team playing short-handed could return to the ice immediately following a goal by the opposing team. This rule was aimed directly at countering a devastating Montreal power play, which was scoring two and three goals in the two minutes that the opposition was short-handed. Toe Blake was coaching the Canadiens now. His punishing power play crew consisted of Harvey and Bernie ("Boom Boom") Geoffrion at the points, Richard and Dickie Moore or Bert Olmstead on the wings, and young Jean Beliveau at center.

"THE RICHARD RIOT"

The major competition of Detroit throughout its glory years was unmistakably French. Between 1949 and 1957, the Red Wings finished first eight times and second once; Montreal was first once, second six times, and third twice. In March of 1955, the two clubs entered

Gordie Howe

their last three games of the season locked in another struggle for the championship. Rocket Richard was gunning for his first NHL scoring title (he had often led in goals but never in total points) when with a high stick he cut the face of Boston defenseman Hal Laycoe. When a linesman tried to intervene, Richard belted him in the eye. President Campbell, who had had his problems with the fiery Richard in the past, suspended the Montreal hero for the remainder of the season and the playoffs.

Canadiens fans went berserk. Campbell's office was besieged by angry telephone calls and letters. A few nights later, when Campbell attended the biggest game of the year, the Canadiens-Detroit game at the Montreal Forum, the president was the constant target of vile names and flying fruit.

Shortly after the first period ended, a fan raced up the stairs and hurled two tomatoes against Campbell's chest. No sooner had the second period started than a tear gas bomb exploded and filled the Forum with smoke and fumes. Fans rushed into the streets, where a mob of more than 10,000 formed and marched through the surrounding area assaulting cab drivers, hurling rocks and bottles, smashing windows, looting stores, and setting newsstands on fire. By the time the Richard Riot had ended, at 3 o'clock in the morning, 37 people had been injured and more than 70 arrested.

As it turned out Richard lost the scoring title, by one point to teammate Bernie Geoffrion, and the Red Wings won the championship by two points over the Canadiens. Where was Richard during the riot? At home, listening to the game on the radio. When someone called and appealed to him to come down and try to quiet the crowd, Richard replied, "No, I should not do that. It would only make matters worse. They would only raise me on their shoulders and march along St. Catherine Street."

The next day the Rocket did go on the radio, pleaded for calm in the city, and said, "I will take my punishment and come back next year to help the club and the younger players to win the Stanley Cup."

The next year, 1955-56, Montreal took the league title as well as the Cup. With Blake behind the bench and Beliveau, Geoffrion, Harvey, Jacques Plante, and Maurice and Henri Richard on the ice, the Canadiens replaced Detroit's dynasty with one of their own. Montreal won six NHL titles in seven years, including five in a row between 1958 and 1962 and a record five straight Stanley Cups (1956 through 1960). General manager Frank Selke and Sam Pollock, his director of player personnel, were filling the ranks with such talent that it looked as if the Canadiens' rule would never end. But Conn Smythe had some surprises for Montreal and the rest of the NHL.

REBIRTH IN TORONTO AND CHICAGO

After his Maple Leafs finished in the basement in 1958, Smythe made George ("Punch") Imlach the Toronto general manager. A week after taking over the Toronto front office, Imlach fired coach Billy Reay and went behind the bench himself. The Leafs rose to fourth place in 1958-59, lost to Montreal in the Stanley Cup finals, then finished in second place the next three years in a row. Spurred by Imlach, players such as Frank Mahovlich, Allan Stanley, Carl Brewer, Bobby Baun, Tim Horton, Red

Kelly, and Johnny Bower took the Leafs to three straight Stanley Cup championships from 1962 through 1964. Montreal was still the team to beat during the regular season, but suddenly Toronto had become masters of the playoffs.

With a former Red Wings coach, Tommy Ivan, in the general manager's chair, the Chicago Black Hawks also showed signs of life. Bobby Hull had arrived in 1957-58, and Stan Mikita was soon to follow. Purchased by multimillionaire James D. Norris in 1952, the Hawks had established a farm system second to none. In the early sixties it paid off. The Hawks won the Stanley Cup—the team's first in 23 years—in 1961. Still, the Canadiens continued to dominate the regular season standings, displaced at the top only by Toronto in '63 and Detroit in '65.

THE BIG EXPANSION

By now hockey was playing to sellout crowds in every league city, including New York and Boston, homes of the now lowly Rangers and Bruins. Television had become a powerful medium in North America. Football, baseball, and basketball had successfully expanded. Rumors of a new hockey league were flying. Hockey had no choice but to loosen its belt, and in 1965, the NHL announced the most dramatic expansion plan in the history of sport: at the start of the 1967-68 season, the league would field six new teams. The first change in the league in a quarter century would double its size. The requirements for franchise applications were formidable: two million dollars to be paid to the league and an arena with a seating capacity of 12,500. Yet within months Campbell had two dozen applications on his desk. They came from all over the United States, four alone from Los Angeles. (Surprisingly, only one came from Canada— from Vancouver, British Columbia.) By February of 1966, franchises had been approved for Philadelphia, Minneapolis-St. Paul, Pittsburgh, Los Angeles, and Oakland. In June, the sixth and final franchise was granted to St. Louis.

The only way to stock these teams was from existing rosters, of course, and on June 6, 1967, more than 200 club officials and newsmen jammed a ballroom at the Queen Elizabeth Hotel in Montreal. Each established team was allowed to protect two goaltenders and 12 other players. When a player was picked, the club that lost him was permitted to protect another of its players. The new clubs would be selecting 20 players for their $2 million ($100,000 a man).

Clarence Campbell determined the order of choice by drawing slips of paper from a hat. When he drew the Los Angeles Kings' number first, owner Jack Kent Cooke promptly selected Terry Sawchuk, the aging, former All-Star goaltender then with Toronto. As the drafting proceeded, it became obvious that the old clubs had done the new ones no favors. Owners such as Weston Adams of Boston had spent years scouting and priming young players for the future, and he and the other owners were not about to part with them for a paltry $100,000 each. When they were finished drafting, the owners of the six new clubs flew home from Montreal pondering how to build competitive teams with the likes of Ken Block, Dave Richardson, Gary Kilpatrick, Dwight Carruthers, Bob Courcy, Keith Wright, Les Hunt, Tom McCarthy, and Max Mastinsek.

There was no doubt that expansion would dilute the quality of hockey. As Clarence Campbell conceded, you can't add a half bottle of water to a half bottle of whiskey and come out with the same product. But at the same time, the established owners argued, the big league game would be brought into new territory and would return to other areas where it had not been seen for years. Hockey had suddenly become a national game in the United States, stretching from harsh New England to summery Malibu. Expansion was going to produce problems; everyone agreed on that. But at the same time it would make hockey more appealing to television (which would mean money in all

the owners' pockets), while opening the doors for future stars and current bench warmers to shine. Without expansion, players such as Bill Goldsworthy, Cesare Maniago, Bill White, and Red Berenson would never have become NHL stars.

Meanwhile in 1966-67, the Black Hawks of Tommy Ivan and Billy Reay were soaring to the regular season championship, their first NHL title since Pete Muldoon had invoked his curse 40 years before. Chicago placed five players on the All-Star team: Stan Mikita, Bobby Hull, Kenny Wharram, Pierre Piote, and goalie Glenn Hall.

In the first year of expansion, 1967-68, the Philadelphia Flyers finished first in the new West Division, losing one more game (32) than they won. But even though none was a potential power, the six new teams did better than expected against the established clubs, winning roughly one of every three games against the East Division. It seemed that the East's players relaxed too much, expecting easy games against the West, and the West's players, many of whom had been slighted or overlooked by the established clubs, played with the dedication of men whose reputations were at stake.

Leafs Bob Baun (21) and John Bower

Expansion star Cesare Maniago

THE BEGINNING OF THE ICE RAGE ERA

The Canadiens hardly faltered on their victorious march through the sixties, winning both the East Division title and the Stanley Cup in 1967-68, Toe Blake's last year as coach. They repeated both accomplishments the following year, under new coach Claude Ruel. At the same time the St. Louis Blues became expansion's Cinderella team under coach Scotty Bowman. With a host of old-timers including former All-Star goalies Glenn Hall and Jacques Plante, the Blues won two straight West Division titles and reached the Stanley Cup finals three years in a row.

The biggest hockey news came from Boston, however, where a much-heralded young defenseman was beginning to supplant Hull as the game's biggest attraction. In 1966-67, his rookie season, Bobby Orr made the second All-Star team; since then he has never failed to make the first team. His rink-long rushes and magical puck-handling feats have left players as well as observers dazed in his wake. And as if one superstar wasn't enough, the Bruins then completed what would later be seen as one of the most one-sided deals in hockey history. The Bruins obtained from Chicago three of the players who would complement and in some cases even outshine the dazzling Orr during the Bruins' rapidly approaching glory years. For the comparatively modest price of a solid defenseman, Gilles Marotte, a diminutive but dynamic centerman, Pit Martin, and a marginal goalie, Jack Norris, the Bruins landed two prolific scorers, Fred Stanfield and Ken Hodge, and the man whose scoring totals would dwarf all others, Phil Esposito.

As the sixties drew to a close with Esposito, Orr, and company scoring like basketball players, Boston appeared to be on the brink of a dynasty. The Bruins finished second in 1968-69 and again in 1969-70, when they won their first Stanley Cup in 29 years. The next year, while roaring to the East Division championship, they set a slew of league

Expansion draft, June 6, 1967

and individual records, including Esposito's 76 goals and 152 points. But in the playoffs, the Canadiens, bolstered by Ken Dryden's spectacular goaltending, upset Boston and won the Cup two rounds later.

After winning the East Division title in 1969-70, the Chicago Black Hawks switched to the West Division, which they ruled for the next three years. The Hawks were a high-scoring team with an All-Star in goal, Tony Esposito, but in 1972, they were seriously wounded when Hull defected to the World Hockey Association.

In 1972-73, the WHA struggled through its first season, making more

news with its outlandish salaries ($2.75 million for Hull, $2.65 million for Derek Sanderson) than it did on the ice. The New England Whalers won the WHA's East Division title and then the World Trophy, the WHA's version of the Stanley Cup, defeating Hull and the Winnipeg Jets, who had captured the West Division title.

The Boston Bruins made a clean sweep of the NHL East Divsion title and the Stanley Cup in 1971-72, but the next year the Canadiens, coached by Bowman and again inspired by Dryden in their nets, lost only 10 games in racing to the East Division title and another Cup.

In 1973-74, the Philadelphia Flyers emerged as expansion's first bona fide contender for the Stanley Cup, grabbing first place in the West Division at the start of the season, challenging the previously unchallenged Black Hawks for the title. After a brief fling with the WHA, Bernie Parent had returned to the Flyers and established himself as clearly the finest young goaltender in hockey. (Dryden had retired when he and the Canadiens failed to agree on a contract.) The Flyers' Bobby Clarke was having another splendid year after winning the Hart Trophy in 1972-73.

Though still struggling, the WHA nevertheless effected still another coup when its Houston Aeros signed Gordie Howe and his sons, Marty and Mark, to contracts totaling two million dollars.

Midway through the 1973-74 season, rumors spread of some sort of impending agreement between the rival leagues. Obviously, the two leagues had begun to negotiate in an attempt to check the near-ruinous competition between them, particularly the spiraling player salaries. As the war between the two leagues abated slightly, yet both geared for further expansion, fans could look back at hockey's primitive origins, and marvel at the game's spectacular growth.

The seventies and early eighties saw considerable upheaval and consolidation within the NHL. In 1970-71, two more clubs were added—the Buffalo Sabres and the Vancouver Cannucks—and the schedule was increased to 78 games. The Atlanta Flames and the New York Islanders were admitted during the 1972-73 season, and the Kansas City Scouts and the Washington Capitals entered two years later. In 1974-75 the schedule increased to 80 games, and the league divided into two conferences—Clarence S. Campbell and Prince of Wales. Each conference consisted of two divisions: the Lester Patrick and Conn Smythe divisions in the Clarence S. Campbell Conference, and the James Norris and Charles F. Adams divisions in the Prince of Wales Conference.

To confuse matters further, in 1981-82 the James Norris Division was moved to the Clarence S. Campbell Conference, and the Lester Patrick Division went over to the Prince of Wales Conference.

In 1976-77, the California Golden Seals were transferred to Cleveland and became the Cleveland Barons. In the sme season, the Kansas City Scouts moved to Denver, Colorado, where they became known as the Colorado Rockies. During the 1978-79 season, the Cleveland club merged with the Minnesota North Stars, and this new club moved from the Conn Smythe

Barry Pederson waits for the drop.

Division to the Charles F. Adams Division. When Edmonton, Hartford, Quebec, and Winnipeg entered the NHL in 1979-80, Hartford was put in the James Norris Division, and the Washington Capitals moved to the Lester Patrick Division.

At this time, 10 of the clubs changed divisions. Chicago, St. Louis, and Winnipeg went from Smythe to Norris. Calgary went from Patrick to Smythe, Hartford and Montreal from Norris to Adams, Los Angeles from Norris to Smythe, Pittsburgh from Norris to Patrick, and Minnesota and Toronto from Adams to Norris. One year later, when the Colorado Rockies became the New Jersey Devils, they were moved from the Conn Smythe Division to the Lester Patrick Division at the same time the Winnipeg Jets went from the James Norris Division to the Conn Smythe Division.

When the 1978-79 season ended, the World Hockey Association called it quits after only seven years. During the Association's lifetime 18 franchises had been granted, two of which had never even played a game—the Dayton Gems and the Miami Screaming Eagles. Other franchises moved around like pawns on a chess board. The New York Raiders became the New York Golden Blades, and moved first to New Jersey and later to San Diego before folding in 1977. The Los Angeles Sharks moved to Detroit (as the Michigan Stags) and then to Baltimore from which they exited in 1975. The Ottawa Nationals went to Toronto and then on to Birmingham. The Philadlephia Blazers moved to Vancouver and then Calgary before quitting in 1977.

Relations between the NHL and the WHA were strained, to say the least. The NHL refused to allow Gerry Cheevers, Bobby Hull, Derek Sanderson, Jean-Claude Tremblay, or any other World Hockey Association player to participate in the Canada-Russia series, although it did relent and allow Hull to play in the Canada Cup series in September, 1976. The signing of under-age juniors aggravated the NHL, and while the World Hockey Association claimed major-league status it never challenged for the Stanley Cup. Instead its members played among themselves for a cup of their own, the Avco World Trophy.

Aloof and uncompromising to the bitter end, NHL president John Ziegler made it very clear that the NHL would not agree to any merger with the World Hockey Association when he stated on March 30, 1979, "We are expanding the NHL by taking in four clubs for the 1979 to 1980 season. We are *not* taking in four World Hockey Association clubs. We will be conducting an expansion draft in June which will give the new clubs some NHL players."

National Hockey League Franchises

Entranced by the Era of Orr, fans forget that a rich hockey tradition was established in Boston long before Bobby was even born. Old line Bruins fans haven't forgotten, however, and neither has anyone else who had the chance to watch Eddie Shore, Milt Schmidt, Dit Clapper, and Tiny Thompson in action. Under the command of crusty Art Ross and owner Charles Francis Adams, the Bruins all but dominated the National Hockey League from 1927 through 1941, winning seven American Division and five league championships, and the Stanley Cup three times. Boston won its first Cup in 1929, with the help of some sharp maneuvering by Adams: when Frank and Lester Patrick's Western Canadian Hockey League was folding, the Bruins' owner bought five players, one of whom was Shore, for a total of $50,000.

Boston was the first American city to be granted an NHL franchise, and its fans have never tarnished the honor. Though it has become grimy and musty, Boston Garden is still a cozy home for the bawdy, raucous capacity crowds, with their wry epithets and humor unheard elsewhere in the league. Boston is a hockey town, even when its Bruins are in decline. The team was mired in the depths of the NHL standings in the late fifties and early sixties, yet their fans kept coming out in overwhelming numbers. Even the Boston Celtics, who at the time were fashioning a magnificent string of National Basketball Association titles and playoff championships, could not match the crowds that the dismal Bruins attracted. If ever an NHL city deserved a hockey winner, it is Boston.

The irrepressible Bruins fans must have gotten their spirit from Shore. In one famous incident Shore emerged from a Boston Garden fracas with one ear hanging precariously from his head. Informed by the team doctor that the dangling ear would have to be removed, Shore stomped into the cold streets outside in search of a doctor with a more promising prognosis. Two more

doctors told him the same thing, but the persistent Shore finally located one who said he would try to save the ear. As the physician prepared to administer an anesthetic, Shore pushed the doctor's hand away and snapped, "Just give me a mirror, Doc. I want to make sure you sew it on right."

Another time Shore got caught in a traffic jam and missed the train the Bruins were taking to Montreal. So Shore left Boston just before midnight, drove all night and the next day in a blinding snowstorm, and checked into the Windsor Hotel a few hours before the team was to leave for the Forum. Art Ross recalled that Shore's eyes were bloodshot from strain and lack of sleep and that he could hardly walk after so

many hours behind the wheel. "He was obviously in no condition to play," Ross said, "but after what he'd done to get there, I had no choice but to let him try." That night Shore scored the only goal in Boston's 1-0 victory.

The Bruins of the thirties had an All-Star goaltender in Thompson, who won the Vezina Trophy four times before another All-Star, Frank ("Mr. Zero") Brimsek, replaced him. Shore anchored a rugged defensive unit, and up front Ross had assembled the high-scoring "Dynamite Trio": Ralph ("Cooney") Weiland at center with Norm ("Dutch") Gainor and Dit Clapper on the wings. Clapper was the first NHL player to play 20 years. Then came "the Kraut Line": Schmidt at center flanked by Woody

Woody Dumart (14) watches Paul Bibeault make save.

Phil Esposito shows typical emotion after typical score.

Boston Bruins

Dumart and Bobby Bauer. Other stalwarts were Flash Hollett and Bill Cowley. In 1941, the Bruins won both the NHL title and the Cup, Boston's last until 1970.

Even when the Bruins floundered, their fans never deserted them. They cheered less often but more lustily for the few bright lights, usually Fern Flaman and "the Uke Line" of Bronco Horvath, Vic Stasiuk, and Johnny Bucyk.

Not until Bobby Orr arrived in 1966 did the Bruins start to reverse their losing trend. The dreamier Boston fans hailed him as the savior who would transform Beantown into a paradise of championship and Stanley Cup champagne. He did but not quite single-handedly. General manager Milt Schmidt made Orr's task considerably easier when on May 15, 1967, he closed a deal with Chicago for Phil Esposito, Fred Stanfield, and Ken Hodge. With veterans Ted Green and John McKenzie and youngsters Derek Sanderson and Wayne Cashman, the Bruins were ready to terrorize the league, at first with their brawling, later with their scoring. Still later they added top-flight defense and goaltending.

In 1967-68 Boston rose to third and the following year to second. In 1969-70 "the Big Bad Bruins," as they were called, tied Chicago for first place with 99 points. The Hawks were awarded the title because they had more wins, but Boston triumphed in the playoffs, taking its first Stanley Cup in 29 years. In 1970-71, the Bruins captured their first league title in 30 years.

In 1971-72, with Esposito scoring 76 goals and 76 assists and Orr as brilliant as ever, the Bruins assaulted the NHL record book and combined their accomplishments of the last two years, winning both the league championship and the Stanley Cup.

The Bruins slipped to second in 1972-73 and were eliminated from the playoffs in the quarterfinals, but they rebounded with another regular season title in 1973-74. After three dreary decades, Beantown was once again basking in the success of its Bruins.

31

Since 1974-75, when the league was divided into four divisions, Boston, playing in the Charles F. Adams Division, has finished first five times and second four times. All the players from their Stanley Cup-winning clubs of 1970 and 1972 are now gone: Esposito was traded to the New York Rangers on November 6, 1975; Orr played 10 games in 1975-76 and signed with the Chicago Black Hawks in June, 1976; Cheevers became Bruins coach in 1080 81; and Wayne Cashman retired after the 1982-83 season.

Although the Bruins remain one of the NHL's strongest clubs, the Stanley Cup continues to elude them. Twice they have reached the finals (in 1977 and 1978) only to lose to the Montreal Canadiens. In 1982, they got by the Buffalo Sabres, but then ran up against a stubborn Quebec club which defeated them in seven hard-fought games. The Quebec Nordiques won the seventh game on Boston ice, and when fighting broke out as the end of the game neared Terry O'Reilly became so frustrated that he punched referee Andy van Hellemond. Needless to say, punching referees is frowned upon by NHL officialdom, and O'Reilly found himself in civvies for the first 10 games of the 1982-83 season.

In 1983, the Bruins at last defeated Quebec, and then once again conquered Buffalo with Brad Park scoring the winning goal in overtime. But when they came up against the New York Islanders, all was lost.

Terry O'Reilly wastes no time in becoming a Bruin.

Team Records

Most Points	121	1970-71
Most Wins	57	1970-71
Most Ties	21	1954-55
Most Loses	47	1961-62
Most Goals	399	1970-71
Most Goals Against	399	1961-62

Individual Records

Most Points	152	Phil Esposito	1970-71
Most Goals	76	Phil Esposiqo	1970-71
Most Assists	102	Bobby Orr	1970-71
Most Penalties in Minutes 265		Terry O'Reilly	1979-80
Most Shutouts	15	Hal Winkler	1927-28

Annual Records

Season	GP	W	L	T	GF	GA	Pts	Finished	Result
1982-83	80	50	20	10	327	228	110	First, Adams Division	Lost Conference
1981-82	80	43	27	10	323	285	96	Second, Adams Division	Lost Division Final
1980-81	80	37	30	13	316	272	87	Second, Adams Division	Lost Preliminary
1979-80	80	46	21	21	310	324	105	Second, Adams Division	Lost Quarter-Final
1978-79	80	43	23	14	316	270	100	First, Adams Division	Lost Semi-Final
1977-78	80	51	18	11	333	218	113	First, Adams Division	Lost Final
1976-77	80	49	23	8	312	240	106	First, Adams Division	Lost Final
1975-76	80	48	15	17	313	237	113	First, Adams Division	Lost Semi-Final
1974-75	80	40	26	14	345	245	94	Second, Adams Division	Lost Preliminary
1973-74	78	52	17	9	349	221	113	First, East Division	Lost Final
1972-73	78	51	22	5	330	225	107	Second, East Division	Lost Quarter-Final
1971-70	78	54	13	11	330	204	119	First, East Division	**Won Stanley Cup**
1970-71	78	57	14	7	399	207	121	First, East Division	Lost Quarter-Final
1969-70	76	40	17	19	277	216	99	Second, East Division	**Won Stanley Cup**
1968-69	76	42	18	16	303	221	100	Second, East Division	Lost Semi-Final
1967-68	74	37	27	10	259	216	84	Third, East Division	Lost Quarter-Final
1966-67	70	17	43	10	182	253	44	Sixth	Out of Playoffs
1965-66	70	21	43	6	174	275	48	Fifth	Out of Playoffs
1964-65	70	21	43	6	166	253	48	Sixth	Out of Playoffs
1963-64	70	18	40	12	170	212	48	Sixth	Out of Playoffs
1962-63	70	14	39	17	198	281	45	Sixth	Out of Playoffs
1961-62	70	15	47	8	177	306	38	Sixth	Out of Playoffs
1960-61	70	15	42	13	176	254	43	Sixth	Out of Playoffs
1959-60	70	28	34	8	220	241	64	Fifth	Out of Playoffs
1958-61	70	32	29	9	205	215	73	Second	Lost Semi-Final
1957-58	70	27	28	15	199	194	69	Fourth	Lost Final
1956-57	70	34	24	12	195	174	80	Third	Lost Final
1955-56	70	23	34	13	147	185	59	Fifth	Out of Playoffs
1954-55	70	23	26	21	169	188	67	Fourth	Lost Semi-Final
1953-54	70	32	28	10	177	181	74	Fourth	Lost Semi-Final
1952-53	70	28	29	13	152	172	69	Third	Lost Final
1951-52	70	25	29	16	162	176	66	Fourth	Lost Semi-Final
1950-51	70	22	30	18	178	197	62	Fourth	Lost Semi-Final
1949-50	70	22	32	16	198	228	60	Fifth	Out of Playoffs
1948-49	60	29	23	8	178	163	66	Second	Lost Semi-Final
1947-48	60	23	24	13	167	168	59	Third	Lost Semi-Final
1946-47	60	26	23	11	190	175	63	Third	Lost Semi-Final
1945-46	50	24	18	8	167	156	56	Second	Lost Final
1944-45	50	16	30	4	179	219	36	Fourth	Lost Semi-Final
1943-44	50	19	26	5	223	268	43	Fifth	Out of Playoffs
1942-43	50	24	17	9	195	176	57	Second	Lost Final
1941-42	48	25	17	6	160	118	56	Third	Lost Semi-Final
1940-41	48	27	8	13	168	102	67	First	**Won Stanley Cup**
1939-40	48	31	12	5	170	98	67	First	Lost Semi-Final
1938-39	48	36	10	2	156	76	74	First	**Won Stanley Cup**
1937-38	48	30	11	7	142	89	67	First, American Division	Lost Semi-Final
1936-37	48	23	18	7	120	110	53	Second, American Division	Lost Quarter-Final
1935-36	48	22	20	6	92	83	50	Second, American Division	Lost Quarter-Final
1934-35	48	26	16	6	129	112	58	First, American Division	Lost Semi-Final
1933-34	48	18	25	5	111	130	41	Fourth, American Division	Out of Playoffs
1932-33	48	25	15	8	124	88	58	First, American Division	Lost Semi-Final
1931-32	48	15	21	12	122	117	42	Fourth, American Division	Out of Playoffs
1930-31	44	28	10	6	143	90	62	First, American Division	Lost Semi-Final
1929-30	44	38	5	1	179	98	77	First, American Division	Lost Final
1928-29	44	26	13	5	89	52	57	First, American Division	**Won Stanley Cup**
1927-28	44	20	13	11	77	70	51	First, American Division	Lost Semi-Final
1926-27	44	21	20	3	97	89	45	Second, American Division	Lost Final
1925-26	36	17	15	4	92	85	38	Fourth	Out of Playoffs
1924-25	30	6	24	0	49	119	12	Sixth	Out of Playoffs

In 1970, when he predicted that his fledgling Buffalo Sabres would be the first expansion team to win the Stanley Cup, Punch Imlach was greeted with predictable skepticism. Punch was acknowledged to be one of the finest coaches and general managers in the history of the game; his record with the Toronto Maple Leafs spoke for itself. But predicting a Stanley Cup for Buffalo seemed more of a ticketselling ploy than a realistic prediction.

Three years later Imlach had no reason to retract his bold prophecy. Not only was Buffalo's War Memorial Auditorium sold out, but Imlach's surprising Sabres had overtaken the Detroit Red Wings for the fourth playoff spot in the NHL's venerable East Division. Buffalo had accumulated more points in the standings (88) than 11 other teams in the league.

A fluke? Hardly. In training camp in St. Catharines, Ontario, before the season began, Imlach had said that the Red Wings could be surpassed, and that his old forces, the Maple Leafs, were in deep trouble. Few paid much attention to him until the Sabres opened

the season with six wins and four ties in their first 10 games. By midseason they were 21-11-7, and at season's end their record was a sparkling 37-27-14.

Buffalo had developed one of the finest lines in the game: Gilbert Perreault at center flanked by Rick Martin and Rene Robert. Aptly labeled "the French Connection," the line could control the puck in the opposing zone with the aplomb most lines barely managed between the blue lines. An even more nifty passing and scoring combination on the power play, Perreault, Martin, and Robert (none more than 25 years old) finished with 105 goals and 244 points among them.

Meanwhile, with 27 goals and 35 assists, Jim Lorentz produced his finest year after undistinguished service with Boston and St. Louis. Gerry Meehan had 31 goals and 29 assists, and Don Luce became a solid two-way player and a dependable part of an excellent penalty-killing unit. On defense, youngsters Tracy Pratt, Mike Robitaille, Jim Schoenfeld, and Larry Carriere were steadied by old pros Larry Hillman and Tim Horton, one of Imlach's favorites

from the glory years in Toronto. With the competent goaltending of Roger Crozier and Dave Dryden, the 1972-73 Buffalo Sabres had no major weaknesses.

Having suffered a heart attack in January of 1972, Imlach was forced to quit his first love—coaching. He yielded the job to an old buddy, Joe Crozier, who alternately coddled, cajoled, berated, and inspired the Sabres to the coveted playoff spot. Understandably, Crozier was named Coach of the Year for his efforts.

Perreault was the key to his club. As befits the fashion for centermen, he is big and strong. To these attributes he adds the speed and puck-handling wizardry of the old-timers. With 92 goals in his first three years, he outscored all other three-year men in NHL history (a record later surpassed by Martin). In his first appearance in the Stanley Cup playoffs, against his boyhood idols, the Montreal Canadiens, Perreault led the series' scorers with 10 points. Though the Sabres lost in six games, he was clearly the dominant player of the round.

The Sabres' fans would rather not think of how close they came to losing Perreault; without Imlach's quick thinking the young superstar might be playing for the Vancouver Canucks today. In the 1970 amateur draft, it was agreed that a spin of a roulette wheel would determine whether Buffalo or Vancouver would choose first. The Sabres picked the high number, the Canucks the low. As several hundred watched, NHL President Clarence Campbell spun the wheel. When it stopped, he adjusted his glasses, peered at it, and announced that the number was one, which meant that Vancouver had won the top pick. Amidst the hubbub that greeted the announcement, Imlach slowly rose, adjusted *his* glasses, and begged Mr. Campbell's pardon. "Wait a minute," he said. "The number isn't one. It's eleven."

Campbell looked at the wheel again, blushed, and admitted, "Mr. Imlach is correct. The number is indeed eleven, and Buffalo wins."

It was only the first of Imlach's triumphs. With Perreault (who signifi-

Buffalo's Haj t keeps the puck in the zone.

Buffalo Sabres

cantly, wears number 11 for the Sabres), and his supporting cast, Buffalo is a bona fide playoff contender despite the team's brief membership in the NHL. And when a team is a playoff contender, it always has a chance to win the Stanley Cup.

But Imlach's prophecy that the Buffalo Sabres would be the first expansion club to win the Stanley Cup quickly fell by the wayside. During his tenure as general manager, the Sabres, playing in the Charles F. Adams Division, finished first once and second three times. In the 1974-75 season, when the club finished first, it entered the Stanley Cup final series, but succumbed to the Philadelphia Flyers four games to two. On December 4, 1978, Punch Imlach was fired.

W. Scott Bowman took over as general manager and coach in 1979-80, and guided the Sabres to a first-place finish in their division, only to see them defeated by the New York Islanders in the Stanley Cup semifinals. In 1980-81, Bowman hired Roger Neilson as coach, and Buffalo again finished first in their division. This time, however, the Minnesota North Stars defeated them in the Stanley Cup quarterfinals. The success that Bowman enjoyed at Montreal has eluded him at Buffalo.

"The French Connection" line no longer exists—Robert was traded to the Colorado Rockies in October, 1979, and Martin was dealt to the Los Angeles Kings in March, 1981.

In 1981-82 and 1982-83, Buffalo finished third in their division, but were eliminated each time by the Boston Bruins.

Annual Records

Season	G	W	L	T	GF	GA	Pts	Finished	Playoff Result
1982-83	80	38	29	13	318	285	89	Third, Adams Division	Lost Division Final
1981-82	80	39	26	15	307	273	93	Third, Adams Division	Lost Division Semi-Final
1980-81	80	39	20	21	327	250	99	First, Adams Division	Lost Quarter-Final
1979-80	80	47	17	16	318	201	110	First, Adams Division	Lost Semi-Final
1978-79	80	36	28	16	280	263	88	Second, Adams Division	Lost Preliminary Round
1977-78	80	44	19	17	288	215	105	Second, Adams Division	Lost Quarter-Final
1976-77	80	48	24	8	301	220	104	Second, Adams Division	Lost Quarter-Final
1975-76	80	46	21	13	339	240	105	Second, Adams Division	Lost Quarter-Final
1974-75	80	49	16	15	354	240	113	First, Adams Division	Lost Final
1973-74	78	32	34	12	242	250	76	Fifth, East Division	Out of Playoffs
1972-73	78	37	7	14	257	219	88	Fourth, East Division	Lost Quarter-Final
1971-70	78	16	43	19	203	289	51	Sixth, East Division	Out of Playoffs
1970-71	78	24	39	15	217	291	63	Fifth, East Division	Out of Playoffs

Team Records
Most Points	113	1974-75
Most Wins	49	1974-75
Most Ties	21	1980-81
Most Loses	43	1971-72
Most Goals	354	1974-75
Most Goals Against	291	1970-71

Individual Records
Most Points	113	Gilbert Perreault 1975-76
Most Goals	56	Daniel Gare 1979-80
Most Assists	69	Gilbert Perreault 1975-76
Most Penalties in Minutes	258	Larry Playfair 1981-82
Most Shutouts	5	Donald Edwards 1977-78

Perreault, Buffalo's all-time point leader.

When major league hockey invaded Dixie in 1972, some speculated that the Southerners would shun the sport as they had the first Northern invaders more than a century before. But Atlantans responded well to the new game and to their new team, fearlessly named the Flames. The fans came to watch at an average of 12,516 per game, and their team responded to the support by producing a better season than the lukewarm year most first year expansion teams are happy to achieve. At season's end the Flames were clearly the hottest show in town.

The Flames didn't make the playoffs in 1972-73, but they did better than anyone expected. With a roaring start they vaulted into second place in the NHL's West Division, and even as late as January they were 20-19-8. When the more experienced teams victimized the Flames in the stretch, Atlanta sank to a seventh-place finish, yet at the end the Flames still showed a better record than did four other clubs in the league.

Among the many things the Flames did right was to hire a crack front office staff, headed by Cliff Fletcher, who, as a native of Montreal, knew little about Atlanta but quite a bit about hockey. He had served as a scout for the Montreal Canadiens and as assistant general manager of the St. Louis Blues before Atlanta beckoned. As general manager of the Flames, Fletcher first hired an old Canadiens hero, Boom Boom Geoffrion, as coach, and then proceeded to build a young aggressive club around a pair of top-flight goaltenders, Phil Muye and Dan Bouchard. Led in scoring by Bob Leiter, who had 26 goals and 34 assists, the first-year Flames had three 20-goal scorers and four players who finished with more than 40 points. They also boasted a potential star in young Jacques Richard.

The Flames' success made Geoffrion a bigger hit in Atlanta than he had been in Montreal, where he was one of the all-time greats as a player. It is generally agreed that no other coach in Atlanta

sports history made quite the impact of "Da Boomer." When he first joined the Flames, the swarthy, black-haired French-Canadian charmed them on Peachtree Street with a hearty handshake and "Y'all come see us now, ya heah?" Now he affects the Dixie vernacular in any one of a dozen radio and television endorsements. He is swamped with requests to appear at a variety of functions, from supermarket openings to dinner banquets.

For their second season the Flames faced the considerable task of proving that their early success had been earned; that it hadn't been the result of the opposition having taken the new

team too lightly, as had happened before in expansion years. The Flames added both size and scoring punch in choosing 6-foot 1-inch, 195-pound Tom Lysiak in the first round of the amateur draft. Lysiak can accelerate quickly with what scouts call "two-stride speed," and he has some fast fists to match. He was everyone's top prospect after he led the Western Amateur Hockey Association in scoring two years in a row. The last player to do that was Philadelphia's All-Star center, Bobby Clarke.

As the Flames began impressively in their second year, Geoffrion allowed himself some cautiously optimistic predictions. "We don't dream in color,"

Larry Romanchych (right) battles Flyers' Andre Dupont.

Calgary Flames

said Geoffrion, "but I think we can do a lot better than we did last year. We've upgraded our roster, and I think we have a great chance to make the playoffs." While Geoffrion motivated his young charges, Fletcher was on the phone to the established clubs in the league, trying to land a player who might bring closer to fruition the team's lofty ambition of making the playoffs in its second year. The bright red seats of the Flames' palatial arena, the Omni, were filled with sellout crowds, and with its fourth major league sports franchise well entrenched, Atlanta had taken another step toward bolstering its status as capital of the New South.

On June 24, 1980, the Atlanta franchise was transferred to Calgary. Major league hockey once again returned to the Western Canadian city where the old Calgary Tigers had played in the Western Canada Hockey League in the early 1920s.

In 1980-81 and 1981-82 the Flames were third in their division and in 1982-83 they rose to second place. G. Clifford Fletcher serves as the club's general manager as he had for the Atlanta Flames during their seven seasons in the NHL. Allister MacNeil coached them for two seasons, 1980-81 and 1981-82, but since then Robert Johnson, former University of Wisconsin coach and father of Mark Johnson, has coached the club.

Calgary played their first three seasons in the old Stampede Corral with its small seating capacity of only 6,479. After starting the 1983-84 season by playing eight of nine games away, Calgary played the St. Louis Blues in the newly built Olympic Saddledome on October 26. Attendance is not a problem for the Flames. The October 26 game was sold out for months ahead of time, and was played before a crowd of 16,674.

Kent Nilsson fights for position.

Annual Records

Season	GP	W	L	T	GF	GA	Pts.	Finished	
1982-83	80	32	34	14	321	317	78	Second, Smythe Division	Lost Division Final
1981-82	80	29	34	17	334	345	75	Third, Smythe Division	Lost Division Semi-Final
1980-81	80	39	27	14	329	298	92	Third, Patrick Division	Lost Semi-Final
1979-80	78	25	38	15	191	239	65	Seventh, West Division	

Team Records

Most Points	92	1980-81
Most Wins	39	1980-81
Most Ties	17	1981-82
Most Losses	34	1981-82; 1982-83
Most Goals	334	1981-82
Most Goals Against	345	1981-82

Individual Records

Most Points	131	Kent Nilsson	1980-8
Most Goals	66	Lanny Mc-Donald	1982-83
Most Assists	82	Kent Nilsson	1980-81
Most Penalties in Minutes	288	Willi Plett	1981-82
Most Shutouts	2	Rejean Lemelin	1980-81
	2	Patrick Riggin	1981-82

Through their first 40 years in the National Hockey League, the Chicago Black Hawks seemed to be laboring under a curse of one kind or another. Usually in the basement or close to it throughout each season, the club subjected its owners to a great deal of torment, not the least of it financial. At first the reasons for the team's failure were thought to be bad luck or lack of talent, but as the decades passed and the Hawks continued to languish, more imaginative theories were advanced. One story began to make the rounds called "the Curse of Muldoon."

The legend had it that Chicago's mysterious problems began after their first year in the National Hockey League. In that year, their first coach, Pete Muldoon, had led the team to a third-place finish in the American Division, behind the New York Rangers and Boston, but ahead of Pittsburgh and Detroit. According to the story, Major Frederic McLaughlin, who owned the club, insisted that the club was good enough to have finished first.

"You're crazy," said Muldoon.

"You're fired," said McLaughlin.

"Fire me, Major, and you'll never finish first," Muldoon reportedly said. "I'll put a curse on this team that will hoodoo it until the end of time."

It is debatable whether such an exchange ever took place, but for the believers certain facts buttressed their contention. Muldoon was fired after his first year; the Hawks, after some early promise, became one of the two worst teams in hockey; and even when they seemed on the verge of winning a league or division title, they wound up losing by a single point (in 1935, 1963, and 1964). By the time the Black Hawks finally won their first NHL championship, in 1967, Chicago fans were convinced that Pete Muldoon was responsible for the team's misfortune.

Chicago finished second five of the six seasons following Muldoon's dismissal. In those early years goalie Charlie Gardiner, Dick Irvin, Hugh Lehman, and George Hay led the club. When a fractured skull abruptly ended

his career, Irvin went behind the Chicago bench and launched a brilliant coaching career that would continue successfully in Toronto and gloriously in Montreal.

Chicago's upper middle class status was primarily the work of Gardiner, who in seven years recorded 42 shutouts and a 2.13 goals-against average. He twice won the Vezina Trophy. But in 1934, a few months after again being named to the All-Star team, Gardiner died of a brain tumor. The Hawks had won their first Stanley Cup that spring with Gardiner in the nets.

Chicago won another Cup in 1938 but during the next 19 years missed the playoffs 14 times, despite the efforts of such stars as Earl Seibert, Doc Romnes, John Mariucci, and Doug and Max Bentley. When Major McLaughlin died in 1944, the franchise was left with virtually no leadership. By the early fifties the club was on the verge of bankruptcy.

Then in 1952, James Norris, Jr., son of the owner of the Detroit Red Wings, and Arthur Wirtz purchased the club. Capitalizing on family ties, Norris lured Tommy Ivan from Detroit in 1954 to become Chicago's general manager. The Hawks finished last four years in a

row and fifth in 1958, but the new regime had laid the foundation for a solid farm system that now produced Bobby Hull and Stan Mikita. With All-Star goalie Glenn Hall, who had been obtained from the Red Wings, these young stars were ready to resurrect the Hawks. The team finished third four straight times and won its first Stanley Cup in 23 years in 1961.

Before he died in 1966, Norris had invested more than two million dollars in the franchise. Attendance at huge Chicago Stadium had leaped from 4,000 per game to more than 20,000. Money was, in fact, no object to Big Jim. During one drinking session in Toronto in 1962, he coolly offered one million dollars for the Maple Leafs' star winger, Frank Mahovlich. The Leafs tentatively agreed, only to back down the next morning. Having thought the deal had been concluded in the evening, Norris was furious when he learned it had not been. By this time, however, the club had no shortage of superstars.

Led by Hull, Mikita, Hall, Ken Wharram, Pierre Pilote, and Elmer ("Moose") Vasko, the Black Hawks became one of the NHL's most exciting teams in the sixties. Billy Reay began as

The Black Hawks' 1934 Stanley Cup winners

38

Chicago Black Hawks

Dennis Hull takes over from departed brother.

Dennis Savard patrols his lane.

coach before the 1963-64 season, and four years later the team finally snapped the Curse of Muldoon with its first league championship.

The Hawks marked 1970, their last year in the NHL's East Divsion, with another title, then dominated the West with three more regular season championships. The loss of Hull to the World Hockey Association was a heavy blow to the club, but the Hawks were strong enough to win even without him. The vociferous patrons of Chicago Stadium had at last forgotten the dire prediction of Pete Muldoon.

In 1973-74, the Hawks reached the semifinals in the Stanley Cup playoffs before losing to the Boston Bruins four games to two. During the next seven seasons they failed to get past the quarterfinals, and on two occasions lost in the preliminary round. From 1974-75 to 1980-81, Chicago finished first four times, second once, and third twice in the Conn Smythe Division. In 1981-82, they were moved to the James Norris Division where they finished fourth; the following season, they jumped to first place. In 1982 and in 1983, the Hawks were defeated in the Clarence S. Campbell Conference championship series, the first year by the Vancouver Canucks, the second by the Edmonton Oilers.

On December 22, 1976, after 13½ seasons as coach for the Hawks, Billy Reay was replaced by William White. Orval Tessier took over the coach's slot in the 1982-83 season. After 23 years as general manager, Tommy Ivan retired at the end of the 1976-77 season, Robert Jesse Pulford has held that position since 1977-78.

Team Records

Most Points 107	. . . . . . 1970-71; 1971-72
Most Wins 49	 1970-71
Most Ties 23	 1973-74
Most Losses 51	 1953-54
Most Goals 338	 1982-83
Most Goals Against . . 363	 1981-82

Individual Records

Most Points 121	Dennis Savard 1982-83
Most Goals 58	Bobby Hull 1968-69
Most Assists 87	Denis Savard 1981-8
Most Penalties in Minutes 303	Alan Second . . . 1981-82
Most Shutouts 15	Tony Esposito . . 1969-70

Annual Records

Season	GP	W	L	T	GF	GA	Pts	Finished	
1982-83	80	47	23	10	338	268	104	First, Norris Division	Lost Conference
1981-82	80	30	38	12	332	363	72	Fourth, Norris Division	Lost Conference
1980-81	80	31	33	16	304	315	78	Second, Smythe Division	Lost Preliminary
1979-80	80	34	27	19	241	250	87	First, Smythe Division	Lost Quarter-Final
1978-79	80	29	36	15	244	277	73	First, Smythe Division	Lost Quarter-Final
1977-78	80	32	29	19	230	220	83	First, Smythe Division	Lost Quarter-Final
1976-77	80	26	43	11	240	298	63	Third, Smythe Division	Lost Preliminary
1975-76	80	32	30	18	254	261	82	First, Smythe Division	Lost Quarter-Final
1974-75	80	37	35	8	268	241	82	Third, Smythe Division	Lost Quarter-Final
1973-74	78	41	14	23	272	164	105	Second, West Division	Lost Semi-Final
1972-73	78	52	27	9	284	225	93	First, West Division	Lost Final
1971-70	78	46	17	15	256	166	107	First, West Division	Lost Semi-Final
1970-71	78	49	20	9	277	184	107	First, West Division	Lost Final
1969-70	76	45	22	9	250	170	99	First, East Division	Lost Semi-Final
1968-69	76	34	33	9	280	246	77	Sixth, East Division	Out of Playoffs
1967-68	74	32	26	16	212	222	80	Fourth, East Division	Lost Semi-Final
1966-67	70	41	17	12	264	170	94	First	Lost Semi-Final
1965-66	70	37	25	8	240	187	82	Second	Lost Semi-Final
1964-65	70	34	28	8	224	176	76	Third	Lost Final
1963-64	70	36	22	12	218	169	84	Second	Lost Semi-Final
1962-63	70	32	21	17	194	178	81	Second	Lost Semi-Final
1961-62	70	31	26	13	217	186	75	Third	Lost Final
1960-61	70	29	24	17	198	180	75	Third	**Won Stanley Cup**
1959-60	70	28	29	13	191	180	69	Third	Lost Semi-Final
1958-61	70	28	29	3	197	200	69	Third	Lost Semi-Final
1957-58	70	24	29	7	163	202	55	Fifth	Out of Playoffs
1956-57	70	16	39	15	169	225	47	Sixth	Out of Playoffs
1955-56	70	19	39	12	155	216	50	Sixth	Out of Playoffs
1954-55	70	13	40	17	161	235	43	Sixth	Out of Playoffs
1953-54	70	12	51	7	133	242	31	Sixth	Out of Playoffs
1952-53	70	27	28	15	169	175	69	Fourth	Lost Semi-Final
1951-52	70	17	44	9	158	241	43	Sixth	Out of Playoffs
1950-51	70	13	47	10	171	280	36	Sixth	Out of Playoffs
1949-50	70	22	38	10	203	244	54	Sixth	Out of Playoffs
1948-49	60	21	31	8	173	211	50	Fifth	Out of Playoffs
1947-48	60	20	34	6	195	225	46	Sixth	Out of Playoffs
1946-47	60	19	37	4	193	274	42	Sixth	Out of Playoffs
1945-46	50	23	20	7	200	178	53	Third	Lost Semi-Final
1944-45	50	13	30	7	141	194	33	Fifth	Out of Playoffs
1943-44	50	22	23	5	178	187	49	Fourth	Lost Final
1942-43	50	17	18	15	179	180	49	Fifth	Out of Playoffs
1941-42	48	22	23	3	145	155	47	Fourth	Lost Quarter-Final
1940-41	48	16	25	7	112	139	39	Fifth	Lost Semi-Final
1939-40	48	23	19	6	112	120	52	Fourth	Lost Quarter-Final
1938-39	48	12	28	8	91	132	32	Seventh	Out of Playoffs
1937-38	48	14	25	9	97	139	37	Third American Division	**Won Stanley Cup**
1936-37	48	14	27	7	99	131	35	Fourth, American Division	Out of Playoffs
1935-36	48	21	19	8	93	92	50	Third, American Division	Lost Quarter-Final
1934-35	48	26	17	5	118	88	57	Second, American Division	Lost Quarter-Final
1933-34	48	20	17	11	88	83	51	Second, American Division	**Won Stanley Cup**
1932-33	48	16	20	12	88	101	44	Fourth, American Division	Out of Playoffs
1931-32	48	18	19	11	86	101	47	Second, American Division	Lost Quarter-Final
1930-31	44	24	17	3	108	78	51	Second, American Division	Lost Final
1929-30	44	21	18	5	117	111	47	Second, American Division	Lost Quarter-Final
1928-29	44	7	29	8	33	65	22	Fifth, American Division	Out of Playoffs
1927-28	44	7	34	3	68	134	17	Fifth, American Division	Out of Playoffs
1926-27	44	19	22	3	115	116	41	Third, American Division	Lost Quarter-Final

One of the saddest things to happen to the National Hockey League over the past 25 years has been the decline of the Detroit Red Wings. A great hockey tradition has been tarnished by palace revolts, misadvised trades, the firing of numerous coaches, and the demise of a once-powerful farm system. As a result, Detroit has frequently failed to make the playoffs, bitterly disappointing their fans, who had gloried in the triumphs of the great Detroit teams of the late forties and fifties, when Gordie Howe, Ted Lindsay, Sid Abel, Terry Sawchuk, and Red Kelly wore Red Wings uniforms with distinction. As these stars grew older, young prospects in the farm system were traded for frontline replacements, and the Red Wings have been struggling ever since.

Professional hockey in the Detroit area began in 1925, when a team called the Cougars played its home games across the river in Windsor's Border City Arena. Hockey languished in the area until one day in 1933 when general manager-coach Jack Adams walked into his office and was informed that the team's new owner, James D. Norris, Sr., was on the phone from Chicago. "Adams?" snapped the gruff voice on the other end of the line. "I'll be in Detroit this afternoon. Meet me with the bankers when I take over that lousy club."

The team, known then as the Falcons, was in such dire financial straits that Adams later recalled, "If Howie Morenz, the great Montreal star, had been available for a dollar ninety-eight, we couldn't have afforded him."

The first thing Norris did was change the name of the team to the Red Wings. As a boy he had played on a team called the Winged Wheelers, and now he borrowed not only part of its name but its emblem. He chose the famous winged wheel emblem because, he said, "it ought to sit well with Henry Ford and the Detroit car people." Then he made his first substantive change by allowing Adams to operate with the financial freedom befitting the fine general manager he was. Adams

immediately bought Syd Howe from the St. Louis Flyers and acquired Hec Kilrea from Toronto. In the next two years, the Red Wings won both the American Division title and the Stanley Cup.

And that was just the beginning. After missing the playoffs in 1938, Detroit was involved in Cup play every spring for the next 20 years. During that time, the Wings won nine league titles (including seven in a row) and five Stanley Cups. During the glory years of Howe, Lindsay, Abel, and company,

Adams would grow red-faced if someone suggested that the Red Wings were the New York Yankees of hockey, "We are not the Yankees of hockey," he insisted. "The Yankees are the Red Wings of baseball."

Adams was stunned by Norris's death in 1952, but he remained as the club's iron ruler under the late owner's daughter, Marguerite Ann. The decline began when one of Norris's sons, Bruce, assumed ownership in the late fifties and decided after the Wings had

Gordie Howe lunges too late to block Mahovlich's shot.

Detroit Red Wings

Terry Sawchuk flops to foil Toronto.

Steve Yzerman looks for the outlet pass.

missed the playoffs in 1962 to dismiss Adams. Adams was shocked, and though well compensated financially for his contributions to the club, he died a bitter man in 1968.

To replace Adams, Norris hired Sid Abel, who had been coaching the Red Wings since 1957-58, but Abel had difficulty as a general manager. Under great pressure from Norris to make the team an annual playoff contender, he mortgaged Detroit's future by dealing away young prospects in the farm system for established players. It worked for a while; from 1963 through 1966 the Red Wings always made the playoffs and in 1965 even won an NHL title. But then the younger clubs matured and ousted the Wings, who have reached the playoffs only once since 1967.

In 1970, Norris hired Ned Harkness, a successful college hockey coach at Rensselaer Polytechnic Institute and Cornell University. As coach of the Wings, Harkness's rah-rah style offended old pros on the club, and one night Gordie Howe informed Norris that the team could no longer play under the new regime. Abel then asked Norris if he, Abel, had the power as general manager to fire Harkness. Told that he did not, Abel quit, and Harkness succeeded him as general manager. Harkness effected a succession of trades that left Red Wings fans confused and bewildered. As if to compound their dismay, the Red Wings were shuffling coaches nearly as often as players.

A semblance of sanity and order was restored in November, 1973, when Alex Delvecchio hung up his skates after 22 years with Detroit and was given a three-year contract as coach. Later in the season, as the Wings continued to lag in the standings, Harkness quit.

Delvecchio coached the club through 1974-75, and in 1975-76 three coaches were used: N. Douglas Barkley, William Dea, and Delvecchio. In 1976-77 Dea coached the first 27 games; then Delvecchio took over, followed by Lawrence Wilson, who coached the final

"Doogie" avoids a boardcheck.

36 games. Lindsay became general manager near the end of that season, and during the summer a promotional blitz proclaimed that "aggressive hockey is back in town." Robert Kromm, who had coached the Trail Smoke Eaters to a World's Amateur Championship and an Allan victory, was named coach. The Red Wings finished second in the James Norris Division, but were eliminated by the Montreal Canadiens in the Stanley Cup playoffs. Since 1978-79, it's been nothing but last-place finishes in the James Norris Division. Kromm was fired near the end of the 1979-80 season. Lindsay's attempt to coach the club in 1980-81 lasted only 20 games, and on November 24 he too was gone.

The Detroit Olympic is situated in an area of the city where muggers abound. Bruce Norris once contemplated moving the club to Pontiac, but since Detroit's Renaissance Center was then being built, city officials were able to persuade him to move the Red Wings temporarily to the Joe Louis Sports Arena, where they first played on December 27, 1979.

After 56 years, the Norris family severed their relationship with the Detroit Red Wings; the club is now owned by Michael Ilitch.

Team Records
Most Points 101 1950-51
Most Wins . . . . 44 . . . . . 1950-51; 1951-52
Most Ties. . . . . 18 . . . . . .1952-53; 1980-81
Most Losses 55 1976-78
Most Goals. 270 1981-82
Most Goals Against . . 351 1981-82
Individual Records
Most Points . . . . 121 Marcel Dionne 1974-75
Most Goals. . . . . 52 Mickey Redmond. 1972-73
Marcel Dionne 1974-75
Most Assists 74
Most Penalties in Minutes
322 Bryan Watson . . 1975-76
Most Shutouts . . . . . . 12 Terry Sawchuk 1951-52;53-54;54-55
12 Glenn Hall 1955-56

Annual Records

Season	GP	W	L	T	GF	GA	Pts	Finished	Playoff Result
1982-83	80	21	44	15	263	344	57	Fifth, Norris Division	Out of Playoffs
1981-82	80	21	47	12	270	351	54	Sixth, Norris Division	Out of Playoffs
1980-81	80	19	43	18	252	339	56	Fifth, Norris Division	Out of Playoffs
1979-80	80	26	43	11	268	306	63	Fifth, Norris Division	Out of Playoffs
1978-79	80	23	41	16	252	295	62	Fifth, Norris Division	Out of Playoffs
1977-78	80	32	34	14	252	266	78	Second, Norris Division	Lost Quarter-Final
1976-77	80	16	55	9	183	309	41	Fifth, Norris Division	Out of Playoffs
1975-76	80	26	44	10	226	300	62	Fourth, Norris Division	Out of Playoffs
1974-75	80	23	45	12	259	335	58	Fourth, Norris Division	Out of Playoffs
1973-74	78	29	39	10	255	319	68	Sixth, East Division	Out of Playoffs
1972-73	78	37	29	12	265	254	86	Fifth, East Division	Out of Playoffs
1971-70	78	33	35	10	261	262	78	Fifth, East Division	Out of Playoffs
1970-71	78	22	45	11	209	308	55	Seventh, East Division	Out of Playoffs
1969-70	76	40	21	15	246	199	95	Third, East Division	Lost Quarter-Final
1968-69	76	33	31	12	239	221	78	Fifth, East Division	Out of Playoffs
1967-68	74	27	35	12	245	257	66	Sixth, East Division	Out of Playoffs
1966-67	70	27	39	4	212	241	58	Fifth	Out of Playoffs
1965-66	70	31	27	12	221	194	74	Fourth	Lost Final
1964-65	70	40	23	7	224	175	87	First	Lost Semi-Final
1963-64	70	30	29	11	191	204	71	Fourth	Lost Final
1962-63	70	32	25	13	200	194	77	Fourth	Lost Final
1961-62	70	23	33	14	184	219	60	Fifth	Out of Playoffs
1960-61	70	25	29	16	195	215	66	Fourt	Lost Final
1959-60	70	26	29	15	186	197	67	Fourt	Lost Semi-Final
1958-61	70	25	37	8	167	218	68	Sixth	Out of Playoffs
1957-58	70	29	29	12	176	207	70	Third	Lost Semi-Final
1956-57	70	38	20	12	198	157	88	First	Lost Semi-Final
1955-56	70	30	24	16	183	148	76	Second	Lost Final
1954-55	70	42	17	11	204	134	95	First	**Won Stanley Cup**
1953-54	70	37	19	14	191	132	88	First	**Won Stanley Cup**
1952-53	70	36	16	18	222	133	90	First	Lost Semi-Final
1951-52	70	44	14	12	215	133	100	First	**Won Stanley Cup**
1950-51	70	44	13	13	236	139	101	First	Lost Semi-Final
1949-50	70	37	19	14	229	164	88	First	**Won Stanley Cup**
1948-49	60	34	19	7	195	145	75	First	Lost Final
1947-48	60	30	18	12	187	148	72	Secoond	Lost Final
1946-47	60	22	27	11	190	193	55	Fourth	Lost Semi-Final
1945-46	50	20	20	10	146	159	50	Fourth	Lost Semi-Final
1944-45	50	31	14	5	218	161	67	Second	Lost Final
1943-44	50	26	18	6	214	177	58	Second	Lost Semi-Final
1942-43	50	25	14	11	169	124	61	First	**Won Stanley Cup**
1941-42	48	19	25	4	140	147	42	Fifth	Lost Final
1940-41	48	21	16	11	112	102	53	Third	Lost Final
1939-40	48	16	26	6	90	126	38	Fifth	Lost Semi-Final
1938-39	48	18	24	6	107	128	42	Fifth	Lost Semi-Final
1937-38	48	12	25	11	99	133	35	Fourth, American Division	Out of Playoffs
1936-37	48	25	14	9	128	102	59	First, American Division	**Won Stanley Cup**
1935-36	48	24	16	8	124	103	56	First, American Division	**Won Stanley Cup**
1934-35	48	19	22	7	127	114	45	Fourth, American Divisio	Out of Playoffs
*1933-34	48	24	14	10	113	98	58	First, American Division	Lost Final
1932-33	48	25	15	8	111	93	58	Second, American Divisio	Lost Semi-Final
1931-32	48	18	20	10	95	108	46	Third, American Division	Lost Quarter Final
**1930-31	44	16	21	7	102	105	39	Fourth, American Division	Out of Playoffs
1929-30	44	14	24	6	117	133	34	Fourth, American Division	Out of Playoffs
1928-29	44	19	16	9	72	63	47	Third, American Division	Lost Quarter-Final
1927-28	44	19	19	6	88	79	44	Fourth, American Division	Out of Playoffs
***1926-27	44	12	28	4	76	105	28	Fifth, American Division	Out of Playoffs

*Team name changed to Red Wings.
**Team name changed to Falcons.
***Team named Cougars.

In 1983, Edmonton went all the way to the Stanley Cup finals before succumbing to the New York Islanders. It wasn't Edmonton's first attempt to win this coveted trophy. Seventy-five years before they had journeyed to Montreal to take on the famous Montreal Wanderers in a two-game, total-goals series. In their zeal to win this prestigious Cup, they had recruited a group of "ringers" that included Bert Lindsay, Harold McNamara, Lester Patrick, Tom Phillips, Pit Pitre, and Steven Vair. in the first game, the Wanderers gave them a sound trouncing for this unsportsmanlike act beating them 7-3. Two nights later, Edmonton appeared on the ice with two of their own players, men who hadn't participated in the first game— Harold Deeton and Hay Millar, Deeton scored three goals and Edmonton won the game 7-6.

Two years later, in 1910, Edmonton was once again back east, this time in Ottawa to challenge the Ottawa Senators. The Senators dispatched them easily by scores of 8-4 and 13-7.

In their first two NHL seasons (1979-80 and 1980-81), playing in the Conn Smythe Division, Edmonton finished fourth. In the next two seasons, they finished first. The Oilers are blessed with the NHL's most outstanding player, Wayne Gretsky, who has won the David A. Hart Memorial Trophy in each of those four seasons and has been the NHL's leading scorer since 1980-81.

Mark Messier leads a frequent charge up ice.

Annual Records

Season	GP	W	L	T	GF	GA	Pts.	Finished	
1982-83	80	47	21	12	424	315	106	First, Smythe Division	Lost Stanley Cup Final
1981-82	80	48	17	15	417	295	111	First, Smythe Division	Lost Division Semi- Final
1980-81	80	29	35	16	328	327	74	Fourth, Smythe Division	Lost Quarter-Final
1979-80	80	28	39	13	301	322	69	Fourth, Smythe Division	Lost Preliminary Round

Team Records
Most Points 111	. . . .	1981-82
Most Wins 48	. . . .	1891-82
Most Ties. 16	. . . .	1980-8
Most Losses. 39	. . . .	1979-80
Most Goals. 424	. . . .	1982-83
Most Goals Against . . 327	. . . .	1980-81

Individual Records
Most Points 212	Wayne Gretzky. .	1981-82
Most Goals. 92	Wayne Gretzky. .	1981-82
Most Assists 125	Wayne Gretzky. .	1982-83
Most Penalties in	Colin Campbel . .	1979-80
Minutes 196	Edward Mio	1979-80
Most Shutouts. 1	D. Andrew Moog.	1982-83

Edmonton Oilers

High-scoring Jari Kurri looks for the puck.

Hartford made their start in the NHL by playing their first 22 home games at Eastern States Coliseum in West Springfield, Massachusetts, while their Civic Center Coliseum was undergoing repairs. They didn't play their first NHL game in Hartford until February 6, 1980. Despite these less than ideal conditions they finished fourth in the James Norris Division. (Actually, with 73 points they were tied with Pittsburgh, but Pittsburgh was awarded third place due to more game wins. In addition, they finished only one point behind the second-place Los Angeles Kings.) The Whalers' coach was J. Donald Blackburn, who was replaced by Lawrence Pleau on February 20 of the following season.

After three seasons of failing to make the Stanley Cup playoffs changes were made. For 1983-84 former bossman of the New York Rangers, Emile Francis, was lured away from the St. Louis Blues; he hired as his coach a man with the nom-de-plume of "Tex": William John "Tex" Evans—born: Garnant, South Wales.

Mark Johnson and goalie Millen fail to stop Canadiens.

Team Records

Most Points 73	. . . .	1979-80
Most Wins 27	. . . .	1979-80
Most Ties 19	. . . .	1979-80
Most Losses 54	. . . .	1982-83
Most Goals 303	. . . .	1979-80
Most Goals Against . . 403	. . . .	1982-83

Individual Records

Most Points 105	Michael Rogers . . .	1979-80; 1980-81
Most Goals 56	Blaine Stoughton	1979-80
Most Assists 65	Michael Rogers . . .	1980-81
Most Penalties in Minutes 242	Garry Howatt . . .	1981-82
Most Shutouts 2	Allan Smith	1979-80

Hartford Whalers

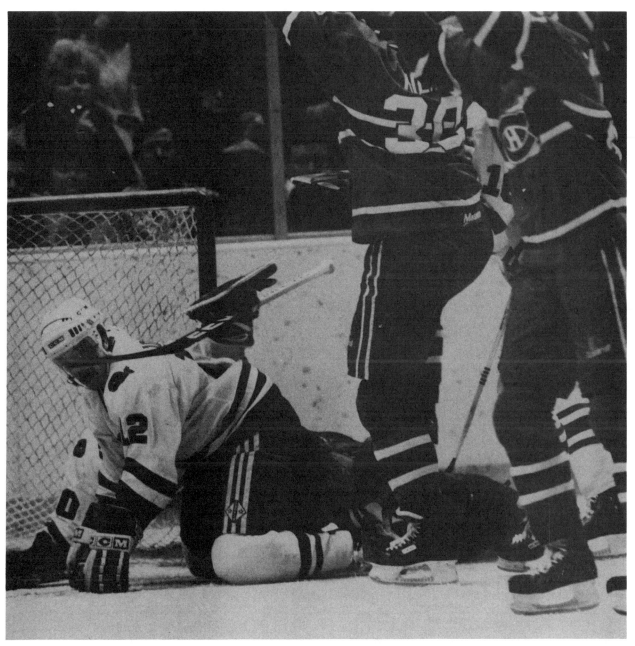

Greg Millen thwarts Winnipeg onslaught.

Annual Records

Season	GP	W	L	T	GF	GA	Pts.	Finished	
1982-83	80	19	54	7	261	403	45	Fifth, Adams Division	Out of Playoffs
1981-82	80	21	41	18	264	351	60	Fifth, Adams Division	Out of Playoffs
1980-81	80	21	41	18	392	372	60	Fourth, Norris Divisin	Out of Playoffs
1979-80	80	27	34	19	303	312	73	Fourth, Norris Division	Lost Preliminary Round

The first owner of the Los Angeles Kings also simultaneously owned the Los Angeles Lakers basketball team and a sizable share in pro football's Washington Redskins. Despite the success of all those teams, the owner, Jack Kent Cooke, who is from Canada, insisted, at least while he owned the Kings, that his first love was hockey. No longer involved with Kings or the Lakers, Cooke is, however, chairman of the board and chief operating executive of Super Bowl's XVII's Champion Redskins.

Nobody fought harder to land a National Hockey League franchise than did Cooke. When the city momentarily thwarted him by denying him use of the Los Angeles Sports Arena for a hockey team, Cooke pledged to build his own arena, and he did. On the day he was awarded the Los Angeles franchise in the NHL, Cooke exclaimed, "I'm an American now, but I feel like I've just been elected King of England!"

At the original expansion draft in June of 1967, Cooke continued to have difficulty controlling his enthusiasm. He mounted a rostrum to proclaim, "The Los Angeles Kings have just made a

deal that will insure them the West division championship." Unfortunately, Cooke had no players to deal—the new teams hadn't even drafted their players yet—so unless he had managed to steal a superstar from an established team, his announcement promised to be anticlimactic. It was. He merely wanted to announce the purchase of Eddie Shore's Springfield Indians as his farm team.

Next he drafted 37-year-old Terry Sawchuk from Toronto as his goaltender, much to the surprise and displeasure of the Maple Leafs. Toronto retaliated by protecting its rights to Red Kelly, even though everyone knew Kelly was retiring as a player and had planned to move to Los Angeles to coach the Kings. Cooke and Toronto owner Stafford Smythe sniped at each other for two days before NHL President Clarence Campbell helped settle the dispute. (The Kings finally got Kelly, and Toronto was compensated with a defenseman, Ken Block.)

Terry Sawchuk was the only quality player the Kings drafted. The rest were fringe major leaguers at best. When he heard of the derisive comments others

were making about his unorthodox choices, Cooke retorted, "Look what Branch Rickey did in 1946 with the Brooklyn Dodgers. Who ever heard of Duke Snider before 1946?" Jack Kent Cooke's goal had been to own an NHL team, and now that he had purchased one for $2 million and would sink another $16 million into a new sports palace, he would brook no interference with his royal whims. Unfortunately, kings are not always blessed with divine rightfulness. After finishing in second place in the first year of expansion and fourth the following season, Cooke's Kings steadily slipped into the depths of the West Division. Through the 1972-73 season, they have missed the playoffs four years in a row. The bottom of the division standings had become almost the exclusive domain of the Kings and their fellow expansionists in Oakland.

Cooke must be admired for his promotional and business genius, his enthusiasm, and his optimism, but his experience with the Kings demonstrated that such qualities are no substitute for shrewd bargaining in the smoke-filled rooms where hockey general managers do business. In his dealings with the game's master traders, Cooke was frisked of players who would star for their new teams: Bill White, Cowboy Bill Flett, and, to a lesser degree, Ross Lonsberry and Dale Rolfe. Even Terry Sawchuk failed woefully for the Kings, on the ice and off it. (It was no secret that he wasn't the public relations ambassador Cooke had somehow envisioned him to be.)

In his best deal Cooke landed goaltender Rogatien Vachon from Montreal. But in February of 1973, with the Kings battling for a playoff berth, Cooke nullified Vachon's noble efforts by trading Ralph Backstrom to Chicago for Dan Maloney. Without Backstrom, a team leader and one of the club's top scorers, the Kings blew their playoff spot to St. Louis in the final weeks of the season. With similarly inexplicable self-destructiveness, Cooke had driven Red Kelly to resign after two consecutive playoff years, having evidently forgotten

Mike Corrigan dents the ice.

Los Angeles Kings

how hard he had fought to get Kelly from Toronto.

After 13 years, Cooke's dream of winning the Stanley Cup vanished, and the ownership of the club was taken over by Jerry Buss. From 1973-74 to 1980-81, the Kings always managed to get to the Stanley Cup playoffs, but in those eight seasons they were able to reach the quarterfinals only three times and were eliminated in the preliminary round five times.

In 1981-82, the Kings improved a little and went to their division's final before losing to the Vancouver Canucks. In 1982-83, they finished last in their division and, therefore, were out of the Stanley Cup playoffs.

On November 26, 1973, Lawrence Regan, the club's original general manager, was replaced by Jake Milford. In 1977-78 Milford went on to the Vancouver Canucks, and George McGuire became the Kings' general manager.

Since Red Kelly's resignation, the Kings have had a succession of coaches—Harold Laycoe, John Wilson, Lawrence Regan, Frederick Glover, Robert Pulford, Ronald Stewart, Robert Berry, C. Parker MacDonald, and Donald Perry. Perry caused a commotion in NHL circles when he ordered Paul Mulvey to leave the bench and enter a brawl during a game in Vancouver on January 24, 1982. Mulvey refused and soon found himself with the New Haven Nighthawks of the minor American Hockey League. On February 3, NHL president John Ziegler suspended Perry for six games, charged him with "being dishonorable and prejudicial to the welfare of the league and the game of hockey," and fined the Los Angeles club $5,000.

Team Records

Most Points	1974-75
Most Wins	1980-81
Most Ties	1974-75
Most Losses	1969-70
Most Goals	1980-81
Most Goals Against	1981-82

Individual Records

Most Points	Marcel Dionne	1979-80
Most Goals	Marcel Dionne	1978-79
Most Assists	Marcel Dionne	1979-80
Most Penalties in Minutes	David Schultz	1976-77
Most Shutouts	Rogatien Vachon	1976-77

Annual Records

Season	GP	W	L	T	GF	GA	Pts	Finished	Playoff Result
1982-83	80	27	41	12	308	365	66	Fifth, Smythe Division	Out of Playoffs
1981-82	80	24	41	15	314	369	63	Fourth, Smythe Division	Lost Division Final
1980-81	80	43	24	13	327	290	99	Second, Norris Division	Lost Preliminary Round
1979-80	80	30	36	14	290	313	74	Second, Norris Division	Lost Preliminary Round
1978-79	80	34	34	12	292	286	80	Third, Norris Division	Lost Preliminary Round
1977-78	80	31	34	15	243	245	77	Third, Norris Division	Lost Preliminary Round
1976-77	80	34	41	15	271	241	83	Second, Norris Divisio	Lost Quarter-Final
1975-76	80	38	33	9	263	265	85	Second, Norris Division	Lost Quarter-Final
1974-75	80	42	17	21	269	185	105	Second, Norris Division	Lost Preliminary Round
1973-74	78	33	33	12	233	231	78	Third, West Division	Lost Quarter-Final
1972-73	78	31	36	11	232	245	83	Sixth, West Division	Out of Playoffs
1971-70	78	20	49	9	206	305	49	Seventh, West Division	Out of Playoffs
1970-71	78	25	40	13	239	303	63	Fifth, West Division	Out of Playoffs
1969-70	76	14	52	10	168	290	78	Sixth, West Division	Out of Playoffs
1968-69	76	24	42	10	185	260	58	Fourth, West Division	Lost Semi-Final
1967-68	74	31	33	10	200	224	72	Second, West Division	Lost Quarter-Final

Charlie Simmer in control.

The National Hockey League was only recognizing the obvious when it selected Minneapolis-St. Paul as an expansion site. The land of summer lakes and winter ice has always been a hotbed of hockey interest, and even as the Metropolitan Sports Center was being built, everyone knew it would be sold out for the North Stars' games.

The NHL acted wisely in selecting a group headed by Walter Bush, Jr., to operate the franchise in the Twin Cities. Bush and his two key partners, Gordon Ritz and Robert McNulty, had run the Minneapolis entry in the Central Hockey League, and all had sound hockey backgrounds. They in turn moved adroitly in hiring Wren Blair to build their hockey club. As director of player personnel for the Boston Bruins, "the Bird," as Blair is called, had perched on the doorstep of the home of Mr. and Mrs. Doug Orr in Parry Sound, Ontario, until he had signed their 14-year-old prodigy. It later earned him the title of "DOBO," or "Discoverer of Bobby Orr."

Blair brought expertise, salesmanship, and color to the Minnesota franchise, and the club began impressively. In the expansion draft Blair

picked future stars Cesare Maniago and Bill Goldsworthy, neither of whom had flourished in the NHL, with New York and Boston respectively. Blair also had the foresight to court Montreal's Sam Pollock, who had more talent in the Canadiens' system than his team needed. Not above begging for a worthy cause, supplicant Blair managed to induce benefactor Pollock to part with Danny Grant, Jude Drouin, Ted Harris, Claude Larose, and Gump Worsley.

Blair also coached the team through its first three years, until a hospital visit forced him to retire from coaching after the 1969-70 season. By then the North Stars were solid playoff contenders. Under new coach Jackie Gordon, the club finished fourth, second, and third before Gordon retired, also because of ill health, and yielded the job to Parker MacDonald early in the 1973-74 season.

Unhindered by attendance considerations, Blair had the freedom to play youngsters in the hope that with the experience they would develop into stars. Some did. From 1969 through 1973, Goldsworthy scored an average of 32 goals a year and, with J. P. Parise, represented the North Stars on Team

Canada in its historic series with the Russians. Parise's 75 points during the 1972-73 season earned him a spot on the 1973 West Division All-Star team. Iron man Danny Grant, who played more than 400 consecutive games through 1973, averaged 29 goals a year. In 1968-69, Grant's 34 goals and 31 assists earned him Rookie of the Year honors. In 1972-73, Drouin blossomed with 27 goals and 46 assists, emerging as one of the NHL's finest centers. Dennis Hextall, obtained from California the year before, led all North Stars scorers with 30 goals and 52 assists. Hometown boy Lou Nanne became one of the team's most popular and effective performers, and Barry Gibbs developed into a rugged, heavy-hitting defenseman.

Although they've done well during the regular season, the North Stars have experienced some bitter luck in the Stanley Cup playoffs, especially against archrival St. Louis. In the 1968 semifinals, Minnesota was eliminated in double overtime of the deciding game when the Blues' Ron Schock scored on a breakaway against Maniago. In the 1971 quarterfinals, the North Stars were again the victims of an overtime goal,

Minnesota North Stars

this one by the Blues' Kevin O'Shea against Maniago.

From 1973-74 to 1978-79, Minnesota made the Stanley Cup playoffs only once (1977), and were eliminated in the preliminary round by the Buffalo Sabres. On February 10, 1978, Louis Nanne replaced John Gordon as general manager. Glen Sonmor took over from Henry ("Harry") Howell as coach on November 17, 1978; Bill Mahoney succeeded Sonmer in the 1983-84 season.

Since 1979-80, the North Stars have been in the Stanley Cup playoffs each season, and in 1980-81, even went as far as the Stanley Cup final series before losing to the New York Islanders. After 15 seasons of NHL action, the North Stars won their first division championship in 1981-82, but were eliminated in the division semifinals by the Chicago Black Hawks. In 1982-83 they were again losers to the Chicago Black Hawks, this time in the division finals.

The North Stars' most tragic loss occurred during a game midway through their initial season. Center Bill Masterton was skating at center ice when he collided with an opposing player, lost his balance, and fell backward, striking his head on the ice. His skull fractured, Masterton died a short time later. He is remembered each year through presentation of the Bill Masterton Memorial Trophy, which the Professional Hockey Writers' Association awards annually to "the National Hockey League player who best exemplifies the qualities of perseverance, sportsmanship, and dedication to hockey."

Bobby Smith flashes his style.

Team Records

Most Points 96	 1982-83
Most Wins 40	 1982-83
Most Ties. 22	 1969-70
Most Losses. 53	. . . . . 1975-76; 1977-78
Most Goals. 356	 1981-82
Most Goals Against . . 341	 1974-75

Individual Records

Most Points 114	Robert SmitH. . . 1981-82
Most Goals. 55	Dino Ciccarelli 1981-82
Most Assists. 71	Robert Smith . . 1981-82
Most Penalties in Minutes 187	Dennis O'Brien. . . .1975-76
Most Shutouts. 6	Cesare Maniago 1967-68

Murray Oliver unloads an off-balance slap shot.

Annual Records

Season	GP	W	L	T	GF	GA	Pts	Finished	Playoff Result
1982-83	80	40	24	16	321	290	96	Second, Norris Division	Lost Division Final
1981-82	80	37	23	20	346	288	94	First, Norris Division	Lost Division Semi-Final
1980-81	80	35	28	17	291	263	87	Third, Adams Division	Lost Final
1979-80	80	36	28	16	311	253	88	Third, Adams Division	Lost Semi-Final
1978-79	80	28	40	12	257	289	68	Fourth, Adams Divisio	Out of Playoffs
1977-78	80	18	53	6	218	325	45	Fifth, Smythe Divisio	Out of Playoffs
1976-77	80	23	39	18	240	310	64	Second, Smythe Division	Lost Preliminary Round
1975-76	80	20	53	7	195	303	47	Fourth, Smythe Division	Out of Playoffs
1974-75	80	23	50	7	221	341	53	Fourth, Smythe Division	Out of Playoffs
1973-74	78	23	38	17	235	275	63	Seventh, West Division	Out of Playoffs
1972-73	78	37	30	11	254	230	85	Third, West Division	Lost Quarter-Final
1971-70	78	37	29	12	212	191	86	Second, West Division	Lost Quarter-Final
1970-71	78	28	34	16	191	223	72	Fourth, West Division	Lost Semi-Final
1969-70	76	19	35	22	224	257	60	Third, West Division	Lost Quarter-Final
1968-69	76	18	43	15	189	270	51	Sixth, West Division	Out of Playoffs
1967-68	74	27	32	15	191	226	69	Fourth, West Division	Lost Semi-Final

The Montreal Canadiens spell their last name with an "e," a subtlety of which even the novice hockey fan need not be reminded. The hallowed name evokes images of toothless grins and champagne flowing from tall green bottles into a large silver bowl; of French-Canadian partisans, bundled in black overcoats and furs, flocking through dark snowy streets to toast yet another Montreal milestone. Anyone who has heard of professional hockey has heard of the triumphant Montreal Canadiens.

The Canadiens have reigned in hockey since Rocket Richard burst to prominence in the mid-forties. Stars such as Boom Boom Geoffrion, Jean Beliveau, Jacques Plante, and Henri Richard have embellished the tradition he began. In the recently renovated Montreal Forum, their home on St. Catherine Street in downtown Montreal,

the Canadiens of today work at their hockey with the diligence and zeal that their loyal but exacting patrons expect and their heritage demands. When they roll in upon their foes in endless waves, the Canadiens inspire their fans to roaring acclaim, which seems only to reinvigorate the players for yet another rush. When they score, the reaction is deafening. On the rare occasions when they dally, the crowd lapses into desultory silence.

From the rows of brilliant red Forum seats rising from the ice at an angle so steep that it is illegal in the United States, the fans peer down at the action with the scrutiny of a scientist examining a specimen. Their dissection of the game is not always pleasant for the home side to bear, especially if it loses. "Lose a game at home," Montreal winger John Ferguson once lamented, "and you just don't feel like going out afterward. It's a case of you preferring

not to see the fans, and of them preferring not to see you."

This hockey craze began innocuously enough one December night in 1909 when a Scottish baker suggested to an Irish contractor that a French-Canadian hockey team might find a following in Montreal. The Scot was James Strachan, who managed the Montreal Wanderers; the Irishman was an heir to railroad riches, Ambrose O'Brien, who owned a hockey team in Renfrew, Ontario. At first he sought to enter the team in the Eastern Canada League. When he was rejected, he founded the Montreal Canadiens, backed them with $5,000 to guarantee player salaries, entered them in a new league called the National Hockey Association, and persuaded Strachan to enter his Wanderers in the new league. The Canadiens played their first game on January 5, 1910, in Montreal's Jubilee Rink before a crowd of 3,000.

The 1930 Stanley Cup champions

Montreal Canadiens

They defeated Cobalt, Ontario, 7-6.

The Canadiens won only 2 of the 12 games they played that season, however, and the next year O'Brien sold the club to George Kennedy, a Montreal wrestler. When Kennedy died, in 1921, Louis Letourneau, Joe Cattarinich, and Leo Dandurand purchased the Canadiens for $11,000. In 1935, during the Depression, Dandurand sold the team for $165,000 to the Canadian Arena Company, which kept it for 22 years before selling to the Molson Brewing Company for more than $1 million.

Among the Canadiens' heroes in those early years were Newsy Lalonde, Howie Morenz, Aurel Joliat, and goalie Georges Vezina, popularly known as "the Chicoutimi Cucumber." The Vezina Trophy was established in his honor after he died of tuberculosis a few months after having collapsed during an NHL game on November 28, 1925.

In 1922, Dandurand, who was coaching the club, angered the team's followers by dealing Lalonde to the Saskatoon Sheiks for Aurel Joliat, a 140-pound forward with ulcers. The anger subsided when Joliat became one of the all-time Montreal heroes. A year after the controversial trade, Howie Morenz joined the team and helped lead it to the Stanley Cup.

On November 29, 1924, a capacity crowd of 9,500 christened the newly built Forum, and the Canadiens defeated the Toronto St. Patricks 7-1. But after a flurry of four league titles and two Stanley Cups in the late twenties and early thirties, the Canadiens slipped both in the standings and in attendance. When the Canadiens drew only 3,000 at one point during the Depression, Dandurand sold them.

In 1940, Dick Irvin was hired as coach after Conn Smythe had banished him from Toronto. Within four years the Canadiens were rising again, with Rocket Richard, Toe Blake, Elmer Lach, Butch Bouchard, and Bill Durnan. Montreal firmly established its winning tradition with four straight league championships and two Stanley Cups

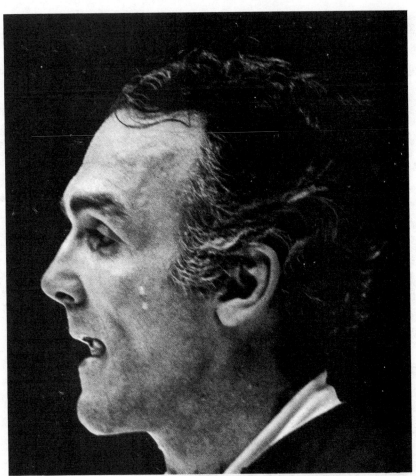

Henri Richard, the link with the past

High-scoring Jacques Lemaire charges goalward against Islanders.

56

from 1943-44 through 1946-47. It reaffirmed its dominance with a host of championship and Cup celebrations in the late fifties and throughout the sixties.

From May, 1964, until his retirement at the end of the 1977-78 season, Samuel Patterson Smyth Pollock was the Canadiens' guiding genius. During that time, Montreal won the Stanley Cup nine times. (They won again in 1979 when Irving Grundman was in charge).

In 1971-72, W. Scott Bowman took over coaching duties from Allister MacNeil, who had coached the Canadiens to a Stanley Cup victory the previous season. Montreal failed to win the Stanley Cup in Bowman's first season, but in 1973 the Canadiens continued their winning tradition by taking their twentieth championship and seventeenth Stanley Cup in 55 years. The Philadelphia Flyers took it in 1974 and 1975, after which Bowman coached the Canadiens to four consecutive Stanley Cup triumphs before departing for Buffalo.

Since then the club has been coached by Geoffrion, Claude Ruel, and Robert Berry, but it has not been able to win the Stanley Cup. In 1980, Montreal was defeated by the Minnesota North Stars when R. Alan MacAdam scored the winning goal in the third period of the seventh game of the quarterfinals. They exited early in 1981 when they lost to the Edmonton Oilers in the preliminary round. Nineteen eight-two saw them knocked out of contention by the Quebec Nordiques in their division semifinals. Again in 1983, they failed to get by their division semifinals when the Buffalo Sabres, recording two shutouts, eliminated them.

Team Records

Most Points	132	1976-77
Most Wins	60	1976-77
Most Ties	23	1962-63
Most Losses	33	1939-40
Most Goals	387	1976-77
Most Goals Against	286	1982-83

Individual Records

Most Points	136	Guy Lafleur 1976-77
		Stephen Shutt .. 1976-77
Most Goals	60	Guy Lafleur 1977-78
Most Assists	60	Peter Mahovlich ...1974-75
Most Penalties in Minutes	82	Christopher Nilan........1980-82
Most Shutouts	22	George Hainsworth..... 1928-29

Annual Records

Season	GP	W	L	T	GF	GA	Pts.	Finished	
1982-83	80	42	24	14	350	286	98	Second, Adams Division	Lost Division Semi-Final
1981-82	80	46	17	17	360	223	109	First, Norris Division	Lost Preliminary Round
1980-81	80	45	22	13	332	232	103	First, Norris Division	Lost Quarter-Final
1979-80	80	47	20	13	328	240	107	First, Norris Division	**Won Stanley Cup**
1978-79	80	50	17	11	337	204	115	First, Norris Division	**Won Stanley Cup**
1977-78	80	59	10	11	359	183	129	First, Norris Division	**Won Stanley Cup**
1976-77	80	60	8	12	387	171	132	First, Norris Division	**Won Stanley Cup**
1975-76	80	58	11	11	337	174	127	First, Norris Division	Lost Semi-Final
1974-75	80	47	14	19	374	225	113	Second, East Division	Lost Quarter-Final
1973-74	78	45	24	9	293	240	99	First, East Division	**Won Stanley Cup**
1972-73	78	52	10	16	329	184	120	First, East Division	**Won Stanley Cup**
1971-72	78	46	16	16	307	205	108	Third, East Division	Lost Quarter-Final
1970-71	78	42	23	13	291	216	97	Third, East Division	**Won Stanley Cup**
1969-70	76	38	22	16	244	201	92	Fifth, East Division	Out of Playoffs
1968-69	76	46	19	11	271	202	103	First, East Division	**Won Stanley Cup**
1967-68	74	42	22	10	236	167	94	First, East Division	**Won Stanley Cup**
1966-67	70	32	25	13	202	188	77	Second	Lost Final
1965-66	70	41	21	8	239	173	90	First	**Won Stanley Cup**
1964-65	70	36	23	11	211	185	83	Second	**Won Stanley Cup**
1963-64	70	36	21	13	209	167	85	First	Lost Semi-Final
1962-63	70	28	19	23	225	183	79	Third	Lost Semi-Final
1961-62	70	42	14	14	259	166	98	First	Lost Semi-Final
1960-61	70	41	19	10	254	188	92	First	Lost Semi-Final
1959-60	70	40	18	12	255	178	92	First	**Won Stanley Cup**
1958-59	70	39	18	13	258	158	91	First	**Won Stanley Cup**
1957-58	70	43	17	10	250	158	96	First	**Won Stanley Cup**
1956-57	70	35	23	12	210	155	82	Second	**Won Stanley Cup**
1955-56	70	45	15	10	222	131	100	First	**Won Stanley Cup**
1954-55	70	41	18	11	228	157	93	Second	Lost Final
1953-54	70	35	24	11	195	141	81	Second	Lost Final
1952-53	70	28	23	19	155	148	75	Second	**Won Stanley Cup**
1951-52	70	34	26	10	195	164	78	Second	Lost Final
1950-51	70	25	30	15	173	184	65	Third	Lost Final
1949-50	70	29	22	19	172	150	77	Second	Lost Semi-Final
1948-49	60	28	23	9	152	126	65	Third	Lost Semi-Final
1947-48	60	20	29	11	147	169	51	Fifth	Out of Playoffs
1946-47	60	34	16	10	189	138	78	First	Lost Final
1945-46	50	28	17	5	172	134	61	First	**Won Stanley Cup**
1944-45	50	38	8	4	228	121	80	First	Lost Semi-Final
1943-44	50	38	5	7	234	109	83	First	**Won Stanley Cup**
1942-43	50	19	19	12	181	191	50	Fourth	Lost Semi-Final
1941-42	48	18	27	3	134	173	39	Sixth	Lost Quarter-Final
1940-41	48	16	26	6	121	147	38	Sixth	Lost Quarter-Final
1939-40	48	10	33	5	90	167	25	Seventh	Out of Playoffs
1938-39	48	15	24	9	115	146	39	Sixth	Lost Quarter-Final
1937-38	48	18	17	13	123	128	49	Third, Canadian Division	Lost Quarter-Final
1936-37	48	24	18	6	115	111	54	First, Canadian Division	Lost Semi-Final
1935-36	48	11	26	11	82	123	33	Fourth, Canadian Division	Out of Playoffs
1934-35	48	19	23	6	110	145	44	Third, Canadian Division	Lost Quarter-Final
1933-34	48	22	20	6	99	101	50	Second, Canadian Division	Lost Quarter-Final
1932-33	48	18	25	5	92	115	41	Third, Canadian Division	Lost Quarter-Final
1931-32	48	25	16	7	128	111	57	First, Canadian Division	Lost Semi-Final
1930-31	44	26	10	8	129	89	60	First, Canadian Division	**Won Stanley Cup**
1929-30	44	21	14	9	142	114	51	Second, Canadian Division	**Won Stanley Cup**
1928-29	44	22	7	15	71	43	59	First, Canadian Division	Lost Semi-Final
1927-28	44	26	11	7	116	48	59	First, Canadian Division	Lost Semi-Final
1926-27	44	28	14	2	99	67	58	Second, Canadian Division	Lost Final
1925-26	36	11	24	1	79	108	23	Seventh	Out of Playoffs
1924-25	30	17	11	2	93	56	36	Third	Lost Cup Playoff
1923-24	24	13	11	0	59	48	26	Second	**Won Stanley Cup**
1922-23	24	13	9	2	73	61	28	Second	Lost NHL Playoff
1921-22	24	12	11	1	88	94	25	Third	Out of Playoffs
1920-21	24	13	11	0	112	99	26	Third	Out of Playoffs
1919-20	24	13	11	0	129	113	26	Second	Out of Playoffs
1918-19	18	10	8	0	88	78	20	Second	Cup Final but no decision
1917-18	22	13	9	0	115	84	26	First and Third*	Lost NHL Final

*Season played in two halves with no combined standing at end.

This franchise may at last have found a permanent home in East Rutherford, New Jersey. Originally granted to Kansas City on June 11, 1974, the Kansas City Scouts played for two seasons in the Crosby Kemper Memorial Arena to an average attendance of only 6,821 for each game. On August 25, 1976, the franchise moved west to Denver, Colorado, where the club was known as the Colorado Rockies. Playing in the McNichols Sports Arena for six seasons, average attendance was 7,451.

The franchise has been less than a success. During its eight seasons, it has made the Stanley Cup playoffs only once (1978), and was eliminated in the preliminary round by the Philadelphia Flyers.

While in Kansas City and in Denver, the club played in the Conn Smythe Division, but since moving to New Jersey it has been in the Lester Patrick Division along with the other New York area clubs—the New York Islanders and the New York Rangers. In the Devils' first season, they finished fifth, three points ahead of the Pittsburgh Penguins; their average attendance in the Byrne Meadowlands Arena was 13,244. William Stewart MacMillan is general manager and coach.

Mel Bridsman eludes pursuing Greschner.

Team Records

Most Points	48	1982-83
Most Wins	17	1982-83
Most Ties	14	1982-83
Most Losses	49	1982-83
Most Goals	230	1982-83
Most Goals Against	338	1982-83

Individual Records

Most Points	55	Aaron Broten	1982-83
Most Goals	25	Steven	
Most Assists	40	Tambellini	1982-83
Most Penalties in Minutes	136	Tapio Levo	1982-83
Most Shutouts	0	Yvon Vautour	1982-83

Annual Records

Season	GP	W	L	T	GF	GA	Pts.	Finished	
1982-83	80	17	49	14	230	338	48	Fifth, Patrick Division	Out of Playoffs

New Jersey Devils

Ken Daneyko lifts the puck free.

Like the first major league settlers on Long Island, baseball's Mets, the New York Islanders began as record-breaking losers. In their first year in the National Hockey League, the Islanders won only 12 games, lost 60, and tied 6. Permitting more than two goals for every one they scored themselves (347 to 170), the Islanders finished a distant last in the NHL's East Division.

In hockey, however, matchless incompetence can have its benefits. Hockey's worst team receives first choice in the next year's amateur draft, if it hasn't traded away the privilege, as Bill Torrey, the Islanders' general manager, was careful not to do. To the Islanders first choice meant Denis Potvin, who was heralded as the finest defenseman to graduate from junior hockey since the New York Rangers' Brad Park. On Long Island Potvin joined another fine young prospect, Billy Harris, whom the Islanders had picked first in the expansion draft the year before. With these and other assets, the Islanders learned to forget their traumatic beginning in the National Hockey League.

Long Island's entrance into the NHL had been an expensive proposition. To join the league it had cost six million dollars for the franchise plus five million dollars indemnity to Manhattan's Rangers. The man behind the Islanders was Roy L. M. Boe, who a few years earlier had established another major league franchise on Long Island, the New York Nets of the American Basketball Association. Boe picked Torrey as the Islanders' general manager, impressed by Torrey's ability and experience with the California (then Oakland) Seals. That club reached the playoffs in Torrey's two years as its executive vice-president. The Islanders would be a more discouraging case. "The first year was a tough one," said Torrey. "Nobody likes to lose, but it kills you to lose as much as we did."

Despite their horrendous play, the Islanders drew well in their first year in the Nassau Veterans Memorial Coliseum. Harris showed flashes of

Denis Potvin, symbol of Islanders' new strength

brilliance in scoring 28 goals and 22 assists. Ed Westfall, after years with the Boston Bruins, was a steadying influence on the younger players. He finished 1972-73 with 46 points—15 goals and 31 assists.

After ruining the coaching debuts of their first two coaches, Phil Goyette and Earl Ingarfield, the Islanders seemed finally to respond to Al Arbour, who presided over a definite improvement in the club in 1973-74. In 15 years as a player and coach, Arbour had never missed the playoffs. Arbour coached the St. Louis Blues for parts of

two seasons, recording a 21-15-14 record before returning as a player in the stretch drive of 1970-71. The following year he took over the Blues in last place in December and boosted them to third by season's end. "Al Arbour," said Torrey, who should know, "is a coach who knows what an expansion club has to go through to mature."

In almost every respect the Islanders were a better team in their second year than they had been in their first. In addition to Denis Potvin, who made the East Division All-Star team, brother Jean Potvin, young Dave Lewis, and veteran

New York Islanders

Bert Marshall gave the team a respectable defense. For the front line the Islanders unveiled two promising rookies: Bob Nystrom and Andre St. Laurent. Ralph Stewart, obtained from Detroit near the end of 1972-73, shone in the early season before an injury sidelined him.

The Islanders were still far from the playoff contenders that Arbour was used to, but their fans were patient, confident of further improvement. Bill Torrey summarized the optimistic mood. ''I got the feeling we learned a lot [in our first year], and we've got a lot of potential,'' he said. ''All we have to do is keep improving and progressing.''

Long Island sports fans needn't have been reminded that it could be done. Baseball's Mets, who had begun no better than the Islanders, had dramatically proved that point. Indeed, in the 1974-75 season, the Islanders finished third in the Lester Patrcik Division, and since then they have won four Lester Patrick Division championships, finished second four times, and won the Stanley Cup four times.

The club's success is partly due to shrewd drafting. In 1975, they chose Clark Gillies and Bryan Trottier, both of whom provod to be outstanding players. Each has been selected twice for the first All-Star Team. Then in 1977 Dwight Foster, who was highly rated by all clubs, was passed over in favor of Mike Bossy. Bossy has scored over 300 goals (never fewer than 50 in a season and on four occasions 60 goals or more), while Foster has yet to score 100. Dennis Potvin, the Islanders' skilled defenseman, has been selected five times for the fisrt All-Star Team, and once for the second All-Star Team.

Annual Records

Season	GP	W	L	T	GF	GA	Pts	Finished	Playoff Result
1982-83								Second, Patrick Division	**Won Stanley Cup**
1981-82	80	42	26	12	302	226	96	First, Patrick Division	**Won Stanley Cup**
1980-81	80	54	16	10	385	250	118	First, Patrick Division	**Won Stanley Cup**
1979-80	80	48	18	14	355	260	110	Second, Patrick Division	**Won Stanley Cup**
1978-79	80	39	28	13	281	247	91	First, Patrick Division	Lost Semi-Final
1977-78	80	51	15	14	358	214	116	First, Patrick Division	Lost Quarter-Final
1976-77	80	48	17	15	334	210	110	Second, Patrick Division	Lost Semi-Final
1975-76	80	47	21	12	288	193	106	Second, Patrick Division	Lost Semi-Final
1974-75	80	42	21	17	297	190	101	Third, Patrick Division	Lost Semi-Final
1973-74	80	33	25	22	264	247	56	Eighth, East Division	Out of Playoffs
1972-73	78	12	60	6	170	347	30	Eighth, East Division	Out of Playoffs

Mike Bossy takes the slot.

Team Records

Most Points 118	. . . .	1981-82
Most Wins 54	. . . .	1981-82
Most Ties. 22	. . . .	1974-75
Most Losses. . . . : . . . 60	. . . .	1972-73
Most Goals. 385	. . . .	1981-82
Most Goals Against . . 347	. . . .	1972-73

Individual Records

Most Points 147	Mike Bossy	1981-82
Most Goals. 69	Mike Bossy	1978-79
Most Assists . . . . . : . . 87	Bryan Trottier . . .	1978-79
Most Penalties in Minutes		
219	Garry Howatt . . .	1979-80
Most Shutouts. 7	Glenn Resch . . .	1975-76

The early seventies have found the New York Rangers in the midst of their most successful period since the early forties, when the era of Frank Boucher, Bill and Bun Cook, and Muzz and Lynn Patrick drew to a close. In almost 60 years of National Hockey League competition, New York had won only three league titles and three Stanley Cups—by far the worst record of any established club. But at last the Rangers were getting themselves invited to that spring wedding party known as the playoffs, and hoping that soon they might surprise everyone with a summer honeymoon.

The man most responsible for the Rangers' revival was Emile Francis, a small former Rangers goaltender who grew in stature when he became their coach and general manager. After taking control of the Rangers in the mid-sixties, Francis built a farm system that produced stars such as Brad Park, Walt Tkaczuk, and Steve Vickers, the 1973 Rookie of the Year. In perhaps his single most important move, he imported from Providence goalie Ed Giacomin, soon to become one of the Rangers' most durable stars as well as one of their most brilliant. Later he acquired savvy and maturity in trades for Pete Stemkowski, Bruce MacGregor, and Bobby Rousseau. As coach, Francis developed the considerable talents of Jean Ratelle, Rod Gilbert, Rod Seiling, and Gilles Villemure.

New York fans had grown impatient with the Rangers for the titles and Cups they had narrowly missed in recent years. In their anger, they sometimes forgot that before Francis arrived they would have been more than content for their then-hapless Rangers to reach the playoffs. That at least Francis had given them.

The New York Rangers are the legacy of George Lewis ("Tex") Rickard, a slick fight promoter who organized the Madison Square Garden Corporation in 1925. Searching for attractions to book in the new arena on Fiftieth Street and Eighth Avenue, Rickard noted with interest the impact that a professional

hockey team called the New York Americans had had on the city. So on November 17, 1926, New York's second hockey team, dubbed "Tex's Rangers," made its debut at the Garden, defeating the Montreal Maroons 1-0. At Rickard's request, Colonel John S. Hammond operated the club. He originally hired Conn Smythe to build the team, then opted for Lester Patrick.

With Frank Boucher, the brothers Cook, and Ching Johnson, the Rangers enjoyed great success in their formative years. They finished in first place in 1926-27 and again in 1931-32, and were always contenders for the NHL's American Division title. After coach

The last New York Stanley Cup winners

Ron Greschner ties up the Devils.

New York Rangers

Patrick made a desperation appearance in goal in the final round of the playoffs against the Montreal Maroons in 1928, the Rangers won their first Stanley Cup. They repeated in 1933.

By this time the rivalry between the Rangers and Americans had grown as intense as the feuding between baseball's Brooklyn Dodgers and New York Giants. From a financial standpoint, the Rangers had a huge advantage in the battle with their Garden competition: the Rangers played rent-free, but the Garden bosses kept raising the rent on the Americans. In 1942, the Americans folded, an unkind fate for a team that had played a vital role in the history of hockey in New York and had inspired the formation of the Rangers.

The Rangers finished in second place from 1938 through 1940 and won their third Cup in 1940. But after the club won the league title in 1941-42, World War II sapped the squad. Thirteen players went to war, and starting in 1942-43, the Rangers finished last five times in seven years. A 15-0 loss to Detroit on January 23, 1944, began a string of 25 games without a victory (21 losses, 4 ties).

The farm system, which Frank Boucher had established, produced youngsters Andy Bathgate, Harry Howell, Dean Prentice, and Lou Fontinato, who lifted the Rangers into the playoffs in 1956, '57, and '58. And in 1961-62, Doug Harvey, the former Montreal star, played and coached the club into the playoffs again. Another woeful period followed, however, and by the time the Rangers finished last in 1965-66, Emile Francis had been given a mandate to refashion the team.

The team Francis commanded at the start was, at its best, artful, but it lacked stamina and hardly intimidated its opponents. Francis immediatley filled Broadway's blue shirts with the muscle of Reg Fleming and Orland Kurtenbach and imparted a winning spirit to youngsters Rod Gilbert and Jean Ratelle. He gambled and won on minor league goaltender Ed Giacomin. As coach and general manager, Francis spurred the Rangers to fourth place in 1966-67 and to second the next year, only four points behind champion Montreal.

After at last reaching the Stanley Club finals against the Boston Bruins in 1972, the Rangers began a steady decline and in 1975-76 and 1976-77 failed to make the Stanley Cup playoffs at all. On January 7, 1976, John Ferguson replaced Emile Francis as general manager. Francis, who was also vice-president of the Rangers, remained until the end of the season and then joined the St. Louis Blues in April 1976. Ferguson left at the end of the 1977-78 seson, and Frederick Shero, who had coached the Philadelphia Flyers to two consecutive Stanley Cup victories in 1974 and 1975, took over as general manager and coach. Two Swedes, Anders Hedberg and Ulf Nilsson, were lured away from the World Hockey Association, and the Rangers again went to the Stanley Cup final series, this time against the Montreal Canadiens.

On November 21, 1980, Craig Patrick (son of Lynn Patrick and grandson of Lester Patrick) replaced Shero; in 1981-82 Herbert Brooks, who had coached the victorious United States Olympic club in 1980, was named coach.

Many of the players so prominent under Francis are gone—Giacomin was waived to Detroit on October 31, 1975; Park and Ratelle were traded to Boston on November 6, 1975; and Gilbert played 19 games in 1977-78 before retiring. Since 1967-68, the Rangers have gone to the Stanley Cup finals only twice and have yet to win a division title. But their loyal patrons continue to pass through the turnstiles at an average rate of 16,885 per game.

Annual Records

Season	GP	W	L	T	GF	GA	Pts	Finished	Playoff Result
1982-83	80	35	35	10	306	287	80	Fourth, Patrick Division	Lost Division Final
1981-82	80	39	27	14	316	306	92	Second, Patrick Division	Lost Division Final
1980-81	80	30	36	14	312	317	74	Fourth, Patrick Division	Lost Semi-Final
1979-80	80	38	32	10	308	284	86	Third, Patrick Division	Lost Quarter-Final
1978-79	80	40	29	11	316	292	91	Third, Patrick Division	Lost Final
1977-78	80	30	37	13	279	280	73	Fourth, Patrick Division	Lost Preliminary Round
1976-77	80	29	37	14	272	310	72	Fourth, Patrick Division	Out of Playoffs
1975-76	80	29	42	9	262	333	67	Fourth, Patrick Division	Out of Playoffs
1974-75	80	37	29	14	319	276	88	Second, Patrick Division	Lost Preliminary Round
1973-74	78	40	24	14	300	251	94		
1972-73	78	47	23	8	297	208	102	Third, East	Lost Semi-Final
1971-70	78	48	17	13	317	192	109	Third, East Division	Lost Semi-Final
1970-71	78	49	18	11	259	177	109	Second, East Division	Lost Final
1969-70	76	38	22	16	246	189	92	Second, East Division	Lost Semi-Final
1968-69	76	41	26	9	231	196	91	Fourth, East Division	Lost Quarter-Final
1967-68	74	39	23	12	226	183	90	Third, East Division	Lost Quarter-Final
1966-67	70	30	28	12	188	189	72	Second, East Division	Lost Quarter-Final
1965-66	70	18	41	11	195	261	47	Fourth	Lost Semi-Final
1964-65	70	20	38	12	179	246	52	Sixth	Out of Playoffs
1963-64	70	22	38	10	186	242	54	Fifth	Out of Playoffs
1962-63	70	22	36	12	211	233	56	Fifth	Out of Playoffs
1961-62	70	26	32	12	195	207	64	Fifth	Out of Playoffs
1960-61	70	22	38	10	204	248	54	Fourth	Lost Semi-Final
1959-60	70	17	38	15	187	247	49	Fifth	Out of Playoffs
1958-61	70	26	32	12	201	217	64	Sixth	Out of Playoffs
1957-58	70	32	25	13	195	188	77	Second	Lost Semi-Final
1956-57	70	26	30	14	184	277	66	Fourth	Lost Semi-Final
1955-56	70	32	28	10	204	203	74	Third	Lost Semi-Final
1954-55	70	17	35	18	150	210	52	Fifth	Out of Playoffs
1953-54	70	29	31	10	161	182	68	Fifth	Out of Playoffs
1952-53	70	17	37	16	152	212	50	Sixth	Out of Playoffs
1951-52	70	23	34	13	192	219	59	Fifth	Out of Playoffs
1950-51	70	20	29	21	169	201	61	Fifth	Out of Playoffs
1949-50	70	28	31	11	170	189	67	Fourth	Lost Final
1948-49	60	18	31	11	133	172	47	Sixth	Out of Playoffs
1947-48	60	21	26	13	176	201	55	Fourth	Lost Semi-Final
1946-47	60	22	32	6	167	186	0	Fifth	Out of Playoffs
1945-46	50	13	28	9	144	191	35	Sixth	Out of Playoffs
1944-45	50	11	29	10	154	247	32	Sixth	Out of Playoffs
1943-44	50	6	39	5	162	310	17	Sixth	Out of Playoffs
1942-43	50	11	31	8	161	253	30	Sixth	Out of Playoffs
1941-42	48	29	17	2	177	143	60	First	Lost Semi-Final
1940-41	48	21	19	8	143	125	50	Fourth	Lost Quarter-Final
1939-40	48	27	11	10	136	77	64	Second	**Won Stanley Cup**
1938-39	48	26	16	6	149	105	58	Second	Lost Semi-Final
1937-38	48	27	15	6	149	96	60	Second, American Division	Lost Quarter-Final
1936-37	48	19	20	9	117	106	47	Third, American Division	Lost Final
1935-36	48	19	17	12	91	96	50	Fourth, American Division	Out of Playoffs
1934-35	48	22	20	6	137	139	50	Third, American Division	Lost Semi-Final
1933-34	48	21	19	8	120	113	50	Third, American Division	Lost Quarter-Final
1932-33	48	23	17	8	135	107	54	Third, American Division	**Won Stanley Cup**
1931-32	48	23	17	8	134	112	54	First, American Division	Lost Final
1930-31	44	9	16	9	106	87	47	Third, American Division	Lost Semi-Final
1929-30	44	17	17	10	136	143	44	Third, American Division	Lost Semi-Final
1928-29	44	21	13	10	t 2	65	52	Second, American Division	Lost Final
1927-28	44	19	16	9	94	79	47	Second, American Division	**Won Stanley Cup**
1926-27	44	25	13	6	95	72	56	First, American Division	Lost Quarter-Final

Although the Philadelphia Flyers had the honor of winning the first West Division title in the National Hockey League, their days of true glory didn't arrive until 1972-73, when they became known as "the Broad Street Bullies" and "the Mad Squad." A young, tough team eager for brawls and undeterred by penalties, Philadelphia finished second to the Chicago Black Hawks that season. Amidst the rowdies, who made up with overenthusiasm what they lacked in skill, a core of equally colorful but more talented players led the Flyers' resurgence. Bobby Clarke became the first player from an expansion team to win the NHL's most valuable player award, the Hart Trophy. Rick MacLeish, a 23-year-old in his first full year in the NHL, scored 50 goals and 50 assists. Bill Barber, the Flyers' top draft pick, led all rookie scorers with 30 goals and 34 assists. Bill Flett got 43 goals, Clarke 37, and Gary Dornhoefer 30. The chief roughnecks were Dave ("the Hammer") Schultz, Bob ("the Hound") Kelly, Don Saleski, and Andre ("Moose") Dupont, each of whom generously contributed to the Flyers' new NHL record for penalty minutes: 1,752.

Before the 1972-73 season, the Flyers had been a lackluster team. They usually made the playoffs, but they did it with a dreary defensive style that emphasized the club's embarrassing lack of scoring punch.

As a team, their most famous exploit was an extracurricular activity: they literally lost their home. In late February of 1968, a strong wind ripped a hole in the roof of the Spectrum, the Flyers' arena. On March 1, another storm left the Spectrum with almost no roof at all, forcing the authorities to close the building. For a while, the homeless Flyers became hockey barnstormers. They played a "home" game in New York's Madison Square Garden and another in Toronto's Maple Leaf Gardens before deciding to complete their season in Quebec City, the site of their top farm club. Despite their mishaps, the Flyers managed to finish in first place. Then the Spectrum

was repaired in time for the Stanley Cup playoffs, and Philadelphia bowed in the quarterfinals to St. Louis.

In its early years Philadelphia simply depended too heavily on the goaltending of Bernie Parent and Doug Favell. Both were prime young prospects, but neither had the experience to stake a firm claim to the number-one job. In 1971, Parent jumped to the World Hockey Association, where he immediately became one of the richest, if not one of the happiest young men in North America. The Flyers reacquired him 2½ years later by

trading Favell to the Toronto Maple Leafs, who had acquired the rights to Parent when he split with the WHA.

"I never wanted to leave the Flyers in the first place," said Parent. "I guess I always considered myself a Flyer, even though I wasn't here." In the first half of 1973-74, the prodigal son made a triumphant return with outstanding goaltending that helped boost the Flyers to the top of the West Division standings. Most of the groundwork for the success of the Flyers had been done in his absence, however. Before the 1971-72 season, Philadelphia had landed coach Fred

Captain Bobby Clarke leads the Flyers.

Philadelphia Flyers

Shero, who had compiled an outstanding record in the farm system of the New York Rangers. Keith Allen, a former Flyers coach, had become a keen general manager. He had slowly but surely filled the ranks by making shrewd trades and organizing a scouting system that discovered Clarke, Barber, and defenseman Tom Bladon.

With the success of 1972-73 and the return of Parent, Philadelphia fans developed a clamorous style in support of their heroes. Their enthusiasm was rewarded when Philadelphia's steady improvement reached its apex in 1974 with the winning of the Stanley Cup. The Atlanta Flames were their first opponents; Philadelphia won that series in four straight games. (On the evening of April 13, coach Shero decided to take a little stroll and, no doubt, contemplate the upcoming fourth game of the series, scheduled for the following night. While on this leisurely walk through the streets of Atlanta he was attacked by hoodlums. Shero fled to the safety of Philadelphia as quickly as possible, leaving assistant coach Michael Nykoluk to coach game number four.

The Flyers' next opponents for the Cup were the New York Rangers; this series went the full seven games. In the fourth game, W. Barry Ashbee lost the use of his right eye when struck by Dale Rolfe's shot. His playing career was over, but Philadelphia retained him as an assistant coach until he died of leukemia in May, 1977.

The next and final series was with the Boston Bruins. This series went six games, with Philadelphia winning the final game 1-0 on Rick MacLeish's goal in the first period.

The Flyers again won the Stanley Cup in 1975. This time the Toronto Maple Leafs were their first opponents. They won four straight games—two of them by shutouts. It took them seven games to down the pesky New York Islanders, and another six before the Buffalo Sabres were eliminated.

After cocahing the Philadelphia Flyers for seven seasons, Fred Shero was lured away by the New York

Annual Records

Season	GP	W	L	T	GF	GA	Pts	Finished	
1982-83	80	49	23	8	326	240	106	First, Patrick Division	Lost Division Semi-Final
1981-82	80	38	31	11	325	313	87	Third, Patrick Division	Lost Division Semi-Final
1980-81	80	41	24	15	313	249	97	Second, Patrick Division	Lost Quarter-Final
1979-80	80	48	12	20	327	254	116	First, Patrick Division	Lost Semi-Final
1978-79	80	40	25	15	281	248	95	Second, Patrick Division	Lost Quarter-Final
1977-78	80	45	20	15	296	200	105	Second, Patrick Division	Lost Semi-Final
1976-77	80	48	16	16	323	213	132	First, Patrick Division	Lost Semi-Final
1975-76	80	51	13	16	348	209	118	First, Patrick Division	Lost Semi-Final
1974-75	80	51	18	11	293	181	113	First, Patrick Division	**Won Stanley Cup**
1973-74	78	50	16	12	273	164	112	First, West Division	**Won Stanley Cup**
1972-73	78	37	30	11	296	256	85	Second, West Division	Lost Semi-Final
1971-70	78	26	38	14	200	236	66	Fifth, West Division	Out of Playoffs
1970-71	78	28	33	17	207	225	73	Third, West Division	Out of Playoffs
1969-70	76	17	35	24	197	225	58	Fifth, West Division	Out of Playoffs
1968-69	76	20	35	21	174	225	61	Third, West Division	Lost Quarter-Final
1967-68	74	31	32	11	173	179	73	First, West Division	Lost Quarter-Final

1983-84 Flyers were the only team to don long pants.

Rangers. (Shero had his troubles in New York, too. On Christmas Day, 1979, just two days before the Rangers were scheduled to host Russia's Central Army club, Shero took a tumble and cracked four ribs. Once again his trusty assistant coach Michael Nykoluk, who had left Philadelphia with him, came to the rescue.

Since Shero's departure, the Flyers have been coached by Robert McCammon, followed by Pat Quinn, and then McCammon again.

Team Records

Most Points 118	. . . .	1975-76
Most Wins 51	. . . .	1974-75
Most Ties. 24	. . . .	1969-70
Most Losses. 38	. . . .	1971-72
Most Goals. 348	. . . .	1975-76
Most Goals Against . . 313	. . . .	1981-82

Individual Records

Most Points 119	Bobby Clarke . . .	1975-76
Most Goals. 61	Reginald Leach . . .	1975-76'
Most Assists 89	Bobby Clarke	1974-75; 1975-76
Most Penalties in Minutes 472	Dave Schultz . . .	1974-75
Most Shutouts. 12	Bernie Parent.	1973-74; 1974-75

The Steel City's National Hockey League Penguins have flopped as often as the unsteady creatures after whom they are named, but the capacity crowds that have filled the Civic Center are proof that the area is interested in hockey. Like so many other cities, it asks only for a contender. Pittsburgh had an NHL franchise, the Pirates, back in the late twenties, and when they contended for the playoffs, the fans supported them. But after the team won a total of 14 games in 1928-29 and 1929-30, few tears were shed when the club moved to Philadelphia.

Then came the Pittsburgh Hornets, an American Hockey League team that won a fair share of games and supporters with youngsters who were being groomed for the NHL's Detroit Red Wings and later the Toronto Maple Leafs. So successful were the Hornets in their last years (they won the AHL title and Calder Cup in 1966-67) that some fans resented the NHL's intrusion into Pittsburgh, which forced the Hornets to depart. Many Pittsburgh hockey fans preferred a minor league winner to the possibility of a big league loser.

Accurately assessing the area's mood, Penguins general manager Jack Reily said, "Our fans aren't interested in a building program. They're used to winners. I think we've got to put a quality product on the ice right from the beginning. I'm aware of some of the potential problems in going for experience, but. . . ."

Experience meant older players, of course. When the Penguins had fininshed drafting, they had the oldest team in the league—an average age of 32. One of their oldest was Andy Bathgate, 35, who had starred for so many years with the New York Rangers. He proved he could still produce when he led all West Division scorers with 20 goals and 59 assists—one of the few bright spots in the Penguins' dismal inaugural season. Though the Penguins won their last four games, they still missed the fourth and final playoff spot in the final week. Critics pointed to the club's season-long inability to win at home. Trying to explain why the club had managed only 15 wins at the Civic Center, Bathgate said, "Maybe we're just too tight at home. We knew how important it was to impress our fans at home, and maybe we just tried too hard."

Rumors that the Penguins were for sale and might even move flourished throughout that first year. Soon after the season ended, the rumors proved to be well founded: a Michigan syndicate headed by banker Donald Parsons purchased 80 percent of the team's stock. Pittsburgh finished fifth again in 1968-69, but then Riley hired Red Kelly as coach. The former NHL All-Star had done wonders with the Los Angeles Kings but was less successful in his relations with his boss, Jack Kent Cooke.

Kelly immediately lifted the Penguins to second place in 1969-70, and as expected, Steel City fans came out to watch and cheer. One of their favorites was a 21-year-old center named Michel Briere, who was clearly a player with enough talent to justify building a team around him. Not long after the Penguins were eliminated from the playoffs, however, Briere was involved in an autombile accident that eventually cost him his life. Shaken by the loss of Briere, the Penguins skidded to sixth

Andy Brown keeps mask off and puck out.

Pittsburgh Penguins

place, and in 1971 were sold again, this time to a Pittsburgh group headed by Thayer Potter. Led by promising youngsters Greg Polis, Jean Pronovost, Syl Apps, Jr., and Bryan Hextall, Jr. (the last two sons of Hall of Famers), Pittsburgh finished fourth in 1971-72. The next year, however, Kelly was fired after a series of disputes with management and replaced by Ken Schinkel, who had played for the Penguins since their inception. The change in coaches produced no improvement, however. In 1972-73, Pittsburgh finished fifth, and when the club continued to flounder through the first half of 1973-74, Schinkel was dispatched.

The Penguins failed to reach the Stanley Cup playoffs in 1973-74, but in 1975 went to the quarterfinals before losing to the New York Islanders. Wren Blair became general manager in 1975-76, but was replaced by Aldege ("Baz") Bastien, a former goaltender whose playing career had ended on December 1, 1976, with the loss of an eye.

Coach Schinkel was replaced by Marc Boileau on February 6, 1974; he in turn was dismissed on January 16, 1976, and the Penguins again turned to Schinkel, who coached the club for the rest of the season and through 1976-77. In 1977-78, John Wilson was named coach and retained the position for three seasons. Another former goaltender, Edward Johnston, became coach in 1980-81.

Bastien was killed in an auto accident in March, 1983, and the Penguins started their 1983-84 season with Johnston as general manager and Louis Angotti as coach. The future won't be easy—Pittsburgh had the worst record of all 21 clubs in 1982-83.

Annual Records

Season	GP	W	L	T	GF	GA	Pts	Finished	Playoff Result
1982-83	80	18	53	9	257	394	45	Sixth, Patrick Division	Out of Playoffs
1981-82	80	31	36	13	310	337	75	Fourth, Patrick Division	Lost Division Semi-Final
1980-81	80	30	37	13	302	345	73	Third, Norris Division	Lost Preliminary Round
1979-80	80	30	37	13	251	303	73	Third, Norris Division	Lost Preliminary Round
1978-79	80	36	31	13	281	279	85	Second, Norris Division	Lost Quarter-Final
1977-78	80	25	37	18	254	321	68	Fourth, Norris Division	Out of Playoffs
1976-77	80	34	33	13	240	252	81	Third, Norris Division	Lost Preliminary Round
1975-76	80	35	33	12	339	303	82	Third, Norris Division	Lost Quarter-Final
1974-75	80	37	28	15	326	289	89	Fifth, West Division	Out of Playoffs
1973-74	78	28	41	9	242	273	65		
1972-73	78	32	37	9	257	265	73	Fifth, West Division	Out of Playoffs
1971-70	78	26	38	14	220	258	66	Fourth, West Division	Out of Playoffs
1970-71	78	21	37	20	221	240	62	Sixth, West Division	Out of Playoffs
1969-70	76	26	38	12	182	238	64	Second, West Division	Lost Semi-Final
1968-69	76	20	45	11	189	252	51	Fifth, West Division	Out of Playoffs
1967-68	74	27	34	13	195	216	67	Fifth, West Division	Out of Playoffs

Team Records

Most Points	89	1974-75
Most Wins	37	1974-75
Most Ties	20	1970-71
Most Losses	53	1982-83
Most Goals	339	1975-76
Most Goals Against	394	1982-83

Individual Records

Most Points	111	Pierre Larouche	1975-76
Most Goals	55	Rick Kehoe	1980-81
Most Assists	67	Syl Apps	1975-76
		Randy Carlyle	1980-81
Most Penalties in Minutes	409	Paul Baxter	1981-82
Most Shutouts	6	Les Binkley	1967-68

The Quebec Bulldogs faded from the NHL scene at the end of the 1919-20 season after finishing last in both halves of a split schedule. The Bulldogs had been one of the clubs granted a franchise when the NHL was formed on November 22, 1917, but they didn't ice a club during the first two seasons. They had been a noted club many years earlier and had won the Stanley Cup for two successive seasons (1912 and 1913) with such famous players as "Bad Joe" Hall, Joe Malone, John Marks, Paddy Moran, and Walter Rooney.

Sixty years later Quebec again entered the NHL with a club called the Nordiques (Northerners). Playing in the Charles F. Adams Division the Nordiques failed to reach the Stanley Cup playoffs in their first season, but finished fourth in each of the next three seasons.

Maurice Filion is their general manager, and since October 20, 1980, Joseph Robert Michel Bergeron has been their coach.

Annual Records

Season	GP	W	L	T	GF	GA	Pts.	Finished	Playoff Result
1982-83	80	34	34	12	343	336	80	Fourth, Adams Division	Lost Semi-Final
1981-82	80	33	31	16	356	345	82	Fourth, Adams Division	Lost Conf. Championship
1980-81	80	30	32	18	314	318	78	Fourth, Adams Division	Lost Perliminary Round
1979-80	80	25	44	11	248	313	61	Fifth, Adams Division	

Czech Marian Stastny provides Nordique punch.

Team Records
Most Points 82 1981-82
Most Wins 34 1982-83
Most Ties 18 1980-81
Most Losses 44 1979-80
Most Goals 356 1981-82
Most Goals Against . . 345 1981-82

Individual Records
Most Points . . . . 139 Peter Stastny . . . 1981-82
Most Goals . . . . 57 Michel Goulet . . . 1982-83
Most Assists . . . . 93 Peter Stastny . . . 1981-82
                            Dale Hunter 1981-82
Most Penalties in Minutes
                    272 Michel Dion 1979-80
                        Daniel
Most Shutouts . . . . 2 Bouchard 1980-81

Quebec Nordiques

Wesley and Bouchard make the stop.

One of the more remarkable stories in the history of the National Hockey League is that of the St. Louis Blues. What originally began as a thinly disguised attemt by the NHL establishment to placate one if its members in good standing, Chicago owner Arthur Wirtz, became, to the surpirse and delight of everyone involved, the most inspirational selection of a franchise site in the NHL's expansion.

In the early summer of 1966, five of the orginal six expansion berths had already been filled. Several cities, each boasting impressive qualifications, were keenly vying for the sixth franchise when word spread that the NHL would choose St. Louis if it could find buyers for both the franchise and a dingy, smelly barn in the city, the Arena. For years the Arena had been used for little more than circuses, and it was anything but a showcase for a hockey team. Its owner, however, was a man with connections—Wirtz, who now saw a chance to unload it at a tidy profit, of course. There were a number of rich hockey nuts in the St. Louis area who were interested in buying a hockey team, but at first sight, or smell, of the building, they lost their interest.

It looked as if the NHL would have to go elsewhere with its franchise and Wirtz would have to keep his malodorous building. But then Sidney Salomon, Jr., and his son, Sid III, stepped forward. A former sportswriter who had forsaken his typewriter for a lucrative career in the insurance business, Salomon had some powerful connections in the St. Louis area. He was the man who had been most responsible for placing a fellow Missourian, Harry S. Truman, on the Democratic ticket in 1944, and he had maintained strong political ties as treasurer of the Democratic National Committee in the early fifties. His sports background was equally impressive. A baseball and golf enthusiast himself, Salomon had served on the board of directors of the St. Louis Cardinals and St. Louis Browns, and in the mid-fifties he had purchased the Syracuse team in the International League and moved it to Miami.

Salomon had been interested in buying a hockey team that would be based in St. Louis, but he had intended to participate merely as a minority partner. Only when it became apparent that the city was about to lose the franchise did he consider heading a group of hockey investors himself.

"The Arena was the stumbling block," he recalled. "But I was familiar with the building. I'd lived in St. Louis most of my life. I ran a quick check on the building and discovered that at the right price it was a good investment, if only for the property upon which it stood."

That settled, Salomon got on the phone to some other investors and in June, 1966, had a hockey franchise for $6.5 million: $2 million for the team, which he named the Blues, and $4.5 million for the building nobody wanted. He and his son then poured thousands of dollars into painting, rustproofing, and parking facilities, and when the

Rob Ramase leads the defense.

1967-68 season opened, the Arena was in remarkably good shape. Unfortunately, the Blues lagged in the standings, and their potential fans stayed away.

In November, with the team near the bottom of the West Division, the Blues made two dramatic moves. Scotty Bowman, a product of the Montreal organization, accepted the coaching reins from Lynn Patrick, and an obscure center, Red Berenson was obtained from the New York Rangers for Ron Stewart, an aging forward. Steadily, the club began to improve, and the city became intrigued. By the time the Blues slipped into the playoffs in the last week of the season, they had inspired a singing, chanting, handclapping following that was the talk of the league. The Arena crowds had swelled from 3,000 in November to 13,000 in April. The partisans became all the more rabid when the Blues progressed to the Stanley Cup finals before the Montreal Canadiens dashed the hopes of the Blues and their fans with a four-game sweep.

The next year, as the Blues skated off with the West Division title and again reached the Cup finals, attendance soared to more than 15,000 per game. Suddenly, the St. Louis Blues were justifying some extravagant investments, past and present. By the end of the next year, when the Blues won their second straight division title, the Salomons had sunk millions into new seats, new ice, more parking, and a posh Arena club. Much to the displeasure of less generous hockey owners and exeutives around the league, the Salomons were now treating their players and families to a two-week spring vacation at the Salomon's Miami Beach hotel.

Through 1973, the Blues were the only NHL club that never missed the playoffs, and they annually top the NHL's official attendance figures with crowds of well over 18,000 per game. Old heroes such as Berenson, Glenn Hall, Jacques Plante, Doug Harvey, Dickie Moore, and Jimmy Roberts are gone, as is Scotty Bowman; when the club is not doing well, the Salomons don't balk at making changes. But a

St. Louis Blues

fairly solid hockey team survives, built around Bob and Barclay Plager, Gary Sabourin (all three original Blues), Greg Polis, and Garry Unger, who was acquired from Detroit in a 1971 trade for Berenson.

Not long ago Sidney Salomon, jr., remarked that the birth and growth of the Blues has been the most exciting thing in his life. Those who live in the high-powered world of presidential politics may find that hard to believe, but then, they have never owned a pro hockey team. But at the end of the 1973-74 season, St. Louis failed to reach the Stanley Cup playoffs for the first time. In 1976-78, Emile Francis became general manager and coach, and directed the club to first place in the Conn Smythe Division. They were then eliminated by the Montreal Canadiens in four staight games.

Ralston-Purina acquired the Blues in 1977-78, and "The Arena" became known as "The Checkerdome." In 1980-81, St. Louis again led the Conn Smythe Division, but after eliminating the Pittsburgh Penguins they themselves were eliminated by the New York Rangers. By 1982-83, St. Louis had slipped to fourth place and Ralston-Purina became disenchanted with the franchise. In several occasions they appeard to have buyers who planned to move the club, but the NHL vetoed any sales, insisting the club remain in St. Louis. At the 1983 draft of junior players, no representatives of the St. Louis Blues were present and, therefore, no juniors were drafted.

Emile Francis left for Hartford after the 1982-83 season, and eventually Ralston-Purina found a buyer satisfactory to the NHL. On July 27, just six weeks before the opening of training camp, Harry Ornest and his associates took control of the Blues. on October 4, the "Checkerdome" sign came down and the "Arena" sign went up again. That evening, 13,502 happy fans passed through the turnstiles to see their Blues defeat the Pittsburgh Penguins 5-3. St. Louis still had major league hockey.

Season	GP	W	L	T	GF	GA	Pts	Finished	Playoff Result
1982-83	80	25	40	15	285	316	65		Lost Division Semi- Final
1981-82	80	32	40	8	315	349	72	Third, Norris Division	Lost Division Final
1980-81	80	45	18	17	352	281	107	First, Smythe Division	Lost Quarter-Final
1979-80	80	34	34	12	266	278	80	Second, Smythe Division	Lost Preliminary Round
1978-79	80	18	50	12	249	348	48	Third, Smythe Division	Out of Playoffs
1977-78	80	20	47	13	195	304	53	Fourth, Smythe Division	Out of Playoffs
1976-77	80	32	39	9	239	276	73	First, Smythe Division	Lost Quarter-Final
1975-76	80	29	37	14	249	290	72	Third, Smythe Division	Lost Preliminary Round
1974-75	80	35	31	14	269	267	84	Second, Smythe Division	Lost Preliminary Round
1973-74	78	26	40	12	206	248	64	Sixth, West Division	Out of Playoffs
1972-73	78	32	34	12	233	251	76	Fourth, West Division	Lost Quarter-Final
1971-70	78	28	29	11	208	247	67	Third, West Division	Lost Semi-Final
1970-71	78	34	25	19	223	208	87	Second, West Division	Lost Quarter-Final
1969-70	76	37	27	12	224	179	86	First, West Division	Lost Final
1968-69	76	37	25	14	204	157	88	First, West Division	Lost Final
1967-68	74	27	31	16	177	191	70	Third, West Division	Lost Final

Nick Harbaruk axes MacGregor.

Team Records

Most Points	107	1980-81
Most Wins	45	1980-81
Most Ties	19	1970-71
Most Losses	50	1978-79
Most Goals	352	1980-81
Most Goals Against	349	1981-82

Individual Records

Most Points	104	Bernard Fedreko	1980-81
Most Goals	54	Wayne Babych	1980-81
Most Assists	73	Bernard Fedreko	1980-81
Most Penalties in Minutes	306	Robert Gassoff	1975-76
Most Shutouts	8	Glenn Hall	1968-69

Although hockey in Canada began in earnest in the nineteenth century, the city of Toronto didn't fully accept the professional game until November 12, 1931. On that night 13,542 people, at the time the largest crowd ever to attend a sports event in the city, poured through the turnstiles of a sparkling new ice palace called Maple Leaf Gardens. There were grand speeches and thunderous bursts of applause, and the bands of the 48th Highlanders and the Royal Grenadiers serenaded the throng with "Happy Days Are Here Again." Then, as the visiting Chicago Black Hawks and hometown Maple Leafs lined up at center ice, each Toronto player was presented with a huge floral horseshoe. The Black Hawks defeated the Leafs 2-1 that night, but as the huge crowd departed, it was obvious that hockey had finally become a prestigious event in Toronto.

The city's first professional hockey team was the Toronto Arenas, which was admitted to the National Hockey League in 1917 and won the Stanley Cup a year later. But then their cantankerous owner, Eddie Livingstone, was squeezed out by owners in Ottawa and Montreal, and the Arenas were supplanted by the Toronto St. Patricks in 1919. The St. Pats won the league title in 1920-21 and the Cup in 1922 but nonetheless didn't develop a solid following.

At this time a World War I hero named Major Conn Smythe was making quite a name for himself as an executive in Toronto's amateur hockey. Tapped by Colonel John S. Hammond, president of the fledgling New York Rangers, Smythe went off to build the Rangers into a solid hockey team. The project aborted, however, when Hammond fired the man he had just hired. Smythe was soon back in Toronto taking a serious look at the flagging St. Pats.

Smythe organized a group of Toronto businessmen who bought the St. Pats for $160,000. In an effort to change the team's lackluster image, Smythe renamed the club the Maple Leafs and changed the uniforms to his old school colors, blue and white. Then he hired an old friend from amateur hockey, Frank Selke, and the two radically changed the team's roster. Two years later only Clarence ("Happy") Day and Ace Bailey remained from the original St. Pats. Despite the changes, Smythe and Selke still needed a star who would anchor their team and draw fans at the same time. So Smythe approached Ottawa with $35,000 and two players and obtained an exciting defenseman named Frank ("King") Clancy. The price was high, but Toronto would never make a better trade.

As Toronto fans flocked to see Clancy play, Smythe surrounded him with hardy performers such as Alex Levinsky, Harold ("Baldy") Cotton, Andy Blair, Frank Finnigan, and Red Horner. He also assembled a fine young scoring line of Joe Primeau at center, and Harvey ("Busher") Jackson and Charlie Conacher on the wings. Selke would write years later in his autobiography, "This threesome was truly a sight to behold. . . . There may have been other great forward lines in hockey but none could match the frenzy that greeted Toronto's 'Kid Line' in the mid-thirties."

As the Leafs prospered, they outgrew their home, the Mutual Street Arena, which seated only 8,000. "We need one that seats twelve thousand at

The first Syl Apps, now a Hall of Famer

Rick Vaive looks for the cross-ice pass.

Toronto Maple Leafs

least," Smythe said, "and even if I have to put up my own building, I'm going to get it in time for next season." That was during the Depression, of course—no time to be talking about erecting a hockey arena. But despite overwhelming odds, Smythe managed to build his Maple Leaf Gardens.

After that opening-night loss to Chicago, the Leafs plummeted to last place. Typically, Smythe scurried about

the NFL trying to trade his team back into contention. He even offered $75,000 for Montreal superstar Howie Morenz, but the Canadiens spurned the offer. When all else failed, he simply replaced coach Art Duncan with Dick Irvin.

As coach of the Chicago Black Hawks, Irvin had shown a flair for developing young players, and he immediately led Toronto's young team into the

thick of the championship fight. The Leafs finished in second place in 1931-32 and eliminated Chicago in the playoff semifinals. Smythe then savored some precious revenge when his Leafs defeated Colonel Hammond's Rangers for the Stanley Cup.

Toronto prospered under Irvin and then under Happy Day through the thirties and forties. The Leafs floundered in the fifties, but then Smythe hired

George ("Punch") Imlach, who as coach and general manager remade the Leafs into solid championship contenders and specialists in winning Stanley Cups—three straight from 1962 through 1964 and another in 1967.

In the 1969 Stanley Cup playoffs the Toronto Maple Leafs opposed the Boston Bruins in the quarterfinals. In Boston the home team won the first two games by scores of 10-0 and 7-0. In the next two games, played in Toronto, the scores were 4-3 and 3-2, both in favor of Boston. As the final buzzer sounded C. Stafford Smythe President of the Maple Leafs, rose from his seat and made his way down a corridor that led to the Maple Leafs' dressing room. There he intercepted Imlach and, motioning him into a small office promptly fired him.

James Gregory was named general manager in May, 1969; ten years later, on July 4, 1979, Imlach would return as general manager. But in late November, 1981, Imlach, who had suffered a heart attack in 1972 while with the Buffalo Sabres, was again having problems with his heart. Gerald McNamara, a former Toronto goaltender, took over the general manager duties.

Toronto has had little to brag about since winning their last Stanley Cup in 1967. They have yet to finish first in their division—in fact, they have yet to finish second. The best they've done is six third-place finishes from 1974-75 to 1978-79 and in 1982-83. In the Stanley Cup playoffs they have reached the semifinal series only once—in 1978—and then they were eliminated by the Montreal Canadiens in four straight games.

Team Records
Most Points 95 1950-51
Most Wins . . . . 41 . . . . . 1950-51; 1977-78
Most Ties. 2 1954-55
Most Losses. 44 1981-82
Most Goals. 322 1980-81
Most Goals Against . . 380 1981-82
Individual Records
Most Points . . . . 117 . . Darryl Sittler. . . . 1977-78
Most Goals. . . . . 54 . . Rick Vaive 1981-82
Most Assists. . . . . . . 72 . . Darryl Sittler. . . . 1977-78
Most Penalties in Minutes . . David Williams 1977-
. . . . 351 78
Most Shutouts. . . . . . 13 . . Harry Lumley . . . 1953-54

Annual Records

Season	GP	W	L	T	GF	GA	Pts	Finished	Playoff Result
1982-83	80	28	40	12	293	330	68	Third, Norris Division	Lost Division Semi
1981-82	80	20	44	16	298	380	56	Fifth, Norris Division	Out of Playoffs
1980-81	80	28	37	15	322	367	71	Fifth, Adams Division	Lost Preliminary
1979-80	80	35	40	5	304	327	75	Fourth, Adams Division	Lost Preliminary
1978-79	80	34	33	13	267	252	81	Third, Adams Division	Lost Quarter-Final
1977-78	80	41	29	10	271	237	82	Third, Adams Division	Lost Semi-Final
1976-77	80	33	32	15	201	285	81	Third, Adams Division	Lost Quarter-Final
1975-76	80	34	31	15	294	276	83	Third, Adams Division	Lost Quarter-Final
1974-75	80	31	33	16	280	209	78	Third, Adams Division	Lost Quarter-Final
1973-74	78	35	27	16	274	230	86	Fourth, East Division	Lost Quarter-Final
1972-73	78	27	41	10	247	279	64	Sixth, East Division	Out of Playoffs
1971-70	78	33	31	14	209	208	80	Fourth, East Division	Lost Quarter-Final
1970-71	78	37	33	8	248	211	82	Fourth, East Division	Lost Quarter-Final
1969-70	76	29	34	13	222	242	71	Sixth, East Division	Out of Playoffs
1968-69	76	35	26	15	234	217	85	Fourth, East Division	Lost Quarter-Final
1967-68	74	33	31	10	209	176	76	Fifth, East Division	Out of Playoffs
1966-67	70	32	27	11	204	211	76	Third	**Won Stanley Cup**
1965-66	70	34	25	11	208	187	79	Third	Lost Semi-Final
1964-65	70	30	26	14	204	173	74	Fourth	Lost Semi-Final
1963-64	70	33	25	12	192	172	78	Third	**Won Stanley Cup**
1962-63	70	35	23	12	221	180	82	First	**Won Stanley Cup**
1961-62	70	37	22	11	232	180	85	Second	**Won Stanley Cup**
1960-61	70	39	19	12	234	176	90	Second	Lost Semi-Final
1959-60	70	35	26	9	199	195	79	Second	Lost Final
1958-59	70	27	32	11	189	201	65	Fourth	Lost Final
1957-58	70	21	38	11	192	226	53	Sixth	Out of Playoffs
1956-57	70	21	34	15	174	192	57	Fifth	Out of Playoffs
1955-56	70	24	33	13	153	181	61	Fourth	Lost Semi-Final
1954-55	70	24	22	22	147	135	70	Third	Lost Semi-Final
1953-54	70	32	24	14	152	131	78	Third	Lost Semi-Final
1952-53	70	27	30	13	156	167	67	Fifth	Out of Playoffs
1951-52	70	29	25	16	168	157	74	Third	Lost Semi-Final
1950-51	70	41	16	13	212	138	95	Second	**Won Stanley Cup**
1949-50	70	31	27	12	176	173	74	Third	Lost Semi-Final
1948-49	60	22	25	13	147	161	57	Fourth	**Won Stanley Cup**
1947-48	60	32	15	13	182	143	77	First	**Won Stanley Cup**
1946-47	60	31	19	10	209	172	72	Second	**Won Stanley Cup**
1945-46	50	19	24	7	174	185	45	Fifth	Out of Playoffs
1944-45	50	24	22	4	183	161	52	Third	**Won Stanley Cup**
1943-44	50	23	23	4	214	174	50	Third	Lost Semi-Final
1942-43	50	22	19	9	198	159	53	Third	Lost Semi-Final
1941-42	48	27	18	3	158	136	57	Second	**Won Stanley Cup**
1940-41	48	28	14	6	145	99	62	Second	Lost Semi-Final
1939-40	48	25	17	6	134	110	56	Third	Lost Final
1938-39	48	19	20	9	114	107	47		Lost Final
1937-38	48	24	15	9	151	127	57	First, Canadian Division	Lost Final
1936-37	48	22	21	5	119	115	49	Third, Canadian Division	Lost Quarter-Final
1935-36	48	23	19	6	126	106	12	Second, Canadian Division	Lost Final
1934-35	48	30	14	4	157	111	64	First, Canadian Division	Lost Final
1933-34	48	26	13	9	174	119	61	First, Canadian Division	Lost Semi-Final
1932-33	48	24	18	6	119	111	54	First, Canadian Division	Lost Final
1931-32	48	23	18	7	155	127	53	Second, Canadian Division	**Won Stanley Cup**
1930-31	44	22	13	9	118	99	53	Second, Canadian Division	Lost Quarter-Final
1929-30	44	17	21	6	116	124	40	Fourth, Canadian Division	Out of Playoffs
1928-29	44	21	18	5	85	69	47	Third, Canadian Division	Lost Semi-Final
1927-28	44	18	18	8	89	88	54	Fourth, Canadian Division	Out of Playoffs
*1926-27	44	15	24	5	79	94	35	Fifth, Canadian Division	Out of Playoffs
1925-26	36	12	21	3	92	114	27	Sixth	Out of Playoffs
1924-25	30	19	11	0	90	84	38	Second	Lost NHL Final
1923-24	24	10	14	0	59	85	30	Third	Out of Playoffs
1922-23	24	13	10	1	82	88	27	Third	Out of Playoffs
1921-22	24	13	10	1	98	97	27	Second	**Won Stanley Cup**
1920-21	24	15	9	0	105	100	30	First	Lost NHL Playoffs
**1919-20	24	12	12	0	119	106	24	Third	Out of Cup Playoffs
1918-19	18	5	13	0	64	92	10	Third	Out of Playoffs
1917-18	22	13	9	0	108	109	26	Second and First	**Won Stanley Cup**

*Name changed from St. Patricks to Maple Leafs.
**Name changed from Arenas to St. Patricks.

Vancouver, British Columbia, welcomed its NHL franchise with enthusiasm bred of years of anticipation. For years fans in that magnificent Western Canadian city had been scheduling Saturday night cocktail parties around "Hockey Night in Canada," hooked on the big league game but with only a minor league club to show for their longing. For various reasons, some of them selfish, the NHL ignored Vancouver in its original expansion plan, but in 1970, the city was, at long last, rewarded with a franchise.

The arrival of the NHL Canucks brought forth bands and banquets, parades and publicity. A spanking new home, the Pacific Coliseum Arena, awaited the team. Solid acceptance at the box office was assured, and former second-stringers from the established clubs were hailed as celebrities.

Although he had yet to touch the puck in NHL competition, the biggest local hero was Dale Tallon, a 6-foot 1-inch, 200-pounder from Noranda, Quebec, who had starred for the Toronto Marlboros in junior hockey. No matter that the Canucks had lost Gilbert Perreault on a spin of a roulette wheel in the amateur draft; Tallon would suffice.

Four years later, the Canucks were still playing to sellout crowds at the Pacific Coliseum. But there were no more bands, banquets, or parades. As the city once longed for a major league franchise, it now longed for a respectable team. All too often the big league Canucks played like their minor league predecessors and namesakes. In their first three years the NHL Canucks finished sixth, seventh, and seventh in the East Division.

Reasonable fans were not surprised that the East Divsion, with its powerhouses in Montreal and Boston and old-line clubs in New York, Detroit, and Toronto, proved inhospitable to the Canucks and their fellow newcomers, the Buffalo Sabres. Vancouver and Buffalo spent most of their first two years scrambling to avoid the basement. But in 1972-73, the Sabres burst to life, overtaking Detroit and

Toronto for the final playoff spot. The Sabres won even more prestige by forcing Montreal through six tough games before surrendering in the Stanley Cup quarterfinal. In stark contrast the Canucks went home after another seventh-place finish, trying to think of an answer to their fans' inevitable question—if Buffalo could do it, why couldn't Vancouver?

Like any other loser, the Canucks have had disillusioning experiences with the shortcuts to success. In their first three years on the NHL scene, they had four coaches and made numerous other front office changes. Bounced out of Philadelphia, Norman ("Bud") Poile was Vancouver's first general manager. To everyone's surprise he hired his old Western Hockey League enemy Hal Laycoe as the team's first coach. Eventually, Laycoe was replaced by Vic Stasiuk, who already had a somewhat checkered past as a coach. The Canucks continued to lose, and when Poile temporarily bowed out for health reasons, Laycoe was elevated to general manager. After the 1972-73 season, Stasiuk was fired and replaced by Bill McCreary, a member of St. Louis's growing list of former coaches. Coley Hall, the Canucks' director claimed, "Bill is exactly the type of person we've been looking for. He's young yet still has plenty of experience. I know he'll be happy in Vancouver."

Indeed, optimism ran high before the start of the 1973-74 season. In the summer, the Canucks had signed all seven of their draft choices and obtained a fine goaltender, Gary Smith, from Chicago in exchange for Tallon. Jerry Korab was expected to add badly needed muscle on defense. Bobby Schmautz had scored 38 goals and 71 points the preceding year, and Andre Boudrias had added 30 goals and 70 points.

But alas, the Canucks once again slipped into the depths of the East Division. Tempers flared in the executive suites, and more changes were made. In mid-January, McCreary was fired and replaced by Phil Maloney. Laycoe said

Hall called him from Hawaii, where the Vancouver boss made his winter home, and told him to dismiss McCreary. McCreary, however, credited the decision to the influence of Poile, who, recovering from his illness, had been given the job of Assistant General Manager. "When you see certain people smiling after a loss and wearing a long face after a win, you begin to wonder what's going on," he said.

Then Laycoe asked for Poile's resignation, and Poile erupted. "I said I had no intention of resigning. You only resign when you know you've done a bad job," said Poile. At that Hall picked up the telephone in Hawaii and demanded that both Laycoe and Poile resign. "We've got to get some people back there who know what they're doing," he said. "We've got to start running this franchise like a business, not a merry-go-round."

Poile then resigned, but Laycoe remained, a few days longer. On January 31, 1974, Laycoe was replaced by Phil Maloney who was now both manager and coach. But the club finished a dismal seventh, only three points ahead of the second-year New York Islanders. in 1974-75, Maloney guided them to the top in the Conn Smythe Division. They faced the Montreal Canadiens in their first Stanley Cup competition and were defeated four games to one. After finishing fourth in 1976-77, Jake Milford became general manager and Orland Kurtenbach was named coach. Harry Neale replaced Kurtenbach the following season. During each of the next five seasons, Vancouver finished either second or third in the Conn Smythe Division.

On March 20, 1982, Vancouver was playing the Quebec Nordiques in Quebec City when a wild brawl erupted. As Neale swapped punches with a spectator, his players invaded the stands to fight with others. Not until Quebec City's gendarmes entered the stands was order restored. NHL president, Ziegler didn't take kindly to this action by the Vancouver club, and on

Vancouver Canucks

March 26 fined several players and their trainer, Larry Ashley, a total of $7,500. He also slapped a 10-game suspension on Harry Neale; since Vancouver had played 75 games up to this point, this meant that Neale wouldn't be able to coach again until the remaining 5 games of the regular season and the first 5 games of the Stanley Cup playoffs—if Vancouver even got that far—had been completed.

Roger Neilson, an assistant coach, took over coaching duties. Vancouver won four and tied one of those remaining five games to move ahead of Calgary and finish second in the Conn Smythe Division. Their first opponent in the Stanley Cup playoffs was Calgary, whom they eliminated in three straight games.

Next Vancouver met Los Angeles, and after two games each had won one by scores of 3-2, and Neale's suspension was over. But Neilson had won eight games, lost one, and tied one—and Neale wasn't about to interrupt success. Neilson would coach Vancouver throughout the Stanley Cup playoffs. Vancouver proceeded to dispose of Los Angeles in the next three games.

Then came Chicago, and the Canucks won the series four games to one. It was during the third period of the one game they lost that white towels came into play. When Denis Savard scored Chicago's fourth goal, Neilson began waving a white towel at referee Robert Myers, which incited several Vancouver players to do likewise. Again the NHL took a dim view of the Vancouver club's actions, ordered it to post a $10,000 performance bond, and fined Neilson $1,000. This, of course, was no deterrence to the Vancouver fans, who waved hundreds of white towels at every home game for the rest of the Stanley Cup playoffs.

Neilson had now won 15 games, lost 2, and tied 1. But their next opponents, the New York Islanders, were to burst the bubble. The Islanders sacked them four games to none.

The following season, Neale became general manager, and Neilson became coach.

Annual Records

Season	GP	W	L	T	GF	GA	Pts	Finished	Playoff Result
1982-83	80	30	35	15	303	309	75	Third, Smythe Division	Lost Semi-Final
1981-82	80	30	33	17	290	286	77	Second, Smythe Division	**Lost Stanley Cup**
1980-81	80	28	32	20	289	301	76	Third, Smythe Division	Lost Preliminary Round
1979-80	80	27	37	16	256	281	70	Third, Smythe Division	Lost Preliminary Round
1978-79	80	25	42	13	217	291	63	Second, Smythe Division	Lost preliminary Round
1977-78	80	20	43	17	239	320	57	Third, Smythe Division	Out of Playoffs
1976-77	80	25	42	13	235	294	63	Fourth, Smythe Division	Out of Playoffs
1975-76	80	33	32	15	271	272	81	Second, Smythe Division	Lost Preliminary Round
1974-75	80	38	32	10	271	254	86	First, Smythe Division	Lost Quarter-Final
1973-74	78	24	43	11	224	296	59	Seventh, East Division	Out of Playoffs
1972-73	78	22	47	9	233	339	53	Seventh, East Division	Out of Playoffs
1971-70	78	20	50	8	203	297	48	Seventh, East Division	Out of Playoffs
1970-71	78	24	48	8	229	296	56	Sixth, East Division	Out of Playoffs

Team Records

Most Points	86	1974-75
Most Wins	38	1974-75
Most Ties	20	1980-81
Most Losses	50	1971-72
Most Goals	303	1982-83
Most Goals Against	339	1972-73

Individual Records

Most Points	88	Stanley Smyl	1982-83
Most Goals	42	Darcy Rota	1982-83
Most Assists	62	Andre Boudrias	1974-7
Most Penalties in Minutes	343	David Williams	1980-81
Most Shutouts	6	Gary Smith	1974-75

Richards Brodeur sprawls for the save.

Washington Capitals

On June 11, 1974, Washington, D.C., was granted an NHL franchise; the Washington Capitals began playing in Capital Center in Landover, Maryland.

No club ever got off to such a bad start: they won a mere 8 games, scored only 181 goals, had 446 scored against them, and at one time lost 17 consecutive games. In their second season, they did little better. The won 11 games and had "only" 394 goals scored against them. This time they had a winless streak that lasted from November 29, 1975, to January 21, 1976, and consisted of 25 games (22 lost, 3 tied).

But they were improving. In 1976-77 the Capitals cut their goals against them to 307, and moved past the Detroit Red Wings in the James Norris Division. In their first eight seasons, the Capitals had never finished higher than fourth and had never been in Stanley Cup playoff. But in 1982-83, the Capitals soared—they won 39 games, held their opponents to 283 goals, and finished third in the Lester Patrick Division with 94 points—14 points more than the New York Rangers. They stormed into their first Stanley Cup playoffs and boldly took on the New York Islanders, who finally defeated them.

Gaetan Duchesne pushes puck up Islander ice.

Team Records

Most Points	94	1982-83
Most Wins	39	1982-83
Most Ties	18	1980-81
Most Losses	67	1974-75
Most Goals	319	1981-82
Most Goals Against	446	1974-75

Individual Records

Most Points	136	Dennis Maruk 1981-82
Most Goals	60	Dennis Maruk . . 1981-82
Most Assists	76	Dennis Maruk . . .81-82
Most Penalties in Minutes	275	S. Randall Holt. . . .1982-83
Most Shutouts	2	Michael Palmateer 1980-81

Annual Records

Season	GP	W	L	T	GF	GA	Pts.	Finished	
1982-83	80	39	25	16	306	283	94	Third, Patrick Division	Lost Division Semi-Final
1981-82	80	26	41	13	319	338	65	Fifth, Patrick Division	Out of Play-Offs
1980-81	80	26	36	18	286	317	70	Fifth, Patrick Division	Out of Play-Offs
1979-80	80	27	40	13	261	293	67	Fifth, Patrick Division	Out of Play-Offs
1978-79	80	24	41	15	273	338	63	Fifth, Patrick Division	Out of Play-Offs
1977-78	80	17	49	14	195	321	48	Fourth, Norris Division	Out of Play-Offs
1976-77	80	24	42	4	221	307	62	Fifth, Norris Division	Out of Play-Offs
1975-76	80	11	59	10	224	394	32	Fourth, Norris Division	Out of Play-Offs

Winnipeg Jets

When Winnipeg was granted an NHL franchise it caused no great excitement. Winnipeg is used to having big-league hockey players around. Many have been born or raised there—Dan Bain, Frank Fredrickson, Chuck Gardiner, Herb Gardiner, Ching Johnson, "Steamer" Maxwell, Billy Mosienko, Babe Pratt, Kenneth Reardon, Jack Ruttan, Terry Sawchuk, "Bullet Joe" Simpson, and many more.

Before the turn of the century Winnipeg had to be reckoned with when it came to producing great hockey clubs. The first club from Western Canada to win the Stanley Cup was the Winnipeg Victorias, who accomplished the feat in February, 1896.

In their first NHL season (1979-80,) the Jets won 20 games, a reasonable number for a first-year club; they had 314 goals scored against them. But in their second season, they seemed to be trying to emulate the Washington Capitals. They won 9 games, had 400 goals scored against them, and had a winless streak of 30 games (23 lost, 7 tied) that lasted from October 19 to December 20, 1980.

In the clubs's third season, 33 games were won, the Jets finished second in the James Norris Division. Although they again won 33 games in 1982-83, they dropped to fourth place when the Vancouver Canucks finished with one point more and the Calgary Flames with four more.

The Jets' first coach was Thomas McVie, who departed during their long winless streak. William Sutherland finished the 1980-81 season, and Thomas Watt took over at the beginning of 1981-82. Former Montreal Canadiens enforcer John Bowie ("Big Bad John") Ferguson, had been their general manager from the start.

Lucien DeBlois keeps his cool.

Team Records

Most Points	80	1980-81
Most Wins	33	1981-82; 1982-83
Most Ties	14	1980-81; 1981-82
Most Losses	57	1980-81
Most Goals	319	1981-82
Most Goals Against	400	1980-81

Individual Records

Most Points	103	Dale Hawerchuk	1981-82
Most Goals	45	Dale Hawerchuk	1981-82
		David Babych	1982-83
Most Assists	61	James Mann	1979-80
Most Penalties in Minutes	287	R. Markus Mattsson	1979-80
Most Shutouts	2	Douglas Soetaert	1981-82

Annual Records

Season	GP	W	L	T	GF	GA	Pts.	Finished	
1982-83	80	33	39	8	331	333	74	Fourth, Smythe Division	Lost Preliminary Round
1981-82	80	33	33	14	319	332	80		
1980-81	80	9	57	14	246	400	32	Second, Norris Division	Lost Division Semi-Final
1979-80	80	20	49	11	214	314	51	Sixth, Smythe Division	Out of Playoffs

Historic Games

New York Rangers versus Montreal Maroons
April 7, 1928

It was the 1928 Stanley Cup finals between the New York Rangers and the Montreal Maroons, and with Madison Square Garden unavailable due to previous commitments, the entire series was being played in the Montreal Forum. The Maroons had blanked the Rangers in the opening game 2-0, and now, with no score in the second period of the second game, New York suddenly found itself in deep trouble; a shot from the stick of Montreal's Nelson Stewart had caught New York's Lorne Chabot in the left eye, and the goalie had been carried from the ice on a stretcher.

Because teams did not carry spare goaltenders in those days, New York coach Lester Patrick was desperate. Peering through the crowd of some 12,000, he spotted a goaltender who had played that year for Ottawa. He approached Eddie Gerard, the Montreal coach, to ask permission to replace Chabot with the Ottawa goalie. With a wry smile Gerard replied, "Suckers were born yesterday, Lester. You're talking to the wrong man. I'm sorry, but I can't hear you."

Gerard's refusal was not very sportsmanlike, especially in view of the fact that several years earlier Patrick had allowed Toronto to replace an injured goaltender—with a player named Eddie Gerard. Forty-four years old, with a long nose and silver hair, Patrick was known as the Silver Fox. A one-time great defenseman, he had become one of hockey's leaders and one of its builders. As the Rangers retired to their dressing room it was clear they would have to come up with a goaltender from among themselves. When nobody volunteered, Frank Boucher said half in jest, "Hey coach, how about you playing goal?"

Boucher had barely finished when Patrrick was strapping on Chabot's pads. "Wait a minute," the players protested, realizing their coach's seriousness. "We'll get somebody else ... anybody."

Now it was too late. Eddie Gerard had made Lester Patrick very mad. "Boys," he said. "I'm going in to play goal. Check as you've never checked before. Help protect an old man."

The Rangers returned to the ice and, as a murmur of surprise swept through the crowd, started lofting practice shots at their white-haired goaltender. Patrick was shaky. He was also unfamiliar with the equipment. But then he announced he was ready, and what followed was a historic moment in New York Rangers history.

Sensing an easy kill, Montreal stormed the New York goal. But every time someone in a maroon sweater got too close, an angry Ranger knocked him to the ice. The New Yorkers were determined to play the game of their lives. At the beginning of the third period, the game was still scoreless.

Thirty seconds into the final period Bill Cook scored, putting the Rangers on top 1-0. The Maroons roared back, but New York was playing tenaciously on defense. The Rangers protected Patrick until Stewart scored with only six minutes to play and sent the game into overtime.

Now even the partisan Montreal crowd was cheering for Patrick and his Rangers. Frustrated, the Maroons responded with rush after futile rush. Play

One-time goalie, 44-year-old Lester Patrick.

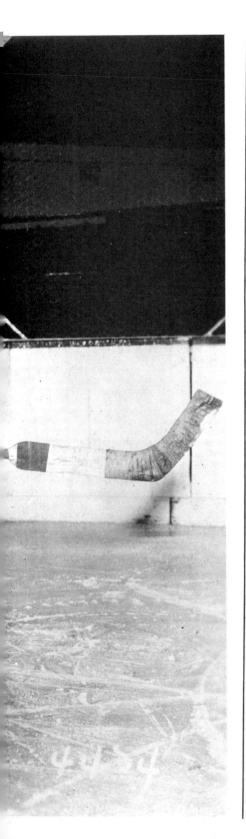

was almost entirely confined to the Rangers' zone until the seven-minute mark of overtime. Then Boucher suddenly stole a Maroons pass and broke down ice in a one-man rush. Weaving across the blue line, he split the Montreal defense, pulled the goaltender, and flipped the puck high into the net for a stirring 2-1 victory. Bone-weary and with tears streaming down his face, Patrick was half carried, half dragged from the ice as the crowd stood and roared its appreciation.

The Rangers hardly looked back after that victory. Granted the use of a substitute goalie, they lost the third game but won the fourth 1-0 on Boucher's goal. Then in the fifth and deciding game, they won their first Stanley Cup with the help of an obscure netminder, Jim ("Red Light") Miller. Again it was Frank Boucher who provided the goals, but everyone realized that without Patrick's gallant move in that second game, the Rangers probably wouldn't have lasted against the powerful Maroons. It was, indeed, one of the most dramatic stories in Stanley Cup history.

Montreal Canadiens versus Toronto Maple Leafs
March 23, 1944

Over the years it has become traditional in hockey to announce three stars at the conclusion of each game. Usually, two are members of the winning team, and the other is a player for the losers. In particularly one-sided games all three may be selected from the winners. On March 23, 1944, a most unusual selection was announced over the public address system of the Montreal Forum. The Canadiens had just defeated the Toronto Maple Leafs 5-1, in a Stanley Cup semifinal game, and as the happy crowd filed out of the Forum, it learned that the three stars for the game were one person—Maurice Richard.

Who could argue? The Rocket had scored all five of Montreal's goals, single-handedly evening the playoff series at one game apiece and thereby starting the Canadiens on the way to their first Stanley Cup in 13 years. Never before and not since has one player so dominated the scoring in a playoff game.

As was their usual strategy, the Maple Leafs had assigned a big forward, Bob Davidson, to check Richard that night. Although he was only 23 years old at the time, Richard had already demonstrated an aptitude for scoring that warranted such an unusual defense. As the teams skated through a scoreless first period, Toronto's ploy seemed to be working. But in the second period Richard exploded.

At 1:48, he took passes from Toe Blake and Mike McMahon and beat Toronto goalie Paul Bibeault, putting the Canadiens on top 1-0. Only 17 seconds later, he scored again, on assists from his "Punch Line" mates, Blake and Elmer Lach.

Down 2-0, Toronto attacked, and at 8:50, the Leafs narrowed their deficit to one goal when Reg Hamilton scored. At 16:46, however, Richard scored his third goal, again on assists from Lach and Blake. Richard had scored quite a remarkable hat trick: three goals in one period, despite the fact that he had spent four minutes of the period in the penalty box. When he left the ice after the second period, Richard was given a standing ovation. As it turned out, however, he wasn't through.

At the one-minute mark of the third period, Richard scored again, Lach and Blake assisting for the third time. Seven minutes later, Rocket added his fifth tally. At first the crowd couldn't believe it, but as the game neared its end, the fans were screaming for still more.

The Leafs lost the next three games, never recovering from Richard's feat. Montreal was inspired by it, and after defeating the Leafs, the Canadiens took the Stanley Cup in the next round. As for Richard, he claimed after the game that he hadn't realized he had set a record. "I only had six or seven shots on net all game," he recalled years later, "and each goal was scored in a different way." The funny thing is that when we beat the Leafs eleven-nothing three games later, I only scored two goals.

"The Leafs always were a close-checking club, and they used to put Bob Davidson out to check me every game. Sometimes he stayed so close to me that I got angry, and that night, I guess, I took it out on him—and the puck."

Bill Mosienko scores his record-setting third goal.

Chicago Black Hawks versus New York Rangers
March 23, 1952

There wasn't much at stake in the game at Madison Square Garden on the night of March 23, 1952. The New York Rangers had long been doomed to a distant last-place finish in the standings, and the visiting Chicago Black Hawks had also been eliminated as a playoff contender. The meaningless game, last of the year for both clubs, attracted a meager turnout of 3,254 fans, who sat scattered throughout the 15,000-seat arena.

Still, there were a few players who were eager to play. Only days before, Chicago's Bill Mosienko had been thumbing through an NHL record book when he remarked to a friend, "Gee, it would be nice to have my name in there with some of the greats."

At least two members of the Rangers had more concrete objectives in mind. Lorne Anderson, a 20-year-old rookie goaltender, wasn't thinking in terms of records; he just wanted to prove he belonged in the NHL, and after permitting 10 goals in his first two starts, he knew that his performance against the Black Hawks might determine his future. And although few knew it at the time, New York's Hy Buller was playing despite a cracked ankle—he was trying to set a new Rangers scoring record for defensemen.

For everyone else it would be a tame game. With nothing at stake, nobody wanted to get hurt. Not a single penalty would be called all night.

With the play sluggish and the defenses unintimidating, it wasn't surprising that goals came early and often. Chicago took a 1-0 lead, then the Rangers came back with three in a row. At the end of the first period, the score was 3-2, New York. Buller had been shut out, Lorne Anderson's job was still insecure, and Mosienko had only an assist on Chicago's first goal to show for his aspirations.

Mosienko displays the symbolic three pucks.

New York scored twice more in the second period to make it 5-2, and Anderson settled down. Early in the third period the Rangers increased their lead to 6-2, and the few spectators comforted themselves with the thought that at least the Rangers would end their dismal season on a winning note.

Then Mosienko stepped onto the ice with linemates Gus Bodnar and George Gee. Bodnar fed a pass to Mosienko and the little right winger skated around Hy Buller and laced a low shot under Anderson's stick. The goal came at 6:09. "It was my twenty-ninth goal," recalled Mosienko, "so I got the puck as a souvenir."

In the faceoff at center ice, Bodnar again controlled the puck, and once again passed to Mosienko. For the second time Mosienko swept past Buller, who was having difficulty pivoting on his bad ankle. Mosienko roared toward Anderson and once more scored low to the stick side. The time was 6:20, the score now 6-4. "That was my thirtieth goal," said Mosienko, "so again I went into the net and got the puck."

On the next faceoff Bodnar drew the puck to Gee along the board on the left side. As Gee started into the Rangers' zone, he spotted Mosienko breaking past Buller once more. "As I reached the blue line I made my move," said Mosienko. "George saw me cutting over the line and laid a perfect pass on my stick."

Bearing down on Anderson again Mosienko figured that the rookie would be looking for another low shot to the stick side. So he switched tactics. Pulling Anderson from the net, he waited for an instant before flipping the puck high over the goalie's left shoulder. Time of goal, 6:30. Bill Mosienko had suddenly realized his dream. He had played in the NHL for years but had failed to set a record. Now in 21 seconds, he had scored the fastest three goals in league history. (In fact, no team had ever scored three as quickly. The team record is 24 seconds, set by the Montreal Maroons in 1932.)

Shaken by the three quick scores, their lead cut to 6-5, the Rangers couldn't do anything right. Less than a munute later Mosienko was again alone in front of Anderson, but with an open net staring him in the face, he shot wide. He had to settle for three goals in 21 seconds instead of four in a little more than a minute. Considering how the other principals fared, Mosienko had no cause to complain. The Rangers blew the game 7-6, Hy Buller failed to score a point, and Lorne Anderson never played another game in the National Hockey League.

Montreal Canadiens versus Toronto Maple Leafs
December 9, 1953

TThe officials whose unenviable task it is to keep the peace in hockey games realize that sometimes fighting is inevitable. At these moments they limit their efforts to containing the hostilities, allowing the principal combatants to battle and persuading others not to intervene. In recent years their work has become considerably easier with the institution of "the third-man rule," which directs the referee to banish from the game any player who intervenes in a two-man fight. "The third-man rule," says the NHL's supervisor of officials, Frank Udvari, "is the best rule to come along in years."

Udvari should know. He was the referee on the night of December 9, 1953, when the biggest fight in hockey history erupted. The battleground was Maple Leaf Gardens, and the participants were practically all the Leafs and Canadiens.

Like all big fights this one was preceded by a preliminary. Montreal's Ed Mazur and Toronto's George Armstrong battled in the first period, and when they continued their fight in the penalty box, Udvari promptly awarded both players game misconducts. As a result, neither would be able to participate in the main event.

Early in the second period, Toronto's Ron Stewart suddenly felt a stick explode against his ribs. Stewart noted that the culprit was Montreal's Bud MacPherson, but he chose not to retaliate, waiting for a more opportune moment. It came at 18:12 of the third period, when Stewart and MacPherson collided again. This time both began shoving and shouting, and before long the two had shed their gloves and begun to pummel one another. At this point Montreal's Tom Johnson came to the aid of his teammate by restraining Stewart with a headlock. His attention momentarily diverted from MacPherson, Stewart freed himself from Johnson's headlock and dispatched a hard right to Johnson's jaw. Now Stewart pursued MacPherson again, emboldened when he saw that Toronto's Eric Nesterenko had already engaged him. When the Canadiens saw MacPherson outnumbered, they came roaring off their bench. Naturally, the Leafs followed suit, and the historic battle was on.

Sticks and gloves littered the ice. Some combatants preferred grappling on the ice, others chose upright boxing stances. No sooner would Udvari and his linesmen pacify one group than others would begin fighting anew. Even the goaltenders (Montreal's Gerry McNeil and Toronto's Harry Lumley) participated, spurning the goalie's usual policy of neutrality.

The only two players who really didn't fight that night were the two who were usually the most belligerent: Montreal's Maurice Richard and Toronto's Tim Horton. Both were willing, experienced battlers, but as mayhem roared about them they must have felt upstaged. They merely grabbed each other's sweaters and engaged in some ritualistic, relatively inconsequential shoving. Horton remembers that Rocket just watched everybody else and muttered, "Crazy . . . crazy . . . crazy. . . ."

The brawl lasted 20 minutes and finally ended in mass exhaustion. Nobody had the strength to throw another punch.

Then Udvari began dealing out penalties. Every player on both teams had been involved in some way, except Mazur and Armstrong (who had long since left), and Doug Harvey, who had been in the penalty box when the brawl erupted (and who had had the good sense to stay there as it continued). Because there were less than two minutes left in the game, Udvari decided to banish all but the minimum eight players necessary to finish the game.

For the game Udvari had assessed 36 penalties for a record 204 minutes. The Canadiens received penalties for 106 minutes, another record, and Toronto 18 for 98. The 26 penalties and 184 minutes in penalties that resulted from the brawl are also records.

Almost incidental in the fights aftermath was the fact that Toronto won the game 3-0.

Richard scores. Suspension of Richard touched off a riot . . .

Detroit Red Wings versus Montreal Canadiens
March 17, 1955

On the last Sunday of the 1954-55 season, the city of Montreal was nearly hysterical with excitement. Its Canadiens were neck-and-neck with the mighty Detroit Red Wings in the race for the National Hockey League championship, and its favorite star, Maurice Richard, appeared to be ready to capture the first scoring championship of his career. It had been nine years since the Canadiens had last finished first, and in four of the last five, they had finished second to the Red Wings. As for Richard, despite his prolific goal scoring, the scoring championship had eluded him. Now he was leading teammate Bernie Geoffrion by four points. So Canadien fans were savoring hopes of a double triumph: Montreal winning the championship and the Rocket winning the scoring title. The story of their disappointment on both counts is the story of the infamous "Richard Riot."

In a Sunday night game in Boston, Richard used his stick to carve up the Bruins' Hal Laycoe in a fight. Then he compounded his error by slugging linesman Cliff Thompson in the eye when the official tried to intervene. The next day NHL President Clarence Campbell looked at Laycoe's scarred face and Thompson's shiner and suspended Richard for the rest of the season— and the playoffs.

Canadiens fans were outraged. Letters and phone calls flooded Campbell's office. Civilized dissidents pleaded that the suspension be lifted; less polite protesters called or wrote Campbell just to swear at him. Campbell's secretary took most of the complaints, including some threatening ones. One caller snapped, "Just tell Campbell I'm an undertaker and he'll be needing me in a few days."

An English-Canadian, Campbell was naturally accused of racism by some French-Canadians. "If Richard's name was Richardson, you'd have given a different verdict," said one. "I was at the morgue this morning to look at a body after an accident. I only wish you had been on the slab—but don't worry, you will be soon."

In the next few days, the city's mood grew even worse. On the night of March 17, 1955, the resentment turned to violence. The Detroit Red Wings were playing the Canadiens in the biggest game of the year, and hundreds in the capacity crowd of 16,000 had come to the Forum in an ugly mood. Campbell had bravely decided to come too, with his equally valiant secretary, who would later become his wife. "If I failed to go, I'd have been branded as a coward," he recalled later. "In any case I'm a season ticket holder and had a right to go. I also felt the police would protect me."

As they took their seats at one end of the arena, Campbell and his secretary were immediately abused. *"Va-t'en,* Campbell! Scram, Campbell!" yelled some fans. Others threw oranges, tomatoes, and pickled pigs' feet at the league president. Campbell remained through the first period, trying his best to concentrate on the game. After the first period ended, one fan (later to be hailed locally as a hero for his "courage") ran up the steps and without speaking rubbed two tomatoes on Campbell's chest.

Early in the second period, with the Red Wings leading 4-1, a full-scale riot erupted. A tear gas bomb exploded, and as the Forum filled with acrid fumes, the crowd poured into the streets. A mob of more than 10,000 rampaged through the area, assaulting cab drivers, hurling rocks and bottles, smashing windows, looting stores, and burning newsstands. Before the authorities brought the riot under control, at 3 A.M., 37 people were injured and 70 arrested.

News of the ugly scene produced a reaction even as far away as London, where the *News Chronicle* commented, "Ice hockey is rough, but it is now a matter of record that Canadian players are spring lambs compared to those who support them." Montreal's director of police claimed it was the worst night he'd seen in 33 years as a cop.

The riot was only one of the setbacks to the city. After the explosion, the game was forfeited to the Red Wings, who a few days later won their seventh straight championship, by two points over the Canadiens. Richard lost his scoring title, by one point to Geoffrion.

Hockey had never experienced anything like it before and, hopefully, never will again.

Protest over suspension took the form of a smoke bomb.

Montreal Canadiens versus New York Rangers
November 1, 1959

Jacques Plante was an innovator. As a young goaltender with the Montreal Canadiens in the early fifties, he used a unique roaming style, which although controversial, was also highly successful for Plante. It earned him the name "Jake the Snake." Today the style is institutionalized; most goalies routinely move from their creases to stop the puck behind the net or to pass it to a teammate.

By 1959, Plante was already one of the game's finest goaltenders. He had won the Vezina Trophy four times, and he had played a major role in Montreal's surge to the top of the standings. His success had not come painlessly, however. Goaltenders wore no masks in those days, and like his colleagues who had played as long as he had, Plante had several hundred stitches in his face. He'd also suffered a broken nose four times, two broken cheekbones, and a fractured skull.

Both cheekbone injuries occurred early in his career, during practice sessions, so as early as 1954, Plante had begun wearing a crude welder's mask during workouts. In 1958, after another shot struck him in the head during a game, Plante and a Montreal businessman set about perfecting a goalie's mask for use in a game. They had one ready for the 1959 season, but coach Toe Blake didn't want his goalie to wear it. "If you have a bad start," he said, "the fans will blame the mask." So Plante continued to wear the mask only in practice sessions.

On the night of November 1, 1959, the Canadiens were playing the Rangers in New York. The game was about eight minutes old and scoreless when Andy Bathgate, New York's high-scoring forward, fired from 25 feet. Screened by players in front of him, Plante never saw the puck, which slammed into his face, knocking him to the ice. Stunned but still conscious, Plante left for the dressing room holding a white towel to his bloody wound. When he reached the dressing room, he went straight to a mirror, "I want to see just how bad this is," he said. Seven stitches were required to close an ugly gash from the side of his nose to his upper lip.

The game was delayed for 20 minutes. Teams didn't carry spare goaltenders in those days, so Blake had no choice but to ask Plante to return to the game. He told his goaltender that he could wear the mask if he wanted to. "Good," said Plante, "because I'm not going back out there without it."

In 1929, Clint Benedict of the Montreal Maroons had experimented briefly with a mask before discarding it. Now Plante was reviving the idea, and this time it would survive and prosper. The Canadiens beat the Rangers 3-1, and as the team continued on an unbeaten streak of 18 games, Plante permitted only 13 goals in 11 straight victories. He wore the mask for each game. "That was good," he said later. "Everyone was skeptical of the mask, and there was pressure for me to show good results or else."

Now, of course, practically every goalie in hockey wears a mask, not out of fear, but out of common sense. As Plante said, "If I jump out of a plane without a parachute, does that make me brave?"

New York Rangers versus Chicago Black Hawks
March 12, 1966

When Maurice Richard scored 50 goals in 1944-45, there were those who thought the feat would never be duplicated. These were the days before expansion was even contemplated, when scoring 20 goals was comparable to hitting .300 in baseball. Even more important, the NHL schedule was limited to 50 games; Richard's pace was a superhuman goal per game. Five years later the NHL expanded its schedule to 70 games, yet not until 1960-61 was Richard's feat equaled, by Montreal's Boom Boom Geoffrion. The next year, when Chicago's Bobby Hull matched the record, he became the people's choice for the future to break it. In the next three seasons, he averaged 37 goals a year with the league's hardest slap shot, which was particularly dangerous when fired from the point on Chicago's devastating power play.

In 1965-66, Hull began with a goal-scoring rush. Though a knee injury sidelined him for 5 games, he reached the 50-goal barrier with 13 games still to play. Even people with only a casual interest in hockey now followed Hull as he stood on the brink of breaking Richard's record. Hull was badgered by radio, television, newspaper, and magazine interviewers as Roger Maris had been while chasing Babe Ruth's record of 60 home runs in 1961.

As the pressure mounted on Hull to score number 51, his teammates abandoned their usual style of play and desperately tried to help him get the big goal. As a result, the entire club suffered. The Hawks were shut out by Toronto, then Montreal, and finally lowly New York. A Chicago newspaper carried the headline, "Will Any Hawk Score?"

On March 12, 1966, Hull and the Hawks took the ice in Chicago Stadium before more than 20,000 fans. The opposition was once again the Rangers, who started lanky Cesare Maniago in goal. The teams played a scoreless first period, which was distinguished only by the expectant hum that swept the huge arena whenever Hull got the puck.

In the second period New York took a 2-0 lead, but early in the third, Chicago's Chico Maki scored on an assist from Hull to make it 2-1. At 4:05, Rangers defenseman Harry Howell drew a two-minute penalty for slashing, but at first Chicago was unable to capitalize. Just as they had in recent games, the Hawks were foiling their attack by trying to set up Hull.

Thirty seconds remained in Howell's penalty when Bill Hay passed to Lou Angotti in the neutral zone. Angotti then gave the puck to Hull and proceeded to the Chicago bench on a line change. Hull swept over the New York blue line and pulled up about 30 feet from Maniago while Eric Nesterenko stormed the net. Then Hull fired a low wrist shot along the ice. Maniago split to make the save, and as Nesterenko sailed past the net, he tipped the goalie's stick. The puck clanged into the back of the net, the red light winked on, and 20,000 people erupted in a mighty roar that shook the building. Hats, programs, confetti, and paper streamers sailed onto the ice. Hull skated toward the section of the stands where his wife was sitting, and through the protective glass, he said to her, "Well, I did it." Then, as teammates swarmed

Bobby Hull beats Detroit's Hank Bassen for goal number 50

Nine long days later, he scores number 51, against New York.

to congratulate him, he picked up one of the hats and plopped it on his head. The crowd loved it, and obviously, so did Bobby.

The official time of the goal was 5:34. The Black Hawks would score two more goals and win the game 4-2. Hull would finish the year with 54 goals, and three years later would set another record with 58.

None of his goals came as hard or was more welcome than number 51.

Detroit Red Wings versus New York Rangers
Montreal Canadiens versus Chicago Black Hawks
April 5, 1970

The most unbelievable season in the history of the National Hockey League ended appropriately enough: unbelievably. The finish, on April 5, 1970, was wild, exciting, bizarre, even comical. Because it was also extremely embarrassing, it forced the NHL to change its rules for breaking deadlocks in the league standings at season's end.

As the final weekend of the season began, a computer calculated that 125 different combinations of finishes were possible in the East Division. With the exception of Toronto, which was doomed to sixth place, each team in the division had a chance to finish in second place, and four as high as first. Chicago and Boston were tied for the league lead with 95 points, Detroit was third with 93, Montreal held fourth with 92, and fifth-place New York had 90. It was definite only that the league rule for determining the final standings would be severely tested. At that time if two teams ended the season tied in points, the rules held that the team with the most victories would finish higher. If the teams had an equal number of victories, most total goals would be the deciding factor. And if the teams were deadlocked in scoring as well as in wins, the club that had permitted the fewest total goals would gain the higher spot in the standings.

As if to make the situation even more dramatic, the schedule for the final weekend listed a series of home-and-home encounters among the contending teams. Chicago was playing in Montreal on Saturday night, and in Chicago Stadium the following night. Likewise, Boston had a home-and-home series with Toronto, and Detroit with New York.

On Saturday night, the Red Wings clinched a playoff berth with a 6-2 victory over the Rangers in Detroit. The Black Hawks surprised the Canadiens in Montreal, winning 4-1, while Boston beat the Maple Leafs in Toronto 4-2. These results left the Rangers still in fifth, two points behind the Canadiens, while the Black Hawks and Bruins were still tied for first.

As the Rangers began their nationally televised game against Detroit in Madison Square Garden on Sunday afternoon, their dilemma was grimly clear: a Rangers victory and a Canadiens loss would still leave the clubs tied for the fourth and final playoff spot with identical 38-22-16 records. Since New York had a cushion in the goals-against column (184 to Montreal's 191), the determining factor would undoubtedly be total goals, and at the beginning of play on Sunday, New York trailed Montreal in that category 237 to 242. So not only did the Rangers have to beat the Wings and depend on the Hawks to defeat Montreal that night; they also had to score at least five more goals than

Montreal scored against the Hawks.

The Red Wings had no such worries. After missing the playoffs three years in a row, they were just happy to be involved again. On their charter flight after Saturday night's game, they popped champagne bottles all the way to New York. Coach Sid Abel had already decided to use Gordie Howe and Alex Delvecchio only sparingly in the Rangers game, resting them for the playoffs. "Mathematically, I didn't think we could make second place because the odds were that Boston would beat Toronto," he would explain later. "Why should I tell my guys to go out and beat their heads against a wall?"

That they did not. Against the Rangers, Abel's forces didn't skate, hit, or check. (Many were, in fact, still feeling the effects of all that champagne.) Meanwhile, New York coach Emile Francis, forced to go all out for victory and goals, decided to send a forechecking forward into each corner and to position his defensemen within 5 feet of the net. This way, he felt, his defensemen could either pass into the corner or receive a pass and shoot on goal like forwards. it was a commitment to total and constant offensive pressure in the Detroit zone, and Francis only hoped that because of it the Wings wouldn't score enough to win.

Francis's strategy and Detroit's lackadaisical play produced a rousing 9-5 victory, which put the Canadiens under extreme pressure that night in Chicago. Not only did the victory pull New York into a tie with Montreal, it also meant that if the Canadiens lost to the Hawks they would have to score at least five goals to bump the Rangers from the final playoff spot.

When the score had reached 9-3 with 3:38 to go, Francis had even pulled goalie Ed Giacomin in a vain attempt to score even more goals. After Detroit scored twice into the empty net, however, Francis returned Giacomin for the rest of the game.

At the other end of the ice, one had to pity poor Roger Crozier. With the Rangers bombarding him from all angles and his teammates interested in nothing more vigorous than an afternoon skate, Crozier was shelled with a record 65 shots on goal. Crozier said later he wasn't playing a hockey game that afternoon; he was playing for his life.

The Rangers' blitz was led by Dave Balon, who had three goals, and Ron Stewart, Rod Gilbert, and Jack Egers, who got two each. "Before the game we were all talking about how many goals we'd get," said Balon. "I think we had half a dozen before we ever got on the ice."

"I just told them they still had a chance and not to let it slip away," said Francis. "I told them hockey is a slippery game. It's played on ice. Funny things can happen."

As far as the Rangers were concerned, the funniest things were yet to come. As the New York players listened on the radio, Montreal took the ice in Chicago knowing it needed either a tie or five goals to make the playoffs. From the outset, it looked as if the Canadiens were playing for the tie. But the Black Hawks were out to win the league title, and they stormed the cautious Canadiens. Chicago seized an early lead, and when with eight minutes left in the game it reached 5-2 on Pit Martin's third goal, Montreal coach Claude Ruel pulled goalie Rogatien Vachon in a desperate attempt to score three more goals. The move only backfired, however. As a capacity crowd of over 20,000 roared and even laughed, the Hawks fired five more goals into

A pummeled Roger Crozier lies tiredly in his net.

ngers fans go wild as Balon scores his third goal of third period.

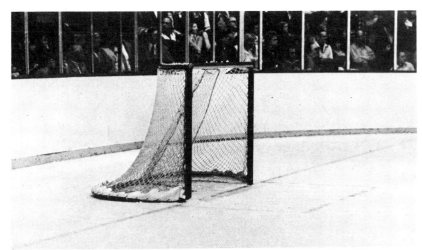

Montreal's net stands open with more than eight minutes to play.

Montreal's vacant net. Vachon would return to his cage only immediately after a Chicago goal or when there was a faceoff in the Montreal zone. When the score rocketed to 10-2 with two minutes remaining, Ruel finally sent Vachon back to finish the game.

After it was all over, Ruel refused to allow the press to interview his players. The portly coach himself didn't feel much like talking, but he did say, "We can't blame Detroit for our problems. But the Red Wings did not work at all. Still we have no one to blame but ourselves for not making the playoffs."

Scotty Bowman, then coach of the West Division champion St. Louis Blues, had attended the game. "I think Montreal played too conservatively, looking for a tie," he said. "That's asking for a lot on Chicago ice. If the Canadiens had gone all-out offensively and forgotten defense, I think they'd have scored five." Who knows? The Hawks, in Tony Esposito, had the year's Vezina Trophy winner and a goalie who set a modern NHL record with 15 shutouts.

Within months the rules concerning ties in the standings were changed. Now when two teams are tied in wins as well as in points at season's end, the situation is resolved by the results of the season series between the tied clubs. But perhaps the unbelievable finish was fitting for a season in which Chicago became the first team to soar from last place to first in one year (the Hawks, though tied in points with Bruins, had 45 victories to Boston's 40), and in which both Canadian teams missed the playoffs for the first time in league history. It was also the first time Montreal missed the playoffs in 22 years.

Chicago's Bobby Hull spoke for everyone in the wild dressing room celebration afterward. "Never saw anything like it," he said, "Never."

(Continued on page 114)

A Portfolio of Action

Hawerchuck tries to push Verbeek off the play

Canadian-American solidarity at Maple Leaf Gardens.

Potvin and Davidson get better acquainted

Philadelphia versus Boston proves that hockey is a swirling mass of colors.

Boston's Dallas Smith bursts between two Islanders, forging a route to goal.

Movement and mood, typifying the game.

Boston Bruins versus St. Louis Blues
May 3, 1970

St. Louis strategy: shadow Orr with two men . . .

In most sports it's up to the defender to prevent the attacker from scoring. Defense is one man's job, putting points on the board is another's. Bobby Orr of the Boston Bruins doesn't recognize the distinction. A defenseman, he's also one of the highest scorers in the National Hockey League.

On a warm Sunday afternoon in the St. Louis Arena, with the Blues playing the Bruins in the first game of the 1970 Stanley Cup finals, St. Louis coach Scotty Bowman became the first coach ever to assign a forward to stop a defenseman. The unorthodox stategy had merit. The Bruins had gunners such as Phil Esposito, Johnny Bucyk, Ken Hodge, and Fred Stanfield, but Orr was the indisputable kingpin of their attack. He set up all of them, and in the 1970 playoffs he was well on his way to establishing new scoring records for a defenseman.

In the days before the opener with the Bruins, Bowman used his blackboard and videotape machine to design a strategy to neutralize Orr. Jimmy Roberts, the Blues' tight-checking left winger, would simply follow Orr wherever he went. Roberts was to totally disregard the puck, except to keep himself between it and Orr. And since Orr was constantly on the ice, Roberts was to be spelled with left wingers Bill McCreary, Terry Crisp, and Tim Ecclestone.

The Blues' maneuver came as a complete surprise to the Bruins and a national television audience as well. Just before the opening faceoff, Roberts skated up to Orr and afterward shadowed him for the entire game. When Boston attacked, Roberts ignored every other white shirt except the one with the black number 4 on the back. When St. Louis rushed, Roberts still stayed with Orr, even though the Bruins' defenseman was trying to break up the attack.

At first Orr didn't know how to react, but before long he realized what the strategy was, concentrated on defense, and abandoned his famed rink-long rushes. The Blues' stratagem to neutralize Orr seemed to be working, but St. Louis was less successful with those other Boston stars. With 15 seconds left in the period, Bucyk scored on a pass from Stanfield to put Boston on top 1-0. At 1:57 of the second period Roberts overskated the puck in front of the Bruins' net but recovered in time to backhand it through Orr's legs and past a startled Gerry Cheevers. That was the high point for the blues.

At 3:57 St. Louis's Jacques Plante was struck between the eyes with a deflected shot and, in spite of the mask he wore, knocked unconscious. He was replaced by Ernie Wakely, who, after a few sparkling saves, was beaten by Bucyk. Roberts was still following Orr all over the ice, but the Bruins simply had too much for the Blues. As someone remarked to Bowman after the game, his strategy worked so well that Orr was on the ice for only five of Boston's six goals in a 6-1 victory.

"I've got to admit that I had more chances today than I've had in a long time," said Bucyk after scoring the hat trick. "What did I get, nine shots?

or one. The strategy failed as Bruins won Cup in four games.

That's a lot. I have to think the way they were checking Bobby had a lot to do with it."

Said Orr, "If they watch me like that in the next game I won't even have to take a shower afterwards. I expected to be watched but not like that. I could have gone out for lunch for all the chances I had to get in the play. So I just stayed out of things."

Over in the losers' quarters, Roberts was saying, "Orr's the one who sets it all up for them. If we can cover him with one man, then it's a good idea. He's more valuable than any one man on our team, so we certainly can sacrifice one man to cover him."

"Every great player in the league has had that kind of attention," agreed Bowman. "It wasn't as effective as I'd hoped, because the other guys didn't accept the drudgery of checking Orr the way Roberts did. But really, how do you practice something like that? We worked on it for six hours, but we don't have Bobby Orr to practice against."

In the second game of the finals two nights later, Roberts was again assigned to Orr. But after the Bruins broke out to a quick 3-0 lead, Bowman abandoned the idea. Capturing their first Stanley Cup since 1941, Boston won that game, 6-2, and swept the Blues in four straight.

After the second game, Bowman was asked for a final comment on his Orr-oriented plot. Looking up from the statistics sheet, he sighed and said, "I did the same thing when I was coaching the Montreal Junior Canadiens and Orr was playing for Oshawa. The only difference was that Bobby was playing sixty minutes then instead of forty. We lost that night too."

Boston Bruins versus Los Angeles Kings
March 12, 1971

It was March 1971, and hockey fans across North America knew it was only a matter of time before Phil Esposito became the greatest goal scorer in hockey history. The big centerman of the Boston Bruins had been on a scoring rampage all year; he had reached 50 goals with incredible ease. And now, with a month remaining in the regular schedule, he was about to tie Bobby Hull's all time record of 58.

Astounding as they were, Esposito's scoring feats were viewed with mixed emotions. Many charged they were a by-product of reckless, mindless expansion, which had left has-beens and never-weres in goal and on defense for most expansion teams. High-scoring games were the rule now, not the exceptions they had been in pre expansion days. Now the fans almost expected a 7-3 or 8-4 game, especially from the Bruins.

On March 11, 1971, Esposito tied Hull's mark before 10,411 people in the Oakland-Alameda Coliseum Arena. The less-than-capacity crowd was in itself a reflection of what expansion meant to hockey, its traditions, and its milestones. In Boston, Montreal, St. Louis, or Minnesota, fans would have been breaking down doors to watch the game's biggest scoring record tied or perhaps even broken. But in Oakland it wasn't much more than another hockey game.

Esposito himself hoped he would tie and/or break the mark in Boston, where fans would appreciate the feat. The Boston fans remembered Rocket Richard's 50 goals in 50 games in 1944-45; Boom Boom Geoffrion's 50 in 1960-61; and Hull's 50 in 1961-62. Boston was among the first of the old-line hockey towns.

Considering the outrageous, postexpansion assault on NHL records, however, it was probably appropriate that Esposito broke Hull's mark the next night, in Los Angeles. At 7:03 of the first period he brought 14,316 fans (also below capacity) to their feet when he tipped Ted Green's shot from the point past Kings goaltender Denis Dejordy. Then, at 15:40 of the second period, he became the first player in history to score 60 goals when he converted passes from Dallas Smith and Ken Hodge. After the game, which the Bruins won by a typically lopsided score, 7-2, Esposito was happy but not elated. He made it a point to say that "Bobby Hull's still the greatest."

"To be honest, I felt more pressure two years ago when I was the first to score more than a hundred points in a season," Esposito said. "No one else had ever done it, and I wanted to be the first. But I'm glad it's over. With eleven games left after this one, I knew that I'd get the record sooner or later, but I still wanted to get number fity-nine in seventy games, so there wouldn't be any asterisk after it in the record books."

And just what happened on the goal? "Nothing much," said Esposito. "I saw Green take the shot, and I know that Teddy shoots low. I knew I could score if I could get my stick on it. But I've been fortunate against the Kings. Denis Dejordy and I both played together in Chicago; I know his moves."

Actually, it was a record-breaking night for all the Bruins, who were soaring to their first NHL title in 30 years. Esposito's pair of goals and an assist gave him 128 points for the season, breaking the record of 126 he had set two years earlier. His sixtieth goal also broke a record set by Montreal's Jean Beliveau in 1955, when he scored 59 goals—47 in 70 league games and 12 during the playoffs.

Orr also got his eighty-sixth, eighty-seventh, and eight-eighth assists in the game, which broke his record of 87 set the year before and which boosted his point total to 123, past the record 120 he had established for defensemen the year before. By scoring his thirty-fifth goal that night, Bobby also raised his own record total of goals for a defenseman.

With Esposito and Orr leading the way, the 1970-71 Bruins shattered 16 NHL team records and 21 individual marks. The team amassed 399 goals, 98 more than any team had ever scored before. Two Bruins scored more than 50 goals, five had 30 or more, and ten had 20 or more. Esposito's hat trick against Montreal on the last day of the regular season gave him seven for the year, three more than any other player had ever managed in one season.

When he was finally through, Esposito had scored 76 goals and 76 assists for 152 points. And during the last game against Montreal, in Boston Garden, 15,000 people rose to their feet and gave him a minute-long standing ovation. They knew full well that Esposito couldn't have accomplished the feat before expansion but were nonetheless acknowledging a remarkable scoring performance in any league.

"For the first time in my life I was shy," Espo said later. "During that ovation I just didn't know how to react. I've never been shy before, but the people in this town are terrific." So was Phil Esposito.

Phil Esposito is congratulated after scoring his fifty-ninth g

Boston Bruins versus Toronto Maple Leafs
February 7, 1976

Boston arrived in Toronto after defeating the Pittsburgh Penguins for their seventh straight victory; they were leading the Charles F. Adams Division with 73 points while Toronto was in third place with only 53. Winning their eighth straight game, therefore, should not have been a very difficult task. John Bucyk, with 1,280 points, was only one point behind Alexander Delvecchio; if he could get a couple of points against Toronto, he would be the NHL's second highest scorer. (Gordie Howe led with 1,809.)

But Darryl Sittler and his wingers, Lanny McDonald and L. Errol Thompson, had other ideas. By 7:01 of the first period, Toronto had scored two goals (McDonald and Turnbull), both assisted by Sittler. At 2:56 of the second period, Sittler scored his first goal of the game; 37 seconds later he assisted on a goal by Salming. Midway in the period Sittler really got rolling when he scored two more goals, at 8:12 and 10:27. Again he asssisted on a goal by Salming at 13:57. Sittler had three goals and two assists in the period, for five points, a feat accomplished by only three other players—Leslie Cunninghams and Maxwell Bentley of Chicago and Leo LaBine of Boston.

At thebeginning of the third period, the score was 8-4 in favor of Toronoto. The game was Sittler. He scored at 0:44, assisted byThompson and Salming, and at 9:27, assisted again byThompson. His third goal of the period came at 16:35, assisted by his other winger, McDonald.

Sittler had scored six goals and assisted on four others, something no other player had ever done. The record had stood at eight points, and only two players had reached that total—M. Bert Olmstead and Rocket Richard, both Montreal Canadiens. Little attention was paid to the fact that by scoring three goals in successive periods he had achieved something else that nobody had ever done before.

Chicago Black Hawks versus Minnesota North Stars
Atlanta Flames versus Pittsburgh Penguins
December 11, 1977

This game, in venerable Chicago Stadium, had barely gotten underway when a goal was scored at 0:19 and the public address announcer extolled over the loudspeaker system, "Goal by Mikita—assists, Pierre Plante and Tony Esposito." The period moved along with few delays. Only one penalty was called. When the period ended Chicago had scored three more goals and led 4-0.

In the second period, Chicago scored twice and Minnesota three times. Near the end of the period, Pierre Plante and Thomas Younghans engaged in an altercation; each drew minor and major penalties. The score was 6-3 as the third period began. There was neither a goal nor a penalty until 13:51

Colorado Rockies versus New York Islanders
November 28, 1979

Playing in Denver, the Colorado Rockies were leading four at the start of the second period when New York Islanders coach, Alger Arbour, decided to replace Glenn Resch with Bill Smith.

A few minutes after the third period got underway, Michael Kaszycki committed an infraction and the referee's arm shot up indicating a delayed penalty (Colorado was controlling the puck). William McKenzie, Colorado's goaltender, raced to the bench to allow the Rockies to get six skaters on the ice. The Rockies attacked; a shot caromed off Smith's chest, passt Islander's defenseman David Lewis, into a corner where Colorado defenseman Rob Ramage controlled it. He shot the puck out but no one intercepted it, and it slid 195 feet into the vacated Colorado net.

At first the goal was given to Lewis, but after the game videotapes showed that Smith had been the last Islander to touch the puck when it deflected off his chest. Although Smith didn't score the goal—he didn't even shoot it—he was awarded it on a technicality, thereby becoming the first goaltender in National Hockey League history to "score" a goal.

Islander's Bill Smith: the first goalie to score a goal

Edmonton Oilers versus WashingtonCapitals
February 15, 1980

There was nothing to indicate that Wayne Gretzky would do anything spectacular as this game progressed in Northlands Coliseum in Edmonton, Alberta. Alan Hangsleben scored at 15:54 for Washingotn. Shortly afterward,, Gretzky received an assist, along with Blair MacDonald, when Brett Callighen-scored for Edmonton at 17:04. Stanley Weir scored at 18:18, and the period ended with Edmonton ahead two goals to one.

In the second period, MacDonald scored at 4:45, Gretzky got another assist, along withCallighen. When MacDonald scored again at 8:56, Gretzky received another assist, and still another 10:56 when Robert Schmautz scored. Edmonton had scored three goals in the second period, and Gretzky had assisted on all of them.

Edmonton had a four-goal lead as the third period began. There was no scoring until 13:14 when David Semenko scored, assisted by Gretzky. Fifty seconds later, Schmautz scored his second goal again as.sisted by Gretzky. Fifty-eight seconds passed before Gretzky got another assist as MacDonald scored his third goal. Gretzky had assisted on three goals in one minute and forty-eight seconds, and had a game total of seven assists. Washington scored their second goal with a little over a minute left to play, ending the game 8-2.

Gretzky didn't break a record with his seven assists, but he tied one that had stood for 33 years. William ("Billy the Kid") Taylor had set while playing for Detroit on March 16, 1947.

Detroit Red Wings versus Vancouver Canucks
February 11, 1982

In this historic game, Vancouver got the first goal when Marc Crawford scored at 3:36 of the first period. Then, as the Detroit spectators watched in awe, their perennial doormat club scored the next four goals.

At 5:28 of the first period, Ted Nolan scored; less than two minutes later, Michael Blaisdell scored. There was only one penalty—a bench penalty to Detroit at 18:15. At the end of the first period, Detroit led two goals to one.

The second period had barely gotten underway when Willie Huber scored. Then, at 8:43 Blaisdell scored his second goal. When the Detroit Red Wings trooped to their dressing room at the end of the second period they were out in front four goals to one, and a victory appeared to be within their grasp.

At 5:55 of the third period, Jody Gage gloved the puck in the crease and immediately, referee Kerry Fraser called for a penalty shot. Thomas of Vancouver's Swedish imports, would take it. As Gilles Gilbert moved across the crease Gradin skated in close, went to his backhand, and slid the puck on the ice into the net. Vancouver successfully killed a penalty to Andy Schliebener at 10:11, and five minutes later Gradin scored again. Detroit saw its lead slip to four goals to three.

The Red Wings managed to stave off Vancouver's attack for over 19 minutes of the third period, but then, at 19:30, Stanley Smyl got a breakaway. Willie Huber, Detroit's German-born defenseman, was able to get his stick to Smyl and trip him from behind; another penalty shot was called. Normally the fouled player would take the shot, but in this case, Smyl had been injured when he crashed into a goal post as he was upended. Vancouver decided to use one of their Czechoslovakian imports—Ivan Hlinka. Hlinia, a veteran of European hockey, fired the puck high into the net as Gilbert moved out toward him.

Although the Detroit spectators had watched a 4-1 lead disappear into a 4-4 tie, they had witnessed something no one else had ever seen. They had watched as two penalty shots were called in one game—not only in one game, but in one period. During an average season, only about 35% of the penalty shots taken result in a score, but in this instance 100% did.

Wayne Gretzky

The Stanley Cup

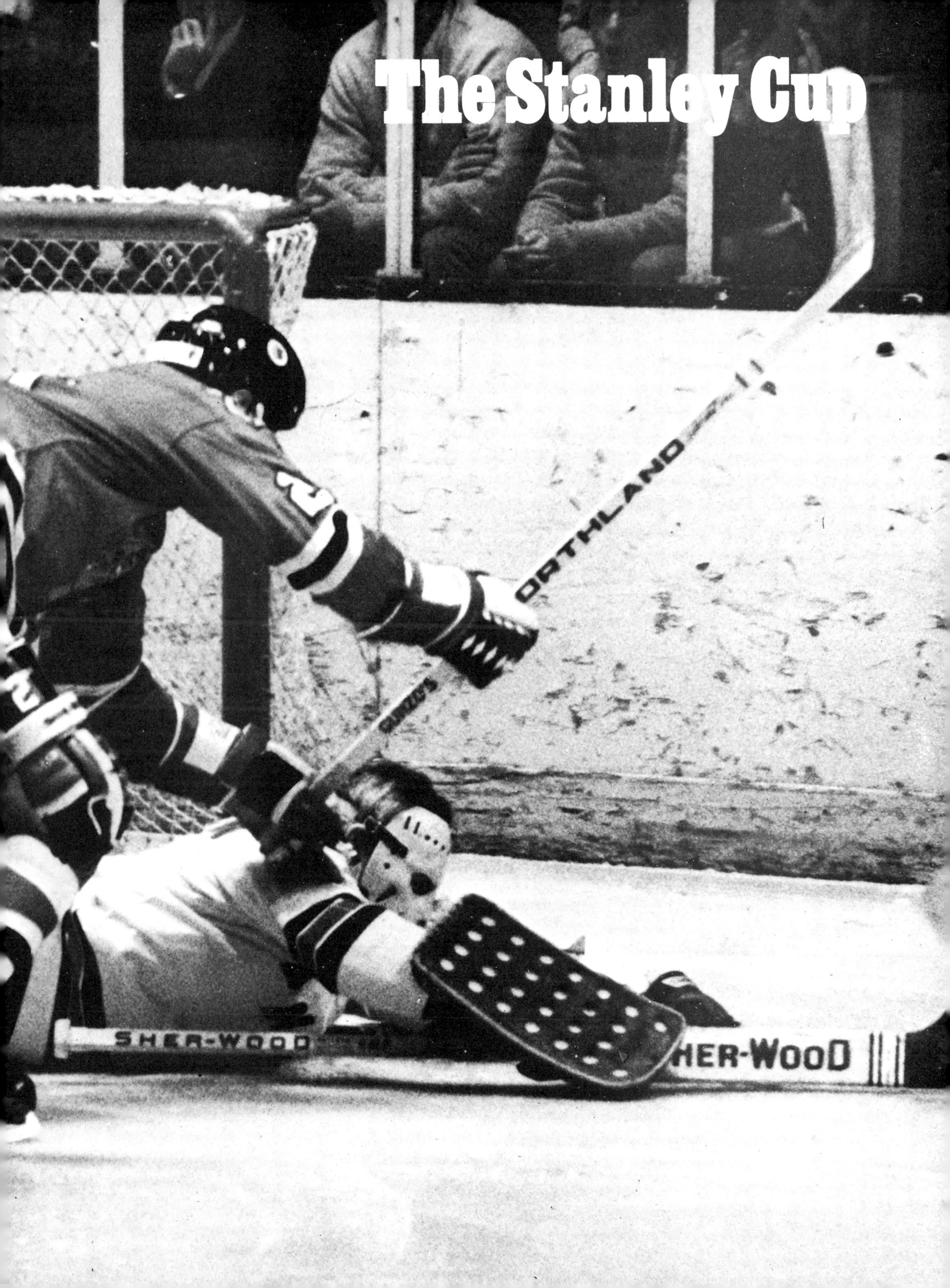

is complete title was Right Honourable Sir Frederick Arthur Stanley, Baron Stanley of Preston, in the County of Lancaster, in the Peerage of Great Britain, Knight Grand Cross of the Most Honourable Order of the Bath. In England he was noted almost as much for his love of horseracing, cricket, and soccer as he was for his breeding, education, and political success. In 1888, he came to Canada to become governor general of the Dominion. It was in this capacity that he donated a silver bowl to a new game that was sweeping the country at the time. Not surprisingly, the bowl would become known as the Stanley Cup.

On March 18, 1892, Lord Stanley intoned, "I have for some time been thinking it would be a good thing if there were a challenge cup. . . It would be worth considering whether [the matches] could not be arranged so that each team would play once at home and once where their opponents hail from." With that a silver bowl worth $48.50, lined with gold and attached to an ebony base, was placed in the hands of trustees. Before parting with his gift, Lord Stanley suggested some ground rules for the proper disposition of it.

   * The winners shall give bond for the return of the cup in good order . . . for the purpose of such bond being given to any other team that may in turn win.
   * Each winning team shall have at their own charge, engraved on a silver ring, fitted on the cup for that purpose, the name of the team and the year won.
   * The cup shall remain a challenge cup, and should not become the property of any team, even if won more than once.
   * In case of any doubt as to the title of any club to claim the

position of champions, the cup shall be held or awarded by the trustees as they may think right, their decision being absolute.

The final rule was to deprive Lord Stanley of his fondest wish—that the first team to have its name inscribed on the Cup would be his hometown favorites from Ottawa. Since Ottawa had been, in its view, "the leading club in Canada" in 1891-92, it claimed the right to hold the Cup, hoping to defend it the next spring. But the trustees had other ideas. They ruled that since there had been no competition for the Cup at the end of the 1891-92 season, some should be arranged and scheduled Ottawa to play the Osgoode Hall club of Toronto. Following Lord Stanley's good intentions that the site for the championship be varied, the trustees scheduled the game for Toronto. Ottawa refused to make the trip, and on February 23, 1893, the trustees announced: "Arrangements have been completed whereby the Lord Stanley Hockey Cup will now pass into the hands of the Montreal Amateur Athletic Association. Some trouble arose last year about the acceptance, and the M.A.A.A. have had it in their possession ever since. The Montreal team will now officially take it over." Thus it was the Montreal club, another powerful team of the era, that was the first to have its name inscribed on the hallowed Cup.

Another irony is that Lord Stanley never saw a Cup game. His term over, he was back in England when the first Cup game was played by defending Montreal against Ottawa at Montreal's Victoria Rink on March 22, 1894. Before more than 5,000 fans, Montreal won 3-1. A Montreal newspaper carried the news the next day.

   In the first half, the play was of the rushing order, with

Montreal getting slightly the best of it. The Ottawas, however, found an opening after about 10 minutes of play, and Russell scored. As soon as the puck was sent off again, Hodgson carried it to the Ottawa end and undertook to score; but the Ottawa defence were on the alert and saved the goal. A hard struggle ensued, and after 10 minutes of rushing and hard hockey, Montreal scored. No other goal was taken in this half, and when the second half commenced, everyone settled down to see a great contest and they were not disappointed. The Ottawas played with much more vim and made it lively for their opponents. The Montrealers were more fortunate, and through the offices of Hodgson and Barlow, two more goals were taken. The match concluded in a victory for the local team by three goals to one. After the match the winners were carried off the rink.

Almost overnight the Stanley Cup became the most coveted trophy in all Canada. Hockey leagues across the country bombarded the trustees with demands that they grant them an opportunity to play for it. Despite the national appeal of the prize, teams from one city dominated the competition. The city of Montreal and three of its teams, the Victorias, the Shamrocks, and the Montreal A.A.A., had a virtual lock on the Cup until 1902, when the Ottawa Silver Seven held it for three years in a row.

In 1905, that Ottawa club accepted the most determined challenge in Stanley Cup history. It came from Dawson City of the Yukon Territory. Financed by Colonel Joe Doyle, a well-heeled local prospector, the Dawson City team embarked on a 23-day trek to Ottawa. By dog sled, boat, and train, the club managed to cover the 4,500 miles to Ottawa. On the third day of the trip, with the temperature well below zero, practically every player had to remove his boots for treatment of cold blisters. After missing a boat connection in Skagway, the team was forced to wait five days before it could book passage from Seattle to Vancouver. Then, following what seemed like an endless train ride, the team straggled into Ottawa the day before the series was to begin.

Alas, they might better have stayed home. Dawson City's gold diggers suffered the most humiliating elimination in Cup history, losing the first game 9-2, and the second and deciding game by 23-3. (In the deciding game, Ottawa's Frank McGee scored a remarkable total of 14 goals, including 8 in eight minutes.)

By 1910, winning the Stanley Cup was no longer possible for Canada's amateur clubs; big money had infiltrated the game at an alarming rate, and the only teams talented enough to compete for the national championship were those stocked with professionals.

In 1913, a series was started between the National Hockey Association and the Pacific Coast Hockey League, but when the PCHL went out of business in 1927, the Cup became the exclusive property of the newly named National Hockey League.

By now the Stanley Cup had already known some irreverent misadventures. It had been kicked into the Rideau Canal by a member of the Ottawa Silver Seven, filled with geraniums by a Montreal housewife, and left on a sidewalk by an absent-minded member of the champion Montreal Canadiens. An executive of the Kenora, Ontario, Thistles had almost thrown the Cup into the Lake of the Woods near Kenora.

More suitable Stanley Cup tradition had also been established, however. When the Cup was at stake, there were never enough tickets for the games and when a team was fortunate enough to capture it, its fans simply went wild. Covering an Ottawa Cup victory in 1909, one

newspaperman described a tumultous celebration.

With the ringing of the gong, spectators leaped to the ice. The old Ottawa cheer which had urged the wearers of the red, white and black to victory . . . again rang out with increasing volume. . . .As the Ottawa players started to leave for the dressing room, they were surrounded. . .Taylor, who had played with a foot bound in batting and lint, snugly encased in a special boot, protected on the inside by a broad welt of hard leather, was seized and raised shoulder-high . . . rooters robbed him of his stick and gloves and retained them as souvenirs . . . far into the night and morning, the rejoicing continued.

Stanley Cup play has inspired some players to perform beyond their capabilities. Others have wilted under the pressure. In 1928, Lester Patrick, coach of the New York Rangers, substituted in goal and inspired his team to win the Cup title. In 1936, the longest

The Ottawa Silver Seven: Cup champions, 1903-05

game in Cup history was won by rookie Modere Bruneteau of the Detroit Red Wings, at 16:30 of the sixth overtime period. In 1951, the Toronto Maple Leafs defeated Montreal in five games, all in overtime. The winning goal in that final game was scored by Bill Barilko, who would die a few months later in a plane crash. A year later, the Red Wings captured the Cup in eight straight games, with goalie Terry Sawchuk yielding only five goals for an amazing 0.62 average. And in 1964, Toronto defeated the Red Wings in seven games, after which it was revealed that defenseman Bobby Baun of the Leafs had played the final two games despite a fractured ankle.

One of the Stanley Cup's supreme competitors was defenseman Tim Horton, who was killed in a car accident in February, 1974, after playing for the Buffalo Sabres in a game at Toronto. Horton had already announced that the 1973-74 season, his twenty-second in the NHL, would be his last. "All I'd like to do," he said, "is play for the Stanley Cup one more time."

Baseball has its World Series, pro football its Super Bowl, college football all those bowls, but no trophy in sport has inspired quite the grit and determination among its competitors as has the Stanley Cup. NHL players now realize as much as $25,000 per man for winning their division championship and the Stanley Cup. Many people may scoff at the suggestion that such financial reward pales when compared with the hallowed ritual of sipping champagne from Lord Stanley's gift of 80 years ago. Let them scoff, say those who have grown up with hockey and who know that the Stanley Cup is not only the oldest but the most cherished trophy in professional sport today.

Coach Hap Day's 1949 champs: Toronto Maple Leafs

STANLEY CUP WINNERS

Season	Champions	Manager	Coach
1982-83	New York Islanders	William Torrey	Alger J. Arbour
1981-82	New York Islanders	William Torrey	Alger J.Arbour
1980-81	New York Islanders	William Torrey	Alger J. Arbour
1979-80	New York Islanders	WilliamTorrey	Alger J. Arbour
1978-79	Montreal Canadiens	Irving Grundman	W. Scott Bowman
1977-78	Montreal Canadiens	Samuel Pollock	W. Scott Bowman
1976-77	Montreal Canadiens	Samuel Pollock	W. Scott Bowman
1975-76	Montreal Canadiens	Samuel Pollock	W. Scott Bowman
1974-75	Philadelphia Flyers	C. Keith Allen	Frederick Shero
1973-74	Philadelphia Flyers	C. Keith Allen	Frederick Shero
1972-73	Montreal Canadiens	Sam Pollock	Scotty Bowman
1971-72	Boston Bruins	Milt Schmidt	Tom Johnson
1970-71	Montreal Canadiens	Sam Pollock	Al MacNeil
1969-70	Boston Bruins	Milt Schmidt	Harry Sinden
1968-69	Montreal Canadiens	Sam Pollock	Claude Ruel
1967-68	Montreal Canadiens	Sam Pollock	Toe Blake
1966-67	Toronto Maple Leafs	Punch Imlach	Punch Imlach
1965-66	Montreal Canadiens	Sam Pollock	Toe Blake
1964-65	Montreal Canadiens	Sam Pollock	Toe Blake
1963-64	Toronto Maple Leafs	Punch Imlach	Punch Imlach
1962-63	Toronto Maple Leafs	Punch Imlach	Punch Imlach
1961-62	Toronto Maple Leafs	Punch Imlach	Punch Imlach
1960-61	Chicago Black Hawks	Tommy Ivan	Rudy Pilous
1959-60	Montreal Canadiens	Frank Selke	Toe Blake
1958-59	Montreal Canadiens	Frank Selke	Toe Blake
1957-58	Montreal Canadiens	Frank Selke	Toe Blake
1956-57	Montreal Canadiens	Frank Selke	Toe Blake
1955-56	Montreal Canadiens	Frank Selke	Toe Blake
1954-55	Detroit Red Wings	Jack Adams	Jimmy Skinner
1953-54	Detroit Red Wings	Jack Adams	Tommy Ivan
1952-53	Montreal Canadiens	Frank Selke	Dick Irvin
1951-52	Detroit Red Wings	Jack Adams	Tommy Ivan
1950-51	Toronto Maple Leafs	Conn Smythe	Joe Primeau
1949-50	Detroit Red Wings	Jack Adams	Tommy Ivan
1948-49	Toronto Maple Leafs	Conn Smythe	Hap Day

1947-48—Toronto Maple Leafs ....Conn Smythe..............Hap Day
1946-47—Toronto Maple Leafs ....Conn Smythe..............Hap Day
1945-46—Montreal Canadiens ....Tommy Gorman..........Dick Irvin
1944-45—Toronto Maple Leafs ....Conn Smythe..............Hap Day
1943-44—Montreal Canadiens ....Tommy Gorman..........Dick Irvin
1942-43—Detroit Red Wings ....Jack Adams ....Jack Adams
1941-42—Toronto Maple Leafs ....Conn Smythe..............Hap Day
1940-41—Boston Bruins ....Art Ross.....................Cooney Weiland
1939-40—New York Rangers ....Lester Patrick............Frank Boucher
1938-39—Boston Bruins ....Art Ross.....................Art Ross
1937-38—Chicago Black Hawks..............Bill Stewart ....Bill Stewart
1936-37—Detroit Red Wings ....Jack Adams ....Jack Adams
1935-36—Detroit Red Wings ....Jack Adams ....Jack Adams
1934-35—Montreal Maroons ....Tommy Gorman..........Tommy Gorman
1933-34—Chicago Black Hawks..............Tommy Gorman..........Tommy Gorman
1932-33—New York Rangers ....Lester Patrick............Lester Patrick
1931-32—Toronto Maple Leafs ....Conn Smythe..............Dick Irvin
1930-31—Montreal Canadiens ....Cecil Hart ....Cecil Hart
1929-30—Montreal Canadiens ....Cecil Hart ....Cecil Hart
1928-29—Boston Bruins ....Art Ross.....................Cy Denneny
1927-28—New York Rangers ....Lester Patrick............Lester Patrick
1926-27—Ottawa Senators ....Dave Gill..................Dave Gill
1925-26—Montreal Maroons ....Eddie Gerard.............Eddie Gerard
1924-25—Victoria Cougars ....Lester Patrick............Lester Patrick
1923-24—Montreal Canadiens ....Leo Dandurand..........Leo Dandurand
1922-23—Ottawa Senators ....Tommy Gorman..........Pete Green
1921-22—Toronto St. Pats ....Charlie Querrie..........Eddie Powers
1920-21—Ottawa Senators ....Tommy Gorman..........Pete Green
1919-20—Ottawa Senators ....Tommy Gorman..........Pete Green
1918-19—No decision
1917-18—Toronto Arenas ....Charlie Querrie..........Dick Carroll
1916-17—Seattle Metropolitans...............Pete Muldoon ....Pete Muldoon
1915-16—Montreal Canadiens ....George Kennedy.........George Kennedy
1914-15—Vancouver Millionaires ....Frank Patrick ....Frank Patrick
1913-14—Toronto Blueshirts ....Jack Marshall............Scotty Davidson
1912-13—Quebec Bulldogs....................M.J. Quinn.................Joe Malone
1911-12—Quebec Bulldogs....................M.J. Quinn ....C. Nolan
1910-11—Ottawa Senators ....   Bruce Stuart
1909-10—Montreal Wanderers................R.R. Boon ....Pud Glass
1908-09—Ottawa Senators ....   Bruce Stuart
1907-08—Montreal Wanderers................R.R. Boon ....Cecil Blachford
1906-07—Montreal Wanderers (March)...R.R. Boon ....Cecil Blachford
1906-07—Kenora Thistles (January) ........F.A. Hudson...............Tommy Phillips
1905-06—Montreal Wanderers................   Cecil Blachford
1904-05—Ottawa Silver Seven ....   A.T. Smith
1903-04—Ottawa Silver Seven ....   A.T. Smith
1902-03—Ottawa Silver Seven ....   A.T. Smith
1901-02—Montreal A.A.A. ....   R.R. Boon
1900-01—Winnipeg Victorias ....   Magnus Flett
1899-1900—Montreal Shamrocks............   H.J. Trihey
1898-99—Montreal Shamrocks ....   H.J. Trihey
1897-98—Montreal Victorias...................   F. Richardson
1896-97—Montreal Victorias...................   Mike Grant
1895-96—Montreal Victorias
            (December, 1896)....................   Mike Grant
1895-96—Winnipeg Victorias (February)..
1894-95—Montreal Victorias...................   Mike Grant
1893-94—Montreal A.A.A. ....
1892-93—Montreal A.A.A. ....

Sir Frederick Arthur Stanley

Line Scores

1927

Ottawa won two games to none.

Game 1

Ottawa 0 0 0 0—0
Boston   0 0 0 0—0

First Period—No scoring

Second Period—No scoring

Third Period—No scoring

Overtime—No scoring

Game 2

Ottawa 2 0 1—3
Boston   0 0 1—1

First Period—1. Ottawa
      2. Ottawa

Second Period—No scoring

Third Period—3. Boston, Oliver;
      4. Ottawa, Denneny (Smith) 19:55

Game 3

Boston   1 0 0 0 0—1
Ottawa 0 1 0 0 0—1

First Period—1. Boston, Herberts (Oliver) 7:00

Second Period—2. Ottawa, Denneny (Clancy) 15:00

Third Period—No scoring

Overtime—No scoring

Game 4

Boston   0 0 1—1
Ottawa 0 2 1—3

First Period—No scoring

Second Period—1. Ottawa, Finnigan (Nighbor) 5:00;
      2. Ottawa, Denneny (unassisted) 7:30

Third Period—3. Ottawa, Denneny (unassisted) 11:00;
      4. Boston, Oliver

1928

New York won three games to two.

Game 1

New York   0 0 0—0
Montreal Maroons 0 1 1—2

First Period—No scoring

Second Period—1. Montreal, Dutton (unassisted) 10:48

Third Period—2. Montreal, Phillips (Munro) 5:56

Game 2

New York   0 1 0 1—2
Montreal Maroons 0 1 0 0—-1

First Period—No scoring

Third Period—1. New York, Bill Cook (unassisted) :30;
      2. Montreal, Steward (Smith) 18:51

Second Period—No scoring

Overtime—3. New York, Boucher (Johnson) 7:05

Game 3

New York   0 0 0—0
Montreal Maroons 0 1 1—2

First Period—No scoring

Second Period—1. Montreal, Stewart (Smith) 14:35

Third Period—2. Montreal, Siebert (unassisted) 12:47

Game 4

New York   0 1 0—1
Montreal Maroons 0 0 0—0

First Period—No scoring

Second Period—1. New York, Boucher (Johnson, Bill Cook)

Third Period—No scoring 13:13

Game 5

New York   1 0 1—2
Montreal Maroons 0 0 1—1

First Period—1. New York, Boucher (Bun Cook) 5:32

Second Period—No scoring

Third Period—2. New York, Boucher (Bill Cook, Abel) 3:35;
      3. Montreal, Phillips (Siebert) 15:00

1929

Boston won two games to none.

Game 1

New York
  0 0 0—0
Boston
  0 2 0—2

First Period—No scoring

Second Period—1. Boston, Clapper (unassisted);
    2. Boston, Gainor (unassisted)

Third Period—No scoring

Game 2

Boston
  0 1 1—2
New York
  0 0 1—1

First Period—No scoring

Second Period—1. Boston, Oliver (unassisted) 14:01

Third Period—2. New York, Keeling (unassisted) 6:48; .
    3. Boston, Carson (Oliver) 18:02

1930

Montreal won two games to none.

Game 1

Montreal
0 2 1—3
Boston
0 0 0—0

First Period—No scoring

Second Period—1. Montreal, Leduc (unassisted) 8:43;
    2. Montreal, S. Mantha (Joliat) 13:17

Third Period—3. Montreal, Lepine (Leduc) 6:27

Game 2

Boston
  0 1 2—3
Montreal
  2 2 0—4

First Period—1. Montreal, McCaffrey (Lepine) 9:10;
    2. Montreal, Wasnie (Burke) 17:36

Second Period—3. Montreal, S. Mantha (Wasnie);
    4. Boston, Shore (unassisted);
    5. Montreal, Morenz (Leduc) 1:00

Third Period—6. Boston, Gailbraith (Oliver);
    7. Boston, Clapper (Weiland)

1931

Montreal won three games to two.

Game 1

Montreal
1 1 0—2
Chicago
0 1 0—1

First Period—1. Montreal, G. Mantha (Gagnon) 4:50

Second Period—2. Montreal, Lepine (unassisted) 2:20;
    3. Chicago, Ripley (Gottselig, Couture) 8:30

Third Period—No scoring

Game 2

Montreal
  0 0 1 0 0—1
Chicago
  0 1 0 0 1—2

First Period—No Scoring

Second Period—1. Chicago, Adams (unassisted) 11:45

Third Period—2. Montreal, Wasnie (Larochelle) 12:10

First Overtime-no scoring

Second Overtime—3. Chicago, Gottselig (unassisted) 4:50

Game 3

Chicago
  0 0 2 0 0 1—3
Montreal
  1 1 0 0 0 0—2

First Period—Montreal, Gagnon (Burke, G. Mantha) 5:15

Second Period—2. Montreal, G. Mantha (Lepine) 7:29

Third Period—3. Chicago, March (Gottselig) 16:20;
    4. Chicago, Adams (Cook) 17:07

First Overtime—No scoring

Second Overtime—No scoring

Third Overtime—5. Chicago, Wentworth (Adams)
    13:50

Game 4

Chicago
  2 0 0—2
Montreal
  0 1 3—4

First Period—1. Chicago, Gottselig (Ripley) 1:33;
    2. Chicago, Arbour (Ingram) 13:58

Second Period—3. Montreal, Gagnon (Leduc) 4:34

Third Period—4. Montreal, Gagnon (Wasnie) 4:25;
    5. Montreal, Lepine (Gagnon) 10:55;
    6. Montreal, Lepine (Joliat) 17:25

Game 5
Chicago
  0 0 0—0
Montreal
  0 1 1—2

First Period—No scoring

Second Period—1. Montreal, Gagnon (Joliat) 9:59

Third Period—2. Montreal, Morenz (unassisted) 15:27

1932
Toronto won three games to none.
Game 1

Toronto
1 4 1—6
New York
1 1 2—4

First Period—1. Toronto, Day (Cotton) 4:25;
    2. New York, Bun Cook (Bill Cook, Boucher) 13:00

Second Period—3. Toronto, Jackson (Day) 3:35
    4. Toronto, Jackson (Horner) 6:45;
    5. Toronto, Conacher (unassisted)
    6. Toronto, Jackson (unassisted)
    7. New York, Dillon (Murdoch)

The Stanley Cup

Third Period—8. New York, Johnson (unassisted) 2:35;
      9. New York, Bun Cook (Boucher) 3:35;
      10. Toronto, Horner (Jackson) 14:37

Game 2

Toronto
0 2 4—6
New York
1 1 0—2

First Period—1. New York, Bun Cook (Bill Cook) 3:53

Second Period—2. New York, Brennan (unassisted) 1:00;
      3.Toronto, Jackson (unassisted)
      4.Toronto, Conacher (unassisted)

Third Period—5. Toronto, Clancy (Primeau) 1:49;
      6. Toronto, Conacher (Jackson)
      7. Toronto, Clancy (Primeau)
      8. Toronto, Cotton (Primeau)

Game 3

New York
0 1 3—4
Toronto
2 1 3—6

First Period—1. Toronto, Blair (Clancy) 5:39
      2. Toronto, Blair (Gracie) 6:11

Second Period—3. Toronto, Jackson (Primeau, Conacher)
10:57;
      4. New York, Boucher (Heller) 15:24

Third Period—5. Toronto, Finnigan (Day) 8:56;
      6. Toronto, Bailey (Conacher, Day) 15:07;
      7. New York, Bun Cook (Boucher) 16:32;
      8. Toronto, Gracie (Finnigan) 17:36;
      9. New York, Boucher (Bun Cook) 18:26;
      10. New York, Boucher (unassisted) 19:26;

1933

New York won three games to one.

Game 1

Toronto
  0 0 1—1
New York
  2 2 1—5

First Period—1. New York, Bun Cook (Bill Cook, Boucher)
12:18;
      2. New York Dillon (Murdoch) 13:11

Second Period—3. New York, Heller (Asmundson,
  Somers) 8:31;

      4. New York, Dillon (unassisted) 14:25

Third Period—5. Toronto, Levinsky (unassisted) 15:53;
      6. New York, Murdoch (Dillon) 16:55

Game 2

New York
  2 0 1—3
Toronto
  1 0 0—1

First Period—1.Toronto, Doraty (Gracie) 1:10;
      2. New York, Heller (Somers) 8:18;
      3. New York, Bill Cook (unassisted) 11:38

Second Period—No scoring

Third Period—4. New York, Seibert (unassisted) 14:39

Game 3

New York
  1 0 1—2
Toronto
  0 1 2—3

First Period—1. New York, Dillon (unassisted) 2:2◀

Second Period—2. Toronto, Doraty (Primeau, Clancy) 7:21

Third Period—3. Toronto, Doraty (unassisted) 5:29;
      4. New York, Keeling (Somers) 7:42;
      5. Toronto, Horner (Cotton, Sands) 8:30

Game 4

New York
  0 0 0-1—1
Toronto
  0 0 0-0—0

First Period—No Scoring

Second Period—No scoring

Third Period—No scoring

Overtime—1. New York, Bill Cook (Keeling) 7:34

1934

Chicago won three games to one.

Game 1

Chicago
  1 0 0 0 1—2
Detroit
  0 0 1 0 0—1

First Period—1. Chicago, Conacher (unassisted) 17:50

Second Period—No scoring

Third Period—2. Detroit, Lewis (Aurie, Graham) 4:40

First Overtime—No scoring

Second Overtime—3. Chicago, Thompson (Romnes) 1-10

Game 2

Chicago
  1 0 3—4
Detroit
  0 1 0—1

First Period—1. Chicago, Couture (unassisted) 17:52

Second Period—2. Detroit, Lewis (Weiland) 9:58

Third Period—3. Chicago, Romnes (Thompson) 1-28;
        4. Chicago, Coulter (Gottselig) 5:34;
        5. Chicago, Gottselig (unassisted) 18:02

Game 3

Detroit
  2 0 3—5
Chicago
  1 1 0—2

First Period—1. Chicago, Thompson (March, Romnes) :28;
        2. Detroit, Pettinger (Starr, Carson) 6:07;
        3. Detroit, Aurie (Buswell) 8:40

Second Period—4. Chicago, Gottselig (Couture, McFadyen) 18:07

Third Period—5. Detroit, Young (unassisted) 13:50;
        6. Detroit, Weiland (Aurie, Lewis) 18:20;
        7. Detroit, Aurie (unassisted) 19:53

Game 4

Detroit
  0 0 0 0 0—0
Chicago
  0 0 0 0 1—1

First Period—No scoring

Second Period—No scoring

Third Period—No scoring

First Overtime—No scoring

Second Overtime—1. Chicago, March (Romnes) 10:05

1935

Montreal Maroons won three games to none.

Game 1

Montreal Maroons
  0 2 0 1—3
Toronto
  0 2 0 0—2

First Period—No scoring

Second Period—1. Montreal, Robinson (Blinco) 3:57;
     2. Toronto, Finnigan (unassisted) 14:28;
     3. Toronto, Clancy (Metz) 18:12;
     4. Montreal, Wentworth (unassisted) 19:12

Third Period—No scoring

Overtime—5. Montreal, Trottier (Robinson) 5:28

Game 2

Montreal Maroons
  1 1 1—3
Toronto
  0 1 0—1

First Period—1. Montreal, Robinson (unassisted) 15:44

Second Period—2. Toronto, Jackson (unassisted) 7:31;
     3. Montreal, Blinco (Shields) 16:47

Third Period—4. Montreal, Northcott (Wentworth) 3:27

Game 3

Toronto
  0 1 0—1
Montreal Maroons
  1 2 1—4

First Period—1. Montreal, Ward (Northcott) 19:35

Second Period—2. Toronto, Thoms (Finnigan) 12:59;
     3. Montreal, Northcott (Ward) 16:18;
     4. Montreal, Wentworth (unassisted) 16:30

Third Period—5. Montreal, Marker (Wentworth) 1:02

1936

Detroit won three games to one.

Game 1

Toronto
  1 0 0—1
Detroit
  3 0 0—3

First Period—1.Detroit, McDonald (unassisted) 4:53;
     2. Detroit, Howe (Young) 5:37;
     3. Detroit, W. Kilrea (Bruneteau) 12:05;
     4. Toronto, Boll (Thoms, Conacher) 12:15

Second Period—No scoring

Third Period—No scoring

Game 2

Toronto
  1 1 2—4
Detroit
  4 2 3—9

First Period—1. Detroit, W. Kilrea (Sorrell) 1:30;
     2. Detroit, Barry (Bowman) 4:25;
     3. Detroit, Lewis (Barry, Aurie) 10:05;
     4. Toronto, Boll (Thoms) 12:35
     5. Detroit, McDonald (H. Kilrea) 16:55

Second Period—6. Detroit, Sorrell (Howe, Barry) 7:15;
     7. Detroit, Pettinger (Howe, Young) 9:10;
     8. Toronto, Primeau (Shill) 14:00

Third Period—9. Detroit, Sorrell (W. Kilrea, Bruneteau)
  7:30;
     10. Toronto, Thoms (Boll, Davidson) 9:40;
     11. Detroit, Pettinger (H. Kilrea, Howe) 12:05;
     12. Toronto, Davidson (Finnigan, H. Jackson) 16:10;
     13. Detroit, McDonald (unassisted) 17:15

Game 3

Detroit
  1 1 1 0—3
Toronto
  0 0 3 1—4

First Period—1.Detroit, Bowman (Pettinger) 9:23

Second Period—2. Detroit, Bruneteau (unassisted) 1:05

Third Period—3. Detroit, Howe (Pettinger, Kelly) 11:15;
     4. Toronto, Primeau (Horner, Davidson, H. Jackson)
  13:09;
     5. Toronto, Kelly (Finnigan) 15:20;
     6. Toronto, Kelly (Primeau) 19:19

Overtime—7. Toronto, Boll (Horner, A. Jackson,
  Thoms) :30

Game 4

Detroit
  0 2 1—3
Toronto
  1 0 1—2

Eddie Shore drinks from 1939 Cup.

First Period—1. Toronto, Primeau (unassisted) 15:10;
Second Period—2. Detroit, Goodfellow (Sorrell) 9:55;
    3. Detroit, Barry (Lewis) 10:38

Third Period—4. Detroit, Kelly (Lewis) 9:45;
    5. Toronto, Thoms (unassisted) 10:57

1937

Detroit won three games to two.

Game 1

Detroit
  0 0 1—1
New York
  3 1 1—5

First Period—1.New York, Keeling (Cooper, Murdoch) 5:23
    2. New York, Patrick (Coulter, Boucher) 9:40;
    3.New York, Cooper, (Keeling, Dillon) 18:43

Second Period—4. New York, Boucher (Johnson) 18:55

Third Period—5. Detroit, Howe (Pettinger, Goodfellow)
  17:12;
    6. New York, Patrick (Boucher, Dillon) 18:22

Game 2

New York
  0 2 0—2
Detroit
  3 1 0—4

First Period—1.Detroit, Sorrell (unassisted) 9:22;

2. Detroit, Bruneteau (Howe) 12:07;
    3. Detroit, Gallagher (W. Kilrea, Sherf) 13:31

Second Period—4. Detroit, Lewis (Howe, Goodfellow)
  11:02;
    5. New York, Pratt (N. Colville, M. Colville) 15:06;
    6. New York, Keeling (Coulter) 18:18

Third Period—No scoring

Game 3

New York
  0 1 0—1
Detroit
  0 0 0—0

First Period—No scoring

Second Period—1. New York, N. Colville (unassisted) :23

Third Period—No scoring

Game 4

New York
  0 0 0—0
Detroit
  0 0 1—1

First Period—No scoring

Second Period—No scoring

Third Period—1. Detroit, Barry (Howe, Sorrell) 12:43

Game 5

New York
  0 0 0—0
Detroit
  1 1 1—3

First Period—1. Detroit, Barry (Howe) 19:22

Second Period—2. Detroit, Sorrell (Barry, H. Kilrea) 9:36

Third Period—3. Detroit, Barry (Sorrell) 2:22

1938

Chicago won three games to one.

Game 1

Chicago
  1 1 1—3
Toronto
  1 0 0—1

First Period—1. Toronto, Drillon (Davidson) 1:54;
   2. Chicago, Gottselig (Dahlstrom, Romnes) 19:08

Second Period—3. Chicago, Thompson (Seibert) 1:51

Third Period—4. Chicago, Gottselig (unassisted) 12:08

Game 2

Chicago
   1 0 0—1
Toronto
   1 1 3—5

First Period—1. Toronto, Drillon (Apps) 1:42;
   2. Chicago, Seibert (unassisted) 8:31

Second Period—3. Toronto, Jackson (Thoms) 6:10

Third Period—4. Toronto, Drillon, (Apps, Hamilton) 9:44;
   5. Toronto, Parsons (Kelly, Fowler) 11:29;
   6. Toronto, Parsons (Kelly, Horner) 12:08

Game 3

Toronto
   1 0 0—1
Chicago
   0 1 1—2

First Period—1. Toronto, Apps, (Driilon, Davidson) 1:35

Second Period—2. Chicago, Voss (Jenkins, Gottselig) 16:02

Third Period—3. Chicago, Romnes (March, Thompson)
   15:55

Game 4

Toronto
   1 0 0—1
Chicago
   1 2 1—4

First Period—1. Chicago, Dahlstrom (Shill, Tindell) 5:52;
   2. Toronto, Drillon (Fowler) 8:26

Second Period—3. Chicago, Voss (Gottselig, Jenkins)
   16:45;
   4. Chicago, Shill (unassisted) 17:58

Third Period—5. Chicago, March (Romnes, Thompson)
   16:24

1939

Boston won four games to one.

Game 1

Toronto
   0 0 1—1
Boston
   1 0 1—2

First Period—1. Boston, Dumart (Shore, Bauer) 16:04

Second Period—No scoring

Third Period—2. Toronto, Horner (Marker, Romnes) 13:54;
   3. Boston, Bauer (unassisted) 16:31

Game 2

Toronto
   2 0 0 1—3
Boston
   0 2 0 0—2

First Period—1. Toronto, Chamberlain (Kampman, Drillon)
   8:55
   2. Toronto, Apps, (Metz, Drillon) 9:29

Second Period—Boston, Conacher (Cowley, Hollett)
   15:05;
   4. Boston, Hill (Cowley, Shore) 16:18

Third Period—No scoring

Overtime—5. Toronto, Romnes (Marker, Jackson)
   10:38

Bruins poster, 1939

Game 3

Boston
  0 0 3—3
Toronto
  0 0 1—1

First Period—No scoring

Second Period—No scoring

Third Period—1. Boston, Bauer (Schmidt) 1:27;
    2. Boston, Conacher (Cowley) 8:12;
    3. Boston, Crawford (Cowley, Conacher) 13:02;
    4. Toronto, Marker (Romnes) 19:10

Game 4

Boston
  1 0 1—1
Toronto
  0 0 0—0

First Period—1. Boston, Conacher (Hill) 2:20

Second Period—No scoring

Third Period—2. Boston, Conacher (Cowley, Hill) 12:55

Game 5

Toronto
  1 0 0—1
Boston
  1 1 1—3

First Period—1. Boston, Hill (Conacher, Cowley) 11:40;
    2. Toronto, Kampman (Romnes) 18:40

Second Period—3. Boston, Conacher (Cowley, Shore)
    17:54

Third Period—4. Boston, Hollett (Schmidt, Crawford)
    19:23

1940

New York won four games to two.

Game 1

Toronto
  1 0 0 0—1
New York
  1 0 0 1—2

First Period—1. New York, Coulter (N. Colville) 9:09;
    2. Toronto, Heron (Schriner) 11:01

Second Period—No scoring

Third Period—No scoring

Overtime—3. New York, Pike (L. Patrick) 15:30

Game 2

Toronto
  2 0 0—2
New York
  1 2 3—6

First Period—1. Toronto, Taylor, (Schriner, Horner) 5:01;
    2. Toronto, Goldup (Langelle, Marker) 6:01;
    3. New York, Hextall (Hiller, Watson) 15:14

Second Period—4. New York, Pratt (N. Colville) 3:57;
    5. New York, Hextall (Heller) 19:48

Third Period—6. New York, Hextall (Watson) 6:26;
    7. New York, Hiller (Watson, Hextall) 12:21;
    8. New York, L. Patrick, (Pratt, Heller) 13:09

Game 3

New York
  1 0 0—1
Toronto
  0 0 2—2

First Period—1. New York, Watson, (unassisted) 18:19

Second Period—No scoring

Third Period—2. Toronto, Drillon (Apps, Horner) 10:32;
    3. Toronto, Goldup (N. Metz) 13:40

Game 4

New York
  0 0 0—0
Toronto
  1 0 2—3

First Period—1. Toronto, Marker (Golup, Langelle) 19:20

Second Period—No scoring

Third Period—2. Toronto, Stanowski (Church) 16:03;
    3. Toronto, Drillon (Apps) 19:26

Game 5

New York
  1 0 0 0 1—2
Toronto
  0 1 0 0 0—1

First Period—1. New York, N. Colville (M. Colville, Shibicky)
    12:21

Second Period—2. Toronto, Apps (unassisted) 16:55

Third Period—No scoring

First Overtime—No scoring

Second Overtime—3. New York, M. Patrick (N. Colville) 11:43

Game 6

New York
  0 0 2 1—3
Toronto
  1 1 0 0—2

First Period—1. Toronto, Apps (Davidson) 6:52

Second Period—2. Toronto, N. Metz (Schriner) 4:51

Third Period—3. New York, N. Colville (Schibicky) 8:08;
    4. New York, Pike, (C. Smith) 10:01

Overtime—5. New York, Hextall (Watson, Hiller) 2:07

1941

Boston won four games to none.

Game 1

Detroit
  0 0 2—2
Boston
  1 1 1—3

First Period—1. Boston, Wiseman (Conacher, Smith) 13:26

Second Period—2. Boston, Schmidt (Dumart, Crawford) 14:45

Third Period—3. Boston, McCreavy (Schmidt, Crawford) 9:1C;
    4. Detroit, Liscombe (Brown, Jennings) 10:55;
    5. Detroit, Howe (Brown, Liscombe) 17:45

Game 2

Detroit
  0 0 1—1
Boston
  0 0 2—2

First Period—No scoring

Second Period—No scoring

Third Period—1. Detroit, M. Bruneteau (Howe, Orlando) 2:41;

    2. Boston, Reardon (Cain, Smith) 13:35;
    3. Boston, Conacher (Schmidt) 17:35

Game 3

Boston
  2 1 1—4
Detroit
  2 0 0—2

First Period—1. Detroit, Jennings, (Grosso, Abel) 3:15;
    2. Boston, Wiseman (Conacher, Hollett) 3:57;
    3. Detroit, Abel (J. Stewart) 7:45;
    4. Boston, Schmidt (Dumart, Bauer) 14:07

Second Period—5. Boston, Schmidt (Clapper, Dumart) :59

Third Period—6. Boston, Jackson (T. Reardon, Clapper) 17:20

Game 4

Boston
  0 3 0—3
Detroit
  1 0 0—1

First Period—1. Detroit, Liscombe (Howe, Giesebrecht) 10:14

Second Period—2. Boston, Hollett (Schmidt) 7:42;
    3. Boston, Bauer (Schmidt) 8:43;
    4. Boston, Wiseman (Conacher, McReavy) 19:32

Third Period—No scoring

1942

Toronto won four games to three.

Game 1
Detroit
  2 1 0—3
Toronto
  2 0 0—2

First Period—1. Detroit, Grosso (Orlando) 1:38;
    2. Toronto, McCreedy (Davidson, Kampman) 6:36;
    3. Detroit, Abel (Grosso) 12:30;
    4. Toronto, Schriner (Taylor) 12:59

Second Period—5. Detroit, Grosso (unassisted) 14:11

Third Period—No scoring

Game 2

Detroit
  2 0 2—4
Toronto
  0 1 1—2

First Period—1. Detroit, Grosso (Wares) 11:48;
    2. Detroit, Bruneteau (Liscombe) 14:17

Second Period—3. Toronto, Schriner (Taylor, Stanowski) 11:13

Third Period—4. Detroit, Grosso (Wares) 4:15;
    5. Detroit, J. Brown, (Bush, Liscombe) 10:08;
    6. Toronto, Stanowski (unassisted) 13:40

Game 3

Toronto
  2 0 0—2
Detroit
  2 2 1—5

First Period—1. Toronto, Carr (Taylor, Kampman) 15:36;
    2. Toronto, Carr (Taylor) 16:06;
    3. Detroit, G. Brown (Bush, Stewart) 18:20;
    4. Detroit, Carveth (Bush, A. Brown) 18:40

Second Period—5. Detroit, McCreavy (Grosso, Bush) 13:12;
    6. Detroit, Howe (Grosso, Bush) 15:11

Third Period—7. Detroit, Bush (Liscombe) 7:11

Game 4

Toronto
  0 2 2—4
Detroit
  0 2 1—3

First Period—No scoring

Second Period—1. Detroit, Bruneteau (Motter) 1:32;
    2. Detroit, Abel, (Grosso, Wares) 9:08;
    3. Toronto, Davidson (Langelle, McCreedy) 13:54;
    4. Toronto, Carr (Taylor, Schriner) 15:20

Third Period—5. Detroit, Liscombe (Howe, Bruneteau) 4:18;
    6. Toronto, Apps (Stanowski, N. Metz) 6:15;
    Toronto, N. Metz (D. Metz, Apps) 12:45

Game 5

Detroit
  0 0 3—3
Toronto
  2 5 2—9

First Period—1. Toronto, N. Metz (Apps, Stanowski) 9:29;
    2. Toronto, Stanowski (unassisted) 15:14

138

Second Period—3. Toronto, Goldham (unassisted) 1:59;
    4. Toronto, Schriner (Taylor) 4:11;
    5. Toronto, D. Metz (Apps, N. Metz) 14:11;
    6. Toronto, Apps (D. Metz, Goldham) 14:28;
    7. Toronto, D. Metz (N. Metz, Stanowski) 16:44

Third Period—8. Detroit, Howe, (McCreavy, Liscombe) 3:08;
    9. Toronto, D. Metz (Apps, Stanowski) 5:36;
    10. Toronto, Apps (D. Metz) 9:25;
    11. Detroit, Motter (Howe) 14:03;
    12. Detroit, Liscombe (Howe) 15:45

Game 6

Toronto
  0 1 2—3
Detroit
  0 0 0—0

First Period—No scoring

Second Period—1. Toronto, D. Metz (unassisted) :14

Third Period—2. Toronto, Goldham (Schriner) 13:32;
    3. Toronto, Taylor (Schriner) 14:04

Game 7

Detroit
  0 1 0—1
Toronto
  0 0 3—3

First Period—No scoring

Second Period—1. Detroit, Howe (Orlando, Abel) 1:45

Third Period—2. Toronto, Schriner (Taylor, Carr) 7:47;
    3. Toronto, Langelle (Goldham, McCreedy) 9:48;
    4. Toronto, Schriner (Taylor, Carr) 16:17

1943

Detroit won four games to none

Game 1

Boston
  1 0 1—2
Detroit
  1 3 2—6

First Period—1.Detroit, J. Stewart (Liscombe, Abel) 1:15;
    2. Boston, A. Jackson (Cain) 18:13

Second Period—3. Detroit, Bruneteau (H. Jackson, Abel) 1:12;
    4. Detroit, Abel, (unassisted) 15:43;
    5. Detroit, Carveth (Douglas) 19:06

Third Period—6. Detroit, Bruneteau (Abel, Liscombe) 1:21;
7. Detroit, Bruneateau (J. Stewart, Abel) 16:24;
8. Detroit. 8 DeMarco (Gallinger, Guidolin) 17:53

Game 2

Boston
0 2 1—3
Detroit
0 1 3—4

First Period—No scoring

Second Period—1. Boston, Crawford (Chamberlain) 10:16;
2. Boston, A. Jackson (Cowley, Cain) 11:04;
3. Detroit, Douglas (Orlando) 17:06

Third Period—4. Detroit, Carveth (Orlando) 5:55;
5. Detroit, Liscombe (Abel) 6:21;
6. Detroit, Howe (Wares) 13:16;
7. Boston, A. Jackson (Cowley, Hollett) 16:38

Game 3

Detroit
2 0 2—4
Boston
0 0 0—0

First Period—1. Detroit, Grosso (Wares) 3:26;
2. Detroit, Grosso (Liscombe) 10:16

Second Period—No scoring

Third Period—3. Detroit, Douglas (Motter) 8:03;
4. Detroit, Grosso (Wares) 18:41

Game 4

Detroit
1 1 0—2
Boston
0 0 0—0

First Period—1. Detroit, Carveth (unassisted) 12:09

Second Period—2. Detroit, Liscombe (unassisted) 2:45

Third Period—No scoring

1944

Montreal won four games to none.

Game 1

Chicago
0 1 0—1
Montreal
1 2 2—5

First Period—1.Montreal, Watson (unassisted) 8:37

Second Period—2. Montreal, Blake (Richard, Lach) 6:35;
3. Chicago, Smith (Bentley, Mosienko) 10:11;
4. Montreal, Getliffe (Heffernan, O'Connor) 10:58

Third Period—5. Montreal, Chamberlain (Watson, Bouchard) 4:47;
6. Montreal, Getliffe (unassisted) 18:07

Game 2

Montreal
0 1 2—3
Chicago
0 0 1—1

First Period—No scoring

Second Period—1. Montreal, Richard (Lach, Blake) 13:00

Third Period—2. Montreal, Richard (Lamoureux) 12:16;
3. Montreal, Richard (Lach) 15:33;
Chicago, Harms (Smith, Allen) 19:59

Game 3

Montreal
0 1 2—3
Chicago
1 0 1—2

First Period—1. Chicago, Allen (Weibe) 5:14

Second Period—2. Montreal, Blake (Richard) 2:02

Third Period—3. Chicago, Harms (Johnson) 4:16;
4. Montreal, McMahon (unassisted) 5:47;
5. Montreal, Watson (Getliffe) 6:42

Game 4

Chicago
1 3 0 0—4
Montreal
1 0 3 1—5

First Period—1. Chicago, Allen (Dahlstrom) 5:12;
2. Montreal, Lach (Blake) 8:48

Second Period—3. Chicago, Harms (Dahlstrom, Allen) 7:30;
4. Chicago, Allen (Smith, Bentley) 9:12;
5. Chicago, Bentley (Smith) 10:09

Third Period—6. Montreal, Lach (Blake) 10:02;
7. Montreal, Richard (Blake) 16:05;
8. Montreal, Richard (Blake, Bouchard) 17:20

Overtime—9. Montreal, Blake (Bouchard) 9:12

1945

Toronto won four games to three

Game 1

Toronto
  1 0 0—1
Detroit
  0 0 0—0

First Period—1. Toronto, Schriner (unassisted) 13:56

Second Period—No scoring

Third Period—No scoring

Game 2

Toronto
  0 1 1—2
Detroit
  0 0 0—0

First Period—No scoring

Second Period—1. Toronto, Kennedy (Pratt) 13:05

Third Period—2. Toronto, Morris (unassisted) 12:03

Game 3

Detroit
  0 0 0—0
Toronto
  0 0 1—1

First Period—No scoring

Second Period—No scoring

Third Period—1. Toronto, Bodnar (Stanowski) 3:01

Game 4

Detroit
  1 1 3—5
Toronto
  2 1 0—3

First Period—1. Detroit, Hollett (E. Bruneteau) 8:35;
    2. Toronto, Kennedy (Hill) 9:19;
    3. Toronto, Kennedy (Hill) 11:44

Second Period—4. Detroit, Armstrong (M. Bruneteau) 9:20;
    5. Toronto, Kennedy (Davidson) 10:21

Third Period—6. Detroit, E. Bruneteau (unassisted) 1:11;
    7. Detroit, Lindsay (unassisted) 3:20;
    8. Detroit, Carveth (Hollett) 17:38

Game 5

Toronto
  0 0 0—0
Detroit
  0 0 2—2

First Period—No scoring

Second Period—No scoring

Third Period—1. Detroit, Hollett (Carveth) 8:21;
    2. Detroit, Carveth (Quackenbush) 16:16

Game 6

Detroit
  0 0 0 1—1
Toronto
  0 0 0 0—0

First Period—No scoring

Second Period—No scoring

Third Period—No scoring

Overtime—1. Detroit, E. Bruneteau (unassisted) 14:16

Game 7

Toronto
  1 0 1—2
Detroit
  0 0 1—1

First Period—1. Toronto, Hill (Kennedy) 5:38

Second Period—No scoring

Third Period—2. Detroit, Armstrong (Hollett) 8:16;
    3. Toronto, Pratt (N. Metz) 12:14

1946

Montreal won four games to one.

Game 1

Boston
  0 2 1 0—3
Montreal
  0 2 1 1—4

First Period—No scoring

Second Period—1. Montreal, Bouchard (unassisted) :21;
    2. Montreal, Fillion (unassisted) 3:19;
    3. Boston, Guidolin (Cain) 5:09;

4. Boston, Dumart (Schmidt) 8:02

Third Period—5. Boston, Crawford (Guidolin) 14:04;
6. Montreal, Chamberlain (Richard) 16:23

Overtime—7. Montreal, Richard (Bouchard) 9:08

Game 2

Boston
  1 1 0 0—2
Montreal
  1 0 1 1—3

First Period—1. Montreal, Lach (Richard) 1:06;
2. Boston, Egan (unassisted) 10:55

Second Period—3. Boston, Bauer (Schmidt) 3:04

Third Period—4. Montreal, Bouchard (unassisted) 10:10

Overtime—5. Montreal, Peters (unassisted) 16:55

Game 3

Montreal
  2 0 2—4
Boston
  1 1 0—2

First Period—1. Montreal, Lach (unassisted) 10:14;
2. Boston, Guidolin (Gallinger, Shill) 11:01;
3. Montreal, Harmon (Chamberlain) 14:13

Second Period—4. Boston, T. Reardon (Cowley, Smith)
18:41

Third Period—5. Montreal, Mosdell (unassisted) 2:45;
6. Montreal, Hiller (Lach) 5:18

Game 4

Montreal
  0 1 1 0—2
Boston
  0 1 1 1—3

First Period—No scoring

Second Period—1. Boston, Henderson (Gallinger) 8:05;
2. Montreal, Richard (Harmon) 13:46

Third Period—3. Boston, Gallinger (Cain) 3:01;
4. Montreal, Richard (Lach) 4:04

Overtime—5. Boston, T. Reardon (Smith, Cowley) 15:13

Game 5

Boston
  2 1 0—3
Montreal
  3 0 3—6

First Period—1. Boston, Cowley (unassisted) 5:42;
2. Montreal, Fillion (Hiller) 9:55;
3. Boston, Bauer (Dumart) 14:01;
4. Montreal, Lach (Eddolls) 15:51;
5. Montreal, Mosdell (Harmon) 18:28

Second Period—6. Boston, Schmidt (unassisted) 7:15

Third Period—7. Montreal, Blake (Lach) 11:06;
8. Montreal, Chamberlain (unassisted) 14:05;
9. Montreal, Hiller (Lach) 17:13

1947

Toronto won four games to two.

Game 1

Toronto
  0 0 0—0
Montreal
  1 2 3—6

First Period—1. Montreal, O'Connor (Leger) 2:20

Second Period—2. Montreal, Reay (Harmon) 8:17;
3. Montreal, Richard (O'Connnor) 9:41

Third Period—4. Montreal, Allen (Bouchard) 5:40;
5. Montreal, Reay (Allen, Bouchard) 11:04;
6. Montreal, Chamberlain (Quilty, Peters) 18:28

Game 2

Toronto
  2 1 1—4
Montreal
  0 0 0—0

First Period—1. Toronto, Kennedy (Lynn, Barilko) 1:12;
2. Toronto, Lynn (Kennedy) 1:36

Second Period—3. Toronto, G. Stewart (D. Metz, Barilko)
6:37

Third Period—4. Toronto, Watson (Mortson) 11:55

Game 3

Montreal
  0 2 0—2
Toronto
  1 2 1—4

141

First Period—1. Toronto, Mortson (unassisted) 9:45

Second Period—2. Toronto, Poile (Stewart, D. Metz) 4:48;
     3. Toronto, Lynn (Meeker) 12:23;
     4. Montreal, Gravelle (O'Connor) 12:33;
     5. Montreal, O'Connor (Blake) 18:30

Third Period—6. Toronto, Kennedy (unassisted) 19:13

Game 4

Montreal
  1 0 0 0—1
Toronto
  1 0 0 1—2

First Period—1. Montreal, Harmon (Blake) 4:38;
     2. Toronto, Watson (Apps) 6:13

Second Period—No scoring

Third Period—No scoring

Overtime—3. Toronto, Apps (Watson) 16:36

Game 5

Toronto
  0 0 1—1
Montreal
  2 1 0—3

First Period—1. Montreal, Richard (Blake, Bouchard) 1:23;
     2. Montreal, Gravelle (Leger) 8:29

Second Period—3. Montreal, Richard (Blake, O'Connor)
  19:32

Third Period—4. Toronto, Poile (Stewart) 13:7

Game 6

Montreal
  1 0 0—1
Toronto
  0 1 1—2

First Period—1. Montreal, O'Connor (unassisted) :25

Second Period—2. Toronto, Lynn (Kennedy, Meeker) 5:39

Third Period—3. Toronto, Kennedy (Meeker) 14:39

1948

Toronto won four games to none.

Game 1

Detroit
  1 0 2—3
Toronto
  3 2 0—5

First Period—1. Detroit, McFadden (Horeck) 7:20;

     2. Toronto, Watson (Apps) 8:21;
     3. Toronto, Klukay (Costello, Bentley) 9:04;
     4. Toronto, Apps (Mortson) 18:24

Second Period—5. Toronto, Mortson (Bentley) 14:31;
     6. Toronto, Meeker (Kennedy, Stanowski) 19:21

Third Period—7. Detroit, Conacher (Quackenbush, Lundy)
  4:28;
     8. Detroit, Lindsay (unassisted) 5:25

Game 2

Detroit
  0 1 1—2
Toronto
  1 3 0—4

First Period—1. Toronto, Bentley (Samis) 13:31

Second Period—2. Toronto, Ezinicki (Apps, Watson) 3:38;
     3. Toronto, Bentley (Costello, Klukay) 17:16;
     4. Detroit, Horeck (Abel) 18:18;
     5. Toronto, Watson (unassisted) 18:50

Third Period—6. Detroit, Gauthier (McFadden) 17:18

Game 3

Toronto
  0 1 1—2
Detroit
  0 0 0—0

First Period—No scoring

Second Period—1. Toronto, Watson (Ezinicki) 19:42

Third Period—2. Toronto, Lynn (Kennedy) 15:16

Game 4

Toronto
  3 3 1—7
Detroit
  0 1 1—2

First Period—1. Toronto, Kennedy (Bentley) 2:51;
     2. Toronto, Boesch (unassisted) 5:03;
     3. Toronto, Watson (unassisted) 11:13

Second Period—4. Detroit, Reise (Pavelich, Horeck) 2:41;
     5. Toronto, Apps (Thompson) 4:26;
     6. Toronto, Kennedy (Lynn) 9:42;
     7. Toronto, Watson (unassisted) 11:38

Third Period—8. Toronto, Costello (Bentley) 14:37;
     9. Detroit, Horeck (Fogolin) 18:48

1949

Toronto won four games to none.

Game 1

Toronto
  1 1 0 1—3
Detroit
  1 0 1 0—2

First Period—1. Detroit, Gee (Lindsay, Howe) 4:15;
      2. Toronto, Bentley (Timgren, Klukay) 13:15

Second Period—3. Toronto, Thompson (Bentley) 16:02

Third Period—4. Detroit, Quackenbush (Lindsay, Gee) 13:56

Overtime—5. Toronto, Klukay (Thompson, Timgren) 17:31

Game 2

Toronto
  2 1 0—3
Detroit
  0 0 1—1

First Period—1. Toronto, Smith (Boesch) 8:50;
      2. Toronto, Smith (Barilko, Kennedy) 9:56

Second Period—3. Toronto, Smith (Kennedy, Mackell)
17:58

Third Period—4. Detroit, Horeck (Stewart, McFadden) 5:50

Game 3

Detroit
  1 0 0—1
Toronto
  0 0 3—3

First Period—1. Detroit, Stewart (Horeck) 4:57

Second Period—2. Toronto, Ezinicki (Gardner, Watson)
11-02;
      3. Toronto, Kennedy (Smith, Mackell) 12:40;
      4. Toronto, Mortson (Thompson, Klukay) 16:18

Third Period—No scoring

Game 4

Detroit
  1 0 0—1
Toronto
  0 2 1—3

First Period—1. Detroit, Lindsay (Gee, Howe) 2:59

Second Period—2. Toronto, Timgren (Bentley) 10:10;
      3. Toronto, Gardner (Thompson, Ezinicki) 19:45

Third Period—4. Toronto, Bentley (Timgren, Mackell) 15:10

1950

Detroit won four games to three.

Game 1

New York
  1 0 0—1
Detroit
  0 4 0—4

First Period—1. New York, O'Connor (Gordon, Mickoski)
5:58

Second Period—2. Detroit, Carveth (Babando, Gee) 4:43;
      3. Detroit, Gee (J. Wilson) 9:32;
      4. Detroit, McFadden (Couture) 10:06;
      5. Detroit, Couture (Pronovost, McFadden) 13:56

Third Period—No scoring

Game 2 (At Toronto)

New York
  0 1 2—3
Detroit
  0 1 0—1

First Period—No scoring

Second Period—1. Detroit, Couture, (Pavelich) 3:05;
      2. New York, Egan (unassisted) 10:39

Third Period—3. New York, Laprade (Stanley) 3:04;
      4. New York, Laprade (unassisted) 11:20

Game 3 (At Toronto)

New York
  0 0 0—0
Detroit
  2 1 1—4

First Period—1. Detroit, Couture (Kelly) 14:14;
      2. Detroit, Gee (Dewsbury) 19:08

Second Period—3. Detroit, Abel (unassisted) 19:16

Third Period—4. Detroit, Pavelich (Kelly) 16:55

Game 4

New York
  0 1 2 1—4
Detroit
  2 0 1 0—3

First Period—1. Detroit, Lindsay (Stewart) 6:31;
      2. Detroit, Abel (Lindsay) 16:48

Second Period—3. New York, O'Connor (Mickoski, Kaleta)
19:59

Third Period—4. Detroit, Pavelich (Peters, Stewart) 3:32;
      5. New York, Laprade (Fisher, Leswick) 8:09;
      6. New York, Kyle (Kaleta) 16:26

Overtime—7. New York, Raleigh (Slowinski) 8:34

Game 5

New York
0 1 0 1—2
Detroit
0 0 1 0—1

First Period—No scoring

Second Period—1. New York, Fisher (Leswick) 7:44

Third Period—2. Detroit, Lindsay (Abel, Carveth) 18:10

Overtime—3. New York, Raleigh (Slowinski, Lund) 1:38

Game 6

New York
2 1 1—4
Detroit
1 2 2—5

First Period—1. New York, Stanley (Kaleta, Mickoski) 3:45;
2. New York, Fisher (Laprade, Leswick) 7:35;
3. Detroit, Lindsay (Stewart) 19:18

Second Period—4. New York, Lund (Egar, Slowinski) 3:18;
5. Detroit, Abel (Carveth, Lindsay) 5:38;
6. Detroit, Couture (Gee, Babando) 16:07

Third Period—7. New York, Leswick (Fisher, Laprade) 1:54;
8. Detroit, Lindsay (Abel) 4:13;
9. Detroit, Abel (Carveth, Dewsbury) 10:34

Game 7

New York
2 1 0 0 0—3
Detroit
0 3 0 0 1—4

First Period—1. New York, Stanley (Leswick) 11:14;
2. New York, Leswick (O'Connor, Laprade) 12:18

Second Period—3. Detroit, Babando (Kelly, Couture) 5:09;
4. Detroit, Abel (Dewsbury) 5:30;
5. New York, O'Connor (Mickoski) 11:42;
6. Detroit, McFadden (Peters) 15:57

Third Period—No scoring

First Overtime—No scoring

Second Overtime—7. Detroit, Babando (Gee) 8:31

1951

Toronto won four games to one.

Game 1

Montreal
1 1 0 0—2
Toronto
2 0 0 1—3

First Period—1. Toronto, Smith (Kennedy, Sloan) :15;
2. Montreal, Richard (unassisted) 15:27;
3. Toronto, Sloan (Mortson) 15:42

Second Period—4. Montreal, Masnick (Reay) 4:02

Third Period—No scoring

Overtime—5. Toronto, Smith (Sloan) 5:51

Game 2

Montreal
1 1 0 1—3
Toronto
0 1 1 0—2

First Period—1. Montreal, Masnick (Meger) 3:44

Second Period—2. Montreal, Reay (Olmstead, Richard) 9:24;
3. Toronto, Smith (Bentley, Kennedy) 16:31

Third Period—4. Toronto, Kennedy (Sloan) 8:16

Overtime—5. Montreal, Richard (Harvey) 2:55

Game 3

Toronto
0 1 0 1—2
Montreal
1 0 0 0—1

First Period—1. Montreal, Richard (Olmstead) 2:18

Second Period—2. Toronto, Smith (Bentley) 5:58

Third Period—No scoring

Overtime—3. Toronto,Kennedy, (Sloan) 4:47

Game 4

Toronto
1 1 0 1—3
Montreal
1 0 1 0—2

First Period—1. Toronto, Smith (Kennedy) :38;
2. Montreal, Richard (Reay, Harvey) 14:41

Second Period—3. Toronto, Meeker (Watson) 1:27

Third Period—4. Montreal, Lach (Richard, Bouchard) 13:49

Overtime—5. Toronto, Watson (Bentley) 5:15

Game 5

Montreal
0 1 1 0—2
Toronto
0 1 1 1—3

First Period—No scoring

Second Period—1. Montreal, Richard (MacPherson) 8:56;
2. Toronto, Sloan (Kennedy) 12:00

Third Period—3. Montreal, Meger (Harvey) 4:47;
4. Toronto, Sloan (Bentley, Smith) 19:28

Overtime—5. Toronto, Barilko (Meeker, Watson) 2:53

1952

Detroit won four games to none.

Game 1

Detroit
0 1 2—3
Montreal
0 0 1—1

First Period—No scoring

Second Period—1. Detroit, Leswick (Pavelich) 3:27

Third Period—2. Detroit, Leswick (Skov) 7:59;
3. Montreal, Johnson (Curry Olmstead) 11:01;
4. Detroit, Lindsay (Abel) 19:44

Game 2

Detroit
1 1 0—2
Montreal
1 0 0—1

First Period—1. Detroit, Pavelich (Leswick, Skov) 16:09;
2. Montreal, Lach (Geoffrion) 18:37

Second Period—3. Detroit, Lindsay (unassisted) :43

Third Period—No scoring

Game 3

Montreal
0 0 0—0
Detroit
1 1 1—3

First Period—1. Detroit, Howe (Stasiuk) 4:31

Second Period—2. Detroit, Lindsay (Howe) 9:13

Third Period—3. Detroit, Howe (Pavelich) 6:54

Game 4

Montreal
0 0 0—0
Detroit
1 1 1—3

First Period—1. Detroit, Prystai (Delvecchio, Wilson) 6:50

Second Period—2. Detroit, Skov (Prystai) 19:39

Third Period—3. Detroit, Prystai (unassisted) 7:35

1953

Montreal won four games to one.

Game 1

Boston
1 0 1—2
Montreal
1 2 1—4

First Period—1. Boston, Armstrong (Mackell) 2:08;
2. Montreal, Moore (unassisted) 13:42

Second Period—3. Montreal, Mosdell (Mazur) 2:37;
4. Montreal, Curry (MacKay, St. Laurent) 16:05

Third Period—5. Boston, Pierson (Mackell, Sanford) 10:11;
6. Montreal, Richard (Mosdell) 11:12

Game 2

Boston
2 1 1—4
Montreal
0 1 0—1

First Period—1. Boston, Labine (Quackenbush) 3:53;
2. Boston, Sanford (Klukay, Chevrefils) 18:13

Second Period—3. Montreal, Olmstead (Curry, Harvey) 1:36;
4. Boston, Sanford (Mackell) 7:26

Third Period—5, Boston, Schmidt (Dumart, Martin) 15:43

Game 3

Montreal
1 1 1—3
Boston
0 0 0—0

First Period—1. Montreal, Johnson (Mosdell) 11:53

Second Period—2. Montreal, Masnick (unassisted) 6:30

Third Period—3. Montreal, Mosdell (Bouchard) 11:27

Game 4

Montreal
3 1 3—7
Boston
1 0 2—3

First Period—1. Montreal, Davis (St. Laurent, MacKay) 3:23;
2. Montreal, Richard (Harvey) 10:58;
3. Montreal, Moore (unassisted) 16:40;
4. Boston, Creighton (Dumart) 18:22

Second Period—5. Montreal, Geoffrion (unassisted) 18:58

Third Period—6. Montreal, Richard (unassisted) 5:33;
      7. Boston, Schmidt (Labine) 7:23;
      8. Boston, McIntyre (Creighton) 16:25;
      9. Montreal, MacKay (unassisted) 17:59;
     10. Montreal, Richard (Olmstead, Lach) 18:27

Game 5

Boston
0 0 0 0—0
Montreal
0 0 0 1—1

First Period—No scoring

Second Period—No scoring

Third Period—No scoring

Overtime—1. Montreal, Lach (Richard) 1:22

1954

Detroit won four games to three.

Game 1

Montreal
0 1 0—1
Detroit
1 0 2—3

First Period—1. Detroit, Lindsay (Reibel, Delvecchio) 13:44

Second Period—2. Montreal, Geoffrion (Harvey, Masnick) 12:16

Third Period—3. Detroit, Reibel (Landsay, Howe) 1:52;
    4. Detroit, Kelly (Pavelich, Leswick) 7:13

Game 2

Montreal
3 0 0—3
Detroit
0 1 0—1

First Period—1. Montreal, Moore (Geoffrion, Beliveau) 15:03;
    2. Montreal, Richard (Moore) 15:28;
    3. Montreal, Richard (Moore) 15:59

Second Period—4. Detroit, Delvecchio (unassisted) 6:37
Third Period—No scoring

Game 3

Detroit
2 1 2—5
Montreal
0 0 2—2

First Period—1. Detroit, Delvecchio (Howe) :42;
    2. Detroit, Lindsay (Kelly) 17:06

Second Period—3. Detroit, Wilson (Prystai, Goldham) 4:57

Third Period—4. Montreal, Johnson (unassisted) 7:19;
    5. Detroit, Prystai (Delvecchio) 7:59;
    6. Detroit, Howe (Delvecchio, Woit) 11:32;
    7. Montreal, St. Laurent (MacKay) 15:02

Game 4

Detroit
0 1 1—2
Montreal
0 0 0—0

First Period—No scoring

Second Period—1. Detroit, Wilson (Prystai) 2:09

Third Period—2. Detroit, Kelly (unassisted) 19:53

Game 5

Montreal
0 0 0 1—1
Detroit
0 0 0 0—0

First Period—No scoring

Second Period—No scoring

Third Period—No scoring

Overtime—1. Montreal, Mosdell (unassisted) 5:45

Game 6

Detroit
0 0 1—1
Montreal
0 3 1—4

First Period—No scoring

Second Period—1. Montreal, Geoffrion (Beliveau) 12:07;
    2. Montreal, Curry (Olmstead, Masnick) 13:07;
    3. Montreal, Curry (Mazur, Lach) 14:25

Third Period—4. Detroit, Prystai (unassisted) 5:11;
    5. Montreal, Richard (Lach) 10:06

Game 7

Montreal
1 0 0 0—1
Detroit
0 1 0 1—2

First Period—1. Montreal, Curry (Masnick) 9:17

Second Period—2. Detroit, Kelly (Lindsay, Delvecchio) 1:17

Third Period—No scoring

Overtime—3. Detroit, Leswick (Skov) 4:29

1955

Detroit won four games to three.

Game 1

Montreal
  0 1 1—2
Detroit
  0 1 3—4

First Period—No scoring

Second Period—1. Montreal, Curry (Mosdell, MacKay) 5:09;
    2. Detroit, Delvecchio (Howe, Lindsay) 14:00

Third Period—3. Montreal, Curry (Mosdell, MacKay) 8:57;
    4. Detroit, Stasiuk (Howe, Lindsay) 13:05;
    5. Detroit, Pavelich (unassisted) 17:07;
    6. Detroit, Lindsay (Howe) 19:42

Game 2

Montreal
  0 0 1—1
Detroit
  4 3 0—7

First Period—1. Detroit, Pronovost (Goldham) 2:15;
    2. Detroit, Lindsay (Howe, Reibel) 9:57;
    3. Detroit, Delvecchio (Stasiuk, Goldham) 16:00;
    4. Detroit, Howe (Reibel) 17:11

Second Period—5. Detroit, Lindsay (Howe, Reibel) 8:10;
    6. Detroit, Lindsay (Delvecchio) 15:48;
    7. Detroit, Lindsay (Reibel, Howe) 19:37

Third Period—8. Montreal, Mosdell (St. Laurent, Curry) 12:32

Game 3

Detroit
  1 1 0—2
Montreal
  2 1 1—4

First Period—1. Montreal, Geoffrion (Beliveau, Olmstead) 8:30;
    2. Montreal, Geoffrion (unassisted) 8:42;
    3. Detroit, Kelly (Stasiuk) 18:13

Second Period—4. Montreal, Geoffrion (Beliveau) 14:23;
    5. Detroit, Stasiuk (Pavelich, Delvecchio) 16:16

Third Period—6. Montreal, Leclair (Moore) 7:50

Game 4

Montreal
  1 3 1—5

Detroit
  1 0 2—3

First Period—1. Montreal, MacKay (Harvey, Mosdell) :40;
    2. Detroit, Reibel (Kelly) 12:38

Second Period—3. Montreal, Geoffrion (unassisted) 3:41;
    4. Montreal, Beliveau (unassisted) 8:25;
    5. Montreal, Johnson (unassisted) 9:07

Third Period—6. Montreal, Curry, (MacKay) 2:33;
    7. Detroit, Reibel (Lindsay, Howe) 3:40;
    8. Detroit, Hay (Reibel) 12:00

Game 5

Montreal
  1 0 0—1
Detroit
  2 2 1—5

First Period—1. Montreal, Beliveau (Harvey, Moore) 8:01;
    2. Detroit, Skov (unassisted) 12:59;
    3. Detroit, Howe (unassisted) 18:59

Second Period—4. Detroit, Howe (Delvecchio, Lindsay) 12:29;
    5. Detroit, Howe (Lindsay, Kelly) 16:20

Third Period—6. Detroit, Stasiuk (Delvecchio, Bonin) 2:09

Game 6

Detroit
  1 1 1—3
Montreal
  1 3 2—6

First Period—1. Montreal, Beliveau (Harvey) 7:30;
    2. Detroit, Delvecchio (Stasiuk) 13:36

Second Period—3. Montreal, Leclair (Harvey, Geoffrion) 3:45;
    4. Montreal, Geoffrion (Beliveau, Harvey) 5:21;
    5. Detroit, Delvecchio (Lindsay, Pronovost) 15:54;
    6. Montreal, Geoffrion (Beliveau, Bouchard) 18:18

Third Period—7. Montreal, Curry (MacKay, Mosdell) :19;
    8. Detroit, Kelly (Leswick, Pavelich) 16:23;
    9. Montreal, MacKay (Mosdell) 18:55

Game 7

Montreal
  0 0 1—1
Detroit
  0 2 1—3

First Period—No scoring

Second Period—1. Detroit, Delvecchio (Kelly) 7:12;
    2. Detroit, Howe (Pronovost) 19:49

Third Period—3. Detroit, Delvecchio (unassisted) 2:59;
    4. Montreal, Curry (Geoffrion, Beliveau) 14:35

Montreal won four games to one.

Game 1

Detroit
 1 3 0—4
Montreal
 0 2 4—6

First Period—1. Detroit, Delvecchio (Reibel, Howe) 8:17

Second Period—2. Montreal, Beliveau (Olmstead) 3:00;
    3. Detroit, Dineen (Ullman, Bucyk) 3:45;
    4. Montreal, H. Richard (M. Richard, Moore) 6:40;
    5. Detroit, Lindsay (Howe) 8:11;
    6. Detroit, Delvecchio (Howe, Ferguson) 11:20

Third Period—7. Montreal, Leclair (Curry, Harvey) 5:20;
    8. Montreal, Geoffrion (Talbot) 6:20;
    9. Montreal, Beliveau (Geoffrion, Olmstead) 7:31;
    10. Montreal, Provost (Leclair, Curry) 10:49

Game 2

Detroit
 0 0 1—1
Montreal
 1 2 2—5

First Period—1. Montreal, Marshall (Olmstead) 7:23

Second Period—2. Montreal, H. Richard (Moore) 11:37;
    3. Montreal, Geoffrion (Olmstead, Beliveau) 14:38

Third Period—4. Detroit, Ullman (Howe, Lindsay) :31;
    5. Montreal, Beliveau (M. Richard, Olmstead) 2:48;
    6. Montreal, M. Richard (H. Richard, Moore) 19:21

Game 3

Montreal
 1 0 0—1
Detroit
 1 0 2—3

First Period—1. Detroit, Kelly (Howe) 14:27;
    2. Montreal, Beliveau (Provost) 19:20

Second Period—No scoring

Third Period—3. Detroit, Lindsay (Pavelich, Arbour) 11:36;
    4. Detroit, Howe (Lindsay, Delvecchio) 18:12

Game 4

Montreal
 1 1 1—3
Detroit
 0 0 0—0

First Period—1. Montreal, Beliveau (Harvey, Olmstead)
 15:52

Second Period—2. Montreal, Beliveau (Geoffrion, Olmstead)
 11:39

Third Period—3. Montreal, Curry (Provost, Mosdell) 11:39

Game 5

Detroit
 0 0 1—1
Montreal
 0 2 1—3

First Period—No scoring

Second Period—1. Montreal, Beliveau (Curry, Harvey)
 14:16;
    2. Montreal, M. Richard (Geoffrion, Beliveau) 15:08

Third Period—3. Montreal, Geoffrion (Beliveau, Olmstead)
 :13;
    4. Detroit, Delvecchio (Lindsay) :25

1957

Montreal won four games to one.

Game 1

Boston
 0 1 0—1
Montreal
 0 4 1—5

First Period—No scoring

Detroit scores in third game of 1952 Cup finals.

Second Period—1. Boston, Mackell (Mohns, Regan) 7:37;
    2. Montreal, M. Richard (Moore, Johnson) 10:39;
    3. Montreal, M. Richard (Harvey) 13:29;
    4. Montreal, Geoffrion (Harvey) 15:35;
    5. Montreal, M. Richard (H. Richard, Harvey) 17:00

Third Period—6. Montreal, M. Richard (H. Richard) 18:17

Game 2

Boston
  0 0 0—0
Montreal
  0 1 0—1

First Period—No scoring

Second Period—1. Montreal, Beliveau (St. Laurent,
  Geoffrion) 2:27

Third Period—No scoring

Game 3

Montreal
  3 0 1—4
Boston
  0 1 1—2

First Period—1. Montreal, Geoffrion (Harvey, Olmstead)
  1:30;
    2. Montreal, Curry (Goyette) 14:39;
    3. Montreal, Geoffrion (Beliveau) 19:54

Second Period—4. Boston, McKenney (Armstrong) 6:16

Third Period—5. Montreal, Goyette (Marshall, Curry) 7:31;
    6. Boston, Mackell (Flaman) 19:16

Game 4

Montreal
  0 0 0—0
Boston
  1 0 1—2

First Period—1. Boston, Mackell (Toppazzini, Regan) 2:56

Second Period—No scoring

Third Period—2. Boston, Mackell (McKenney, Labine)
  19:40

Game 5

Boston
  0 0 1—1
Montreal
  1 2 2—5

First Period—1. Montreal, Pronovost (Provost, Marshall)
  18:11

Second Period—2. Montreal, Moore (Geoffrion, Harvey) :14;
    3. Montreal, Geoffrion (Olmstead, Johnson) 15:12

Third Period—4. Boston, Labine (Boivin) 13:43;
    5. Montreal, Marshall (Moore, Curry) 17:38;
    6. Montreal, Curry (Moore, Broden) 18:31

1958

Montreal won four games to two.

Game 1

Boston
  0 1 0—1
Montreal
  1 1 0—2

First Period—1. Montreal, Geoffrion (Marshall, Harvey)
  12:24

Second Period—2. Boston, Stanley (McKenney, Mackell)
  5:54;
    3. Montreal, Moore (Beliveau, M. Richard) 13:52

Third Period—No scoring

Game 2

Boston
  3 1 1—5
Montreal
  1 1 0—2

First Period—1. Boston, Johnson (Regan, Labine) :20;
    2. Montreal, Geoffrion (Harvey, Moore) 3:12;
    3. Boston, McKenney (Mackell, Regan) 6:58;
    4. Boston, Horvath (Boone) 17:23

Second Period—5. Boston, Regan (Stanley) 5:00;
    6. Montreal, Harvey (Moore) 7:00

Third Period—7. Boston, Horvath (Stasiuk, Mohns) 16:52

Game 3

Montreal
  1 0 2—3
Boston
  0 0 0—0

First Period—1. Montreal, M. Richard (Geoffrion, Harvey)
  18:20

Second Period—No scoring

Third Period—2. Montreal, H. Richard (Harvey) 3:00;
  3. Montreal, M. Richard (H. Richard, Moore) 15:06

Game 4

Montreal
  0 0 1—1
Boston
  1 1 1—3

First Period—1. Boston, McKenney (Mackell, Regan) 5:35

Second Period—2. Boston, McKenney (Horvath, Stasiuk) 3:30

Third Period—3. Boston, Toppazzini (Mackell) 2:30;
  4. Montreal, Provost (Beliveau, Bonin) 12:57

Game 5

Boston
  1 0 1 0—2
Montreal
  0 2 0 1—3

First Period—1. Boston, Mackell (Stanley, Toppazzini) 18:43

Second Period—2. Montreal, Geoffrion (Beliveau) 2:20;
  3. Montreal, Beliveau (Geoffrion) 3:02

Third Period—4. Boston, Horvath (Stasiuk, Boivin) 10:35

Overtime—5. Montreal, M. Richard (Moore, H. Richard) 5:45

Game 6

Montreal
  2 2 1—5
Boston
  1 0 2—3

First Period—1. Montreal, Geoffrion (Beliveau, Olmstead) :46;
  2. Montreal, M. Richard (Moore) 1:54;
  3. Boston, McKenney (Mohns) 18:35

Second Period—4. Montreal, Beliveau (Geoffrion, Harvey) 6:42;
  5. Montreal, Geoffrion (unassisted) 19:26

Third Period—6. Boston, N. Johnson (Regan) 5:20;
  7. Boston, Regan, (Flaman, Labine) 13:41;
  8. Montreal, Harvey (unassisted) 19:00

1959

Montreal won four games to one.

Game 1

Toronto
  2 1 0—3
Montreal
  2 1 2—5

First Period—1. Montreal, H. Richard (Moore, Talbot) :36;
  2. Toronto, Duff (unassisted) 4:53;
  3. Toronto, Harris (Horton) 6:24;
  4. Montreal, Backstrom (Provost) 15:41

Second Period—5. Montreal, Pronovost (Goyette, Provost) 16:28;
  6. Toronto, Stewart, (Brewer, Olmstead) 18:26

Third Period—7. Montreal, Bonin (H. Richard, Harvey) 11:59;
  8. Montreal, Moore (Bonin, H. Richard) 15:02

Game 2

Toronto
  0 1 0—1
Montreal
  1 0 2—3

First Period—1. Montreal, Johnson (H. Richard, Moore) 5:12

Second Period—2. Toronto, Stewart (Creighton, Pulford) 11:41

Third Period—3. Montreal, Provost (Harvey) 5:02;
  4. Montreal, Provost (Goyette, Harvey) 18:33

Game 3

Montreal
  1 0 1 0—2
Toronto
  1 1 0 1—3

First Period—1. Toronto, Harris (Stanley, Mahovlich) 16:29;
  2. Montreal, Bonin (Harvey, Geoffrion) 17:31

Second Period—3. Toronto, Olmstead (Pulford, Stewart) 17:11

Third Period—4. Montreal, Moore (Turner, Marshall) 1:30

Overtime—5. Toronto, Duff (Armstrong) 10:06

Game 4

Montreal
 0 0 3—3
Toronto
 0 0 2—2

First Period—No scoring

Second Period—No scoring

Third Period—1. Toronto, Harris (Ehman, Duff) 3:45;
2. Montreal, McDonald (Backstrom, Geoffrion) 9:54;
3. Montreal, Backstrom (McDonald, Geoffrion) 13:01;
4. Montreal, Geoffrion (H. Richard, Bonin) 15:56;
5. Toronto, Mahovlich (Ehman) 18:36

Game 5

Toronto
 0 1 2—3
Montreal
 3 2 0—5

First Period—1. Montreal, Backstrom, (Geoffrion, Moore) 4:13;
2. Montreal, Geoffrion (Harvey, Backstrom) 13:42;
3. Montreal, Johnson (Backstrom) 16:26

Second Period—4. Toronto, Pulford (Armstrong, Brewer) 4:27;
5. Montreal, Bonin (H. Richard, Harvey) 9:55;
6. Montreal, Geoffrion (Backstrom, Johnson) 19:25

Third Period—7. Toronto, Mahovlich (Harris, Ehman) 12:07;
8. Toronto, Olmstead (Ehman, Mahovlich) 16:19

1960

Montreal won four games to none.

Game 1

Toronto
 0 2 0—2
Montreal
 3 0 1—4

First Period—1. Montreal, Moore (H. Richard, Geoffrion) 2:27;
2. Montreal, Harvey (H. Richard) 8:55;
3. Montreal, Beliveau (Geoffrion, H. Richard) 11:56

Second Period—4. Toronto, Baun (Armstrong, Regan) 5:23;
5. Toronto, Olmstead (Kelly, Horton) 17:35

Third Period—6. Montreal, H. Richard (Moore, Geoffrion) 1:30

Game 2

Toronto
 1 0 0—1
Montreal
 2 0 0—2

First Period—1. Montreal, Moore (M. Richard, H. Richard) 1:26;
2. Montreal, Beliveau (Talbot, Bonin) 5:56;
3. Toronto, Regan (Armstrong, Duff) 19:32

Second Period—No scoring

Third Period—No scoring

Game 3

Montreal
 1 2 2—5
Toronto
 0 1 1—2

First Period—1. Montreal, Marshall (Hicke) 13:54

Second Period—2. Montreal, Goyette (Provost, Pronovost) :21;
3. Montreal, H. Richard (unassisted) 15:27;
4. Toronto, Wilson (Harris, Brewer) 16:19

Third Period—5. Montreal, Goyette (unassisted) 8:57;
6. Montreal, M. Richard (H. Richard, Moore) 10:07;
7. Toronto, Olmstead (Kelly, Edmundson) 19:47

Game 4

Montreal
 2 1 1—4
Toronto
 0 0 0—0

First Period—1. Montreal, Beliveau (Langlois, Geoffrion) 8:16;
2. Montreal, Harvey (Geoffrion, Langlois) 8:45

Second Period—3. Montreal, H. Richard (M. Richard, Moore) 16:40

Third Period—4. Montreal, Beliveau (Bonin, Geoffrion) 1:21

1961

Chicago won four games to two.

Game 1

Detroit
  0 1 1—2
Chicago
  3 0 0—3

First Period—1. Chicago, Hull (M. Balfour, Mikita) 9:39;
        2. Chicago, Wharram (McDonald, Mikita) 10:10;
        3. Chicago, Hull (Pilote, M. Balfour) 13:15

Second Period—4. Detroit, Lunde (Howe) 16:14

Third Period—5. Detroit, Johnson (Howe, Ullman) 19:18

Game 2

Chicago
  0 1 0—1
Detroit
  2 0 1—3

First Period—1. Detroit, Young (Stasiuk, Delvecchio) 8:10;
        2. Detroit, Delvecchio (Howe, Johnson) 17:39

Second Period—3. Chicago, Pilote (unassisted) :41

Third Period—4. Detroit, Delvecchio (Stasiuk, Howe) 19:22

Game 3

Detroit
  0 0 1—1
Chicago
  0 3 0—3

First Period—No scoring

Second Period—1. Chicago, Mikita (Hull, Pilote) 11:54;
        2. Chicago, Murphy (Litzenberger, Pilote) 14:19;
        3. Chicago, M. Balfour (Hull, Hay) 18:16

Third Period—4. Detroit, Howe (Delvecchio, Young) 9:28

Game 4

Chicago
  0 1 0—1
Detroit
  0 1 1—2

First Period—No scoring

Second Period—1. Chicago, Hay (Hull, M. Balfour) 7:34;
        2. Detroit, Delvecchio (MacGregor, Howe) 8:48

Third Period—3. Detroit, MacGregor (Fonteyne, Godfrey)
13:10

Game 5

Detroit
  2 1 0—3
Chicago
  2 1 3—6

First Period—1. Detroit, Labine (Johnson, Ullman) 2:14;
        2. Chicago, M. Balfour (Hay, Hull) 9:36;
        3. Chicago, Murphy (St. Laurent, Nesterenko) 10:04;
        4. Detroit, Glover (MacGregor, Fonteyne) 15:35

Second Period—5. Chicago, M. Balfour (Pilote, Hay)
16:23;

        6. Detroit, Stasiuk (Howe, Pronovost) 18:49

Third Period—7. Chicago, Mikita (Pilote, Vasko) 2:51;
        8. Chicago, Pilote (Wharram, Mikita) 7:02;
        9. Chicago, Mikita (Murphy) 13:27

Game 6

Chicago
  0 2 3—5
Detroit
  1 0 0—1

First Period—1. Detroit, MacDonald (Howe, Delvecchio)
15:24

Second Period—2. Chicago, Fleming (unassisted) 6:45;
        3. Chicago, McDonald (Hull, Mikita) 18:49

Third Period—4. Chicago, Nesterenko (Sloan, Pilote) :57;
        5. Chicago, Evans (unassisted) 6:27;
        6. Chicago, Wharram (unassisted) 18:00

1962

Toronto won four games to two.

Game 1

Chicago
  1 0 0—1
Toronto
  0 2 2—4

First Period—1. Chicago, Hull (Pilote, Mikita) 3:35

Second Period—2. Toronto, Keon (Duff, Armstrong) 1:32;
        3. Toronto, Mahovlich (Horton, Stewart) 13:54

Third Period—4. Toronto, Armstrong (Duff) 6:03;
        5. Toronto, Horton (Armstrong, Keon) 14:32

Game 2

Chicago
0 0 2—2
Toronto
1 0 2—3

First Period—1. Toronto, Harris (Horton, Stewart) 2:35

Second Period—No scoring

Third Period—2. Chicago, Mikita (McDonald, Wharram) 8:47;
    3. Toronto, Mahovlich (Stewart, Kelly) 9:47;
    4. Toronto, Armstrong (Duff, Stanley) 16:08;
    5. Chicago, Mikita (Pilote) 18:27

Game 3

Toronto
0 0 0—0
Chicago
0 2 1—3

First Period—No scoring

Second Period—1. Chicago, Mikita (Pilote, McDonald) 4:35;
    2. Chicago, McDonald (Pilote, Hay) 8:33

Third Period—3. Chicago, Horvath (Nesterenko) 19:21

Game 4

Toronto
1 0 0—1
Chicago
2 2 0—4

First Period—1. Chicago, Hull (Mikita) 10:35;
    2. Chicago, Fleming (Nesterenko) 15:41;
    3. Toronto, Kelly (Armstrong, Duff) 18:08

Second Period—4. Chicago, Hull (Hay, Mikita) :46;
    5. Chicago, Fleming (Nesterenko, Hovrath) 7:31

Third Period—No scoring

Game 5

Toronto
2 3 3—8
Chicago
1 2 1—4

First Period—1. Toronto, Pulford (Nevin, Olmstead) :17;
    2. Toronto, Pulford (unassisted) 17:45;
    3. Chicago, Balfour (Hay, Hull) 18:05

Second Period—4. Chicago, McDonald (Mikita, Hull) :59;
    5. Chicago, McDonald (Hull, Mikita) 3:07;

    6. Toronto, Harris (Mahovlich, Horton) 8:31;
    7. Toronto, Keon (Horton, Mahovlich) 9:50;
    8. Toronto, Mahovlich (Kelly, Stewart) 13:24

Third Period—9. Toronto, Armstrong (Brewer, Baun) 4:41;
    10. Toronto, Mahovlich (Stewart, Baun) 6:31;
    11. Chicago, Turner (St. Laurent, Nesterenko) 10:31;
    12. Toronto, Pulford (Harris, Horton) 13:51

Game 6

Toronto
0 0 2—2
Chicago
0 0 1—1

First Period—No scoring

Second Period—No scoring

Third Period—1. Chicago, Hull (Balfour, Hay) 8:56;
    2. Toronto, Nevin (Baun, Mahovlich) 10:29;
    3. Toronto, Duff (Horton, Armstrong) 14:14

1963

Toronto won four games to one.

Game 1

Detroit
0 2 0—2
Toronto
3 0 1—4

First Period—1. Toronto, Duff, (Keon, Stanley) :49;
    2. Toronto, Duff (Horton, Stanley) 1:08;
    3. Toronto, Nevin (unassisted) 14:42

Second Period—4. Detroit, Jeffrey (Ullman, Smith) 5:36;
    5. Detroit, Jeffrey (Howe, Ullman) 8:05

Third Period—6. Toronto, Nevin (Pulford, Shack) 5:08

Game 2

Detroit
0 1 1—2
Toronto
2 2 0—4

First Period—1. Toronto, Litzenberger (Pulford, Horton) 5:31;
    2. Toronto, Stewart (Litzenberger, Kelly) 18:42

Second Period—3. Toronto, Nevin (Stanley, Horton) :49;
    4. Detroit, Howe (Delvecchio, M. Pronovost) 1:32;
    5. Toronto, Stewart (Litzenberger, Harris) 8:55

Third Period—6. Detroit, Howe (Jeffrey, Ullman) 2:03

Game 3

Toronto
  1 1 0—2
Detroit
  1 2 0—3

First Period—1. Detroit, Stasiuk (Ullman, Smith) :33;
      2. Toronto, Keon (Brewer, Duff) 14:56

Second Period—3. Detroit, Faulkner (M. Pronovost, MacGregor) 8:13;
      4. Toronto, Horton (Kelly) 13:06;
      5. Detroit, Faulkner (M. Pronovost, A. Pronovost) 13:39

Third Period—No scoring

Game 4

Toronto
  0 2 2—4
Detroit
  1 1 0—2

First Period—1. Detroit, Howe (Delvecchio, MacDonald) 2:54

Second Period—2. Toronto, Armstrong (Keon) 1:17;
      3. Detroit, Joyal (Howe) 2:38;
      4. Toronto, Kelly (Baun, Mahovlich) 17:41

Third Period—5. Toronto, Keon (unassisted) 9:42;
      6. Toronto, Kelly (unassisted) 17:45

Game 5

Detroit
  0 1 0—1
Toronto
  1 0 2—3

First Period—1. Toronto, Keon (Armstrong) 17:44

Second Period—2. Detroit, Delvecchio (Howe, M. Pronovost) :49

Third Period—3. Toronto, Shack (Douglas, Pulford) 13:28;
      4. Toronto, Keon (Armstrong, Stanley) 19:55

1964

Toronto won four games to three.

Game 1

Detroit
  2 0 0—2
Toronto
  1 0 2—3

First Period—1. Detroit, MacGregor (Barkley) 4:31;
      2. Toronto, Armstrong (Stanley, McKenney) 4:44;
      3. Detroit, Howe (MacDonald, Delvecchio) 10:25

Second Period—No scoring.

Third Period—4. Toronto, Armstrong (Kelly, McKenney) 4:02;
      5. Toronto, Pulford (unassisted) 19:58

Game 2

Detroit
  1 2 0 1—4
Toronto
  1 0 2 0—3

First Period—1. Toronto, Stanley (Kelly, (Mahovlich) 4:41;
      2. Detroit, Ullman (Gadsby, Jeffrey) 12:43

Second Period—3. Detroit, Joyal (Barkley) 3:19;
      4. Detroit, Smith (Howe) 16:15

Third Period—5. Toronto, Kelly (Baun, Mahovlich) 11:57;
      6. Toronto, Ehman (Bathgate, Stewart) 19:17

Overtime—7. Detroit, Jeffrey (Howe, Ullman) 7:52

Game 3

Toronto
  0 1 2—3
Detroit
  3 0 1—4

First Period—1. Detroit, Smith (unassisted) 2:40;
      2. Detroit, MacGregor (Barkley, Martin) 3:38;
      3. Detroit, Smith (Ullman, Delvecchio) 14:47

Second Period—4. Toronto, Bathgate (Mahovlich, Kelly) 4:16

Third Period—5. Toronto, Keon (McKenney, Armstrong) 7:34;
      6. Toronto, McKenney (Horton, Keon) 18:47;
      7. Detroit, Delvecchio (Howe, A. Pronovost) 19:43

Game 4

Toronto
  1 1 2—4
Detroit
  0 2 0—2

First Period—1. Toronto, Keon (Horton, McKenney) 5:45

Second Period—2. Detroit, MacGregor (Joyal) 5:57;
      3. Detroit, Howe (Jeffrey, Ullman)13:05;
      4. Toronto, Keon (McKenney, Armstrong) 16:09

Third Period—5. Toronto, Bathgate (Mahovlich, Kelly) 10:55;
6. Toronto, Mahovlich (Stewart, Pulford) 18:09

Game 5

Detroit
1 0 1—2
Toronto
0 0 1—1

First Period—1. Detroit, Howe (Delvecchio) 10:52

Second Period—No scoring

Third Period—2. Detroit, Joyal (A. Pronovost) 7:50;
3. Toronto, Armstrong (Bathgate, Mahovlich) 14:57

Game 6

Toronto
1 2 0 1—4
Detroit
0 3 0 0—3

First Period—1. Toronto, Pulford (Stanley) 17:01

Second Period—2. Detroit, Henderson (Martin) 4:20;
3. Detroit, Martin (Howe, McMillan) 10:56;
4. Toronto, Pulford, (Stewart, Brewer) 14:36;
5. Detroit, Howe (Delvecchio, Gadsby) 15:56;
6. Toronto, Harris (Armstrong, Baun) 17:48

Third Period—No scoring

Overtime—7. Toronto, Baun (Pulford) 1:43

Game 7

Detroit
0 0 0—0
Toronto
1 0 3—4

First Period—1. Toronto, Bathgate (unassisted) 3:04

Second Period—No scoring

Third Period—2. Toronto, Keon (Harris) 4:26;
3. Toronto, Kelly (Stanley, Mahovlich) 5:53;
4. Toronto, Armstrong (Mahovlich) 15:26

1965

Montreal won four games to three.

Game 1

Chicago
0 1 1—2
Montreal
0 2 1—3

First Period—No scoring

Second Period—1. Montreal, Richard (Berenson) 2:39;
2. Chicago, Henry (B. Hull) 4:47;
3. Montreal, Ferguson (unassisted) 5:26

Third Period—4. Chicago, Ravlich (Maki, Mikita) 2:28;
5. Montreal, Cournoyer (Harris, Beliveau) 8:59

Game 2

Chicago
0 0 0—0
Montreal
0 1 1—2

First Period—No scoring

Second Period—1. Montreal, Beliveau (Picard, Provost)
2:55

Third Period—2. Montreal, Duff (Beliveau, J. C. Tremblay)
8:07

Game 3

Montreal
0 1 0—1
Chicago
0 1 2—3

First Period—No scoring

Second Period—1. Montreal, Ferguson (J. C. Tremblay,
Backstrom) 4:16;
2. Chicago, Esposito (Maki, Pilote) 5:03

Third Period—3. Chicago, Wharram (Mikita) 2:08;
4. Chicago, Maki (Esposito, B. Hull) 19:24

Game 4

Montreal
0 1 0—1
Chicago
1 0 4—5

First Period—1. Chicago, Stanfield (unassisted) 2:57

Second Period—2. Montreal, Beliveau (Duff, J. C. Tremblay)
6:29

Third Period—3. Chicago, Hull (Pilote) :26;

4. Chicago, Hay (Stanfield) 15:20;
5. Chicago, Hull (Maki) 18:48;
6. Chicago, Jarrett (Vasko) 19:57

Game 5

Chicago
  0 0 0—0
Montreal
  2 1 3—6

First Period—1. Montreal, Beliveau (Rousseau, Duff) 7:14;
    2. Montreal, Duff (Beliveau, Rousseau) 16:36

Second Period—3. Montreal, Rousseau (Beliveau, J. C. Tremblay) 2:38

Third Period—4. Montreal, Beliveau (Duff, J. C. Tremblay) 4:29;
    5. Montreal, Richard (Provost) 16:46;
    6. Montreal, J. C. Tremblay (unassisted) 19:55

Game 6

Montreal
  0 1 0—1
Chicago
  0 0 2—2

First Period—No scoring

Second Period—1. Montreal, Backstrom (Harris, Ferguson) 16:57

Third Period—2. Chicago, Vasko (Mohns, Ravlich) 6:06;
    3. Chicago, Mohns (Mikita, Pilote) 8:15

Game 7

Chicago
  0 0 0—0
Montreal
  4 0 0—4

First Period—1. Montreal, Beliveau (Duff, Rousseau) :14;
    2. Montreal, Duff (Beliveau, Rousseau) 5:03;
    3. Montreal, Cournoyer (Duff, Rousseau) 16:29;
    4. Montreal, Richard (Harris) 18:45

Second Period—No scoring

Third Period—No scoring

1966

Montreal won four games to two.

Game 1

Detroit
  1 1 1—3
Montreal
  0 1 1—2

First Period—1. Detroit, Smith (Bathgate) 13:25

Second Period—2. Montreal, Backstrom (J. C. Tremblay) 4:23;
    3. Detroit, Gadsby (McDonald) 5:14

Third Period—4. Detroit, Henderson (Marshall) 2:14;
    5. Montreal, Harper (Rousseau) 2:36

Game 2

Detroit
  1 0 4—5
Montreal
  1 0 1—2

First Period—1. Montreal, J. C. Tremblay (Beliveau, Cournoyer) 6:55;
    2. Detroit, Bathgate (Prentice, Ullman) 18:39

Second Period—No scoring

Third Period—3. Detroit, MacGregor (Henderson, Ullman) 1:51;
    4. Detroit, McDonald (Gadsby, Smith) 2:45;
    5. Montreal, Cournoyer (Harper, Price) 12:00;
    6. Detroit, Smith (Bathgate) 12:28;
    7. Detroit, Prentice (Delvecchio) 16:25

Game 3

Montreal
  2 0 2—4
Detroit
  1 0 1—2

First Period—1. Detroit, Ullman (unassisted) 4:20;
    2. Montreal, Balon (Harper, Richard) 15:40;
    3. Montreal, Beliveau (unassisted) 19:12

Second Period—No scoring

Third Period—4. Montreal, G. Tremblay (Beliveau) 1:45;
    5. Montreal, G. Tremblay (J. C. Tremblay, Rouseau) 3:21;
    6. Detroit, Howe (Delvecchio, Marshall) 19:59

Game 4

Montreal
   0 1 1—2
Detroit
   0 1 0—1

First Period—No scoring

Second Period—1. Detroit, Ullman (MacGregor, Henderson) 11:24;
      2. Montreal, Beliveau (Duff, J. C. Tremblay) 19:51

Third Period—3. Montreal, Backstrom (Duff, Roberts) 13:37

Game 5

Detroit
   0 1 0—1
Montreal
   2 2 1—5

First Period—1. Montreal, Provost (Backstrom, J. C. Tremblay) 1:06;
      2. Montreal, Cournoyer (J. C. Tremblay, G. Tremblay) 19:21

Second Period—3. Montreal, Balon (Richard, Rochefort) 1:05;
      4. Montreal, Rousseau (Duff, Backstrom) 11:22;
      5. Detroit, Ullman (Henderson, Bathgate) 14:22

Third Period—6. Montreal, Duff (Richard) 5:31

Game 6

Montreal
   1 1 0 1—3
Detroit
   0 1 1 0—2

First Period—1. Montreal, Beliveau (G. Tremblay, Provost) 9:08

Second Period—2. Montreal, Rochefort (Richard, Balon) 10:11;
      3. Detroit, Ullman (Delvecchio, Howe) 11:55

Third Period—4. Detroit, Smith (Bergman, McDonald) 10:30

Overtime—5. Montreal, Richard (Balon, Talbot) 2:20

1967

Toronto won four games to two.

Game 1

Toronto
   1 1 0—2
Montreal
   2 2 2—6

First Period—1. Montreal, Cournoyer (Beliveau, Rouseau) 6:25;
      2. Toronto, Hillman (Pappin) 6:40;
      3. Montreal, Richard (Rochefort, Balon) 11:19

Second Period—4. Montreal, Cournoyer (Rousseau, Richard) 5:03;
      5. Montreal, Beliveau (G. Tremblay) 6:36;
      6. Toronto, Pappin (Horton, Pulford) 12:59

Third Period—7. Montreal, Richard (Balon) 4:53;
      8. Montreal, Richard (J. C. Tremblay) 8:21

Game 2

Toronto
   1 2 0—3
Montreal
   0 0 0—0

First Period—1. Toronto, Stemkowski (Pulford, Walton) 12:14

Second Period—2. Toronto, Walton (Pappin, Mahovlich) 19:12;
      3. Toronto, Horton (Stemkowski, Conacher) 16:57

Third Period—No scoring

Game 3

Montreal
   1 1 0 0 0—2
Toronto
   1 1 0 0 1—3

First Period—1. Montreal, Beliveau (Rousseau, Duff) 2:27;
      2. Toronto, Stemkowski (Hillman, Pappin) 8:39

Second Period—3. Toronto, Pappin (Horton, Pulford) 10:34;
      4. Montreal, Ferguson (Beliveau) 19:10

Third Period—No scoring

First Overtime—No scoring

Second Overtime—5. Toronto, Pulford (Stemkowski, Pappin) 8:26

Game 4

Montreal
2 3 1—6
Toronto
0 2 0—2

First Period—1. Montreal, Backstrom (Larose) 12:25;
    2. Montreal, Beliveau (Rousseau, Cournoyer) 13:08

Second Period—3. Toronto, Walton (Stemkowski, Pulford)
2:09;
        4. Montreal, Richard (unassisted) 2:26;
        5. Toronto, Horton (unassisted) 12:16;
        6. Montreal, Beliveau (Ferguson, Cournoyer) 13:41;
        7. Montreal, Backstrom (J. C. Tremblay) 15:58

Third Period—8. Montreal, Roberts (Richard) 15:17

Game 5

Toronto
1 3 0—4
Montreal
1 0 0—1

First Period—1. Montreal, Rochefort (Duff, Richard) 6:03;
    2. Toronto, Pappin (Keon, Mahovlich) 15:06

Second Period—3. Toronto, Conacher (Kelly, Ellis) 3:07;
        4. Toronto, Pronovost (unassisted) 12:02;
        5. Toronto, Keon (Horton) 19:27

Third Period—No scoring

Game 6

Montreal
0 0 1—1
Toronto
0 2 1—3

First Period—No scoring

Second Period—1. Toronto, Ellis (Kelly, Stanley) 6:25;
    2. Toronto, Pappin (Stemkowski, Pulford) 19:24

Third Period—3. Montreal, Duff (Harris) 5:28;
        4. Toronto, Armstrong (Pulford, Kelly) 19:13

1968

Montreal won four games to none.

Game 1

Montreal
1 1 0 1—3
St. Louis
1 1 0 0—2

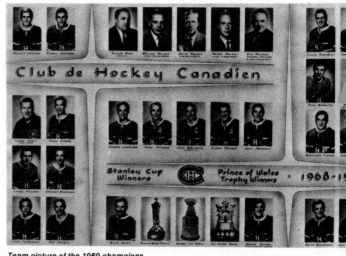

Team picture of the 1969 champions

First Period—1. St. Louis, Barclay Plager (unassisted)
9:19;
        2. Montreal, Richard (Larose) 9:42

Second Period—3. St. Louis, Moore (Barclay Plager, Berenson) 8:16;
        4. Montreal, Cournoyer (Harris, Ferguson) 18:14

Third Period—No scoring

Overtime—5. Montreal, Lemaire (unassisted) 1:41

Game 2

Montreal
0 0 1—1
St. Louis
0 0 0—0

First Period—No scoring

Second Period—No scoring

Third Period—1. Montreal, Savard (Provost) 2:17

Game 3

St. Louis
1 1 1 0—3
Montreal
1 1 1 1—4

First Period—1. St. Louis, St. Marseille (Picard, Harvey)
10:22;
        2. Montreal, Cournoyer (Richard, Ferguson) 14:24

Second Period—3. Montreal, Savard (unassisted) 1:23;
        4. St. Louis, Berenson (Talbot) 3:37

Third Period—5. Montreal, Backstrom (Cournoyer, Ferguson) 11:43;
   6. St. Louis, Berenson (unassisted) 17:25

Overtime—7. Montreal, Rousseau (Duff) 1:13

Game 4

St. Louis
 0 2 0—2
Montreal
 1 0 2—3

First Period—1. Montreal, Duff (Lemaire) 16:47

Second Period—2. St. Louis, Cameron (Ecclestone, Arbour) 6:53;
   3. St. Louis, Sabourin (Veneruzzo, St. Marseille) 7:50

Third Period—4. Montreal, Richard (J. C. Tremblay) 7:24;
   5. Montreal, J. C. Tremblay (Cournoyer, Backstrom) 11:40

1969

Montreal won four games to none.

Game 1

St. Louis
 1 0 0—1
Montreal
 2 0 1—3

First Period—1. Montreal, Duff (Cournoyer, Beliveau) 3:39;
   2. Montreal, Rouseau (Provost) 4:17;
   3. St. Louis, St. Marseille (McCreary, Picard) 18:24

Second Period—No scoring

Third Period—4. Montreal, Ferguson (Richard) 19:46

Game 2

St. Louis
 0 0 1—1
Montreal
 1 2 0—3

First Period—1. Montreal, Backstrom (J. C. Tremblay) 17:26

Second Period—2. Montreal, Duff (Beliveau, Savard) 9:07;
   3. Montreal, Cournoyer (Beliveau) 14:11

Third Period—4. St. Louis, Keenan (Roberts, Barclay
  Plager) 9:20

Game 3

Montreal
 1 2 1—4
St. Louis
 0 0 0—0

First Period—1. Montreal, Savard (Duff) 12:34

Second Period—2. Montreal, Lemaire (Redmond) 8:16;
   3. Montreal, Duff (Cournoyer, Beliveau) 13:38

Third Period—4. Montreal, Duff (Beliveau, Cournoyer) 18:35

Game 4

Montreal
 0 0 2—2
St. Louis
 0 1 0—1

First Period—No scoring

Second Period—1. St. Louis, Gray (St. Marseille, Crisp) 10:50

Third Period—2. Montreal, Harris (Duff, J. C. Tremblay) :42;
   3. Montreal, Ferguson (Backstrom) 3:02

1970

Boston won four games to none.

Game 1

Boston
 1 1 4—6
St. Louis
 0 1 0—1

First Period—1. Boston, Bucyk (Stanfield) 19:45

Second Period—2. St. Louis, Roberts (B. McCreary) 1:52;
   3. Boston, Bucyk (McKenzie, Esposito) 5:16

Third Period—4. Boston, Carleton (Sanderson, Awrey) 4:59;
   5. Boston, Bucyk (R. Smith, McKenzie) 5:31;
   6. Boston, Sanderson (Orr) 17:20;
   7. Boston, Esposito (unassisted) 18:58

Game 2

Boston
 3 1 2—6
St. Louis
 0 1 1—2

First Period—1. Boston, Stanfield (Orr, Esposito) 8:10;

2. Boston, Westfall (R. Smith) 13:38;
3. Boston, Westfall (Orr) 19:15

Second Period—4. Boston, Sanderson (Esposito, Carleton) 9:37;
5. St. Louis, Gray (Picard) 17:26

Third Period—6. Boston, Sanderson (D. Smith, Westfall) :58;
7. St. Louis, Marseille (Goyette, McDonald) 4:15;
8. Boston, Bucyk (McKenzie) 15:00

Game 3

St. Louis
  1 0 0—1
Boston
  2 0 2—4

First Period—1. St. Louis, St. Marseille (unassisted) 5:32;
2. Boston, Bucyk (Esposito, Stanfield) 13:23;
3. Boston, McKenzie (Orr, Stanfield) 18:23

Second Period—No scoring

Third Period—4. Boston, Cashman (Hodge, Esposito) 3:20;
5. Boston, Cashman (Hodge, Esposito) 14:26

Game 4

St. Louis
  1 1 1 0—3
Boston
  1 1 1 1—4

First Period—1. Boston, R. Smith (Sanderson) 5:28;
2. St. Louis, Berenson (Bob Plager, Ecclestone) 19:17

Second Period—3. St. Louis, Sabourin (St. Marseille) 3:22;
4. Boston, Esposito (Hodge) 14:22

Third Period—5. St. Louis, Keenan (Goyette, Roberts) :19;
6. Boston, Bucyk (McKenzie, R. Smith) 13:28

Overtime—Boston, Orr (Sanderson) :40

1971

Montreal won four games to three.

Game 1

Montreal
  0 1 0 0 0—1
Chicago
  0 0 1 0 1—2

First Period—No scoring

Second Period—1. Montreal, Lemaire (Tremblay, Mahovlich) 12:29

Third Period—2. Chicago, B. Hull (Pappin, Stapleton) 7:54

First Overtime—No scoring

Second Overtime—3. Chicago, Pappin (Mikita, White) 1:11

Game 2

Montreal
  2 0 1—3
Chicago
  1 2 2—5

First Period—1. Chicago, B. Hull (Maki, Angotti) 4:39;
2. Montreal, Lemaire (Tremblay) 9:06
3. Montreal, P. Mahovlich (Tremblay, Laperriere) 17:58

Second Period—4. Chicago, Maki (Angotti, B. Hull) 11:58;
5. Chicago, Pappin (O'Shea, Foley) 13:50

Third Period—6. Chicago, Angotti (unassisted) 7:27;
7. Montreal, F. Mahovlich (unassisted) 8:56;
8. Chicago, Angotti (unassisted) 16:47

Game 3

Chicago
  2 0 0—2
Montreal
  0 2 2—4

First Period—1. Chicago, Koroll (B. Hull, Mikita) 4:26;
2. Chicago, B. Hull (Pappin, Martin) 13:38

Second Period—3. Montreal, P. Mahovlich (unassisted) 5:56;
4. Montreal, F. Mahovlich (Beliveau, Cournoyer) 17:34

Third Period—5. Montreal, Cournoyer (Harper) 6:23;
6. Montreal, F. Mahovlich (Lapointe) 12:13

Game 4

Chicago
  1 1 0—2
Montreal
  3 2 0—5

First Period—1. Montreal, P. Mahovlich (Harper, Laperriere) 1:00;
2. Chicago, Mikita (Koroll, Stapleton) 3:09;
3. Montreal, Beliveau (Cournoyer, F. Mahovlich) 6:55;
4. Montreal, Lapointe (Houle, Richard) 16:33

Second Period—5. Montreal, Cournoyer (unassisted) 9:07;
6. Chicago, D. Hull (Mikita) 12:30;
7. Montreal, Cournoyer (F. Mahovlich, P. Mahovlich) 15:53

Third Period—No scoring

Game 5

Montreal
  0 0 0—0
Chicago
  1 1 0—2

First Period—1. Chicago, D. Hull (Koroll, B. Hull) 10:57

Second Period—2. Chicago, Koroll (D. Hull, Mikita) 11:26

Third Period—No scoring

Game 6

Chicago
  1 2 0—3
Montreal
  1 1 2—4

First Period—1. Chicago, Pappin (unassisted) 11:25;
    2. Montreal, Cournoyer (Beliveau, F. Mahovlich) 12:33

Second Period—3. Montreal, P. Mahovlich (Houle, Ferguson) 5:04;
    4. Chicago, Maki (White, B. Hull) 17:40;
    5. Chicago, Pappin (Jarrett, B. Hull) 18:48

Third Period—6. Montreal, F. Mahovlich (Beliveau) 5:10;
    7. Montreal, P. Mahovlich (F. Mahovlich) 8:56

Game 7

Montreal
  0 2 1—3
Chicago
  1 1 0—2

First Period—1. Chicago, D. Hull (Koroll, B. Hull) 19:12

Second Period—2. Chicago, O'Shea (Martin) 7:33;
    3. Montreal, Lemaire (Laperriere) 14:18;
    4. Montreal, Richard (Lemaire) 18:20

Third Period—5. Montreal, Richard (Houle, Lapointe) 2:34

1972

Boston won four games to two.

Game 1

New York
  1 1 3—5
Boston
  4 1 1—6

First Period—1. New York, Rolfe (Gilbert, Park) 3:52;

    2. Boston, Stanfield, (McKenzie) 5:07;
    3. Boston, Hodge (Esposito, Walton) 15:48;
    4. Boston, Sanderson, (Westfall) 17:29;
    5. Boston, Hodge (Esposito) 18:14

Second Period—6. Boston, Hodge (Esposito, Orr) 10:46;
    7. New York, Gilbert (Hadfield, Ratelle) 11:54

Third Period—8. New York, Hadfield (Tkaczuk, Gilbert) 1:56;
    9. New York, Tkaczuk (unassisted) 7:48;
    10. New York, MacGregor (Irvine, Stemkowski) 9:17;
    11. Boston, Bailey (Walton, Westfall) 17:44

Game 2

New York
  0 1 0—1
Boston
  1 0 1—2

First Period—1. Boston, Bucyk (Orr, Stanfield) 16:15

Second Period—2. New York, Gilbert (Neilson, Hadfield) 7:23

Third Period—3. Boston, Hodge (Walton, Esposito) 11:53

Game 3

Boston
  1 1 0—2
New York
  3 2 0—5

First Period—1. New York, Park (Hadfield, Fairbairn) 1:22;
    2. New York, Gilbert (Park, Rousseau) 11:19;
    3. New York, Park (Gilbert) 13:00;
    4. Boston, Walton (Vadnais) 14:04

Second Period—5. Boston, Orr (D. Smith, Cashman) 1:10;
    6. New York, Gilbert (Rousseau, Park) 3:46;
    7. New York, Stemkowski (MacGregor, Irvine) 19:23

Third Period—No scoring

Game 4

Boston
  2 1 0—3
New York
  0 1 1—2

First Period—1. Boston, Orr (Walton) 5:26;
    2. Boston, Orr (McKenzie, Bucyk) 8:17

Second Period—3. Boston, Marcotte (Orr) 16:33;
    4. New York, Irvine (Stemkowski, Seiling) 18:38

Third Period—5. New York, Seiling (Irvine, Stemkowski) 18:35

Game 5

New York
 1 0 2—3
Boston
 2 0 0—2

First Period—1. Boston, Cashman (Hodge, Esposito) 3:55;
2. New York, Rolfe (Tkaczuk, Fairbairn) 13:45;
3. Boston, Hodge (Stanfield, Esposito) 16:07

Second Period—No scoring

Third Period—4. New York, Rousseau (Park, MacGregor) 2:56;
5. New York, Rousseau (Irvine) 12:45

Game 6

Boston
 1 0 2—3
New York
 0 0 0—0

First Period—1. Boston, Orr (Hodge, Bucyk) 11:18

Second Period—No scoring

Third Period—2. Boston, Cashman (Esposito, Orr) 5:10;
3. Boston, Cashman (Hodge, Esposito) 18:11

1973

Montreal won four games to two.

Game 1

Chicago
 3 0 0—3
Montreal
 2 2 4—8

First Period—1. Chicago, Martin (Stapleton, Hull) :35;
2. Chicago, Backstrom (Stapleton) 1:02;
3. Montreal, Laperriere (unassisted) 2:28;
4. Montreal, Tardif (Lefleur, Houle) 8:07
5. Chicago, Martin (Stapleton, White) 12:07

Second Period—6. Montreal, Lefley (Cournoyer, Lemaire) 3:01;
7. Montreal, Lemaire (Richard, Tardif) 16:23

Third Period—8. Montreal, Lemaire (F. Mahovlich, P. Ma-hovlich) 8:38;
9. Montreal, P. Mahovlich (unassisted) 12:36;

10. Montreal, F. Mahovlich (Lafleur, Houle) 13:34;
11. Montreal, Lefley (Lemaire, Cournoyer) 14:35

Game 2

Chicago
 0 1 0—1
Montreal
 1 1 2—4

First Period—1. Montreal, Bouchard (Larose, P. Mahovlich) 5:36

Second Period—2. Chicago, Koroll (Redmond, Angotti) 7:28;
3. Montreal, Cournoyer (F. Mahovlich) 12:08

Third Period—4. Montreal, Cournoyer (Lapointe, Lemaire) 5:01;
5. Montreal, F. Mahovlich (unassisted) 19:26

Game 3

Montreal
 0 1 3—4
Chicago
 4 1 2—7

First Period—1. Chicago, Hull (Pappin, Stapleton) 1:59;
2. Chicago, J. P. Bordeleau (Mikita, Koroll) 11:44;
3. Chicago, White (Stapleton, Backstrom) 13:20;
4. Chicago, Mikita) Koroll, White) 14:20

Second Period—5. Chicago, Marks (Frig, Mikita) 2:08;
6. Montreal, F. Mahovlich (P. Mahovlich, Robinson) 10:25

Third Period—7. Montreal, Cournoyer (Lemaire, Lefley) 1:20;
8. Montreal, Lapointe (F. Mahovlich, Larose) 7:15;
9. Montreal, Lemaire (Cournoyer, Tardif) 8:01;
10. Chicago, Hull (unassisted) 19:29;
11. Chicago, Pappin (Hull) 19:49

Game 4

Montreal
 1 2 1—4
Chicago
 0 0 0—0

First Period—1. Montreal, Tardif (Cournoyer, Lemaire) 1:08

Second Period—2. Montreal, Cournoyer (Tardif) 14:13;
3. Montreal, Lefley (P. Mahovlich, Larose) 15:43

Third Period—4. Montreal, Larose (Lemaire) 3:45

Phil Esposito leads 1972 Bruins.

First Period—1. Chicago, Martin (Mikita, Stapleton) 10:35;
2. Chicago, Martin (Pappin) 11:31;
3. Montreal, Richard (F. Mahovlich) 19:48

Second Period—4. Montreal, P. Mahovlich (Laperriere, Lefley) 5:05;
5. Montreal, Houle (P. Mahovlich, Lefley) 6:37;
6. Chicago, Kryskow (Maki, Backstrom) 8:32;
7. Montreal, F. Mahovlich (Lapointe, Cournoyer) 10:54;
8. Chicago, Martin, (Hull) 17:05

Third Period—9. Montreal, Cournoyer (Lemaire) 8:13;
10. Montreal, Tardif (Cournoyer, Lemaire) 12:42

1974

Philadelphia won four games to two.

Game 1

Boston
  2 0 1—3
Philadelphia
  0 1 1—2

First Period—1. Boston, Cashman (Orr, Vadnais) 12:05;
2. Sheppard (Forbes, D. Smith) 13:01

Second Period—3. Philadelphia, Kindrachuk (Joseph Watson, Saleski) 7:47

Third Period—4. Philadelphia, Clarke (Joseph Watson, Nolet)   5:32;
5. Boston, Orr (Hodge, Cashman) 19:38

Game 2

Boston
  2 0 0 0—2
Philadelphia
  0 1 1 1—3

First Period—1. Boston Cashman (Vadnais, P. Esposito) 14:24;
2. Boston, P. Esposito (Hodge-Cashman) 17:22

Second Period—3. Philadelphia, Clarke (Flett, Schultz) 1:08

Third Period—4. Philadelphia, Dupont (MacLeish, Clarke) 19:08

Overtime—5. Philadelphia, Clarke (Flett, Schultz) 12:01

Game 5

Chicago
  2 5 1—8
Montreal
  2 3 2—7

First Period—1. Montreal, F. Mahovlich (unassisted) 2:47;
2. Chicago, Hull (Jarrett, Russell) 9:34;
3. Chicago, Mikita (Stapleton) 11:24;
4. Montreal, P. Mahovlich (F. Mahovlich, Robinson) 14:52

Second Period—5. Montreal, Larose (unassisted) :37;
6. Chicago, Kryskow (Backstrom, Maki) 3:10;
7. Montreal, Larose (Wilson) 4:23;
8. Chicago, Mikita (Stapleton, Marks) 6:21;
9. Montreal, Cournoyer (Lemaire, Lapointe) 7:09;
10. Chicago, Pappin (unassisted) 11:24;
11. Chicago, Frig (Mikita) 16:21;
12. Chicago, Pappin (Mikita, Hull) 19:03

Third Period—13. Montreal, Savard (Wilson, Larose) 1:15;
14. Chicago, Angotti (White) 4:06;
15. Montreal, Richard (F. Mahovlich) 11:43

Game 6

Montreal
  1 3 2—6
Chicago
  2 2 0—4

Game 3

Boston
  1 0 0—1
Philadelphia
  2 0 2—4

First Period—1. Boston, Bucyk (Sheppard, Orr) 1:03;
    2. Philadelphia, Bladon (Clarke, MacLeish) 10:27;
    3. Philadelphia, Crisp 15:43

Second Period—No scoring

Third Period—4. Philadelphia, Kindrachuk (Saleski, Barber)
7:53
    5. Philadelphia, Lonsberry (MacLeish) 14:19

Game 4

Boston
  2 0 0—2
Philadelphia
  2 0 2—4

First Period—1. Philadelphia, MacLeish (Bladon) 4:40;
    2. Boston, Schultz (Saleski, Van Impe) 5:30;
    3. Boston, P. Esposito (Bucyk, Hodge) 7:12;
    4. Boston, A. Savard (Orr, Vadnais) 11:24

Second Period—No scoring

Third Period—5. Philadelphia, Barber (Lonsberry, James
Watson) 14:25;
    6. Philadelphia, Dupont (Clarke, Crisp) 16:40

Game 5

Boston
  1 2 2—5
Philadelphia
  0 1 0-1

First Period—1. Boston, Sheppard (Orr) 8:14

Second Period—2. Philadelphia, Clement (Flett, Van Impe)
6:04;
    3. Boston, Orr (Sheppard, Bucyk) 12:06;
    4. Boston, Orr (Hodge, D. Smith)16:55

Third Period—5. Boston, Hodge (Sheppard, Bucyk) 0:39;
    6. Boston, Marcotte (A. Savard, O'Reilly) 18:59

Game 6

Boston
  0 0 0—0
Philadelphia
  1 0 0—1

First Period—1. Philadelphia, MacLeish (Dupont) 14:48

Second Period—No scoring

Third Period—No scoring

1975

Philadelphia won four games to two.

Game 1

Philadelphia
  0 0 4—4
Buffalo
  0 0 1—1

First Period—No scoring

Second Period—No scoring

Third Period—1. Philadelphia, Barber (Van Impe, MacLeish)
3:42;
    2. Philadelphia, Lonsberry (Bladon, Clarke) 7:29;
    3. Buffalo, R. Martin (Lorentz) 11:07;
    4. Philadelphia, Clarke 11:41;
    5. Philadelphia, Barber (Clarke) 19:02

Game 2

Philadelphia
  0 1 1—2
Buffalo
  0 0 1—1

First Period—No scoring

Second Period—1. Philadelphia, Leach (Clarke), Lonsberry)
8:24

Third Period—2. Buffalo, Korab (Lorentz, Spencer) 2:18;
    3. Philadelphia, Clarke (Barber, MacLeish) 6:43

Game 3

Philadelphia
  3 1 0 0—4
Buffalo
  2 1 1 1—5

First Period—1. Philadelphia, Dornhoefer (Barber) 0:39;
    2. Philadelphia, Saleski (E. Harris) 3:09;
    3. Buffalo, Gare (Ramsay, Luce) 11:46;
    4. Buffalo, R. Martin (Guevremont) 12:03;
    5. Philadelphia, MacLeish (Barber) 14:13

Second Period—6. Buffalo, Luce (Korab) 0:29;
    7. Philadelphia, Leach (Crisp, R. Kelly) 14:30

Third Period—8. Buffalo, Hajt (R. Martin, Luce) 9:56

Overtime—9. Buffalo, Robert (R. Martin, Perreault) 18:29

Game 4

Philadelphia
  1 1 0—2
Buffalo
  0 3 1—4

First Period—1. Philadelphia, Dupont (R. Kelly, Crisp) 11:28

Second Period—2. Buffalo, Korab (R. Martin, Robert) 3:46;
        3. Philadelphia, Lonsberry (MacLeish) 4:20;
        4. Buffalo, Perreault (Robert, R. Martin) 10:07;
        5. Buffalo, Lorentz (Dudley, Schoenfeld) 15:07

Third Period—6. Buffalo, Gare (Luce, Schoenfeld) 19:28

Game 5

Philadelphia
  3 2 0—5
Buffalo
  0 0 1—1 ·

First Period—1. Philadelphia, Shultz (Saleski, Kindrachuk) 3:12;
        2. Philadelphia, Dornhoefer (Crisp, Van Impe) 12:31;
        3. Philadelphia, R. Kelly (Crisp, James Watson) 12:50

Second Period—4. Philadelphia, Leach (Barber, Goodenough) 1:55;
        5. Philadelphia, Schultz (Goodenough, E. Harris) 9:56

Third Period—6. Buffalo, Luce (Ramsay, Gare) 14:02

Game 6

Philadelphia
  0 0 2—2
Buffalo
  0 0 0—0

First Period—No scoring

Second Period—No scoring
Third Period—1. Philadelphia, R. Kelly (Leach, James Watson) 0:11;
        2. Philadelphia, Clement (Kindarchuk) 17:13

1976

Montreal won four games to none.

Game 1

Philadelphia
  2 0 1—3
Montreal
  0 2 2—4

First Period—No scoring

Second Period—1. Montreal, Lemaire 15:19

Third Period—2. Montreal, Lafleur 2:41;
        3. Philadelphia, Schultz (Bladon) 17:35

Game 3

Philadelphia
  2 0 0—2
Montreal
  1 1 1—3

First Period—1. Montreal, Shutt (Lafleur) 3:17;
        2. Philadelphia, Leach (Clarke, Goodenough) 8:40;
        3. Philadelphia, Leach 18:14

Second Period—4. Montreal, Shutt (Lafleur, Mahovlich) 1:09

Third Period—5. Montreal, P. Bouchard (M. Wilson) 9:16

Game 4

Philadelphia
  2 1 0—3
Montreal
  2 1 2—5

First Period—1. Philadelphia, Leach (Bridgman) 0:41;
        2. Montreal, Shutt (Cournoyer, Mahovlich) 5:35;
        3. Montreal, P. Bouchard (Risebrough) 11:48;
        4. Philadelphia, Barber (Dupont, Bladon) 18:20

Second Period—5. Philadelphia, Dupont (Barber, Clarke) 13:59;
        6. Montreal, Cournoyer (Robinson, Lafleur) 19:49

Third Period—7. Montreal, Lafleur (Mahovlich, Shutt) 14:18
        8. Montreal, Mahovlich (Lafleur, Shutt) 15:16

1977

Montreal won four games to none.

Game 1

Boston
  1 2 0—3
Montreal
  3 1 3—7

First Period—1. Montreal, Risenbrough (Lambert, G. Lapointe) 1:45;

    2. Montreal, Lambert (Robinson, Jarvis) 4:23;

    3. Boston, Park (Ratelle) 5:23;

    4. Montreal, Tremblay (S. Savard, G. Lapointe) 14:35

Second Period—5. Montreal, Lemaire (Lafleur) 5:08;

    6. Boston, O'Reilly (Park) 11:54;

    7. Boston, Schmautz (Park) 16:35

Third Period—8. Montreal, Chartraw (Mahovlich, W. Wilson) 0:59;

    9. Montreal, Tremblay (Mahovlich, Lambert) 2:04;

    10. Montreal, Lambert (Risebrough, S. Savard) 13:58

Game 2

Boston

  0 0 0—0

Montreal

  0 2 1—3

First Period—No scoring

Second Period—1. Montreal, Mahovlich (Shutt, Robinson) 7:43;

    2. Montreal, Risebrough (Lafleur, Shutt) 12:07

Third Period—3. Montreal, Shutt (Lafleur, P. Bouchard) 5:40

Game 3

Boston

  0 1 1—2

Montreal

  3 0 1—4

First Period—1. Montreal, Lafleur (G. Lapointe, Mahovlich) 4:08;

    2. Montreal, Shutt (Lamaire, Lafleur) 7:58;

    3. Montreal, Lemaire (G. Lapointe, Lafleur) 18:29

Second Period—4. Boston, Sheppard (Middleton, Cashman) 6:32

Third Period—5. Montreal, Lafleur (Shutt, Lemaire) 12:52;

    6. Boston, McNab (Middleton, Park) 18:34

Game 4

Boston

  1 0 0 0—1

Montreal

  0 1 0 1—2

First Period—1. Boston, Schmautz (Park) 11:38

Second Period—2. Montreal, Lemaire (Lafleur, Robinson) 1:34

Third Period—No scoring

Overtime—3. Montreal, Lemaire (Lafleur) 4:32

1978

Montreal won four games to two.

Game 1

Montreal

  2 1 1—4

Boston

  1 0 0—1

First Period—1. Boston, Park (Schmautz, Ratelle) 2:31;

    2. Montreal, Lafleur (G. Lapointe) 4:31;

    3. Montreal, Lambert (Lafleur, Shutt) 9:53

Second Period—4. Montreal, Shutt (Lemaire, Lafleur) 13:54

Third Period—5. Montreal, Cournoyer (Jarvis, Lambert) 3:55

Game 2

Montreal

  0 1 1 1—3

Boston

  0 1 1 0—2

First Period—No scoring

Second Period—1. Boston, Park (O'Reilly, McNab) 3:57;

    2. Montreal, Shutt (Cornoyer, Robinson) 7:00

Third Period—3. Montreal Gainey (Jarvis, Houle) 12:12;

    4. Boston, R. Smith (Cashman, McNab) 15:48

Overtime—5. Montreal, Lafleur (Robinson) 13:09

Game 3

Montreal

  0 0 0—0

Boston

  2 0 2—4

First Period—1. Boston, Doak (Ratelle) 0:59;

    2. Boston, Middleton (Ratelle) 5:11

Second Period—No scoring

Third Period—3. Boston, McNab (Milbury) 2:54;

    4. Boston, O'Reilly (McNab, Milbury) 15:39

Game 4

Montreal

  1 1 1 0—3

Boston

  1 0 2 1—4

First Period—1. Boston, Sheppard (Marcotte) 0:25;
2. Montreal Risebrough (Tremblay, Gainey) 3:26

Second Period—3. Montreal Robinson (Mondou) 7:00

Third Period—4. Boston, McNab (Cashman, O'Reilly) 9:19;
5. Boston, Park (Milbury, Sheppard) 13:20;
6. Montreal, Lafleur (G. Lapointe, Lemaire) 19:27

Overtime—7. Schmautz (Sheppard, Park) 6:22

Game 5

Montreal
2 2 0—4
Boston
0 0 1—1

First Period—1. Montreal, Robinson (S. Savard) 7:46;
2. Montreal, Mondou (S. Savard) 11:10

Second Period—3. Montreal Larouche (Cournoyer, S. Savard) 13:04;
4. Montreal, Lemaire (Nyrop) 18:42

Third Period—5. Boston, Marcotte (Schmautz, R. Miller) 11:22

Game 6

Montreal
2 2 0—4
Boston
1 0 0—1

First Period—1. Boston, Park (Marcotte, Sheppard) 4:05;
2. Montreal Shutt (Mondou, Robinson) 7:01;
3. Montreal Tremblay (Mondou, Robinson) 9:20

Second Period—4. Montreal, Tremblay (Lambert, Nyrop) 13:37
5. Montreal, Houle (Jarvis) 17:46

Third Period—No scoring

1979

Montreal won four games to one.

Game 1

New York
2 2 0—4
Montreal
0 1 0—1

First Period—1. New York Rangers, Vickers (Hedberg) 6:28;
2. New York Rangers, Greschner 14:27

Second Period—3. Montreal, Lafleur (Lemaire, Lambert) 7:07;
4. New York Rangers, P. Esposito (McEwen) 9:30;
5. New York Rangers, David Maloney (Hedberg, Tkaczuk) 12:32

Third Period—No scoring

Game 2

New York
2 0 0—2
Montreal
3 2 1—6

First Period—1. New York Rangers, Hedberg (Vickers) 1:02;
2. New York Rangers, Duguay (McEwen, Hickey) 6:21;
3. Montreal, Lambert (M. Tremblay, Risebrough) 8:34;
4. Montreal, Lafleur (Lemaire, Shutt) 12:24;
5. Montreal, Gainey (Jarvis, Chartraw) 16:27

Second Period—6. Montreal, Shutt 6:51;
7. Montreal, Lemaire (S. Savard, Shutt) 17:35

Third Period—8. Montreal, Napier (Gainey) 4:38

Game 3

New York
0 0 1—1
Montreal
2 0 2—4

First Period—1. Montreal, Shutt (Lemaire, Robinson) 7:27;
2. Risebrough (Lambert, S. Savard) 15:44

Second Period—No scoring

Third Period—3. New York Rangers, Duguay 6:06;
4. Montreal, M. Tremblay (Lambert, Risebrough) 14:48;
5. Lemaire (Shutt, Dryden) 17:10

Game 4

New York
2 0 1 0—3
Montreal
1 1 1 1—4

First Period—1. New York Rangers, Hickey (David Maloney, Sheehan) 1:19;
2. Montreal, Houle (Gainey) 2:39;
3. New York Rangers, D. Murdoch (P. Esposito, Hickey) 17:03

Second Period—4. Montreal, Lambert (Houle) 18:05

Third Period—5. New York Rangers, P. Esposito (Donald

Maloney, David Maloney) 4:26;
        6. Montreal, Gainey 6:27

Overtime—7. Montreal, S. Savard (Lafleur, Shutt) 7:25

Game 5

New York
  1 0 0—1
Montreal
  1 3 0—4

First Period—1. Montreal, Chartraw (Houle, Lambert) 10:36;
        2. New York Rangers, Vadnais (D. Murdoch) 16:52

Second Period—3. Montreal, Lemaire 1:02;
        4. Montreal, Gainey (Jarvis, Houle) 11:01
        5. Montreal, Lemaire (Houle) 18:49

Third Period—No scoring

1980

New York Islanders won four games to two.

Game 1

Philadelphia
  1 1 1 0—3
New York
  1 1 1 1—4

First Period—1. Philadelphia, Bridgman 10:31;
        2. New York Islanders, Bossy (Trottier) 12.02

Second Period—3. New York Islanders, D. Potvin (Gillies, Goring) 2:20;
        4. Philadelphia, Clarke (Barber, Leach) 17:08

Third Period—5. Philadelphia, MacLeish (Holmgren) 13:10;
        6. New York Islanders, Persson (Bossy, D. Potvin) 16:18

Overtime—7. New York Islanders, D. Potvin (Tonelli, Nystrom) 4:07

Game 2

Philadelphia
  3 3 2—8
New York
  1 1 1—3

First Period—1. New York Islanders, Goring (Gillies, Duane Sutter) 3:23;
        2. Philadelphia, Holmgren (Propp, Dailey) 7:22;
        3. Philadelphia, R. Kelley (Behn Wilson, Clarke) 8:37;
        4. , Clarke (J. Watson, Barber) 17:23

Second Period—5. Philadelphia, Barber (Clarke, Leach) 1:06;
        6. New York Islanders, Trottier (Bossy) 3:28;
        7. Philadelphia, Holmgren (Linseman, Barber) 4:13;
        8. Philadelphia, Propp (Dailey, Clarke) 15:47

Third Period—9. Philadelphia, Gorence (Dailey, Bridgman) 1:40;
        10. Philadelphia, Holmgren (Linseman, Behn Wilson) 4:19;
        11. New York Islanders, Goring (Bourne, Persson) 15:00

Game 3

Philadelphia
  0 0 2—2
New York
  4 2 0—6

First Period—1. New York Islanders, Henning (Bourne) 2:38;
        2. New York Islanders, D. Potvin 7:43;
        3. New York Islanders, Trottier (Bossy, D. Potvin) 13:04;
        4. New York Islanders, Bossy (Gillies, D. Potvin) 14:29

Second Period—5. New York Islanders, Gillies (Persson) 15:41;

        6. New York Islanders, D. Potvin (Persson, Bossy) 17:25

Third Period—7. Philadelphia, Clarke (Leach, Busniuk) 9:48;
        8. Philadelphia, Busniuk (Bridgman) 11:32

Game 4

Philadelphia
  0 1 1—2
New York
  2 0 3—5

First Period—1. New York Islanders, Bossy (Gillies, Trottier) 7:23;
        2. New York Islanders, Goring (Gillies, Duane Sutter) 13:06

Second Period—3. Philadelphia, Paddock (MacLeish, Behn Wilson) 1:35

Third Period—4. New York Islanders, Trottier (Howatt) 6:06;
        5. Philadelphia, Linseman (Propp, Gorence) 11:53;
        6. New York Islanders, Nystrom (Bourne) 12:35;
        7. New York Islanders, Gillies (Duane Sutter) 14:08

Game 5

Philadelphia
  0 3 3—6
New York
  1 1 1—3

First Period—1. New York Islanders, Persson (Bossy) 10:58

Second Period—Clarke (Leach, Behn Wilson) 1:35;
        3. Philadelphia, MacLeish 5:55;
        4. New York Islanders, Trottier (Bossy, Persson) 16:16;
        5. Philadelphia, Busniuk (Propp, Linseman) 17:04

Third Period—6. Philadelphia, MacLeish (Bridgman) 9:43;
        7. Philadelphia, Propp (Linseman, Holmgren) 12:33;
        8. New York Islanders, Persson (Goring, D. Potvin) 14:57;
        9. Philadelphia, Holmgren (Linseman) 17:26

Game 6

Philadelphia
  2 0 2 0—4
New York
  2 2 0 1—5

First Period—1. Philadelphia, Leach (Macleish, Barber) 7:21;
        2. New York Islanders, D. Potvin (Bossy, Trottier) 11:56;
        3. New York Islanders, Duane Sutter (Gillies, Goring) 14:08;
        4. Philadelphia, Propp (Holmgren, Linseman) 18:58

Second Period—5. New York Islanders, Bossy (Bourne, Trottier) 7:34;
        6. New York Islanders, Nystrom (Tonelli) 19:46

Third Period—7. Philadelphia, Dailey (Linseman, Holmgren) 1:47;
        8. Philadelphia, Paddock (A. Dupont, MacLeish) 6:02

Overtime—9. New York Islanders, Nystrom (Henning, Tonelli) 7:11

1981

New York Islanders won four games to one.

Game 1

New York
  3 1 2—6
Minnesota
  0 1 2—3

First Period—New York Islanders, Kallur (Langevin, Goring) 2:54;

2. New York Islanders, Trottier (Carroll) 14:38;
3.New York Islanders, Kallur (Trottier) 15:25

Second Period—4. New York Islanders, Merrick 9:58;
        5. Minnesota, Anderson (Ciccarelli) 13:04

Third Period—6. New York Islanders, Merrick 0:58;
        7. Minnesota, Payne (Hartsburg, R. D. Smith)3:08;
        8. New York Islanders, Merrick (Langevin, Tonelli) 13:15;
        9. Minnesota, Ciccarelli (T. McCarthy) 15:14

Game 2

First period—1. Minnesota, Ciccarelli (Hartsburg, Christoff) 3:38;
        2. New York Islanders, Bossy (McEwen, D. Potvin) 4:33;
        3. New York Islanders, Nystrom (Merrick, Tonelli) 14:39;
        4. New York Islanders, D. Potvin (Merrick) 17:48

Second Period—5. Minnesota, B. Palmer (N. Broten, G. Smith) 9:15

Third Period—6. Minnesota, Payne (T. Young, Roberts) 0:30;
        7. New York Islanders, D. Potvin (Goring) 8:00;
        8. New York Islanders, Morrow (Merrick, D. Potvin) 11:57;
        9. New York Islanders, Bossy (Trottier, Bourne) 16:22

Game 3

New York
  2 3 3—8
Minnesota
  2 0 2—4

First Period—1. Minnesota, Christoff (Hartsburg, Ciccarelli) 3:25;
        2. Minnesota, Payne (T. Young, MacAdam) 14:09;
        3. New York Islanders, Bossy (Gillies) 14:47;
        4.Minnesota , R. D. Smith (Hartsburg, Payne) 16:30

Second Period—5. New York Islanders, Nystrom (Tonelli, Merrick) 4:10;
        6. New York Islanders, Goring (D. Potvin, Bossy) 7:16;
        7. New York Islanders, Goring (Gillies) 11:51

Third Period—8. Minnesota, Payne (T. Young, Christoff) 1:11;
        9. New York Islanders, Bossy (Trottier) 2:05;
        10. New York Islanders, Goring (Carroll, D. Potvin) 6:34;
        11. Minnesota, Ciccarelli (R. D. Smith) 13:35
        12. New York Islanders, Trottier (Bossy, Merrick) 19:16

Game 4

New York
  1 1 0—2
Minnesota
  1 1 2—4

First Period—1. New York Islanders, Lane (Bossy, Trottier) 3:47;

2. Minnesota, Hartsburg, (R. D. Smith, Brad Maxwell) 11:34

Second Period—3. Minnesota, MacAdam (Payne, Brad Maxwell) 5:15;
   4. New York Islanders, McEwen (Tonelli, Kallur) 7:37

Third Period—5. Minnesota, Payne (Brad Maxwell, MacAdam) 12:26;
   6. Minnesota, R. D. Smith (MacAdam, Brad Maxwell) 18:12

Game 5

New York
   3 1 1—5
Minnesota
   1 0 0—1

First Period—1. New York Islanders, Goring (Bourne) 5:12;
   2. New York Islanders, Merrick (Tonelli, Nystrom) 5:37;
   3. New York Islanders, Goring (Gillies, Bossy) 10:03;
   4. Minnesota, Christoff 16:06

Second Period—5. New York Islanders, Bourne (Carroll, Kallur) 19:21

Third Period—6. New York Islanders, McEwen (Trottier) 17:06

1982

New York Islanders won four games to none.

Game 1

Vancouver
   2 2 1 0—5
New York
   3 1 1 1—6

First Period—1. Vancouver, Gradin (Molin) 1:29;
   2. New York Islanders, Gillies (Potvin, Trottier) 11:35;
   3. New York Islanders, Bossy (Gillies, Carroll) 15:52;
   4. Vancouver, Gradin (Fraser, Molin) 17:40;
   5. New York Islanders, Potvin (Goring) 19:51

Second Period—6. New York Islanders, Potvin (Trottier, Persson) 3:15;
   7. Vancouver, Smyl (Gradin, Fraser) 5:06;
   8. Vancouver, Boldirev (D. Williams) 9:27

Third Period—9. Vancouver, Nill (Minor, D. Williams) 13:06;
   10 New York Islanders, Bossy (Tonelli, Trottier) 15:14

Overtime—11. New York Islanders, Bossy 19:58

Game 2

Vancouver
   0 3 1—4
New York
   1 1 4—6

First Period—1. New York Islanders, Carroll (Bourne) 15:55

Second Period—2. Vancouver, Gradin (Molin, Fraser) 8:28;
   3. Vancouver, Boldirev (Molin, Halward) 13:12;
   4. New York Islanders, Bossy (Persson, Potvin) 17:06;
   5. Vancouver, Lindgren (Gradin) 19:42

Third Period—6. New York Islanders, Bourne (Persson, Bossy) 0:32;
   7. New York Islanders, Duane Sutter (Brent Sutter, Potvin) 1:19;
   8. Vancouver, Minor (D. Williams) 2:27;
   9. New York Islanders, Trottier (Jonsson, Potvin) 7:18;
   10. New York Islanders, Nystrom (Tonelli, Merrick) 14:10

Game 3

Vancouver
   0 0 0—0
New York
   0 2 1—3

First Period—No scoring

Second Period—1. New York Islanders, Gillies (Brent, Sutter) 2:56;
   2. New York Islanders, Bossy (Persson, Trottier) 12-30

Third Period—3. New York Islanders, Nystrom (Goring, Potvin) 18:40

Game 4

Vancouver
   1 0 0—1
New York
   1 2 0—3

First Period—1. New York Islanders, Goring (Potvin) 11:38;
   2. Vancouver, Smyl (Minor, C. Campbell) 18:09

Second Period—3. New York Islanders, Bossy (Trottier, Potvin) 5:00;
   4. New York Islanders, Bossy (Trottier, Persson) 8:00

Third Period—No scoring

1983

New York Islanders won four games to none.

Game 1

New York
1 0 1—2
Edmonton
0 0 0—0

First Period—1. New York Islanders, Duane Sutter (Bourne, Persson) 5:36

Second Period—No scoring

Third Period—2. New York Islanders, Morrow (Potvin) 19:48

Game 2

New York
3 2 1—6
Edmonton
1 1 1—3

First Period—1. Edmonton, Semenko (Roulston, Huddy) 8:39;
    2. New York Islanders, Jonsson (Duane Sutter, Brent Sutter) 14:21;
    3. New York Islanders, Nystrom (Trottier) 17:55;
    4. New York Islanders, Bossy (Potvin) 19:17

Second Period—5. Edmonton, Kurri (G. Anderson, Gretzky) 5:07;
    6. New York Islanders, Bourne (Duane Sutter) 8:03;
    7. New York Islanders, Brent Sutter (Morrow) 8:41

Third Period—8. Edmonton, G. Anderson (Fogolin, Gretzky) 4:48;
    9. New York Islanders, Brent Sutter (Duane Sutter, Jonsson) 14:11

Game 3

New York
1 0 4—5
Edmonton
0 1 0—1

First Period—1. New York Islanders, Kallur (Bossy, Morrow) 19:41

Second Period—2. Edmonton, Kurri (Gretzky) 1:05

Third Period—3. New York Islanders, Bourne (Persson, Langevin) 5:11;
    4. New York Islanders, Morrow (Trottier, Kallur) 6:21;
    5. New York Islanders, Duane Sutter (Bourne, Brent Sutter) 16:43;

Bossy takes Sutter off the play in 1983 game.

    6. New York Islanders, Brent Sutter (Potvin, Duane Sutter) 19:02

Game 4

New York
3 0 1—4
Edmonton
0 2 0—2

First Period—1. New York Islanders, Trottier (Gillies, Bossy) 11:02;
    2. New York Islanders, Tonelli (Nystrom) 11:45;
    3. New York Islanders, Bossy (Trottier) 12:39

Second Period—4. Edmonton, Kurri (Gretzky) 0:35;
    5. Edmonton, Messier (Fogolin, Coffey) 19:39

Third Period—6. New York Islanders, Morrow 18:51

All - Star Games

The first of the National Hockey League's annual All-Star games was played on October 13, 1947, in Toronto's Maple Leaf Gardens before 14,169 spectators, who watched the All-Stars defeat the defending Stanley Cup champion Maple Leafs 4-3. There had been three all-star games before this one, but none were official league affairs.

On February 14, 1934 in Toronto, the Maple Leafs played a collection of stars from the other seven teams for the benefit of Ace Bailey, whose brilliant career with the Leafs had come to an abrupt end the year before when he suffered a skull fracture at the hands of Boston's Eddie Shore. The Leafs won that game 7-3.

On November 3, 1937, in the Montreal Forum, an all-star game was played in memory of Howie Morenz, the Canadiens' star who died March 8, 1937, from an embolism that resulted from a broken leg he suffered in a game several weeks earlier. In this all-star game the All-Stars defeated a team comprised of Montreal Canadiens and Montreal Maroons, 6-5.

The Forum was again the site of such a game October 29, 1939, in memory of the Canadiens' Albert ("Babe") Siebert, who had drowned in Lake Huron the previous August. The All-Stars defeated the Canadiens 5-2.

For the first annual All-Star game in 1947, it was decided that the Stanley Cup champions of the previous year would oppose a team comprised of the previous season's first- and second-team All-Stars, augmented by players from the NHL's five other teams. The game would be played each year on the home ice of the Stanley Cup champions. This format was followed for nearly 20 years except in 1948, when the game was played at Chicago Stadium, and in 1951 and 1952, when the first All-Star team and players from the four United States teams played the second All-Star team and players from Montreal and Toronto. This revision was abandoned, however, after both games ended in ties.

In 1966-67, the All-Star game was rescheduled and played in January instead of at the start of the regular season. Two years later the league adopted the current format, in which stars of the West Division oppose those of the East Division. Members of the NHL Writers' Association select 12 players for each team, and each coach chooses the remainder of his roster. All-Star coaches are the two who coached the previous season's division champions.

In an effort to give the game more exposure, it was decided in 1969-70 that the annual attraction would be rotated among NHL cities. Since then, St. Louis, Boston, Minnesota, and New York each have had the All-Star game for the first time.

All-Star games are never hard-hitting, competitive affairs, because players are wary of incurring injuries. The games are popular spectacles, however, for they are the only times when so many stars play together. The popularity of the All-Star game has been reflected in its attendance figures, which rose steadily to the record crowd of 17,085 at Chicago Stadium in 1974.

Since its official inception, the game has been a money-maker for the players. Members of the winning team get only $500 and the losers $250, but from 1947 through 1957, two-thirds of the gross receipts of each game have gone to the NHL Players Pension Fund. Since 1957, when matching contributions to the Pension Fund were instituted, receipts have been used to cover expenses incurred for the game (including $2,000 for each first-team player and $1,000 for each second-team member) and administration expenses for the Pension Fund.

Leafs, All-Stars, and officials who staged 1934 benefit game

1947-48
At Toronto, October 13, 1947
All-Stars 4, Toronto 3

First Period
1—Toronto, Watson (Ezinicki) 12:29
    Penalties: Mortson, Leswick, Ezinicki (2), Reardon
Second Period
2—Toronto, Ezinicki (Apps, Watson) 1:03
3—All-Stars, M. Bentley (Reardon) 4:39
4—Toronto, Apps (Watson), Morton 5:01
5—All-Stars, Warwick (Laprade), Reardon 17:35
    Penalties: Lynn, Reardon (minor and major)
Third Period
6—All-Stars, Richard ....:28
7—All-Stars, D. Bentley (Schmidt, Richard) 1:26
    Penalties: Mortson (2), Bouchard, Ezinicki, Schmidt

Referee: King Clancy
Linesmen: Jim Primeau, Eddie Nepham

1948-49
At Chicago, November 3, 1948
All-Stars 3, Toronto 1

First Period
No score
Penalties: Ezinicki, Reardon.
Second Period
1—All-Stars, Lindsay (Richard, Lach) 1:35
2—All-Stars, Dumart 3:06
3—Toronto, M. Bentley (Costello) 5:13
4—All-Stars, G. Stewart (D. Bentley) 19:32
    Penalties: Mortson (major), Howe (major), J. Stewart,
    Bouchard, Juzda
Third Period
No score
Penalties: Bouchard

Referee: Bill Chadwick
Linesmen: Sam Babcock, Mush March

1949-50
At Toronto, October 10, 1949
All-Stars 3, Toronto 1

First Period
1—Toronto, Barilko (Watson, Gardner) 15:22
2—All-Stars, Goldham (Laprade) 18:03
    Penalties: Richard, Meeker, Thomson, Howe
Second Period
3—All-Stars, Ronty (Goldham) 14:42
    Penalties: Harmon, Thomson, Boesch, Egan, Smith
Third Period
4—All-Stars, D. Bentley (Quackenbush) 2:38
    No penalties

Referee: Bill Chadwick
Linesmen: Ed Mepham, Jim Primeau

1950-51
At Detroit, October 8, 1950
Detroit 7, All-Stars 1

First Period
1—Detroit, Lindsay (Howe) 19
2—Detroit, Lindsay (Abel) 17:12
    Penalties: Richard, 7:57; Leswick, 9:00; Abel, 9:15; Pro-
novost, 11:45; Bentley, 15:13; Leswick, 16:54
Second Period
3—Detroit, Howe (Lindsay, Kelly) 11:12
4—Detroit, Peters (Kelly, Prystai) 18:36
5—Detroit, Pavelich (Prystai, Peters) 19:44
    Penalties: Couture, 4:30
Third Period
6—Detroit, Prystai (Pavelich) 7:36
7—Detroit, Lindsay 14:28
8—All-Stars, Smith (Peirson) 18:27
    Penalties: Peters, 5:03; Stewart, 13:10

Referee: George Gravel
Linesmen: George Hayes, Doug Young

1951-52
At Toronto, October 9, 1951
First Team 2, Second Team 2

First Period
1—First Team, Howe (Lindsay, Schmidt) 7:59
    Penalties: Curry, 6:38; Eddols, 10:41, Sloan, 15:58
Second Period
2—Second Team, Sloan (Watson, M. Bentley) 2:26
3—First Team, Peirson (Stewart, Raleigh) 16:49
    Penalties: Raleigh, 1:46; Lindsay, 13:26
Third Period
4—Second Team, Mosdell (Sloan, Mortson) 9:25
    Penalties: Lindsay, 1:25; Howe, 5:53

Referee: Bill Chadwick
Linesmen: Sam Babcock, William Morrison

1952-53
At Detroit, October 5, 1952
First Team 1, Second Team 1

First Period
No score
Penalties: Buller, :23; Sanford, 3:51; Thomson, 12:46;
    Richard, 18:03
Second Period
1—First Team, Pavelich (Mosienko, Creighton) 9:57
    Penalties: Bouchard, 4:53; Thomson, 7:50; Thomson,
16:39; Howe, 6:34
Third Period
2—Second Team, Richard (Buller) 1:36
    Penalties: Lach, 15:09

Referee: Bill Chadwick
Linesmen: Doug Young, George Hayes

All-Stars for 1947 game

1953-54
At Montreal, October 3, 1953
All-Stars 3, Montreal 1

First Period
1—All-Stars, Hergesheimer (Ronty, Kelly) 4:06
2—All-Stars, Hergesheimer (Kelly) 5:25
   Penalties: Meger, 4:00; McPherson, 4:37; Lindsay, 8:55
Second Period
No score
Penalties: Mortson, 5:03; St. Laurent, 11:28; Howe, 12:52;
Richard, 15:18; Mosdell, 19:58
Third Period
3—Montreal, Richard (Harvey, Beliveau) 4:30
4—All-Stars, Delvecchio 19:27
   Penalties: Kelly, 2:34 (major); Olmstead, 2:34 (major);
   Smith, 3:30

Referee: Red Storey
Linesmen: Sam Babcock, Doug Davies

1954-55
At Detroit, October 2, 1954
All-Stars 2, Detroit 2

First Period
1—Detroit, Delvecchio (Lindsay, Reibel) 9:50
2—Detroit, Howe (Reibel, Kelly) 19:55
   Penalties: Mortson, 1:37; Bonin, 5:48; Mackell, 8:30;
   Bonin, 13:18; Howell, 18:03; Horton, 18:26
Second Period
2—All-Stars, Mortson (Gadsby, Kennedy) 4:19
3—All-Stars, Mohns (Beliveau) 13:10
   Penalties: Dineen, 4:01; Bonin, 7:53; Howell, 7:53; San-
   ford, 13:27; Mohns, 19:51
Third Period
No score
Penalties: Lindsay, 1:09; Mortson, 3:57; Woit, 9:09

Referee: Bill Chadwick
Linesmen: William Morrison, George Hayes

1955-56
At Detroit, October 2, 1955
Detroit 3, All-Stars 1

First Period
No score
Penalties: Flaman, 1:28; Corcoran, 8:46; Geoffrion, 9:04;
Stewart, 10:32; Bucyk, 15:16; Stanley, 16:14; Morrison, 19:14
Second Period
1—Detroit, Howe (Reibel, Delvecchio) ....:57
2—Detroit, Reibel (Howe, Lindsay) 5:43
   Penalties: Corcoran, 6:40; Hollingworth, 16:01
Third Period
3—All-Stars, Harvey (Beliveau, Smith) 16:38
4—Detroit, Reibel (Lindsay, Goldham) 19:33
   Penalties: Hollingworth, 10:54; Harvey, 12:28

Referee: Frank Udvari
Linesmen: George Hayes, William Morrison

1956-57
At Montreal, October 9, 1956
All-Stars 1, Montreal 1

First Period
No score
Penalties: Flaman, 1:42; Beliveau, 7:44; Beliveau, 18:29
Second Period
1—Montreal, M. Richard (Olmstead, Harvey) 14:58
2—All Stars, Lindsay (Mortson) 18:48
   Penalties: Mortson, 8:14, Sullivan, 14:25
Third Period
No score
Penalties: Labine, 2:17; Mortson, 9:42

Referee: Red Storey
Linesmen: Doug Davies, Bill Roberts

1957-58
At Montreal, October 5, 1957
All-Stars 5, Montreal 3

First Period

1—All-Stars, Kelly 1:06
2—Montreal, M. Richard (H. Richard, Moore) 10:53
3—All-Stars, Stanley (Prentice, Migay) 19:55
    Penalties: Migay, 5:36; Talbot, 14:25; Howe, 15:55, Harvey, 16:05, Howe, 19:14

Second Period

4—Montreal, Olmstead (Johnson) 33
5—Montreal, Smrke (Bonin) 9:13
6—All-Stars, Bathgate (Litzenberger, Prentice) 18:14
    Penalties: Talbot, 5:54; Chevrefils, 12:36; Johnson, 18:59

Third Period

7—All-Stars, Howe (Chevrefils, Morrison) 8:11
8—All-Stars, Prentice (Bathgate, Litzenberger) 16:50
    Penalties: Flaman, 5:48; Olmstead, 6:24; Flaman, 9:46

Referee: Red Storey
Linesmen: Doug Davies, Bill Morrison

1958-59
At Montreal, October 4, 1958
Montreal 6, All-Stars 3

First Period

1—Montreal, M. Richard (Harvey, Moore) 9:19
2—Montreal, Geoffrion (H. Richard) 16:20
    Penalties: Henry, 7:29; Harvey, 11:41

Second Period

3—Montreal, Marshall (Provost) 2:33
4—Montreal, H. Richard (Talbot, Moore) 5:08
5—All-Stars, Pulford (Toppazzini, Harris) 11:39
    Penalties: Turner, 2:24

Third Period

6—All-Stars, Bathgate (Litzenberger, Henry) 3:55
7—Montreal, MacDonald (Provost, Marshall) 7:43
8—All-Stars, Bathgate (Pulford, Sullivan) 13:54
9—Montreal, M. Richard (Moore, H. Richard) 16:04
    Penalties: Mohns, 4:25; Duff, 7:36; Provost, 12:52

Referee: Eddie Powers
Linesmen: George Hayes, Bill Morrison

1959-60
At Montreal, October 3, 1959
Montreal 6, All-Stars1

First Period

No score
No penalties

Second Period

1—Montreal, Beliveau (Hicke, Harvey) 4:25
2—Montreal, McDonald (Backstrom, Geoffrion) 13:43
3—All-Stars, McKenney (Litzenberger) 18:30
No Penalties

Third Period

4—Montreal, Moore (H. Richard, Johnson) 7:44
5—Montreal, H. Richard (Moore, Harvey) 9:31
6—Montreal, Beliveau (Hicke, Bonin) 11:54
7—Montreal, Pronovost (Harvey) 15:51
    Penalties: Tremblay, 8:43; Bathgate, 9:21; Turner, 12:45

Referee: Frank Udvari
Linesmen: George Hayes, Bob Frampton

1960-61
At Montreal, October 1, 1960
All-Stars 2, Montreal 1

First Period

No score
Penalties: Talbot, 7:22

Second Period

1—All-Stars, Mahovlich (Pilote, Kelly) ....:40
2—Montreal, Provost (Backstrom, A. Pronovost) 11:40
3—All-Stars, Hebenton (Sullivan) 15:51
    Penalties: Sullivan, 12:17; Hull, 14:47; Johnson, 17:03

Third Period

No score
Penalties: Hicke, 2:58; Gadsby, 5:44; Pilote, 6:54; Harvey, 10:20

Referee: Eddie Powers
Linesmen: George Hayes, Neil Armstrong

1961-62
At Chicago, October 7, 1961
All-Stars 3, Chicago 1

First Period

1—All-Stars, Delvecchio (Howe, Ullman) 11:37
    Penalties: Mahovlich, 8:26; Hay, 15:02; Vasko, 19:15

Second Period

2—All-Stars, McKenney (Bathgate, Pronovost) 2:37
3—Chicago, Nesterenko (Hull, Pilote) 6:26
4—All-Stars, Howe (Delvecchio, Ullman) 11:38
    Penalties: Goyette, 4:46; Mahovlich, Nesterenko (double minors each), 7:36; Nesterenko, 16:21; McKenney, 19:47

Third Period

No score
Penalties: Pilote, 1:38; Richard, 11:49; Hull, 19:24

Referee: Frank Udvari
Linesmen: Neil Armstrong, George Hayes

Goalie Lumley repulses Wings' Delvecchio in 1955 game.

1962-63
At Toronto, October 6, 1962
Toronto 4, All-Stars 1

First Period
1—Toronto, Duff (Douglas, Armstrong) 5:22
2—All-Stars, Howe (Delvecchio, Pilote) 7:26
3—Toronto, Pulford (Stewart) 10:45
4—Toronto, Mahovlich (Stanley) 13:03
5—Toronto, Shack (Keon) 19:32
Penalties: Mohns, 4:32; Nevin, 6:16, McKenney, 12:41; Brewer, 12:41; Howe, 15:39; Shack, 15:39
Second Period
No score
Penalties: Kelly, 1:56; Howe, 16:33; Brewer, 18:30
Third Period
No score
Penalties: Baun, 13:03; Boivin, 17:35; Shack, 19:21

Referee: Eddie Powers
Linesmen: Matt Pavelich, Ron Wicks

1963-64
At Toronto, October 5, 1963
All-Stars 3, Toronto 3

First Period
1—Toronto, Mahovlich (Armstrong, Baun) 2:22

2—All-Stars, Richard (Henry, Howe) 4:08
3—Toronto, Mahovlich (Keon, Litzenberger) 12:11
4—All-Stars, Hull (Geoffrion) 19:27
Penalties: Stanley, 2:42; Howell, 15:18; Duff, 18:15
Second Period
No Score
Penalties: Pronovost, 11:47, Horton, 16:32, Baun, 18:55, Hull, 19:27, Horton, 19:27
Third Period
5—Toronto, Litzenberger (Mahovlich, Kelly) 2:56
6—All-Stars, Pronovost (Bucyk, Oliver) 3:23
Penalties: Stanley, 17:04

Referee: Frank Udvari
Linesmen: Matt Pavelich, Neil Armstrong

1964-65
At Toronto, October 10, 1964
All-Stars 3, Toronto 2

First Period
No score
Penalties: Bathgate, 1:05; Howell, 7:25; Baun, 15:38; Douglas, 17:42; Oliver, 17:42
Second Period
1—All-Stars, Boivin (Laperriere, Oliver) 10:47

Penalties: Stewart, 5:32; Pilote, 5:43; Douglas, 8:35; Provost, 10:51

Referee: Frank Udvari
Linesmen: Neil Armstrong, Ron Wicks

1965-66
At Montreal, October 20, 1965
All-Stars 5, Montreal 2

First Period
No score
Penalties: Gadsby, :48; Beliveau, 7:13; Harris, 9:48; Larose, 13:27; Pronovost, 16:08; Harris, 16:33
Second Period
1—Montreal, Beliveau (Duff, Rousseau) 6:48
2—Montreal, Laperriere (Backstrom, Larose).............11:00
3—All-Stars, Ullman (Hull, Howe) 12:40
4—All-Stars, Hull (Howe, Oliver) 16:35
5—All-Stars, Howe (Ullman, Baun) 19:19
Penalties: Balon, 16:31
Third Period
6—All-Stars, Bucyk (Gadsby, Oliver) 10:01
7—All-Stars, Howe 18:39
Penalties: Ellis, 6:20; Ferguson, 11:57; Howell, 14:31; Howell, 18:31

Referee: Art Skov
Linesmen: Neil Armstrong, Matt Pavelich

1966-67
At Montreal, January 18, 1967
Montreal 3, All-Stars 0

First Period
1—Montreal, Richard (Rousseau, Harper) 14:03
2—Montreal, Ferguson (Larose) 15:59
No penalties
Second Period
No score
Penalties: Howell, 6:58; Richard, 7:19; Ferguson, 10:00
Third Period
3—Montreal, Ferguson (Richard, Rousseau) 19:52
No penalties

Referee: Vern Buffey
Linesmen: Neil Armstrong, Matt Pavelich

1967-68
At Toronto, January 16, 1968
Toronto 4, All-Stars 3

First Period
1—Toronto, Oliver (Mahovlich, Hillman) 5:56
2—All Stars, Mikita (B. Hull, J. C. Tremblay) 19:53
Penalties: Stemkowski, 14:10; Howell, 17:54

Second Period
3—All-Stars, Wharram (Mikita) ....:35
4—Toronto, Stanley (Stemkowski, Carleton) 7:56
5—Toronto, Stemkowski (Carleton, Rupp) 16:36
Penalties: Howe, 3:53
Third Period
6—Toronto, Ellis (Mahovlich, Hillman) 3:31
2—Toronto, Douglas (Bathgate, Mahovlich) 11:45
3—All-Stars, Beliveau (Hull, Howe) 13:51
Penalties: Laperriere, 2:27; Mikita, 9:43; Baun, 9:43, Howell, 11:03, Hodge, 15:31
Third Period
4—All-Stars, Oliver (Bucyk, Howell) 6:11
5—Toronto, Pappin (Ehman) 13:35
7—All-Stars, Ullman (Howe, Orr) 8:23
Penalties: Howe, 14:42; Walton, 14:42

Referee: Bill Friday
Linesmen: Pat Shetler, Brent Casselman

1968-69
At Montreal, January 21, 1969
East 3, West 3

First Period
1—West, Berenson (Harvey, Picard) 4:43
2—East, F. Mahovlich (Rousseau, Stapleton) 17:32
Penalties: Vadnais, 12:55
Second Period
3—West, J. Roberts (Berenson, Picard) 1:53
Penalties: Horton, 11:44; White, 17:50
Third Period
4—East, F. Mahovlich (T. Harris, Gilbert) 3:11
5—East, Nevin (Ullman) 7:20
6—West, Larose (Grant, O'Shea) 17:07
Penalties: White, 10:18; Harvey, 11:55; Horton, 18:46

Referee: John Ashley
Linesmen: Neil Armstrong, Matt Pavelich

1969-70
At St. Louis, January 20, 1970
East 4, West 1

First Period
1—East, Laperriere ....:20
2—West, Prentice (Berenson, Woytowich) ....:37
3—East, Howe (Hull, Lemaire) 7:20
Penalties: Park, 1:52; St. Marseille, 6:00
Second Period
4—East, Hull (Brewer) 3:26
5—East, Tkaczuk (McKenzie, Bucyk) 9:37
Penalties: Woytowich, 15:47
Third Period
No score
Penalties: Woytowich, 2:12

Referee: Art Skov
Linesmen: Matt Pavelich, Claude Bechard

1970-71
At Boston, January 19, 1971
West 2, East 1

First Period
1—West, C. Maki ....:36
2—West, B. Hull (Flett) 4:38
3—East, Cournoyer (D. Smith, Balon) 6:19
    Penalties; Harris, 2:17; F. Mahovlich, 3:09; B. Hull, 11:14
Second Period
No score
Penalties: Bucyk, 1:22
Third Period
No score
Penalties: Stapleton, 2:48; Magnuson, 8:34

Referee: Bill Friday
Linesmen: Neil Armstrong, John D'Amico

1971-72
At Minnesota, January 25, 1972
East 3, West 2

First Period
1—West, B. Hull (P. Martin, Maki) 17:01
    Penalties: Hadfield, 6:22
Second Period
2—West, Nolet (D. Hull) 1:11
3—East, Ratelle (Tremblay, Gilbert) 3:48
4—East, McKenzie (Park, Seiling) 18:45
    Penalties: White, 5:26
Third Period
5—East, Esposito (D. Smith, Orr) 1:09
    Penalties: White, 2:28; Esposito, 5:34; Tremblay, 8:42;
Mohns, 19:05

Referee: Bruce Hood
Linesmen: Matt Pavelich, Claude Bechard

1972-73
At New York, January 30, 1973
East 5, West 4

First Period
No score
Penalties: Orr, 11:11; Bergman, 14:52
Second Period
1—West, Polis (Clarke, MacDonald) ....:55
2—East, Robert (Park) 3:56
3—East, F. Mahovlich 16:27
4—East, Henderson (Esposito, Hodge) 19:12
5—West, Martin (D. Hull, Pappin) 19:29
    Penalties: Hodge, 6:26

Third Period
6—East, Lemaire (F. Mahovlich, Lapointe) 3:19
7—West, Polis (Harper) 4:27
8—West, Harper (Mikita) 9:23
9—East, Schmautz (Savard) 13:59
    Penalties: White, 10:03

Referee: Lloyd Gilmour
Linesmen: Neil Armstrong, John D'Amico

1973-74
At Chicago, January 29, 1974
East 4, West 6

First Period
1—East Division, F. Mahovlich (Cournoyer-Ullman) 3:33
2—East Division, Cournoyer (Ullman) 16:20
    Penalty: H. Martin, 11:17
Second Period
3—West Division, Berry (Mikita) 5:59
4—West Division, McDonough (Clarke, MacDonald) 13:55
5—West Division, MacDonald (B. Plager, Awrey) 19:07
    Penalties: D. Hextall, (7:42); Berenson, 18:35
Third Period
6—West Division, Mikita (Unger, White) 2:25
7—West Division, Unger (Mikita, White) 7:54
8—East Division, D. Potvin 9:55
9—East Division, M. Redmond (Berenson) 14:55
10—West Division, H. Martin (Pappin) 19:13
    Penalty: B. Plager 6:27

Referee: Arthur Skov
Linesmen: Willard William Norris, Matthew Pavelich

1974-75
At Montreal, January 21, 1975
Clarence S. Campbell Conference 1, Prince of Wales Conference 7

First Period
1—Prince of Wales, Apps (J. Johnston, Vadnais) 9:38
2—Prince of Wales, Luce (O'Reilly, Dupere) 12:03
3—Prince of Wales, Sittler (Lafleur) 14:22
4—Campbell, D. Potvin (Unger) 19:41
    Penalties: None
Second Period
5—Prince of Wales, P. Esposito (Lafleur, Murdoch) 19:16
    Penalties: Vickers, 0:16; Luce, 4:51; Harper, 12:11; Korab, 19:37
Third Period
6—Prince of Wales, Apps (Robert, R. Martin) 3:25
7—Prince of Wales, O'Reilly 5:43
8—Prince of Wales, Orr (Lafleur, Sittler) 7:19
    Penalties: James Watson, 6:42; Clarke, 13:32

Referee: Wally Harris
Linesmen: Joseph Claude Bechard, Leon Stickle

1975-76
At Philadelphia, January 20, 1976
Clarence S. Campbell conference 5, Prince of Wales Conference 7

First Period

1—Prince of Wales, R. Martin (P. Mahovlich, Lafleur) 6:01
2—Campbell, C. Bennet (Dupont) 16:59
3—Prince of Wales, P. Mahovlich (G. Lapointe, Lafleur) 18:31
4—Prince of Wales, Park, (R. Martin, P. Mahovlich) 19:00
    Penalties: None

Second Period

5—Prince of Wales, MacAdam (Daniel Maloney) 9:34
6—Prince of Wales, Lafleur (P. Mahovlich, R. Martin) 11:57
7—Prince of Wales, Dionne 13:51
8—Prince of Wales, Daniel Maloney (Larouche, MacAdam) 16:59
    Penalty: Barber, 17:24

Third Period

9—Campbell, Ververgaert (Trottier, W. Harris) 4:33

10—Campbell, Ververgaert (Trottier, W. Harris) 4:43
11—Campbell, D. Potvin 14:17
12—Campbell, Vickers (Unger, D. Potvin) 14:46
    Penalty: Marks, 15:26

Referee: Lloyd Gilmour
Linesmen: Neil Armstrong, John D'Amico

1976-77
At Vancouver, January 25, 1977
Clarenece S. Campbell Conference 3, Prince of Wales Conference 4

First Period

1—Campbell, Vail (D. Potvin) 2:54
2—Prince of Wales, McDonald (Gainey, McNab) 6:22
    Penalties: Campbell (too many players on ice) served by R. Gilbert,
15:32; Dornhoefer, G. Lapointe, 16:24

Second Period

3—Campbell, MacLeish (Nystrom, D. Potvin) 11:56
4—Prince of Wales, McDonald (Perreault, Robinson) 19:27
      Penalties: D. Potvin, 4:11; G. Lapointe, 5:08; Paiement, 8:34; Joseph Watson, 14:02

Third Period

5—Prince of Wales, R. Martin (Dionne, Robinson) 4:00
6—Campbell, P. Esposito (R. Gilbert, Dornhoefer) 12-23
7—Prince of Wales, R. Martin (Dionne, Lafleur) 18:04
      Penalties: Russel, 13:17; Salming, 15:48

Referee: Ronald Wicks

Linesmen: Ron Finn, Matthew Pavelich

1977-78
At Buffalo, January 24, 1978
Clarence S. Campbell Conference 2, Prince of Wales Conference 3

First Period

1—Campbell, Barber 1:25
2—Campbell, D. Potvin (Clarke) 12:12
      Penalties: Salming, 7-42; Gillies, 18:30

Second Period

3—Prince of Wales, Sittler (Park, Robinson) 19:32
      Penalties: Dailey, 2:25; McDonald, W. Smith, (served by Barber, 3:36); Vadnais, 18:12

Third Period

4—Prince of Wales, R. Martin (Dionne, O'Reilly) 18:21
      Penalties: None

Overtime

5—Prince of Wales, Perreault (Shutt, Salming) 3:55
      Penalties: None

Referee: Bruce Hood

Linesmen: John D'Amico, Leon Stickle

1978-79

No game played.
NHL played series with Russia on February 8, 10, and 11, 1979. *See* International Games

1979-80
At Detroit, February 5, 1980
Clarence S. Campbell Conference 3, Prince of Wales Conference 6

First Period

1—Prince of Wales, L. Robinson 3:58
2—Prince of Wales, Payne (Murphy, Goring) 4:19
3—Campbell, Leach (McEwen) 7:15
      Penalty: Hartsburg, 12:23

Second Period

4—Campbell, K. Nilsson (Federko, MacLeish) 6:03
      Penalties: None

Third Period

5—Campbell, Propp (P. Esposito, Leach) 4:14
6—Prince of Wales, Stackhouse (Sittler, Lafleur) 11:40
7—Prince of Wales, Hartsburg (Real Cloutier, Ratelle) 12:40
8—Prince of Wales, Larson (Payne, Perreault) 13:12
9—Prince of Wales, Real Cloutier (G. Howe) 16:06
      Penalties: None

Referee: Dave Newell

Linesmen: John D'Amico, Raymond Angelo Joseph Sacpinello

1980-81
At Inglewood, California, February 10, 1981
Clarence S. Campbell Conference 4, Prince of Wales Conference 1

First Period

1—Campbell, K. Nilsson (Barber, Holmgren) 0:45
2—Campbell, Barber (Johnstone) 8:02
      Penalties: Bourne, 7:47; Williams, 10:27

Second Period

3—Campbell, W. Babych (Johnstone, Federko) 16:12
      Penalties: None

Third Period

4—Prince of Wales, Ogrodnick (Mark Howe, Kehoe) 6:13
5—Campbell, Behn Wilson (Bossy, Gretzky) 10:18
      Penalties: None

Referee: Bryan Howard Lewis

Linesmen: James Edward Chirstison, Gerard Gauthier

1981-82
At Landover, Maryland, February 9, 1982
Clarence S. Campbell Conference 2, Prince of Wales Conference 4
First Period

1—Campbell, Vaive (Brian Sutter) 2:32
2—Prince of Wales, Bourque (Maruk, Carlyle) 12-03
3—Prince of Wales, Tardif (Middleton, P. Stastny) 13:27
      Penalties: Tardif, 5:40; Hartsburg, 10:36

Second Period

4—Campbell, Gretzky (Coffey, Ciccarelli) 0-26
5—Prince of Wales, Bossy (Beck, Tonelli) 17:10
      Penalties: Hawerchuk, 3:52; Tardif, 13:13

Third Period

6—Prince of Wales, Bossy (Robinson) 1:19
      Penalty: Stoughton, 2:37
      Referee: Wally Harris
      Linesmen: Ron Finn, Swede Knox

1982-83
At Uniondale, New York, February 8, 1983
Clarence S. Campbell Conference 9, Prince of Wales Conference 3

First Period

1—Prince of Wales, Goulet (P. Satstny) 3:41
2—Campbell, D. Babych (McDonald, Brian Sutter) 11:37
3—Prince of Wales, Bourque 19:01
      Penalties: Brian Sutter, 6:26; Langevin, 10:58

Second Period

4—Campbell, Ciccarelli (N. Broten, Secord) 3:01
5—Campbell, T. McCarthy (Ciccarelli, R. Murray) 14:51
      Penalties: None

Third Period

6—Campbell, Gretzky (Kurri, Coffey) 6:20
7—Campbell, McDonald (Brian Sutter, Dionne) 7:29
8—Campbell, Gretzky (Messier, Kurri) 10:31
9—Prince of Wales, Donald Maloney (Marini) 14:04
10—Campbell, Gretzky (D. Wilson, Messier) 15:32
11—Campbell, Vaive 17:15
12—Campbell, Gretzky (Messier) 19:18
      Penalty: Ramsey, 3:33

Referee: Robert Graham Myers

Linesmen: Ryan Bozak, Leon Stickle

Bossy takes Sutter off the play in 1983 game.

Coaches and General Managers

Jack Adams poses for 1961 publicity release.

With the exception of Gordie Howe, nobody had a greater impact on the Detroit Red Wings than John James ("Jack") Adams. Bold, defiant, hard-headed, Adams flew the Red Wings above the clouds after they had encountered years of turbulence. In 35 years as coach and general manager, Adams directed the Red Wings to a dozen first-place finishes and seven Stanley Cups. His reign included a record seven straight National Hockey League titles from 1948-49 through 1954-55.

Adams arrived in Detroit in 1927, after helping manage the Ottawa Senators to a Stanley Cup victory over the Boston Bruins. Success did not arrive with him, however, for Adams's clever hockey instincts did little to alleviate the major problem that plagued the Detroit franchise—lack of money. The financial situation deteriorated further when the Depression hit two years later.

Then in 1933, James Norris Sr., a Chicago millionaire, purchased the Detroit club. Norris immediately changed the team's name from the Falcons to the Red Wings and gave Adams the money to start wheeling and dealing. "Pops was the bankroll and the boss, and after he took over, Detroit hockey never looked back," recalled Adams.

The Red Wings rose to first place in the NHL's American Division in 1933-34, and two years later, after Adams obtained Syd Howe from St. Louis, Hec Kilrea from Toronto, and Marty Barry from Boston, the team finished first and won its first Stanley Cup. When Detroit repeated both triumphs in 1936-67, it marked the first time in NHL history that a team had won both the division title and the Cup in successive seasons.

Adams coached the team himself for 20 seasons. He was a hard-driving taskmaster who usually wasn't afraid to make changes. In 1934-5, for example, he shocked the NHL by switching his star forward, Ebbie Goodfellow, to defense. No matter that Goodfellow had led the American Division in scoring a few years earlier; Detroit still hadn't won the Cup. Goodfellow then became an All-Star on defense and played a major role in Detroit's spurt to the top. Apparently impressed with the Wings' unprecedented second sweep of the division title and the Cup in 1936-37, Adams decided not to trade to improve his squad. In addition to Goodfellow, Barry, and Howe, he already had Larry Aurie, Herbie Lewis, Johnny Sorrell, Bucko McDonald, and Mud Bruneteau. But the next year Detroit sank to last. "I should have been dealing," he conceded. "After this flop, I'll never hesitate to bust up championship clubs."

In 1938-39, Detroit began its record 20 years of never missing the

184

Jack Adams

playoffs. The golden age was dawning. Adams's scouts had signed a 14-year-old, Terry Sawchuk, in East Kildonan, Manitoba, and a gangly 13-year-old, Gordie Howe, in Saskatoon, Saskatchewan. In Toronto two more youngsters, Red Kelly and Ted Lindsay, were signed mere blocks from Maple Leaf Gardens. When these young men burst into the league in the late forties, Detroit began its matchless streak of seven straight NHL titles. By then Adams had confined his duties to those of general manager, overseeing the most powerful farm system in hockey.

James Norris died in 1952, but under Adam, the Wings continued to prevail into the mid-fifties. Then Bruce Norris, the former owner's son, inherited the franchise, and when the Red Wings slipped from championship prominence, he began scrutinizing his front office. After Detroit missed the playoffs in 1961-62, Adams was eased out and replaced by Sid Abel.

On May 2, 1968, Adams died a bitter man at his desk in Detroit, his final hockey assignment the lackluster task of running the Central Professional Hockey League.

Adams keeps track of his players.

Alger Joseph Arbour's professional playing career has spanned 19 years, four NHL clubs, and several clubs in the minor professional American, Quebec, and Western hockey leagues. As a player, he was a well-traveled defenseman, for one main reason—he wore glasses. Coaches shy away from players with glasses for fear these players will be hit by the puck or struck by a stick.

Arbour's nomadic career may be the reason he is such a successful coach, for during his travels he played for some fine coaches and undoubtedly took note of their methods. While playing for Detroit, he learned from Thomas Ivan, James Skinner, and Sid Abel. Rudolph Pilous was his mentor in Chicago, Punch Imlach in Toronto, and J. Lynn Patrick and Scotty Bowman in St. Louis.

When the NHL expanded in 1967-68, Arbour was drafted from Toronto to play for St. Louis. He was chosen to captain the Blues, and played in three successive Stanley Cup finals. His first opportunity to coach came late in the 1969-70 season when general manager and coach Bowman was away on a scouting trip. Arbour coached three games; won one and lost 2. He was named coach for the 1970-71 season, but after 50 games Bowman returned to his coaching position, sending Arbour back to the ice. The next season Bowman left for Montreal, and Arbour was named assistant general manager to J. Lynn Patrick. On December 24, 1971, he replaced Bill McCreary and coached St. Louis in the final 44 games of the season. After 13 games in the 1972-73 season, in which he won two, lost six, and tied five, Arbour was replaced by Jean-Guy Talbot.

Arbour came to the New York Islanders in 1973-74, and although the club finished last in the East Division, they won seven more games and increased their point total from 30 to 56. Arbour's success as the Islander's coach is partly attributable to the way his players play for him. Islanders do not gripe; they put their faith in Arbour's judgment and play their game his way—-and as a result they can now put four Stanley Cup rings on their fingers.

This belief in Arbour probably began during the 1975 Stanley Cup playoffs when the Pittsburgh Penguins won the first three games of their series. With the Islanders one game away from elimination, Arbour convinced his players they could win the next four games—and they did. Arbour has molded the Islanders into a disciplined club that consistently plays well. When the chips are down they rise to the occasion. in the last two Stanley Cup final series the Islanders have taken their opponents—Vancouver and Edmonton—in four straight games.

The Islanders started slowly in

Arbour signals last-minute instructions.

Al Arbour

1983-84, and at the end of October, with a six-won six-lost record, were trailing the New York Rangers and Philadelphia in their division. But Arbour got the Islanders back on course, and by mid-December they were out in front in the Lester Patric Division—and rolling.

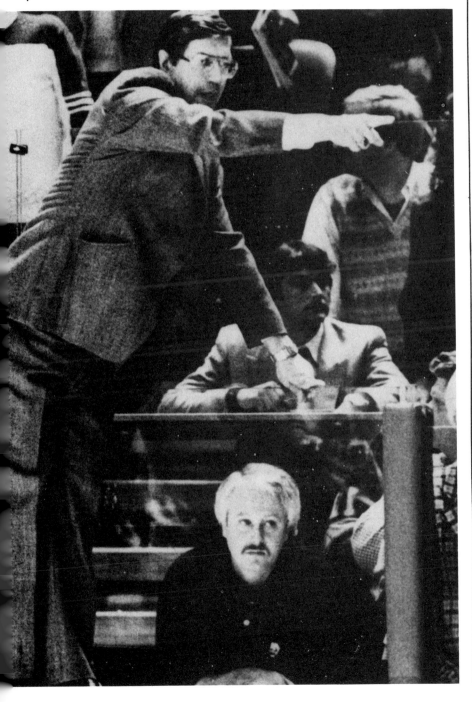

WScott Bowman's career as a hockey player came to an end when he suffered a head injury in 1951-52 during a junior hockey game. He then served for almost a decade in various capacities for the Montreal Canadiens, including two seasons spent assisting Samuel Pollack in the management and coaching of the Hull-Ottawa Jr. Canadiens. In 1961, Bowman was named head scout for Eastern Canada.

When the St. Louis Blues entered the NHL, general manager and coach J. Lynn Patrick recruited Bowman as his assistant. Bowman took over the coaching duties on November 22, 1967, and guided the blues to the Stanley Cup finals. Before the start of the 1968-69 season he replaced Patrick as general manager, and directed St. Louis to two West Division titles and the Stanley Cup finals in 1968-69 and 1969-70.

When Montreal's Claude Ruel relinquished coaching duties after winning the Stanley Cup in 1971, Bowman returned to Montreal—and Pollock. In his second season there he guided the Canadiens to the East Division title and a Stanley Cup victory.

During the late 1970's, a number of outstanding players, skated for Montreal including goaltenders Kenneth Dryden and ""Bunny" Larocque; defensemen Guy Lapointe, Larry Robinson, and Serge Savard; and forwards Yvan Cournoyer, Robert Gainey, Guy Lafleur, Yvon Lambert, Jacques Lemaire, Douglas Risebrough, Stephen Shutt, and Mario Tremblay. With this nucleus, Bowman won a James Norris Division title in 1974-75, followed by four successive James Norris Division titles and Stanley Cup victories.

Samuel Pollock retired after the 1977-78 season, and Irving Grundman was named general manager. Bowman departed after the following season leaving an impressive record of six Division titles and five Stanley Cups in eight years.

George ""Punch" Imlach had been fired as general manager of the Buffalo Sabres and in 1979-80 Bowman took over as both general manager and coach. He nearly guided Buffalo to two successive Charles F. Adams Division titles. In 1981-82 and 1982-83, however,

Scotty Bowman accepts job with Sabres.

Scotty Bowman

Bowman directs Canadien strategy.

the Sabres dropped to third place in the Charles F. Adams Division, and were eliminated from the Stanley Cup playoffs by the Boston Bruins each time.

T oe Blake was an unremitting perfectionist. He simply believed his team could win every game it played or at least the National Hockey League championship every year. Blake's Montreal Canadiens powerhouses never achieved such perfection—they did lose a game here and there and even a few league titles—but their magnificent record under Blake suggests that he was one of the least disappointed perfectionists in the history of hockey.

In the 13 years he paced behind the Canadiens' bench, Montreal won an astounding total of nine NHL titles and eight Stanley Cups. From 1956 through 1960, the Canadiens reeled off a record five Cups in a row. Only once did they finish lower than second—in 1962-63, when they finished third, three points behind the champion Toronto Maple Leafs.

Blake became a winner as a star center for Rocket Richard and Elmer Lach on Montreal's fabled "Punch Line." When he was promoted to coach, his winning habit became a near obsession. He never permitted himself to agree to more than a one-year contract, apparently reasoning that job insecurity would keep him at his best. "I'm not our for security," he explained. "I'm out to win. I get scared when we lose, and I don't like being scared. In 1955, I was bloody well scared half to death when I took over this team. It had *too* many good players that year, and I had played with several of them. How was I to know how they would react to me as their coach? I get more tense and nervous every year, and it is making me a bitter man. People say, 'Calm down, Toe,' but I can't calm down. If the day ever comes when I can swallow defeat, I will quit."

It was nerves, not defeat, that drove Blake into self-imposed retirement. His quest for unattainable excellence made him morose and moody,

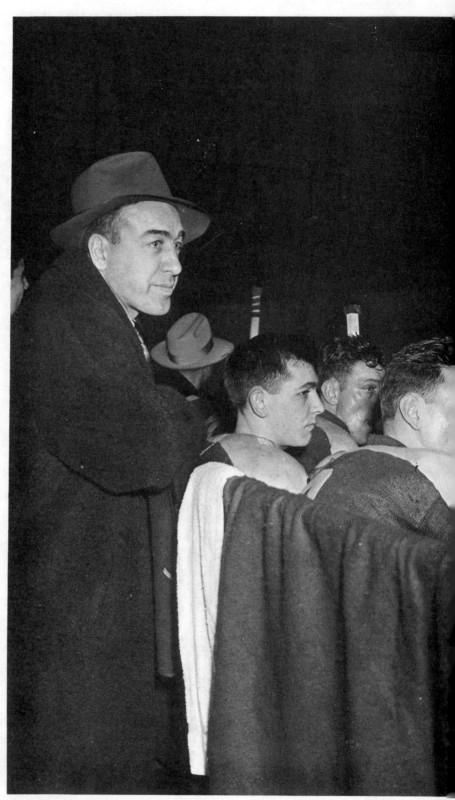

Blake behind the bench in 1949

190

Toe Blake

unable to escape the pressure for constant victory even in the summers. There were always thoughts of next season to plague him. Next season still another Canadiens team would be favored to win the NHL title and the Stanley Cup, and Blake would spend the off-season worrying that something might go wrong. When the Canadiens lost or played less than their best in winning, Toe Blake would quietly close the door to the dressing room in the Montreal Forum and berate his players until they would remember, either through fear or understanding of him, how important it was for the Canadiens to be winners. "Get mad!" Blake would rage. "You're better than they are! Look up! Up!"

And the Habs would look up and see the Montreal heroes whose portraits hung from the walls. Below the paintings was a passage from a poem written during World War I: "To you from failing hands we throw the torch,/Be yours to hold it high. . . ."

"Nobody grabbed that message quite like Blake," recalled Montreal winger Dick Duff. "We always knew if we didn't catch that torch, he'd light it under us."

Although the Canadiens may sometimes have resented their coach for the superhuman demands he made on them, a strong bond existed between Blake and his players. They not only feared and respected their coach but felt free to discuss their deepest problems with him. And in his way Blake showed respect for them. He never ran bed checks and even in hockey's jet age would book his team on trains whenever possible. "The best you can get on a plane is a three-handed poker game," he said. "That's no good."

Blake's final year, 1967-68, began as his most disappointing, but ended as his most satisfying. Hobbled by injuries to key players such as Jean Beliveau, Henri Richard, and Yvan Cournoyer, the Canadiens floundered in last place until early January. Then the wounded began to return, and driven by their fiery

coach, the Canadiens produced one of the longest winning streaks (12 games) in NHL history. In five weeks the Habs soared from last place to first, and after winning the title, they quite naturally captured another Stanley Cup.

During the wild celebration afterward, Blake announced he was quitting.

"I think this is it," he said. "I'd like to coach the Canadiens for a hundred years, but the tension is too terrific. I don't think I could take it anymore. Why, on days of some games this year I was almost not human."

A glance at Toe Blake's coaching record indeed makes one wonder.

As a superior defenseman and Toronto team captain in the twenties and thirties, Clarence ("Happy") Day learned the hockey coach's trade from Dick Irvin, then coach of the Maple Leafs. Like Irvin, Day shunned tobacco and liquor and concentrated fiercely on hockey. As a coach he would inspire his players to make nearly as great a commitment to the game.

After finishing his playing career with the New York Americans in 1937-38, Day turned to refereeing. Then Conn Smythe asked him to coach the Maple Leafs. In 10 years in Toronto, Day would win five Stanley Cups, including three in a row (1947 through 1949). Day's teams would finish first once and second three times. Only once under Day, in 1945-46, would Toronto miss the playoffs.

As a player, Day had been a master of the clutch-and-grab style—holding without getting caught. But if the referees rarely detected his defensive transgressions, the players knew them only too well. "When Hap was on defense," recalled one former teammate, "it used to cost the opposition triple money for sweaters. There were times he'd rip them right off their backs."

Not surprisingly, the Leafs adopted Day's style when he returned to Toronto as coach. Often their tactics were so infuriatingly successful that their opponents spent more time complaining to the referee than playing the Maple Leafs. Toronto perfected more creditable defensive techniques also. The Leafs would drop to the ice to block shots and would kill penalties with stern forechecking as well as conservative positional play. They had few stars and no superstars but as a result, they worked together more closely than any other team in the league. When Toronto fans joked about the fact that no Leafs had been selected for the All-Star team in 1948, though Toronto had won the Stanley Cup the previous spring, Day observed, "We may not have the All-Stars, but we have the champions."

Above all, Hap Day had the respect

Clarence ("Happy") Day

Happy Day

Day took Toronto to the Cup three straight years.

of his players. It enabled him to conduct rigorous practice sessions with a minimum of grumbling from them. Once, Pat Egan, a Boston player, happened to catch the last few moments of a Toronto practice session at Maple Leaf Gardens. As the Leafs struggled through a grueling series of starts and stops, Egan said, "That's why they're going to win everything. Day could tell those kids to go through the wall headfirst, and they'd do it."

In Day's second year as coach, the Leafs showed the spirit that Day had imbued in them. After eliminating the New York Rangers in the first round of the Stanley Cup playoffs, Toronto was favored to take the Detroit Red Wings in the finals. After three games, however, Detroit led the series 3-0. As Toronto

fans lapsed into despair, Day calmly told his Leafs, "You have to forget the idea that you have to win four games in a row."

Then Day juggled his lineup. In two totally unorthodox moves, he benched high-scoring Gordie Dillion and defenseman Bucko McDonald and replaced them with two unknowns, brothers Don and Nick Metz. When the Red Wings opened a 2-0 lead in the second period of the fourth game and the Toronto coach refused to alter his revised lineup, Leafs fans concluded that he had lost his senses. But the Leafs persevered, rallied, and eventually won 4-3 on a goal by Nick Metz. Toronto bombed the Wings in the fifth game 9-3 and blanked them in the sixth 3-0. Then, on April 18, 1942, Toronto

defeated Detroit 3-1 and became the first NHL team ever to win a playoff series after losing the first three games. It was an accomplishment of inspiration as well as strategy. Hap Day could take credit for both.

In 1951-52, Emile Percy ("The Cat") Francis tended goal in 14 games for the New York Rangers—and then disappeared from the major league scene. He resurfaced nine years later when the Rangers announced they had signed him to coach the Guelph Royals, their junior club in the Ontario Hockey Association, and Francis has been around ever since.

In 1962-63, F. Murray Patrick, the Rangers general manager, brought Francis to New York as his assistant. Two years later, on October 30, 1964, Francis was named general manager after Patrick left to become vice-president of Madison Square Garden Center which was then under construction.

By December, 1965, the Rangers had won only five games under coach George ("Red") Sullivan. Francis decided it was time for a change and installed himself as coach. He held this position until the 1968-69 season when he brought in Boom Boom Geoffrion to take over. But when Geoffrion collapsed in the dressing room during a game in Oakland, California, on January 17, Francis again assumed coaching duties. It would be the 1973-74 season before he would hire another coach, Lawrence Popein . . . only to take *his* place on January 11. Two years later Francis started the season with Ronald Stewart as coach.

On January 7, 1976, the tumult ended when the New York Rangers brought in John Ferguson as general manager and coach. Francis had been with the Rangers for almost 14 years, 11½ as general manager. There had been no Stanley Cup (although they had come close in 1972) and no Division title. Nonetheless, Francis had brought something special to New York. He had created hope in the hearts of the fans— something that had been lacking since the days of Lester Patrick. Tickets to see the Rangers are now at a premium, and the value of the franchise has increased dramatically. New York has become a hockey town in the same class as Montreal, Toronto, and Boston. The feisty little guy behind the bench is

missed by many of the Rangers' regular patrons.

But Francis's career was far from over. The very next season he was with St. Louis, and he guided the Blues to a Conn Smythe Division title. St. Louis failed to reach the Stanley Cup playoffs in 1977-78 and 1978-79, and by December 7 of the following season St. Louis had won only 8 games, lost 16, and tied 4. Barclay Plager resigned as coach, and Francis replaced him with Gordon ("Red") Berenson. The next season (1980-81), the Blues won another Conn Smythe Division title, and Berenson won the Jack Adams Award as coach of the year.

In 1983-84 Francis was on the move again, this time to Hartford, Connecticut, where he was named general manager of the Hartford Whalers.

Emile Francis

"The Cat" exhorts his sometimes-frustrating Blues.

George ("Punch") Imlach admits that as a coach he was abrasive, stubborn, and arrogant; in short, an SOB. To his players he was a merciless taskmaster, to the Maple Leafs' fans an incorrigible traditionalist. Perhaps the only things he did better than making himself unpopular were driving his team to the playoffs and winning Stanley Cups. His Leafs, the best since the days of Happy Day, took three straight Cups and four in six years. In 10 years they won only one league championship, in 1962-63, but only once did they miss the playoffs.

It was his methods more than the results that rankled his critics. As general manager as well as coach of the Leafs, Imlach had an unshakeable faith in his aging players: Allan Stanley, Johnny Bower, Red Kelly, and George Armstrong, for instance. When the Leafs failed to win the Stanley Cup in 1965 and '66 with these players, after having won three consecutive Cups with them, the usually reserved Toronto patrons clamored for a shakeup. But Imlach stubbornly refused to concede. He clung to the players who had produced for him in the past, and in 1967, they did again, vindicating him with one of the most emotional Cup victories in history.

Unquestionably, he had a knack for getting the most out of his players. Perhaps it was partly because they thrived on punishment. Sometimes when the Leafs returned to Toronto after all-night train trips or weather-delayed flights, Imlach would bus them straight to Maple Leaf Gardens for practice. Not a workout, but *practice*—a solid 2½ hours of scrimmages, sprints, and starts-and-stops.

And there was no relief in his dressing rooms. Punch spouted coaches' cliches about extra effort, desire, determination, and conditioning. He was an insistent though not always an inspirational orator. He once admitted that there were times when he must have sounded like a nagging wife. "There were players who had been around for ten years," he said, "and they'd see me coming into the room and think, 'Here

comes lecture number twelve again. Or number fifteen. Or eighteen.' I probably could have taped some of those spiels and saved myself a lot of breath."

Before one playoff game, he had $2,500 in small bills stacked in the middle of the dressing room floor. As his team trooped in after the warmup for the game, Imlach pointed to the pile of money and told his men, "Now look, that's your money. Don't let the other guy put his hand in your pocket." Toronto won that game.

Before another game, Imlach purchased some books on the power of positive thinking, personally autographed them, and gave them to his Leafs. "Read it, *believe* it," he said. Again the Leafs won.

Beneath his tough exterior, however, Imlach had his soft spots. The late Tim Horton, a mainstay on the Leafs and later on Imlach's Buffalo Sabres, once recalled a particular 10-game losing streak in 1967 during which Punch's true colors came through. "He

Imlach ready for the formal inauguration of the Seattle Coliseum

Punch Imlach

could have blasted us in the papers, made a lot of lineup changes, and taken us apart behind closed doors,'' Horton said. ''But instead of criticizing us, he went out of his way to build up our confidence. He kept impressing us with the fact that we had too much ability to keep skidding. In view of all the pressure on him to make changes, it took real patience and courage on his part to wait out the slump.'' That was the year that Imlach's aging Leafs won their fourth Cup in six years. Today he concedes that he may have stayed too long with some aging performers, but overall, he's convinced that the strategy was sound.

In January, 1972, a heart attack forced Imlach to retire from coaching. Now, as general manager at Buffalo, he isn't doing badly, but he still fondly recalls his coaching days. ''I'll always miss coaching,'' Imlach says. ''There's no way you can pour twenty-five years of your life into something and not miss it.''

He became general manager of the Buffalo Sabres, and predicted that Buffalo would be the first expansion club to win the Stanley Cup. They weren't. Although the Sabres did win one division title during Imlach's tenure, in the 1974-75 season, they lost to Philadelphia—another expansion club—in the Stanley Cup finals four games to two.

On December 4, 1978, Imlach was fired by the Sabres. He returned to the Toronto Maple Leafs as general manager in 1979-80, but in late November, 1981, heart problems began to plague him again, and he was forced to leave.

Punch commands the Leafs in Maple Leaf Gardens.

In 1940, Major Conn Smythe, World War I hero and owner of the Toronto Maple Leafs, was headed back to war. As a man who knew the dangers of battle better than most, he realized he might not return. So he moved to protect his investments, particularly his beloved Maple Leafs, lest anything befall him in World War II. Having made a successful practice of dealing established players for potential stars, Smythe now cast a critical eye on his coach, Dick Irvin. Smythe thought Irvin, then 50, would be over the hill in a few years. He would explain later, "If something happened to me, I wanted a younger man to coach the Leafs and make the decisions." So Smythe decided to let his coach go.

Irvin had first caught Smythe's eye by directing the Chicago Black Hawks to second place and the Stanley Cup finals in 1930-31, his first year as their coach. With the Hawks he introduced the strategy of using three quick forward lines, which he kept fresh by severely limiting their time on the ice.

When the innovative Irvin came to Toronto, Smythe dealt for the talent that would help make him successful. As a result, Irvin began his tenure at Toronto with three straight Canadian Division titles and, after finishing second and third, added another in 1937-38. The only thing Irvin could't win with the Leafs, it seemed, was the Stanley Cup; six times in eight years he directed the Leafs to the playoff finals, but each time they failed there.

After Smythe dismissed him as coach on the eve of World War II, Irvin immediately signed as head coach of the Montreal Canadiens. For years to come he would return to haunt the Leafs—and Smythe. In 15 years with Montreal, Irvin would win four NHL titles. Were it not for the Detroit Red Wings, who were on a rampage of their own, his record would have been even better. (Irvin's Canadiens teams finished second to Detroit five times.) Also in Montreal, Irvin would shake his playoff jinx by winning three Stanley Cups.

When Irvin arrived in Montreal, he took control of a team that had

Irvin gets full attention during practice session.

Dick Irvin

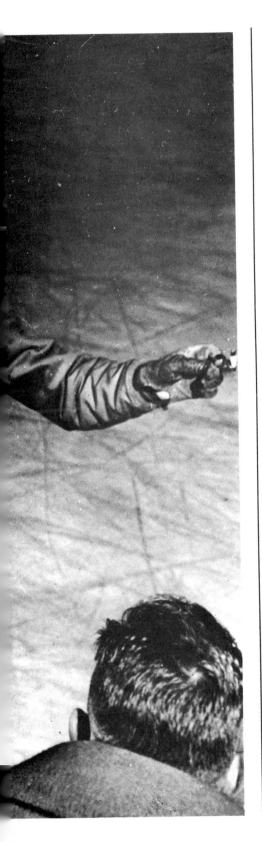

staggered through the late thirties with a series of mediocre seasons. In 1939-40, the Habs had managed only 10 victories and a seventh-place finish. Irvin's efforts to revive the team's old spirit and pride took effect only gradually. The Canadiens finished sixth in Irvin's first two years but showed signs of revival in 1942-43.

Then a young, bull-strong forward named Maurice Richard propelled the Canadiens to the top. Irvin ignored convention and placed Richard, a left-handed shooter, at right wing on a line with Toe Blake and Elmer Lach. It was a masterful stroke. Instantly the trio became one of the highest scoring lines in the game, winning the nickname "the Punch Line" and leading Montreal to four NHL titles in a row. To further please their coach, the Canadiens bagged Stanley Cups in 1944, 1946, and again in 1953.

Irvin was a slight, gaunt man who in World War I had suffered devastating wounds, the pain from which continued to plague him long afterward, allowing him to sleep on only one side. Like most successful coaches, he was intensely dedicated to hockey and the Spartan regimen that success required. Like Toe Blake, who succeeded him as coach of the Candiens, Irvin couldn't tolerate even the thought of defeat. The stretch from 1951 to 1955 was particularly frustrating to him. In that period, despite their talent, the Canadiens couldn't overhaul mighty Detroit, finishing second to the Red Wings four years in a row. Irvin's tantrums were loud and well publicized in these years, and eventually management decided the team needed a new coach. In 1954-55, Montreal finished second to Detroit with 41 wins, only 18 losses, and 11 ties, then reached the Cup finals before losing, to Detroit, of course. Not long afterward, Montreal general manager Frank Selke announced that Toe Blake was replacing Dick Irvin. His reason for firing Irvin? "Bad-tempered coaching."

At that time the Chicago Black Hawks were doing poorly. They had finished last seven times in nine

seasons and didn't care about tempers or anything else, they wanted a coach, and when Montreal fired Irvin, he was welcomed to Chicago.

So Dick Irvin returned to the city where he had played for three season and where his coaching career had begun. The 1955-56 season would prove to be another last-place finish for Chicago, but there was a glimmer of hope. Although many players would soon be replaced, a couple would stay—Pierre Pilote and Kenneth Wharram.

The next fall, with Eric Nesterenko (who had recently been acquired from the Toronto Maple Leafs) in training camp, Irvin began readying the Black Hawks for the coming campaign. But Irvin was not well and as opening night of the season drew near he knew he wouldn't be able to go on. On September 30 he resigned and returned to his home in Montreal. Thomas Ivan, the general manager, took over the coaching duties.

The NHL doesn't easily forget the men who have spent their lives among the various clubs of the league, and they didn't forget Irvin. On November 11, 1956, the NHL Governors, in appreciation of Irvin's long service in the league (3 seasons as a player, 26 seasons as a coach), named him their good-will ambassador. In this job created especially for him, Irvin would make public speeches, appear on television and radio, and conduct schools for coaches throughout Canada).

It's not likely that he fulfilled any of those assignments, and less likely that the NHL Governors minded, for on May 16, 1957, in Montreal, James Dickenson Irvin passed away.

From 1947-48 through 1953-54, Tommy Ivan coached the Detroit Red Wings to six NHL championships and three Stanley Cups. In those seven years the Wings missed finishing first only once; in 1947-48, they finished second. Ivan is the first to admit that any coach blessed as he was with Gordie Howe, Sid Abel, Ted Lindsay, and Terry Sawchuk is not likely to be a loser. But although other coaches have had teams as talented as Ivan's, no coach has matched Ivan's six consecutive regular season titles. It is a record that is unlikely to be surpassed.

Ivan's coaching career came to an abrupt end in 1954 when James Norris, Jr., son of the Red Wings' owner, bought the Chicago Black Hawks, having been assured that the NHL's stronger clubs would help him resurrect the hapless team. As part of the deal, Ivan was permitted to shift his allegiance from Norris, Sr., to Norris, Jr. In doing so, he won a promotion of sorts—from coach of the lordly Red Wings to general manager of the impoverished Black Hawks.

When Ivan came to the Black Hawks, Chicago fans were so disenchanted with them that the Hawks had difficulty filling a quarter of the 16,000 seats in huge Chicago Stadium. For the franchise to survive, it was clear that the Black Hawks would have to become a winner. As a first step in effecting the transformation, Ivan found a common element in the success of Detroit, Montreal, and Toronto: each club had first established a solid farm system. Now Ivan began to build one for the Hawks.

"When I came to Chicago," he recalled, "the Black Hawks had but one-half of a sponsored club. When sponsorships were abolished in 1970, we had nine. It took a lot of money, sweat, and hustle to establish that farm system. Jim said money was no object, but in the beginning not that many clubs were anxious to be sponsored by Chicago. Nobody wants to be associated with a loser. But I was always on the lookout for a club that might be

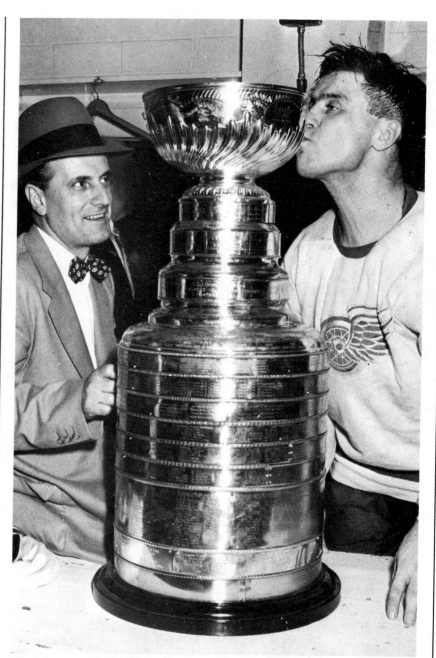

With winning-goal scorer Leswick in 1954

200

Tommy Ivan

interested, and when I heard of one, I was on a plane the next day."

The Hawks remained mired in the depths of the standings through 1957-58, but Ivan's farm system produced two promising youngsters for the next two seasons: first Bobby Hull, a young left winger with an explosive slap shot, and the next year, Stan Mikita, a promising playmaker. When Glenn Hall, an All-Star goaltender, was acquired from the Detroit Red Wings, Chicago had laid the foundation for an era of success. Beginning in 1958-59, the Hawks finished third four years in a row. In 1961, they won their first Stanley Cup in 23 years.

Ivan installed Billy Reay as coach for the 1963-64 season, and with an ever increasing flow of talent, Chicago soon joined the elite of the NHL. The Hawks won their first league title in 1966-67 and another in 1969-70, their last season as a member of the NHL's East Division. With the addition of two former American college players, defenseman Keith Magnuson and forward Cliff Koroll, the Black Hawks soared to three straight West Division titles and twice reached the Stanley Cup finals.

After 23 seasons as the general manager of the Chicago Black Hawks, Ivan retired at the end of the 1976-77 season. He now has time to reflect on two extraordinary hockey careers: coach of one championship team, architect of another.

Ivan heeds his superstar, Bobby Hull.

Around the National Hockey League, Sam Pollock is known as "the Godfather:" he makes deals that weaker teams can't refuse. His trading formula is simple and foolproof. The overstocked Canadiens surrender proven major leaguers who can help marginal or floundering teams gain respectability. In return Montreal receives draft choices that will keep the Canadiens abundantly supplied for years to come. Pollock's greatest asset is his ability to recognize talent and then to obtain it through complex trades. The chubby little general manager of the Montreal Canadiens goes to the amateur draft each June with more choices than any other general manager in the league, and Montreal's success is all but assured.

The main job of the general manager is to supply talent, and no one in hockey does that as well as Pollock. Since Pollock became general manager in 1963, Yuan Cournoyer, Guy Lafleur, Jacques Lemaire, Jacques Laperriere, Guy Lapointe, Serge Savard, and Ken Dryden have all risen through the Montreal farm system. In trades Pollock has landed Frank and Peter Mahovlich, and one shudders to think how close he came to getting the draft choice that would have brought Gilbert Perreault to Montreal.

For a while it was said that Pollock simply inherited a powerful club from Frank Selke, Sr., but as the years passed and the Canadiens have continued to thrive, it has become obvious that Pollock has independently achieved his success. "I've seen others inherit the talent and kick it away," said one GM, "but I personally think Sam's as sharp as they come."

Pollock rose the hard way. After coaching the Montreal Junior Canadiens from 1947 through 1953, he took control of the Canadiens' entire farm system. He maintained the system as the league's finest, and in 1960, Montreal general manager Frank Selke rewarded him by appointing him general manager of Montreal's Hull-Ottawa entry in the Eastern Professional

Hockey League. It was obvious that Selke was grooming Pollock to succeed him. The transition took place in 1963, and since then, the Canadiens have won five NHL titles and six Stanley Cups.

In addition to his other skills, Pollock is a master at guiding his legislation through the NHL Board of Governors. When some of it then benefits the Canadiens, there is some predictable grumbling in executive suites around the league. NHL President Clarence Campbell, a Pollock-watcher for years, says, "I don't know if he studied Branch Rickey or not, but Sam's very much like him. All of Rickey's rivals feared him because they felt he would get them sooner or later. I think the same feeling exists with regard to Mr. Pollock."

Says Pollock, "You work around the clock to get what you have, then you work around the clock to keep it. When you're down, maybe you're inclined to gamble. When you're on top, you're inclined to be selfish.

"We've had some down years since I've been here. In 1969-70, we finished out of the playoffs for the first time in twenty-two years. But we didn't panic. We didn't trade away the whole team in an attempt to finish first in 1970-71 We looked at what we had, made the adjustments we felt were necessary, and let things take care of themselves. Never, ever, will I mortgage our future for a short-term gain."

It's a credo more easily proclaimed than held to. Pollock is one of the few general managers who, through skill

Sam Pollock, "the Godfather"

Sam Pollock

With Rejean Houle, another rookie sensation

and good fortune, has done both.
He retired after the 1977-78 season
Pollock had been the Canadiens
general manager since May, 1964, and
had, in 14 seasons, brought the Stanley
Cup to Montreal nine times.

illy Reay is not a spectacular coach. There is little color or excitement in what he says or does, and he often communicates most effectively with nothing more than a cold stare. If there is any spark to Reay's presence it's in his attire. Both he and Chicago general manager Tommy Ivan favor striped suits, fedoras, glistening cuff links, and in general a sartorial style that well-heeled Chicagoans flaunted 50 years ago.

Fortunately, Reay is judged not on his style but on his record: the 10 most successful years in the previously sad history of Chicago hockey. Led by Bobby Hull and Stan Mikita, the Black Hawks had shown signs of life in the late fifties and early sixties. Yet even then they finished no higher than second, and that high only once. But since Reay arrived in 1963, Chicago has almost always contended for the division title and the Stanley Cup. It was under Reay, in 1966-67, that the Hawks finally won their first league championship.

The Black Hawks descended to fourth in 1967-68 and last place in 1968-69, but the following year they rebounded more strongly than ever, becoming the first team ever to progress from last place one season to first place the next. In 1970-71, Reay's Hawks moved to the NHL's West Division, where they won three titles in a row and were fighting for it through 1972-73.

Reay guided the Black Hawks to success even in years of adversity. He won when Hull was holding out, when Mikita was injured, and after defensive stalwart Pierre Pilote and goalie Glenn Hall had moved on. He did it with resourcefulness and faith in his players. When hockey purists ridiculed Tony Esposito's unorthodox fall-down, spread-eagle style, Reay defended his goalie. "All I know is that he keeps the puck out of the net. That's his job, and as long as he gets it done, the job's his," Reay insisted. It is now no longer contested that in Esposito the Hawks have one of the finest goaltenders in Hockey.

Reay also showed extraordinary faith in two untested American college players who arrived at Chicago's training camp in 1969. At that time few American college players had survived in the NHL, but under Reay, Cliff Koroll on right wing and Keith Magnuson on defense not only survived but starred. Depite Magnuson's league-leading 213 minutes in penalties (or perhaps to some degree because of it), Chicago made its record jump from last place in 1968-69 to first in 1969-70. "With those kids," Reay said, all too modestly, "we were kissed by angels."

It was also in 1969-70 that Bobby Hull missed a number of early games over a contract squabble, then returned to discover that Reay had introduced a new, disciplined style for the Hawks. "I'm just not used to this," Hull protested. "I'm used to carrying the puck and free-wheeling all over the ice. Going up and down my wing like a guy on a string is just not my style." Bobby soon adjusted, however, and Reay's

Billy Reay, Chicago's finest coach

Billy Reay

new strategy proved to benefit more than hamper him. The stress on positional play left him fresher for the next game and, at the end of the regular season, for the playoffs. Though he missed 17 games through holdout and injury, Hull still managed 38 big goals in the regular season.

Billy Reay also helped Hull's brother, Dennis, become one of the biggest scorers in the game today, which is another reason the dapper little coach has become something of a fixture with Chicago. In fact, as coach of the Black Hawks, he has held an NHL coaching job longer than any coach in the league today. Over the years he has grown no more flamboyant, only more successful.

Chicago enjoyed great success during the regular seasons. They won four straight division titles from 1969-70 to 1972-73, and another in 1975-76. It was in Stanley Cup play that they faltered. Chicago hadn't been able to get by the quarterfinals since 1974. When the Black Hawks got off to a poor start in 1976-77 (won 10, lost 19, tied 5), Reay was replaced by William E. White. Upon his departure, Reay had held his NHL coaching job longer than any coach in the league.

Reay frets during loss to Canadiens.

When Art Ross was coach, chief scout, general manager, and eventually owner of the Boston Bruins, he had some famous encounters with his chief rivals, Toronto's Conn Smythe and New York's Lester Patrick. Once, Patrick was coveting Boston's star defenseman, Eddie Shore, at the time the biggest name in hockey. For him Patrick offered Ross an obscure defenseman, Myles Lane. Because Lane had been raised in the Boston area and educated in New England, at Dartmouth, Patrick blithely suggested to Ross that he would be a natural attraction in Boston.

Never one to affect diplomacy when a blunt putdown would do, Ross replied to Patrick's offer with a brief telegram. It read, "Lester, you're so many Myles away from Shore you need a life preserver."

Ross steered the Bruins through their most successful days prior to the modern era of Bobby Orr and Phil Esposito. He coached the Bruins from 1924 through 1934, during which time they won five American Division titles and a Stanley Cup. In 1936, he returned to the helm and produced two championships and another Cup in three years. Led by goalie Frank Brimsek, Dit Clapper, Cooney Weiland, Bobby Bauer, Woody Dumart, and Milt Schmidt, Boston then won two more titles, in 1940 and '41, and added another Cup.

One of Ross's greatest attributes was his willingness to innovate. He was the first coach ever to pull his goaltender in favor of a sixth attacker. (The maneuver has since become standard hockey strategy, though it usually fails, as it did the night Ross first tried it, in a 1-0 loss to the Montreal Canadiens.) It was also Ross who suggested that limp mesh be used for a goal's nets, and who once devised an elaborate four-man defensive front.

Perhaps Ross's most famous trait was his impetuousness. When a rookie goalie named Frank Brimsek challenged All-Star Tiny Thompson in Boston's 1938 training camp, Ross quickly contrived a

Ross as coach of the 1924 Bruins

With Bobby Bauer of the Kraut Line

test to settle the issue. He fired 25 shots at each from point-blank range. After six eluded Thompson, and none got by Brimsek, Ross traded Thompson to Detroit. Boston fans were outraged, but Brimsek vindicated Ross by becoming an All-Star himself.

Ross's antics have become hockey legends, especially in Boston. Old-line Bruins fans can still see Eddie Shore (at Ross's orders) skating onto the ice with a bullfighter's cape on his shoulders and a servant behind him while the band played "Hail to the Chief." When he reached center ice, Shore would remove the cape and hand it to the servant. The ritual completed, Shore would then join the Bruins in their warmup, and the crowd would erupt in applause.

In 1947, Ross gave the National Hockey League a trophy to be awarded each year to the player who leads the NHL in scoring. Through that trophy, hockey remembers Art Ross of the Boston Bruins, one of the finest coaches, general managers, and showmen in hockey history.

Frank Selke, Sr., started out as an electrician in Kitchener, Ontario. As an amateur hockey buff who lived not far from Toronto, he made the acquaintance of Major Conn Smythe and eventually joined him as the Maple Leafs were growing into a National Hockey League power. When Maple Leaf Gardens opened, Selke gained executive status and various administrative duties. His real goal, however, was to run his own hockey club. When Smythe returned from World War II, a mild personality clash with him helped Selke realize his ambition. He left the Leafs, and on June 25, 1946, Selke was named managing director of the Montreal Canadiens.

Thanks largely to the talents of Maurice ("Rocket") Richard, the organization that Selke joined was already prospering. Selke's duty was to maintain the club's surge toward dominance of the NHL standings and the Stanley Cup playoffs.

Despite the Canadiens' triumphs, Selke was worried. He studied Montreal's roster, then went to see the owners. "I told them that no other team could match their top six players: Bill Durnan in goal, Ken Reardon and Butch Bouchard on defense, and 'the Punch Line' of Toe Blake, Richard, and Elmer Lach. But there were no reserves, no farm system," Selke said.

Asked for his suggestions, Selke replied, "We must build a chain of farms in every Canadian province, just like Toronto has. It will take money."

The Canadiens' owners provided it, and Selke began to build. In one year alone he spent $300,000 to keep the farm clubs operating. To acquire the rights to a youngster named Jean Beliveau, he purchased the whole Quebec Senior Amateur League. At one time no less than six of the teams contending for Canada's amateur trophy (the Memorial Cup) were Montreal farm clubs. Eventually, they would produce stars such as Beliveau, Boom Boom Geoffrion, and Dickie Moore for the parent club.

Selke had learned his lessons well in Toronto. With the Canadiens he

A name on the door . . .

Frank Selke, Sr.

gained the reputation for being an excellent organizer, a sound judge of talent, a cautious administrator who never made a decision before thoroughly examining all aspects of it, and, unlike Smythe, a congenial sort. When Selke arrived in Montreal, the coach of the Canadiens was Dick Irvin, whom Selke had befriended when they were both with Toronto. Irvin was a moody, volatile man, and at times the rigors of contention brought out the worst in him, but Selke was a steadying influence. The two blessed the Canadiens with cohesive executive direction until Selke grew tired of his intemperate caoch. He hired another one, Toe Blake, to replace him.

Under Blake and Selke the Canadiens established a dynasty that has hardly every faltered. Selke culled his extensive farm system for the talent that Blake would parlay into championships. When he finally retired in 1962, Selke could recall a plethora of obscure youngsters whom he had brought to the big leagues, where they became legends in Montreal history: Doug Harvey, Jacques Plante, Henri Richard, Tom Johnson, J. C. Tremblay, Jean Guy Talbot.

The Canadiens were already at the top when Frank Selke arrived, and when he departed, leaving the reins to Sam Pollack, who became general manager in May, 1964, they were as firmly entrenched there as ever.

Selke with the beloved trophy

Major Conn Smythe was a battler. He returned from World War I draped with medals: a member of the Royal Canadian Air Force, he had been shot down and captured. Then he had escaped, only to be recaptured as he tried to rescue a buddy.

After the war, Smythe brought his battling spirit to the growing world of hockey. After becoming an outstanding amateur hockey coach and manager in and around Toronto, his hometown, he was hired by Colonel John S. Hammond to build the newly born New York Rangers. However, he quarreled with Hammond, and less than a year after he began in New York, he was fired and returned to Toronto.

By this time the city's National Hockey League entry, the St. Patricks, were for sale. Smythe was interested but could not match the $200,000 that a group from Philadelphia had offered. Smythe's syndicate of World War I veterans managed to scrape up only $160,000. He made up the difference by taunting the St. Pats' owners. "Surely you don't want to walk down the street in your hometown and have your neighbors snub you because you sold out to foreigners," he told them. "Haven't you any civic pride?" Smythe's group eventually got the franchise, for $160,000.

Smythe immediatley changed the team's name to the Maple Leafs and ordered new uniforms of blue and white with the now-traditional maple leaf on the jersey. Then he and assistant Frank Selke, whom he had known from his amateur hockey days, set about building a contender. The Leafs soon had stars such as King Clancy, Joe Primeau, Charlie Conacher, and Harvey ("Busher") Jackson, and with them a winning team.

Perhaps Smythe's most amazing feat was building Maple Leaf Gardens during the Depression. He had become convinced that he needed an arena that would seat at least 12,000, as well as one that would give prestige to hockey in Toronto. He was undeterred when critics advised him that no money was

Smythe wins enthusiastically.

available, that unemployment was high, and that banks were trying to collect money, not loan it. Smythe insisted that building costs were low and that the construction of a new building would create new jobs. In the long run it would give the entire community a badly needed boost, he argued.

Somehow, Smythe and his associates raised $1 million and broke ground for the new building. When costs began to exceed estimates, Smythe convinced laborers and suppliers to accept 20 percent of their wages or bill payments in Garden stock. It was a brilliant maneuver, and Maple Leaf Gardens was erected with almost unbelievable speed. It was ready in less than a year, for the 1931-32 season. Toronto hockey hasn't been the same since.

The Leafs enjoyed great success

through the thirties, with Smythe changing players constantly. "You can't win this year on what you did last year," he explained. In the late forties he would ship no fewer than five players to Chicago for the high-scoring Max Bentley.

When World War II broke out, the ever-patriotic Smythe organized an antiaircraft battery and departed for Europe. In France a German plane dropped flares over his battery's headquarters. One of them fell into an ammunition truck, which exploded, killing two men. Shrapnel grazed the spine of Smythe and only narrowly missed paralyzing him. Despite his wounds, he continued to bark orders until the fire from the explosion had been extinguished.

As he had after World War I, Smythe

Conn Smythe

returned from World War II eager to turn his energies to hockey. This time he had a foundation on which to build and a new formula for success. "I should have figured it out years ago," he said. "Youth is the answer to this game. Put the kids in with a few old pappy guys who still like to win, and the combination is unbeatable." Smythe's combination was goalie Turk Broda, Syl Apps, Nick and Don Metz, Wally Stanowski, Bill Barilko, "Wild Bill" Ezinicki, Gus Mortson, Howie Meeker, Ted Kennedy, and Max Bentley.

As Smythe thirsted for a winning team, he openly scorned those who seemed complacent or uncompetitive. Once, after the Boston Bruins played a particularly listless game in Toronto, Smythe accompanied his Leafs on their next trip to Boston and took out an ad in a local paper. "Attention hockey fans," it read. "If you're tired of seeing the kind of hockey the Boston Bruins are playing, come to the Garden tonight and see a real hockey club, the Toronto Maple Leafs." Such antics did nothing to enhance his reputation among his fellow owners. Yet even they had to admit that as prime architect of the Toronto Maple Leafs, Major Conn Smythe gave hockey one of its most venerable institutions.

Smythe sold his interest in Maple Leaf Gardens on November 23, 1961, and his son, C. Stafford Smythe, along with Harold E. Ballard, and John F. Bassett acquired control. The younger Smythe replaced his father as president of Maple Leaf Gardens, but Conn Smythe remained a director and continued to serve on the Hockey Hall of Fame Committee.

At that time candidates for election to the Hall of Fame had to meet the following qualifications—"playing ability, integrity, character, and their contribution to their club and the game of hockey in general."

Harvey ("Busher") Jackson was the left winger on the Maple Leafs fabled "Kid Line" that electrified NHL spectators in the early 1930s. He was a gifted skater and led the NHL in scoring (points) in 1931-32 at the tender age of 21 years and 2 months (Bobby Hull

With Toronto's Harvey Jackson

211

came close—he was 21 years and 3 months when he led the league in 1959-60). When Jackson's name came before the Hall of Fame selection committee Smythe protested, arguing that Jackson didn't meet all of the qualifications. When the committee elected him despite this protest, Smythe resigned.

Smythe had strong convictions about what a man should be and how he should act, many of which would be considered outdated today. He believed a man should serve his country for whatever the cause—right or wrong. He had served his in two world wars, was the recipient of the Military Cross for action in World War I, and still walked with a limp caused by the shrapnel wound he received in World War II.

He was still a director of Maple Leaf Gardens when Cassius Clay (Muhammad Ali) was scheduled to fight there. At that time Clay was making a concerted effort to avoid induction into the U.S. Army. Again Smythe protested, claiming Clay was unfit to appear in Maple Leaf Gardens or any other arena, for that matter. Again he was overruled, and again his response was to resign.

Conn Smythe had now severed his last link with Maple Leaf Gardens—and with hockey. He continued his involvement with thoroughbred racing until November 18, 1980, when he died on his farm in Caledon, Ontario. The death of Constantine Falkland Karrys Smythe ended an era, the likes of which Toronto will never see again.

William Arthur Torrey

Born in Montreal, Quebec, on June 23, 1934, William Arthur Torrey attended St. Lawrence University in Canton, New York, where he played varsity hockey and from which he graduated in 1957.

In the early 1960s, Torrey was director of public relations for the Pittsburgh Hornets of the minor American Hockey League; he later served as the Hornets' business manager. In the 1968-69 season, he joined the Oakland Seals as executive vice-president. For two weeks in 1970-71 he was their general manager: when Frank D. Selke resigned as the Seals' general manager on November 12, 1970, Torrey replaced him . . . only to resign himself on November 25. Charles O. Finley was not an owner who endeared himself to his employees.

The New York Islanders entered the NHL in 1972-73, and Torrey has been their general manager right from the beginning. But stability has not existed in the case of their coaches. For their first season, Philippe Goyette was signed as coach, but on January 29 he was succeeded by Earl Ingarfield. The season was a disaster—the club won only 12 games and finished a distant last in the East Division scoring a mere 170 goals but having 347 scored against them. The next season, Alger Arbour arrived to coach the Islanders, and although the club again finished last in the East Division they at least held their goals-against to 247—exactly 100 fewer than the year before.

In 1974-75, the Islanders qualified for the Stanley Cup playoffs, and they have never looked back. Part of their success has to be the result of Torrey's decision not to trade away their draft choices. Through the draft they acquired Lorne Henning, Denis Potvin, Clark Gillies, Bryan Trottier, Michael Bossy, John Tonelli, Brent and Duane Sutter, and William Carroll. The trade with Los Angeles for Butch Goring and the acquisition of L. Wayne Merrick from the Cleveland Barons gave them two fine centers.

After 11 seasons in the NHL, Torrey can look back at four Lester Patrick Division titles and the winning of four Stanley Cups.

Hall of Fame

The Hockey Hall of Fame and Museum, located in Exhibition Place on the shore of Lake Erie in Toronto, was officially opened August 26, 1961, by the Prime Minister of Canada, John F. Diefenbaker. The six National Hockey League clubs at the time financed construction of the building, and the city of Toronto furnished the land. Hockey exhibits are provided and financed by the NHL and the Canadian Amateur Hockey Association. Administrative costs are underwritten by the National Hockey League.

Any person who has distinguished himself in hockey as a player, executive, or referee is eligible for election to the Hockey Hall of Fame. Successful player and referee candidates normally have completed their active careers three years prior to election, but in exceptional cases this period can be shortened by the Hockey Hall of Fame Committee.

Candidates for election as executives and referees can be nominated only by the Hockey Hall of Fame and Museum Board of Governors and upon election are known as "Builders." Player candidates are chosen on the basis of "playing ability, integrity, character, and their contribution to their team and the game of hockey in general."

There are 247 members of the Hockey Hall of Fame: 173 players, 65 builders, 9 referees.

M. H. (Lefty) Reid is Director and Curator of the Hockey Hall of Fame and Museum.

PLAYERS

Abel, Sidney Gerald ("Sid")   Left Wing and Center
Detroit, Chicago   1969

Bailey, Irvin Wallace ("Ace")   Right Wing
Toronto   1975

Bathgate, Andrew James ("Andy")   Right Wing
New York, Rangers, Toronto, Detroit, Pittsburgh   1978

Adams, John James ("Jack")   Center
Vancouver, Toronto. Ottawa   1959

Bain, Donald H.   Center
Winnipeg   1945

Beliveau, Jean Arthur   Center
Montreal   1972

Apps, Charles Joseph Sylvanus ("Syl")   Center
Toronto   1961

Baker, Hobart Amery Hare ("Hobey")   Rover
St. Nicholas Hockey Club, New York   1945

Bentley, Douglas Wagner   Left Wing and Center
Chicago, New York   1964

Armstrong, George Edward   Center and Right Wing
Toronto   1975

Barry, Martin J. ("Marty")   Center
New York Americans, Boston, Detroit, Montreal   1965

Bentley, Maxwell Herbert Lloyd ("Max")   Center
Chicago, Toronto, New York   1966

218

Blake, Hector ("Ioe")   Left Wing
Montreal Maroons, Montreal Canadiens   1966

Boucher, George ("Buck")   Defense
Ottawa, Montreal Maroons, Chicago   1960

Burch, H. William   Center
Hamilton, New York Americans, Boston, Chicago 1974

Boon, Richard R. ("Dickie")   Rover
Montreal A. A. A., Montreal Wanderers   1952

Bowie, Russell   Rover
Montreal Victorias   1945

Cameron, Harold Hugh ("Harry")   Defense
Toronto, Ottawa, Montreal   1962

Bouchard, Emile Joseph ("Butch")   Defense
Montreal   1966

Broadbent, Harry L. ("Punchy")   Right Wing
Ottawa, Montreal Maroons, New York Americans   1962

Clancey, Francis Michael ("King")   Defense
Ottawa, Toronto   1958

Boucher, Frank Xavier   Center
Ottawa, Vancouver, New York   1958

Bucyk, John Paul   Left Wing
Detroit, Boston   1981

Clapper, Aubrey Victor ("Dit")   Right Wing and Defense
Boston   1945 219

Cleghorn, Sprague   Defense
Renfrew, Montreal Wanderers, Ottawa, Toronto,
Montreal Canadiens, Boston   1958

Coulter, Arthur Edmund   Defense
Quebec, Ottawa, Toronto, Saskatoon, Calgary,
Vancouver   1974

Darragh, John Proctor ("Jack")   Right Wing
Ottawa   1962

Colville, Neil MacNeil   Center and Defense
New York   1967

Cournoyer, Yvan Serge   Center
Chicago, New York   1982

Davidson, Allan M. ("Scotty")   Right Wing
Toronto   1950

Conacher, Charles William   Right Wing
Toronto, Detroit, New York Americans   1961

Cowley, William Mailes ("Bill")   Left Wing
Montreal   1968

Day, Clarence Henry ("Hap")   Defense
Toronto, New York Americans   1961

Cook, William Osser ("Bill")   Right Wing
Saskatoon, New York   1952

Crawford, Samuel Russell ("Rusty")   Right Wing
St. Louis, Boston   1962

Delvecchio, Alexander Peter   Center and Left Wing
Detroit   1977

Denneny, Cyril Joseph ("Cy")   Left Wing
Toronto Ontarios, Toronto Shamrocks,
Toronto Blueshirts, Ottawa, Boston   1959

Dutton, Mervyn Alexander ("Red")   Defense
Calgary, Montreal Maroons, New York Americans 1958

Foyston, Frank C.   Left Wing
Toronto, Seattle, Victoria, Detroit   1958

Drillon, Gordon Arthur   Right Wing
Toronto, Montreal   1975

Dye, Cecil Henry ("Babe")   Right Wing
Toronto, Hamilton, Chicago, New York Americans 1970

Fredrickson, Frank   Center
Victoria, Detroit, Boston, Pittsburgh   1958

Drinkwater, Charles Graham   Cover-Point
Montreal Victorias   1950

Phil Esposito   Center
Sault Ste. Marie, St. Louis, Chicago,   1984
Boston, New York Rangers

Dunderdale, Thomas   Center
Montreal Shamrocks, Quebec, Victoria,
Portland, Edmonton, Saskatoon   1974

Farrell, Arthur F.   Wing
Montreal Shamrocks   1965

Gadsby, William Alexander ("Bill")   Defense
Chicago, New York, Detroit   1970

Gardiner, Herbert Martin   Defense
Calgary, Montreal, Chicago   1958   221

Gardner, James Henry ("Jimmy")   Left Wing
Montreal A. A. A., Calumet, Pittsburgh, 1962
Montreal Shamrocks,

Gilmour, Hamilton Livingstone ("Billy") Rover 1962
Ottawa Silver Seven, Montreal Victorias, Ottawa Senators

Green, Wilfred Thomas ("Shorty")   Right Wing
Hamilton. New York Americans   1962

Geoffrion, Joseph Andre Bernard ("Boom Boom")
Montreal Wanderers. New Westminster,   Right Wing
Montreal Canadiens Montreal, New York   1972

Goheen. Francis Xavier ("Moose")   Defense
1920 Olympic club (U.S.A.)   1952

Griffis, Silas Seth ("Si")   Cover-Point
Rat Portage (Kenora)   1950

Gerard, Edward George ("Eddie")   Defense
Ottawa   1945

Goodfellow, Ebenezer Ralston ("Ebbie")   Defense
Detroit   1963

Hall, Joseph Henry ("Joe")   Defense
Kenora, Brandon, Quebec, Montreal   1961

Gilbert, Rodrigue Gabriel ("Rod")   Right Wing
New York Rangers   1982

Grant, Michael ("Mike")   Point
Montreal Victorias   1950

Harvey, Douglas Norman   Defense
Montreal, New York, Detroit, St. Louis.   1973

Hay, George William   *Left Wing*
Regina, Portland, Chicago, Detroit   1958

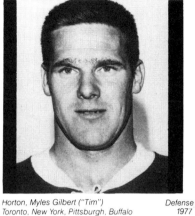

Horton, Myles Gilbert ("Tim")   *Defense*
Toronto, New York, Pittsburgh, Buffalo   1977

Hull, Robert Marvin ("Golden Jet")   *Left Wing*
Chicago, Winnipeg, Hartford   1983

Hextall, Bryan Aldwin   *Right Wing*
New York   1969

Howe, Gordon ("Gordie")   *Right Wing*
Detroit, Hartford   1972

Hyland, Harry M.   *Right Wing*
Montreal Shamrocks, Montreal Wanderers,   1962
New Westminster, Ottawa

Hooper, Charles Thomas ("Tom")   *Rover*
Rat Portage (Kenora), Montreal Wanderers   1962

Howe, Sydney Harris ("Syd")   *Defense*
Ottawa, Philadelphia, St. Louis, Detroit   1965

Irvin, James Dickeson   *Center*
Portland, Regina, Chicago   1958

Horner, George Reginald ("Red")   *Defense*
Toronto   1965

Howell, Henry Vernon ("Harry") Left Wing and Center
New York, Oakland, Los Angeles   1979

Jackson, Harvey ("Busher")   *Left Wing*
Toronto, New York Americans, Boston   1971

223

Continued on page 242

A Portfolio of Superstars

Brad Park

John Bucyk

Gump Worsley and Milt Schmidt

Johnson, Ernest ("Moose")   Left Wing   1958
Montreal A.A.A., Montreal Wanderers, New Westminster,
Portland, Victoria

Keats, Gordon Blanchard ("Duke")   Center   1958
Toronto Blueshirts, Edmonton, Boston, Detroit, Chicago

Lalonde, Edouard Charles ("Newsy")   Center   1950
Cornwall, Sault Ste. Marie (Ontario), Toronto, Montreal,
Renfrew, Vancouver, Saskatoon, New York Americans

Johnson, Ivan Wilfred ("Ching")   Defense
New York Rangers, New York Americans   1970

Kelly, Leonard Patrick ("Red")   Defense
Detroit, Toronto   1969

Laviolette, Jean Baptiste ("Jack")   Left Wing
Sault Ste. Marie (Michigan), Montreal Shamrocks,
Montreal Canadiens   1962

Johnson, Thomas Christian ("Tom")   Defense
Montreal, Boston   1952

Kennedy, Theodore Samuel ("Teeder")   Center
Toronto   1966

Jacques LaMaire   Center
Quebec, Houston, Montreal   1984

Joliat, Aurel Emile   Left Wing
Montreal   1945

Lach, Elmer James   Center
Montreal   1966

Lindsay, Robert Blake Theodore   Left Wing
Detroit, Chicago   1966

MacKay, Duncan McMillan ("Mickey")   Center
Vancouver, Chicago, Pittsburgh, Boston   1952

Marshall, John C. ("Jack")   Center   1965
Winnipeg, Montreal A.A.A.,Montreal Wanderers, Montreal

McNamara, George A.   Defense   1958
Sault Ste. Marie (Michigan), Montreal Shamrocks, Halifax,
Toronto Tecumsehs, Ottawa, Toronto Ontarios, 228th Battalion

Mahovlich, Francis William ("Frank")   Left Wing
Toronto, Detroit, Montreal   1981

Maxwell, Fred G. ("Steamer")   Rover
Shamrocks, Toronto   amateur   1962

Mikita, Stanley ("Stosh")   Center
Chicago   1983

Malone, Maurice Joseph ("Joe")   Center
Quebec, Waterloo, Montreal, Hamilton   1950

McGee, Francis C. ("Frank")   Center
Ottawa   1945

Moore, Richard Winston ("Dickie")   Left Wing
Montreal, Toronto, St. Louis   1974

Mantha, Sylvio   Defense
Montreal, Boston   1960

McGimsie, William George ("Billy")   Center
Rat Portage (Kenora)   1962

Morenz, Howarth William ("Howie")   Center
Montreal, Chicago, New York   1945

Mosienko, William ("Billy") — Right Wing
Chicago — 1965

Orr, Robert Gordon ("Bobby") — Defense
Boston, Chicago — 1979

Phillips, Thomas Neil ("Tom") — 1975 — Left Wing
Rat Portage (Kenora), Montreal A. A. A., Toronto, Ottawa,
Edmonton, Vancouver

Nighbor, Frank J. — Center
Port Arthur, Vancouver, Ottawa, Toronto — 1945

Bernard Parent, Goalie
Oklahoma City, Toronto, Boston. — 1984

Pilote, Joseph Albert Pierre Paul — 1962 — Defense
Montreal Nationals, Montreal Shamrocks, Edmonton,
Montreal Canadiens, Vancouver

Noble, Edward Reginald ("Reg") — Left Wing and
Toronto, Montreal Maroons, Detroit — Defense 1962

Patrick, Joseph Lynn — Left Wing
New York Rangers — 1980

Pitre, Didier ("Pit") — Right Wing
Chicago, Toronto — 1966

Oliver, Harold ("Harry") — Right Wing
Calgary, Boston, New York Americans — 1967

Patrick, Lester ("The Silver Fox") — Rover
Brandon, Montreal Wanderers. Edmonton, Renfrew,
Victoria, Spokane, Seattle, New York — 1945

Pratt, Walter Basil ("Babe") — Defense
New York, Toronto, Boston — 1963

Primeau, A. Joseph ("Joe")　　　Center
Toronto　　　　　　　　　　　　1978

Rankin, Frank　　　　　　　　Rover
amateur　　　　　　　　　　　1966

Richardson, George Taylor
Queen's University

Pronovost, Joseph Rene Marcel　　Defense
Detroit, Toronto　　　　　　　　　1945

Reardon, Kenneth Joseph ("Kenny")　Defense
Montreal　　　　　　　　　　　　1979

Roberts, Gordon　　　　　　　　Left Wing
Ottawa, Montreal Wanderers, Vancouver, Seattle　1971

Pulford, Harvey E.　　　　　　Point
Ottawa　　　　　　　　　　　1976

Richard, Joseph Henri　　　　Center
Montreal　　　　　　　　　　1961

Ross, Arthur Howey　　　　　　Cover-Point
Brandon, Kenora, Montreal Wanderers,　1945
Haileybury, Ottawa

Quackenbush, Hubert George ("Bill")　Defense
Detroit, Boston　　　　　　　　　1961

Richard, Joseph Henri Maurice ("The Rocket")　1950
Montreal　　　　　　　　　　　　Right Wing

Russell, Blair　　　　　　　　Center
Montreal Victorias　　　　　　1965

245

Russell, Ernest   Right Wing
Montreal Wanderers   1965

Schriner, David ("Sweeney")   Defense
New York, Americans, Toronto   1961

Siebert, Albert Charles ("Babe")
Montreal Maroons, New York, Boston,
Montreal Canadiens

Ruttan, J. D. ("Jack")   Wing
amateur   1961

Seibert, Earl Walter   Forward
New York, Chicago, Detroit   1945

Simpson, Harold Joseph ("Bullet Joe")   Defense
Edmonton, New York Americans   1962

Scanlan, Frederick   Center
Montreal Shamrocks, Winnipeg   1962

Seibert, Oliver Levi   Defense
Houghton, London, Guelph   1964

Smith, Alfred Edward ("Alf")   Right Wing
Pittsburgh, Ottawa, Kenora

Schmidt, Milton Conrad ("Milt")   Left Wing
Boston   1963

Shor, Edward William   Left Wing and Defense
Regina, Edmonton, Boston, New York Americans   1962

Smith, Reginald Joseph ("Hooley")   1972   Center
Ottawa, Montreal Maroons, Boston, New York Americans

Smith, Thomas James   1973   *Center*
Quebec, Toronto Ontarios, Montreal Canadiens

Stewart, Nelson Robert   *Center*
Montreal Maroons, Boston, New York Americans 1962

Trihey, Henry Judah ("Harry")   *Center*
Montreal Shamrocks   1950

Stanley, Allan Herbert   *Defense*
New York, Chicago, Boston, Toronto,   1981
Philadelphia

Stuart, Bruce   *Rover*
Ottawa, Quebec, Pittsburgh, Houghton, 1961
Montreal Wanderers

Ullman, Norman Victor Alexander   *Center*
Detroit, Toronto   1982

Stanley, Russell ("Barney")   *Right Wing*
Vancouver, Calgary, Regina, Edmonton, Chicago 1962

Stuart, William Hodgson ("Hod")   *Cover-Point*
Ottawa, Quebec. Calumet, Pittsburgh,   1945
Montreal Wanderers

Walker. John Phillip ("Jack")   *Rover*
Moncton, Toronto, Seattle, Victoria, Detroit   1960

Stewart, John Sherratt ("Black Jack")   *Defense*
Detroit, Chicago   1964

Taylor, Frederic Wellington ("Cyclone")   *Rover*
Portage la Prairie, Hougnton, Ottawa,   1945
Renfrew, Vancouver

Walsh, Martin   *Center*
Queen's University, Ottawa   1962

247

Watson, Harry E.   Center
1924 Olympic club (Canada)   1962

Wilson, Gordon Allan ("Phat")   Defense
amateur   1962

Weiland, Ralph ("Cooney")   Center
Boston, Ottawa, Detroit   1971

Westwick, Harry ("Rat")   Rover
Ottawa   1962

Whitcroft, Frederick   Rover
Kenora, Edmonton, Renfrew   1962

248

GOALTENDERS

Benedict, Clinton S. ("Benny")   1965
Ottawa Senators, Montreal Maroons

Connell, Alexander   1983
Ottawa Senators, Detroit Falcons, New York Americans,
Montreal Maroons

Hainsworth, George   1975
Montreal Canadiens, Toronto Maple Leafs

Bower, John William ("Johnny")   1976
New York Rangers, Toronto Maple Leafs

Dryden, Kenneth Wayne ("Ken")   1964
Montreal Canadiens

Hall, Glenn Henry
Detroit Red Wings, Chicago Black Hawks,
St. Louis Blues

Brimsek, Francis Charles   1966
Boston Bruins, Chicago Black Hawks

Durnan, William Ronald ("Bill")
Montreal Canadiens

Hern, William Milton ("Riley")   1962
Houghton, Montreal Wanderers

Broda, Walter Edward ("Turk")   1967
Toronto Maple Leafs

Gardiner. Charles Robert ("Chuck")   1945
Chicago Black Hawks

Holmes, Harry ("Hap")   1972
Toronto, Seatle Metropolitans, Victoria Cougars, Detroit
Cougars

249

Hutton, John Bower ("Bouse")   1962
Ottawa Silver Seven

Moran, Patrick Joseph ("Paddy")   1978
Quebec Bulldogs, Haileybury

Thompson, Cecil Ralph ("Tiny")   1959
Boston Bruins, Detroit Red Wings

Lehman, Frederick Hugh   1961
Sault Ste. Marie (Ontario), Berlin (Kitchener), Galt, New
Westminster Royals, Vancouver, Chicago Black Hawks

Plante, Joseph Jacques Omer
Montreal Canadiens, New York Rangers, St. Louis Blues,
Toronto Maple Leafs

Vezina, Georges
Montreal Canadiens

LeSueur, Percy   1980
Smiths Falls, Ottawa, Toronto Ontarios

Rayner, Claude Earl ("Chuck")   1973
New York Americans, New York Rangers

Worsely, Lorne John ("Gump")   1980
New York Rangers, Montreal Canadiens,
Minnesota North Stars

Lumley, Harry   1958
Detroit Red Wings, New York Rangers, Chicago Black
Hawks, Toronto Maple Leafs, Boston Bruins

Sawchuk, Terrance Gordon ("Terry")   1971
Detroit Red Wings Boston Bruins, Toronto Maple Leafs,
Los Angeles Kings, New York Rangers

Worters, Roy   1969
Pittsburgh Pirates, New York Americans, Montreal
Canadiens

REFEREES

Ashley, John   *1981*

Ion, Frederick James ("Mickey")   *1961*

Udvari, Frank Joseph   *1973*

Chadwick, William L. ("Bill")   *1964*

Rodden, Michael J. ("Mike")   *1962*

Elliott, Edwin S. ("Chaucer")   *1961*

Smeaton, J. Cooper   *1961*

Hewitson, Robert W. ("Bobby")   *1963*

Storey, Roy Alvin ("Red")   *1967*

251

BUILDERS

Adams, Charles Francis   1960

Allan, Sir H. Montague   1945

Brown, Walter A.   1962

Adams, Weston W., Sr.   1972

Ballard, Harold Edwin   1977

Buckland, Frank   1975

Ahearn, Thomas Franklyn   1962

Bickell, John Paris   1978

Butterfield, Jack Arlington   1980

Ahearne, John Francis ("Bunny")   1977

Brown, George V.   1961

Frank Calder

Campbell, Angus Daniel   1964

Dudley, George S.   1958

Gorman, Thomas Patrick   1963

Campbell, Clarence Sutherland   1966

Dunn, James A.   1968

Hay, Charles   1974

Cattarinich, M. Joseph   1977

Francis, Emile Percy   1982

Hendy, James Cecil Valdamar   1968

Dilio, Francis Paul   1964

Gibson, John L. ("Jack")   1976

Hewitt, Foster William   1965

253

Hewitt, William Abraham   1945

Jennings, William M.   1975

LeBel, Robert   1970

Hume, Fred J.   1962

Juckes, Gordon W.   1979

Lockhart, Thomas F.   1965

George "Punch" Imlach   1984

Kilpatrick, Gen. John Reed   1960

Loicq, Paul   1961

Ivan, Thomas Nathaniel   1974

Leader, George Alfred   1969

McLaughlin, Major Frederic W.   1963

254

John Caverly Milford   1984

Norris, James D., Sr.   1958

Pickard, Allan W.   1958

Molson, Senator Hartland de Montarville   1973

Northey, William M.   1945

Pollock, Samuel Patterson Smyth   1978

Nelson, Francis   1945

O'Brien, John Ambrose   1962

Raymond, Senator Donat   1958

Norris, Bruce A.   1969

Patrick, Frank A.   1958

Robertson, John Ross   1945

255

Robinson, Claude C.   1945

Smith, Frank Donald   1962

Tarasov, Anatoli V.   1974

Ross, Philip Danken   1976

Smythe, Conn   1958

Turner, Lloyd   1958

Selke, Frank J.   1960

Stanley of Preston, Lord   1945

Tutt, William Thayer   1978

Sinden, Harry Jarhes   1983

Sutherland, Captain James T.   1945

Voss, Carl Potter   1974

256

Waghorne, Fred C.   *1961*

Wirtz, Arthur Michael, Sr.   *1971*

Wirtz, William W.   *1976*

Each year of NHL hockey produces regular season champions and a Stanley Cup winner. Following are those teams that have won regular season titles and/or Stanley Cups with consistency unmatched in the history of the NHL.

Boston Bruins 1929-41

The Boston Bruins were such a disappointment to their fans through the forties, fifties, and sixties largely because in the thirties, they had been so very good. Indeed between 1926 and 1941, the Bruins finished in first place 10 times and won three Stanley Cups; they virtually dominated the NHL's American Division, capturing the title in 7 of the 12 years the division existed.

Boston's hockey heritage was founded on names such as Eddie Shore and Milt Schmidt, Cooney Weiland and Dit Clapper, Woody Dumart and Bobby Bauer, Tiny Thompson and Frank Brimsek, all of whom starred for the Bruins through the thirties.

In 1929-30, the Bruins swept to 38 victories in 44 games, including 14 in a row. They, more than any other team, capitalized on new rules permitting passing in all three zones. And while Weiland was leading the league in scoring with 73 points, goalie Thompson was permitting the fewest goals to the opposition. For Thompson it was just a hint of things to come: he would win the coveted Vezina Trophy four times, before being sold to the Detroit Red Wings eight years later.

Usually at or near the top, those Bruins were a strong, fast team that could both score goals and play defense. In Shore they had not only one of the league's premier players (who won the MVP trophy four times in six years) but also the dirtiest: in 1933 it was Shore who ended the career of Toronto's Ace Bailey with one wicked check—from behind.

In 1937, Art Ross assembled Boston's famed "Kraut Line": Schmidt at center with Dumart and Bauer on the wings. Three years later the trio finished 1-2-3 in league scoring. In 1938, Boston fans were stunned when Ross sent their favorite, Tiny Thompson, to Detroit. Ross knew what he was doing; he simply had to make room in the Bruins' nets for a rookie, Frank Brimsek. Brimsek turned in 10 shutouts in 41 games, and during one stretch did not give up a goal in 231 minutes and 54 seconds. Then Brimsek went on another binge and wasn't scored upon for 220 minutes, 47 seconds. (During each of the streaks, he recorded three shutouts.) He won the Vezina Trophy, Rookie of the Year, a berth on the All-Star team, and the nickname "Mr. Zero." Naturally, the Bruins won the NHL championship and the Stanley Cup.

Boston swept into the forties with two more NHL championships and, in 1941, a Cup victory, but after that it was downhill. The Boston Garden would remain sold out year after pitiful year, but the faithful wouldn't be rewarded with anything close to a comparable era until 25 years later, when superstars Bobby Orr and Phil Esposito led a revival.

Goalie Tiny Thompson in 1930 practice session

Left to right, Hitchman, Lane, Owens, and Shore of '29 Brui

Montreal Canadiens 1943-47

In Montreal they say *"Les Canadiens sont la,"* which means "The Canadiens are there." "There" is almost always first place, or very close to it. No other players have guzzled so much champagne from Lord Stanley's grand old cup as have *Les Candiens*.

Before the forties the Canadiens had known success with immortals Howie Morenz, Newsy Lalonde, Aurel Joliat, Georges Vezina, and George Hainsworth. The endeavors of these men and their mates inspired in Quebec the most rabid following in hockey. But as *Les Canadiens* cooled off in the thirties, so did their fans. It wasn't until the arrival of one of the game's greatest goal scorers, Maurice ("Rocket") Richard that those Forum fires blazed once more.

Richard first joined the Canadiens in 1942, but after scoring five goals in 16 games, he was suddenly gone for the rest of the season with a broken ankle. When Richard came back the next year, coach Dick Irvin placed him on a line with Toe Blake at center and Elmer Lach on left wing. "The Punch Line" ignited the Canadiens, who streaked to the NHL title, losing but 5 of 50 games, and then won the Cup in 9 games. Richard pumped in a record 12 goals, 5 in a 5-1 triumph over Toronto.

The Canadiens won four straight titles and two Stanley Cups. In 1944-45, Rocket Richard became the first player to score 50 goals in one season. Though the total was later equaled and then surpassed, he is still the only man to have scored 50 times in a 50-game season. At one point he scored 15 goals in nine games, including once again, 5 in one contest. Ten times he scored 2 or more goals the same night.

Richard had plenty of help from the rest of the club and particularly from his linemates on the Punch Line, which occupied the top three spots in NHL scoring at season's end. Lach won the Art Ross and Hart Trophies. Butch Bouchard, Kenny Reardon, and goalie Bill Durnan (who was to win the Vezina four years in a row, and six years in seven) all played important roles in the victory streak.

In 1946-47, the NHL established the bonus system for All-Star players and trophy winners—strictly, it seemed, for the Canadiens' benefit. No less than four Canadiens—Richard, Bouchard, Reardon, and Durnan—made the six-man All-Star team; Durnan became the first goalie to win four straight Vezinas, and Richard took the Hart. Montreal won its fourth championship in succession but lost to playoff-potent Toronto in the Cup finals.

Lach won another scoring title in 1947-48, and Richard joined him on the All-Star first team, but the Canadiens mysteriously slipped to fifth place and missed the playoffs. Dissolution of the dynasty? Hardly. Everyone knew the Canadiens would be back, and eight years later they were, better than ever.

The 1946 Stanley Cup champions

"The Punch Line:" left to right, Richard, Lach, and Blake

Toronto Maple Leafs 1942-51

The winner of an NHL regular season title today is the best team in a division over an arduous 78-game schedule. Ironically, however, a regular season champion has never won quite as much prestige as the Stanley Cup winners, who occasionally have been lesser teams that happened to get hot in the playoffs.

It seems the Cup brings out the best in some teams, the worst in others. With the exception of the Montreal Canadiens, no NHL team has been as productive in playoff competition as have the Toronto Maple Leafs. Since 1927, the Maple Leafs have won 11 Stanley Cups, 6 of which they captured during a 10-year span. The regular season championships of that era were largely the property of powerhouses from Montreal and Detroit. In 1947, '48 and '49, Toronto won three straight Cups (a record at the time). In 1950, the Leafs lost in the Cup semifinals to Detroit. Then they recaptured the Cup in 1951, their fourth Stanley Cup in five years.

The key members of that Toronto team, which won only one regular season championship, were wing Max Bentley, center Ted ("Teeder") Kennedy, defensemen Gus Mortson and Jim Thompson, and goalie Turk Broda, who was especially hard on Detroit's "Production Line" in the 1948 finals and '51 semifinals.

One of the most stirring Cup finals in history was the Toronto triumph over the Canadiens in 1951, when every game was decided in sudden death overtime. Toronto won the first 3-2 on Sid Smith's goal at 5:51 of overtime. Montreal took the second, also 3-2, on Rocket Richard's winner at 2:55 of overtime. Then the series moved to the Forum, where Kennedy won the third game, 2-1, at 4:47 of overtime. Harry Watson put Toronto on top three games

to one with an overtime goal at 5:15 for another 3-2 victory. In the fifth game, back in Maple Leaf Gardens, the Canadiens carried a 2-1 lead into the final minute. Toronto coach Joe Primeau pulled his goaltender, and Tod Sloan tied the game with only 32 seconds to go. Then a relatively unsung defenseman, Bill Barilko, who had neither a goal nor an assist in the series, scored at 2:53 of overtime, and the Leafs had their fourth Cup in five years. That 1951 Cup title was to be the last for the Maple Leafs for 11 years. Then abrasive, outspoken, balding general manager-coach Punch Imlach would be running the show, and Toronto would be at its playoff best once again.

Kenny Reardon

Turk Broda pushes puck away from Chicago.

Detroit Red Wings 1947-57

Until the 1947-48 season, the Detroit Red Wings had flown at comparatively low altitudes. They had finished in first place a few times and in 1937, 1938, and 1943 succeeded in winning both their league title and the Stanley Cup. But those were modest achievements compared to those of their dynasty to come.

In 1947-48, the Wings finished second to Toronto in the regular season and lost to the Maple Leafs in the Cup finals. Still, it didn't take an expert to appreciate the extraordinary happenings down at Grand River and McGraw in Motor City. A new line had been assembled—Sid Abel at center and Gordie Howe and Ted Lindsay on the wings—soon to become known as ''the Production Line.''

Soon Detroit was off on a victory rampage that numbed the rest of the NHL. Even powerful Montreal found itself outclassed, relegated to second place season after season despite its nucleus of stars who had developed in the forties. (In 1954-55, for example, the Canadiens lost only 18 games but still finished second to the Red Wings, who lost only 17 and then reemphasized their supremacy by defeating Montreal for the Stanley Cup.) From 1948-49 through 1956-57, Detroit finished in first place a record seven times in a row and eight times in nine years. Four times they celebrated with Stanley Cups.

The names of players on those devastating teams became household words. In addition to Howe, Lindsay, and Abel, there were annual All-Stars such as Red Kelly and Terry Sawchuk. Leo Reise, Marcel Pronovost, Alex Delvecchio, and Glenn Hall won recognition too, despite the fact that the stars' achievements outshone theirs.

In 1949-50, when the Production Line finished 1-2-3 in league scoring, manager Jack Adams observed, ''Those guys could score goals in their sleep.''

A year later Adams brought up a rookie named Sawchuk, and the kid responded with a 1.98 goals-against average and 11 shutouts. The Wings became the first team in history to produce more than 100 points (101 to be exact) in the league standings. The next year Detroit finished with an even 100 points, 22 ahead of second-place Montreal. In the playoffs Sawchuk permitted a total of only five goals, and Howe and Abel bombarded the Canadiens with five goals each in the finals. The Wings reached the champagne in back-to-back, four-game sweeps.

A youngster, Alex Delvecchio, replaced Abel between Howe and Lindsay in 1952-53, and again Detroit roared to the NHL title, becoming the first team ever to win five in succession. In 1954-55, Howe became the first player to win the scoring championship four years in a row, and the Red Wings made it an unprecedented seven championships in seven years. Naturally, they added the Cup.

By now there were rumblings in Montreal. In 1955-56, a young Canadiens team collected 100 points in winning the NHL title by 24 over the second-place Wings. Then Montreal took the Stanley Cup. Detroit captured the championship the next year but bowed out in the Cup semifinals and thereafter disappeared among the also-rans. Since 1956-57, Detroit has finished first only in 1964-65, when Sid Abel, then a coach, persuaded ex-linemate Lindsay to leave retirement for a last nostalgic fling with him and Gordie Howe.

Aggressive Lindsay battles Fern Flaman (12) in Toronto cre

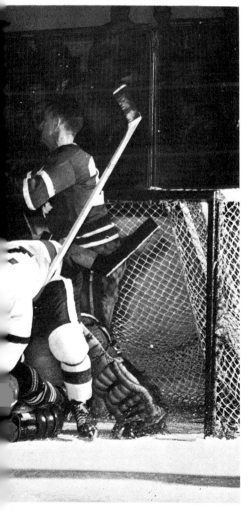

Production Line:" left to right, Howe, Abel, and Lindsay

Montreal Canadiens 1955-

The Montreal Canadiens began their second dynasty with the 1955-56 season, when they finished with 100 points in the league standings for the first time in their history. Far behind in second place, with 76 points, were the mighty Detroit Red Wings, who knew better than anyone else that their days at the top were numbered. These Canadiens were fast, talented, and young, with new heroes such as Jean Beliveau, Boom Boom Geoffrion, Doug Harvey, and Bert Olmstead. The Candadiens skewered even the most ferocious opposition in the Canadiens' den, the Montreal Forum, and were almost as devastating on the road. And the Rocket—well, 10 years had hardly drained him. He still perennially made the All-Star team.

With Toe Blake now behind the bench, the Canadiens were a storming, swarming team that strafed the opposing goal from every angle and guarded its own like a fort. Harvey quarterbacked a power play that scored so frequently it eventually forced the league to change its rules to permit a short-handed team to regain its penalized player after it had been scored on.

The Montreal team that soared to the top, pausing only when Detroit won the NHL title in 1956-57, was fiercely proud. When every other team was out to get them, hoping to catch them on an off night, the Canadiens continued to find the strength and stamina to win. Jacques Plante recalls, "Toe Blake used to tell us, 'Second place for the Canadiens is as bad as last place for any other team.' So you had the pressure of winning every game. You were the best and every other team played a hundred percent against you. If we knew we had a key game coming up, we could give more than a hundred percent. That's why we stayed on top."

Montreal regulars had no choice but to be up for every game; if they weren't, they might be gone for the next. In 1955-56, after they had finished second to Detroit by only two points the year before, no less than three young-sters (Jean Guy Talbot, Claude Provost, and Richard's younger brother, Henri) stuck with the Montreal team, although it was already loaded with talent. That year the Canadiens first unseated the Red Wings and won their first of five straight Stanley Cups. Montreal regulars have been conscious of what's growing down on the farm ever since.

From 1957-58 through 1962-62, the Canadiens led the league, so in seven years, they swept six titles. From 1956 through 1960, the Stanley Cup was theirs alone. (When Blake retired in 1968, admitting that his intense desire to win had left his nerves and disposi-tion in disarray, he had driven the Canadiens to nine titles and eight Cups in 13 years.)

Great coach though he was, Blake had the prime ingredient for producing a dynasty: talent. From 1955 through 1961, Montreal had five scoring champions—Beliveau once, Dickie Moore and Geoffrion twice each. In 1961, Geoffrion matched Richard's record 50 goals. Plante won the Vezina a record five times in a row from 1956 through 1960. Harvey took the James Norris Trophy as the NHL's best defenseman a record seven times (six of those times with Montreal, the last time with New York). Beliveau won the Hart Trophy in 1956, Geoffrion in '61, Plante in '62, Beliveau again in '64. Montreal had the Rookie of the Year in 1959 (Ralph Backstrom), 1962 (Bobby Rousseau), and 1964, Jacques Laper-riere). From 1954-55 through 1960-61, the Canadiens twice placed four players on the All-Star team, and in two other years placed three.

The winning tradition carried through the sixties to the present. In the sixties the Canadiens finished in first place seven times and won five Cups. Only the names have changed; now it is Yvan Cournoyer, Frank and Peter Mahovlich, Jacques Lemaire, Guy Lapointe, Henri Richard, and Laperriere who are keeping the Canadiens superior. (Before he quit in 1973, when the Canadiens refused to renegotiate his contract, Ken Dryden was one of the finest goaltenders in hockey.)

In 1973-74, the Boston Bruins finished first in the East Division, and then the Canadiens took over. For the next eight seasons they were their division's leader. Although they relinquished the Stanley Cup to the Philadelphia Flyers in 1974 and in 1975 they didn't relinquish it for very long. With Kenneth Dryden back in goal, Guy Lafleur, Guy Lapointe, Jacques Lemaire, Larry Robinson, Serge Savard, and Stephen Shutt from their 1973 Stanley Cup-winning club, along with newcomers Raymond Chartraw, Robert Gainey, Douglas Jarvis, Yvon

Bower, Stanley (26), and Horton defend the Cup.

Lambert, Douglas Risebrough, and Mario Tremblay, the Montreal Canadiens rolled to four consecutive Stanley Cup triumphs.

And so what began back in the forties continues today, making a truism of that little French phrase, *"Les Canadiens sont la."*

Toronto Maple Leafs 1959-67

Major Conn Smythe, who gave the Toronto Maple Leafs their name, their colors, and their beautiful home on Carlton Street, also instilled in them a passion for the Stanley Cup. George ("Punch") Imlach, who became Toronto's general manager and coach in 1959, shared the passion. He liked to finish in first place, but he was perfectly willing to shoot for the Cup and not lose sleep over the regular season championship.

Imlach's priorities are reflected in his record at Toronto. In his 10 years, the Leafs missed the playoffs only once, reached the finals twice, and won four Stanley Cups, including three straight, in 1962, '63, and '64. A conservative, close-checking style is recommended procedure in playoff competition, and under Imlach the Leafs practiced it all year long. It wasn't the most exciting style in the league—"clutch and grab," many called it—but from 1959-60 through 1962-63, it proved to be a workable strategy for regular season play as well as the playoffs. The Leafs finished first once and second to mighty Montreal three times.

With the exception of Frank Mahovlich and Red Kelly, Toronto didn't have much firepower. But forwards George Armstrong, Bob Pulford, Dave Keon, and Kelly, a former defenseman and a superior two-way player, were all marvelous forecheckers. If the opposition overcame their efforts, it paid its dues in the Toronto zone, where one of the finest defensive foursomes in the history of the game—Carl Brewer and Bobby Baun, Tim Horton and Allan Stanley—were masters at jarring an attacker loose from the puck at the most opportune moment. Then, when the Leafs recovered the puck, they didn't give it back before dumping it on goal and forcing the opposition to reform its attack.

"People accused Toronto of going out and getting a one-goal lead and then sitting on it," Imlach recalls. "Well I don't think we were *that* defensive-minded, but we did sit on leads. And why not? The name of the game is winning, isn't it?"

In 1962-63, Toronto won the regular season title by one point over the Chicago Black Hawks, who were laden with stars Bobby Hull, Stan Mikita, Pierre Pilote, and Glenn Hall. The Maple Leafs had defeated the Hawks in the Stanley Cup finals the previous spring. Then in 1963 and '64, the Red Wings were their victims.

The Leafs finished fourth and bowed out in the 1965 Cup semifinals. The following year they were third, but once again lost in the semifinals. Convinced by now that the Leafs were too old, all Toronto demanded that the club be shaken up. Imlach was the only one who wasn't convinced, however, and as general manager, he refused to revamp his team. In 1966-67 the Leafs once again finished third, then rewarded Imlach's stubborn faith in them by winning their fourth Cup in six years in a stirring final against Montreal. On the ice in the last seconds of that deciding game were Kelly, Armstrong, Pulford, Horton, Baun, and goalie Johnny Bower—the very players the fans had claimed had outlived their usefulness. It was, for Imlach and his aging Leafs, the most satisfying Cup of all.

New York Islanders 1977–

The possibility that the New York Islanders would someday be a great club was first recognized in the statistics for 1973-74. That season they had 247 goals-against—100 fewer than the previous season. In 1974-75 they reduced the number further to 221, and scored and additional 82 more goals to finish third in the Lester Patrick Division.

In the meantime, the Islanders were also acquiring a solid core of god players—Michael Bossy, Robert Bourne, clark Gillies, L. Wayne Merrick, T. Robert Nystrom, Denis Potvin, Bill Smith, and Bryan Trottier. With these players and with the astute coaching of Alger Arbour they took the Lester Patrick Division title in both 1977-78 and 1978-79. The Islanders were now a club to be reckoned with.

Despite the fact that the Islanders finished second to the Philadelphia Flyers in the Lester Patrick division in 1979-80, they went on to win the Stanlyey Cup. They disposed of the Los Angles Kings quite handily, winning the first game 8-1 and the fourth game 6-0. In the quater finals they found the Boston Bruins a little tougher when they were forced to go to overtime to win three of the games. In the semifinals, they defeated the Buffalo Sabres four

games to two. In the final series the Islanders opposed the Philadelphia Flyers and, although Philadelphia won two games by scored of 8-3 and 6-3, the Isalnders won the other four., two of them in overtime.

In 1981, the Toronto Maple Leafs gave the Islanders little trouble in their first series. They scored 20 goals while Toronto was scoring 4. In the quarterfinals the Islanders defeated the Edmonton Oilers after six games. In the semifinals they handled the New York Rangers quite easily in four straight games—scoring 22 goals to the Rangers' eight. The Minnesota North Stars were no problem in the finals and the New York Islanders had won their second consecutive Stanley Cup.

Nineteen eight-two saw the Islanders facing the Pittsburgh Penguins in their first series, and the stubborn Penguins forced the series to the limit. The Islanders won the first two games at Uniondale, New York by the scores of 8-1 and 7-2. But at Pittsburgh the Penguins thrashed back and won the next two games 2-1 and 5-2. In the Lester Patrick Division final the New York Rangers weren't as easy as they had been the previous season, with the series going to six games. In the Prince of Wales Conference final they disposed

of the Quebec Nordiques in four games and did likewise to the Vancouver Canucks, to win their third consecutive Stanley Cup.

In their first series in 1983, the New York Islanders eliminated the Washington Capitals and then ran up against the New York Rangers. The Rangers again forced the series to six games. Next came the boston Bruins and another six games before they were gone. The Edmonton Oilers followed, and the Islanders romped over them in four straight games. They had now won their fourth consecutive Stanley Cup, and indeed become one of hockey's great clubs.

All-Star Teams
By Decade
1930-40
G—Charlie Gardiner, Chicago
D—Eddie Shore, Boston
D—King Clancy, Toronto
C—Frank Boucher, New York
LW—Harvey Jackson, Toronto
RW—Bill Cook, New York

1940-50
G-Bill Durnan, Montreal
D—Earl Seibert, Chicago
D—Jack Stewart, Detroit
C—Elmer Lach, Montreal
LW—Doug Bentley, Chicago
RW—Maurice Richard, Montreal

1950-60
G—Terry Sawchuk, Detroit
D—Doug Harvey, Montreal
D—Red Kelly, Detroit
C—Jean Beliveau, Montreal
LW—Ted Lindsay, Detroit
RW—Gordie Howe, Detroit

1960-1970
G—Glenn Hall, Chicago and St. Louis
D—Bobby Orr, Boston
D—Pierre Pilote, Chicago
C—Phil Esposito, Boston
LW—Bobby Hull, Chicago
RW—Gordie Howe, Detroit

1970-1980
G — Ken Dryden, Montreal
D — Denis Potvin, New York Islanders
D — Brad Park, Boston
C — Phil Esposito, Boston
LW — Bill Barber, Philadelphia
RW — Guy Lafleur, Montreal

ottier controls the tempo for Islanders.

Arenas

National Hockey League Arenas

Team	Arena	Capacity
Boston Bruins	Boston Garden	14,673
Buffalo Sabres	Memorial Audiorium	16,433 *
Calgary Flames	The Sadledome	16,200 *
Chicago Black Hawks	Chicago Stadim	17,263
Detroit Red Wings	Joe Louis Sports Arena	19,275
Edmonton Oilers	Northlands Coliseum	17,300
Hartford Whalers	Civic Center Coliseum	14,557
Los Angeles Kings	The Forum	16,005
Minnesota North Stars	Met Center	15,184
Montreal Canadiens	Montreal Forum	16,074
New Jersey Devils	Byrne Meadowlands Arna	19,051
New York Islanders	Nassau Veterans Memorial Coliseum	15,230
New York Rangers	Madison Square Garden	17,500
Philadelphia Flyers	The Spectrum	17,147
Pittsburgh Penguins	Civic Arena	16,033
Quebec Noridques	Quebec Coliseum	15,250
St. Louis Blues	The Arena	17,967
Toronto Maple Leafs	Maple Leaf Gardens	16,182
Vancouver Canucks	Pacific Coliseum	15,613
Washington Capitals	Capital Center	18,130
Winnipeg Jets	Winnipeg Arena	15,250

Dates and Results of First Game Played in Each Arena

Boston Garden (Boston) November 20, 1928; Boston 0, Montreal 1

Memorial Auditorium (Buffalo) October 15, 1970; Buffalo 0, Montreal 3

The Sadledome (Calgary) October 15, 1983; Calgary 3, Edmonton 4

Chicago Stadium (Chicago) December 15, 1929; Chicago 3, Pittsburgh 1

Joe Louis Sports Stadium (Detroit) December 27, 1979; Detroit 2, St. Louis 3

Northlands Colisum (Edmonton) October 13, 1979; Edmonton 3, Detroit 3

Civic Center Coliseum (Hartford) February 6, 1980; Hartford 7, Los Angeles 3

The Forum (Inglewood, California) December 30, 1967; Los Angeles 0, Phildalephia 2

Met Center (Bloominton, Minnesota) October 21, 1967; Minnesota 3, California 1

Montreal Forum (Montreal) November 29, 1924; Montreal 7, Toronto 1

Byrne Meadowlands Arena (East Rutherford, New Jersey) October 5. 1982; New Jersey 3, Pittsburgh 3

Nassau Veterans Memorial Colisuem (Uniondale, New York) February 19, 1968; Rangers 3, phi∗ephia 1

The Spectrum (Philadelphia) October 19, 1967; Philadelphia 1, Pittsburgh 0

Civic Arena (Pittsburgh) October 11, 1967; Pittsburgh 1, Montreal 2

Quebec Coliseum (Quebec City) October 10, 1979; Quebec 3, Atlanta 5

The Arean (St. louis) October 11, 1967; St. Louis 2, Minnesota 2

Madison Square Garden in 1974

Madison Square Garden, vintage 1931

Maple Leaf Gardens (Toronto) November 12, 1931; Toronto 1, Chicago 2

Pacific Coliseum (Vancouver) October 9, 1970; Vancouver 1, Los Angeles 3

Capital Center (Landover, Maryland) October 15, 1974; Washington 1, Los Angeles 1

Winnipeg Arena (Winnipeg) October 14, 1979; Winnipeg 4, Colorado 2

Maple Leaf Gardens

Public dining room in Buffalo's "Aud"

Rule Book

REPRINTED WITH THE PERMISSION
OF THE NATIONAL HOCKEY LEAGUE

RULE BOOK INDEX

SECTION ONE ....THE RINK
SECTION TWO ....TEAMS
SECTION THREE ....EQUIPMENT
SECTION FOUR ....PENALTIES
SECTION FIVE ....OFFICIALS
SECTION SIX ....PLAYING RULES
(alphabetical)

Jockeying for position—no penalty.

SIGNALS

BOARDING

Pounding the closed fist of one hand into the open palm of the other hand.

CHARGING

Rotating clenched fists around one another in front of chest.

ELBOWING

Tapping the elbow of the "whistle hand" with the opposite hand.

CROSS-CHECKING

A forward and backward motion with both fists clenched extending from the chest.

DELAYED CALL-ING OF PENALTY

Referee extends arm and points to penalized player.

HIGH-STICKING

Holding both fists, clenched, one above the other at the side of the head.

HOLDING

Clasping the wrists of the "whistle hand" well in front of the chest.

HOOKING

A tugging motion with both arms, as if pulling something toward the stomach.

ICING

Linesman's arms folded across the upper chest.

INTERFERENCE

Crossed arms stationary in front of chest with fists closed.

KNEEING

Slapping the knee with palm of hand while keeping both skates on the ice.

MISCONDUCT

Place both hands on hips.

SPEARING

A jabbing motion with both hands thrust out in front of the body.

TRIPPING

Striking the right leg with the right hand below the knee, keeping both skates on the ice.

ROUGHING

A thrusting motion with the arm extending from the side.

SLOW WHISTLE

Arm in which whistle is not held extended above head. If play returns to neutral zone without stoppage of play arm is drawn down the instant the puck crosses the line.

UNSPORTSMAN-LIKE CONDUCT

Use both hands to form a "T" in front of the chest.

SLASHING

A chopping motion with the edge of one hand across the opposite forearm.

WASH-OUT

Both arms swung laterally at shoulder level with palms down. When used by the linesman it means no icing or no off-side.

278

SECTION ONE—THE RINK

Rule 1. Rink

The game of "Ice Hockey" shall be played on an ice surface known as a "RINK."

(NOTE) *There shall be no markings on the ice except as provided under these rules without the express written permission of the League.*

Rule 2. Dimensions of Rink

(a)

The official size of the rink shall be two hundred feet long and eighty-five feet wide. The corners shall be rounded in the arc of a circle with radius of twenty-eight feet.

The rink shall be surrounded by a wooden or fibreglass wall or fence known as the "boards" which shall extend not less that forty inches and not more than forty-eight inches above the level of the ice surface. The ideal height of the boards above the ice surface shall be forty-two inches. Except for the official markings provided for in these rules the entire playing surface and the boards shall be white in color except the kick plate at the bottom of the board which shall be light blue or light yellow in color.

Any variations from any of the foregoing dimensions shall require official authorization by the League.

(b)

The boards shall be constructed in such manner that the surface facing the ice shall be smooth and free of any obstruction or any object that could cause injury to players.

All doors giving access to the playing surface must swing away from the ice surface.

All glass, wire or other types of protective screens and gear used to hold them in position shall be mounted on the boards on the side away from the playing surface.

Rule 3. Goal Posts and Nets

(a)

Ten feet from each end of the rink and in the center of a red line two inches wide, drawn completely across the width of the ice and continued vertically up the side of the boards, regulation goal posts and nets shall be set in such manner as to remain stationary during the progress of a game. The goal posts shall be kept in position by means of metal rods or pipes affixed in the ice or floor and projecting a minimum of eight inches above the ice surface.

Where the length of the playing surface exceeds two hundred feet the goal line and goal posts may be placed not more that fifteen feet from the end of the rink.

(b)

The goal posts shall be of approved design and material, extending vertically four feet above the surface of the ice and set six feet apart measured from the inside of the posts. A crossbar of the same material as the goal posts shall extend from the top of one post to the top of the other.

(NOTE) *For League games the "NHL Official Goal Frame and Net" are approved and adopted. The design and specifications set out in the Plan of Goal printed in this Rule Book are official.*

(c)

There shall be attached to each goal frame a net of approved design made of white nylon cord which shall be draped in such a manner as to prevent the puck coming to rest on the outside of it.

A skirt of heavy white nylon fabric or heavy-weight white canvas shall be laced around the "3" base plate of the goal frame in such a way as to protect the net from being cut or broken. This skirt shall not project more than one inch above the base plate.

(NOTE) *The frame of the goal including the small "3" attached to the top crossbar shall be draped with a nylon mesh net so as to completely enclose the back of the frame. The net shall be made of three-ply twisted twine (O.130-inch diameter) or equivalent braided twine of multifilament white nylon with an appropriate tensile strength of 700 pounds. The size of the mesh shall be two and one-half inches (inside measurement) from each knot to each diagonal knot when fully stretched. Knotting shall be made so as to ensure no sliding of the twine. The net shall be laced to the frame with medium white nylon cord no smaller in size than No. 21.*

(d)

The goal posts and crossbar shall be painted in red and all other exterior surfaces shall be painted in white.

(e)

The red line, two inches wide, between the goal posts on the ice and extended completely across the rink, shall be known as the "GOAL LINE."

(f)

The Goal area, enclosed by the goal line and the base of the goal, shall be painted white.

Rule 4. Goal Crease

(a)

In front of each goal a "GOAL CREASE" area shall be marked by a red line two inches in width.

(b)

The goal crease shall be laid out as follows: One foot from the outside of each goal post, lines four feet in length and two inches in width shall be drawn at right angles to the goal line and the points of these lines farthest from the goal line shall be joined by another line, two inches in width.

(c)

The goal crease area shall include all the space outlined by the crease lines and extending vertically four feet to the level of the top of the goal frame.

Rule 5. Division of Ice Surface

(a)

The ice area between the two goals shall be divided into three parts by lines, twelve inches in width, and blue in color, drawn sixty feet out from the goal lines, and extended completely across the rink, parallel with the goal lines, and continued vertically up the side of boards.

(b)

That portion of the ice surface in which the goal is situated shall be called the "DEFENDING ZONE" of the team defending that goal; the central portion shall be known as the "NEUTRAL ZONE," and the portion farthest from the defended goal as the "ATTACKING ZONE."

(c)

There shall also be a line, twelve inches in width, and red in color, drawn completely across the rink in center ice, parallel with the goal lines and continued vertically up the side of the boards, known as the "CENTER LINE." This line shall contain at regular intervals markings of a uniform distinctive design which will easily distinguish it from the two blue lines . . . the outer edges of which must be continuous.

Rule 6. Center Ice Spot and Circle

A circular blue spot, twelve inches in diameter, shall be marked exactly in the center of the rink: and with this spot as a center a circle of fifteen feet radius shall be marked with a blue line two inches in width.

Rule 7. Face-off Spots in Neutral Zone

Two red spots two feet in diameter shall be marked on the ice in the Neutral Zone five feet from each blue line. The spots shall be forty-four feet apart and each shall be a uniform distance from the adjacent boards.

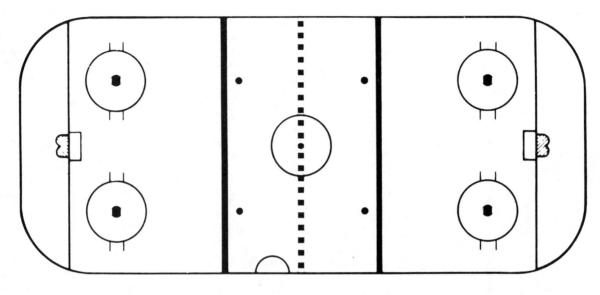

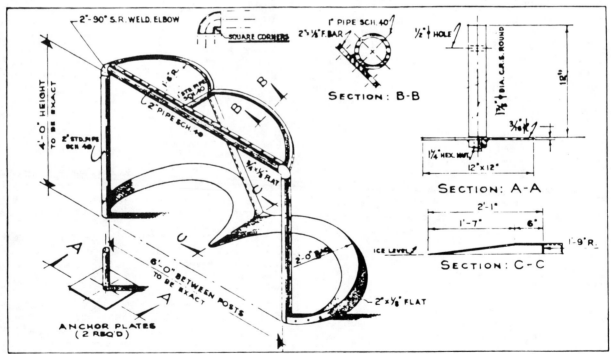

SQUARE CORNERS

1" PIPE SCH. 40
2½ × ⅛ F. BAR

SECTION: B-B

2"-90° S.R. WELD. ELBOW

2" PIPE SCH. 40

4'-0" HEIGHT
TO BE EXACT

2" STD. PIPE
SCH. 40

¾ × ½ FLAT

2'-0" RAD.

6'-0" BETWEEN POSTS
TO BE EXACT

ANCHOR PLATES
(2 REQ'D)

2" × ⅛" FLAT

½" ⌀ HOLE

1⅜" DIA. C.R.S. ROUND

12"

3/16"R

1¼ HEX NUT
12" × 12"

SECTION: A-A

2'-1"
1'-7"   6"
ICE LEVEL

1'-9" R.

SECTION: C-C

Rule 8. End Zone Face-off Spots and Circles

(a)

In both end zones and on both sides of each goal, red face-off spots and circles shall be marked on the ice. The face-off spots shall be two feet in diameter. Within the face-off spot, draw two parallel lines three inches from the top and bottom of the spot. The area within the two lines shall be painted red, the remainder shall be painted white.

The circles shall be two inches wide with a radius of fifteen feet from the center of the face-off spots. At the outer edge of both sides of each face-off circle and parallel to the goal line shall be marked two red lines, two inches wide and two feet in length and three feet apart.

(b)

The location of the face-offs shall be fixed in the following manner:

Along a line of twenty feet from each goal line and parallel to it, mark two points twenty-two feet on both sides of the straight line joining the centers of the two goals. Each such point shall be the center of a face-off spot and circle.

Rule 9. Players' Bench

(a)

Each rink shall be provided with seats or benches for the use of players of both teams and the accommodations provided including benches and doors shall be uniform for both teams. Such seats or benches shall have accommodation for at least fourteen persons of each team, and shall be placed immediately alongside the ice, in the Neutral Zone, as near to the center of the rink as possible with doors opening in the Neutral Zone and convenient to the dressing rooms.

Each players' bench should be twenty-four feet in length and when situated in the spectator area they shall be separated from the spectators by a protective glass of sufficient height so as to afford the necessary protection of the players. The players' benches shall be on the same side of the playing surface opposite the penalty bench and should be separated by a substantial distance.

(NOTE) *Those buildings that were built prior to the introduction of this Rule and in which players' benches were installed on opposite sides of the rink are exempt from this Rule.*

Where physically possible each Players' Bench shall have two doors opening in the Neutral Zone and all doors opening to the playing surface shall be constructed so that they swing inward.

(b)

None but players in uniform, Manager, Coach and Trainer shall be permitted to occupy the benches so provided.

Rule 10. Penalty Bench

(a)

Each rink must be provided with benches or seats to be known as the "PENALTY BENCH." These benches or seats must be capable of accommodating a total of ten persons including the Penalty Timekeepers. Separate penalty benches shall be provided for each team and they shall be situated on opposite sides of the Timekeeper's area. The penalty bench(es) must be situated in the Neutral Zone.

(b)

On the ice immediately in front of the Penalty Timekeeper's seat there shall be marked in red on the ice a semi-circle of ten feet radius and two inches in width which shall be known as the "REFEREE'S CREASE."

(c)

Each "Penalty Bench" shall be protected from the spectator area by means of a glass partition which shall be not less than five feet above the height of the boards.

Rule 11. Signal and Timing Devices

(a)

Each rink must be provided with a siren, or other suitable sound device, for the use of Timekeepers.

(b)

Each rink shall be provided with some form of electrical clock for the purpose of keeping the spectators, players and game officials accurately informed as to all time elements at all stages of the game including the time remaining to be played in any period and the time remaining to be served by at least five penalized players on each team.

Time recording for both game time and penalty time shall show time remaining to be played or served.

(c)

Behind each goal electrical lights shall be set up for the use of the Goal Judges. A red light will signify the scoring of a goal. Where automatic lights are available, a green light will signify the end of a period or a game.

(NOTE) *A goal cannot be scored when a green light is showing.*

Rule 12. Police Protection

All clubs shall provide adequate police or other protection for all players and officials at all times.

The Referee shall report to the President any failure of this protection observed by him or reported to him with particulars of such failure.

SECTION TWO—TEAMS

Rule 13. Composition of Team

(a)

A team shall be composed of six players, who shall be under contract to the club they represent.

(b)

Each player and each goalkeeper listed in the line-up of each team shall wear an individual identifying number at least ten inches high on the back of his sweater and, in addition, each player and goalkeeper shall wear his surname in full, in block letters 3 inches high, across the back of his sweater at shoulder height.

All players of each team shall be dressed uniformly in conformity with approved design and color of their helmets, sweaters, short pants, stockings and boots. Any player or goalkeeper not complying with this provision shall not be permitted to participate in the game.

Each Member Club shall design and wear distinctive and contrasting uniforms for their home and road games, no parts of which shall be interchangeable except the pants.

Rule 14. Captain of Team

(a)

One Captain shall be appointed by each team, and he alone shall have the privilege of discussing with the Referee any questions relating to interpretation of rules which may arise during the progress of a game. He shall wear the letter "C," approximately three inches in height and in contrasting color, in a conspicuous position on the front of his sweater.

(b)

The Referee and Official Scorer shall be advised prior to the start of each game, the name of the Captain of the team and the designated substitute.

(c)

No goalkeeper shall be entitled to exercise the privilege of Captain.

(d)

Only the Captain, when invited to do so by the Referee, shall have the privilege of discussing any point relating to the interpretation of rules. Any Captain or player who comes off the bench and makes any protest or

Goalkeeper's equipment may be used by him only.

intervention with the Officials for any purpose must be assessed a misconduct penalty in addition to a minor penalty under Rule 42. (b) —Abuse of Officials.

A complaint about a penalty is NOT a matter "relating to the interpretation of the rules" and a minor penalty shall be imposed against any Captain or other player making such a complaint.

(e)

No playing Coach or playing Manager shall be permitted to act as Captain.

Rule 15. Players in Uniform

(a)

At the beginning of each game the Manager or Coach of each team shall list the players and goalkeepers who shall be eligible to play in the game. Not more than eighteen players, exclusive of goalkeepers, shall be permitted.

(b)

A list of names and numbers of all eligible players and goalkeepers must be handed to the Referee or Official Scorer before the game, and no change shall be permitted in the list or addition thereto shall be permitted after the commencement of the game.

(c)

Each team shall be allowed one goalkeeper on the ice at one time. The goalkeeper may be removed and another "player" substituted. Such substitute shall not be permitted the privileges of the goalkeeper.

(d)

Each team shall have on its bench, or on a chair immediately beside the bench, a substitute Goalkeeper who shall at all times be fully dressed and equipped ready to play.

(e)

Except when both goalkeepers are incapacitated, no player on the playing roster in that game shall be permitted to wear the equipment of the goalkeeper.

(f)

In regular League and Play-off games if both listed goalkeepers are incapacitated, that team shall be entitled to dress and play any available goalkeeper who is eligible. No delay shall be permitted in taking his position in the goal, and he shall be permitted a two-minute warm-up. However, the warm-up is not permitted in the event a goalkeeper is substituted for a penalty shot.

(NOTE) *The two-minute warm-up for a substitute goalkeeper shall be limited to one warm-up per game per goalkeeper.*

(g)

The Referee shall report to the President for disciplinary action any delay in making a substitution of goalkeepers.

Rule 16. Starting Line-Up

(a)

Prior to the start of the game, at the request of the Referee, the Manager or Coach of the visiting team is required to name the starting line-up to the Referee or the Official Scorer. At any time in the game at the request of the Referee, made to the Captain, the visiting team must place a playing line-up on the ice and promptly commence play.

(b)

Prior to the start of the game the Manager or Coach of the home team, having been advised by the Official Scorer or the Referee the names of the starting line-up of the visiting team, shall name the starting line-up ofthe home team which information shall be conveyed by the Official Scorer or the Referee to the Coach of the visiting team.

(c)

No change in the starting line-up of either team as given to the Referee or Official Scorer, or in the playing line-up on the ice, shall be made until the game is actually in progress. For an infraction of this rule a bench minor penalty shall be imposed upon the offending team, provided such infraction is called to the attention of the Referee before the second face-off in the first period takes place.

(d)

Following the stoppage of play the visiting team shall promptly place a line-up on the ice ready for play and no substitution shall be made from that time until play has been resumed. The home team may then make any desired substitution which does not result in the delay of the game.

If there is any undue delay by either team in changing lines the Referee shall order the offending team or teams to take their positions immediately and not permit a line change.

(NOTE) *When a substitution has been made under the above rule no additional substitution may be made until play commences.*

(e)

The Referee shall give the Visiting Team a reasonable amount of time to make their change after which he shall put up his hand to indicate that no further change shall be made by the Visiting Club. At this point, the Home Team may change immediately. Any attempt by the Visiting Team to make a change after the Referee's signal shall result in the assessment of a bench minor penalty for delay of game.

Rule 17. Equalizing of Teams
DELETED

Rule 18. Change of Players

(a)

Players may be changed at any time from the players' bench, provided that the player or players leaving the ice shall always be at the players' bench and out of the play before any change is made.

A goalkeeper may be changed for another player at any time under the conditions set out in this section.

(NOTE 1) *When a goalkeeper leaves his goal area and proceeds to his players' bench for the purpose of substituting another player, the rear Linesman shall be responsible to see that the substitution made is not illegal by reason of the premature departure of the substitute from the bench (before the goalkeeper is within ten feet of the bench). If the substitution is made prematurely, the Linesman shall stop the play immediately by blowing his whistle unless the non-offending team has possession of the puck in which event the stoppage will be delayed until the puck*

changes hands. There shall be no time penalty to the team making the premature substitution but the resulting face-off will take place on the center "face-off spot."

(NOTE 2) *The referee shall request that the public address announcer make the following announcement: "Play has been stopped due to premature entry of a player from the players' bench." If in the course of making a substitution the player entering the game plays the puck with his stick, skates or hands or who checks or makes any physical contact with an opposing player while the retiring player is actually on the ice then the infraction of "too many men on the ice" will be called.*

If in the course of a substitution either the player entering the play or the player retiring is struck by the puck accidentally the play will not be stopped and no penalty will be called.

(b)

If by reason of insufficient playing time remaining, or by reason of penalties already imposed, a bench minor penalty is imposed for deliberate illegal substitution (too many men on the ice) which cannot be served in its entirety within the legal playing time, a penalty shot shall be awarded against the offending team.

(c)

A player serving a penalty on the penalty bench, who is to be changed after the penalty has been served, must proceed at once by way of the ice and be at his own players' bench before any change can be made.

For any violation of this rule a bench minor penalty shall be imposed.

Rule 19. Injured Players

(a)

When a player, other than a goalkeeper, is injured or compelled to leave the ice during a game, he may retire from the game and be replaced by a substitute, but play must continue without the teams leaving the ice.

(b)

If a goalkeeper sustains an injury or becomes ill he must be ready to resume play immediately or be replaced by a substitute goalkeeper and NO additional time shall be allowed by the referee for the purpose of enabling the injured or ill goalkeeper to resume his position. (See also Section (d).)

(c)

The Referee shall report to the President for disciplinary action any delay in making a goalkeeper substitution.

The substitute goalkeeper shall be subject to the regular rules governing goalkeepers and shall be entitled to the same privileges.

(d)

When a substitution for the regular goalkeeper has been made, such regular goalkeeper shall not resume his position until the first stoppage of play thereafter.

(e)

If a penalized player has been injured he may proceed to the dressing room without the necessity of taking a seat on the penalty bench. If the injured player receives a minor penalty the penalized team shall immediately put a substitute player without change. If the injured player receives a major penalty the penalized team shall place a substitute player on the penalty bench before the penalty expires and no other replacement for the penalized player shall be permitted to enter the game except from the penalty bench. For violation of this rule a bench minor penalty shall be imposed.

The penalized player who has been injured and been replaced on the penalty bench shall not be eligible to play until his penalty has expired.

(f)

When a player is injured so that he cannot continue play or go to his bench, the play shall not be stopped until the injured player's team has

secured possession of the puck; if the player's team is in possession of the puck at the time of injury, play shall be stopped immediately, unless his team is in a scoring position.

(NOTE) *In the case where it is obvious that a player has sustained a serious injury the Referee and/or Linesman may stop the play immediately.*

(g)

When play has been stopped by the Referee or Linesman due to an injured player, such player must be substituted for immediately (except goalkeeper).

If when the attacking team has control of the puck in its attacking zone, play is stopped by reason of any injury to a player on the defending team, the face-off shall take place in the defending team's end zone face-off spot.

SECTION THREE—EQUIPMENT

Rule 20. Sticks

(a)

The sticks shall be made of wood or other material approved by the Rules Committee, and must not have any projections. Adhesive tape of any color may be wrapped around the stick at any place for the purpose of reinforcement or to improve control of the puck. In the case of a goalkeeper's stick, there shall be a knob of white tape or some other protective material approved by the League not less than one-half inch (½") thick at the top of the shaft.

(b)

No stick shall exceed fifty-eight inches (58") in length from heel to the end of the shaft nor more than twelve and one-half inches (12½") from the heel to the end of the blade.

The blade of the stick shall not be more than three inches in width at any point nor less than two inches. All edges of the blade shall be bevelled. The curvature of the blade of the stick shall be restricted in such a way that the distance of a perpendicular line measured from a straight line drawn from any point at the heel to the end of the blade to the point of maximum curvature shall not exceed one-half inch.

(c)

The blade of the goalkeeper's stick shall not exceed three and one-half inches in width at any point except at the heel where it must not exceed four and one-half inches in width; nor shall the goalkeepers' stick exceed fifteen and one-half inches in length from the heel to the end of the blade.

The widened portion of the goalkeeper's stick extending up the shaft from the blade shall not extend more than twenty-six inches from the heel and shall not exceed three and one-half inches in width.

(d)

A minor penalty plus a fine of two hundred dollars ($200.00) shall be imposed on any player or goalkeeper who uses a stick not conforming to the provisions of this rule.

(NOTE 1) *When a formal complaint is made by the Captain or designated substitute of a team, against the dimensions of any stick, the Referee shall take the stick to the Timekeeper's bench where the necessary measurement shall be made immediately. The result shall be reported to the Penalty Timekeeper who shall record it on the back of the penalty period.*

If the complaint is not sustained a bench minor penalty shall be imposed against the complaining Club in addition to a fine of $100.

(NOTE 2) *A player who participates in the play while taking a replacement stick to his goalkeeper shall incur a minor penalty under this rule but the automatic fine of two hundred dollars ($200.00) shall not be imposed. If his participation causes a foul resulting in a minor or major penalty the*

A seriously injured player may cause immediate stoppage of play.

referee shall report the incident to the President for disciplinary action.

(e)

In the event that a player scores on a penalty shot while using an illegal stick the goal shall be disallowed and no further penalty imposed. However, if no goal is scored the player taking the penalty shot shall receive a minor penalty.

(f)

A minor penalty plus a ten-minute misconduct penalty shall be imposed on any player who refuses to surrender his stick for measurement when requested to do so by the Referee. In addition this player shall be subject to a $200 fine.

Rule 21. Skates

(a)

All hockey skates shall be of a design approved by the Rules Committee. All skates worn by players (but not goalkeepers) and by the Referee and Linesmen shall be equipped with safety heel tips.

When the Referee becomes aware that any person is wearing a skate in which the protective heel tip is missing or broken, he shall direct its replacement at the next intermission. If such replacement is not carried out, the Referee shall report the incident to the President for disciplinary action.

(b)

The use of speed skates or fancy skates or any skate so designed that it may cause injury is prohibited.

Rule 22. Goalkeeper's Equipment

(a)

With the exception of skates and stick, all the equipment worn by the goalkeeper must be constructed soley for the purpose of protecting the head or body, and he must not wear any garment or use any contrivance which would give him undue assistance in keeping goal.

(NOTE) *Cages on gloves and abdominal aprons extending down the front of the thighs on the outside of the pants are prohibited. "Cage" shall mean any lacing or webbing or other material in the goalkeeper's glove joining the thumb and index finger which is in excess of the minimum necessary to fill the gap when the goalkeeper's thumb and forefinger in the glove are fully extended and spread and includes any pocket or pouch effect produced by excess lacing or webbing or other material between the thumb and forefinger when fully extended or spread.*

Protective padding attached to the back or forming part of goalkeepers' gloves shall not exceed eight inches in width nor more than sixteen inches in length at any point.

(b)

The leg guards worn by goalkeepers shall not exceed ten inches in extreme width when on the leg of the player.

(NOTE) *At the commencement of each season and prior to play-offs, goalkeepers' leg guards shall be checked by League Staff and any violation of this rule shall be reported to the Club involved and to the President of the League.*

(c)

Protective masks of a design approved by the Rules Committee may be worn by goalkeepers.

Rule 23. Protective Equipment

(a)

All protective equipment, except gloves, headgear and goalkeepers' leg guards must be worn under the uniform. For violation of this rule, after warning by the Referee, a minor penalty shall be imposed.

(NOTE) *Players including the goalkeeper violating this rule shall not be permitted to participate in game until such equipment has been corrected or removed.*

(b)

All players of both teams shall wear a helmet of design, material and construction approved by the Rules Committee at all times while participating in a game, either on the playing surface or the players' or penalty benches.

Players, who have been under Standard Player's contract to a Member Club of the League, at any time prior to June 1, 1979, may elect for exemption from the operation of this sub-section (b) by execution of an approved Request and Release form and filing it with the League office.

Rule 24. Dangerous Equipment

(a)

The use of pads or protectors made of metal, or of any other material likely to cause injury to a player, is prohibited.

(b)

A mask or protector of a design approved by the rules Committee may be worn by a player who has sustained a facial injury.

(NOTE) *All elbow pads which do not have a soft protective outer covering of sponge-rubber or similar material at least ½ inch thick shall be considered dangerous equipment.*

In the first instance the injured player shall be entitled to wear any protective device prescribed by the Club doctor. If any opposing Club objects to the device it may record its objection with the President who shall promptly poll the Rules Committee for approval or otherwise.

(c)

A glove from which all or part of the palm has been removed or cut to permit the use of the bare hand shall be considered illegal equipment and if any player wears such a glove in play a minor penalty shall be imposed on him.

(NOTE) *The Officiating Department is specifically authorized to make a check of each team's equipment to ensure the compliance with this rule. It shall report its findings to the President for his disciplinary action.*

Rule 25. Puck

(a)

The puck shall be made of vulcanized rubber, or other approved material, one inch thick and three inches in diameter and shall weigh between five and a half ounces and six ounces. All pucks used in competition must be approved by the Rules Committee.

(b)

The home team shall be responsible for providing an adequate supply of official pucks which shall be kept in a frozen condition. This supply of pucks shall be kept at the penalty bench under the control of one of the regular minor officials or a special attendant.

(NOTE TO SECTION THREE) *A request for measurement of any equipment covered by this section shall be limited to one request by each Club during the course of any stoppage of play.*

The Referee may, at his own discretion, measure any equipment used for the first time in the game.

Equipment must protect the goalkeeper, not the goal.

Misconduct penalty removes offender from ice for ten minutes.

SECTION FOUR—PENALTIES

Rule 26. Penalties

Penalties shall be actual playing time and shall be divided into the following classes:

(1) Minor Penalties
(2) Bench Minor Penalties
(3) Major Penalties
(4) Misconduct Penalties
(5) Match Penalties
(6) Penalty Shot.

Where coincident penalties are imposed on players of both teams the penalized players of the visiting team shall take their positions on the penalty bench first in the place designated for visiting players.

(NOTE) *When play is not actually in progress and an offense is committed by any player, the same penalty shall apply as though play were actually in progress.*

Rule 27. Minor Penalties

(a)

For a "MINOR PENALTY," any player, other than a goalkeeper, shall be ruled off the ice for two minutes during which time no substitute shall be permitted.

(b)

A "BENCH MINOR" penalty involves the removal from the ice of one player of the team against which the penalty is awarded for a period of two minutes. Any player except a goalkeeper of the team may be designated to serve the penalty by the Manager or Coach through the playing Captain and such player shall take his place on the penalty bench promptly and serve the penalty as if it was a minor penalty imposed upon him.

(c)

If while a team is "short-handed" by one or more minor or bench minor penalties the opposing team scores a goal, the first of such penalties shall automatically terminate.

(NOTE) *"Short-handed" means that the team must be below the numerical strength of its opponents on the ice at the time the goal is scored. The minor or bench minor penalty which terminates automatically is the one which causes the team scored against to be "short-handed." Thus coincident minor penalties to both teams do NOT cause either side to be "short-handed."*

This rule shall also apply when a goal is scored on a penalty shot.

When the minor penalties of two players of the same team terminate at the same time the Captain of that team shall designate to the Referee which of such players will return to the ice first and the Referee will instruct the Penalty Timekeeper accordingly.

When a player receives a major penalty and a minor penalty at the same time the major penalty shall be served first by the penalized player except under Rule 28 (c) in which case the minor penalty will be recorded and served first.

(NOTE) *This applies to the case where BOTH penalties are imposed on the SAME player.*

See also Note to Rule 33.

(d)

If while a team is short-handed by one penalty (minor or major), coincident minor penalties of equal duration are imposed against a player of each team, then immediate substitution shall be made for such players.

Rule 28. Major Penalties

(a)

For the first "MAJOR PENALTY" in any one game, the offender, except the goalkeeper, shall be ruled off the ice for five minutes, during which time no substitute shall be permitted.

An automatic fine of fifty dollars ($50.00) shall also be added when a major penalty is imposed for any foul causing injury to the face or head of an opponent by means of a stick.

(b)

For the third major penalty in the same game, to the same player, he shall be ruled off the ice for the balance of the playing time, but a substitute shall be permitted to replace the player so suspended after five minutes shall have elapsed. (Major penalty plus game misconduct penalty with automatic fine of one hundred dollars ($100.00).)

(c)

When coincident major penalties or coincident penalties of equal duration, including a major penalty, are imposed against players of both teams, the penalized players shall all take their places on the penalty benches and such penalized players shall not leave the penalty bench until the first stoppage of play following the expiry of their respective penalties. Immediate substitutions shall be made for an equal number of major penalties or *coincident penalties of equal duration including a major penalty to* each team so penalized and the penalties of the players *for* which substitution have been made shall not be taken into account for the purpose of the delayed Rule 33.

Where it is required to determine which of the penalized players shall be designated to serve the delayed penalty under Rule 33 the penalized team shall have the right to make such designation not in conflict with Rule 27.

Rule 29. Misconduct Penalties

(a)

"MISCONDUCT" penalties to all players except the goalkeeper, involve removal from the game for a period of ten minutes each. A substitute player is permitted to immediately replace a player serving a misconduct penalty. A player whose misconduct penalty has expired shall remain in the penalty box until the next stoppage of play.

When a player receives a minor penalty and a misconduct penalty at the same time, the penalized team shall immediately put a substitute player on the penalty bench and he shall serve the minor penalty without change.

When a player receives a major penalty and a misconduct penalty at the same time, the penalized team shall place a substitute player on the penalty bench before the major penalty expires and no replacement for the penalized player shall be permitted to enter the game except from the penalty bench. Any violation of this provision shall be treated as an illegal substitution under Rule 18 calling for a bench minor penalty.

(b)

A misconduct penalty imposed on any player at any time, shall be accompanied with an automatic fine of fifty dollars ($50.00).

(c)

A "GAME MISCONDUCT" penalty involves the suspension of a player for the balance of the game but a substitute is permitted to replace immediately the player so removed. A player incurring a game misconduct penalty shall incur an automatic fine of one hundred dollars ($100.00) and the case shall be reported to the President who shall have full power to impose such further penalties by way of suspension or fine on the penalized player or any other player involved in the altercation.

Against penalty shot, goalkeeper stands alone.

(d)

A Game Misconduct penalty shall be imposed on any player or goal-keeper who is the first to intervene in an altercation then in progress. This penalty is in addition to any other penalty incurred in the same incident.

(e)

The Referee may impose a "GROSS MISCONDUCT" penalty on any player, Manager, Coach or Trainer who is guilty of gross misconduct of any kind. Any person incurring a "Gross Misconduct" penalty shall be suspended for the balance of the game and shall incur an automatic fine of one hundred dollars ($100) and the case shall be referred to the President of the League for further disciplinary action.

(NOTE) *For all "Game Misconduct" and "Gross Misconduct" penalties regardless of when imposed, a total of ten minutes shall be charged in the records against the offending player.*

(f)

In regular League games, any player who incurs a total of three Game Misconduct penalties shall be suspended automatically for the next League game of his team. For each subsequent Game Misconduct penalty the automatic suspension shall be increased by one game. For each suspension of a player his Club shall be fined one thousand dollars ($1000).

In Play-off games any player who incurs a total of two Game Misconduct penalties shall be suspended automatically for the next Play-off game of his team. For each subsequent Game Misconduct penalty during the Play-offs the automatic suspension shall be increased by one game. For each suspension of a player during Play-offs his Club shall be fined one thousand dollars ($1000).

(NOTE) *Any Game Misconduct penalty for which a player has been assessed an automatic suspension or supplementary discipline in the form of game suspension(s) by the President shall NOT be taken into account when calculating the total number of offenses under this subsection.*

The automatic suspensions incurred under this subsection in respect to League games shall have no effect with respect to violations during Play-off games.

Rule 30. Match Penalties

A "MATCH" penalty involves the suspension of a player for the balance of the game, and the offender shall be ordered to the dressing room immediately. A substitute player is permitted to replace the penalized player after ten minutes playing time has elapsed when the penalty is imposed under Rule 49, and after five minutes actual playing time has elapsed when the penalty is imposed under Rule 44.

(NOTE 1) *Regulations regarding additional penalties and substitutes are specifically covered in individual Rules 44, 49 and 64 any additional penalty shall be served by a player to be designated by the Manager or Coach of the offending team through the playing Captain such player to take his place in the penalty box immediately.*

For all "MATCH" penalties, regardless of when imposed, or prescribed additional penalties, a total of ten minutes shall be charged in the records against the offending player.

(NOTE 2) *When the coincident match penalties have been imposed under Rule 44, Rule 49 or Rule 64 to a player on both teams Rule 28 (c) covering coincident major penalties will be applicable with respect to player substitution.*

(NOTE 3) *The Referee is required to report all match penalties and the surrounding circumstances to the President of the League immediately following the game in which they occur.*

Rule 31. Penalty Shot

(a)

Any infraction of the rules which calls for a "Penalty Shot" shall be taken as follows:—

The Referee shall cause to be announced over the public address system the name of the player designated by him or selected by the team entitled to take the shot (as appropriate) and shall then place the puck on the center face-off spot and the player taking the shot will, on the instruction of the Referee, play the puck from there and shall attempt to score on the goalkeeper. The player taking the shot may carry the puck in any part of the Neutral Zone of his own Defending Zone but once the puck has crossed the Attacking Blue Line it must be kept in motion towards the opponents' goal line and once it is shot the play shall be considered complete. No goal can be scored on a rebound of any kind and any time the puck crosses the goal line the shot shall be considered complete.

Only a player designated as a Goalkeeper or Alternate Goalkeeper may defend against the penalty shot.

(b)

The Goalkeeper must remain in his crease until the player taking the penalty shot has touched the puck and in the event of violation of this rule or any foul committed by a Goalkeeper the Referee shall allow the shot to be taken and if the shot fails he shall permit the penalty shot to be taken over again.

The Goalkeeper may attempt to stop the shot in any manner except by throwing his stick or any object, in which case a goal shall be awarded.

(NOTE) *See Rule 80.*

(c)

In cases where a penalty shot has been awarded under Rule 50 (c)—deliberately displacing goal post during course of breakaway—under Rule 62 (g)—interference, under Rule 66 (k)—for illegal entry into the game, under Rule 80 (a)—for throwing a stick and under Rule 83 (b)—for fouling from behind, the Referee shall designate the player who has been fouled as the player who shall take the penalty shot.

In cases where a penalty shot has been awarded under Rule 18 (b)—deliberate illegal substitution with insufficient playing time remaining or Rule 50 (d)—deliberately displacing goal post or Rule 53 (c)—falling on the puck from the crease area—the penalty shot shall be taken by a player selected by the Captain of the non-offending team from the players on the ice at the time when the foul was committed. Such selection shall be reported to the Referee and cannot be changed.

If by reason of injury the player designated by the Referee to take the penalty shot is unable to do so within a reasonable time, the shot may be taken by a player selected by the Captain of the non-offending team from the players on the ice when the foul was committed. Such selection shall be reported to the Referee and cannot be changed.

(d)

Should the player in respect to whom a penalty shot has been awarded himself commit a foul in connection with the same play or circumstances, either before or after the penalty shot penalty has been awarded, be designated to take the shot he shall first be permitted to do so before being sent to the penalty bench to serve the penalty except when such a penalty is for a game misconduct, gross misconduct or match penalty in which case the penalty shot shall be taken by a player selected by the Captain of the non-offending team from the players on the ice at the time when the foul was committed.

If at the time a penalty shot is awarded the goalkeeper of the penalized team has been removed from the ice to substitute another player the goalkeeper shall be permitted to return to the ice before the penalty shot is taken.

(e)

While the penalty shot is being taken, players of both sides shall withdraw to the sides of the rink and beyond the center red line.

(f)

If, while the penalty shot is being taken, any player of the opposing team shall have by some action interfered with or distracted the player taking the shot and because of such action the shot should have failed, a second attempt shall be permitted and the Referee shall impose a misconduct penalty on the player so interfering or distracting.

(g)

If a goal is scored from a penalty shot the puck shall be faced at center ice in the usual way. If a goal is not scored the puck shall be faced at either of the end face-off spots in the zone in which the penalty shot has been tried.

(h)

Should a goal be scored from a penalty shot, a further penalty to the offending player shall not be applied unless the offense for which the penalty shot was awarded was such as to incur a major or match penalty or misconduct penalty, in which case the penalty prescribed for the particular offense, shall be imposed.

If the offense for which the penalty shot was awarded was such as would normally incur a minor penalty, then regardless of whether the penalty shot results in a goal or not, no further minor penalty shall be served.

(i)

If the foul upon which the penalty shot is based occurs during actual playing time the penalty shot shall be awarded and taken immediately in the usual manner notwithstanding any delay occasioned by a slow whistle by the Referee to permit the play to be completed which delay results in the expiry of the regular playing time in any period.

The time required for the taking of a penalty shot shall not be included in the regular playing time of any overtime.

Rule 32: Goalkeeper's Penalties

(a)

A goalkeeper shall not be sent to the penalty bench for an offense which incurs a minor penalty, but instead the minor penalty shall be served by another member of his team who was on the ice when the offense was committed, said player to be designated by the Manager or Coach of the offending team through the playing Captain and such substitute shall not be changed.

(b)

Same as 32 (a) above except change "minor" to "major."

(c)

Should a goalkeeper incur three major penalties in one game he shall be ruled off the ice for the balance of the playing time and his place will be taken by a member of his own Club, or by a regular substitute goalkeeper who is available. (Major penalty plus game misconduct penalty and automatic fine of one hundred dollars ($100.00).)

(d)

Should a goalkeeper on the ice incur a misconduct penalty, this penalty shall be served by another member of his team who was on the ice when the offense was committed, said player to be designated by the Manager or Coach of the offending team through the Captain and, in addition, fined fifty dollars ($50.00).

(e)

Should a goalkeeper incur a game misconduct penalty, his place then will be taken by a member of his own Club, or by a regular substitute goalkeeper who is available, and such player will be allowed the goalkeeper's full equipment. In addition the goalkeeper shall be fined one hundred dollars ($100.00).

(f)

Should a goalkeeper incur a match penalty, his place then will be taken by a member of his own Club, or by a substitute goalkeeper who is available, and such player will be allowed the goalkeeper's equipment. However, any additional penalties as specifically called for by the individual rules covering match penalties, will apply, and the offending team shall be penalized accordingly; such additional penalty to be served by another member of the team on the ice at the time the offense was committed, said player to be designated by the Manager or Coach of the offending team through the Captain. (See Rules 44, 49 and 64.)

(g)

A goalkeeper incurring a match penalty shall incur an automatic fine of two hundred dollars ($200.00) and the case shall be investigated promptly by the President who shall have full power to impose such further penalty by way of suspension or fine on the penalized goalkeeper or any

Goalkeeper joins the fight—and will receive penalty.

other player in the altercation.

(h)

A minor penalty shall be imposed on a goalkeeper who leaves the immediate vicinity of his crease during an altercation. In addition, he shall be subject to a fine of one hundred dollars ($100.00) and this incident shall be reported to the President for such further disciplinary action as may be required.

(NOTE) *All penalties imposed on goalkeeper regardless of who serves penalty or any substitution shall be charged in the records against the goalkeeper.*

(i)

If a goalkeeper participates in the play in any manner when he is beyond the center red line a minor penalty shall be imposed upon him.

Rule 33. Delayed Penalties

(a)

If a third player of any team shall be penalized while two players of the same team are serving penalties, the penalty time of the third player shall not commence until the penalty time of one of the two players already penalized shall have elapsed. Nevertheless, the third player penalized must at once proceed to the penalty bench but may be replaced by a substitute until such time as the penalty time of the penalized player shall commence.

(b)

When any team shall have three players serving penalties at the same time and because of the delayed penalty rule, a substitute for the third offender is on the ice, none of the three penalized players on the penalty bench may return to the ice until play has stopped. When play has been stopped, the player whose full penalty has expired, may return to the play.

Provided however that the Penalty Timekeeper shall permit the return to the ice in the order of expiry of their penalties, of a player or players when by reason of the expiration of their penalties the penalized team is entitled to have more than four players on the ice.

(c)

In the case of delayed penalties, the Referee shall instruct the Penalty Timekeeper that penalized players whose penalties have expired shall only be allowed to return to the ice when there is a stoppage of play.

When the penalties of two players of the same team will expire at the same time the Captain of that team will designate to the Referee which of such players will return to the ice first and the Referee will instruct the Penalty Timekeeper accordingly.

When a major and a minor penalty are imposed at the same time on players of the same team the Penalty Timekeeper shall record the minor as being the first of such penalties.

(NOTE) *This applies to the case where the two penalties are imposed on DIFFERENT players of the same team. See also Note to Rule 27.*

Rule 34. Calling of Penalties

(a)

Should an infraction of the rules which call for a minor, major, misconduct, game misconduct or match penalty be committed by a player of the side in possession of the puck, the Referee shall immediately blow his whistle and give the penalties to the deserving players.

The resulting face-off shall be made at the place where the play was stopped unless the stoppage occurs in the Attacking Zone of the player penalized in which case the face-off shall be made at the nearest face-off spot in the Neutral Zone.

(b)

Should an infraction of the rules which would call for a minor, major, misconduct, game misconduct or match penalty be committed by a

player of the team not in possession of the puck, the Referee will blow his whistle and impose the penalty on the offending player upon completion of the play by the team in possession of the puck.

(NOTE) *There shall be no signal given by the Referee for a misconduct or Game Misconduct penalty under this section.*

The resulting face-off shall be made at the place where the play was stopped, unless during the period of a delayed whistle due to a foul by a player of the side NOT in possession, the side in possession ices the puck, shoots the puck so that it goes out of bounds or is unplayable then the face-off following the stoppage shall take place in the Neutral Zone near the Defending Blue Line of the team shooting the puck.

If the penalty or penalties to be imposed are minor penalties and a goal is scored on the play by the non-offending side the minor penalty or penalties shall not be imposed but major and match penalties shall be imposed in the normal manner regardless of whether a goal is scored or not.

(NOTE 1) *"Completion of the play by the team in possession" in this rule means that the puck must have come into the possession and control of an opposing player or has been "frozen." This does not mean a rebound off the goalkeeper, the goal or the boards or any accidental contact with the body or equipment of an opposing player.*

Linesman must be alert and mobile.

Penalties are served in penalty box—"the cooler."

(NOTE 2) *If after the Referee has signalled a penalty but before the whistle has been blown the puck shall enter the goal of the non-offending team as the direct result of the action of a player of that team, the goal shall be allowed and the penalty signalled shall be imposed in the normal manner.*

If when a team is "short-handed" by reason of one or more minor or bench minor penalties the Referee signals a further minor penalty or penalties against the "short-handed" team and a goal is scored by the non-offending side before the whistle is blown then the goal shall be allowed, the penalty or penalties signalled shall be washed out and the first of the minor penalties already being served shall automatically terminate under Rule 27 (c).

(c)

Should the same offending player commit other fouls on the same play, either before or after the Referee has blown his whistle, the offending player shall serve such penalties consecutively.

Rule 34A. Supplementary Discipline

In addition to the automatic fines and suspensions imposed under these Rules, the President may, at his discretion, investigate any incident that occurs in connection with any Exhibition, League or Play-off game and may assess additional fines and/or suspensions for any offense committed during the course of a game or any aftermath thereof by a player, Trainer, Manager, Coach or Club Executive whether or not such offense has been penalized by the Referee.

Rule 34B. Suspensions Arising from Exhibition Games

Whenever suspensions are imposed as a result of infractions occurring during exibition games, the President shall exercise his discretion in scheduling the suspensions to ensure that no team shall be short more players in any regular League game that it would have been had the infractions occurred in regular League games.

SECTION FIVE—OFFICIALS

Rule 35. Appointment of Officials

(a)

The President shall appoint a Referee, two Linesmen, Game Timekeeper, Penalty Timekeeper, Official Scorer and two Goal Judges for each game.

(b)

The President shall forward to all clubs a list of Referees, and Off-Ice Officials, all of whom must be treated with proper respect at all times during the season by all players and officials of clubs.

Rule 36. Referee

(a)

The REFEREE shall have general supervision of the game, and shall have full control of all game officials and players during the game, including stoppages; and in case of any dispute, his decision shall be final. The Referee shall remain on the ice at the conclusion of each period until all players have proceeded to their dressing rooms.

(b)

All Referees and Linesmen shall be garbed in black trousers and official sweaters.

(c)

The Referee shall order the teams on the ice at the appointed time for the beginning of a game, and at the commencement of each period. If for any reason there be more than fifteen minutes' delay in the commencement of the game or any undue delay in resuming play after the fifteen-minute intervals between periods, the Referee shall state in his report to the President the cause of the delay, and the club or clubs which were at fault.

(d)

It shall be his duty to see to it that all players are properly dressed, and that the approved regulation equipment is in use at all times during the game.

(e)

The Referee shall, before starting the game, see that the appointed Game Timekeeper, Penalty Timekeeper, Official Scorer and Goal Judges are in their respective places, and satisfy himself that the timing and signalling equipment are in order.

(f)

It shall be his duty to impose such penalties as are prescribed by the rules for infractions thereof, and he shall give the final decision in matters of disputed goals. The Referee may consult with the Linesmen or Goal Judge before making his decision.

(g)

The Referee shall announce to the Official Scorer or Penalty Timekeeper all goals legally scored as well as penalties, and for what infractions such penalties are imposed.

The Referee shall cause to be announced over the public address system the reason for not allowing a goal every time the goal signal light is turned on in the course of play. This shall be done at the first stoppage of play regardless of any standard signal given by the Referee when the goal signal light was put on in error.

The Referee shall report to the Official Scorer the name or number of the goal scorer but he shall *not* give any information or advice with respect to assist.

(NOTE) *The name of the scorer and any player entitled to an assist will be announced on the public address system. In the event that the Referee disallows a goal for any violation of the rules, he shall report the reason for disallowance to the Official Scorer who shall announce the Referee's decision correctly over the public address system.*

The infraction of the rules for which each penalty has been imposed will be announced correctly as reported by the Referee, over the public address system. Where players of both teams are penalized on the same play, the penalty to the visiting player will be announced first.

Where a penalty is imposed by the Referee which calls for a mandatory or automatic fine, only the time portion of the penalty will be reported by the Referee to the Official Scorer and announced on the public address system, and the fine will be collected through the League office.

(h)

The Referee shall see to it that players of opposing teams are separated on the penalty bench to prevent feuding.

(i)

He shall not halt the game for any infractions of the rules concerning offside play at the blue line, or center line or any violation of the "Icing the puck" rule which shall be the function of the Linesman alone, unless the Linesman shall be prevented by some accident from doing so, in which case the duties of the Linesman shall be assumed by the Referee until play is stopped.

(j)

Should a Referee accidentally leave the ice or receive an injury which incapacitates him from discharging his duties while play is in progress the game shall be automatically stopped.

(k)

If, through misadventure or sickness, the Referee and Linesmen appointed are prevented from appearing, the Managers or Coaches of the two clubs shall agree on a Referee and Linesman. If they are unable to agree, they shall appoint a player from each side who shall act as Referee and Linesman; the player of the home club acting as Referee, and the player of the visiting club as Linesman.

(l)

If the regularly appointed officials appear during the progress of the game, they shall at once replace the temporary officials.

(m)

Should a Linesman appointed be unable to act at the last minute or through sickness or accident be unable to finish the game, the Referee shall have the power to appoint another, in his stead, if he deems it necessary, or if required to do so by the Manager or Coach of either of the competing teams.

(n)

If, owing to illness or accident, the Referee is unable to continue to officiate, one of the Linesmen shall perform such duties as devolved upon the Referee during the balance of the game, the Linesman to be selected by the Referee.

(o)

The Referee shall check Club's rosters and all players in uniform before signing reports of the game.

(p)

The Referee shall report to the President promptly and in detail the circumstances of any of the following incidents:

(1) When a stick or part thereof is thrown outside the playing area;

(2) Every obscene gesture made by any person involved in the playing or conduct of the game whether as a participant or as an official of either team or of the League, which gesture he has personally observed or which has been brought to his attention by any game official;

(3) When any player, trainer, coach or Club executive becomes involved in an altercation with a spectator.

(4) Every infraction under Rule 77 (c) (slashing).

Rule 37. Linesman

(a)

The duty of the LINESMAN is to determine any infractions of the rules concerning off-side play at the blue line, or center line, or any violation of the "Icing the Puck" rule.

He shall stop the play when the puck goes outside the playing area and when it is interfered with by any ineligible person and when it is struck above the height of the shoulder and when the goal post has been displaced from its normal position. He shall stop the play for off-sides occurring on face-offs circles. He shall stop the play when he has observed that a goal has been scored but the referee did not. He shall stop the play when there has been a premature substitution for a goalkeeper under Rule 18 (a) and for injured players under Rule 19 (f) and for a player batting the puck forward to a teammate under Rule 57 (e) and interference by spectators under Rule 63 (a).

(b)

He shall face the puck at all times, except at the start of the game, at the beginning of each period and after a goal has been scored.

The Referee may call upon a Linesman to conduct a face-off at any time.

(c)

He shall, when requested to do so by the Referee, give his version of any incident that may have taken place during the playing of the game.

(d)

He shall not stop the play to impose any penalty except when a major penalty is warranted to a player on the ice when a serious incident has been observed by him but not by the referee and any violation of the Rule 18 (a) & (c)—Change of Players (too many men on the ice) and any

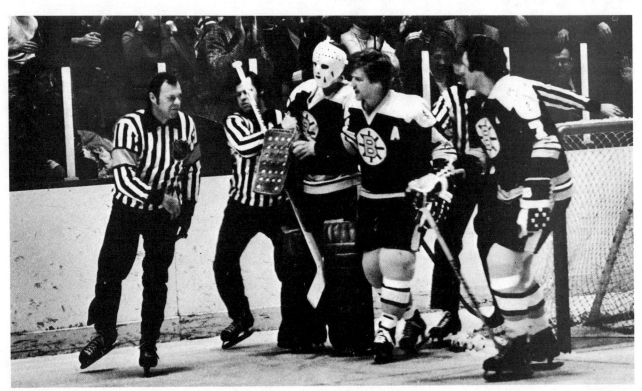

Bruins players flirt with misconduct penalties.

violation of Rule 42 (k) (articles thrown on the ice from vicinity of players' or penalty bench) and Rule 42 (l) (interference by Player, Coach, Trainer, or Club executive who interferes with game official) and Rule 46 (c) (stick thrown on ice from players' bench) and he shall report such violation to the Referee who shall impose a bench minor penalty against the offending team.

He shall report immediately to the Referee his version of the circumstances with respect to Rule 50 (c)—Delaying the game by deliberately displacing post from its normal position.

He shall report immediately to the Referee his version of any infraction of the rules constituting a major or match foul or Game Misconduct or any conduct calling for a bench minor penalty or misconduct penalty under these rules.

Rule 38. Goal Judge

(a)

There shall be one GOAL JUDGE at each goal. They shall not be members of either club engaged in a game, nor shall they be replaced during its progress, unless after the commencement of the game it becomes apparent that either Goal Judge, on account of partisanship or any other cause, is guilty of giving unjust decisions, when the Referee may appoint another Goal Judge to act in his stead.

(b)

Goal Judges shall be stationed behind the goals, during the progress of play, in properly screened cages, so that there can be no interference with their activities; and they shall not change goals during the game.

(c)

In the event of a goal being claimed, the Goal Judge of that goal shall decide whether or not the puck has passed between the goal posts and entirely over the goal line, his decision simply being "goal" or "no goal."

Rule 39. Penalty Timekeeper

(a)

The PENALTY TIMEKEEPER shall keep, on the official forms provided, a correct record of all penalties imposed by the officials including the names of the players penalized, the infractions penalized, the duration of each penalty and the time at which each penalty was imposed. He shall report in the Penalty Record each penalty shot awarded, the name of the player taking the shot and the result of the shot.

(b)

The Penalty Timekeeper shall check and ensure that the time served by all penalized players is correct. He shall be responsible for the correct posting of penalties on the scoreboard at all times and shall promptly call to the attention of the Referee any discrepancy between the time recorded on the clock and the official correct time and he shall be responsible for making any adjustments ordered by the Referee.

He shall upon request give a penalized player correct information as to the unexpired time of his penalty.

(NOTE 1) *The infraction of the rules for which each penalty has been imposed will be announced twice over the public address system as reported by the Referee. Where players of both teams are penalized on the same play, the penalty to the visiting player will be announced first.*

(NOTE 2) *Misconduct penalties and coincident major penalties should not be recorded on the timing device but such penalized players should be alerted and released at the first stoppage of play following the expiration of their penalties.*

(c)

Upon the completion of each game, the Penalty Timekeeper shall complete and sign three copies of the Penalty Record to be distributed as quickly as possible to the following persons:—

(1) One copy to the Official Scorer for transmission to the League President;

(2) One copy to the visiting Coach or Manager.

(3) One copy to the home Coach or Manager.

(d)

The Officiating Department shall be entitled to inspect, collect and forward to the League headquarters the actual work sheets used by the Penalty Timekeeper in any game.

Rule 40. Official Scorer

(a)

Before the start of the game, the Official Scorer shall obtain from the Manager or Coach of both teams a list of all eligible players and the starting line-up of each team which information shall be made known to the opposing team Manager or Coach before the start of play either personally or through the Referee.

The Official Scorer shall secure the names of the Captain, from the Manager or Coach at the time the line-ups are collected and will indicate those nominated by placing the letter "C" opposite their names on the Referee's Report of Match. All of this information shall be presented to the Referee for his signature at the completion of the game.

(b)

The Official Scorer shall keep a record of the goals scored, the scorers, and players to whom assists have been credited, and shall indicate those players on the lists who have actually taken part in the game. He shall also record the time of entry into the game of any substitute goalkeeper. He shall record on the Official Score Sheet a notation where a goal is scored when the goalkeeper has been removed from the ice.

Referee has final decision on all goals.

297

(c)

The Official Scorer shall award the points for goals and assists and his decision shall be final. The awards of points for goals and assists shall be announced twice over the public address system and all changes in such awards shall also be announced in the same manner.

No requests for changes in any award of points shall be considered unless they are made at or before the conclusion of actual play in the game by the team Captain.

(d)

At the conclusion of the game the Official Scorer shall complete and sign three copies of the Official Score Sheet for distribution as quickly as possible to the following persons:—

(1) One copy to the League President;

(2) One copy to the visiting Coach or Manager;

(3) One copy to the home Coach or Manager.

(e)

The Official Scorer shall also prepare the Official Report of Match for signature by the Referee and forward it to the League President together with the Official Score Sheet and the Penalty Record.

(f)

The Official Scorer should be in an elevated position, well away from the Players' Benches, with house telephone communication to the Public Address Announcer.

Rule 41. Game Timekeeper

(a)

The Game Timekeeper shall record the time of starting and finishing of each period in the game and all playing time during the game.

(b)

The Game Timekeeper shall signal the Referee and the competing teams for the start of the game and each succeeding period and the Referee shall start the play promptly in accordance with Rule 81.

To assist in assuring the prompt return to the ice of the teams and the officials the Game Timekeeper shall give a preliminary warning three minutes prior to the resumption of play in each period.

(c)

If the rink is not equipped with an automatic gong or bell or siren or, if such device fails to function, the Game Timekeeper shall signal the end of each period by ringing a gong or bell or by blowing a whistle.

(d)

He shall cause to be announced on the public address system at the nineteenth minute in each period that there is one minute remaining to be played in the period.

(e)

In the event of any dispute regarding time, the matter shall be referred to the Referee for adjustment, and his decision shall be final.

Rule 41A. Statistician

(a)

There shall be appointed for duty at every game played in the League a Statistician and such assistants or alternates as may be deemed necessary.

(b)

The duty of the Statistician(s) is to correctly record on the official League forms supplied all of the data therein provided for concerning the performance of the individual players and the participating team.

(c)

These records shall be compiled and recorded in strict conformity with the instructions printed on the forms supplied and shall be completed as

to totals where required and with such accuracy as to ensure that the data supplied is "in balance."

(d)

At the conclusion of each game the Statisticion shall sign and distribute three copies of the final and correct Game Statisticion's Report to each of the following persons:—

(1) One copy to the League President (through the Official Scorer if possible—otherwise by direct mail);

(2) One copy to the visiting Coach or Manager;

(3) One copy to the home Coach or Manager.$

SECTION SIX—PLAYING RULES

Rule 42. Abuse of Officials and other Misconduct

(NOTE) *In the enforcement of this rule the Referee has, in many instances, the option of imposing a "misconduct penalty" or a "bench minor penalty." In principle the Referee is directed to impose a "bench minor penalty" in respect to the violations which occur on or in the immediate vicinity of the players' bench but off the playing surface, and in all cases affecting non-playing personnel or players. A "misconduct penalty" should be imposed for violations which occur on the playing surface or in the penalty bench area and where the penalized player is readily identifiable.*

(a)

A misconduct penalty shall be imposed on any player who uses obscene, profane or abusive language to any person or who intentionally knocks or shoots the puck out of the reach of an official who is retrieving it or who deliberately throws any equipment out of the playing area.

(b)

A minor penalty shall be assessed to any player who challenges or disputes the rulings of any official during a game. If the player persists in such challenge or dispute he shall be assessed a misconduct penalty and any further dispute will result in a Game Misconduct Penalty being assessed to the offending player.

(c)

A misconduct penalty shall be imposed on any player or players who bang the boards with their sticks or other instruments any time.

In the event that the Coach, Trainer, Manager or Club Executive commits an infraction under this Rule a bench minor penalty shall be imposed.

(d)

A bench minor penalty shall be imposed on the team of any penalized player who does not proceed directly and immediately to the penalty box and take his place on the penalty bench or to the dressing room when so ordered by the Referee.

Where coincident penalties are imposed on players on both teams the penalized players of the visiting team shall take their positions on the penalty bench first in the place designated for visiting players, or where there is no special designation then on the bench farthest from the gate.

(e)

Any player who (following a fight or other altercation in which he has been involved is broken up, and for which he is penalized) fails to proceed directly and immediately to the penalty bench; or who causes any delay by retrieving his equipment (gloves, sticks, etc., shall be delivered to him at the penalty bench by his teammates), shall incur an automatic fine of one hundred dollars ($100.00) in addition to all other penalties or fines incurred.

(f)

Any player who persists in continuing or attempting to continue the fight or altercation after he has been ordered by the Referee to stop, or, who resists a Linesman in the discharge of his duties shall, at the discretion of the Referee, incur a Misconduct or a Game Misconduct penalty in addition to any penalties imposed.

(g)

A misconduct penalty shall be imposed on any player who, after warning by the Referee, persists in any course of conduct (including threatening or abusive language or gestures or similar actions) designed to incite an opponent into incurring a penalty.

If, after the assessment of a Misconduct Penalty, a player persists in any course of conduct for which he was previously assessed a Misconduct Penalty, he shall be assessed a Game Misconduct Penalty.

(h)

In the case of any Club Executive, Manager, Coach or Trainer being guilty of such misconduct, he is to be removed from the bench by order of the Referee, and his case reported to the President for further action.

(i)

If any Club Executive, Manager, Coach or Trainer is removed from the bench by order of the Referee, he must not sit near the bench of his club, nor in any way direct or attempt to direct the play of his club.

(j)

A bench minor penalty shall be imposed against the offending team if any player, any Club Executive, Manager, Coach or Trainer uses obscene, profane or abusive language or gesture to any person or uses the name of any official coupled with any vociferous remarks.

(k)

A bench minor penalty shall be imposed against the offending team if any player, Trainer, Coach, Manager or Club Executive in the vicinity of the players' bench or penalty bench throws anything on the ice during the progress of the game or during stoppage of play.

(NOTE) *The penalty provided under this rule is in addition to any penalty imposed under Rule 46 (c) "Broken Stick."*

(l)

A bench minor penalty shall be imposed against the offending team if any player, Trainer, Coach, Manager or Club Executive interferes in any manner with any game official including Referee, Linesmen, Timekeepers or Goal Judges in the performance of their duties.

The Referee may assess further penalties under Rule 67 (Abuse of Officials) if he deems them to be warranted.

(m)

A misconduct penalty shall be imposed on any player or players who, except for the purpose of taking their positions on the penalty bench, enter or remain in the Referee's crease while he is reporting to or consulting with any game official including Linesmen, Timekeeper, Penalty Timekeeper, Official Scorer or Announcer.

(n)

A minor penalty shall be imposed on any player who is guilty of unsportsmanlike conduct including, but not limited to, hair-pulling, biting, grabbing hold of face mask, etc.

Rule 43. Adjustment to Clothing and Equipment

(a)

Play shall not be stopped nor the game delayed by reason of adjustments to clothing, equipment, shoes, skates or sticks.

For an infringement of this rule, a minor penalty shall be given.

(b)

The onus of maintaining clothing and equipment in proper condition shall be upon the player. If adjustments are required, the player shall retire from the ice and play shall continue uninterruptedly with a substitute.

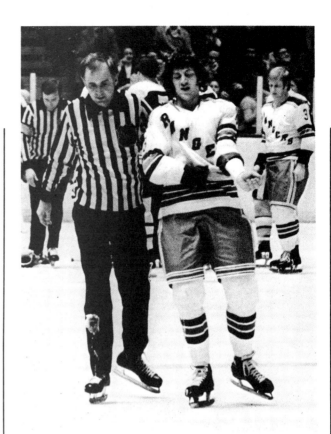

Players "should" proceed directly to penalty box.

(c)

No delay shall be permitted for the repair or adjustment of goalkeeper's equipment. If adjustments are required the goalkeeper will retire from the ice and his place will be taken by the substitute goalkeeper immediately.

(d)

For an infraction of this rule by a goalkeeper, a minor penalty shall be imposed.

Rule 44. Attempt to Injure

(a)

A match penalty shall be imposed on any player who deliberately attempts to injure an opponent and the circumstances shall be reported to the President for further action. A substitute for the penalized player shall be permitted at the end of the fifth minute.

In addition to the match penalty, the player shall be automatically suspended from further competition until the President has ruled on the issue.

(b)

A Game Misconduct penalty shall be imposed on any player who deliberately attempts to injure an Official, Manager, Coach or Trainer in any manner and the circumstances shall be reported to the President for further action.

(NOTE) *The President, upon preliminary investigation indicating the probable imposition of supplementary disciplinary action, may order the immediate suspension of a player, who has incurred a match penalty under this rule, pending the final determination of such supplementary disciplinary action.*

Rule 45. Board-Checking

(a)

A minor or major penalty, at the discretion of the Referee based upon the degree of violence of the impact with the boards, shall be imposed on any player who bodychecks, cross-checks, elbows, charges or trips an opponent in such a manner that causes the opponent to be thrown violently into the boards.

(NOTE) *Any unnecessary contact with a player playing the puck on an obvious "icing" or "off-side" play which results in that player being knocked into the fence is "boarding" and must be penalized as such. In other instances where there is no contact with the fence it should be treated as "charging."*

"Rolling" an opponent (if he is the puck carrier) along the fence where he is endeavoring to go through too small an opening is not boarding. However, if the opponent is not the puck carrier, then such action should be penalized as boarding, charging, interference or if the arms or stick are employed it should be called holding or hooking.

(b)
When a major penalty is imposed under this Rule for a foul resulting in injury to the face or head of an opponent an automatic fine of fifty dollars ($50.00) shall be imposed.

Rule 46. Broken Stick

(a)
A player without a stick may participate in the game. A player whose stick is broken may participate in the game provided he drops the broken portion. A minor penalty shall be imposed for an infraction of this rule.

(NOTE) *A broken stick is one which, in the opinion of the Referee, is unfit for normal play.*

(b)
A goalkeeper may continue to play with a broken stick until stoppage of play or until he has been legally provided with a stick.

(c)
A player whose stick is broken may not receive a stick thrown on the ice from any part of the rink but must obtain same at his players' bench. A goalkeeper whose stick is broken may not receive a stick thrown on the ice from any part of the rink but may receive a stick from a teammate without proceeding to his players' bench. A minor penalty shall be imposed on the player or goalkeeper receiving a stick illegally under this rule.

(d)
A goalkeeper whose stick is broken or illegal may not go to the players' bench for a replacement but must receive his stick from a teammate.

For an infraction of this rule a minor penalty shall be imposed on the goalkeeper.

Rule 47. Charging

(a)
A minor or major penalty shall be imposed on a player who runs or jumps into or charges an opponent.

(b)
When a major penalty is imposed under this rule for a foul, resulting in injury to the face or head of an opponent, an automatic fine of fifty dollars ($50.00) shall be imposed.

(c)
A minor or major penalty shall be imposed on a player who charges a goalkeeper while the goalkeeper is within his goal crease.

(NOTE) *If more than two steps or strides are taken it shall be considered a charge.*

A goalkeeper is NOT "fair game" just because he is outside the goal crease area. A penalty for interference or charging (minor or major) should be called in every case where an opposing player makes unnecessary contact with a goalkeeper.

Likewise Referees should be alert to penalize goalkeepers for tripping, slashing or spearing in the vicinity of the goal.

Rule 48. Cross-Checking and Butt-Ending

(a)
A minor or major penalty, at the discretion of the Referee, shall be imposed on a player who "cross-checks" an opponent.

(b)
A major penalty shall be imposed on any player who "butt-ends" or attempts to "butt-end" an opponent.

(NOTE) *Attempt to "butt-end" shall include all cases where a "butt-end" gesture is made regardless whether body contact is made or not.*

(c)
When a major penalty is imposed under this rule an automatic fine of fifty dollars ($50.00) shall also be imposed.

(NOTE) *Cross-check shall mean a check delivered with both hands on the stick and no part of the stick on the ice.*

Rule 49. Deliberate Injury of Opponents

(a)
A match penalty shall be imposed on a player who deliberately injures an opponent in any manner.

(NOTE) *Any player wearing tape or any other material on his hands who cuts or injures an opponent during an altercation shall receive a match penalty under this rule.*

(b)
In addition to the match penalty, the player shall be automatically suspended from further competition until the President has ruled on the issue.

(c)
No substitute shall be permitted to take the place of the penalized player until ten minutes actual playing time shall have elapsed, from the time the penalty was imposed.

(d)
A Game Misconduct penalty shall be imposed on any player who deliberately injures an Official, Manager, Coach or Trainer in any manner and the circumstances shall be reported to the President for further action

Rule 50. Delaying the Game

(a)
A minor penalty shall be imposed on any player or goalkeeper who delays the game by deliberately shooting or batting the puck with his stick outside the playing area.

(NOTE) *This penalty shall apply also when a player or goalkeeper deliberately bats or shoots the puck with his stick outside the playing area after a stoppage of play.*

(b)
A minor penalty shall be imposed on any player or goalkeeper who throws or deliberately bats the puck with his hand or stick outside the playing area.

(c)
A minor penalty shall be imposed on any player (including goalkeeper) who delays the game by deliberately displacing a goal post from its normal position. The Referee or Linesmen shall stop play immediately when a goal post has been displaced.

If the goal post is deliberately displaced by a goalkeeper or player during the course of a "breakaway" a penalty shot will be awarded to the non-offending team, which shot shall be taken by the player last in possession of the puck.

(NOTE) *A player with a "breakaway" is defined as a player in control of the puck with no opposition between him and the opposing goal and with a reasonable scoring opportunity.*

(d)
If by reason of insufficient time in the regular playing time or by reason of

Cross-checking and high sticking by Gilbert.

penalties already imposed the minor penalty awarded to a player for deliberately displacing his own goal post cannot be served in its entirety within the regular playing time of the game or at any time in overtime, a penalty shot shall be awarded against the offending team.

(e)

A bench minor penalty shall be imposed upon any team which, after warning by the Referee to its Captain or designated substitute to place the correct number of players on the ice and commence play, fails to comply with the Referee's direction and thereby causes any delay by making additional substitutions, by persisting in having its players off-side, or in any other manner.

Rule 51. Elbowing, Kneeing and Head-Butting

(a)

A minor or major penalty, at the discretion of the Referee, shall be imposed on any player who uses his elbow or knee in such a manner as to in any way foul an opponent.

(b)

When a major penalty is imposed under this rule for a foul resulting in an injury to an opponent an automatic fine of fifty dollars ($50.00) shall also be imposed.

(c)

A match penalty shall be imposed on any player who deliberately "head-butts" or attempts to "head-butt" an opponent during an altercation and the circumstances shall be reported to the President for further action. A substitute shall be permitted at the end of the fifth minute. In the event there is an injury to an opponent resulting from the foul no substitute shall be permitted to take the place of the penalized player until ten minutes time shall be elapsed.

Rule 52. Face-Offs

(a)

The puck shall be "faced-off" by the Referee or the Linesman dropping the puck on the ice between the sticks of the players "facing-off." Players facing-off will stand squarely facing their opponents' end of the rink approximately one stick length apart with the blade of their sticks on the ice.

When the face-off takes place in any of the end face-off circles the players taking part shall take their position so that they will stand squarely facing their opponent's end of the rink. The sticks on both players facing-off shall have the blade on the ice within the designated white area. The visiting player shall place his stick within the designated white area first.

No other player shall be allowed to enter the face-off circle or come within fifteen feet of the players facing-off the puck, and must stand on side on all face-offs.

If a violation of this sub-section of this rule occurs the Referee or Linesman shall re-face the puck.

(b)

If after warning by the Referee or Linesman either of the players fails to take his proper position for the face-off promptly, the official shall be entitled to face-off the puck notwithstanding such default.

(c)

In the conduct of any face-off anywhere on the playing surface no player facing-off shall make any physical contact with his opponent's body by means of his own body or by his stick except in the course of playing the puck after the face-off has been completed.

For violation of this Rule the Referee shall impose a minor penalty or penalties on the player(s) whose action(s) caused the physical contact.

(NOTE) *"Conduct of any face-off" commences when the Referee des-*

Deliberate injury draws a match penalty.

ignates the place of the face-off and he (or the Linesman) takes up his position to drop the puck.

(d)

If a player facing-off fails to take his proper position immediately when directed by the Official, the Official may order him replaced for that face-off by any teammate then on the ice.

No substitution of players shall be permitted until the face-off has been completed and play has been resumed except when a penalty is imposed which will affect the on-ice strength of either team.

(e)

A second violation of any of the provisions of subsection (a) hereof by the same team during the same face-off shall be penalized with a minor penalty to the player who commits the second violation of the rule.

(f)

When an infringement of a rule has been committed or a stoppage of play has been caused by any player of the attacking side in the Attacking Zone the ensuing face-off shall be made in the Neutral Zone on the nearest face-off spot.

(NOTE) *This includes stoppage of play caused by player of attacking side shooting the puck on the back of the defending team's net without any intervening action by the defending team.*

(g)

When an infringement of a rule has been committed by players of both sides in the play resulting in the stoppage, the ensuing face-off will be made at the place of such infringement or at the place where play is stopped.

(h)

When stoppage occurs between the end face-off spots and near the end of rink the puck shall be faced-off at the end face-off spot, on the side where the stoppage occurs unless otherwise expressly provided by these rules.

(i)

No face-off shall be made within fifteen feet of the goal or sidebaords.

(j)

When a goal is illegally scored as a result of a puck being deflected directly from an official anywhere in the defending zone the resulting face-off shall be made at the end face-off spot in the defending zone.

(k)

When the game is stopped for any reason not specifically covered in the official rules, the puck must be faced-off where it was last played.

(l)

The whistle will not be blown by the official to start play. Playing time will commence from the instant the puck is faced-off and will stop when the whistle is blown.

(m)

Following a stoppage of play, should one of both defensemen, who are the point players or any player coming from the bench of the attcking team enter into the attacking zone beyond the outer edge of the corner face-off circle, the ensuing face-off shall take place at the nearest spot in the neutral zone near the blue line of the defending team.

Rule 53. Falling on Puck

(a)

A minor penalty shall be imposed on a player other than the goalkeeper who deliberately falls on or gathers a puck into his body.

(NOTE) *Any player who drops to his knees to block shots should not be penalized if the puck is shot under them or becomes lodged in their clothing or equipment but any use of the hands to make the puck unplayable should be penalized promptly.*

(b)

A minor penalty shall be imposed on a goalkeeper who (when he is in his own goal crease) deliberately falls on or gathers the puck into his body or who holds or places the puck against any part of the goal in such a manner as to cause a stoppage of play unless he is actually being checked by an opponent.

(NOTE) *Refer to Rule 73 (c) for Rule governing freezing of puck by goalkeeper outside of his crease area.*

(c)

No defending player, except the goalkeeper, will be permitted to fall on the puck or hold the puck or gather a puck into the body or hands when the puck is within the goal crease.

For infringement of this rule, play shall immediately be stopped and a penalty shot shall be ordered against the offending team, but no other penalty shall be given.

(NOTE) *This rule shall be interpreted so that a penalty shot will be awarded only when the puck is in the crease at the instant the offense occurs. However, in cases where the puck is outside the crease, Rule 53 (a) may still apply and a minor penalty may be imposed, even though no penalty shot is awarded.*

Rule 54. Fisticuffs

(a)

A major or a minor and a Game Misconduct penalty, at the discretion of the Referee, shall be imposed on any player who starts fisticuffs.

(b)

A minor penalty shall be imposed on a player who, having been struck, shall retaliate with a blow or attempted blow. However, at the discretion of the Referee a major or a double minor penalty or a Game Misconduct penalty may be imposed if such player continues the altercation.

(NOTE 1) *It is the intent and purpose of this Rule that the Referee shall impose the "Major and Game Misconduct" penalty in all cases when the instigator or retaliator of the fight is the aggressor and is plainly doing so for the purpose of intimidation or punishment.*

Face-offs start play after every whistle.

303

Fighting draws a major, double minor, or minor penalty.

(NOTE 2) *The Referee is provided very wide latitude in the penalties which he may impose under this rule. This is done intentionally to enable him to differentiate between the obvious degrees of responsiblity of the participants either for starting the fighting or persisting in continuing the fighting. The discretion provided should be exercised realistically.*

(NOTE 3) *Referees are directed to employ every means provided by these Rules to stop "brawling" and should use this Rule and Rules 42 (e) and (f) for this purpose.*

(c)

A Misconduct or Game Misconduct penalty shall be imposed on any player involved in fisticffs off the playing surface or with another player who is off the playing surface.

(d)

A Game Misconduct penalty, at the discretion of the Referee, shall be imposed on any player or goalkeeper who is the first to intervene in an altercation then in progress except when a match penalty is being imposed in the original altercation. This penalty is in addition to any other penalty incurred in the same incident.

(e)

When a fight occurs all players not engaged in the altercation shall separate and clear the zone i in which the altercation is taking place and shall move to areas designated by the Referee upon his command.

Failure to comply with instructions of the Referee will result in a club fine of one thousand dollars ($1,000) for the first offense, three thousand dollars ($3,000) for the second offense and five thousand dollars ($5,000) for each subsequent offense.

(NOTE) *In the case of those buildings where the benches are on the same side of the rink the visiting team will proceed to the vicinity of the penalty bench and the home team to the vicinity of its players' bench. In the case where the benches are on opposite sides of the rink each Club will proceed to its own players' bench. However, in the event that the altercation takes place in the neutral zone each Club will proceed to its own defensive zone.*

(f)

A Game Misconduct penalty shall be imposed on any player who is assessed a major penalty for fighting following the original altercaation.

Notwithstanding this rule, at the discretion of the Referee the automatic Game Misconduct penalty may be waived for a player in the altercation, if the opposing player was clearly the instigator of the altercation.

Rule 55.   Goals and Assists

(NOTE) *It is the responsibility of the official Scorer to award goals and assists, and his decision in this respect is final notwithstanding the report of the Referee or any other game official. Such awards shall be made or withheld strictly in accordance with the provisions of this rule. Therefore, it is essential that the Official Scorer shall be thoroughly familiar with every aspect of this rule, be alert to observe all actions which could affect the making of an award and, above all, the awards must be made or withheld with absolute impartiality.*

In case of an obvious error in awarding a goal or an assist which has been announced, it should be corrected promptly but changes should nott be made in the official scoring summary after the Referee has signed the Game Report.

(a)

A goal shall be scored when the puck shall have been put between the goal posts by the stick of a player of the attacking side, from in front, and below the cross bar, and entirely across a red line, the width of the diameter of the goal posts drawn on the ice from one goal post to the other.

(b)

A goal shall be scored if the puck is put into the goal in any way by a player of the defending side. The player of the attacking side who last played the puck shall be credited with the goal but no assist shall be awarded.

(c)

If an attacking player kicks the puck and it is deflected into the net by any player of the defending side except the goalkeeper, the goal shall be allowed. The player who kicked the puck shall be credited with the goal but no assist shall be awarded.

(d)

If the puck shall have been deflected into the goal from the shot of an attacking player by striking any part of the person of a player of the same side, a goal shall be allowed. The player who deflected the puck shall be credited with the goal. The goal shall not be allowed if the puck has been kicked, thrown or otherwise deliberately directed into the goal by any means other than a stick.

(e)

If a goal is scored as a result of a puck being deflected directly into the net from an official, the goal shall not be allowed.

(f)

Should a player legally propel a puck into the goal crease of the opponent club and the puck should become loose and available to another player of the attacking side, a goal scored on the play shall be legal.

(g)

Any goal scored, other than as covered by the official rules, shall not be allowed.

(h)

A "goal" shall be credited in the scoring records to a player who shall have propelled the puck into the opponents' goal. Each "goal" shall count one point in the player's record.

(i)

When a player scores a goal an "assist" shall be credited to the player or players taking part in the play immediately preceeding the goal, but not more than two assists can be given on any goal. Each "assist" so credited shall count one point in the player's record.

(j)

Only one point can be credited to any one player on a goal.

Rule 56.   Gross Misconduct

Refer to Rule 9—Misconduct Penalty

Rule 57.   Handling Puck With Hands

(a)

If a player, except the goalkeeper, closes his hand on the puck the play shall be stopped and a minor penalty shall be imposed on him. A goalkeeper who holds the puck with his hands for longer than three seconds shall be given a minor penalty unless he is actually boing checked by an opponent.

(b)

A goalkeeper must not deliberately hold the puck in any manner which in the opinion of the Referee causes a stoppage of play, nor throw the puck k forward towards the opponents' goal, nor deliberately pile up snow or obstacles at or near his net, that in the opinion of the referee would tend to prevent the scoring of a goal.

(NOTE) *The object of this entire rule is to keep the puck in play continuously and any action taken by the goalkeeper which causes an unncessary stoppage must be penalized without warning.*

(c)

The penalty for infringement of this rule by the goalkeeper shall be a minor penalty.

(NOTE) *In the case of puck thrown forward by the goalkeeper being taken by an opponent, the Referee shall allow the resulting play to be completed, and if a goal is scored by the non-offending team, it shall be*

Hooking or tripping may be called here—it's the referee's decision.

allowed and no penalty given; but if a goal is not scored, play shall be stopped and a minor penalty shall be imposed against the goalkeeper.

(d)

A minor penalty shall be imposed on a player except the goalkeeper who, while play is in progress, picks up the puck off the ice with his hand.

If a player, except the goalkeeper, picks up the puck with hand while play is in progress, from the ice in the goal crease area the play shall be stopped immediately and a penalty shot shall be awarded to the non-offending team.

(e)

A player shall be permitted to stop or "bat" a puck in the air with his open hand, or push it along the ice with his hand, and the play shall not be stopped unless in the opinion of the Referee he has deliberately directed the puck to a teammate, in which case the play shall be stopped and the puck faced-off at the spot where the offense occurred.

(NOTE) *The object of this rule is to ensure continuous action and the referee should NOT stop play unless he is satisfied that the directing of the puck to a teammate was in fact DELIBERATE.*

into the net at any time, but a goal shall be allowed when the puck has been legally "batted" or is deflected into the the goal by a defending player except the goalkeeper.

Rule 58.   High Sticks

(a)

The carrying of sticks above the normal height of the shoulder is prohibited, and a minor or major penalty may be imposed on a player violating this Rule, at the discretion of the Referee.

(b)

A goal scored from a stick so carried shall not be allowed, except by a player of the defending team.

(c)

When a player carries or holds any part of his stick above the height of his shoulder so that injury to the face or head of an opposing player results, the Referee shall have no alternative but to impose a major penalty on the offending player.

When a major penalty is imposed under this rule for a foul resulting in injury to the face or head of an opponent, an automatic fine of fifty dollars ($50.00) shall also be imposed.

(d)

Batting the puck with the stick above the normal height of the shoulders is prohibited and when it occurs there shall be a whistle and ensuing face-off at the spot where the offense occured unless:

1.   the puck is batted to an opponent in which case the play shall continue.

2.   a player of the defending side shall bat the puck into his own goal in which case the goal shall be allowed.

(NOTE) *When a player bats the puck to an opponent under sub-section 1 the Referee shall give the "washout" signal immediately. Otherwise he will stop the play.*

(e)

When either team is below the numerical strength of its opponent and a player of the team of greater numerical strength causes a stoppage of play by striking the puck with his stick above the height of his shoulder, the resulting face-off shall be made at one of the end face-off spots adjacent to the goal of the team causing the stoppage.

Rule 59.   Holding an Opponent

A minor penalty shall be imposed on a player who holds an opponent with hands or stick or in any other way.

Rule 60.   Hooking

(a)

A minor penalty shall be imposed on player who impedes or seeks to impede the progress of an opponent by "hooking" with his stick.

(b) A major penalty shall be imposed on any player who injures an opponent by "hooking."

When a major penalty is imposed under this rule for a foul resulting in injury to the face or head of an opponent, an automatic fine of fifty dollars ($50.00) shall also be imposed.

(NOTE) *When a player is checking another in such a way that there is only stick-to-stick contact such action is NOT either hooking or holding.*

Rule 61.   Icing the Puck

(a)

For the purpose of this rule, the center line will divide the ice into halves. Should any player of a team, equal or superior in numerical strength to the opposing team, shoot, bat, or deflect the puck from his own half of the ice, beyond the goal line of the opposing team, play shall be stopped and the puck faced off at the end face-off spot of the offending team, unless on the play the puck shall have entered the net of the opposing team, in which case the goal shall be allowed.

For the purpose of this rule the point of last contact with the puck by the team in possession shall be used to determine whether icing has occurred or not.

(NOTE 1) *If during the period of a delayed whistle due to a foul by a player of the side NOT in possession, the side in possession "ices" the puck, then the face-off following the stoppage of play shall take place in the Neutral zone near the Defending Blue Line of the team "icing" the puck.*

(NOTE 2) *When a team is "short-handed" as the result of penalty and the penalty is about to expire, the decision as to whether there has been an "icing" shall be determined at the instant the penalty expires. The action of the penalized player remaining in the penalty box will not alter the ruling.*

(NOTE 3) *For the purpose of interpretation of this rule "Icing the Puck" is completed, the instant the puck is touched first by a defending player (other than the goalkeeper) after it has crossed the Goal Line and if in the action of so touching the puck it is knocked or deflected into the net it is NO goal.*

(NOTE 4) *When the puck is shot and rebounds from the body or stick of an opponent in his own half of the ice so as to cross the goal line of the player shooting it shall not be considered as "icing."*

(NOTE 5) *Notwithstanding the provisions of this section concerning "batting" the puck in respect to the "icing the puck" rule, the provisions of the final paragraph of Rule 57 (e) apply and NO goal can be scored by batting the puck with the hand into the opponent's goal whether intended or not.*

(NOTE 6) *If while the Linesman has signalled a slow whistle for a clean interception unde Rule 71 (c), the player intercepting shoots or bats the puck beyond the opponent's goal line in such a manner as to consti-tute "icing the puck," the Linesman's "slow whistle" shall be considered exhausted the instant the puck crosses the blue line and "icing" shall be called in the usual manner.*

(b)

If a player of the side shooting the puck down the ice who is on-side and eligible to play the puck does so before it is touched by an opposing player, the play shall continue and it shall not be considered a violation of this rule.

Tripping is not always as obvious or as purposeful as it is here.

(NOTE) *If the team returns to full strength following a shot by one of its players, play shall continue and the face-off shall not take place.*

(d)

If, however, the puck shall go beyond the goal line in the opposite half of the ice directly from either of the players while facing off, it shall not be considered a violation of the rule.

(e)

If, in the opinion of the Linesman, a player of the opposing team excepting the goalkeeper is able to play the puck before it passes his goal line, but has not done so, the face-off shall not be allowed and play shall continue. If, in the opinion of the referee, the defending side intentionally abstains from playing the puck promptly when they are in a position to do so, he shall stop the play and order the resulting face-off on the adjacent corner face-off spot nearest the goal of the team at fault.

(NOTE) *The purpose of this section is to enforce continuous action and both Referee and Linesmen should interpret and apply the rule to produce this result.*

(f)

If the puck shall touch any part of a player of the opposing side or his skates or his stick, or if it passes through any part of the goal crease before it shall have reached his goal line, or shall have touched the goalkeeper or his skates or his stick or any time before or after crossing his goal line, it shall not be considered as "icing the puck" and play shall continue.

(NOTE) *If the goaltender takes any action to dislodge the puck from back of the nets the icing shall be washed out.*

(g)

If the Linesman shall have erred in calling an "icing the puck" infraction (regardless of whether either team is short-handed) the puck shall be faced on the center ice face-off spot.

(c)

If the puck was so shot by a player of a side below the numerical strength of the opposing team, play shall continue and the face-off shall not take place.

Rule 62. Interference

(a)

A minor penalty shall be imposed on a player who interferes with or impedes the progress of an opponent who is not in possession of the puck, or who deliberately knocks a stick out of an opponent's hand or who prevents a player who has dropped his stick or any other piece of equipment from regaining possession of it or who knocks or shoots any abandoned or broken stick or illegal puck or other debris towards an opposing puck carrier in a manner that could cause him to be distracted. (See also Rule 80 (a).)

(NOTE) *The last player to touch the puck—other than a goalkeeper— shall be considered the player in possession. In interpreting this rule the Referee should make sure which of the players is the one creating the interference—often it is the action and movement of the attacking player which causes the interference since the defending players are entitled to "stand their ground" or "shadow" the attacking players. Players of the side in possession shall not be allowed to "run" deliberate interference for the puck carrier.*

(b)

A minor penalty shall be imposed on any player on the players' bench or on the penalty bench who by means of his stick or his body interferes with the movements of the puck or of any opponent on the ice during the progress of play.

(c)

A minor penalty shall be imposed on a player who, by means of his stick or his body, interferes with or impedes the movements of the goalkeeper by actual physical contact, while he is in his goal crease area unless the puck is already in that area.

(d)

Unless the puck is in the goal crease area, a player of the attacking side may not stand on the goal crease line or in the goal crease or hold his stick in the goal crease area, and if the puck should enter the net while such condition prevails, a goal shall not be allowed, and the puck shall be faced in the neutral zone at face-off spot nearest the attacking zone of the offending team.

A minor penalty shall be imposed on any player of the attacking team who deliberately stands in the goal crease area.

(e)

If a player of the attacking side has been physically interfered with by the action of any defending player so as to cause him to be in the goal crease, and the puck should enter the net while the player so interfered with, is still within the goal crease, the "goal" shall be allowed.

(f)

If when the goalkeeper has been removed from the ice any member of his team (including the goalkeeper) not legally on the ice, including the Manager, Coach or Trainer interferes by means of his body or stick or any other object with the movements of the puck or an opposing player, the Referee shall immediately award a goal to the non-offending team.

(g)

When a player, in control of the puck in the opponent's side of the center red line, and having no other opponent to pass than the goalkeeper, is interfered with by a stick or any part thereof or any other object thrown or shot by any member of the defending team including the Manager, Coach or Trainer, a penalty shot shall be awarded to the non-offending side.

(NOTE) *The attention of Referees is directed particularly to three types of offensive interference which should be penalized;*
(1)When the defending team secures possession of the puck in its own end and the other players of that team run interference for the puck carrier by forming a protective screen against forechecker;
(2)When a player facing off obstructs his opposite number after the face-off when the opponent is not in possession of the puck;
(3)When the puck carrier makes a drop pass and follows through so as to make bodily contact with an opposing player.

Defensive interference consists of bodily contact with an opposing player who is not in possession of the puck.

Rule 63. Interference by/with Spectators

(a)

In the event of a player being held or interfered with by a spectator, the Referee or Linesman shall blow the whistle and play shall be stopped, unless the team of the player interfered with is in possession of the puck at this time when the play shall be allowed to be completed before blowing the whistle, and the puck shall be faced at the spot where last played at time of stoppage.

(b)

Any player who physically interferes with the spectators shall automatically incur a Gross Misconduct penalty and the Referee shall report all such infractions to the President who shall have full power to impose such further penalty as he shall deem appropriate.

(c)

In the event that objects are thrown on the ice which interfere with the progress of the game the Referee shall blow the whistle and stop the play, and the puck shall be faced-off at the spot play is stopped.

(NOTE) *The Referee shall report to the President for disciplinary action, all cases in which a player becomes involved in an altercation with a spectator.*

Rule 64. Kicking Player

A match penalty shall be imposed on any player who kicks or attempts to kick another player.

(NOTE) *Whether or not an injury occurs the Referee may, at his discretion, impose a ten-minute time penalty under this rule.*

Rule 65. Kicking Puck

Kicking the puck shall be permitted in all zones, but a goal may not be scored by the kick of an attacking player except if an attacking player kicks the puck and it is deflected into the net by any players of the defending side except the goalkeeper.

Rule 66. Leaving Players' Bench or Penalty Bench

(a)

No player may leave the players' bench or penalty bench at any time during an altercation, or for the purpose of starting an altercation. Substitutions made prior to the altercation shall be permitted provided the players so substituting do not enter the altercation.

(b)

For violation of this rule a Double Minor penalty shall be imposed on the player of the team who was first to leave the players' bench or penalty bench during an altercation. If players of both teams leave their respective benches at the same time, the first identifiable player of each team to do so shall incur a Double Minor penalty. A Game Misconduct penalty shall also be imposed on any player who is penalized under this sub-section and the Club of a player(s) incurring the Game Misconduct penalty shall incur a fine of one thousand dollars ($1000) for the first such incident, three thousand dollars ($3000) for the second such incident and five thousand dollars ($5000) for the third and each subsequent such incident.

(c)

Any player (other than those dealt with under sub-section (b) hereof) who leaves his players' bench during an altercation and is assessed any penalty for his actions, shall also incur an automatic Game Misconduct penalty.

(d)

A player (other than those dealt with under subsection (b) hereof) who leaves his players' bench during an altercation, shall be subject to an automatic fine of one hundred dollars ($100.00) and the Referee shall

report all such infractions to the President who shall have full power to impose such further penalty as he shall deem appropriate.

(NOTE 1) *This automatic fine shall be imposed in addition to the normal penalties imposed for fouls committed by the player after he has left the players' bench.*

(NOTE 2) *For the purpose of determining which player was first to leave his players' bench during an altercation the Referee may consult with the Linesmen or Off-Ice Officials.*

(e)

In regular League, Exhibition and Play-off games any player who incurs a penalty under sub-section (a) hereof (for leaving the players' bench or penalty bench first) shall be suspended automatically for the next three (3) regular League games of his team. For each subsequent violation by the same player the automatic suspension shall be increased by three (3) games.

Suspensions incurred during regular League play shall carry into the Play-offs.

(f)

Except at the end of each period, or on expiration of penalty, no player may at any time leave the penalty bench.

(g)

A penalized player who leaves the penalty bench before his penalty has expired, whether play is in progress or not, shall incur an addition minor penalty, after serving his unexpired penalty.

(h)

Any penalized player leaving the penalty bench during stoppage of play and during an altercation shall incur a minor penalty plus a Game Misconduct penalty after serving his unexpired time.

(i)

If a player leaves the penalty bench before his penalty is fully served, the Penalty Timekeeper shall note the time and signal the Referee who will immediately stop play.

(j)

In the case of a player returning to the ice before his time has expired through an error of the Penalty Timekeeper, he is not to serve an additional penalty, but must serve his unexpired time.

(k)

If a player of an attacking side in possession of the puck shall be in such a position as to have no opposition between him and the opposing goalkeeper, and while in such position he shall be interfered with by a player of the opposing side who shall have illegally entered the game, the Referee shall impose a penalty shot against the side to which the offending player belongs.

(l)

If the opposing goalkeeper has been removed and an attacking player in possession of the puck shall have no player of the defending team to pass and a stick or a part thereof or any other object is thrown or shot by an opposing player or the player is fouled from behind thereby being prevented from having a clear shot on an open goal, a goal shall be awarded against the offending team.

If when the opposing goalkeeper has been removed from the ice a player of the side attacking the unattended goal is interfered with by a player who shall have entered the game illegally, the Referee shall immediately award a goal to the non-offending team.

(m)

If a Coach or Manager gets on the ice after the start of a period and before that period is ended the Referee shall impose a bench minor penalty against the team and report the incident to the President for disciplinary action.

Elbowing on both players—two minutes each.

Legal attack: puck precedes the player over blue line.

(n)

Any Club Executive or Manager committing the same offense, will be automatically fined two hundred dollars ($200.00).

(o)

If a penalized player returns to the ice from the penalty bench before his penalty has expired by his own error or the error of the Penalty Timekeeper, any goal scored by his own team while he is illegally on the ice shall be disallowed, but all penalties imposed on either team shall be served as regular penalties.

(p)

If a player shall illegally enter the game from his own players' bench or from the penalty bench, any goal scored by his own team while he is illegally on the ice shall be disallowed, but all penalties imposed against either team shall be served as regular penalties.

(q)

A bench minor penalty shall be imposed on a team whose player(s) leave the players' bench for any purpose other than a change of players and when no altercation is in progress.

Rule 67. Physical Abuse of Officials

(a)

Any player who deliberately strikes an official, deliberately applies physical force in any manner against an official, deliberately makes contact with an official, physically demeans an official or deliberately applies physical force to an official solely for the purpose of getting free of such an official during or immediately following an altercation shall receive a Game Misconduct penalty.

In addition, the following automatic game suspensions shall apply:

Category I

Any player who deliberately strikes an official or who deliberately applies physical force in any manner against an official shall be suspended for 20 games.

Category II

Any player who by his actions physically demeans an official or who deliberately applies physical force to an official solely for the purpose of getting free of such an official during an altercation with another player shall be suspended for three games.

The Referee, immediately after the game in which any such Game Misconduct penalty is imposed, shall after consultation with the linesmen decide the category of the offense. He shall make an oral report to the President and advise of the category of the offense.

The player and club involved shall be notified by the League of said decision the morning following the game.

(b)

Any Club Executive, Manager, Coach or Trainer who holds or strikes an official, shall be automatically suspended from the game, ordered to the dressing room, and a substantial fine shall be imposed by the President.

Rule 68. Obscene or Profane Language or Gestures

(a)

Players shall not use obscene gestures on the ice or anywhere in the rink before, during or after the game. For a violation of this rule a Game Misconduct penalty shall be imposed and the Referee shall report the circumstances to the President of the League for further disciplinary action.

(b)

Players shall not use profane language on the ice or anywhere in the rink before, during or after a game. For violation of this Rule, a Misconduct Penalty shall be imposed except when the violation occurs in the vicinity of the players' bench in which case a bench minor penalty shall be imposed.

(NOTE) *It is the responsibility of all game officials and all Club officials to send a confidential report to the President setting out the full details concerning the use of obscene gestures or language by any player, Coach or other official. The President shall take such further disciplinary action as he shall deem appropriate.*

(c)

Club Executives, Managers, Coaches and Trainers shall not use obscene or profane language or gestures anywhere in the rink. For violation of this rule a bench minor penalty shall be imposed.

Rule 69. Off-Sides

(a)

The position of the player's skates and not that of his stick shall be the determining factor in all instances in deciding an "off-side." A player is off-side when both skates are completely over the outer edge of the determining center line or blue line involved in the play.

(NOTE 1) *A player is "on-side" when "either" of his skates are in contact with or on his own side of the line at the instant the puck completely crosses the outer edge of that line regardless of the position of his stick.*

(NOTE 2) *It should be noted that while the position of the player's skates is what determines whether a player is "off-side" nevertheless the question of "off-side" never arises until the puck has completely crossed the outer edge of the line at which time the decision is to be made.*

(b)

If in the opinion of the Linesman an intentional off-side play has been made, the puck shall be faced-off at the end face-off spot in the defending zone of the offending team.

(NOTE 3) *This rule does not apply to a team below the numerical strength of its opponent. In such cases the puck shall be faced-off at the spot from which the pass was made.*

(NOTE 4) *An intentional off-side is one which is made for the purpose of securing a stoppage of play regardless of the reason, or where an off-side play is made under conditions where there is no possibility of completing a legal pass.*

(c)

If the Linesmen shall have erred in calling an off-side pass infraction (regardless of whether either team is short-handed) the puck shall be faced on the center ice face-off spot.

Rule 70. Passes

(a)

The puck may be passed by any player to a player of the same side within any one of the three zones into which the ice is divided, but may not be passed forward from a player in one zone to a player of the same side in another zone, except by a player on the defending team, who may make and take forward passes from their own defending zone to the center line without incurring an off-side penalty. This "forward pass" from the Defending Zone must be completed by the pass receiver who is preceded by the puck across the center line, otherwise play shall be stopped and the face-off shall be at the point from which the pass was made.

(NOTE 1) *The position of the puck (not the player's skates) shall be the determining factor in deciding from which zone the pass was made.*

(NOTE 2) *Passes may be completed legally at the center red line in exactly the same manner as passes at the attacking blue line.*

(b)

Should the puck, having been passed, contact any part of the body, stick or skates of a player of the same side who is legally on-side, the pass shall be considered to have been completed.

Forward passing is permitted within zones.

(c)

The player last touched by the puck shall be deemed to be in possession.

Rebounds off goalkeeper's pads or other equipment shall not be considered as a change of possession or the completion of the play by the team when applying Rule 34 (b).

(d)

If a player in the Neutral Zone is preceded into the Attacking Zone by the puck passed from the Neutral Zone he shall be eligible to take possession of the puck anywhere in the Attacking Zone except when the "Icing the Puck" rule applies.

(e)

If a player in the same zone from which a pass is made is preceded by the puck into succeeding zones he shall be eligile to take possession of the puck in that zone except where the "Icing the Puck" rule applies.

(f)

If an attacking player passes the puck backward toward his own goal from the Attacking Zone, an opponent may play the puck anywhere regardless of whether he (the opponent) was in the same zone at the time the puck was passed or not. *(No "slow whistle.")*

Rule 71. Preceding Puck into Attacking Zone
(a)
Players of an attacking team must not precede the puck into the Attacking Zone.
(b)
For violation of this rule, the play is stopped, and puck shall be faced-off in the Neutral Zone at face-off spot nearest the Attacking Zone of the offending team.

(NOTE) *A player actually controlling the puck who shall cross the line ahead of the puck, shall not be considered "off-side."*
(c)
If, however, notwithstanding the fact that a member of the attacking team shall have preceded the puck into the Attacking Zone, the puck be cleanly intercepted by a member of the defending team at or near the blue line, and be carried or passed by them into the Neutral Zone, the "off-side" shall be ignored and play permitted to continue.

(Officials will carry out this rule by means of the "slow whistle.")
(d)
If a player legally carries or passes the puck back into his own Defending Zone while a player of the opposing team is in such Defending Zone, the "off-side" shall be ignored and play permitted to continue.

(No "slow whistle.")

Rule 72. Puck Out of Bounds or Unplayable
(a)
When the puck goes outside the playing area at either end, or either side of the rink or strikes any obstacles above the playing surface other than the boards, glass or wire it shall be faced-off from whence it was shot or deflected, unless otherwise expressly provided in these rules.
(b)
When the puck becomes lodged in the netting on the outside of either goal so as to make it unplayable, or if it is frozen between opposing players intentionally or otherwise the Referee shall stop the play and face-off the puck at either of the adjacent face-off spots unless in the opinion of the Referee the stoppage was caused by a player of the attacking team, in which case the resulting face-off shall be conducted in the Neutral Zone.

(NOTE) *This includes stoppage of play caused by player of attacking side shooting the puck on to the back of the defending team's net without any intervening action by the defending team.*

The defending team and/or the attacking team may play the puck off the net at any time. However, should the puck remain on the net for longer than three seconds, play shall be stopped and the face-off shall take place in the end face-off zone except when the stoppage is caused by the attacking team, then the face-off shall take place on a face-off spot in the neutral zone.
(c)
A minor penalty shall be imposed on a goalkeeper who deliberately drops the puck on the goal netting to cause a stoppage of play.
(d)
If the puck comes to rest on top of the boards surrounding the playing area it shall be considered to be in play and may be played legally by hand or stick.

Rule 73. Puck Must Be Kept in Motion
(a)
The puck must at all times be kept in motion.

(b)
Except to carry the puck behind its goal once, a side in possession of the puck in its own defense area shall always advance the puck towards the opposing goal, except if it shall be prevented from so doing by players of the opposing side.

For the first infraction of this rule play shall be stopped and a face-off shall be made at either end face-off spot adjacent to the goal of the team causing the stoppage and the Referee shall warn the Captain or designated substitute of the offending team of the reason for the face-off. For a second violation by any player of the same team in the same period a minor penalty shall be imposed on the player violating the rule.
(c)
A minor penalty shall be imposed on any player including the goalkeeper who holds, freezes or plays the puck with his stick, skates or body in such a manner as to deliberately cause a stoppage of play.

(NOTE) *With regard to a goalkeeper this rule applies outside of his goal crease only.*
(d)
A player beyond his defense area shall not pass nor carry the puck backward into his Defense Zone for the purpose of delaying the game except when his team is below the numerical strength of the opponents on the ice.
(e)
For an infringement of this rule, the face-off shall be at the nearest end face-off spot in the Defending Zone of the offending team.

Rule 74. Puck Out of Sight and Illegal Puck
(a)
Should a scramble take place, or a player accidentally fall on the puck, and the puck be out of sight of the Referee, he shall immediatley blow his

Player is in perfect pass-receiving position.

whistle and stop the play. The puck shall then be "faced-off" at the point where the play was stopped, unless otherwise provided for in the rules.

(b)

If, at any time while play is in progress, a puck other than the one legally in play shall appear on the playing surface, the play shall not be stopped but shall continue with the legal puck until the play then in progress is completed by change of possession.

Rule 75. Puck Striking Official

Play shall not be stopped if the puck touches an official anywhere on the rink, regardless of whether a team is short-handed or not.

Rule 76. Refusing to Start Play

(a)

If, when both teams are on the ice, one team for any reason shall refuse to play when ordered to do so by the Referee, he shall warn the Captain and allow the team so refusing fifteen seconds within which to begin the game or resume play. If at the end of that time the team shall still refuse to play, the Referee shall impose a two-minute penalty on a player of the offending team to be designated by the Manager or Coach of that team, through the playing Captain; and should there be a repetition of the same incident the Referee shall notify the Manager or Coach that he has been fined the sum of two hundred dollars ($200.00). Should the offending team still refuse to play, the Referee shall have no alternative but to declare that the game be forfeited to the non-offending club, and the case shall be reported to the President for further action.

(b)

If a team, when ordered to do so by the Referee, through its Club Executive, Manager or Coach, fails to go on the ice, and start play within five minutes, the Club Executive, Manager or Coach shall be fined five hundred dollars ($500.00); the game shall be forfeited, and the case shall be reported to the President for further action.

(NOTE) *The President of the League shall issue instructions pertaining to records, etc., of a forfeited game.*

Rule 77. Slashing

(a)

A minor or major penalty, at the discretion of the Referee, shall be imposed on any player who impedes or seeks to impede the progress of an opponent by "slashing" with his stick.

(b)

A major penalty shall be imposed on any player who injures an opponent by slashing. When a major penalty is imposed under this rule for a foul resulting in injury to the face or head of an opponent, an automatic fine of fifty dollars ($50.00) shall also be imposed.

(NOTE) *Referees should penalize as "slashing" any player who swings his stick at any opposing player (whether in or out of range) without actually striking him or where a player on the pretext of playing the puck makes a wild swing at the puck with the object of intimidating an opponent.*

(c)

Any player who swings his stick at another player in the course of any altercation shall be subject to a fine of not less than two hundred dollars ·($200.00), with or without suspension, to be imposed by the President.

(NOTE) *The Referee shall impose the normal appropriate penalty provided in the other section of this rule and shall in addition report promptly to the President all infractions under this section.*

Rule 78. Spearing

(a)

A major penalty shall be imposed on a player who spears or attempts to spear an opponent.

Player precedes puck across the blue line—off-sides.

315

(NOTE) *"Attempt to spear" shall include all cases where a spearing gesture is made regardless whether bodily contact is made or not.*
(b)
In addition to the major penalty imposed under this rule an automatic fine of fifty dollars ($50.00) will also be imposed.

(NOTE 1) *"Spearing" shall mean stabbing an opponent with the point of the stick blade while the stick is being carried with one hand or both hands.*

(NOTE 2) *Spearing may also be treated as a "deliberate attempt to injure" under Rule 44.*

Rule 79. Start of Game and Periods

(a)
The game shall be commenced at the time scheduled by a "face-off" in the center of the rink and shall be renewed promptly at the conclusion of each intermission in the same manner.

No delay shall be permitted by reason of any ceremony, exhibition, demonstration or presentation unless consented to reasonably in advance by the visiting team.

(b)
Home clubs shall have the choice of goals to defend at the start of the game except where both players' benches are on the same side of the rink, in which case the home club shall start the game defending the goal nearest to its own bench. The teams shall change ends for each succeeding regular or overtime period.

(c)
During the pre-game warm-up (which shall not exceed twenty minutes in duration) and before the commencement of play in any period each team shall confine its activity to its own end of the rink so as to leave clear any area thirty feet wide across the center of the Neutral Zone.

(NOTE 1) *The Game Timekeeper shall be responsible for signalling the commencement and termination of the pre-game warm-up and any violation of this rule by the players shall be reported to the President by the Supervisor when in attendance at a game.*

(NOTE 2) *Players shall not be permitted to come on the ice during a stoppage in play or at the end of the first and second periods for the purpose of warming-up. The Referee will report any violation of this rule to the President for disciplinary action.*

(d)
Fifteen minutes before the time scheduled for the start of the game both teams shall vacate the ice and proceed to their dressing rooms while the ice is being flooded. Both teams shall be signalled by the Game Timekeeper to return to the ice together in time for the scheduled start of the game.

(e)
When a team fails to appear on the ice promptly without proper justification a fine shall be assessed against the offending team. The amount of the fine to be decided by the President.

Rule 80. Throwing Stick

(a)
When any player of the defending side, or Manager, Coach or Trainer, deliberately throws or shoots a stick or any part thereof or any other object, at the puck in his Defending Zone, the Referee shall allow the play to be completed and if a goal is not scored a penalty shot shall be awarded to the non-offending side, which shot shall be taken by the player designated by the Referee as the player fouled.

If, however, the goal being unattended and the attacking player having no defending player to pass and having a chance to score on an "open net," a stick or part thereof or any other object be thrown or shot by any member of the defending team, including the Manager, Coach or Trainer thereby preventing a shot on the "open net", a goal shall be awarded to the attacking side.

(NOTE 1) *If the officials are unable to determine the person against whom the offense was made the offended team through the Captain shall designate the player on the ice at the time the offense was committed who will take the shot.*

(NOTE 2) *For the purpose of this rule, an open net is defined as one from which a goalkeeper has been removed for an additional attacking player.*

(b)
A major penalty shall be imposed on any player *on the ice* who throws his stick or any part thereof or any other object in the direction of the puck in any zone, except when such act has been penalized by the assessment of a penalty shot or the award of a goal.

(NOTE) *When a player discards the broken portion of a stick by tossing it to the side of the ice (and not over the boards) in such a way as will not interfere with play or opposing player, no penalty will be imposed for so doing.*

(c)
A Misconduct or Game Misconduct penalty, at the discretion of the Referee, shall be imposed on a player who throws his stick or any part thereof outside the playing area. If the offense is committed in protest of an official's decision a minor penalty for unsportsmanlike conduct plus a Game Misconduct penalty shall be assessed to the offending player.

Rule 81. Time of Match

(a)
The time allowed for a game shall be three twenty-minute periods of actual play with a rest intermission between periods.

Play shall be resumed promptly following each intermission upon the expiry of fifteen minutes from the completion of play in the preceding period. A preliminary warning shall be given by the Game Timekeeper to the officials and to both teams three minutes prior to the resumption of play in each period and the final warning shall be given in sufficient time to enable the teams to resume play promptly.

(NOTE) *For the purpose of keeping the spectators informed as to the time remaining during intermission the Game Timekeeper will use the electric clock to record length of intermissions.*

(b)
The team scoring the greatest number of goals during the three twenty-minute periods shall be the winner, and shall be credited with two points in the League standing.

(c)
In the intervals between periods, the ice surface shall be flooded unless mutually agreed to the contrary.

(d)
If any unusual delay occurs within five minutes of the end of the first or second periods the Referee may order the next regular intermission to be taken immediately and the balance of the period will be completed on the resumption of play with the teams defending the same goals, after which the teams will change ends and resume play of the ensuing period without delay.

(NOTE) *If a delay takes place with more than five minutes remaining in the first or second period, the Referee will order the next regular intermission to be taken immediately only when requested to do so by the Home Club.*

Rule 82. Tied Games

(a)
If, at the end of three (3) regular twenty-minute periods, the score shall be

tied, the teams will play an additional period of not more than five (5) minutes with the team scoring first being declared the winner. If, at the end of the overtime period, the score remains tied, each team shall be credited with one point in the League standing.

(NOTE) *The overtime period will be commenced immediately following a two-minute rest period during which the players will remain on the ice. The teams will switch ends for the overtime period.*

(b)
Special conditions for duration and number of periods of play-off games, shall be arranged by the Board of Governors.

Rule 83. Tripping

(a)
A minor penalty shall be imposed on any player who shall place his stick, knee, foot, arm, hand or elbow in such a manner that it shall cause his opponent to trip or fall.

(NOTE 1) *If in the opinion of the Referee a player is unquestionably hook-checking the puck and obtains possession of it, thereby tripping puck carrier, no penalty shall be imposed.*

(NOTE 2) *Accidental trips occurring simultaneously with or after stoppage of play will not be penalized.*

(b)
When a player, in control of the puck in the opponent's side of the center red line, and having no other opponent to pass than the goalkeeper, is tripped or otherwise fouled from behind thus preventing a reasonable scoring opportunity a penalty shot shall be awarded to the non-offending side. Nevertheless the Referee shall not stop the play until the attacking side has lost possession of the puck to the defending side.

(NOTE) *The intention of this rule is to restore a reasonable scoring opportunity which has been lost by reason of a foul from behind when the foul is committed in the opponent's side of the center red line.*

By "control of the Puck" is meant the act of propelling the puck with the stick. If while it is being propelled the puck is touched by another player or his equipment or hits the goal or goes free the player shall no longer be considered to be "in control of the puck."

(c)
If, when the opposing goalkeeper has been removed from the ice, a player in control of the puck is tripped or otherwise fouled with no opposition between him and the opposing goal, thus preventing a reasonable scoring opportunity, the Referee shall immediately stop the play and award a goal to the attacking team.

Rule 84. Unnecessary Roughness

At the discretion of the Referee, a minor penalty or double minor penalty may be imposed on any player deemed guilty of unnecessary roughness.

Rule 85. Time-Outs

Each team shall be permitted to take one time-out of thirty seconds duration during the course of regular time or overtime in the case of a play-off game and which must be taken during a normal stoppage of play. Any player designated by the Coach will indicate to the Referee that his team is exercising its option and the Referee will report the time-out to the Game Timekeeper who shall be responsible for signalling the termination of the time-out.

(NOTE) *All players including the goalkeepers on the ice at the time of the time-out will be allowed to go to their respective benches. Only one time-out can be taken at a stoppage and no time-out will be allowed after a reasonable amount of time has elapsed during a normal stoppage of play.$*

Fighting draws at least two minutes, often five.

317

Rosters

In some cases, a player may have performed for another NHL and/or minor league team in years cited.

BOSTON BRUINS

Players

Adduono, Rick 1975-76
Aldcorn, Gary 1960-61
Anderson, Earl 1974-77
Arbour, John 1965-66; 1967-68
Armstrong, Robert. 1950-62
Ashbee, W. Barry. 1965-66
Atkinson, Steven 1968-69
Aubuchon, Oscar 1942-44
Awrey, Donald 1963-73
Babando, Peter 1947-49
Bailey, Garnet 1968-73
Balfour, Murray 1964-65
Baluik, Stanley 1959-60
Barr, David 1981-83
Barry, Edward 1946-47
Barry, Martin 1929-35
Barry, William R. "Ray" 1951-52
Bartlett, James 1960-61
Bauer, Robert 1935-42;
1945-47; 1951-52
Beattie, John "Red". 1930-31; 1932-38
Beckett, Robert. 1956-58;
1961-62; 1963-64
Bennett, William. 1978-79
Benson, Robert 1924-25
Bergdinon, Fred 1925-26
Besler, Philip 1935-36
Bettio, Silvio "Sam" 1949-50
Beverley, Nicholas. 1966-67;
1969-70; 1971-74
Bionda, Jack 1956-59
Blackburn, J. Donald 1962-63
Blake, L. Robert. 1935-36
Bodnar, August "Gus". 1953-55
Boivin, Leo 1954-66
Boldirev, Ivan 1970-72
Boll, Frank "Buzz" 1942-44
Bonin, Marcel 1955-56
Boone, Carl 1957-58
Boucher, William 1926-27
Bourque, Raymond 1979-83
Boyd, Irvin "Yank" 1931-32; 1942-44
Brackenborough, John 1925-26
Bradley, Barton 1949-50
Brennan, Thomas 1943-45
Briden, Archibald 1926-27
Brown, Adam 1951-52
Bruce, A. Gordon 1940-42; 1945-46
Buchanan, Ronald 1966-67
Bucyk, John 1957-78
Burch, H. William 1932-33
Burke, Edward. 1931-32
Burns, Charles. 1959-63
Byers, Gordon 1949-50
Caffery, John "Jack" 1956-58
Cahill, Charles 1925-26
Cain, Herbert. 1939-46

Calladine, Norman. 1942-45
Carleton K. Wayne. 1969-71
Carroll, George 1924-25
Carson, William 1928-30
Carter, William 1960-61
Carveth, Joseph 1946-48
Cashman, Wayne 1964-65; 1967-83
Chamberlain, Erwin "Murph" 1942-43
Chapman, Arthur 1930-34
Cherry, Richard "Dick" 1956-57
Chevrefils Real 1951-59
Chisholm, Arthur 1960-61
Church, John "Jack" 1945-46
Clapper, Aubrey "Dit" 1927-47
Clark, Gordon 1974-76
Cleghorn, Sprague 1925-28
Conacher, Roy. 1938-42; 1945-46
Connelly, Wayne 1961-64; 1966-67
Connor, Harry 1927-28; 1929-30
Cook, Alexander 1931-32
Cook, Frederick "Bun". 1936-37
Cook, Lloyd 1924-25
Cooper, Carson 1924-27
Corcoran, Norman. 1949-50;
1952-53; 1954-55
Costello, J. Murray. 1954-56
Coutu, William "Billy". 1926-27
Cowley, William 1935-47
Crawford, John 1937-50
Creighton, David 1948-54
Crisp, Terrance 1965-66
Crowder, Bruce 1981-83
Crowder, Keith. 1980-83
Cupolo, William 1944-45
Darragh, Harold. 1930-31
Davie, Robert "Pinkie". 1933-36
Davis, Lorne 1955-56; 1959-60
Davison, Murray 1965-66
Delmonte, Armand "Dutch". 1945-46
DeMarco, Albert "Ab" 1942-44
DeMarco, Albert T. 1978-79
Denneny, Cyril "Cy" 1928-29
Desrosiers, Gerry 1942-43
Dillabough, Robert 1965-67
Doak, Gary 1965-70; 1972-81
Dornhoefer, Gerhardt 1963-66
Dufour, Luc 1982-83
Duguid, Lorne 1935-37
Dumart, Woodrow 1935-42; 1945-54
Edestrand, Darryl 1973-78
Egan, Martin "Pat". 1943-49
Ehman, Gerald 1957-58
Emms, Leighton "Hap" 1934-35
Erickson, Autry 1959-61
Erickson, Grant 1968-69
Esposito, Philip 1967-76
Ezinicki, William 1950-52
Fergus, Tom. 1981-83
Ferguson, Lorne 1949-52; 1954-56
Fillion, Marcel 1944-45
Filmore, Thomas 1932-34
Finnigan, Edward 1935-36

Fisher, Duncan 1950-53
Flaman, Ferdinand 1944-51; 1954-61
Fleming, Reginald 1964-66
Forbes, David 1973-77
Forbes, Michael. 1977-78
Foster, Dwight 1977-81
Foster, Harry 1931-32
Fredrickson, Frank. 1926-29
Frost, Harry 1938-39
Gagne, Arthur 1929-30
Gagne, Pierre 1959-60
Gagnon, Jean 1934-35
Gainor, Norman "Dutch" 1927-31
Galbraith, W. Percival "Perk". 1926-34
Gallinger, Donald 1942-44; 1945-48
Gardner, Calvin 1953-57
Gariepy, Raymond. 1953-54
Gaudreault, Armand 1944-45
Gauthier, Jean. 1968-69
Gendron, Jean-Guy 1958-61; 1962-64
Geran, George "Gerry" 1925-26
Getliffe, Raymond 1935-39
Gibbs, Barry 1967-69
Gibson, Douglas 1973-74; 1975-76
Gilbert, Jeannot. 1962-63; 1964-65
Gillis, Michael 1980-83
Giroux, Arthur 1934-35
Gladu, Jean-Paul 1944-45
Godfrey, Warren 1952-55; 1962-63
Goldsworthy, Leroy 1936-38
Goldsworthy, William. 1964-67
Gordon, Fred. 1927-28
Gracie, Robert. 1933-34
Graham, Edward "Ted" 1935-36
Graham, Rodney. 1974-75
Gray, Terrence 1961-62
Green, Edward "Ted" 1960-69; 1970-72
Green, Redvers "Red" 1928-29
Gronsdahl, Lloyd 1941-42
Gross, Lloyd 1933-34
Grosso, Donald 1946-47
Gryp, Robert 1973-74
Guidolin, Armand 1942-44; 1945-47
Hagman, Matti 1976-78

Halward, Douglas 1975-78
Hamill, Robert "Red" 1937-42
Harnott, Walter "Happy" 1933-34
Harrington, Leland 1925-26; 1927-28
Harris, Fred "Smokey" 1924-25
Harris, Henry. 1930-31
Harrison, Edward 1947-51
Harrison, James 1968-70
Haynes, Paul 1934-35
Headley, Fern "Curley" 1924-25
Hebenton, Andrew 1963-64
Heinrich, Lionel 1955-56
Henderson J. Murray. 1944-52
Herberts, James 1924-28
Hergesheimer, Philip 1941-42
Heximer, Orville "Obs" 1932-33
Hicks, Wayne 1962-63
Hill, J. Melvin 1937-41

Hiller, Wilbert "Dutch" 1941-43
Hillier, Randy 1981-83
Hillman, Floyd 1956-57
Hillman, Lawrence 1957-60
Hitchman, F. Lionel 1924-34
Hodge, Kenneth 1967-73
Hodgson, Edward "Ted" 1966-67
Hollet, William "Flash" 1935-44
Horeck, Peter 1949-51
Horvath, Bronco 1957-61
Howe, Marty 1982-83
Hurley, Paul 1968-69
Hutton, William 1929-31
Hynes, David 1973-75
Ingram, Frank 1924-25
Irvine, Edward "Ted" 1963-64
Jackson, Arthur 1937-38; 1939-45
Jackson, Harvey "Busher" 1941-44
Jackson, Stanton 1924-26
Jackson, Walter 1935-36
Jenkins, Roger 1935-36
Jennings, Joseph W. "Bill" 1944-45
Jeremiah, Edward 1931-32
Jerwa, Frank 1931-35
Jerwa, Joseph 1931-32;
                           1933-34; 1936-37
Johnson, Norman B. 1957-59
Johnson, Thomas 1963-65
Jonathan, Stanley 1975-83
Jones, Ronald 1971-73
Kalbfleisch, Walter 1936-37
Kaminsky, Max 1934-36
Kasper, Stephen 1980-83
Keats, Gordon "Duke" 1926-27
Kennedy, Forbes 1962-66
Klein, Lloyd 1928-29; 1931-32
Klukay, Joseph 1952-55
Kluzak, Gord 1982-83
Knibbs, William 1964-65
Kopak, Russel 1943-44
Kraftcheck, Stephen 1950-51
Krake, Philip "Skip" 1963-64; 1965-68
Krushelnyski, Michael 1981-83
Kryzanowski, Edward 1948-52
Kullman, Arnold 1947-48; 1949-50
Kurtenbach, Orland 1961-62; 1963-65
Kyle, Walter "Gus" 1951-52
LaBine, Leo 1951-61
Labrie, Guy 1943-44
Lalonde, Robert 1979-81
Lamb, Joseph 1932-34
Lane, Myles 1928-30; 1933-34
Langdon, Stephen 1974-76; 1977-78
Langlois, Albert 1965-66
Larose, Charles 1925-26
Lauder, Martin 1927-28
Laycoe, Harold 1950-56
Leach, Lawrence 1958-60; 1961-62
Leach, Reginald 1970-72
Leduc, Richard 1972-74
Leiter, Robert 1962-66; 1968-69
Lesuk, William 1968-70

Leswick, Peter 1944-45
Leveille, Normand 1981-83
Lonsberry, D. Ross 1966-69
Lorentz, James 1968-70
Lowe, Ross 1949-51
Lund, Pentti 1951-53
Lynn, Victor 1950-52
Lyon, Ronald "Peaches" 1930-31
Macdonald, C. Parker 1965-66
MacKay, Duncan "Mickey" 1928-30
Mackell, Fleming 1951-60
MacTavish, Craig 1979-83
Maloney, Philip 1949-51
Maluta, Raymond 1975-77
Manson, Raymond 1947-48
Mantha, Sylvio 1936-7
Marcotte, Donald 1965-66; 1968-82
Mario, Frank 1941-42; 1944-45
Marotte, Gilles 1965-67
Marquess, Clarence "Mark" 1946-47
Martin, Francis 1952-54
Martin, George Clare 1941-42; 1946-48
Martin, Hubert "Pit" 1965-67
Matte, Joseph 1925-26
Maxner, Wayne 1964-66
McAtee, Norman 1946-47
McCarthy, Thomas P. F. 1960-61
McCord, Robert 1963-65
McCrimmon, B. Brad 1979-82
McDonald, Alvin "Ab" 1964-65
McGill, John 1941-42; 1944-47
McInenly, Bertram "Bert" 1933-36
McIntyre, John "Jake" 1949-50; 1951-53
McKechnie, Walter 1974-75
McKenney, Donald 1954-63
McKenzie, John 1965-72
McLellan, Scott 1982-83
McMahon, Michael C. 1945-46
McManus, Samuel 1936-37
McNab, Peter 1976-83
McReavy, Patrick 1938-42
Meeking, Harry 1926-27
Meissner, Richard "Dick" 1959-62
Melnyk, Larry 1980-83
Mickoski, Nicholas 1959-60
Middleton, Richard 1976-83
Milbury, Michael 1975-83
Miller, Robert 1977-81
Mitchell, Herbert 1924-26
Mohns, Douglas 1953-64
Morris, Bernard 1924-25
Morrison, Douglas 1979-82
Morrison, James 1951-52; 1958-59
Motter, Alexander 1934-36
Murphy, R. Ronald 1965-70
Nicholson, Allan "Al" 1955-57
Nicolson, Graeme 1978-79
Nowak, Henry 1974-77
O'Brien, Dennis 1977-80
O'Brien, Ellard 1955-56
O'Connell, Michael 1980-83
Oddleifson, Chistopher 1972-74

O'Donnell, Frederick 1972-74
Oliver, Harold "Harry" 1926-34
Oliver, Murray 1960-67
O'Neil, James "Peggy" 1933-37
O'Neil, Paul 1975-76
O'Ree, William 1957-58; 1960-61
O'Reilly, J. J. Terence 1971-83
Orr, Robert, "Bobby" 1966-76
Ouellette, Gerald 1960-61
Owen, George 1928-33
Pachal, Clayton 1976-78
Palazzari, Aldo 1943-44
Palmer, Brad 1982-83
Panagabko, Edwin "Ed" 1955-57
Parise, Jean-Paul 1965-67
Park, D. Bradford "Brad" 1975-83
Patterson, George 1933-34
Pederson, Barry 1980-83
Peirson, John 1946-54; 1955-58
Pennington, Clifford 1961-63
Peters, Garry 1971-72
Peters, James M. 1947-49
Pettinger, Eric 1928-29
Pettinger, Gordon 1937-40
Pidhirny, Harry 1957-58
Poile, Norman "Bud" 1949-50
Poliziani, Daniel 1958-59
Popiel, Poul 1965-66
Portland, John "Jack" 1934-40
Pratt, Jack 1930-32
Pratt, Walter "Babe" 1946-47
Prentice, Dean 1962-66
Pronovost, J. A. Andre 1960-63
Pusie, Jean 1934-35
Quackenbush, Hubert "Bill" 1949-56
Quackenbush, Maxwell 1950-51
Quilty, John 1947-48
Ranieri, George 1956-57
Ratelle, J. G. Y. Jean 1975-81
Rathwell, John "Jake" 1974-75
Ravlich, Matthew 1962-63; 1971-73
Reardon, Terrence 1938-39; 1940-41;
                           1945-47
Redahl, Gordon 1958-59
Redding, George 1924-26
Redmond, Richard "Dick" 1978-82
Regan, Lawrence "Larry" 1956-59
Reibel, Earl 1958-59
Reigle, Edmond 1950-51
Riley, Jack 1935-46
Ripley, Victor 1932-34
Rittinger, Alan 1943-44
Rivers, J. Wayne 1963-67
Roberts, Douglas "Doug" 1971-74
Roche, Earl 1932-33
Rodden, Edmund 1928-29
Rolfe, Dale 1959-60
Ronty, Paul 1947-51
Rowe, Robert "Bobby" 1924-25
Rozzini, Gino 1944-45
Ruhnke, Kent 1975-76
Runge, Paul 1930-32; 1935-36

Sanderson, Derek 1965-74
Sandford, Edward 1947-55
Sands, Charles 1934-39
Sarner, Craig. 1974-75
Sather, Glen 1966-69
Savage, Gordon 1934-35
Savard, Andre 1973-76
Scherza, Charles. 1943-44
Schmautz, Robert "Bobby" 1973-80
Schmidt, Clarence. 1943-44
Schmidt, John 1942-43
Schmidt, Joseph 1943-44
Schmidt, Milton 1936-42; 1945-55
Schnarr, Werner 1924-26
Schock, Daniel 1970-71
Schock, Ronald. 1963-67
Secord, Alan "Al" 1978-81
Shack, Edward 1967-69
Shanahan, Sean 1977-78
Shannon, Gerald "Jerry" 1934-36
Shay, Norman 1924-26
Sheppard, Gregory 1972-78
Sheppard, Jake "Johnny" 1933-34
Shields, Albert 1936-37
Shill, John "Jack" 1934-35
Shill, William 1942-43; 1945-47
Shore, Edward. 1926-40
Siebet, Albert "Babe" 1933-36
Simmons, Allan "Al" 1973-74; 1975-76
Sims, Allan "Al" 1973-79
Skinner, Alfred 1924-25
Smillie, Donald 1933-34
Smith, Alexander 1932-34
Smith, Barry 1975-76
Smith, Dallas 1959-62; 1965-77
Smith, Desmond 1939-42
Smith, Floyd 1954-55; 1956-57
Smith, Kenneth 1944-51
Smith, Reginald "Hooley" 1936-37
Smith, Richard. 1968-72; 1976-80
Songin, Thomas 1978-81
Sparrow, Emory "Spunk" 1924-25
Speer, F. William "Bill" 1969-71
Spencer, J. Irvin 1962-63
Spring, Franklin 1969-70
Stanfield, Frederic 1967-73
Stanley, Allan. 1956-58
Stapleton, Patrick. 1961-63
Stasiuk, Victor 1955-61
Stevens, Philip. 1925-26
Stewart, Nelson 1932-35; 1936-37
Stewart, Robert 1971-72
Stewart, Ronald. 1965-67
Stuart, William "Red" 1924-27
Sullivan, George "Red" 1949-53
Sutherland, Max 1931-32
Taylor, Robert 1929-30
Taylor, William J. 1947-48
Teal, Allan "Skip" 1954-55
Tessier, Orval. 1955-56; 1960-61
Thompson, Clifford 1941-42; 1948-49
Thomas, William 1944-45

Toppazzini, Gerald 1952-54; 1955-64
Toppazzini, Zellio. 1948-51
Touhey, William 1931-32
Turlik, Gordon 1959-60
Vadnais, Carol 1971-76
Walton, Michael. 1970-73; 1978-79
Ward, Donald 1959-60
Warwick, Grant 1947-49
Watson, Joseph 1964-65; 1966-67
Webster, Thomas. 1968-70
Weiland, Ralph "Cooney" 1928-32; 1935-
                                                       39
Wensink, John. 1976-80
Westfall, V. Edwin "Ed" 1961-72
Wilcox, Archibald. 1933-34
Wilkins, Barry 1966-67; 1968-70
Wilkinson, John 1943-44
Williams, Burr 1934-35
Williams, Thomas M. 1961-69
Wilson, Wallace 1947-48
Wiseman, Edward 1939-42
Woytowich, Robert 1964-67
Yackel, Kenneth. 1958-59
Zanussi, Joseph "Joe" 1975-77

Goaltenders

Abott, George 1943-44
Adams, John 1972-73
Baron, Marco. 1979-83
Belanger, Yves 1979-80
Bennett, Harvey. 1944-45
Bibeault, Paul 1944-46
Bittner, Richard 1949-50
Brimsek, Francis 1938-41; 1945-49
Broderick, Kenneth 1973-75
Brooks, D. Ross. 1972-75
Chadwick, Edwin. 1961-62
Cheevers, Gerald 1965-72; 1975-80
Colvin, Lester 1948-49
Courteau, Maurice. 1943-44
Craig, James. 1980-81
Cude, Wilfred 1931-32
Damore, Nicholas 1941-42
DeFelice, Norman 1956-57
Evans, Claude 1957-58
Fowler, Norman "Hec" 1924-25
Franks, James 1943-44
Gamble, Bruce 1960-62
Gardiner, Wilbert "Bert". 1943-44
Gelineau, John "Jack" 1948-51
Gilbert, Gilles 1973-80
Gill, Andre. 1967-68
Grahame, Ronald 1977-78
Grant, Benjamin 1943-44
Head, Donald 1961-62
Henderson, John. 1954-56
Henry, Gordon "Red" 1948-50
Henry, Samuel James 1951-55
Jackson, Percy 1931-32; 1935-36
Johnston, Edward 1962-73
Junkin, Joseph 1968-69

Keenan, Donald 1958-59
Lockhart, Howard "Holes". 1924-25
Lumley, Harry 1957-60
Millar, F. Allan "Al". 1957-58
Moffat, Michael "Mike". 1981-83
Norris, Jack 1964-65
Parent, Bernard 1965-67
Peeters, Peter "Pete" 1982-83
Perreault, Robert 1962-63
Pettie, James "Jim" 1976-79
Plante, J. Jacques 1972-73
Pronovost, Claude. 1955-56
Reece, David "Dave". 1975-76
Ring, Robert 1965-66
Roberts, Morris 1925-26
Sawchuc, Terrance 1955-57
Simmons, Donald 1956-61
Stewart, Charles "Doc". 1924-27
Stewart, Jim. 1979-80
Thompson, Cecil "Tiny". 1928-39
Vachon, Rogatien 1980-82
Wilson, Ross "Lefty" 1957-58
Winkler, Harold 1926-28

BUFFALO SABRES
Players
Anderson, Ronald C. G. 1970-72
Andrea, Paul 1970-71
Andreychuk, David 1982-83
Atkinson, Steven 1970-74
Ball, Terry. 1970-72
Barrie, Douglas 1970-72
Boland, Michael J. 1978-79
Breitenback, Ken 1975-77; 1978-79
Busniuk, Ronald. 1972-74
Byers, Michael 1971-72
Carriere, Larry 1972-75; 1977-78
Cunneyworth, Randy 1980-82
Cyr, Paul 1982-83
Davis, Malcolm "Mal" 1982-83
Deadmarsh, Ernest "Butch" 1970-73
Dudley, Richard 1972-75; 1978-81
Duff, T. Richard "Dick' 1970-72
Dunn, Richard "Richie". 1977-82
Eatough, Jeff 1981-82
Evans, Christopher 1971-72
Fenyves, David 1982-83
Fischer, Ronald 1981-83
Fleming, Reginald 1970-71
Fogolin, Lee 1974-79
Foligno, Mike. 1981-83
Gare, Daniel 1974-82
Gillis, Jere 1982-83
Gould, John 1971-74; 1979-80
Goyette, J. G. Philippe 1970-72
Gratton, Normand "Norm". 1972-75
Guevremont, Jocelyn "Josh". 1974-79
Hajt, William 1973-83
Hamel, Gilles 1980-83
Hamilton, Allan. 1970-72
Harris, Hugh. 1972-73
Haworth, Alan 1980-82

322

Hess, Robert	1981-82
Hillman, Lawrence	1971-73
Horton, Myles "Tim"	1972-74
Housley, Phil	1982-83
Inglis, William	1970-71
James, Valmore	1981-82
Keenan, Lawrence	1970-72
Korab, Gerald "Jerry"	1973-80
Kowal, Joseph	1976-78
Krake, Philip "Skip"	1970-71
Lacombe, Francois	1970-71
Lagace, Jean-Guy	1970-71
Lambert, Yvon	1981-82
Lawson, Daniel	1971-72
Lemieux, Real	1973-74
Lorentz, James	1971-78
Luce, Donald	1971-81
Marshall, Donald	1970-71
Martin, Richard	1971-81
Martin, Terry	1975-79
McAdam, Gary	1975-79; 1982-83
McClanahan, Rob	1979-81
McCourt, Dale	1981-83
McDonald, Brian	1970-71
McIntosh, Paul	1974-76
McKay, Raymond	1971-73
McKegney, Anthony	1978-83
McKenna, Sean	1981-83
McMahon, Michael W.	1970-71
McNab, Peter	1973-76
McSheffrey, Bryan	1974-75
Meehan, Gerald "Gerry"	1970-75
Mickey, R. Larry	1971-75
Moller, Michael "Mike"	1980-83
Mongrain, Robert	1979-82
Myers, Harold "Hap"	1970-71
Noris, Joseph	1973-74
O'Shea, Kevin	1970-72
Patrick, Stephen	1980-83
Perreault, Gilbert	1970-83
Perry, Brian	1970-71
Peterson, Brent	1981-83
Playfair, Larry	1978-83
Pratt, Tracy	1970-74
Ramsay, Craig	1971-83
Ramsey, Michael	1979-83
Ramsey, Wayne	1977-78
Richard, Jacques	1975-77; 1978-79
Richer, Robert	1972-73
Robert, Rene	1971-79
Robertson, Geordie	1982-83
Robitaille, Michael	1971-75
Rombough, Douglas	1972-74
Ruff, Lindy	1979-83
Sauve, Jean-Francois	1980-83
Savard, Andre	1976-83
Schmautz, Clifford "Cliff"	1970-71
Schock, Ronald	1977-78
Schoenfeld, James "Jim"	1972-82
Schultz, David	1978-80
Seiling, Richard "Ric"	1977-83
Shack, Edward	1970-72

Smith, Derek	1976-82
Smith, Floyd	1970-72
Spencer, Brian	1973-77
Stanfield, Frederic	1974-78
Stewart, William	1977-79
Suikkanen, Kai	1981-83
Talbot, Jean-Guy	1970-71
Terbenche, Paul	1970-74
Tidey, Alexander	1976-78
Titanic, Morris	1974-76
Van Boxmeer, John	1979-83
Virta, Hannu	1981-83
Walsh, James "Jim"	1981-82
Watson, James A.	1970-72
Wyrozub, W. Randall "Randy"	1970-74
Zaine, Rodney	1971-72

Goaltenders

Bromley, Gary	1973-76
Cloutier, Jacques	1981-83
Crozier, Roger	1970-76
Daley, T. Joseph "Joe"	1970-71
Desjardins, Gerard	1974-78
Dryden, David	1970-74
Edwards, Donald	1976-82
Farr, Norman "Rocky"	1972-75
Harrison, Paul	1981-82
Ireland, Randolph "Randy"	1978-79
Myre, L. Philippe "Phil"	1982-83
Sauve, Robert	1976-83
Smith, Allan "Al"	1975-77

CALGARY FLAMES
Players

Beers, Edward	1981-83
Bourgeois, Charles	1981-83
Bridgman, Melvin	1981-83
Chouinard, Guy	1980-83
Christoff, Steve	1982-83
Clement, William	1980-82
Curtale, Tony	1980-81
Cyr, Denis	1980-83
Dunn, Richard "Richie"	1982-83
Dwyer, Michael	1980-82
Eakin, Bruce	1981-82
Eloranta, Kari	1981-83
Gould, Robert	1980-82
Hampson, Gordon	1982-83
Harrer, Tim	1982-83
Hindmarch, David	1980-83
Hislop, James	1980-83
Holt, S. Randall "Randy"	1980-82
Houston, Kenneth	1980-82
Hunter, Timothy "Tim"	1981-83
Ingarfield, Earl, Jr.	1980-81
Jackson, James	1982-83
Jalonen, Kari	1982-83
Konroyd, Stephen	1980-83
Labraaten, Daniel	1980-82
Lalonde, Robert	1981-82

Lavallee, Kevin	1980-83
Lever, Donald	1980-82
MacInnis, Allan	1981-83
MacMillan, Robert	1980-82
Macoun, Jamie	1982-83
Marsh, C. Bradley "Brad"	1980-82
McAdam, Gary	1981-82
McDonald, Lanny	1981-83
McKendry, Alex	1980-81
Meredith, Gregory	1982-83
Mokosak, Carl	1981-83
Murdoch, Robert J.	1980-82
Nilsson, Kent	1980-83
Peplinski, James	1980-83
Plett, Willi	1980-82
Rautakallio, Pekka	1980-82
Reinhart, Paul	1980-83
Ribble, Patrick	1981-83
Rioux, Pierre	1982-83
Risebrough, Douglas	1982-83
Russell, Philip	1980-83
Smith, Brad	1980-81
Turnbull, Randy	1981-82
Vail, Eric	1980-82
Walker, Howard	1982-83
Wappel, Gordon	1980-82
Wilson, Bertwin "Bert"	1980-81

Goaltenders

Bernhardt, Tim	1982-83
Bouchard, Daniel	1980-81
Edwards, Donald	1982-83
Lemelin, Rejean "Reggie"	1980-83
Riggin, Patrick	1980-82
Vernon, Michael	1982-83

CHICAGO BLACK HAWKS
Players

Abel, Clarence	1929-34
Abel, Sidney	1952-54
Adams, Stewart	1929-32
Allen, George	1939-44; 1945-46
Angotti, Louis	1965-67; 1969-73
Arbour, Alger "Al"	1958-61
Arbour, Ernest	1927-31
Archambault, Michel	1976-77
Ashworth, Frank	1946-47
Babando, Peter	1950-53
Backstrom, Ralph	1972-73
Bailey, Robert	1957-58
Baldwin, Douglas	1947-48
Balfour, Earl	1958-61
Balfour, Murray	1959-64
Barkley, N. Douglas	1957-58; 1959-60
Bedard, James	1949-51
Bentley, Douglas	1939-44; 1945-52
Bentley, Maxwell	1940-43; 1945-48
Bentley, Reginald	1942-43
Besler, Philip	1938-39
Black, Stephen	1950-51
Blade, Henry	1946-48

Blair, Andrew 1936-37
Blinco, Russell 1938-39
Bodnar, August "Gus" 1947-54
Boldirev, Evan 1974-79
Bordeleau, Christian 1971-72
Bordeleau, Jean-Pierre 1971-80
Bostrom, Helge 1929-33
Boucher, George 1931-32
Boudrias, Andre 1968-69
Bowman, R. Kirk 1976-78
Boyer, Walter "Wally" 1966-67
Brayshaw, Russell 1944-45
Brenneman, John 1964-65
Bretto, Joseph 1944-45
Brink, Milton 1936-37
Brown, Adam 1946-51
Brown, Keith 1979-83
Browne, Cecil 1927-28
Brydson, Glenn 1935-38
Buchanan, Michael 1951-52
Bulley, Edward "Ted" 1976-82
Burch, H. William 1932-33
Burke, Martin 1934-38
Burns, Robert 1928-30
Butler, John 1947-48
Buttrey, Gordon 1943-44
Caffery, Terrance 1969-70
Campbell, Bryan 1969-72
Campbell, Donald 1943-44
Carbol, Leo 1942-43
Carse, Robert 1939-43
Carse, William 1939-42
Chad, John 1939-41; 1945-46
Check, Lude 1944-45
Ciesla, Henry 1955-57
Coflin, Hugh 1950-51
Conacher, Charles, Jr. 1951-55
Conacher, James 1948-52
Conacher, Lionel 1933-34
Conacher, Roy 1947-52
Connolly, Albert 1937-38
Cook, Thomas 1929-37
Cooper, Joseph 1938-46
Corcoran, Norman 1955-56
Costello, J. Murray 1953-54
Coulter, Arthur 1931-36
Couture, Gerald 1952-54
Couture, Rosario 1928-35
Creighton, David 1954-55
Crossman, Douglas 1980-83
Cunningham, Leslie 1939-40
Cushenan, Ian 1956-58

Cyr, Denis 1982-83
Dahlstrom, Carl 1937-45
Daigle, Alain 1974-80
Davis, Lorne 1954-55
Dea, William 1957-58
DeMarco, Albert "Ab" 1938-40
Denneny, Corbett 1927-28
Desilets, Joffre 1938-40
Desjardins, Victor 1930-31
Dewsbury, Albert 1950-56

Dick, Harry 1946-47
Dickens, Ernest 1947-51
Dineen, William 1957-58
Donaldson, R. Gary 1973-74
Doraty, Kenneth 1926-27
Dupont, Jerome 1981-83
Dutkowski, Laudes 1926-27; 1929-31;
                                    1933-34
Dye, Cecil "Babe" 1926-28
Dyte, John 1943-44
Erickson, Autry 1962-64
Esposito, Philip 1963-67
Evans, W. John 1958-63
Farrant, Walter 1943-44
Fashoway, Gordon 1950-51
Feamster, David 1981-83
Ferguson, Lorne 1957-59
Fidler, Michael 1982-83
Field, Wilfred 1944-45
Fielder, Guyle 1950-51
Finney, Joseph 1951-54
Fleming, Reginald 1960-64
Fogolin, Lidio 1950-56
Foley, Gilbert 1970-71
Fowler, Thomas 1946-47
Fox, Gregory 1978-83
Fraser, Curt 1982-83
Fraser, Gordon 1926-28
Fraser, Harvey 1944-45
Frig, Leonard 1973-74
Gadsby, William 1946-55
Gagnon, Germain 1973-76
Gamble, Richard "Dick" 1954-55
Gardiner, Herbert "Herb" 1928-29
Gardner, Calvin 1952-53
Gardner, William 1980-83
Gee, George 1945-49; 1951-54
Glover, Frederick 1952-53
Glover, Howard 1958-59
Goldham, Robert 1947-50
Goldsworthy, Leroy 1933-35
Gottselig, John 1928-45
Goyer, Gerald 1967-68
Gracie, Robert 1938-39
Graham, Edward 1927-33
Grigor, George 1943-44
Grosso, Donald 1944-46
Guidolin, Armand 1948-52
Hall, Murray 1961-62; 1963-64
Hamill, Robert 1941-43; 1945-51
Hamilton, Reginald 1945-47
Hanson, Oscar 1937-38
Harms, John 1943-45
Harrison, James 1976-79
Hassard, Robert 1954-55
Hay, George 1926-27
Hay, William 1959-67
Henry, Camille 1964-65
Hergesheimer, Philip 1939-43
Hergesheimer, Walter 1956-57
Heyliger, Victor 1937-38; 1943-44
Hicks, Douglas 1977-79

Hicks, Wayne 1960-61
Higgins, Tim 1978-83
Hildebrand, Isaac "Ike" 1953-55
Hillman, Wayne 1961-65
Hinton, Daniel 1976-77
Hodge, Kenneth 1964-67
Hoffinger, Val 1927-29
Hoffmeyer, Robert 1977-79
Hollingworth, Gordon 1954-55
Holmes, Louis 1931-32
Holt, S. Randall "Randy" 1974-78
Horeck, Peter 1944-47; 1951-52
Horvath, Bronco 1961-62
Hrymnak, Stephen 1951-52
Hucul, Frederick 1950-54
Hull, Dennis 1964-77
Hull, Robert 1957-72
Hutchison, David 1979-82
Ingram, Frank 1929-32
Ingram, Ronald 1956-57
Irvin, James Dickenson 1926-29
Jackson, Harold 1936-38
Jackson, John 1946-47
Jankowski, Louis 1953-55
Jarrett, Douglas 1964-75
Jenkins, Roger 1930-34; 1937-39
Johnson, Norman B. 1958-59
Johnson, Virgil 1937-38; 1943-45
Johnston, George 1941-43; 1945-47
Johnston, Joseph "Joey" 1975-76
Kachur, Edward 1956-58
Kaleta, Alexander 1941-42; 1945-48
Keats, Gordon 1927-29
Kelly, J. Robert 1977-79
Kelly, Regis 1936-37; 1940-41
Kendall, William 1933-38
Kennedy, Forbes 1956-57
Kenny, William 1934-35
Kerr, Reginald 1977-82
Klingbeil, Ernest 1936-37
Korab, Gerald "Jerry" 1970-73
Koroll, Clifford 1969-80
Kryskow, David 1972-74
Kryzanowski, Edward 1952-53
L'Abbe, Maurice 1972-73
Lacroix, Andre 1971-72
LaFrance, Leo 1927-28
Lalonde, Hector 1953-54; 1955-57
LaPrairie, Bernard "Bun" 1936-37
Larmer, Steve 1980-83
Larochelle, Wildore 1935-37
Leblanc, Jean-Paul 1968-69
Lecuyer, Douglas 1978-81
Ledingham, Walter 1972-73
Leier, Edward 1949-51
Leisient, Arthur 1928-29
Lewsick, Anthony "Tony" 1955-56
Lewsick, Jack 1933-34
Levinsky, Alexander 1934-39
Lewicki, Daniel 1958-59
Lindsay, Theodore 1957-60
Litzenberger, Edward 1954-61

Locking, Norman 1934-36
Logan, David 1975-80
Loughlin, Clement 1928-29
Lowrey, Gerald 1931-32
Ludzik, Steve 1981-83
Lunde, Leonard 1962-63; 1965-66
Lundy, Patrick 1950-51
Lynn, Victor 1952-54
Lysiak, Thomas 1978-83
MacKay, David 1940-41
MacKay, Duncan 1926-28
MacKenzie, William 1932-33; 1937-40
MacNeil, Allister "Al" 1962-66
Maggs, Darryl 1971-73
Magnuson, Keith 1969-80
Maki, Ronald "Chico" 1961-74; 1975-76
Maki, Wayne 1967-69
Maloney, Daniel 1970-71; 1972-73
Maloney, Philip 1958-60
March, Harold 1928-45
Marucci, John 1940-42; 1945-48
Marks, John 1972-82
Marotte, Jean-Gilles 1967-70
Marsh, Peter 1980-83
Martin, Francis 1954-58
Martin, George Clare 1951-52
Martin, Hubert "Pit" 1967-78
Masnick, Paul 1954-55
Mason, Charles 1938-39
Matte, Joseph 1942-43
Mazur, Edward 1956-57
McBurney, James 1952-53
McCaig, Douglas 1948-51
McCalmon, Edward 1927-28
McCormack, John 1954-55
McDill, Jeffrey 1976-77
McDonald, Alvin 1960-64
McDonald, Byron 1944-45
McFadden, James 1951-54
McFadyen, Donald 1932-36
McIntyre, John "Jake" 1953-58
McKay, Raymond 1968-71
McKegney, Ian 1976-77
McKenzie, John 1958-59; 1963-65
McKinnon, Alexander 1928-29
McKinnon, Robert 1928-29
McMahon, Michael W. 1968-69
McVeigh, Charles 1926-28
Melnyk, M. Gerald 1961-62
Menard, Hillary 1953-54
Menard, Howard 1969-70
Michaluk, Arthur 1947-48
Michaluk, John 1950-51
Mickey, R. Larry 1964-65
Mickoski, Nicholas 1954-58
Mikita, Stanley 1958-80
Miller, Earl 1927-32
Miller, Jack 1949-51
Miszuk, John 1965-67
Mitchell, William 1941-43; 1944-45
Mohns, Douglas 1964-71
Moran, Ambrose 1927-28
Morenz, Howarth 1934-36

Morrison, Donald 1950-51
Mortson, J. Angus "Gus" 1952-58
Mosdell, Kenneth 1956-57
Mosienko, William 1941-55
Mulvey, Grant 1974-83
Murphy, R. Ronald 1957-64
Murray, Robert 1975-83
Murray, Troy 1981-83
Nattrass, Ralph 1946-50
Nesterenko, Eric 1956-72
Nicholson, John 1937-38
Northcott, Lawrence 1938-39
O'Callahan, Jack 1982-83
O'Connell, Michael 1977-81
Ogilvie, Brian 1972-73
Olmstead, M. Bert 1948-51
Orban, William 1967-69
Orr, Robert 1976-77; 1978-79
O'Shea, Daniel 1970-72
Ouellette, Adeland 1935-36
Palangio, Peter 1936-38
Palmer, Robert "Rob" 1973-76
Papike, Joseph 1940-42; 1944-45
Pappin, James 1968-75
Paterson, Rick 1979-83
Peters, James M. 1951-54
Phillipoff, Harold 1978-80
Pilote, J. A. Pierre 1955-68
Pinder, A. Gerald 1969-71
Plante, Pierre 1977-78
Poeta, Anthony 1951-52
Poile, Norman "Bud" 1947-49
Portland, John 1939-41
Powell, Raymond 1950-51
Powis, Geoffrey 1967-68
Powis, T. Lynn 1973-74
Preston, Richard 1979-83
Price, John 1951-54
Prystai, Metro 1947-50; 1954-56
Purpur, Clifford 1941-45
Quackenbush, Maxwell 1951-52
Raglan, Clarence 1951-53
Ramsay, Leslie 1944-45
Ravlich, Matthew 1964-67; 1968-69
Redmond, Richard "Dick" 1972-77
Reibel, Earl "Dutch" 1957-58
Reid, A. Thomas "Tom" 1967-69
Reise, Leo, Jr. 1945-47
Ribble, Patrick 1978-80
Richardson, David 1965-66
Riley, James 1926-27
Ripley, Victor 1928-33
Robidoux, Florent 1980-82
Robinson, Douglas 1964-65
Robinson, Earl 1938-39
Rodden, Edmund 1926-28
Romanchych, Larry 1970-71
Romnes, Elwin "Doc" 1930-39
Rota, Darcy 1973-79
Ruskowski, Terry 1979-83
Russell, Philip 1972-79
St. Laurent, Dollard 1958-62
Sandford, Edward 1955-56

Sasakamoose, Fred 1953-54
Savard, Denis 1980-83
Savard, Jean 1977-79
Schaefer, Paul 1936-37
Schmautz, Robert "Bobby" 1967-69
Sclisizzi, James Enio 1952-53
Secord, Alan "Al" 1980-83
Sedlbauer, Ronald 1979-81
Seibert, Earl 1935-45
Sharpley, Glen 1980-82
Shea, Francis 1931-32
Sheehan, Robert "Bobby" 1975-76
Shelton, W. Douglas 1967-68
Sheppard, Jake "John" 1933-34
Shill, John 1937-39
Shmyr, Paul 1968-71
Simon, John 1944-45
Skov, Glen 1955-60
Sleaver, John 1953-54; 1956-57
Sloan, Aloysius 1958-61
Smith, Clinton 1943-47
Smith, Desmond 1939-40
Smith, Glen 1950-51
Smith, Wayne 1966-67
Solheim, Kenneth 1980-81
Somers, Arthur 1929-31
Stanfield, Frederic 1964-67
Stanley, Allan 1954-56
Stanley, Russell 1927-28
Stapleton, Patrick 1965-73
Stasiuk, Victor 1949-51
Stewart, James Gaye 1947-50
Stewart, John 1950-52
Stewart, Kenneth 1941-42
Stratton, Arthur 1965-66
Sullivan, Frank 1954-56
Sullivan, George 1954-56
Suomi, Albert 1936-37
Sutter, Darryl 1979-83
Tallon, M. Dale 1973-78
Tanti, Tony 1981-83
Taylor, Harry 1951-52
Taylor, Ralph 1927-30
Terbenche, Paul 1967-68
Thomas, Cyril 1947-48
Thompson, Paul 1931-39
Thoms, William 1938-45
Thomson, James 1957-58
Thomson, William 1943-44
Timgren, Raymond 1954-55
Toppazzini, Gerald 1953-55
Toppazzini, Zellio 1956-57
Toupin, Jacques 1943-44
Townsend, Arthur 1926-27
Trapp, Robert 1926-28
Traub, Percy 1926-27
Trimper, Timothy 1979-80
Trudel, Louis 1933-38
Turner, Robert 1961-63
Tuten, Audley 1941-43
Ubriaco, Eugene 1969-70
Van Impe, Edward 1966-67
Vasko, Elmer 1956-66

Vaydik, Gregory "Greg" 1976-77
Vokes, —- 1930-31
Voss, Carl 1937-38
Walton, Michael 1978-79
Ward, Donald 1957-58
Wares, Edward 1945-47
Wasnie, Nicholas. 1927-28
Watson, Harry 1954-57
Wentworth, Marvin. 1927-32
Wharram, Kenneth. 1951-52; 1953-54;
1955-56; 1958-69
White, William 1969-73
Wiebe, Arthur 1932-33; 1934-44
Wilson, Carol 1926-27
Wilson, Douglas 1977-83
Wilson, John 1955-57
Wilson, Lawrence 1953-56
Wilson, Robert. 1953-54
Wilson, Roger 1974-75
Wiste, James. 1968-70
Witiuk, Stephen 1951-52
Woit, Benedict. 1955-57
Wylie, Duane 1974-75; 1976-77
Young, Brian 1980-81
Young, Howard 1963-64; 1968-69
Zaharko, Miles. 1978-79; 1980-82
Zeidel, Lazarus "Larry" 1953-54
Zobrosky, Martin 1944-45

Goaltenders

Almas, Ralph. 1950-51
Bannerman, Murray. 1980-83
Bassen, Henry "Hank" 1954-56
Bibeault, Paul 1946-47
Brimsek, Francis 1949-50
Brown, Kenneth. 1970-71
Chabot, Lorne 1934-35
Cude, Wilfred 1931-32
DeJordy, Denis 1962-70
Desjardins, Gerard 1969-72
Dickie, William. 1941-42
Dryden, David. 1965-66; 1967-69
Dumas, Michel "Mike". . . .1974-75; 1976-77
Esposito, Anthony "Tony" 1969-83
Francis, Emile 1946-48
Frederick, Raymond 1954-55
Gardiner, Charles 1927-34
Gardiner, Wilbert. 1942-43
Gelineau, John 1953-54
Goodman, Paul. 1939-41
Hall, Glenn 1957-67
Henry, Samuel James 1948-49
Highton, Hector. 1943-44
Jackson, Douglas 1947-48
Johnston, Edward "Eddie" 1977-78
Karakas, Michael. 1935-40; 1943-46
Lehman, F. Hugh 1926-28
LoPresti, Samuel 1940-42
Lumley, Harry 1950-52
Marois, Jean 1953-54
Meloche, Gilles 1970-71
Norris, Jack. 1967-69

Pelletier, Marcel. 1950-51
Roberts, Morris 1951-52
Rollins, Elwin "Al" 1952-57
Sorodenski, Warren 1981-82
Smith, Gary. 1971-73
Stevenson, Douglas 1944-46
Veisor, Michael 1973-75; 1976-80
Villemure, Gilles. 1975-77

DETROIT RED WINGS
Players
Abel, Gerald 1966-67
Abel, Sidney 1938-43; 1945-52
Achtymichuck, Eugene 1958-59
Aldcorn, Gary 1959-61
Allen, C. Keith 1953-55
Amadio, David. 1957-58
Anderson, Dale 1956-57
Anderson, Earl 1974-75
Anderson, Ronald 1967-69
Anderson, Thomas 1934-35
Arbour, Alger "Al" 1953-54; 1956-58
Arbour, John "Jack" 1926-27
Armstrong, Murray. 1943-46
Asmundson, Oscar 1934-35
Aurie, Lawrence 1927-39
Babando, Peter 1949-50
Bailey, Garnet 1972-74
Bailey, Robert 1957-58
Baldwin, Douglas 1946-47
Barkley, N. Douglas "Doug" 1962-66
Barrett, John 1980-83
Barry, Martin 1935-39
Bathe, Francis 1974-76
Bathgate, Andrew 1965-67
Baun, Robert 1968-71
Beattie, John "Red". 1937-38
Behling, Richard 1940-41; 1942-43
Bellefeuille, Peter. 1926-27; 1928-30
Bennett, Frank 1943-44
Berenson, Gordon "Red" 1970-75
Bergeron, Michel. 1974-78
Bergman, Gary 1964-75
Bergman, L. Thommie 1972-75; 1977-80
Berry, Frederick. 1976-77
Besler, Philip 1938-39
Bessone, Peter 1937-38
Black, Stephen 1949-51
Bladon, Thomas 1980-81
Blaisdell, Michael 1980-83
Bloom, Michael 1974-77
Boileau, J. R. C. Marc 1961-62
Boivin, Leo 1965-67
Boldirev, Ivan 1982-83
Bolduc, Daniel. 1978-80
Bonin, Marcel 1952-55
Boucha, Henry 1971-74
Bowman, Ralph "Scotty". 1934-40
Bowness, Richard "Rick" 1977-78
Boyd, Irvin "Yank" 1934-35
Brenneman, John 1967-68
Brewer, Carl 1969-70
Briden, Archibald 1926-27

Brophy, Bernard 1928-30
Brown, Adam . . . 1941-42; 1943-44; 1945-47
Brown, Gerald 1941-42; 1945-46
Brown, Larry 1970-71
Brown, P. Conway "Connie". 1938-43
Brown, Stanley 1927-28
Brown, S. Arnold 1970-72
Bruneteau, Edward 1940-41; 1943-49
Bruneteau, Modere "Mud". 1935-46
Brydge, William. 1928-29
Bucyk, John 1955-57
Bukovich, Anthony. 1943-45
Buller, Hyman 1943-45
Burns, Charles. 1958-59
Burton, Cumming 1955-56; 1957-59
Bush, Edward 1938-39; 1941-42
Buswell, Walter 1932-35
Cameron, Alan 1975-79
Cameron, Craig. 1966-67
Campbell, Colin. 1982-83
Carroll, Gregory. 1978-79
Carruthers, G. Dwight 1965-66
Carson, Francis 1931-34
Carveth, Joseph 1940-46; 1949-51
Charron, Guy. 1970-75
Check, Lude 1943-44
Chevrefils, Real 1955-56
Cloutier, Rejean. 1979-80; 1981-82
Cloutier, Roland. 1977-79
Coates, Stephen 1976-77
Collins, William 1970-74
Conacher, Brian 1971-72
Conacher, Charles. 1938-39
Conacher, James 1945-49
Conacher, Roy. 1946-47
Connelly, Wayne 1968-71
Connors, Robert 1928-30
Cook, Robert 1972-73
Cooper, Carson 1927-32
Corcoran, Norman. 1955-56
Costello, J. Murray. 1955-57
Couture, Gerald. 1945-51
Cox, Daniel 1931-32
Crashley, W. Barton 1965-69; 1974-75
Craven, Murray 1982-83
Crawford, Robert. 1982-83
Creighton, James 1930-31
Croteau, Gary 1969-70
Cullen, Charles "Barry" 1959-60
Cullen, Raymond. 1966-67
Cushenan, Ian. 1963-64
Daley, Frank. 1928-29
Davis, Lorne 1954-55
Davis, Malcolm 1978-79; 1980-81
Davis, Robert. 1932-33
Dea, William 1956-58; 1969-71
Deacon, Donald 1936-37; 1938-40
Debenedet, Nelson 1973-74
Delvecchio, Alexander 1950-74
Dewsbury, Albert. 1946-47; 1949-50
Diachuk, Edward. 1960-61
Dillabough, Robert 1961-62; 1964-65
Dillon, Cecil. 1939-40

Dineen, William 1953-58
Dionne, Marcel 1971-75
Doak, Gary 1965-66; 1972-73
Doran, John "Red" 1937-38
Doran, Lloyd 1946-47
Doraty, Kenneth. 1937-38
Douglas, Kent 1967-69
Douglas, Lester. . . . 1940-41; 1942-43; 1945-
47
Drolet, Rene 1974-75
Drouillard, Clarence 1937-38
Duguid, Lorne. 1934-36
Duncan, W. J. Arthur 1926-27
Ecclestone, Timothy 1970-74
Egan, Martin "Pat". 1943-44
Ehman, Gerald 1958-59
Elik, Boris "Bo" 1962-63
Emms, Leighton "Hap" 1931-34
Enio—*see Sclisizzi*
Evans, Christopher 1973-74
Evans, Stewart. 1930-31; 1932-34
Falkenberg, Robert 1966-69; 1970-72
Faulkner, S. Alexander. 1962-64
Ferguson, Lorne 1955-58
Fielder, Guyle 1957-58
Filmore, Thomas 1930-32
Fisher, Duncan 1958-59
Fisher, Joseph. 1939-43
Fogolin, Lidio "Lee". 1948-51
Foley, Gilbert 1973-74
Foligno, Mike. 1979-82
Folk, William 1951-53
Fontaine, Leonard 1972-74
Fonteyne, Valere 1959-63; 64-67
Foster, Dwight 1982-83
Foster, Harry "Yip" 1933-35
Foyston, Frank 1926-28
Francis, Robert 1982-83
Fraser, Gordon 1927-29
Fredrickson, Frank. 1926-27; 1930-31
Ftorek, Robert "Robbie" 1972-74
Gadsby, William. 1961-66
Gago, Joseph "Jody" 1980-82
Gagne, Arthur 1931-32
Gallagher, John. 1932-33; 1936-37
Gare, Daniel 1981-83
Gauthier, R. Fernand "Fern" 1945-49
Gee, George 1948-51
Giesebrecht, Roy "Gus" 1938-42
Giroux, Arthur 1935-36
Giroux, Larry 1974-78
Gloeckner, Lorry 1978-79
Glover, Frederick. 1949-50; 1951-52
Glover, Howard 1960-62
Godfrey, Warren 1955-62; 1963-68
Goegan, Peter. 1957-67
Goldham, Robert. 1950-56
Goldsworthy, Leroy 1930-31; 1932-33
Goodfellow, Ebenezer "Ebbie" 1929-43
Gordon, Fred 1926-27
Graham, Edward "Ted" 1933-35
Grant, Daniel 1974-78
Gravelle, J. G. Leo. 1950-51

Gross, Lloyd 1933-35
Grosso, Donald. 1938-45
Gruen, Daniel 1972-74
Guidolin, Armand "Bep" 1947-49
Haddon, Lloyd. 1959-60
Halderson, Harold 1926-27
Haley, Leonard 1959-61
Hall, Murray. 1965-67
Hamel, Jean 1973-81
Hampson, Edward. 1963-65; 1966-68
Hanson, David. 1978-79
Hanson, Emil. 1932-33
Harper, Terrance 1975-79
Harris, Edward "Ted". 1973-74
Harris, Ronald 1962-64; 1968-72
Harris, William 1965-66
Hart, Gerald 1968-72
Harvey, Douglas 1966-67
Harvey, Frederick 1975-77
Hatoum, Edward 1968-70
Hay, George 1927-31; 1932-33
Hay, James 1952-55
Head, Galen 1967-68
Healey, Richard. 1960-61
Henderson, Paul 1962-68
Hendrickson, John 1957-59; 1961-62
Herberts, James 1928-30
Herchenratter, Arthur. 1940-41
Hextall, Bryan 1975-76
Hextall, Dennis 1975-79
Hicks, Glenn 1979-81
Hicks, Harold. 1929-31
Hiller, Wilbert "Dutch" 1941-42
Hillman, Lawrence. 1954-57
Hilworth, John 1977-80
Hogaboam, William 1972-76; 1978-80
Hollett, William "Flash" 1943-46
Hollingsworth, Gordon "Bucky". 1955-58
Holmes, Charles 1958-59; 1961-62
Holota, John 1942-43; 1945-46
Horeck, Peter 1946-49
Howe, Gordon 1946-71
Howe, Sydney. 1934-46
Huber, Wilhelm "Willie" 1978-83
Hudson, Ronald 1937-38; 1939-40
Hughes, Brenton 1973-74
Hughes, James "Rusty" 1929-30
Hull, Dennis. 1977-78
Ingarfield, Earl, Jr. 1980-81
Ingram, Ronald 1963-64
Jackson, Harold 1940-41; 1942-47
Jankowski, Louis. 1950-51; 1952-53
Jarrett, Gary 1966-68
Jarry, Pierre 1973-75
Jeffrey, Lawrence "Larry" 1961-65
Jennings, Joseph W. "Bill". 1940-44
Johnson, Allan. 1960-63
Johnson, Daniel 1971-72
Johnson, Earl 1953-54
Johnston, Lawrence 1971-74
Jones, Alvin "Buck". 1938-40; 1941-42
Joly, Gregory. 1976-83
Joyal, Edward 1962-65

Kane, Francis "Red" 1943-44
Karlander, Allan. 1969-73
Keating, John T. 1938-40
Keats, Gordon "Duke". 1926-28
Kelly, David 1976-77
Kelly, Leonard "Red". 1947-60
Kelly, Peter 1935-39
Kennedy, Forbes 1957-60; 1961-62
Kilrea, Brian. 1957-58
Kilrea, Hector 1931-32; 1935-40
Kilrea, Kenneth 1938-42; 1943-44
Kilrea, Walter "Wally" 1934-38
Kirton, Mark. 1980-83
Kisio, Kelly. 1982-83
Kitchen, C. Hobart "Hobie" 1926-27
Korn, James 1979-82
Korney, Michael. 1973-76
Krulicki, James 1970-71
Kryskow, David 1974-75
LaBine, Leo. 1960-62
Labraaten, Daniel 1978-81
Ladouceur, Randy. 1982-83
LaForge, Claude . . . 1958-59; 1960-62; 1963-
65
Lafreniere, Roger. 1962-63
Lajeunesse, Serge 1970-73
Lalande, Hector 1957-58
Lamb, Joseph. 1937-38
Langolis, Albert 1963-65
Lapointe, Richard "Rick" 1975-77
Larson, Reed. 1976-83
Lavender, Brian. 1972-74
Lawson, Daniel 1967-69
Leach, Reginald 1982-83
Leblanc, Fernand 1976-79
Leblanc, Jean-Paul 1975-79
LeClerc, Renald. 1968-69; 1970-71
Lemieux, Real 1966-67
Leswick, Anthony 1951-55; 1957-58
Lewis, Herbert. 1928-39
Libett, L. Nicholas 1967-79
Lecari, Anthony. 1946-47
Lindsay, Theodore. 1944-57; 1964-65
Liscombe, H. Carl 1937-46
Litzenberger, Edward 1961-62
Lochead, William. 1974-79
Lofthouse, Mark. 1981-83
Loiselle, Claude. 1981-83
Long, Barry. 1979-80
Loughlin, Clement 1926-28
Lucas, David 1962-63
Luce, Donald. 1970-71
Lunde, Leonard. 1958-62
Lundstrom, Tord 1973-74
Lundy, Patrick 1945-49
Lyle, George 1979-82
Lynch, John "Jack". 1973-75
Lynn, Victor 1943-44
MacDonald, C. Parker. 1960-67
MacDonald, Lowell 1961-65
MacGregor, Bruce. 1960-71
MacKay, Calum 1946-47; 1948-49
Mackie, Howard 1936-38

MacMillan, John 1963-65
Mahovlich, Francis. 1967-71
Mahovlich, Peter 1965-69; 1979-81
Maloney, Daniel. 1975-78
Manery, Randy 1970-72
Mann, Kenneth 1975-76
Marcon, Louis 1958-60; 1962-63
Marker, August "Gus" 1932-34
Marsh, Gary 1967-68
Marshall, Albert "Bert". 1965-68
Martin, George Clare. 1949-51
Martin, Hubert "Pit" 1961-62; 1963-66
Martineau, Donald. 1975-77
Mason, Charles. 1938-39
Matte, Roland 1929-30
McAdam, Gary 1980-81
McAtee, Jerome "Jud" 1942-45
McCabe, Stanley 1929-31
McCaig, Douglas 1941-42; 1945-49
McCann, Richard 1967-72; 1974-75
McCarthy, Thomas P. F. 1956-59
McCord, Robert. 1965-68
McCourt, Dale 1977-82
McCrary, William "Bill". 1957-58
McCutcheon, Brian 1974-77
McDonald, Alvin 1965-67; 1971-72
McDonald, Byron. 1939-40; 1944-45
McDonald, Wilfred "Bucko". 1934-39
McDonough, J. Allison "Al". 1977-78
McFadden, James. 1947-51
McInenly, Bertram "Bert". 1930-32
McIntyre, John "Jake" 1957-60
McKechnie, Walter 1974-77; 1981-83
McKenney, Donald 1965-66
McKenzie, John. 1959-61
McLenahan, Roland 1945-46
McLeod, Allan "Al" 1973-74
McMahon, Michael W. 1969-70
McNab, Maxwell 1947-50
McNeill, Stuart. 1957-60
McNeill, William. 1956-60; 1962-64
McReavy, Patrick. 1941-42
Meeking, Harry 1926-27
Mellor, Thomas 1973-75
Melnyk, M. Gerald. 1959-61
Menard, Howard 1963-64
Mickoski, Nicholas 1957-59
Millar, Hugh. 1946-47
Miller, Perry 1977-81
Miller, Thomas 1970-71
Miszuk, John 1963-64
Mitchell, William D. 1963-64
Moffatt, Ronald 1932-35
Monahan, Garry 1969-70
Monteith, Henry "Hank". 1968-71
Morrison, Donald. 1947-49
Morrison, James 1959-60
Morrison, Roderick 1947-48
Mortson, J. Angus "Gus". 1958-59
Motter, Alexander 1937-43
Muloin, J. Wayne 1963-64
Murdoch, Donald 1981-82

Murphy, Brian 1974-75
Murphy, R. Ronald. 1964-66
Murray, Kenneth 1972-73
Murray, Terry 1976-77
Nahrgang, James 1974-77
Nedomansky, Vaclav "Big Ned". 1977-82
Newell, G. Richard 1972-74
Newman, John 1930-31
Nicholson, Edward 1947-48
Niekamp, James 1970-72
Noble, E. Reginald 1927-33
Nolan, Theodore "Ted" 1981-82
Nowak, Henry "Hank" 1974-75
Oatman, Warren Russell 1926-27
Odrowski, Gerald 1960-63
Ogrodnick, John 1979-83
Oliver, Murray 1957-58; 1959-61
Olson, Dennis 1957-58
Orlando, James. 1936-38; 1939-43
Osborne, Mark 1981-83
Palangio, Peter 1927-28
Paterson, Joseph. 1980-83
Patterson, George 1934-35
Paul, Arthur "Butch" 1964-65
Pavelich, Martin. 1947-57
Peer, Bert 1939-40
Peters, James M.. . . . . 1949-51; 1953-54
Peters, James S. 1964-68
Peterson, Brent 1978-82
Pettinger, Gordon 1933-38
Pirus, J. Alexander 1979-80
Plumb, Robert 1977-79
Podolsky, Nelson 1948-49
Poile, Donald 1954-55; 1957-58
Poile, Norman "Bud" 1948-49
Polonich, Dennis 1974-81; 1982-83
Popiel, Poul 1968-70
Prentice, Dean 1965-69
Price, G. Noel 1961-62
Pronovost, J. A. Andre. 1962-65
Pronovost, J. R. Marcel 1950-65
Prystai, Metro 1950-58
Pyatt, Nelson 1973-75
Quackenbush, Hubert "Bill" 1942-49
Raglan, Clarence 1950-51
Ravlich, Matthew "Matt" 1969-70
Reaume, Marc. 1959-61
Reay, William. 1943-45
Redmond, Michael "Mickey". 1970-76
Reibel, Earl "Dutch" 1953-58
Reise, Leo, Jr. 1946-52
Richardson, David. 1967-68
Riley, James 1926-27
Ritchie, Robert 1976-78
Rivers, J. Wayne 1961-62
Roberto, Philip. 1974-76
Roberts, Douglas 1965-68; 1973-75
Robertson, Fred 1933-34
Robitaille, Michael 1970-71
Roche, Desmond "Desse" 1934-35
Roche, Earl 1934-35
Rochefort, David 1966-67

Rochefort, Leon. 1971-73
Rockburn, Harvey 1929-31
Rolfe, Dale. 1969-71
Rossignol, Roland 1943-44; 1945-46
Roulston, W. Orville "Rolly" 1935-38
Rowe, Thomas 1982-83
Ruelle, Bernard 1943-44
St. Laurent, Andre 1977-79
Salovaara, John. 1974-76
Sandford, Edward 1955-56
Schamehorn, Kevin 1976-77; 1979-80
Schoenfeld, James 1981-83
Schofield, Dwight 1976-77
Sclisizzi, James Enio 1947-50; 1951-52
Seibert, Earl 1944-46
Sheehan, Robert "Bobby" 1976-77
Sheehy, Timothy 1977-78
Sheppard, Frank 1927-28
Sheppard, Jake "John" 1926-28
Sherf, John 1935-39; 1943-44
Sherritt, Gordon. 1943-44
Shires, James 1970-71
Short, Steven 1978-79
Simon, John "Cully". 1942-45
Simon, Thain 1946-47
Simpson, Clifford 1946-47
Sincalir, Reginald 1952-53
Skaare, Bjorne 1978-79
Skov, Glen. 1949-55
Smith, Alexander. 1931-32
Smith, Brad 1980-83
Smith, Brian S.. . . . . 1957-58; 1959-61
Smith, Carl 1943-44
Smith, Dalton "Nakina" 1943-44
Smith, Derek 1981-83
Smith, Floyd 1962-68
Smith, Gregory 1981-83
Smith, Richard "Rick" 1980-81
Snell, H. Edward 1974-75
Snow, W. Alexander "Sandy". 1968-69
Sobchuk, Dennis 1979-80
Solheim, Kenneth 1982-83
Solinger, Robert 1959-60
Sorrell, John 1930-38
Speck, Frederick 1968-70
Spencer, J. Irvin 1963-64; 1967-68
Stackhouse, Ronald 1971-74
Stankiewicz, Edward 1953-54; 1955-56
Starr, Wilfred 1933-36
Stasiuk, Victor 1950-55; 1960-63
Steele, Frank 1930-31
Stemkowski, Peter 1967-71
Stewart, Blair 1973-75
Stewart, James Gaye. 1950-51
Stewart, John. 1938-43; 1945-50
Strate, Gordon 1956-59
Stratton Arthur 1963-64
Sullivan, Barry 1947-48
Sutherland, William 1971-72
Taft, John. 1978-79
Talbot, Jean-Guy 1967-68
Taylor, Edward "Ted" 1966-67

Taylor, William J. 1946-47	Gardner, George 1965-68	Driscoll, Peter 1980-83
Thibeault, Lawrence 1944-45	Gatherum, David 1953-54	Flett, William 1979-80
Thompson, L. Errol 1977-81	Giacomin, Edward. 1975-78	Fogolin, Lee 1979-81
Thomson, William 1938-39; 1943-44	Gilbert, Gilles 1980-83	Forbes, Michael 1979-80
Toppazzini, Gerald 1955-56	Grant, Douglas 1973-76	Gregg, Randy 1979-80
Trader, Larry 1982-83	Gray, Gerald 1970-71	Gretzky, Wayne 1979-83
Traub, Percy 1927-29	Gray, Harrison 1963-64	Habscheid, Marc 1979-80
Trottier, David 1938-39	Hall, Glenn 1952-53; 1954-57	Hagman, Matti 1980-81
Ullman, Norman. 1955-68	Holmes, Harry 1926-28	Hamilton, Allan ("Al") 1982-83
Unger, Garry 1967-71	Jensen, Allan "Al" 1980-81	Harrison, James 1981-83
Vail, Eric 1981-82	Legris, Claude. 1980-82	Hicks, Douglas 1980-82
Vasko, Richard 1977-78; 1979-81	Low, Ronald "Ron" 1977-78	Huddy, Charles 1979-80
Volmar, Douglas 1970-72	Lozinski, Larry. 1980-81	Hughes, John 1979-80
Voss, Carl 1932-34	Lumley, Harry 1943-50	Hughes, Patrick · · · · · · · · · · · 1972-74
Walker, John "Jack". 1926-28	McDuffe, Peter 1975-76	Hunter, David · · · · · · · · · · · · · 1978-79
Wall, Robert. 1964-67; 1971-72	McGratton, Thomas. 1947-48	Jackson, Donald · · · · · · · · · · · 1981-83
Wares, Edward 1937-43	McKenzie, William "Bill" 1973-75	Kurri, Jari 1980-83
Watson, Bryan 1965-67; 1973-77	McLeod, Donald 1970-71	Lariviere, Garry 1980-83
Watson, Harry 1942-43; 1945-46	Micalef, Corrado 1981-83	Lindstrom, Bo M. Willy . . 1982-83
Watson, James A. 1963-66; 1967-70	Moore, Alfred 1939-40	Linseman, Ken 1982-83
Watts, Brian. 1975-76	Mowers, John 1940-43; 1946-47	Lowe, Kevin. 1979-83
Webster, Thomas. 1970-72; 1979-80	Perreault, Robert 1958-59	Lumley, David 1979-83
Weiland, Ralph "Cooney" 1933-35	Richardson, Terrance 1973-77	MacDonald, Blair 1979-81
Weir, Stanley 1982-83	Riggin, Dennis. 1959-60; 1962-63	Makkonen, Kari 1979-80
Whitelaw, Robert. 1940-42	Roach, John Ross 1932-35	Messier, Mark 1979-83
Wilder, Archibald. 1940-41	Rupp, Patrick. 1963-64	Murdoch, Donalad 1979-81
Williams, Burr 1933-34; 1936-37	Rutherford, James 1970-71; 1973-81;	Nachbaur, Donald 1982-83
Williams, Frederick 1976-77	 1982-83	Nethery, Lance 1981-82
Wilson, John 1949-50; 1951-55; 1957-59	Sauve, Robert "Bob". 1981-82	Newman, Daniel 1979-80
Wilson, Lawrence 1949-50; 1951-53	Sawchuk, Terrance 1949-55; 1957-64;	Poddubny, Walter 1981-82
Wilson, Richard G. "Rick" 1976-77	 1968-69	Popiel, Poul ("Paul") 1979-80
Wing, Murray. 1973-74	Smith, Allan. 1971-72	Pouzar, Jaroslav 1982-83
Wiseman, Edward 1932-36	Smith, Norman. 1934-39; 1943-45	Price, S. Patrick 1979-81
Wochy, Stephen. 1944-45; 1946-47	Stefan, Gregory "Greg". 1981-83	Roulston, Thomas 1980-83
Woods, Paul 1977-83	Stuart, Herbert. 1926-27	Schmautz, Robert ("Bobby") 1979-80
Woit, Benedict. 1950-55	Teno, Harvey 1938-39	Semenko, David 1979-83
Wong, Michael. 1975-76	Thompson, Cecil "Tiny". 1938-40	Siltanen, Risto 1979-82
Wright, Larry 1977-78	Turner, Joseph. 1941-42	Sommer, Roy 1980-81
Young, Douglas. 1931-39	Vachon, Rogatien 1978-80	Strueby, Todd 1981-83
Young, Howard 1960-63; 1966-68	Wetzel, Carl 1964-65	Tidey, Alexander 1979-80
Zeidel, Lazarus "Larry" 1951-53	Wilson, Ross "Lefty" 1953-54	Toal, Michael 1979-80
Zeniuk, Edward 1954-55		Unger, Garry 1980-83
Zunich, Rudy. 1943-44		Wier, Stanley 1979-82

Goaltenders

EDMONTON OILERS
Players

Goaltenders

Almas, Ralph. 1946-47; 1952-53	Anderson, Glenn. 1980-83	Corsi, James. 1979-80
Bassen, Henry "Hank" 1960-64; 1965-67	Areshenkoff, Ronald 1979-80	Cutts, Donald 1979-80
Beveridge, William. 1929-30	Ashby, Donald 1979-81	Dryden, David 1979-80
Boisvert, Gilles 1959-60	Baltimore, Bryon 1979-80	Dupuis, Robert 1979-80
Bourque, Claude. 1939-40	Bednarski, John. 1979-80	Edwards, Gary 1980-81
Brown, Andrew "Andy" 1971-73	Berry, Kenneth 1981-82	Fuhr, Grant 1981-83
Connell, Alexander 1931-32	Bianchin, Wayne 1979-80	LoPresti, Peter 1980-81
Cox, Abbie 1933-34	Bladon, Thomas 1980-81	Low, Ronald 1979-83
Crozier, Roger. 1963-70	Blum, John 1982-83	Middlebrook, Lindsay 1982-83
Cude, Wilfred 1933-34	Boschman, Laurie. 1981-83	Mio, Edward 1979-81
Daley, T. Joseph "Joe" 1971-72	Brackenbury, J. Curtis. 1980-82	Moog, D. Andrew ("Andy 1980-83
DeJordy, Denis 1972-74	Callighen, Brett 1979-80	
Dion, Conrad. 1943-45	Campbell, Colin 1979-80	
Dolson, Clarence "Dolly". 1928-31	Carter, Ronald. 1979-82	## HARTFORD WHALERS
Edwards, A. Roy 1967-71; 1972-74	Chipperfield. Ronald 1980-83	### Players
Franks, James. 1937-38; 1943-44	Coffey, Paul. 1980-81	Abrahamsson, Thommy 1960-81
	Connor, Cameron 1980-83	Adams, Gregory. 1982-83

Alley, Steve 1979-81
Allison, Raymond 1979-81
Anderson, Russell 1981-83
Antonovich, Michael 1979-80
Arthur, Frederick 1980-81
Barnes, Norman 1980-82
Bennett, William 1979-80
Bourbonnais, Dan 1981-82
Boutette, Patrick 1979-81
Brownschidle, Jeffrey 1981-83
Brubaker, Jeffrey 1979-81
Carroll, Gregory 1979-80
DeBol, David 1979-81
Douglas, Jordy 1979-82
Fidler, Michael 1980-82
Fotiu, Nicholas 1979-81
Francis, Ronald 1981-83
Fridgen, Dan 1981-83
Galarneau, Michel 1980-83
Gilhen, Randy 1982-83
Gillen, Donald 1981-82
Giroux, Larry 1979-80
Hangsleben, Alan 1979-80
Henderson, Archie 1982-83
Hill, Brian 1979-80
Hodgson, Richard 1979-80
Hoffman, Michael 1982-83
Hospodar, Edward 1982-83
Howatt, Garry 1981-82
Howe, Gordon 1979-80
Howe, Mark 1979-82
Howe, Marty 1979-82
Hull, Robert ("Bobby") 1979-80
Johnson, Mark 1982-83
Johnston, Bernard 1979-81
Kemp, Kevin 1980-81
Keon, David 1979-82
Kotsopoulos, Christopher 1981-83
Lacroix, Andre 1979-80
Lacroix, Pierre 1982-83
Larouche, Pierre 1981-83
Lawless, Paul 1982-83
Ley, Richard 1979-81
Luksa, Charles 1979-80
Lupien, Gilles 1980-82
Lyle, George 1981-83
MacDermid, Paul 1981-83
MacGregor, Randy 1981-82
MacLeish, Richard ("Rick") 1981-82
Malinowski, Merlin 1982-83
Marshall, Paul 1982-83
McClanahan, Rob 1981-82
McDonald, Girard 1981-82
McDougal, Michael 1981-83
McIlhargey, John ("Jack") 1980-82
Meagher, Richard 1980-83
Merkosky, Glenn 1981-82
Miller, Warren 1980-83
Nachbaur, Donald 1980-82
Neufeld, Ray 1979-83
Paterson, Mark 1982-83
Plumb, Ronald 1979-80

Renaud, Mark 1979-83
Roberts, Gordon 1979-81
Rogers, Michael 1979-81
Rowe, Thomas 1979-82
Savard, Jean 1979-80
Schurman, Maynard 1979-80
Sheehy, Timothy "Tim" 1979-80
Shmyr, Paul 1981-82
Siltanen, Risto 1982-83
Sims, Allan "Al" 1979-81
Smith, Stuart G. 1979-83
Stephenson, Robert 1979-80
Stoughton, Blaine 1979-83
Sulliman, S. Douglas 1981-83
Sullivan, Robert 1982-83
Volcan, Michael 1980-83
Warner, James 1979-80
Wesley, T. Blake 1981-83

Goaltenders

Garrett, John 1979-82
Holland, Kenneth 1980-81
Millen, Greg 1981-83
Smith, Allan "Al" 1979-80
Veisor, Michael 1980-83

LOS ANGELES KINGS
Players

Abgrall, Dennis 1975-76
Amadio, David 1967-69
Anderson, James 1967-68
Anderson, Ronald C. G. 1968-69
Apps, Sylvanus M. 1977-80
Backstrom, Ralph 1970-73
Barnes, Blair 1982-83
Barrie, Douglas 1971-72
Bernier, Serge 1971-73
Berry, Robert 1970-77
Beverley, Nicholas 1978-79
Blight, Richard "Rick" 1982-83
Bonar, Daniel 1980-83
Bozek, Steven 1981-83
Brown, Jim 1982-83
Brown, Larry 1972-78
Byers, Michael 1970-72
Cahan, Lawrence 1968-71
Campbell, Bryan 1967-70
Carlin, Brian 1971-72
Carlson, Steve 1979-80
Carr, Eugene 1973-78
Carriere, Larry 1977-78
Chartraw, R. Richard 1980-83
Clippingdale, Steve 1976-77
Corrigan, Michael 1967-68; 1969-70;
. . . . 1971-76
Crashley, W. Barton "Bart" 1975-76
Croteau, Gary 1968-70
Curtis, Paul 1970-73
DeMarco, Albert T. 1975-77
Dionne, Marcel 1975-83

Duff, T. Richard 1969-71
Dufour, Marc 1968-69
Edestrand, Darryl 1977-79
Evans, Daryl 1981-83
Flett, William 1967-72
Foley, Gerald 1968-69
Fox, James 1980-83
Gans, David 1982-83
Garland, S. Scott 1978-79
Gibbs, Barry 1979-80
Gibson, John 1980-82
Giroux, Pierre 1982-83
Gladney, Robert "Bob" 1982-83
Glennie, Brian 1978-79
Goldup, Glenn 1976-82
Goring, Robert "Butch" 1969-80
Grant, Daniel 1977-79
Gray, Terrence 1967-68
Grenier, Lucien 1970-72
Gruhl, Scott 1981-83
Halward, Douglas 1978-81
Hampton, Richard 1978-80
Hangsleben, Alan "Al" 1981-82
Hardy, Mark 1979-83
Harper, Terrance 1972-75
Harris, William "Bill" 1979-82
Heaslip, Mark 1978-79
Helander, Peter 1982-83
Hextall, Dennis 1969-70
Hicke, Ernest 1977-78
Hillman, Lawrence 1971-72
Hoene, Phil 1972-75
Hoganson, Dale 1969-72
Holmes, Warren 1981-83
Holt, S. Randall "Randy" 1978-80
Hopkins, Dean 1979-83
Howell, Henry "Harry" 1970-73
Howse, Donald 1979-80
Hughes, Brenton "Brent" 1967-70
Hughes, Howard 1967-70
Hutchison, David 1974-78
Inglis, William 1967-69
Irvine, Edward "Ted" 1967-70
Isaksson, Ulf 1982-83
Jensen, Steven 1978-82
Johansen, Trevor 1981-82
Johnson, N. James "Jim" 1971-72
Johnston, Lawrence 1967-68
Joyal, Edward 1967-72
Kannegiesser, Sheldon 1973-77
Kelly, John-Paul 1979-83
Kennedy, E. Dean 1982-83
Kilrea, Brian 1967-68
Komadoski, Neil 1972-78
Korab, Gerald "Jerry" 1979-83
Kozak, Don 1972-78
Krake, Philip "Skip" 1968-70
Labossiere, W. Gordon 1970-71
Lemieux, Jacques 1969-70
Lemieux, Real 1967-74
Lesuk, William 1971-74
Lewis, David 1979-83

Long, Barry 1972-74
Lonsberry, D. Ross 1969-72
Luce, Donald. 1980-81
MacDonald, Lowell 1967-69
MacLellan, Brian 1982-83
Maloney, Daniel 1972-75
Manery, Randy 1977-80
Marotte, Jean-Gilles 1969-74
Marson, Michael 1979-80
Martin, Richard 1980-82
McDonough, J. Allison ("Al") 1970-72
Menard, Howard 1967-69
Mickey, R. La 1970-71
Mikkelson, William 1971-72
Monahan, Garry 1969-70
Monahan, Hartland 1977-78
Morrison, David 1980-83
Moxey, James 1976-77
Mulhern, Richard 1978-80
Mulvey, Paul 1981-82
Murdoch, Robert J. 1973-79
Murphy, Lawrence. 1980-83
Murphy, Michael ("Mike") 1973-83
Murray, James. 1967-68
Nechaev, Victor 1982-83
Nevin, Robert 1973-76
Nicholls, Bernie 1981-83
Palmer, Robert ("Rob") 1977-82
Peters, James S. 1972-75
Popiel, Poul ("Paul") 1967-68
Potvin, Jean 1970-72
Price, G. Noel 1970-71
Pulford, Robert 1970-72
Ravlich, Matthew ("Matt") 1969-71
Robinson, Douglas 1970-71
Rochefort, Leon 1969-70
Rolfe, Dale. 1967-70
Rota, Randy 1973-74
Ruskowski, Terry 1982-83
St. Laurent, Andre 1979-82
St. Marseille, Francis 1972-77
Sargent, Gary 1975-78
Schamehorn, Kevin. 1980-81
Schultz, David. 1976-78
Scruton, Howard 1982 83
Selwood, Bradley "Brad" 1979-80
Shack, Edward 1969-71
Sheehan, Robert "Bobby" 1981-82
Short, Steven 1977-78
Simmer, Charles 1977-83
Sims, Allan "Al" 1981-83
Smith, Brian 1967-68
Smith, Douglas 1981-83
Stamler, Lorne 1976-78
Stanfield, James 1969-72
Stemkowski, Peter 1977-78
Sykes, Phil 1982-83
Taylor, David 1977-83
Terrion, Greg. 1980-82
Turnbull, Ian 1981-82
Turner, Dean 1982-83
Unger, Garry 1980-81
Venasky, Victor 1972-79

Volmar, Douglas 1972-73
Waddell, Donald 1980-81
Walker, Russell 1976-78
Wall, Robert 1967-70
Wells, G. Jay 1979-83
White, William 1967-70
Widing, Juha 1969-77
Williams, Thomas C. 1973-79
Wilson, Bertwin "Bert" 1975-80
Wilson, Murray 1978-79
Witherspoon, James 1975-76
Woytowich, Robert 1971-72

Goaltenders

Blake, Michael. 1981-83
Caron, Jacques 1967-69
DeJordy, Denis 1969-72
Desjardins, Gerard 1968-70
Edwards, Gary 1971-77
Grahame, Ronald 1978-81
Keans, Douglas 1979-83
Laskoski, Gary 1982-83
Lessard, Mario 1978-83
Mattsson, R. Markus 1982-83
Norris, Jack 1970-71
Pageau, Paul 1980-81
Rutherford, James 1980-82
Rutledge, Wayne. 1967-70
Sawchuk, Terrance "Terry" 1967-68
Simmons, Gary. 1976-78
Smith, William 1971-72
Vachon, Rogatien 1971-78

MINNESOTA NORTH STARS
Players
Ahrens, Chris. 1973-78
Andersson, Kent-Erik 1977-82
Antonovich, Michael 1975-76; 1981-82
Arnason, E. Charles. 1978-79
Baby, John 1978-79
Balon, David 1967-68
Barlow, Robert 1969-71
Barrett, Frederick. 1970-71; 1972-83
Beaudin, Norman 1970-71
Bellows, Brian 1982-83
Bennett, Harvey 1977-78
Bergloff, Robert 1982-83
Bergman, Gary 1973-74
Beverley, Nicholas 1976-78
Bialowas, Dwight 1974-77
Blackburn, J. Donald 1972-73
Boivin, Leo 1968-70
Boo, James 1977-78
Boucha, Henry 1974-75
Boudrias, Andre 1967-69
Brasar, Per-Olav 1977-80
Broten, Neal 1980-83
Brumwell, J. Murray 1980-82
Burns, Charles. 1969-73
Butters, William 1977-79
Byers, Jerry. 1972-74

Caffery, Terrance 1970-71
Cameron, Craig 1971-72; 1974-76
Carlson, Jack 1978-79; 1980-82
Charlebois, Robert 1967-68
Chernoff, Michael 1968-69
Chicoine, Daniel 1978-80
Chinnick, Richard "Rick" 1973-75
Christoff, Steve 1980-82
Ciccarelli, Dino 1980-83
Colley, Thomas 1974-75
Collins, William 1967-70
Connelly, Wayne 1967-69
Contini, Joseph "Joe" 1980-81
Cook, Robert 1974-75
Cressman, David 1974-76
Cullen, Raymond 1967-70
Dineen, Gary 1968-69
Dobson, James "Jim" 1979-82
Douglas, Jordy 1982-83
Drouin, Jude 1970-75
Dunlop, Blake 1973-77
Eaves, Michael 1978-83
Engele, Jerome "Jerry" 1975-78
Erickson, Grant 1969-70
Eriksson, B. Roland 1976-78
Fairbairn, William 1976-78
Featherstone, Anthony "Tony" 1973-74
Ferguson, George 1982-83
Fidler, Michael 1978-81
Fitzpatrick, Alexander 1967-68
Flesch, John. 1974-76
Flockhart, Robert "Rob" 1979-81
Fontas, Jon 1979-81
Friest, Ronald 1980-83
Gallimore, James "Jamie" 1977-78
Gambucci, Gary 1973-74
Geldart, Gary 1970-71
Gibbs, Barry 1969-75
Giles, Curt. 1979-83
Goegan, Peter 1967-68
Goldsworthy, William. 1967-74
Grant, Daniel 1968-74
Gratton, Normand "Norm" 1974-76
Hakansson, Anders. 1981-83
Hall, Murray 1967-68
Hampson, Edward "Ted 1970-72
Hanson, David 1979-80
Harris, Edward "Ted" 1970-74
Harris, George. 1967-68
Hartsburg, Craig 1979-83
Harvey, Frederick "Buster" 1972-74
Hayek, Peter 1981-82
Heindl, William 1970-72
Henderson, Archie. 1981-82
Hextall, Bryan L. 1975-76
Hextall, Dennis 1971-76
Hicke, Ernest 1974-77
Hicks, Douglas 1974-78
Hillman, Lawrence 1968-69
Hillman, Wayne 1968-69
Hogaboam, William 1975-79
Holbrook, Terry 1972-74
Horvath, Bronco 1967-68

Jackson, Donald 1977-81
Jarry, Pierre 1975-78
Jarvis, Wesley "Wes" 1982-83
Jensen, Steven 1975-78
Johns, Donald 1967-68
Johnson, Mark 1981-82
Johnston, Joseph "Joey" 1968-69
Johnston, Marshall. 1967-71
Kiessling, Udo 1981-82
Labossiere, W. Gordon. 1970-72
Laird, Robbie 1979-80
Langlais, J. A. Alain 1973-75
Larose, Claude D. 1968-70
Lawson, Daniel 1968-71
Lunde, Leonard 1967-68
MacAdam, R. Alan "Al" 1978-83
MacDonald, C. Parker 1967-69
MacDougall, Kim 1974-75
MacKenzie, J. Barry 1968-69
Magee, Dean 1977-78
Mandich, Daniel "Dan" 1982-83
Manery, Kris 1978-80
Marcetta, Milan 1967-69
Martineau, Donald 1974-75
Maruk, Dennis 1978-79
Masterton, William 1967-68
Maxwell, Kevin. 1980-82
McCarthy, Tom. 1979-83
McCaskill, Edward "Ted" 1967-68
McCord, Robert. 1967-69
McElmury, James. 1972-73
McIntosh, Bruce 1972-73
McKechnie, Walter 1967-71
McKenny, James 1978-79
McMahon, Michael W. 1967-69
Meighan, Ron 1981-82
Meissner, Barrie. 1967-69
Melin, Roger 1980-82
Miszuk, John 1969-70
Mohns, Douglas. 1970-73
Muloin, John Wayne 1970-71
Nanne, Louis 1967-78
Nantais, Richard 1974-77
Nevin, Robert. 1971-73
Norrish, Rod 1973-75
Nyrop, William 1981-82
O'Brien, Dennis 1970-78
Oliver, Murray 1970-75
Orban, William. 1968-70
O'Shea, Daniel. 1968-71
Palmer, Brad 1980-82
Paradise, Robert 1971-72
Parise, Jean-Paul. 1978-89
Payne, Steven 1978-83
Pirus, J. Alexander 1976-79
Plager, William 1967-68; 1973-76
Plett, Willi 1982-83
Polanic, Thomas 1969-71
Polich, Michael 1978-81
Potvin, Jean 1978-79
Poulin, Daniel 1981-82
Prentice, Dean 1971-74

Pronovost, J. A. Andre 1967-68
Redmond, Richard "Dick". 1969-71
Reid, A. Thomas 1968-78
Richter, Dave 1981-83
Roberts, Gordon 1980-83
Roberts, James D.. 1976-79
Rogers, A. John 1973-75
Rombough, Douglas 1974-76
Rousseau, J. J. Robert 1970-71
Rupp, Duane. 1968-69
Sargent, Gary 1978-83
Sather, Glen. 1975-76
Seguin, Daniel 1970-71
Sharpley, Glen 1976-81
Shmyr, Paul. 1979-81
Sly, Darryl 1969-70
Smith, Brian D.. 1968-69
Smith, Gregory. 1978-81
Smith, Robert 1978-83
Solheim, Kenneth 1980-83
Standing, George. 1967-68
Stanfield, Frederick 1973-75
Talafous, Dean 1974-78
Talbot, Jean-Guy 1967-68
Taylor, Edward "Ted" 1967-68
Vasko, Elmer 1967-70
Velischek, Randy 1982-83
White, Anthony "Tony" 1979-80
Whitlock, Robert. 1969-70
Williams, Thomas M.. 1969-71
Woytowich, R. 1967-68
Young, Timothy "Tim" 1975-83
Young, Warren 1981-83
Younghans, Thomas. 1976-82
Zanussi, Ronald 1977-81

Goaltenders

Bauman, Garry 1967-69
Beaupre, Donald 1980-83
Broderick, Kenneth 1969-70
Edwards, Gary 1978-80
Gilbert, Gilles 1969-73
Harrison, Paul 1975-78
Janaszak, Steven 1979-80
Levasseur, Jean-Louis 1979-80
LoPresti, Peter 1974-79
Maniago, Cesare 1967-76
Mattsson, R. Markus 1982-83
Meloche, Gilles. 1978-83
Middlebrook, Lindsay 1981-82
Rivard, Fernand 1968-70; 1973-75
Smith, Gary 1976-78
Wetzel, Carl 1969-70
Worsley, Lorne "Gump". 1969-70

MONTREAL CANADIENS
Players

Abbott, Reginald 1952-53
Achtymichuk, Eugene. . . .1951-52; 1956-58
Acton, Keith 1979-83

Adams, John E. 1940-41
Alexandre, Arthur. 1931-33
Allen, George. 1946-47
Andruff, Ronald 1974-76
Arbour, Amos. 1918-21
Arnason, E. Charles "Chuck" 1971-73
Asmundson, Oscar 1937-38
Awrey, Donald 1974-76
Backstrom, Ralph. 1956-71
Baker, William. 1980-81
Balfour, Murray 1956-58
Balon, David. 1963-67
Barry, Martin 1939-40
Bartlett, James 1954-55
Beliveau, Jean 1950-51; 1952-71
Bell, William 1917-19; 1920-24
Bennett, Max 1935-36
Benoit, Joseph 1940-43; 1945-47
Berenson, Gordon "Red" 1961-66
Berlinquette, Louis 1917-23
Berry, Robert 1968-69
Blaine, Gary 1954-55
Blake, Hector "Toe" 1935-48
Bonin, Marcel 1957-62
Bordeleau, Christian. 1968-70
Bouchard, Edmond 1921-22; 1923-24
Bouchard, Emile "Butch" 1941-56
Bouchard, Pierre 1970-78
Boucher, Robert 1923-24
Boucher, William. 1921-27
Boucier, Conrad 1935-36
Boucier, Jean-Louis 1935-36
Boudrias, Andre 1963-65; 1966-67
Bourgault, Leo 1932-35
Bownass, John "Jack" 1957-58
Brisson, Gerald 1962-63
Broden, Connell 1955-56; 1957-58
Brown, George. 1936-39
Brubaker, Jeffrey 1981-82
Burchell, Frederick 1950-51; 1953-54
Burke, Martin 1927-34; 1937-38
Buswell, Walter 1935-40
Cain, Herbert 1938-39
Cameron, Harold "Harry" 1919-20
Cameron, William. 1923-24
Campbell, David. 1920-21
Campeau, Jean "Tod" . . .1943-44; 1947-49
Carbonneau, Guy. 1980-81; 1982-83
Caron, Alain 1968-69
Carse, Robert. 1947-48
Carson, Gerald. . . . . ,1928-30; 1932-35
Carter, William 1957-58; 1961-62
Carveth, Joseph. 1947-50
Chamberlain, Erwin 1940-42; 1943-49
Charron, Guy 1969-71
Chartraw, R. Richard 1974-81
Cleghorn, J. Ogilvie "Odie" 1918-25
Cleghorn, Sprague. 1921-25
Clune, Walter 1955-56
Collings, Norman 1934-35
Collins, William. 1970-71
Comeau, Reynald. 1971-72

Comier, Roger 1925-26
Connelly, Wayne 1960-61
Connor, Cameron 1978-79
Cooper, Carson 1926-27
Corbeau, Bert 1917-22
Corriveau, F. Andre 1953-54
Coughlin, Jack 1919-20
Cournoyer, Yvan 1963-79
Coutu, William 1917-20; 1921-26
Couture, Gerald 1951-52
Couture, Rosario 1935-36
Cressman, Glen 1956-57
Crutchfield, Nelson 1934-35
Currie, Hugh 1950-51
Curry, Floyd 1947-48; 1949-58
Curtis, Paul 1969-70
Cushenan, Ian 1958-59
Dame, Aurelia "Bunny" 1941-42
Daoust, Daniel 1982-83
Davis, Lorne 1951-52; 1953-54
Dawes, Robert 1950-51
Delorme, Gilbert 1981-83
Demers, Antonio 1937-38; 1939-43
Denis, Louis "Lulu" 1949-51
Desaulniers, Gerard 1950-51; 1952-54
Desilets, Joffre 1935-38
Deslauriers, Jacques 1955-56
Dheere, Marcel 1942-43
Doherty, Fred 1918-19
Doran, John "Red" 1939-40
Dorohoy, Edward 1948-49
Drillon, Gordon 1942-43
Drouin, Jude 1968-70
Drouin, Paul "Polly" 1935-41
Dube, J. Gilles 1949-50
Duff, T. Richard "Dick" 1964-70
Dupont, Normand 1979-80
Dussault, J. Normand 1947-51
Eddolls, Frank 1944-47
Edmundson, Garry 1951-52
Engblom, Brian 1977-82
Evans, Stewart 1938-39
Ferguson, John 1963-71
Field, Wilfred 1944-45
Fillion, Robert 1943-50
Fleming, Reginald 1959-60
Fontinato, Louis 1961-63
Fortier, Charles 1923-24
Frampton, Robert 1949-50
Fraser, Gordon 1929-30
Frew, Irvine 1935-36
Fryday, Robert 1949-50; 1951-52
Gagne, Arthur 1926-29
Gagnon, Germain 1971-72
Gagnon, Jean 1939-40
Gainey, Robert 1973-83
Gamble, Richard 1950-54; 1955-56
Gardiner, Herbert "Herb" 1926-29
Gardner, David 1972-74
Gaudreault, Leo 1927-29; 1932-33
Gauthier, Arthur 1926-27
Gauthier, Jean . 1960-64; 1965-67; 1969-70

Gauthier, R. Fernand "Fern" 1944-45
Gendron, Jean-Guy 1960-61
Goeffrion, Daniel 1979-80
Geoffrion, J. A. Bernard 1950-64
Getliffe, Raymond 1939-45
Gingras, Gaston 1979-83
Giroux, Arthur 1932-33
Glover, Howard 1968-69
Godin, H. Gabriel "Sam" 1933-34
Goldsworthy, Leroy 1934-36
Goldup, Glenn 1973-76
Goupille, Clifford 1935-43
Goyette, J. G. Philippe 1956-63
Graboski, Anthony 1940-43
Gracie, Robert 1938-39
Grant, Daniel 1965-66; 1967-68
Gravelle, J. G. Leo 1946-50
Gray, Terrence 1963-64
Green, Richard 1982-83
Grenier, Lucien 1969-70
Grosvenor, Leonard 1932-33
Haggarty, James 1941-42
Hall, Joseph 1917-19
Hamilton, Charles "Chuck" 1961-62
Hanna, John 1963-64
Harmon, Glen 1942-51
Harper, Terrance 1962-72
Harrington, Leland "Hago" 1932-33
Harris, Edward "Ted" 1963-70
Hart, Harold 1926-28; 1932-33
Harvey, Douglas 1947-61
Haynes, Paul 1935-41
Headley, Fern "Curley" 1924-25
Heffernan, Gerald 1941-42; 1943-44
Heron, Robert 1941-42
Hicke, William 1959-65
Hicks, Wayne 1963-64
Hiller, Wilbert 1942-43; 1944-46
Hillman, Lawrence 1968-69
Hirschfeld, John "Bert" 1949-51
Hoekstra, Cecil 1959-60
Hoganson, Dale 1971-73
Holmes, William 1925-26
Horvath, Bronco 1956-57
Houle, Rejean 1969-73; 1976-83
Huck, A. Francis "Fran" 1969-71
Hughes, Patrick 1977-79
Hunter, Mark 1981-83
Irwin, Ivan 1952-53
Jarvis, Douglas 1975-82
Jenkins, Roger 1934-35; 1936-37
Joanette, Rosario 1944-45
Johns, Donald 1965-66
Johnson, Allan "Al" 1956-57
Johnson, Thomas 1947-48; 1950-63
Joliat, Aurel 1922-38
Joliat, Rene "Bobby" 1924-25
Joly, Yvan 1980-81; 1982-83
Kaiser, Vernon 1950-51
King, Frank 1950-51
Kitchen, William 1981-83
Lach, Elmer 1940-54

Lafleur, Guy 1971-83
Lafleur, Rene 1924-25
LaForce, Ernest 1942-43
LaForge, Claude 1957-58
LaFrance, Adelard 1933-34
LaFrance, Leo 1926-28
Lalonde, Edouard "Newsy" 1917-22
Lamb, Joseph 1934-35
Lambert, Yvon 1972-81
Lamirande, Jean-Paul 1954-55
Lamoureux, Leo 1941-47
Langlois, Albert 1957-61
Langlois, Charles 1927-28
Langway, Rod 1978-82
Laperriere, J. Jacques 1962-74
Lapointe, Guy 1968-82
Larochelle, Wildore 1925-36
Larose, Claude D. 1962-68; 1970-75
Larouche, Pierre 1977-82
Laughlin, Craig 1981-82
Laviolette, Jean "Jack" 1917-18
Laycoe, Harold 1947-51
Leclair, John "Jackie" 1954-57
Leduc, J. Albert 1925-33; 1934-35
Lee, Robert 1942-43
Lefley, Charles "Chuck" 1970-75
Leger, Roger 1946-50
Lemaire, Jacques 1967-79
Lepine, Alfred "Pit" 1925-38
Lepine, Hector 1925-26
Leroux, G. 1935-36
Lesieur, Arthur . 1928-29; 1930-32; 1935-36
Lewis, Douglas 1946-47
Litzenberger, Edward 1952-55
Locas, Jacques 1947-49
Lorrain, Rodrigue 1935-40; 1941-42
Lowe, Ross 1951-52
Ludwig, Craig 1982-83
Lumley, David 1978-79
Lupien, Gilles 1977-80
Lynn, Victor 1945-46
Macey, Hubert 1946-47
MacKay, Calum 1949-52; 1953-55
MacKay, Murdo 1945-46; 1947-48
MacKenzie, William 1936-38
MacNeil, Allister "Al" 1961-62
MacPherson,
James 1948-49; 1950-55; 1956-57
Mahaffy, John 1942-43
Mahovlich, Francis 1970-74
Mahovlich, Peter 1969-78
Mailley, Frank 1942-43
Majeau, Fernand 1943-45
Malone, Clifford 1951-52
Malone, M. Joseph 1917-19; 1922-24
Manastersky, Timothy "Tom" 1950-51
Mancuso, Felix "Gus" 1937-40
Mantha, Leon-Georges 1928-41
Mantha, Sylvio 1923-36
Marshall, Donald 1951-52; 1954-63
Masnick, Paul 1950-55
Matz, Jean 1924-25

333

Mazur, Edward 1953-55	Quilty, John 1940-42; 1946-48	Tremblay, Marcel 1938-39
McCaffrey, Albert 1929-31	Raymond, Armand 1937-38; 1939-40	Tremblay, Mario 1974-83
McCartney, R. 1932-33	Raymond, Paul-Marcel 1932-35	Tremblay, Nils 1944-45
McCormack, John 1951-54	Reardon, Kenneth 1940-42; 1945-50	Trudel, Louis. 1938-41
McCreary, Vernon. 1964-65	Reardon, Terrence 1941-43	Tudin, Conny 1941-42
McCreary, William "Bill" 1962-63	Réaume, Marc 1963-64	Turner, Robert. 1955-61
McDonald, Alvin "Ab". 1958-60	Reay, William 1945-53	Vadnais, Carol 1966-68
McDonald, "Jack" 1920-22	Redmond, Michael "Mickey" 1967-71	Van Boxmeer, John. 1973-77
McGibbon, Irving 1942-43	Richard, J. Henri. 1955-75	Walter, Ryan 1982-83
McGill, Jack 1934-37	Richard, H. H. Maurice. 1942-60	Walton, Robert 1943-44
McKinnon, John 1925-26	Riley, Jack 1933-35	Ward, James 1938-39
McMahon, Michael C. 1945-46	Riopelle, Howard "Rip". 1947-50	Warwick, Grant. 1949-50
McNamara, Howard 1919-20	Risebrough, Douglas 1974-82	Wasnie, Nicholas 1929-32
Meagher, Richard. 1979-80	Ritchie, David. 1920-21; 1924-26	Watson, Bryan 1963-65; 1967-68
Meager, Paul 1950-55	Rivers, Gustave "Gus" 1929-32	Watson, Phillipe 1943-44
Meroneck, William 1939-40; 1942-43	Robert, Claude. 1950-51	Wentworth, Marvin 1938-40
Mickey, R. Larry 1969-70	Roberto, Phillip. 1969-72	White, Leonard "Moe" 1945-46
Miller, Wiliam 1935-37	Roberts, James W. 1963-67; 1971-77	Wickenheiser, Douglas. 1980-83
Nonahan, Garry 1967-69	Robertson, George. 1947-49	Willson, Donald 1937-39
Mondou, Armand 1928-40	Robinson, Earl 1939-40	Wilson, Carol "Cully" 1920-21
Mondou, Pierre. 1977-83	Robinson, Larry 1972-83	Wilson, Gerald 1956-57
Moore, Richard "Dickie". 1951-63	Robinson, Morris 1979-80	Wilson, Murray 1972-78
Moran, Ambrose. 1926-27	Roche, Desmond "Desse" 34-35	Wilson, Richard g. "Rick" 1973-74
Morenz, Howarth 1923-34; 1936-37	Roche, Ernest. 1950-51	Young, Douglas 1939-41
Morin, Peter 1941-42	Rochefort, Leon 1963-67; 1970-71	
Mosdell, Kenneth 1944-56; 1957-58	Ronty, Paul 1954-55	
Mummery, Harry. 1920-21	Root, William 1982-83	Goaltenders
Munro, Duncan 1931-32	Rossignol, Roland 1944-45	Aiken, John 1957-58
Murdoch, Robert J. 1970-73	Rota, Randy 1972-73	Bauman, Garry. 1966-67
Murray, Leo 1932-33	Rousseau, Guy. 1954-55; 1956-57	Bibeault, Paul 1940-43; 1945-46
Napier, R. Mark 1978-83	Rousseau, J. J. Robert 1960-70	Binette, Andre 1954-55
Maslund, Mats 1982-83	Grousseau, Roland. 1952-53	Bourque, Claude 1938-40
Nattress, Ric. 1982-83	Runge, Paul 1934-37	Broderick, Leonard. 1957-58
Newman, Daniel 1978-79	St. Laurent, Dollard. 1950-58	Chabot, Lorne 1933-34
Milan, Christopher 1979:83	Sands, Charles. 1939-43	Cox, Abbie 1935-36
Nyrop, William 1975-78	Sather, Glen 1974-75	Cude, Wilfred 1933-41
O'Connor, Herbert "Buddy" 1941-47	Savage, Gordon 1934-35	Cyr, Claude 1958-59
Olmstead, M. Bert 1950-58	Savard, Serge 1966-81	DeJordy, Dennis 1971-72
O'Neil, James "Peggy" 140-42	Schoefiled, Dwight. 1982-83	Dryden, Kenneth 1970-73; 1974-79
Orleski, David. 1980-82	Schutt, Rodney. 1977-78	Durnan, William 1943-50
Palangio, Peter. 1926-27; 1928-29	Shanahan, Sean 1975-77	Esposito, Anthony "Tony" 1968-69
Pargeter, George 1946-47	Sheehan, Robert "Bobby"69-719	Evans, Claude 1954-55
Patterson,George 1927-29	Shutt, Stephen 1972-83	Gardiner, Wilbert "Bert" 1940-42
Paulhus, Roalnd 1925-26	Siebert, Albert 1936-39	Gauthier, Paul. 1937-38
Payer, ... 1917-18	Singbush, Alexander 1940-41	Hainsworth, George 1926-33; 1936-37
Pennington, Clifford 1960-61	Skov, Glen 1960-61	Erron, Denis 1979-82
Peters, Garry . . . 1964-65; 1966-671966-67	Smart, Alexander 142-43	Hodge, Charles 1954-55; 1957-61; 1963-67
Peters, James. 1945-48	Smith, Desmond. 1938-39	Holden, Mark 1981-83
Phillips, Charles 1942-43	Smith, Donald. 1919-20	Karakas, Michael 1939-40
Picard, Jean-No 1964-65	Smith, Stuart. 1940-42	Lecroix, Alphonse 1925-26
Picard, Robert 1980-83	Smrke, Stanley 1956-58	Larocque, Michel "Bunny" 1973-81
Pitre, Didier 1917-23	Starr, Harold 1932-33	Maniago, Cesare 1962-63
Plamondon, Gerard 1947-51	Stevens, Philip 1921-22	McNeil, Gerard. 1947-48; 1949-54; 1956-57
Pleau, Lawrence. 1969-72	Stewart, James Gaye 1952-53	Moriessette, Jean-Guy 1963-64
Poirier, Gordon 1939-40	Summerhill, William 1938-40	Murphy, Hal 1952-53
Polich, Michael. 1977-78	Talbot, Jean-Guy 1954-67	Murray, Thomas 1929-30
Portland, John 1933-35; 1040-43	Tardif, Marc 1969-73	Myre, L. Philippe 1969-72
Price, G. Noel 1965-67	Tessier, Orval 1954-55	Perreault, Robert 1955-56
Prodgers, George "Goldy" 1925-26	Thibeault, Lawrence 1945-46	Plante, J. Jacques 1952-63
Pronovost, J. A. Andre 1956-61	Thomson, Rhys 1939-40	Plasse, Michel 1972-74
Provost, J. A. claude. 1955-70	Tremblay, Jean-Claude 1959-72	Pronovost, Claude 1958-59
Pusie, Jean. 1930-32; 1935-36	Tremblay, J. Jean-Gilles 1960-69	Rheaume, Herbert 1925-26

334

Sevigny, Richard 1979-83	Cook, Robert 1972-74	Tambellini, Steven 1978-81
Taugher, William 1925-26	Crisp, Terrance 1972-73	Teal, Victor 1973-74
Thomas, R. Wayne 1972-74	Devine, Kevin 1982-83	Tonelli, John 1978-83
Vachon, Rogatien 1966-72	Dineen, Gordon 1982-83	Trottier, Bryan 1975-83
Vezina, Georges 1917-26	Drouin, Jude 1974-78	Vautour, Yvon 1979-80
Wakely, Ernest 1962-63; 1968-69	Fortier, David 1974-76	Westfall, V. Edwin "Eddie" 1972-79
Wamsley, Richard 1980-83	Gagnon, Germain 1972-74	
Worsley, Lorne "Gump" 1963-70	Gilbert, Gregory 1981-83	
Worters, Roy 1929-30	Gillies, Clark 1974-83	**Goaltenders**
	Goring, Robert 1979-83	
NEW JERSEY DEVILS	Grenier, Richard 1972-73	Brodeur, Richard 1979-80
Players	Hallin, Mats 1982-83	Desjardins, Gerard 1972-74
Antonovich, Michael 1982-83	Hansen, Richard 1976-79	Gray, Gerald "Gerry" 1972-73
Ashton, Brent 1982-83	Harris, William "Bill" 1972-80	Hogosta, Goran 1977-78
Broten, Aaron 1982-83	Hart, Gerald "Gerry" 1972-79	Melanson, Roland "Rollie" 1980-83
Brumwell, J. Murray 1982-83	Hawryliw, Neil 1981-82	Resch, Glenn "Chico" 1973-81
Cameron, David 1982-83	Henning, Lorne 1972-81	Smith, William 1972-83
Cirella, Joe 1982-83	Hicke, Ernest 1972-75	
Floyd, Larry 1982-83	Hordy, Michael 1978-80	**RANGERS**
Foster, Dwight 1982-83	Howatt, Garry 1972-81	Abel, Clarence "Taffy" 1926-29
Gagne, Paul 1982-83	Hudson, David 1972-74	Adam, Douglas 1949-50
Howatt, Garry 1982-83	Johnston, Randy 1979-80	Ailsby, Lloyd 1951-52
Hutchison, David 1982-83	Jonsson, Tomas 1981-83	Albright, Clinton 1948-49
Kitchen, Michael 1982-83	Kallur, Anders 1979-83	Allen, George 1938-39
Larmer, Jeff 1982-83	Kaszycki, Michael 1977-80	Allison, Michael 1980-83
Lever, Donald. 1982-83	Lane, Gordon 1979-83	Allum, William 1940-41
Levo, Tapio 1982-83	Langevin, David. 1979-83	Andersson, Kent-Erik. 1982-83
Lorimer, Robert 1982-83	Lavender, Brian 1972-73	Andrea, Paul 1965-66
Ludvig, Jan 1982-83	Ledingham, Walter 1976-77	Angotti, Louis 1964-66
MacMillan, Robert 1982-83	Lefley, Bryan 1972-74	Anslow, Hubert 1947-48
Malinowski, Merlin 1982-83	Lewis, David 1973-80	Apps, Sylvanus M. 1970-71
Marini, Hector 1982-83	Lorimer, Robert. 1976-81	Asmundson, Oscar 1932-34
Meagher, Richard 1982-83	MacGuigan, Garth 1979-80	Atanas, Walter 1944-45
Merkosky, Glenn 1982-83	MacMillan, William 1973-77	Attwell, Ronald 1967-68
Moher, Mike 1982-83	Mair, James 1972-73	Aubuchon, Oscar 1943-44
Palmer, Robert "Rob" 1982-83	Marchinko, Brian 1972-74	Awrey, Donald 1977-78
Pierce, Randy 1982-83	Marini, Hector 1978-79; 1980-82	Ayres, Thomas. 1935-36
Porvari, Jukka 1982-83	Marshall, Albert ("Bert") 1973-79	Babando, Peter 1952-53
Quenneville, Joel 1982-83	McEwen, Michael 1980-83	Backman, Michael 1981-83
Tambellini, Steven 1982-83	McKendry, Alex 1977-80	Baker, William 1982-83
Vadnais, Carol 1982-83	Merrick, L. Wayne 1977-83	Balon, David 1959-63; 1968-72
Vautour, Yvon 1982-83	Mikkelson, William 1972-73	Bandura, Jeff. 1980-81
Verbeek, Patrick 1982-83	Miller, Thomas 1972-75	Bartlett, James 1955-56; 1958-60
Wenslnk, John 1982-83	Morrow, Ken. 1979-83	Barton, Clifford 1939-40
	Murray, Kennoth 1972-73	Bathgate, Andrew 1952-64
	Nicholson, Neil 1977-78	Bathgate, Frank 1952-53
Goaltenders	Nystrom, T. Robert. 1972-83	Beaton, A. Francis "Frank" 1978-80
	Parise, Jean-Paul 1974-78	Beck, Barry. 1979-83
Low, Ronald 1982-83	Persson, Stefan 1977-83	Bednarski, John 1974-77
MacKenzie, Shawn 1982-83	Potvin, Denis 1973-83	Belisle, Daniel 1960-61
Middlebrook, Lindsay 1982-83	Potvin, Jean 1979-81	Bell, Harry. 1946-47
Resch, Glenn "Chico". 1982-83	Price, S. Patrick 1975-79	Bell, Joseph 1942-43; 1946-47
	Pulkkinen, David 1972-73	Bend, J. Linthwaite 1942-43
NEW YORK ISLANDERS	Regier, Darcy 1982-83	Bennett, Curt. 1972-73
Players	Rombough, Douglas 1973-75	Bentley, Douglas 1953-54
Bergeron, Michel 1977-78	St. Laurent, Andre 1973-78	Bentley, Maxwell 1953-54
Blackburn, J. Donald 1972-73	Smith, Ronald 1972-73	Berenson, Gordon. 1966-68
Bossy, Michael 1977-83	Spencer, Brian 1972-74	Beverley, Nicholas. 1974-77
Bourne, Robert 1974-83	Stewart, Ralph 1972-76	Blackburn, J. Donald. 1969-71
Boutilier, Paul 1981-83	Stewart, Ronald 1972-73	Blackburn, Robert 1968-69
Brown, S. Arnold. 1972-73	Sutter, Brent 1980-83	Bothwell, Timothy 1978-82
Cameron, Craig 1972-75	Sutter, Duane 1979-83	Bouchard, Richard 1954-55
Carroll, William 1980-83		Boucher, Frank 1926-38; 1943-44

Bourgault, Leo 1926-31
Bownass, John 1958-60; 1961-62
Boyd, William. 1926-29
Brennan, Douglas 1931-34
Brenneman, John 1964-66
Brown, Harold 1945-46
Brown, Larry 1969-71
Brown, Stanley 1926-27
Brown, S. Arnold 1964-71
Brydson, Glenn 1935-36
Buchanan, Ralph "Bucky" 1948-49
Buller, Hyman 1951-54
Burnett, J. Kelvin "Kelly" 1952-53
Burns, Gary. 1980-81
Burns, Norman 1941-42
Butler, Jerome "Jerry" 1972-75
Byers, Jerry 1977-78
Cahan, Lawrence 1956-59; 1961-65
Callighen, Francis "Patsy" 1927-28
Cameron, Angus 1942-43
Carr, Eugene 1971-74
Carr, Lorne 1933-34
Carrigan, Eugene 1930-31
Carse, William 1938-39
Carson, Gerald 1928-29
Chalmers, William 1953-54
Chartraw, R. Richard 1982-83
Chrystal, Robert 1953-55
Ciesla, Henry "Hank" 1957-59
Clark, Dan 1978-79
Cline, Bruce 1956-57
Collins, William 1975-76
Colville, Matthew 1935-42; 1945-47
Colville, Neil 1935-42; 1944-49
Colwill, Leslie 1958-59
Conacher, Charles, Jr. 1954-56
Conacher, James 1951-53
Conacher, Patrick 1979-80; 1982-83
Connolly, Albert "Bert". 1934-36
Connor, Cameron 1979-81; 1982-83
Cook, Frederick "Bun". 1926-36
Cook, William 1926-37
Cooper, Harold 1944-45
Cooper, Joseph. 1935-38; 1946-47
Coulter, Arthur 1935-42
Cox, Daniel 1933-34
Creighton, David 1955-58
Cullen, Brian 1959-61
Cullen, Raymond. 1965-66
Cunningham, Robert 1960-62
Cushenan, Ian. 1959-60
Damore, Henry "Hank" 1943-44
Davidson, Gordon 1942-44
Dea, William 1953-54
DeBlois, Lucien 1977-80
DeLory, Valentine. 1948-49
DeMarco, Albert "Ab" 1943-47
DeMarco, Albert T. 1969-73
Demers, Antonio "Tony" 1943-44
Denis, Jean-Paul 1946-47; 1949-50
Desjardins, Victor 1931-32
Dewar, Thomas 1943-44

Dickenson, John H. "Herb" 1951-53
Dill, Robert 1943-45
Dillon, Cecil. 1930-39
Dillon, G. Wayne 1975-78
Doak, Gary 1971-72
Dore, Andre. 1978-83
Dorey, R. James 1971-72
Drummond, James 1944-45
Duff, T. Richard "Dick" 1963-65
Dufour, Marc 1963-65
Duguay, Ronald. 1977-83
Dupont, Andre. 1970-71
Dutkowski, Laudes "Duke" 1933-34
Dyck, Henry 1943-44
Eddolls, Frank 1947-52
Egan, Martin "Pat". 1949-51
Egers, John "Jack" 1969-72; 1973-74
Esposito, Philip 1975-81
Evans, W. John 1948-52; 1953-58
Ezinicki, William. 1954-55
Fahey, J. Trevor 1964-65
Fairbairn, William 1968-77
Farrish, David 1976-79
Fisher, Duncan 1948-51
Fitzpatrick, Alexander 1964-65
Fleming, Reginald 1965-69
Foley, Gerald 1956-58
Fonteyne, Valere 1963-65
Fontinato, Louis. 1954-61
Foster, Harry "Yip" 1929-30
Foster, Herbert 1940-41; 1947-48
Fotiu, Nicholas. 1976-79; 1980-83
Fraser, Archibald 1943-44
Ftorek, Robert "Robbie" 1981-83
Gadsby, William. 1954-61
Gainor, Norman "Dutch" 1931-32
Gardner, Calvin 1945-48
Garrett, Dudley 1942-43
Gauthier, R. Fernand "Fern" 1943-44
Gendron, Jean-Guy. 1955-58; 1961-62
Geoffrion, J. A. Bernard 1966-68
Gilbert, Rodrigue "Rod" 1960-78
Gillis, Jere 1980-82
Glover, Howard 1963-64
Goegan, Peter. 1961-62
Goldsworthy, Leroy 1929-30
Goldsworthy, William 1976-78
Goldup, Henry. 1942-43; 1944-46
Gooden, William 1942-44
Gordon, John "Jackie" 1948-51
Gosselin, Benoit 1977-78
Goyette, Philippe. 1963-69; 1971-78
Gratton, Normand 1971-72
Gray, Alexander. 1927-28
Greschner, Ronald 1974-83
Guevremont, Jocelyn "Josh" 1979-80
Hadfield, Victor 1961-74
Hall, G. Wayne. 1960-61
Hamilton, Allan 1965-66; 1967-70
Hampson, Edward "Ted" 1960-63
Hanna, John 1958-61
Hannigan, Patrick "Pat" 1960-62

Harris, Ronald 1972-76
Harrison, Edward. 1950-51
Harvey, Douglas 1961-64
Haworth, Gordon. 1952-53
Heaslip, Mark 1976-78
Hebenton, Andrew 1955-63
Hedberg, Anders 1978-83
Heindl, William. 1972-73
Heller, Ehrhardt "Ott". 1931-46
Henry, Camille. . . 1953-55; 1956-65; 1967-68
Hergesheimer, Walter 1951-56; 1958-59
Heximer, Orville. 1929-30
Hextall, Bryan A. 1936-44; 1945-48
Hextall, Bryan L. 1962-63
Hextall, Dennis 1968-69
Hicke, William 1964-67
Hickey, Greg 1977-78
Hickey, Patrick 1975-80; 1981-82
Hildebrand, Isaac "Ike" 1953-54
Hiller, Wilbert 1937-41; 1943-44
Hillman, Wayne 1964-68
Hodge, Kenneth 1976-78
Holland, Jerry 1974-76
Holst, Greg 1975-78
Horton, Myles "Tim" 1969-71
Horvath, Bronco 1955-57; 1962-63
Hospodar, Edward 1979-82
Howe, Victor 1950-51; 1953-55
Howell, Henry "Harry". 1952-69
Howell, Ronald 1954-56
Hunt, Frederick 1944-45
Huras, Larry 1976-77
Hutchinson, Ronald. 1960-61
Ingarfield, Earl. 1958-67
Ingram, Ronald 1963-65
Irvine, Edward "Ted" 1969-75
Irwin, Ivan 1953-56; 1957-58
Jamieson, James. 1943-44
Jarrett, Douglas. 1975-77
Jarry, Pierre 1971-72
Jeffrey, Lawrence "Larry" 1967-69
Jerwa, Joseph 1930-31
Johns, Donald 1960-61; 1962-65
Johnson, Ivan "Ching". 1926-37
Johnson, N. James "Jim". 1964-67
Johnstone, Edward 1975-76; 1977-83
Jones, Robert 1968-69
Juckes, Winston 1947-48; 1949-50
Juzda, William. 1940-42; 1945-48
Kabel, Robert 1959-61
Kaleta, Alexander 1948-51
Kannegiesser, Sheldon 1972-74
Keating, Michael 1977-78
Keeling, Melville "Butch" 1928-38
Keller, Ralph 1962-63
Kenny, William 1930-31
Kirk, Robert 1937-38
Kirkpatrick, Robert 1942-43
Kleinendorst, Scot 1982-83
Kontos, Chris. 1982-83
Korney, Michael. 1978-79
Kotanen, Enio 1948-49; 1950-51

Kotsopoulos, Christopher 1980-81
Kraftcheck, Stephen 1951-53
Krol, Joseph 1936-37; 1938-39
Krulicki, James 1970-71
Kukulowicz, Adolph. 1952-54
Kullman, Edward 1947-49; 1950-54
Kuntz, Alan . . . . 1941-42; 1945-46$
Kurtenbach, Orland 1960-61; 1966-70
Kwong, Lawrence 1947-48
Kyle, Walter "Gus". 1949-51
Kyle, William 1949-51
Labadie, J. G. Michel. 1952-53
Labossiere, W. Gordon 1963-65
Labovich, Max. 1943-44
Labrie, Guy 1944-45
Laidlaw, Thomas 1980-83
Lamirande, Jean-Paul 1946-48; 1949-50
Lancien, John "Jack" 1946-47; 1949-51
Lane, Myles. 1928-29
Langlois, Albert. 1961-64
Laprade, Edgar. 1945-55
Larose, Claude 1979-80
Larson, Norman. 1946-47
Latreille, Philip. 1960-61
Laycoe, Harold 1945-47
Lebrun, Albert 1960-61; 1965-66
Leduc, J. Albert. 1933-34
Leger, Roger 1943-44
Legge, N. Randall "Randy" 1972-73
Leinonen, Mikko 1981-83
Lemieux, Real 1969-70; 1973-74
Leswick, Anthony "Tony" 1945-51
Levandoski, Joseph 1946-47
Levinsky, Alexander 1934-35
Lewicki, Daniel 1954-58
Lewis, Robert 1975-76
Lochead, William. 1979-80
Lorentz, James 1971-72
Lowe, Norman "Odie" 1948-50
Luce, Donald. 1969-71
Lund, Pentti. 1948-51
MacDonald, C. Parker 1956-58; 1959-60
MacDonald, J. Kilby 1939-41; 1943-45
Macey, Hubert. 1941-43
MacGregor, Bruce. 1970-74
MacKenzie, William 1934-35
Mackey, Reginald 1926-27
MacKintosh, Ian "Mickey" 1952-53
MacMillan, Robert 1974-75
MacNeil, Allister "Al". 1966-67
Mahaffy, John 1943-44
Maloney, David 1974-83
Maloney, Donald 1978-83
Mancuso, Felix "Gus" 1942-43
Mann, John "Jack" 1943-45
Manson, Raymond 1948-49
Maracle, Henry 1930-31
Markham, Ray 1979-80
Marois, Mario. 1977-81
Marotte, Jean-Gilles 1973-76
Marshall, Albert "Bert" 1972-73
Marshall, Donald 1963-70

Martin, George Clare 1951-52
Mason, Charles 1934-36
Mayer, James 1979-80
McAdam, Samuel 1930-31
McCallum, Duncan 1965-66
McCarthy, Daniel. 1980-81
McClanahan, Rob 1981-83
McCreary, William "Bill". 1953-55
McDonagh, William 1949-50
McDonald, John A. 1943-44
McDonald, Robert. 1943-44
McDonald, Wilfred "Bucko" 1943-45
McDougal, Michael 1978-79; 1980-81
McEwen, Michael 1976-80
McGregor, Donald "Sandy". 1963-64
McKenney, Donald . . . . . . : 1962-64
McKenzie, John. 1965-66
McLeod, R. John. 1949-53; 1954-55
McMahon, Michael W. 1963-66; 1971-72
Meissner, Richard "Dick" 1963-65
Mickey, R. Larry. 1965-68
Mickoski, Nicholas 1948-55
Middleton, Richard 1974-76
Mikol, John "Jim". 1964-65
Milks, Hibbert "Hib" 1931-32
Miller, Warren. 1979-80
Moe, William 1944-49
Mohns, Lloyd. 1943-44
Molyneaux, Lawrence 1937-39
Monahan, Hartland 1974-75
Morenz, Howarth 1935-36
Morris, Elwyn. 1948-49
Morrison, James 1960-61
Morrison, Mark 1981-82
Murdoch, Donald 1976-80
Murdoch, J. Murray 1926-37
Murphy, Michael "Mike". 1972-74
Murphy, R. Ronald. 1952-57
Myles, Victor 1942-43
Nedomansky, Vaclav "Big Ned". 1982-83
Neilson, James 1962-74
Nethery, Lance 1980-82
Nevin, Robert 1963-71
Newman, Daniel 1976-78
Nicolson, Graeme 1982-83
Nilsson, Ulf 1978-81; 1982-83
Oatman, Warren Russell 1928-29
O'Connor, Herbert "Buddy". 1947-51
Palazzari, Aldo 1943-44
Park, D. Bradford "Brad". 1968-76
Patrick F. Murray 1937-41; 1945-46
Patrick J. Lynn. 1934-43; 1945-46
Patrick, Lester 1926-27
Pavelich, Mark. 1981-83
Pearson, G. Melvin 1959-60; 1961-63;
. . . . 1964-65
Perreault, Fernand. 1947-48; 1949-50
Peters, Frank 1930-31
Peters, Garry. 1965-66
Pettinger, Gordon 1932-33
Pike, Alfred "Alf" 1939-43; 1945-47
Plager, Robert 1964-67

Plante, Pierre. 1978-79
Poile, Norman "Bud". 1949-50
Polich, John. 1939-41
Polis, Gregory 1974-79
Popein, Lawrence 1954-61
Pratt, Walter "Babe". 1935-43
Prentice, Dean 1952-63
Price, G. Noel 1959-61
Pusie, Jean 1933-34
Quenneville, Leo 1929-30
Raleigh, J. Donald 1943-44; 1947-56
Ratelle, J. G. Y. Jean 1960-76
Read, Melvin. 1946-47
Regan, William . . . . ·1929-31
Reinikka, Oliver 1926-27
Reise, Leo. 1929-30
Reise, Leo, Jr. 1952-54
Richardson, David. 1963-65
Ripley, Victor 1933-35
Ritson, Alexander 1944-45
Rivers, J. Wayne 1968-69
Robinson, Douglas 1964-67
Robitaille, Michael 1969-71
Rochefort, Leon. 1960-61; 1962-63
Rodden, Edmund 1930-31
Rogers, Michael 1981-83
Rolfe, Dale. 1970-75
Ronson, Leonard "Len". 1960-61
Ronty, Paul 1951-55
Ross, James 1951-53
Rousseau, J. J. Robert. 1971-75
Rowe, Ronald 1947-48
Ruotsalainen, Reijo 1981-83
Rupp, Duane. 1962-63
Russell, Churchill. 1945-48
Sacharuk, Lawrence 1972-77
Sanderson, Derek 1974-76
Sands, Charles 1943-44
Sather, Glen 1970-74
Scherza, Charles. 1943-45
Schinkel, Kenneth 1959-64; 1966-67
Scott, Lawrence 1927-28
Seiling, Rodney. 1963-75
Senick George 1952-53
Shack, Edward 1958-61
Shack, Josepph. 1942-43; 1944-45
Shero, Frederick 1947-50
Shibicky, Alexander. 1935-42; 1945-46
Siebert, Albert "Babe". 1932-34
Silk, David 1979-83
Sinclair, Reginald 1950-52
Slowinski, Edward 1947-53
Smith, Clinton 1936-43
Smith, Dallas, ... 1977-78
Smith, Donald 1949-50
Smith, Floyd 1960-61
Smith, Stanford 1939-41
Somers, Arthur 1931-35
Sonmor, Glen 1953-55
Spencer, J. Irvin 1959-62
Staley, Allan "Red". 1948-49
Stanley, Allan. 1948-55

Stanowski, Walter 1948-51
Starr, Harold 1934-36
Stefanski, Ed "Bud". 1977-78
Stemkowski, Peter. 1970-77
Sterner, Ulf 1964-65
Stewart, James Gaye. 1951-53
Stewart, Ronald. 1967-73
Stoddard, John "Jack" 1951-53
Strain, Neil. 1952-53
Stratton, Arthur 1959-60
Strobel, Arthur. 1943-44
Sulliman, S. Douglas 1979-81
Sullivan, George "Red" 1956-61
Sweeney, William. 1959-60
Talafous, Dean. 1978-82
Tatchell, Spencer. 1942-43
Taylor, Edward "Ted" 1964-66
Taylor, G. William 1964-65
Taylor, Ralph 1929-30
Taylor, William J. 1947-48
Thompson, Paul 1926-31
Thurier, Alfred 1944-45
Tkaczuk, Walter. 1967-81
Toppazzini, Zellio. 1950-52
Trainor, Thomas W. "Wes" 1948-49
Trottier, Guy 1968-69
Trudell, Rene. 1945-48
Turner, Dean 1978-79
Tustin, Norman 1941-42
Vadnais, Carol. 1975-82
Vail, Melville "Sparky" 1928-30
Vickers, Stephen 1972-82
Voss, Carl 1932-33
Waite, Frank. 1930-31
Wallin, Peter 1980-82
Wares, Edward 1936-37
Warwick, Grant 1941-48
Warwick, William 1942-44
Watson, Phillipe. 1935-43; 1944-48
Webster, John 1949-50
White, Sherman. 1946-47; 1949-50
Widing, Juha. 1969-70
Williams, Thomas, C. 1971-74
Wilson, Bertwin "Bert". 1973-75
Wilson, John 1960-62
Wood, Robert 1950-51
Wylie, William 1950-51
Younghans, Thomas 1981-82
Zanussi, Joseph 1974-75

Goaltenders

Aitkenhead, Andrew 1932-35
Anderson, Lorne 1951-52
Astrom, Hardy. 1977-78
Baker, Steven "Steve" 1979-83
Beveridge, William. 1942-43
Bouvrette, Lionel 1942-43
Bower, John 1953-55; 1956-57
Buzinski, Stephen 1942-43
Chabot, Lorne 1926-28

Davidson, John 1975-83
DeCourcy, Robert 1947-48
Dryden, David. 1961-62
Francis, Emile 1948-52
Franks, James. 1942-43
Gamble, Bruce 1958-59
Gardiner, Wilbert "Bert". 1935-36
Giacomin, Edward. 1965-76
Gratton, Gilles 1976-77
Hanlon, Glen 1982-83
Henry, Samuel James 1941-42; 1945-48
Jackson, Percy 1934-35
Kerr, David 1934-41
Klymkiw, Julian 1958-59
Lumley, Harry 1943-44
Maniago, Cesare. 1965-67
McAuley, Kenneth 1943-45
McCartan, John "Jack" 1959-61
McDuffe, Peter 1972-74
Mio, Edward "Eddie". 1981-83
Olesevich, Daniel 1961-62
Paille, Marcel. 1957-63; 1964-65
Pelletier, Marcel. 1962-63
Plante, J. Jacques 1963-65
Rayner, Claude "Chuck" 1945-53
Ridley, C. Curtis "Curt" 1974-75
Roach, John Ross 1928-32
Rollins, Elwin "Al" 1959-60
Sawchuk, Terrance 1969-70
Schaefer, Joseph. 1959-61
Simmons, Donald 1965-66; 1967-69
Soetaert, Douglas "Doug". 1975-81
Stevenson, Douglas 1944-45
Tataryn, David 1976-77
Thomas, R. Wayne. 1977-81
Vanbiesbrouck, John 1981-82
Villemure, Gilles. . . . 1963-64; 1967-69; 1970-75
Weeks, Stephen "Steve" 1980-83
Wilson, Duncan. 1974-76
Winkler, Harold 1926-27
Worsley, Lorne "Gump". . . . 1952-53; 1954-63

PHILDAELPHIA FLYERS
Players

Adams, Gregory 1980-82
Allison, Raymond. 1981-83
Angotti, Louis 1967-68
Arthur, Frederick 1981-83
Ashbee, W. Barry 1970-74
Bailey, Reid 1980-82
Ball, Terry 1967-68; 1969-70
Barber, William. 1972-73
Barnes, Norman 1976-77; 1979-81
Bathe, Francis. 1977-83
Bennett, Harvey 1976-78
Bernier, Serge 1968-72
Blackburn, J. Donald 1967-69
Bladon, Thomas. 1972-78
Boland, Michael A.. 1974-75
Botell, Mark 1981-82
Brickley, Andy 1982-83

Bridgman, Melvin 1975-82
Brossart, William "Willie" 1971-73
Brown, David 1982-83
Brown, Larry 1971-72
Busniuk, Michael. 1979-81
Byers, Michael 1968-69
Callander, L. Drew 1976-79
Carruthers, G. Dwight 1967-68
Carson, Lindsay 1981-83
Cherry, Richard "Dick" 1968-70
Clarke, Robert. 1969-83
Clement, William 1971-75
Cochrane, Glen 1978-79; 1980-83
Collins, William 1976-77
Crisp, Terrance 1972-77
Cunningham, James 1977-78
Dailey, Robert 1976-82
Dean, Barry 1977-79
Dornhoefer, Gerhardt "Gary" 1967-78
Drolet, Rene 1971-72
Dunlop, Blake 1977-79
Dupont Andre 1972-80
Dvorak, Miroslav 1982-83
Edestrand, Darryl 1969-70
Eriksson, Thomas 1980-82
Evans, J. Paul . . . 1978-79; 1980-81; 1982-83
Fitzpatrick, Ross 1982-83
Fleming, Reginald 1969-70
Flett, William 1971-74
Flockhart, Ronald 1980-83
Foley, Gilbert "Rick" 1971-72
Gardner, David 1979-80
Gauthier, Jean 1967-68
Gendron, Jean-Guy 1967-72
Gillen, Donald 1979-80
Goodenough, Larry 1974-77
Gorence, Thomas 1978-83
Hale, Larry 1968-72
Hanna, John. 1967-68
Hannigan, Patrick 1967-69
Harris, Edward "Ted" 1974-75
Heiskala, Earl 1968-71
Hicks, Wayne 1967-68
Hill, Alan "Al" 1976-82
Hillman, Lawrence 1969-71
Hillman, Wayne 1969-73
Hoekstra, Edward 1967-68
Hoffmeyer, Robert 1981-83
Holmgren, Paul 1975-83
Howe, Mark. 1982-83
Hoyda, David. 1977-79
Hughes, Brenton "Brent" 1970-73
Johnson, N. James "Jim" 1967-72
Joyal, Edward 1971-72
Keenan, Lawrence 1971-72
Kelly, Robert 1970-80
Kennedy, Forbes 1967-69
Kerr, Tim 1980-83
Kindrachuk, Orest 1972-78
Lacroix, Andre 1967-71
LaForge, Claude 1967-69
Lajeunesse, Serge 1973-75

338

Lapointe, Richard "Rick" 1976-79
Leach, Reginald 1974-82
Lesuk, William 1970-72
Linseman, Ken 1978-82
Lonsberry, D. Ross 1971-78
Lucas, Daniel 1978-79
MacAdam, R. Alan "Al" 1973-74
MacLeish, Richard "Rick" 1970-81
MacSweyn, D. Ralph 1967-70; 1971-72
Mair, James 1970-72
Marsh, C. Bradley "Brad" 1981-83
McCarthy, Kevin 1977-79
McCrimmon, B. Brad 1982-83
McIlhargey, John 1974-77; 1979-81
Meehan, Gerald "Gerry" 1968-69
Michayluk, David 1981-83
Mickey, R. Larry 1971-72
Miszuk, John 1967-69
Morrison, Gary 1979-82
Morrison, H. Lewis "Lew" 1969-72
Murray, Terry 1975-77; 1978-79; 1980-81)
Nolet, Simon 1967-74
Osburn, Ran 1974-75
Paddock, A. John 1976-77; 1979-80; 1982-83
Paiement, J. W. Rosaire "Rosie" ...1967-70
Parizeau, Michel "Mike" 1971-72
Patterson, Dennis 1979-80
Pelletier, J. G. Roger 1967-68
Peters, Garry 1967-71
Plante, Pierre 1971-73
Potvin, Jean 1971-73
Poulin, Dave 1982-83
Preston, Yves 1978-79; 1980-81
Propp, Briar 1979-83
Ritchie, Robert 1976-77
Rochefort, Leon 1967-69
Saleski, Donald 1971-79
Sarrazin, Richard "Dick" 1968-70; 1971-72
Schmautz, Clifford "Cliff" 1970-71
Schock, Daniel 1970-71
Schultz, David 1971-76
Selby, R. Briton "Brit" 1967-69
Sinisalo, Ilkka 1981-83
Sirois, Robert 1974-76
Sittler, Darryl 1981-83
Smith, Steve 1981-82
Stankiewicz, Myron 1968-69
Stanley, Allan 1968-69
Stratton, Arthur 1967-68
Sutherland, William 1967-71
Sutter, Ronald 1982-83
Suzor, Mark 1976-77
Swarbrick, George 1970-71
Taylor, Mark 1981-83
Van Impe, Edward 1967-76
Ververgaert, Dennis 1978-80
Watson, James C. 1972-82
Watson, Joseph 1967-78
Wesley, T. Blake 1979-81
Williams, Gordon 1981-83
Wilson, Behn 1978-83
Wright, Keith 1967-68

Wright, Larry 1971-73; 1975-76
Zeidel, Lazarus "Larry" 1967-69

Goaltenders

Belhumeur, Michel 1972-73
Favell, Douglas 1967-73
Froese, Robert "Bob" 1982-83
Gamble, Bruce 1970-72
Inness, Gary 1975-77
Larocque, Michel "Bunny" 1982-83
Lindbergh, Per-Erik "Pelle" 1981-83
McLeod, Donald "Smokey" 1971-72
Moore, Robert "Robbie" 1978-79
Mrazek, Jerome 1975-76
Myre, L. Philippe 1979-81
Parent, Bernard 1973-79
Peeters, Peter "Pete" 1978-82
St. Croix, Rick 1977-83
Stephenson, R. Wayne 1974-79
Taylor, Robert 1971-76
Wilson, Duncan 1969-70

PITTSBURGH PENGUINS
Players
Anderson, Russell 1976-82
Andrea, Paul 1967-69
Angotti, Louis 1968-69
Apps, Sylvanus M. 1970-78
Arbour, John G. 1968-69
Arnason, E. Charles "Chuck" 1973-76
Awrey, Donald 1976-77
Barrie, Douglas 1968-69
Bathgate, Andrew 1967-68; 1970-71
Baxter, Paul 1980-83
Bennett, Harvey 1974-76
Bergeron, Yves 1974-75; 1976-77
Beverley, Nicholas 1973-74
Bianchin, Wayne 1973-79
Bignell, Larry 1973-74
Blackburn, Robert 1969-71
Bladon, Thomas 1978-80
Boivin, Leo 1967-69
Boutette, Patrick 1981-83
Boyd, Randy 1981-83
Boyer, Walter 1968-72
Briere, Michel 1969-70
Bullard, Michael 1980-83
Burns, Charles 1968-69
Burns, Robert "Robin" 1970-73
Burrows, David 1971-78; 1980-81
Buskas, Rod 1982-83
Campbell, Colin 1974-76; 77-79
Cardwell, Stephen 1970-73
Carlyle, Randy 1978-83
Carr, Eugene 1977-78
Cassidy, Thomas 1977-78
Chapman, Blair 1976-80
Chorney, Marc 1980-83
Clackson, Kimbel 1979-80
Corrigan, Michael 1976-78
Cossette, Jacques ... 1975-76; 1977-79

Davis, Kim 1977-81
Dea, William 1967-69
Debenedet, Nelson 1974-75
DeMarco, Albert T. 1973-75
Dillabough, Robert 1967-69
Durbano, H. Steven 1973-76
Edestrand, Darryl 1971-74
Edur, Thomas 1977-78
Faubert, Mario 1974-78; 1979-82
Feltrin, Anthony "Tony" 1980-83
Ferguson, George 1978-83
Flesch, John 1977-78
Fonteyne, Valere 1967-72
Gardner, Paul 1980-83
Garner, Robert "Rob" 1982-83
Gatzos, Steve 1981-83
Gilbert, Edward 1975-77
Gilbertson, Stanley 1975-77
Graham, Patrick 1981-83
Hadfield, Victor 1974-77
Hakansson, Anders 1982-83
Hamilton, James 1977-83
Hannan, David 1981-83
Harbaruk, M. Nickolas "Nick" 1969-73
Harris, William "Hinky" 1968-69
Hextall, Bryan L. 1969-74
Hicke, William 1971-72
Hicks, Wayne 1967-68
Horton, Myles "Tim" 1971-72
Hotham, Gregory 1981-83
Hrynewich, Tim 1982-83
Hudson, Alexander "Lex" 1978-79
Hughes, Patrick 1979-81
Ingarfield, Earl 1967-69
Johnson, Mark 1979-82
Jonathan, Stanley 1982-83
Jones, Ronald 1973-74
Kannegiesser, Sheldon 1970-73
Kehoe, Rick 1974-83
Kelly, John "Battleship" 1973-77
Kessell, Richard "Rick" 1969-73
Kindrachuk, Orest 1978-81
Konik, George 1967-68
Labre, Yvon 1970-71; 1973-74
Laframboise, Peter 1974-75
Lagace, Jean-Guy 1968-69; 1972-75
Lalonde, Ronald 1972-75
Lanyon, Edward "Ted" 1967-68
Larouche, Pierre 1974-78
LeCaine, William 1968-69
Lecuyer, Douglas 1982-83
Lee, Peter 1977-83
Leiter, Robert 1971-72
Libett, L. Nicholas 1979-81
Lonsberry, D. Ross 1978-81
Lukowich, Bernard 1973-74
Lundberg, Brian 1982-83
Lupien, Gilles 1980-81
Lynch, John 1972-74
Lyon, Steve 1976-77
MacDonald, Lowell 1970-71; 1972-78
MacLeish, Richard "Rick" 1981-83
MacNeil, Allister "Al" 1967-68

339

Mahovlich, P. 1977-79
Malone, W. G. 1976-83
Marshall, Paul. 1979-81
Mattiussi, Richard 1967-69
McAdam, Gary 1978-81
McCallum, Duncan 1967-71
McClelland, Kevin 1981-83
McCreary, V. Keith 1967-72
McDonald, Alvin 1967-68
McDonough, J. Allison 1971-74
KcKenzie, Brian 1971-72
McMahon, Michael 1969-70
McManama, Robert 1973-76
Meeker, Michael 1978-79
Meighan, Ron 1982-83
Monahan, Hartland 1977-78
Morrison, H. Lewis "Lew" 1974-78
Morrison, James 1969-71
Mulvey, Paul 1981-82
Nolet, Simon 1975-76
Noris, Joseph 1971-72
Nowak, Henry "Hank" 1973-74
Owchar, Dennis 1974-78
Paradise, Robert 1977-79
Pearson, G. A. Melvin "Mel" 1967-68
Polis, Gregory 1970-74
Pratt, Kelly 1974-75
Pratt, Tracy 1968-70
Prentice, Dean 1969-71
Price, G. Noel 1967-69
Price, S. Patrick 1980-83
Price, Thomas 1976-79
Pronovost, J. Jean 1968-78
Rissling, Gary 1980-83
Rivard, J. Robert "Bobby" 1967-68
Robert, Rene 1971-72
Rupp, Duane 1968-73
St. Laurent Andre 1981-83
Sanderson, Derek 1977-78
Sather, Glen 1969-71
Schinkel, Kenneth 1967-73
Schock, Ronald 1969-77
Schultz, David 1977-79
Schutt, Rodney 1978-83
Shack, Edward 1971-73
Shedden, Douglas 1981-83
Sheppard, Gregory 1978-82
Shires, James 1972-73
Simpson, Robert "Bobby" 1981-83
Snell, H. Edward "Ted" 1973-74
Snell, Ronald 1968-70
Speer, F. William "Bill" 1967-69
Spencer, Brian 1977-79
Stackhouse, Ronald 1973-82
Stewart, John 1970-72
Stewart, Robert 1979-80
Stoughton, Blaine 1973-74
Stratton, Arthur 1967-68
Stumpf, Robert 1974-75
Sutter, Richard 1982-83
Swain, Garth "Garry" 1968-69
Swarbrick, George 1968-70

Tallon, M. Dale 1978-80
Thompson, L. Errol. 1980-81
Turnbull, Ian 1982-83
Ubriaco, Eugene 1967-69
Van Impe, Edward 1975-77
Watson, Bryan 1968-74
Wiley, T. James 1972-74
Wilkins, Barry 1974-76
Wolf, Bennett 1980-83
Woytowich, Robert 1968-72
Zaine, Rodney 1970-71

Goaltenders

Bassen, Henry "Hank" 1967-68
Binkley, Leslie 1967-72
Brown, Andrew 1972-74
Daley, T. Joseph "Joe" 1968-70
Dion, Michel 1981-83
Edwards, A. Roy 1971-72
Edwards, Gary 1981-82
Edwards, Marvin 1968-69
Harrison, Paul 1981-82
Herron, Denis . . .1972-75; 1976-79; 1982-83
Hoganson, Paul 1970-71
Holland, Robert 1979-81
Inness, Gary 1973-76
Johnson, Robert 1974-75
Laxton, Gordon 1975-79
Millen, Greg 1978-81
Newton, Cameron 1970-71; 1972-73
Plasse, Michel 1974-76
Redquest, Greg 1977-78
Ricci, Nick 1979-83
Romano, Roberto 1982-83
Rutherford, James 1971-74
Smith, Allan "Al" 1969-71
Taylor, Robert 1975-76
Wilson, Duncan 1976-78

QUEBEC NORDIQUES
Players
Aubrey, Pierre 1980-83
Baxter, Paul 1979-80
Bernier, Serge 1979-81
Bilodeau, Gilles. 1979-80
Bolduc, Michel 1981-83
Brackenbury, J. Curtis. 1979-80
Chipperfield, Ronald 1979-81
Clackson, Kimbel 1980-81
Cloutier, Real 1979-83
Cloutier, Roland 1979-80
Cote, Alain 1979-83
David, Richard 1979-80; 1981-83
Dupont, Andre 1980-83
Eagles, Michael 1982-83
Eldebrink, Anders 1982-83
Farrish, David 1979-80
Fitchner, Robert. 1979-81
Frycer, Miroslav 1981-82
Ftorek, Robert "Robbie" 1979-82
Gaulin, Jean-Marc 1982-83
Gillis, Jere 1981-82

Gillis, Paul. 1982-83
Goulet, Michel 1979-83
Hamel, Jean 1981-83
Hart, Gerald "Gerry". 1979-81
Hickey, Patrick 1981-82
Hislop, James "Jamie" 1979-81
Hoganson, Dale 1979-82
Hunter, Dale 1980-83
Johnson, Terrance 1979-83
Lacombe, Francois 1979-80
Lacroix, Pierre 1979-83
Lapointe, Richard "Rick" 1982-83
Lariviere, Garry 1979-81
Leduc, Richard 1979-81
Legge, Barry 1979-80
Marois, Mario 1980-83
Martin, Terry 1979-80
McRae, Basil 1981-83
Moller, Randy 1982-83
Norwood, Lee 1980-82
Paddock, A. John 1980-81
Paiement, Wilfrid 1981-83
Pichette, Dave 1980-83
Plante, Pierre 1979-80
Price, S. Patrick 1982-83
Richard, Jacques 1979-83
Rochefort, Normand 1980-83
Saunders, Bernie 1979-81
Shaw, David 1982-83
Sleigher, Louis 1981-83
Smrke, John 1979-80
Sobchuk, Dennis 1982-83
Stastny, Anton 1980-83
Stastny, Marian 1981-83
Stastny, Peter 1980-83
Stewart, Blair 1979-80
Stewart, John 1979-80
Stewart, Paul 1979-80
Tanguay, Christian 1981-82
Tardif, Marc 1979-83
Tebutt, Greg 1979-80
Therrien, Gaston 1980-83
Thomas, Reginald 1979-80
Tookey, Timothy "Tim" 1982-83
Weir, Wally 1979-83
Wensink, John 1980-81
Wesley, T. Blake 1982-83

Goaltenders
Bouchard, Daniel 1980-83
Dion, Michel 1979-81
Garrett, John 1981-83
Grahame, Ronald 1980-81
Hogosta, Goran 1979-80
Low, Ronald 1979-80
Malarchuk, Clint 1981-83
Plasse, Michel 1980-82

ST. LOUIS BLUES
Players
Affleck, R. Bruce 1974-79
Anderson, Perry 1981-83
Anderson, Ronald 1969-70

Angotti, Louis 1973-74
Arbour, Alger "Al" 1967-71
Arbour, John 1970-72
Attwell, Ronald 1967-68
Awrey, Donald 1973-75
Babin, Mitch 1975-76
Babych, Wayne 1978-83
Bailey, Garnet 1973-75
Baker, William "Bill" 1981-82
Beaudin, Norman 1967-68
Bennett, Curt 1970-72; 1977-79
Bennett, Harvey 1978-79
Berenson, Gordon "Red" 1967-71; 1974-
                                              78
Bordeleau, Christian 1970-72
Borotsik, Jack 1974-75
Bothwell, Timothy 1982-83
Boudrias, Andre 1969-70
Bourbonnais, Rick 1975-78
Bowness, Richard "Rick" 1978-80
Brackenbury, J. Curtis 1982-83
Brewer, Carl 1970-72
Brooks, Gordon 1971-72; 1973-74
Brownschidle, John "Jack" 1977-83
Buchanan, Ronald 1969-70
Butler, Jerome "Jerry" 1975-78
Buynak, Gordon 1974-75
Cameron, Craig 1967-69; 1970-71
Campbell, G. Scott 1981-82
Cardin, Claude 1967-68
Carlson, Jack 1982-83
Carr, Eugene 1971-72
Chapman, Blair 1979-83
Collins, William 1973-75
Collyard, Robert 1973-74
Connelly, Wayne 1970-72
Cowick, R. Bruce 1975-76
Crawford, Robert R. 1979-80; 1981-83
Crisp, Terrance 1967-72
Crombeen, Michael "Mike" 1978-83
Currie, Tony 1977-82
Curtis, Paul 1972-73
DeMarco, Albert T. 1972-74
Dennis, Norman 1968-72
Dore, Andre 1982-83
Dunlop, Blake 1979-83
Dupere, Denis 1974-75
Dupont, Andre 1971-73
Durbano, H. Steven 1972-74; 1978-79
Ecclestone, Timothy 1967-71
Edestrand, Darryl 1967-68
Egers, John "Jack" 1971-74
Eloranta, Kari 1981-82
Evans, Christopher 1971-75
Fairbairn, William 1977-79
Federko, Bernard 1976-83
Forey, Conley "Connie" 1973-74
Fortin, Raymond 1967-70
Frig, Leonard 1977-78; 1979-80
Gardner, David 1973-75
Gassoff, Robert 1973-77
Gibbs, Barry 1977-79

Gilbertson, Stanley 1974-75
Giroux, Larry 1973-74; 1978-80
Goyette, J. G. Philippe 1969-70
Gray, Terrence 1968-70
Hamel, Jean 1972-74
Hamilton, Charles "Chuck" 1972-73
Hammarstrom, H. Inge 1977-79
Hansen, Richie 1981-82
Harbaruk, M. Nickolas "Nick" 1973-74
Harper, Terrance 1979-80
Harris, Edward "Ted" 1973-74
Hart, Gerald "Gerry" 1980-83
Harvey, Douglas 1968-69
Henry, Camille 1968-70
Hess, Robert "Bob" 1974-79; 1980-81
Hickey, Patrick 1982-83
Holt, Gareth "Gary" 1977-78
Hornung, Larry 1970-72
Hrechkosy, David 1975-77
Huck, A. Francis 1970-71; 1972-73
Hucul, Fredrick 1967-68
Hughes, Brenton "Brent" 1972-74
Irvine, Edward "Ted" 1975-77
Jirik, Jaroslav 1969-70
Kannegiesser, Gordon 1967-68; 1971-72
Kea, Adrian "Ed" 1979-83
Keenan, Lawrence 1967-71
Kelly, John "Battleship" 1973-74
Klassen, Ralph 1979-83
Komadoski, Neil 1977-80
Kuntz, Murray 1974-75
Labatte, Neil 1978-79; 1981-82
Lafreniere, Roger 1972-73
Lamby, Richard "Dick" 1978-81
Lampman, Michael 1972-74
Lapointe, Guy 1981-83
Lapointe, Richard "Rick" 1979-82
Larose, Claude 1974-78
Laurence, Don "Red" 1979-80
Lavender, Brian 1971-72
Lefley, Charles 1974-77; 1979-81
Lemieux, Alain 1981-83
Lorentz, James 1970-72
Lukowich, Bernard 1974-75
MacLean, Paul 1980-81
MacMillan, Robert 1975-78
MacNeil, S. Bernard 1973-74
Madigan, Cornelius "Connie" 1972-73
Maki, Wayne 1969-70
Marotte, Jean-Gilles 1976-77
Masters, James "Jamie" . . .1975-77; 1978-79
Maxwell, Bryan 1979-81
McCord, Robert 1972-73
McCreary, William 1967-71
McCrimmon, John 1974-75
McDonald, Alvin "Ab" 1968-71
McKenney, Donald 1967-68
McTavish, Gordon 1978-79
Melnyk, M. Gerald 1967-68
Merrick, L. Wayne 1972-76
Micheletti, Joseph "Joe" 1979-82
Monahan, Hartland 1979-81

Moore, Richard "Dickie" 1967-68
Morrison, George 1970-72
Mullen, Joseph 1981-83
Murdoch, Robert L. 1978-79
Murphy, Michael "Mike" 1971-73
Nedomansky, Vaclav "Big Ned" 1982-83
Nill, James "Jim" 1981-82
Noris, Joseph 1972-73
Norwich, Craig 1980-81
Odrowski, Gerald 1971-72
Ogilvie, Brian 1974-79
O'Shea, Daniel 1971-73
O'Shea, Kevin 1971-73
Palazzari, Douglas 1974-75; 1976-79
Parizeau, Michel "Mike" 1971-72
Patey, Larry 1975-83
Patrick, Craig 1974-75
Patrick, Glenn 1973-74
Pavese, James "Jim" 1981-83
Pettersson, Jorgen 1980-83
Picard, A. Roger 1967-68
Picard, Jean-Noel 1967-73
Plager, Barclay 1967-77
Plager, Robert 1967-78
Plager, William 1968-72
Plante, Pierre 1972-77
Polis, Gregory 1973-74
Ramage, G. Rob 1982-83
Redmond, Richard "Dick" 1977-78
Reeds, Mark 1981-83
Richardson, Kenneth 1974-75; 1977-79
Rivers, J. Wayne 1967-68
Roberto, Phillip 1971-75
Roberts, James W. 1967-72; 1977-78
Sabourin, Gary 1967-74
Sacharuk, Lawrence 1974-75
St. Marseille, Francis 1967-73
Sanderson, Derek 1975-77
Sather, Glen 1973-74
Schock, Ronald 1967-69
Seiling, Rodney 1976-79
Selby, R. Briton 1970-72
Shinske, Richard "Rick" 1978-79
Shires, James "Jim" 1971-72
Simpson, Robert "Bobby" 1979-80
Smith, Richard "Rick" 1975-77
Smrke, John 1977-79
Spring, Franklin 1973-75
Stankiewicz, Myron 1968-69
Stewart, Robert 1978-80
Stewart, Ronald 1967-68
Stewart, William 1980-83
Stumpf, Robert 1974-75
Sutherland, William 1970-72
Sutter, Brian 1976-83
Talbot, Jean-Guy 1967-71
Thomson, Floyd 1971-78; 1979-80
Tudor, Robert "Rob" 1982-83
Turnbull, Perry 1979-83
Unger, Garry 1970-79
Veneruzzo, Gary 1967-68; 1971-72
Vigneault, Alain 1981-83

Wall, Robert 1970-71
Walton, Michael 1978-79
Watson, Bryan 1973-74
Wensink, John 1973-74
Whelden, Donald 1974-75
Williams, Warren 1973-74
Wilson, Bertwin "Bert" 1975-76
Wilson, Richard G. "Rick" 1974-76
Wilson, Richard W. "Rik" 1981-83
Wright, John 1973-74
Zanussi, Joseph "Joe" 1976-77
Zuke, Michael "Mike" 1978-83

Goaltenders

Belanger, Yves 1974-78
Caley, Donald 1967-68
Caron, Jacques 1971-73
Davidson, John 1973-75
Edwards, Gary 1968-70; 1981-82
Grant, Douglas 1976-80
Gratton, Gilles 1975-76
Hall, Glenn 1967-71
Hanlon, Glen 1981-83
Heinz, Richard "Rick" 1980-83
Irons, Robert "Robbie" 1968-69
Johnson, Robert 1972-73
Johnston, Edward 1974-78
Liut, Michael "Mike" 1979-83
Martin, Seth 1967-68
McDuffe, Peter 1971-72
McLeod, James 1971-72
Myre, L. Philoppe 1977-79
Ouimet, Edward "Ted" 1968-69
Plante, J. Jacques 1968-70
Plasse, Michel 1970-71
Richardson, Terrance 1978-79
Skidmore, Paul 1981-82
Staniowski, Edward 1975-81
Stephenson, F. Wayne 1971-74
Wakely, Ernest 1969-72
Watt, James . . . . 1973-74$

TORONTO MAPLE LEAFS

Acomb, Douglas 1969-70
Adam, Russ 1982-83
Adams, John "Jack" 1917-19; 1922-26
Adams, Stewart 1932-33
Aldcorn, Gary 1956-59
Alexander, Claire 1974-77
Anderson, John 1977-83
Andrews, Lloyd 1921-25
Apps, C. Sylvanus 1936-43; 1945-48
Arbour, Alger "Al" 1961-64; 1965-66
Arbour, Amos 1923-24
Arbour, John "Jack" 1928-29
Armstrong, George 1949-50; 1951-71
Armstrong, Murray 1937-39
Armstrong, Norman "Red" 1962-63
Arundel, John 1949-50
Ashby, Donald 1975-79
Aubin, Normand 1981-83

Backor, Peter 1944-45
Bailey, Irvin "Ace" 1926-34
Bailey, Reid 1982-83
Bailey, Robert 1953-56
Baldwin, Douglas 1945-46
Balfour, Earl 1951-52; 1953-54; 1955-56;
                                                    1957-58
Barbe, Andre "Andy" 1950-51
Barilko, William 1946-51
Bathgate, Andrew 1963-65
Baun, Robert 1956-67; 1970-73
Belanger, Alain 1977-78
Bellefeuille, Peter 1925-27
Benning, James 1981-83
Bentley, Maxwell 1947-53
Bionda, Jack 1955-56
Blair, Andrew 1928-36
Blair, Charles "Chuck" 1948-49
Blair, George "Dusty" 1950-51
Blake, Francis 1935-36
Bodnar, August "Gus" 1943-47
Boesch, Garth 1946-50
Boimistruck, Fred 1981-83
Boisvert, Serge 1982-83
Boivin, Leo 1951-55
Boll, Frank "Buzz" 1933-39
Bolton, Hugh 1949-57
Boothman, George 1942-44
Boschman, Laurie 1979-82
Boudreau, Bruce 1976-82
Bourgault, Leo 1926-27
Boutette, Patrick 1975-80
Boyer, Walter "Wally" 1965-66
Brenneman, John 1966-67
Brewer, Carl 1957-65; 1979-80
Brindley, Douglas 1970-71
Brossart, William 1973-75
Brown, S. Arnold 1961-62; 1963-64
Brydge, William 1926-27
Brydson, Gordon 1929-30
Buchanan, Allaster 1948-50
Burega, William 1955-56
Burrows, David 1978-81
Butler, Jerome "Jerry" 1977-80
Byers, Michael 1967-69
Caffery, John "Jack" 1954-55
Cahan, Lawrence 1954-56
Cain, James "Dutch" 1925-26
Cameron, Harold "Harry" 1917-23
Carey, George 1923-24
Carleton, K. Wayne 1965-70
Carlyle, Randy 1976-78
Carr, Alfred 1943-44
Carr, Lorne 1941-46
Carriere, Larry 1979-80
Carson, William 1926-29
Ceresino, Raymond 1948-49
Chamberlain, Erwin "Murph" 1937-40
Champagne, Andre 1962-63
Chisholm, Alexander "Lex" 1939-41
Church, John "Jack" 1938-42
Clancy, Francis "King" 1930-37

Clancy, Terrance 1968-70; 1972-73
Cleghorn, Sprague 1920-21
Conacher, Brian 1961-62; 1965-68
Conacher, Charles 1929-38
Conacher, Charles, Jr. 1957-58
Copp, Robert 1942-43; 1950-51
Corbeau, Bert 1923-27
Corrigan, Charles 1937-38
Costello, Lester 1948-49
Cotton, E. Harold 1928-35
Coughlin, Jack 1917-18
Cox, Daniel 1926-30
Crawford, Samuel "Rusty" 1917-19
Creighton, David 1954-55; 1958-60
Crozier, Joseph 1959-60
Cullen, Brian 1954-59
Cullen, Charles "Barry" 1955-59
Daoust, Daniel 1982-83
Darragh, Harold 1931-33
Davidson, Robert 1934-46
Davis, Kim 1980-81
Dawes, Robert 1946-47; 1948-50
Day, Clarence "Hap" 1924-37
DeMarco, Albert "Ab" 1942-43
Denneny, Corbett 1917-23; 1926-27
Denoird, Gerald 1922-23
Derlago, William 1979-83
Dickens, Ernest 1941-42; 1945-46
Doraty, Kenneth 1932-35
Dorey, R. James 1968-72
Douglas, Kent 1962-67
Downie, David 1932-33
Draper, Bruce 1962-63
Drillon, Gordon 1936-42
Duff, T. Richard "Dick" 1954-64
Duncan, Arthur 1927-31
Dunlap, Frank 1943-44
Dunn, David 1974-76
Dupere, Denis 1970-74
Duris, Vitezslav 1980-81; 1982-83
Dye, Cecil "Babe" 1919-26; 1930-31
Ecclestone, Timothy 1973-75
Edmundson, Garry 1959-61
Ehman, Gerald 1958-61; 1963-64
Ellis, Ronald 1963-75; 1977-81
Evans, Christopher 1969-70
Evans, Paul 1976-78
Ezinicki, William 1944-50
Farrish, David 1979-81; 1982-83
Faulkner, S. Alexander 1961-62
Ferguson, George 1972-78
Finnigan, Frank 1931-32; 1934-37
Fisher, Alvin 1924-25
Flaman, Ferdinand 1950-54
Flett, William 1974-75
Foley, Gerald 1954-55
Forsey, Jack 1942-43
Fortier, David 1972-73
Fowler, James 1936-39
Frycer, Miroslav 1981-83
Gamble, Richard "Dick" 1965-67
Gardner, Calvin 1948-52

Gardner, Paul 1978-80	Jarry, Pierre 1971-74	Marshall, Paul 1980-82
Gariepy, Raymond. 1955-56	Jarvis, James 1936-37	Marshall, Willmott . . 1952-53; 1954-56; 1958-59
Garland, S. Scott. 1975-77	Jeffrey, Lawrence "Larry" 1965-67	
Gavin, R. Stewart. 1980-83	Jenkins, Roger 1930-31	Martin, Jack. 1960-61
Gibson, John. 1981-82	Johansen, Trevor 1977-79; 1981-82	Martin, Terry 1979-83
Gingras, Gaston 1982-83	Johnson, Daniel. 1969-70	Martin, Thomas 1967-68
Girard, Kenneth. 1956-58; 1959-60	Johnson (Johansen), William. 1949-50	Masnick, Paul 1957-58
Glennie, Brian 1969-78	Johnstone, R. Ross 1943-45	Mathers, Frank. 1948-50; 1951-52
Godden, Ernie. 1981-82	Jones, Alvin. 1942-43	Matte, Joseph 1919-20
Goldham, Robert. 1941-42; 1945-47	Jones, James 1977-80	Maxwell, Wally. 1952-53
Goldup, Henry "Hank" 1939-43	Joyal, Edward 1965-66	Mayer, Sheppard. 1942-43
Gorman, Edwin 1927-28	Juzda, William 1948-52	McCaffrey, Albert. 1924-28
Gracie, Robert. 1930-33	Kampman, Rudolph "Bingo" 1937-42	McCormack, John. 1947-51
Gray, Alexander. 1928-29	Kaszycki, Michael 1979-81; 1982-83	McCreary, William 1980-81
Grisdale, John. 1972-73; 1974-75	Keeling, Melville 1926-28	McCreedy, John 1941-42; 1944-45
Gross, Lloyd 1926-27	Keenan, Lawrence "Larry" 1961-62	McCutcheon, Darwin. 1981-82
Halderson, Harold 1926-27	Kehoe, Rick. 1971-74	McDonald, Lanny 1973-80
Hamel, Herbert 1930-31	Kelly, Leonard "Red". 1959-67	McDonald, Wilfred "Bucko". 1938-44
Hamilton, John 1942-44; 1945-46	Kelly, Regis 1934-40	McGill, Robert. 1981-83
Hamilton, Reginald 1935-45	Kemp, Stanley. 1948-49	McIntyre, Lawrence. 1969-70; 1972-73
Hammarstrom, H. Inge 1973-78	Kendall, William. 1936-37	McKechnie, Walter 1978-80
Hampson, Edward "Ted" 1959-60	Kennedy, Forbes 1968-69	McKenney, Donald 1963-65
Hannigan, J. Gordon 1952-56	Kennedy, Theodore 1942-55; 1956-57	McKenny, James 1965-78
Hannigan, Patrick "Pat" 1959-60	Keon, David. 1960-75	McLean, Jack 1942-45
Hannigan, Raymond 1948-49	Kilrea, Hector 1933-35	McLellan, D. John 1951-52
Harris, George "Duke" 1967-68	Kirton, Mark. 1979-81	Meehan, Gerald 1968-69
Harris, William "Hinky" 1955-65	Klukay, Joseph 1946-52; 1954-56	Meeker, Howard 1946-54
Harris, William "Bill". 1981-83	Knox, Paul. 1954-55	Meeking, Harry 1917-19
Harrison, James 1969-72	Korn, James 1981-83	Melrose, Barry. . . . . 1980-83$
Hassard, Robert 1949-51; 1952-54	Kozak, Lester 1961-62	Metz. Donald. 1938-42; 1945-49
Heffernan, Frank 1919-20	Kraftcheck, Stephen 1958-59	Metz, Nicholas 1934-42; 1944-48
Henderson, Paul 1967-74	Kurtenbach, Orland. 1965-66	Mickey, R. Larry. 1968-69
Herberts, James 1927-28	Langelle, Peter 1938-42	Migay, Rudolph 1949-50; 1951-60
Heron, Robert 1938-41	Levinsky, Alexander 1930-34	Mikol, John "Jim". 1962-63
Hickey, Patrick. 1979-82	Lewicki, Daniel 1950-54	Miller, Earl. 1931-32
Higgins, Paul. 1981-83	Ley, Richard 1968-72	Moffat, Lyle 1972-73; 1974-75
Hill, J. Melvin. 1942-46	Liddington, Robert 1970-71	Monahan, Garry 1970-75; 1978-79
Hillman, Lawrence. 1960-68	Litzenberger, Edward 1961-64	Moore, Richard "Dickie" 1964-65
Hinse, Andre. 1967-68	Loughlin, Wilfred 1923-24	Morris, Elwyn. 1943-46
Hollett, William. 1933-36	Lowrey, Gerald 1927-29	Morrison, James 1951-58
Holway, Albert "Toots". 1923-26	Luce, Donald. 1981-82	Mortson, J. Angus "Gus". 1946-52
Hopkins, Larry. 1977-78	Lundrigan, Joseph 1972-73	Mulhern, Richard. 1979-80
Horne, George 1928-29	Lynn, Victor. 1946-50	Mummery, Harry 1917-19
Horner, G. Reginald. 1928-40	Macdonald, C. Parker 1952-53; 1954-55	Muni, Craig 1981-83
Horton, Myles 1949-50; 1951-70	Mackasey, Blair. 1976-77	Munro, Gerald 1925-26
Horvath, Bronco 1962-63	Mackell, Fleming 1947-52	Murray, Kenneth 1969-71
Hotham, Gregory. 1979-82	MacMillan, John 1960-64	Murray, Randall 1969-70
Howard, Jack 1936-37	MacMillan, William. 1970-72	Neely, Robert. 1973-78
Howe, Sydney 1931-32	MacNeil, Allister "Al". 1955-60	Nelson, Gordon. 1969-70
Huard, Roland. 1930-31	Maggs, Darryl 1979-80	Nesterenko, Eric 1951-56
Hubick, Gregory 1975-76	Magnan, Marc 1982-83	Neville, Michael. 1917-18; 1924-26
Hurst, Ronald 1955-57	Mahovlich, Francis. 1956-68	Nevin, Robert 1957-59; 1960-64
Hutchinson, David. 1978-80	Maloney, Daniel. 1977-82	Nighbor, Frank J. 1929-30
Ihnacak, Peter. 1982-83	Maloney, Philip 1950-51; 1952-53	Nigro, Frank. 1982-83
Imlach, Brent. 1965-67	Mann, Norman. 1938-39; 1940-41	Noble, E. Reginald 1917-25
Ingoldsby, John. 1942-44	Manno, Robert 1981-82	Nolan, Patrick 1921-22
Jackson, Arthur 1934-37; 1944-45	Marchinko, Brian 1970-72	Nykoluk, Michael 1956-57
Jackson, Harvey "Busher". 1929-39	Marker, August "Gus" 1938-41	Nylund, Gary. 1982-83
Jackson, Stanton, ...1921-22; 1923-25	Markle, John 1935-36	O'Flaherty, Gerard "Gerry" 1971-72
Jacobs— 1918-19	Marks, John "Jack". 1917-18	Oliver, Murray 1967-70
James, Gerald 1954-58; 1959-60	Marsh, Gary 1968-69	Olmstead, M. Bert 1958-62
Jarrett, Gary 1960-61	Marshall, Donald 1971-72	O'Neill, Thomas. 1943-45

Brasar, Per-Olov 1979-82
Bubla, Jiri 1981-83
Butcher, Garth 1981-83
Butler, Jerome "Jerry" 1979-82
Callander, L. Drew............. 1978-80
Campbell, Colin 1980-82
Carriere, Larry 1976-78
Christie, Michael 1980-81
Connelly, Wayne 1971-72
Cook, Robert 1970-71
Corrigan, Michael 1970-72
Crawford, Marc............... 1981-83
Cullen, Raymond 1970-71
Currie, Tony................... 1981-83
Dailey, Robert 1973-77
Delorme, Ronald 1981-83
DeMarco, Albert T. 1974-76
Derlago, William.............. 1978-80
Doak, Gary 1970-72
Dunn, David................... 1973-75
Eldebrink, Anders 1981-83
Eriksson, B. Roland 1978-79
Flockhart, Robert "Rob".......1976-79
Folco, Peter 1973-74
Fortier, David 1976-77
Fraser, Curt 1978-83
Gassoff, H. Bradley "Brad" 1975-79
Gillis, Jere 1977-81
Gloor, Daniel 1973-74
Goodenough, Larry 1976-80
Gould, John 1973-77
Gould, Larry.................. 1973-74
Gradin, Thomas 1978-83
Graves, Hilliard 1976-79
Grisdale, John 1974-79
Guevremont...................1971-75
Hall, Murray 1970-72
Halward, Douglas...............1980-83
Hargreaves, James 1970-71; 1972-73
Hatoum, Edward 1970-71
Hazlett, Steven 1979-80
Hlinka, Ivan 1981-83
Holt, S. Randall "Randy".........1978-79
Homenuke, Ronald 1972-73
Hubick, Gregory 1979-80
Hughes, John 1979-80
Hurlburt, Robert "Bob".........1974-75
Johnson, Daniel ("Danny".........1970-72
Kannegiesser, Sheldon 1977-78
Kearns, Dennis 1971-81
Kirton, Mark 1982-83
Korab, Gerald ("Jerry")..........1973-74
Kozak, Don 1978-79
Kulak, Stuart ("Stu'.............1982-83
Kurtenbach, Orland 1970-74
Lalonde, Robert................1971-77
Lampman, Michael 1973-74
Lanz, Rick 1980-83
Lemay, Maurice ("Moe").........1981-83
Lemieux, Richard...............1971-74
Lever, Donald 1972-80
Lindgren, Lars 1978-83
Logan, David 1979-81

Lunde, Leonard 1970-71
Lupul, Gary.................... 1979-83
MacDonald, Blair 1980-83
Mair, James 1972-75
Maki, Wayne 1970-73
Manery, Kris 1979-80
Manno, Robert 1976-81
Marois, Mario 1980-81
Martin, Hubert "Pit".............. 1981-83
McCarthy, Kevin 1974-76
McCord, Dennis................ 1973-74
McDonnell, Joseph 1981-82
McIlhargey, John "Jack".......... 1976-80
McSheffrey, Bryan 1972-74
Meehan, Gerald "Gerry".......... 1974-75
Minor, Gerald 1979-83
Molin, Lars 1981-83
Monahan, Garry 1974-78
Murray, Robert 1974-77
Nill, James "Jim' 1981-83
Oddleifson, Christopher 1973-81
O'Flaherty, Gerard "Gerry'........ 1972-78
O'Neil, Paul 1973-74
Paiement, J. W. Rosaire "Rosie" 1970-72
Petit, Michel 1982-83
Popiel, Poul "Paul" 1970-72
Pratt, Tracy 1973-76
Primeau, Kevin 1980-81
Quinn, J. B. Patrick 1970-72
Reaume, Marc 1970-71
Richardson, Glen 1975-76
Rizzuto, Garth 1970-71
Robitaille, Michael 1974-77
Rochefort, Leon 1974-76
Rota, Darcy 1979-83
Sanderson, Derek 1976-77
Schella, John 1970-72
Schliebener, Andreas "Andy" 1981-82
Schmautz, Robert 1980-81
Sedlbauer, Ronald 1974-80
Seguin, Daniel 1973-74
Sly, Darryl.................... 1970-71
Smith, Brad 1978-80
Smyl, Stanley 1978-83
Snepsts, Harold 1974-83
Sobchuk, Eugene 1973-74
Speck, Frederick 1971-72
Spruce, Andrew 1976-77
Stewart, Ralph 1970-71; 1976-78
Stewart, Ronald 1971-72
Stone, Stephen 1973-74
Sundstrom, Patrik.............. 1982-83
Tallon, M. Dale................. 1970-73
Tannahill, Donald 1972-74
Tanti, Tony 1982-83
Taylor, Edward "Ted" 1970-72
Tudor, Robert 1978-80
Vaive, Rick 1979-80
Ververgaert, Dennis 1973-79
Veysey, Sidney................ 1977-78
Walton, Michael 1975-78
Ward, Ronald 1971-72
Wilcox, Barry 1974-75

Wiley, T. James 1974-77
Wilkins, Barry 1970-75
Williams, David 1979-83
Wiste, James 1970-71
Wright, John 1972-74
Young, Howard 1970-71
Zetterstrom, Lars 1978-79

Goaltenders

Bannerman, Murray 1977-78
Brodeur, Richard 1980-83
Bromley, Gary 1978-81
Bullock, Bruce 1976-77
Caprice, Frank 1982-83
Caron, Jacques................1973-74
Dyck, Edwin..................1971-74
Ellacott, Ken 1982-83
Kardner, George "Bud" 1970-72
Garrett, John 1982-83
Hanlon, Glen 1977-82
Heinz, Richard "Rick" 1981-82
Hodge, Charles 1970-71
Lockett, Kenneth 1974-76
Maniago, Cesare 1976-78
McLelland, David 1972-73
Ridley, C. Curtis 1975-78; 1979-80
Smith, Gary...................1973-76
Wilson, Duncan 1970-73; 1978-79

WASHINGTON CAPITALS
Players

Anderson, Murray 1974-7
Anderson, Ronald 1974-75
Arnason, E. Charles "Chuck" 1978-79
Atkinson, Steven 1974-75
Bailey, Garnet 1974-78
Bennett, Harvey............... 1975-77
Bergeron, Michel 1978-79
Bidner, R. Todd 1981-82
Blomqvist, Timo............... 1981-83
Bloom, Michael 1974-75
Bolonchuk, Larry 1975-78
Bouchard, Pierre 1978-82
Bragnalo, Richard 1975-79
Brooks, Gordon 1974-75
Brossart, William "Willie"......... 1974-76
Bulley, Edward "Ted" 1982-83
Burton, Nelson................ 1977-79
Calder, Eric 1981-83
Camazzola, Anthony "Tony" 1981-82
Carpenter, Robert "Bobby" 1981-83
Carroll, Gregory............... 1978-79
Cassolato, Anthony "Tony" 1979-82
Charron, Guy 1976-81
Clement, William 1975-76
Clippingdale, Steve 1979-80
Collins, William 1976-78
Coulis, Tim................... 1979-80
Cowick, R. Bruce 1974-75
Currie, Glen 1979-83
Duchesne, Gaetan 1981-83

345

Dupere, Denis 1974-75	Murray, Terry 1981-82	**WINNIPEG JETS**
Edberg, Rolf 1978-81	Nicholson, Paul 1974-77	**Players**

Stamler, Lorne 1979-80
Steen, Anders 1980-81
Steen, Thomas 1981-83
Sullivan, Peter 1979-81
Tomalty, Glenn 1979-80
Trimper, Timothy "Tim" 1980-83
Watters, Timothy "Tim 1981-83
Whelton, William 1980-81
Wilson, Ronald Lee 1979-83

Goaltenders

Dion, Michel 1980-81
Hamel, Pierre 1979-81
Hayward, Brian 1982-83
Loustel, Ron 1980-81
Mattsson, R. Markus 1979-81
Middlebrook, Lindsay 1979-81
Smith, Gary 1979-80
Soetaert, Douglas 1981-83
Staniowski, Edward 1981-83

Records

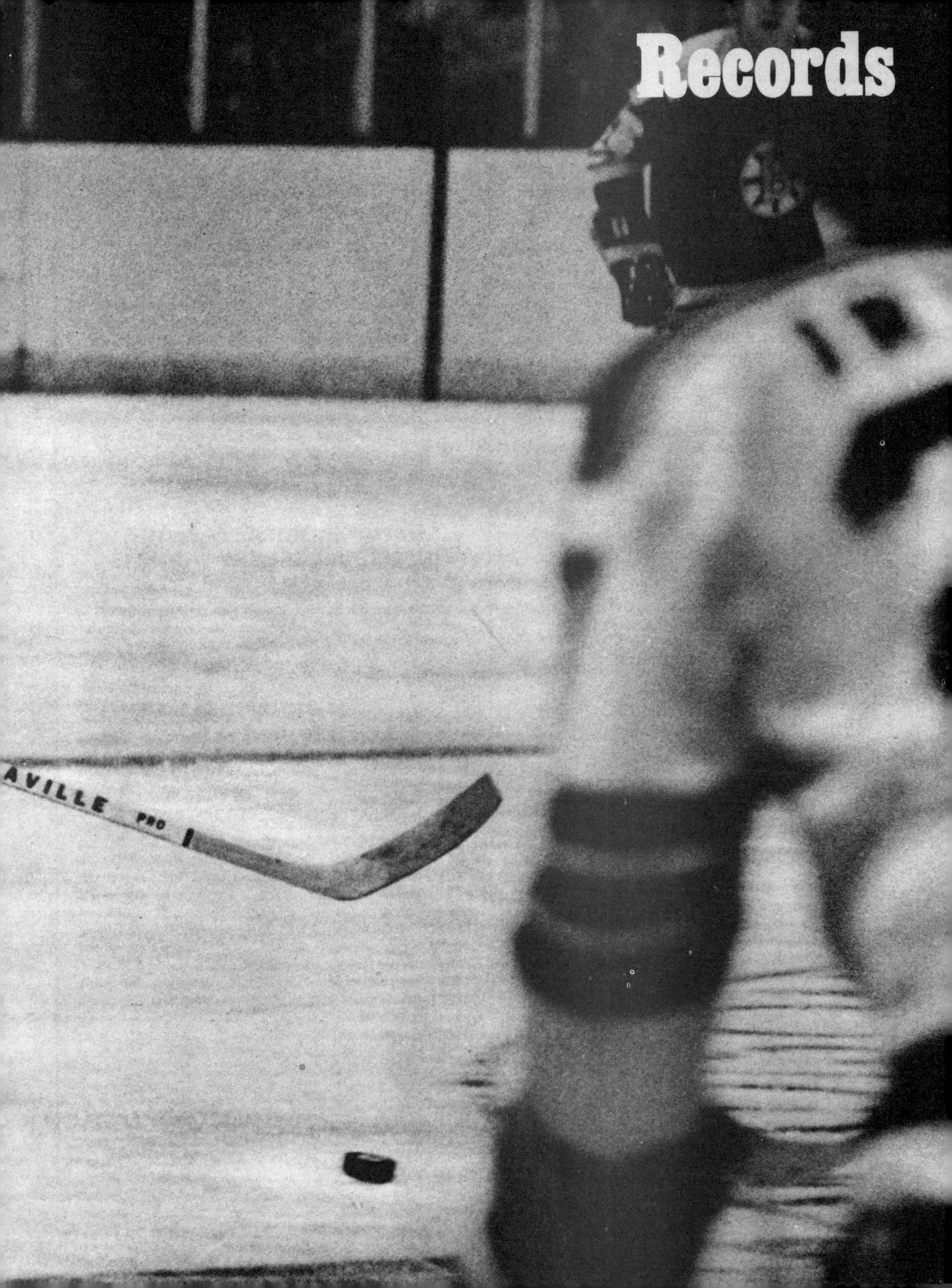

CLARENCE S. CAMPBELL BOWL

This trophy was presented by the NHL clubs in recognition of Clarence S. Campbell's long service in their behalf. It is made of sterling silver and was crafted in 1878 by a British silversmith. Until 1974-75, the trophy was awarded to the club finishing first in the West Division.

1967-68	Philadelphia Flyers
1968-69	St. Louis Blues
1969-70	St. Louis Blues
1970-71	Chicago Black Hawks
1971-72	Chicago Black Hawks
1972-73	Chicago Black Hawks
1973-74	Philadelphia Flyers

In 1974-75, the NHL divided into four divisions and two conferences. From that time until 1981-82, the trophy was awarded to the club with the best record in the Clarence S. Campbell Conference.

1974-75	Philadelphia Flyers
1975-76	Philadelphia Flyers
1976-77	Philadelphia Flyers
1977-78	New York Islanders
1978-79	New York Islanders
1979-80	Philadelphia Flyers
1980-81	New York Islanders

Since 1981-82 the trophy has been awarded to the Clarence S. Campbell Conference club that advances through the Stanley Cup playoffs to face the Prince of Wales conference club in the final Stanley Cup series.

1981-82	Vancouver Canucks
1982-83	Edmonton Oilers

PRINCE OF WALES TROPHY

This trophy was presented to the NHL by His Royal Highness, the Prince of Wales (later King Edward VIII) in 1924, and was awarded to the league champions.

1924-25	Montreal Canadiens
1925-26	Montreal Canadiens
1926-27	Ottawa Senators

From 1927-28 to 1937-38 it was awarded to the club finishing first in the American Division.

1927-28	Boston Bruins
1928-29	Boston Bruins
1929-30	Boston Bruins
1930-31	Boston Bruins
1931-32	New York Rangers
1932-33	Boston Bruins
1933-34	Detroit Red Wings
1934-35	Boston Bruins
1935-36	Detroit Red Wings
1936-37	Detroit Red Wings
1937-38	Boston Bruins

With the abandonment of the two-division system this trophy was again awarded to the league champions.

1938-39	Boston Bruins
1939-40	Boston Bruins

1940-41	Boston Bruins
1941-42	New York Rangers
1942-43	Detroit Red Wings
1943-44	Montreal Canadiens
1944-45	Montreal Canadiens
1945-46	Montreal Canadiens
1946-47	Montreal Canadiens
1947-48	Toronto Maple Leafs
1948-49	Detroit Red Wings
1949-50	Detroit Red Wings
1950-51	Detroit Red Wings
1951-52	Detroit Red Wings
1952-53	Detroit Red Wings
1953-54	Detroit Red Wings
1954-55	Detroit Red Wings
1955-56	Montreal Canadiens
1956-57	Detroit Red Wings
1957-58	Montreal Canadiens
1958-59	Montreal Canadiens
1959-60	Montreal Canadiens
1960-61	Montreal Canadiens
1961-62	Montreal Canadiens
1962-63	Toronto Maple Leafs
1963-64	Montreal Canadiens
1964-65	Detroit Red Wings
1965-66	Montreal Canadiens
1966-67	Chicago Black Hawks

With the return of the two-division system, the Prince of Wales trophy was awarded to the club finishing first in the East Division.

1967-68	Montreal Canadiens
1968-69	Montreal Canadiens
1969-70	Chicgao Black Hawks
1970-71	Boston Bruins
1971-72	Boston Bruins
1972-73	Montreal Canadiens
1973-74	Boston Bruins

In 1974-75 the NHL divided into four divisions and two conferences. From that time until 1981-82, the trophy was awarded to the club with the best record in the Prince of Wales Conference.

1974-75	Buffalo Sabres
1975-76	Montreal Canadiens
1976-77	Montreal Canadiens
1977-78	Montreal Canadiens
1978-79	Montreal Canadiens
1979-80	Buffalo Sabres
1980-81	Montreal Canadiens

Since 1981-82 it has been awarded to the Prince of Wales Conference club that advances through the Stanley Cup playoffs to face the Clarence S. Campbell club in the final Stanley Cup series.

1981-82	New York Islanders
1982-83	New York Islanders

JACK ADAMS AWARD

Presented by the National Hockey League Broadcasters' Association in 1974 to commemorate John J. ("Jack") Adams, former manager of the Detroit Red Wings, it is awarded to the "National Hockey League coach adjudged to have contributed the most to his club's success."

1973-74	Frederick A. Shero	Philadelphia Flyers
1974-75	Robert J. Pulford	Los Angeles Kings
1975-76	Donald S. Cherry	Boston Bruins
1976-77	W. Scott Bowman	Montreal Canadiens
1977-78	Robert D. Kromm	Detroit Red Wings
1978-79	Alger J. ("Al") Arbour	New York Islanders
1979-80	J. B. Patrick Quinn	Philadelphia Flyers
1980-81	Gordon A. ("Red") Berenson	St. Louis Blues
1981-82	Thomas Watt	Winnipeg Jets
1982-83	Orval R. Tessier	Chicago Black Hawks

LADY BYNG TROPHY

In 1925 Lady Byng, wife of the then governor-general of Canada, presented this trophy. It is awarded to "the player adjudged to have exhibited the best type of sportsmanship and gentlemanly conduct combined with a high standard of playing ability."

1924-25	Frank Nighbor	Ottawa Senators
1925-26	Frank Nighbor	Ottawa Senators
1926-27	H. William Burch	New York Americans
1927-28	Frank Boucher	New York Rangers
1928-29	Frank Boucher	New York Rangers
1929-30	Frank Boucher	New York Rangers
1930-31,	Frank Boucher	New York Rangers
1931-32	A. Joseph Primeau	Toronto Maple Leafs
1932-33	Frank Boucher	New York Rangers
1933-34	Frank Boucher	New York Rangers
1934-35	Frank Boucher	New York Rangers

After winning this trophy seven times in eight seasons, Frank Boucher was given permanent possession of it and Lady Byng presented another.

1935-36	Elwin ("Doc")Romnes	Chicago Black Hawks
1936-37	Martin Barry	Detroit Red Wings
1937-38	Gordon Drillon	Toronto Maple Leafs
1938-39	Clinton Smith	New York Rangers
1939-40	Robert Bauer	Boston Bruins
1940-41	Robert Bauer	Boston Bruins
1941-42	C. J. Sylvanus Apps	Toronto Maple Leafs
1942-43	Maxwell Bentley	Chicago Black Hawks
1943-44	Clinton Smith	Chicago Black Hawks
1944-45	William Mosienko	Chicago Black Hawks
1945-46,	Hector ("Toe") Blake	Montreal Canadiens
1946-47	Robert Bauer	Boston Bruins
1947-48	Herbert ("Buddy") O'Connor	New York Rangers
1948-49	Hubert ("Bill") Quackenbush	Detroit Red Wings
1949-50	Edgar Laprade	New York Rangers

Lady Byng died in June, 1949, and the NHL presented a new trophy named the Lady Byng Memorial Trophy.

Winners

1950-51	Leonard ("Red") Kelly	Detroit Red Wings
1951-52	Sidney Smith	Toronto Maple Leafs
1952-53	Leonard ("Red") Kelly	Detroit Red Wings
1953-54	Leonard ("Red") Kelly	Detroit Red Wings
1954-55	Sidney Smith	Toronto Maple Leafs
1955-56	Earl ("Dutch") Reibel	Detroit Red Wings
1956-57	Andrew Hebenton	New York Rangers
1957-58	Camille Henry	New York Rangers
1958-59	Alexander Delvecchio	Detroit Red Wings
1959-60	Donald McKenney	Boston Bruins
1960-61	Leonard ("Red")Kelly	Toronto Maple Leafs
1961-62	David Keon	Toronto Maple Leafs
1962-63	David Keon	Toronto Maple Leafs
1963-64	Kenneth Wharram	Chicago Black Hawks
1964-65	Robert Hull	Chicago Black Hawks
1965-66	Alexander Delvecchio	Detroit Red Wings
1966-67	Stanley Mikita	Chicago Black Hawks
1967-68	Stanley Mikita	Chicago Black Hawks
1968-69	Alexander Delvecchio	Detroit Red Wings
1969-70	J. G. Philippe Goyette	St. Louis Blues
1970-71	John Bucyk	Boston Bruins
1971-72	J. G. Y. Jean Ratelle	New York Rangers
1972-73	Gilbert Perreault	Buffalo Sabres
1973-74	John Bucyk	Boston Bruins
1974-75	Marcel Dionne	Detroit Red Wings
1975-76	J. G. Y. Jean Ratelle	N. Y. Rangers, Boston
1976-77	Marcel Dionne	Los Angeles Kings
1977-78	Robert ("Butch") Goring	Los Angeles Kings
1978-79	Robert MacMillan	Atlanta Flames
1979-80	Wayne Gretzky	Edmonton Oilers
1980-81	Rick Kehoe	Pittsburgh Penguins
1981-82	Richard Middleton	Boston Bruins
1982-83	Michael Bossy	New York Islanders

FRANK CALDER TROPHY

When the 1932-33 season ended, Carl Voss of the Detroit Red Wings (who had begun the season with the New York Rangers but had been sold to Detroit on December 12) was voted "rookie of the year" by hockey writers in a poll taken by the Canadian Press. The following year the writers chose Russell Blinco of the Montreal Maroons. In 1934-35, they chose David ("Sweeney") Schriner of the New York Americans, and in 1935-36 selected Michael Karakas of the Chicago Black Hawks. When the writers chose their "rookie of the year" for 1936-37, Frank Calder bought a trophy and presented it to the winner. Calder continued this tradition every year until his death.

1936-37	C. J. Sylvannus Apps	Toronto Maple Leafs
1937-38	Carl Dahlstrom	Chicago Black Hawks
1938-39	Francis Brimsek	Boston Bruins
1939-40	J. A. Kilby MacDonald	New York Rangers
1940-41	John Quilty	Montreal Canadiens
1941-42	Grant Warwick	New York Rangers
1942-43	J. Gaye Stewart	Toronto Maple Leafs

Calder died in 1943 and the NHL perpetuated his memory with the presentation of the Frank Calder Memorial Trophy.

FRANK CALDER MEMORIAL TROPHY

1943-44	August ("Gus") Bodnar	Toronto Maple Leafs
1944-45	Frank McCool	Toronto Maple Leafs
1945-46	Edgar Laprade	New York Rangers
1946-47	Howard Meeker	Toronto Maple Leafs
1947-48	James McFadden	Detroit Red Wings
1948-49	Pentti Lund	New York Rangers

1949-50	John ("Jack") Gelineau	Boston Bruins
1950-51	Terrance Sawchuk	Detroit Red Wings
1951-52	J. A. Bernard Geoffrion	Montreal Canadiens
1952-53	Lorne Worsley	New York Rangers
1953-54	Camille Henry	New York Rangers
1954-55	Edward Litzenberger	Montreal, Chicago
1955-56	Glenn Hall	Detroit Red Wings
1956-57	Lawrence Regan	Boston Bruins
1957-58	Francis Mahovlich	Toronto Maple Leafs
1958-59	Ralph Backstrom	Montreal Canadiens
1959-60	William Hay	Chicago Black Hawks
1960-61	David Keon	Toronto Maple Leafs
1961-62	J. J. Robert Rousseau	Montreal Canadiens
1962-63	Kent Douglas	Toronto Maple Leafs
1963-64	J. Jacques Laperriere	Montreal Canadiens
1964-65	Roger Crozier	Detroit Red Wings
1965-66	R. Briton ("Brit") Selby	Toronto Maple Leafs
1966-67	Robert Orr	Boston Bruins
1967-68	Derek Sanderson	Boston Bruins
1968-69	Daniel Grant	Minnesota North Stars
1969-70	Anthony ("Tony") Esposito	Chicago Black Hawks
1970-71	Gilbert Perreault	Buffalo Sabres
1971-72	Kenneth Dryden	Montreal Canadiens
1972-73	Stephen Vickers	New York Rangers
1973-74	Denis Potvin	New York Islanders
1974-75	Eric Vail	Altanta Flames
1975-76	Bryan Trottier	New York Islanders
1976-77	Willi Plett	Atlanta Flames
1977-78	Michael Bossy	New York Islanders
1978-79	Robert Smith	Minnesota North Stars
1979-80	Raymond Bourque	Boston Bruins
1980-81	Peter Stastny	Quebec Nordiques
1981-82	Dale Hawerchuk	Winnipeg Jets
1982-83	Steve Larmer	Chicago Black Hawks

DR. DAVID A. HART TROPHY

This trophy was presented to the NHL in 1923 by Dr. David A. Hart, father of Cecil M. Hart, former manager of the Montreal Canadiens. It is awarded to "the player adjudged to be the most valuable to his club."

1923-24	Frank Nighbor	Ottawa Senators
1924-25	H. William Burch	Hamilton Tigers
1925-26	Nelson Stewart	Montreal Maroons
1926-27	Herbert Gardiner	Montreal Canadiens
1927-28	Howarth Morenz	Montreal Canadiens
1928-29	Roy Worters	New York Americans
1929-30	Nelson Stewart	Montreal Maroons
1930-31	Howarth Morenz	Montreal Canadiens
1931-32	Howarth Morenz	Boston Bruins
1932-33	Edward Shore	Montreal Canadiens
1933-34	Aurele Joliat	Boston Bruins
1934-35	Edward Shore	Boston Bruins
1935-36	Edward Shore	Montreal Canadiens
1936-37	Albert ("Babe") Siebert	Boston Bruins
1937-38	Edward Shore	Montreal Canadiens
1938-39	Hector ("Toe") Blake	Detroit Red Wings
1939-40	Ebenezer Goodfellow	Boston Bruins
1940-41	William Cowley	Brooklyn Americans
1941-42	Thomas Anderson	Boston Bruins
1942-43	William Cowley	Toronto Maple Leafs

1943-44	Walter ("Babe") Pratt	Montreal Canadiens
1944-45	Elmer Lach	Chicago Black Hawks
1945-46	Maxwell Bentley	Montreal Canadiens
1946-47	J. H. Maurice Richard	New York Rangers
1947-48	Herbert ("Buddy") O'Connor	Detroit Red Wings
1948-49	Sidney Abel	New York Rangers
1949-50	Claude ("Chuck") Rayner	Boston Bruins
1950-51	Milton Schmidt	Detroit Red Wings
1951-52	Gordon Howe	Detroit Red Wings
1952-53	Gordon Howe	Chicago Black Hawks
1953-54	Elwin ("Al") Rollins	Toronto Maple Leafs
1954-55	Theodore Kennedy	Montreal Canadiens
1955-56	Jean Beliveau	Detroit Red Wings
1956-57	Gordon Howe	Detroit Red Wings
1957-58	Gordon Howe	New York Rangers
1958-59	Andrew Bathgate	

This trophy was given to Hockey's Hall of Fame, and in 1960 the NHL presented the Dr. David A. Hart Memorial Trophy.

DR. DAVID A. HART MEMORIAL TROPHY

1959-60	Gordon Howe	Detroit Red Wings
1960-61	J. A. Bernard Geoffrion	Montreal Canadiens
1961-62	J. Jacques Plante	Montreal Canadiens
1962-63	Gordon Howe	Detroit Red Wings
1963-64	Jean Beliveau	Montreal Canadiens
1964-65	Robert Hull	Chicago Black Hawks
1965-66	Robert Hull	Chicago Black Hawks
1966-67	Stanley Mikita	Chicago Black Hawks
1967-68	Stanley Mikita	Chicago Black Hawks
1968-69	Philip Esposito	Boston Bruins
1969-70	Robert Orr	Boston Bruins
1970-71	Robert Orr	Boston Bruins
1971-72	Robert Orr	Boston Bruins
1972-73	Robert Clarke	Philadelphia Flyers
1973-74	Philip Esposito	Boston Bruins
1974-75	Robert Clarke	Philadelphia Flyers
1975-76	Robert Clarke	Philadelphia Flyers
1976-77	Guy Lafleur	Montreal Canadiens
1977-78	Guy Lafleur	Montreal Canadiens
1978-79	Bryan Trottier	New York Islanders
1979-80	Wayne Gretzky	Edmonton Oilers
1980-81	Wayne Gretzky	Edmonton Oilers
1981-82	Wayne Gretzky	Edmonton Oilers
1982-83	Wayne Gretzky	Edmonton Oilers

WILLIAM M. JENNINGS TROPHY

This trophy was presented by the Board of Governors of the National Hockey League to honor William J. Jennings. Jennings was president of the New York Rangers from the 1962-63 season until his death on August 17, 1981. It is awarded to the goaltender(s) playing for the club with the fewest goals-against during the regular season.

1981-82	Denis Herron and Richard Wamsley	Montreal Canadiens
1982-83	Roland Melanson and William Smith	New York Islanders

BILL MASTERTON MEMORIAL TROPHY

This trophy was presented by the National Hockey League Writers' Association (later called the Professional Hockey Writers' Association) to honor the memory of William ("Bat") Masterton of the Minnesota North Stars. Masterton was fatally injured in a game with the Oakland Seals in Bloomington, Minnesota, on January 13, 1968, and died two days later. The trophy is awarded to "the National Hockey League player who best exemplifies the qualities of perseverance, sportsmanship, and dedication to hockey."

1967-68	J. A. Claude Provost	Montreal Canadiens
1968-69	Edward ("Ted") Hampson	Oakland Seals
1969-70	Hubert ("Pit") Martin	Chicago Black Hawks
1970-71	J. G. Y. Jean Ratelle	New York Rangers
1971-72	Robert Clarke	Philadelphia Flyers
1972-73	Lowell MacDonald	Pittsburgh Penguins
1973-74	J. Henri Richard	Montreal Canadiens
1974-75	Donald Luce	Buffalo Sabres
1975-76	Rodrigue Gilbert	New York Rangers
1976-77	V. Edwin Westfall	New York Islanders
1977-78	Robert ("Butch") Goring	Los Angeles Kings
1978-79	Serge Savard	Montreal Canadiens
1979-80	R. Alan ("Al") MacAdam	Minnesota North Stars
1980-81	Blake Dunlop	St. Louis Blues
1981-82	Glenn ("Chico") Resch	Colorado Rockies
1982-83	Lanny McDonald	Calgary Flames

JAMES NORRIS MEMORIAL TROPHY

James Norris, former owner of the Detroit Red Wings, died on December 4, 1952. His four children, Bruce, James, Eleanore, and Marguerite Ann, presented this trophy to the NHL in memory of their father. It is awarded to "the defense player who demonstrates throughout the season the greatest all-around ability in the position."

1953-54	Leonard (Red") Kelly	Detroit Red Wings
1954-55	Douglas Harvey	Montreal Canadiens
1955-56	Douglas Harvey	Montreal Canadiens
1956-57	Douglas Harvey	Montreal Canadiens
1957-58	Douglas Harvey	Montreal Canadiens
1958-59	Thomas Johnson	Montreal Canadiens
1959-60	Douglas Harvey	Montreal Canadiens
1960-61	Douglas Harvey	Montreal Canadiens
1961-62	Douglas Harvey	Montreal Canadiens
1962-63	J. A. Pierre Pilote	Chicago Black Hawks
1963-64	J. A. Pierre Pilote	Chicago Black Hawks
1964-65	J. A. Pierre Pilote	Chicago Black Hawks
1965-66	J. Jacques Laperriere	Montreal Canadiens
1966-67	Henry ("Harry") Howell	New York Rangers
1967-68	Robert Orr	Boston Bruins
1968-69	Robert Orr	Boston Bruins
1969-70	Robert Orr	Boston Bruins
1970-71	Robert Orr	Boston Bruins
1971-72	Robert Orr	Boston Bruins
1972-73	Robert Orr	Boston Bruins
1973-74	Robert Orr	Boston Bruins
1974-75	Robert Orr	Boston Bruins
1975-76	Denis Potvin	New York Islanders
1976-77	Larry Robinson	Montreal Canadiens
1977-78	Denis Potvin	New York Islanders
1978-79	Denis Potvin	New York Islanders

1979-80	Larry Robinson	Montreal Canadiens
1980-81	Randy Carlyle	Pittsburgh Penguins
1981-82	Douglas Wilson	Chicago Black Hawks
1982-83	Rod Langway	Washington Capitals

LESTER PATRICK MEMORIAL TROPHY

This trophy was presented by the New York Rangers in 1966 to honor Lester Patrick, their first manager. It is awarded for "outstanding service to hockey in the United States."

1966
    John J. ("Jack") Adams
1967
    Charles F. Adams
    Gordon Howe
    James Norris, Sr.
1968
    Walter A. Brown
    Gen. John Reed Kilpatrick
    Thomas F. Lockhart
1969
    Robert M. Hull
    Edward J. Jeremiah
1970
    James C. V. (Jim") Hendy
    Edward W. Shore
1971
    William M. Jennings
    Terrence G. Sawchuk
    John B. Sollenberger
1972
    Clarence S. Campbell
    John H. ("Jack") Kelly
    James Duggan Norris
    Ralph ("Cooney") Weiland
1973
    Walter L. Bush, Jr.
1974
    Weston W. Adams, Sr.
    Charles L. Crovat
    Alexander Delvecchio
    J. Murray Murdoch
1975
    William L. Chadwick
    Donald M. Clark
    Thomas Ivan
1976
    George A. Leader
    Stanley Mikita
    Bruce A. Norris
1977
    Murray A. Armstrong
    John Paul Bucyk
    John P. Mariucci
1978
    Philip A. Esposito
    Tom Fitzgerald
    William Thayer Tutt
    William W. ("Bill") Wirtz
1979
    Robert Gordon Orr

1980
  Robert E. Clarke
  Frederick A. Shero
  Edward M. Snyder
  1980 U.S. Olympic Hockey Club
1981
  Charles M. Schulz
1982
  Emile Percy Francis
1983
  William Arthur Torrey

ARTHUR H. ROSS TROPHY

In 1947 Arthur Ross, former manager of the Boston Bruin, presented this trophy to the NHL. It is awarded to "the player who leads the league in scoring (points) at the end of the regular season." If a tie results, the trophy is given to the player with the most goals. (Twice this has occurred. In 1961-62, Robert Hull tied with Andrew Bathgate of the New York Rangers—Hull had the most goals. In 1979-80, Dionne tied with Wayne Gretzky of the Edmonton Oilers—Dionne had the most goals.)

1947-48	Elmer Lach	Montreal Canadiens
1948-49	Roy Conacher	Chicago Black Hawks
1949-50	R. B. Theodore Lindsay	Detroit Red Wings
1950-51	Gordon Howe	Detroit Red Wings
1951-52	Gordon Howe	Detroit Red Wings
1952-53	Gordon Howe	Detroit Red Wings
1953-54	Gordon Howe	Detroit Red Wings
1954-55	J. A. Bernard Geoffrion	Montreal Canadiens
1955-56	Jean Beliveau	Montreal Canadiens
1956-57	Gordon Howe	Detroit Red Wings
1957-58	Richard ("Dickie") Moore	Montreal Canadiens
1958-59	Richard ("Dickie") Moore	Montreal Canadiens
1959-60	Robert Hull	Chicago Black Hawks
1960-61	J. A. Bernard Geoffrion	Montreal Canadiens
1961-62	Robert Hull	Chicago Black Hawks
1962-63	Gordon Howe	Detroit Red Wings
1963-64	Stanley Mikita	Chicago Black Hawks
1964-65	Stanley Mikita	Chicago Black Hawks
1965-66	Robert Hull	Chicago Black Hawks
1966-67	Stanley Mikita	Chicago Black Hawks
1967-68	Stanley Mikita	Chicago Black Hawks
1968-69	Philip Esposito	Boston Bruins
1969-70	Robert Orr	Boston Bruins
1970-71	Philip Esposito	Boston Bruins
1971-72	Philip Esposito	Boston Bruins
1972-73	Philip Esposito	Boston Bruins
1973-74	Philip Esposito	Boston Bruins
1974-75	Robert Orr	Boston Bruins
1975-76	Guy Lafleur	Montreal Canadiens
1976-77	Guy Lafleur	Montreal Canadiens
1977-78	Guy Lafleur	Montreal Canadiens
1978-79	Bryan Trottier	New York Islanders
1979-80	Marcel Dionne	Los Angeles Kings
1980-81	Wayne Gretzky	Edmonton Oilers
1981-82	Wayne Gretzky	Edmonton Oilers
1982-83	Wayne Gretzky	Edmonton Oilers

FRANK J. SELKE TROPHY

This trophy was presented to the NHL by the Board of Governors of the National Hockey League in 1977, in honor of Frank Selke. It is awarded to "the forward who best excels in the defensive aspects of the game."

1977-78	Robert Gainey	Montreal Canadiens
1978-79	Robert Gainey	Montreal Canadiens
1979-80	Robert Gainey	Montreal Canadiens
1980-81	Robert Gainey	Montreal Canadiens
1981-82	Stephen Kasper	Boston Bruins
1982-83	Robert Clarke	Philadelphia Flyers

CONN SMYTHE TROPHY

In 1964, Maple Leaf Gardens Limited presented this trophy to honor Conn Smythe. It is awarded to "the most valuable player for his club in the Stanley Cup play-offs."

1965	Jean Beliveau	Montreal Canadiens
1966	Roger Crozier	Detroit Red Wings
1967	David Keon	Toronto Maple Leafs
1968	Glenn Hall	St. Louis Blues
1969	Serge Savard	Montreal Canadiens
1970	Robert Orr	Boston Bruins
1971	Keneth Dryden	Montreal Canadiens
1972	Robert Orr	Boston Bruins
1973	Yvan Cournoyer	Montreal Canadiens
1974	Bernard Parent	Philadelphia Flyers
1975	Bernard Parent	Philadelphia Flyers
1976	Reginald Leach	Philadelphia Flyers
1977	Guy Lafleur	Montreal Canadiens
1978	Larry Robinson	Montreal Canadiens
1979	Robert Gainey	Montreal Canadiens
1980	Bryan Trottier	New York Islanders
1981	Robert ("Butch") Goring	New York Islanders
1982	Michael Bossy	New York Islanders
1983	William Smith	New York Islanders

GEORGES VEZINA MEMORIAL TROPHY

This trophy was presented to the NHL in memory of Georges Vezina by Joseph M. ("Joe") Cattarinich, Joseph Viateur ("Leo") Dandurand, and Louis Letourneau, former owners of the Montreal Canadiens. Vezina was the Montreal Canadiens' goaltender from the 1910-11 season until he collapsed on November 28, 1925, during the Canadiens' first game of that season. He died of tuberculosis four months later, on March 27, 1926, in Chicoutimi, Quebec. This trophy was originally awarded to the goaltender(s) playing for the club with the fewest goals-against during the regular season.

1926-27	George Hainsworth	Montreal Canadiens
1927-28	George Hainsworth	Montreal Canadiens
1928-29	George Hainsworth	Montreal Canadiens
1929-30	Cecil ("Tiny") Thompson	Boston Bruins
1930-31	Roy Worters	New York Americans
1931-32	Charles Gardiner	Chicago Black Hawks
1932-33	Cecil ("Tiny") Thompson	Boston Bruins
1933-34	Charles Gardiner	Chicago Black Hawks
1934-35	Lorne Chabot	Chicago Black Hawks
1935-36	Cecil ("Tiny") Thompson	

1936-37	Norman Smith	Boston Bruins
1937-38	Cecil ("Tiny") Thompson	Detroit Red Wings
1938-39	Francis Brimsek	Boston Bruins
1939-40	David Kerr	Boston Bruins
1940-41	Walter ("Turk") Broda	New York Rangers
1941-42	Francis Brimsek	Toronto Maple Leafs
1942-43	John Mowers	Boston Bruins
1943-44	William Durnan	Detroit Red Wings
1944-45	William Durnan	Montreal Canadiens
1945-46	William Durnan	Montreal Canadiens
1946-47	William Durnan	Montreal Canadiens
1947-48	Walter ("Turk") Broda	Montreal Canadiens
1948-49	William Durnan	Toronto Maple Leafs
1949-50	William Durnan	Montreal Canadiens
1950-51	Elwin ("Al") Rollins	Montreal Canadiens
1951-52	Terrance Sawchuk	Toronto Maple Leafs
1952-53	Terrance Sawchuk	Detroit Red Wings
1953-54	Harry Lumley	Detroit Red Wings
1954-55	Terrance Sawchuk	Toronto Maple Leafs
1955-56	J. Jacques Plante	Detroit Red Wings
1956-57	J. Jacques Plante	Montreal Canadiens
1957-58	J. Jacques Plante	Montreal Canadiens
1958-59	J. Jacques Plante	Montreal Canadiens
1959-60	J. Jacques Plante	Montreal Canadiens
1960-61	John Bower	Montreal Canadiens
1961-62	J. Jacques Plante	Toronto Maple Leafs
1962-63	Glenn Hall	Montreal Canadiens
1963-64	Charles Hodge	Chicago Black Hawks
1964-65	John Bower and Terrance Sawchuk	Montreal Canadiens
1965-66	Charles Hodge and Lorne Worsley	Toronto Maple Leafs
1966-67	Denis DeJordy and Glenn Hall	Montreal Canadiens
1967-68	Rogatien Vachon and Lorne Worsley	Chicago Black Hawks
1968-69	Glenn Hall and J. Jacques Plante	Montreal Canadiens
1969-70	Anthony (Tony") Esposito	St. Louis Blues
1970-71	Edward Giacomin and Gilles Villemure	Chicago Black Hawks
1971-72	Anthony ("Tony") Esposito and Gary Smith	New York Rangers
1972-73	Kenneth Dryden	Chicago Black Hawks
1973-74	Anthony ("Tony") Esposito	Montreal Canadiens
1974-75	Bernard Parent	Chicago Black Hawks
1975-76	Kenneth Dryden	Philadelphia Flyers
1976-77	Kenneth Dryden and Michel Larocque	Philadelphia Flyers
1977-78	Kenneth Dryden and Michel Larocque	Montreal Canadiens
1978-79	Kenneth Dryden and Michel Larocque	Montreal Canadiens
1979-80	Donald Edwards and Robert Sauve	Buffalo Sabres
1980-81	Denis Herron, Michel Larocque and Richard Sevigny	Montreal Canadiens

Since 1981-82, this trophy has been awarded to "the goaltender adjudged to be the best at his position" by the NHL general managers. Note: see William M. Jennings Trophy

William Smith	New York Islanders
Peter Peeters	Boston Bruins

NHL TEAM RECORDS

CLUB RECORDS
Most Wins

1976-77	Montreal Canadiens	60
1977-78	Montreal Canadiens	59
1975-76	Montreal Canadiens	58
1970-71	Boston Bruins	57
1971-72	Boston Bruins	54
1981-82	New York Islanders	54
1972-73	Montreal Canadiens	52
1973-74	Boston Bruins	52
1978-79	Montreal Canadiens	52
1972-73	Boston Bruins	51
1974-75	Philadelphia Flyers	51
1975-76	Philadelphia Flyers	51
1977-78	Boston Bruins	51
1978-79	New York Islanders	51
1973-74	Philadelphia Flyers	50
1982-83	Boston Bruins	50
1970-71	Chicago Black Hawks	49
1970-71	New York Rangers	49
1974-75	Buffalo Sabres	49
1976-77	Boston Bruins	49
1982-83	Philadelphia Flyers	49

Most Losses

1974-75	Washington Capitals	67
1972-73	New York Islanders	60
1975-76	Washington Capitals	59
1980-81	Winnipeg Jets	57
1975-76	Kansas City Scouts	56
1973-74	California Golden Seals	55
1976-77	Detroit Red Wings	55
1974-75	Kansas City Scouts	54
1982-83	Hartford Whalers	54
1970-71	California Golden Seals	53
1975-76	Minnesota North Stars	53
1977-78	Minnesota North Stars	53
1978-79	Colorado Rockies	53
1982-83	Pittsburgh Penguins	53
1969-70	Los Angeles Kings	52
1953-54	Chicago Black Hawks	51
1971-72	Vancouver Canucks	50
1974-75	Minnesota North Stars	50
1978-79	St. Louis Blues	50
1971-72	Los Angeles Kings	49
1977-78	Washington Capitals	49
1979-80	Winnipeg Jets	49
1981-82	Colorado Rockies	49
1982-83	New Jersey Devils	49

Most Ties

1969-70	Philadelphia Flyers	24
1962-63	Montreal Canadiens	23
1973-74	Chicago Black Hawks	23
1954-55	Toronto Maple Leafs	22
1969-70	Minnesota North Stars	22
1974-75	New York Islanders	22
1950-51	New York Rangers	21
1954-55	Boston Bruins	21
1968-69	Philadelphia Flyers	21
1974-75	Los Angeles Kings	21
1977-78	Colorado Rockies	21
1980-81	Buffalo Sabres	21
1970-71	Pittsburgh Penguins	20
1979-80	Philadelphia Flyers	20
1980-81	Vancouver Canucks	20
1981-82	Minnesota North Stars	20
1949-50	Montreal Canadiens	19
1952-53	Montreal Canadiens	19
1969-70	Boston Bruins	19
1970-71	St. Louis Blues	19
1971-72	Buffalo Sabres	19
1974-75	Montreal Canadiens	19
1977-78	Atlanta Flames	19
1977-78	Chicago Black Hawks	19
1979-80	Chicago Black Hawks	19
1979-80	Hartford Whalers	19

Most Points

1976-77	Montreal Canadiens	(won 60, lost 8, tied 12)	132
1977-78	Montreal Canadiens	(won 59, lost 10, tied 11)	129
1975-76	Montreal Canadiens	(won 58, lost 11, tied 11)	127
1970-71	Boston Bruins	(won 57, lost 14, tied 7)	121
1972-73	Montreal Canadiens	(won 52, lost 10, tied 16)	120
1971-72	Boston Bruins	(won 54, lost 13, tied 11)	119
1975-76	Philadelphia Flyers	(won 51, lost 13, tied 16)	118
1981-82	New York Islanders	(won 54, lost 16, tied 10)	118
1978-79	New York Islanders	(won 51, lost 15, tied 14)	116
1979-80	Philadelphia Flyers	(won 48, lost 12, tied 20)	116
1978-79	Montreal Canadiens	(won 52, lost 17, lost 11)	115
1973-74	Boston Bruins	(won 52, lost 17, tied 9)	113
1974-75	Philadelphia Flyers	(won 51, lost 18, tied 11)	113
1974-75	Buffalo Sabres	(won 49, lost 16, tied 15)	113
1974-75	Montreal Canadiens	(won 47, lost 14, tied 19)	113
1975-76	Boston Bruins	(won 48, lost 15, tied 17)	113
1977-78	Boston Bruins	(won 51, lost 18, tied 11)	113
1973-74	Philadelphia Flyers	(won 50, lost 16, tied 12)	112
1976-77	Philadelphia Flyers	(won 48, lost 16, tied 16)	112
1977-78	New York Islanders	(won 48, lost 17, tied 15)	111
1981-82	Edmonton Oilers	(won 48, lost 17, tied 15)	111
1979-80	Buffalo Sabres	(won 47, lost 17, tied 16)	110
1980-81	New York Islanders	(won 48, lost 18, tied 14)	110
1982-83	Boston Bruins	(won 50, lost 20, tied 10)	110

Most Goals

1982-83	Edmonton Oilers	424
1981-82	Edmonton Oilers	417
1970-71	Boston Bruins	399
1976-77	Montreal Canadiens	387
1981-82	New York Islanders	385
1974-75	Montreal Canadiens	374
1981-82	Montreal Canadiens	360
1977-78	Montreal Canadiens	359
1978-79	New York Islanders	358
1981-82	Quebec Nordiques	356
1980-81	New York Islanders	355
1974-75	Buffalo Sabres	354
1980-81	St. Louis Blues	352
1982-83	Montreal Canadiens	350
1973-74	Boston Bruins	349
1975-76	Philadelphia Flyers	348
1981-82	Minnesota North Stars	346
1974-75	Boston Bruins	345
1982-83	Quebec Nordiques	343
1975-76	Buffalo Sabres	339
1975-76	Pittsburgh Penguins	339
1982-83	Chicago Black Hawks	338
1975-76	Montreal Canadiens	337
1978-79	Montreal Canadiens	337
1980-81	Los Angeles Kings	337

Most Assists (one club)

1981-82	Edmonton Oilers	697
1970-71	Boston Bruins	678
1982-83	Edmonton Oilers	652
1981-82	New York Islanders	621
1976-77	Montreal Canadiens	616
1978 79	New York Islanders	608
1981-82	Quebec Nordiques	605
1974-75	Montreal Canadiens	594
1981-82	Montreal Canadiens	581
1981-82	Minnesota North Stars	577
1980-81	St. Louis Blues	572
1980-81	New York Islanders	570
1973-74	Boston Bruins	569
1974-75	Buffalo Sabres	569
1977-78	New York Islanders	569
1981-82	Calgary Flames	569
1982-83	Quebec Nordiques	567
1975-76	Pittsburgh Penquins	563
1977-78	Montreal Canadiens	563
1982-83	Philadelphia Flyers	560
1971-72	Boston Bruins	560
1972-73	Boston Bruins	558
1977-78	Boston Bruins	556
1975-76	Montreal Canadiens	

Most wins, one season, Montreal Canadiens

Most goals, one season, Edmonton Oilers

357

Most points, one season, Edmonton Oilers

Most Points (Scoring)

1981-82	Edmonton Oilers	(417 goals, 706 assists)	1123
1982-83	Edmonton Oilers	(424 goals, 678 assists)	1102
1970-71	Boston Bruins	(399 goals, 697 assists)	1096
1981-82	New York Islanders	(385 goals, 652 assists)	1037
1976-77	Montreal Canadiens	(387 goals, 621 assists)	1008
1974-75	Montreal Canadiens	(374 goals, 605 assists)	979
1978-79	New York Islanders	(358 goals, 616 assists)	974
1981-82	Quebec Nordiques	(356 goals, 608 assists)	964
1981-82	Montreal Canadiens	(360 goals, 594 assists)	954
1980-81	St. Louis Blues	(352 goals, 577 assists)	929
1980-81	New York Islanders	(355 goals, 572 assists)	927
1981-82	Minnesota North Stars	(346 goals, 581 assists)	927
1974-75	Buffalo Sabres	(354 goals, 569 assists)	923
1977-78	Montreal Canadiens	(359 goals, 563 assists)	922
1973-74	Boston Bruins	(349 goals, 570 assists)	919
1982-83	Quebec Nordiques	(343 goals, 569 assists)	912
1975-76	Pittsburgh Penguins	(339 goals, 567 assists)	906
1975-76	Philadelphia Flyers	(348 goals, 555 assists)	903
1977-78	New York Islanders	(334 goals, 569 assists)	903
1981-82	Calgary Flames	(334 goals, 569 assists)	903
1982-83	Montreal Canadiens	(350 goals, 552 assists)	902
1974-75	Boston Bruins	(345 goals, 550 assists)	895
1975-76	'Montreal Canadiens	(337 goals, 556 assists)	893
1982-83	Chicago Black Hawks	(338 goals, 555 assists)	893
1977-78	Boston Bruins	(333 goals, 558 assists)	891

Most Goals-Against

1974-75	Washington Capitals	446
1982-83	Hartford Whalers	403
1980-81	Winnipeg Jets	400
1975-76	Washington Capitals	394
1982-83	Pittsburgh Penguins	394
1981-82	Toronto Maple Leafs	380
1980-81	Hartford Whalers	372
1981-82	Los Angeles Kings	369
1980-81	Toronto Maple Leafs	367
1982-83	Los Angeles Kings	365
1981-82	Chicago Black Hawks	363
1981-82	Colorado Rockies	362
1975-76	Kansas City Scouts	351
1981-82	Detroit Red Wings	351
1981-82	Hartford Whalers	351
1981-82	St. Louis Blues	349
1978-79	St. Louis Blues	348
1972-73	New York Islanders	347
1980-81	Pittsburgh Penguins	345
1981-82	Calgary Flames	345
1981-82	Quebec Nordiques	341
1980-81	Colorado Rockies	344
1982-83	Detroit Red Wings	344
1973-74	California Golden Seals	342
1974-75	Minnesota North Stars	341

Most Penalties in Minutes

1980-81	Philadelphia Flyers	2621
1981-82	Philadelphia Flyers	2493
1981-82	Pittsburgh Penguins	2212
1980-81	New York Rangers	1981
1975-76	Philadelphia Flyers	1980
1974-75	Philadelphia Flyers	1969
1981-82	Washington Capitals	1932
1975-76	Detroit Red Wings	1922
1980-81	Vancouver Canucks	1892
1981-82	Toronto Maple Leafs	1888
1980-81	Washington Capitals	1872
1982-83	Pittsburgh Penguins	1859
1979-80	Philadelphia Flyers	1844
1981-82	Vancouver Canucks	1840
1980-81	Boston Bruins	1836
1980-81	Toronto Maple Leafs	1830
1979-80	Vancouver Canucks	1808
1980-81	Pittsburgh Penguins	1808
1981-82	Chicago Black Hawks	1775
1982-83	Edmonton Oilers	1771
1981-82	Quebec Nordiques	1757
1972-73	Philadelphia Flyers	1756
1973-74	Philadelphia Flyers	1750
1981-82	Los Angeles Kings	1730
1980-81	Detroit Red Wings	1687

Most Shutouts

1928-29	Montreal Canadiens	22
1928-29	New York Americans	16
1925-26	Ottawa Senators	15
1927-28	Boston Bruins	15
1927-28	Ottawa Senators	15
1969-70	Chicago Black Hawks	15
1926-27	Montreal Canadiens	14
1971-72	Chicago Black Hawks	14
1976-77	Montreal Canadiens	14
1926-27	Montreal Maroons	13
1926-27	Ottawa Senators	13
1927-28	Montreal Canadiens	13
1928-29	New York Rangers	13
1953-54	Detroit Red Wings	13
1953-54	Toronto Maple Leafs	13
1968-69	St. Louis Blues	13

GAME
Most Goals (both clubs)

January 10, 1920	Montreal Canadiens (14)	and Toronto St. Patricks (7)	21
January 4, 1984	Edmonton Oilers (12)	and Minnesota North Stars (8)	20
December 19, 1917	Montreal Wanderers (10)	and Toronto Arenas (9)	19
March 3, 1920	Montreal Canadiens (16)	and Quebec Bulldogs (3)	19
February 26, 1921	Hamilton Tigers (6)	and Montreal Canadiens (13)	19
March 4, 1944	Boston Bruins (10)	and New York Rangers (9)	19
March 16, 1944	Boston Bruins (9)	and Detroit Red Wings (10)	19
October 7, 1983	Minnesota North Stars (9)	and Vancouver Canucks (10)	19
January 11, 1938	Montreal Canadiens (7)	and Montreal Maroons (11)	18
March 17, 1946	Detroit Red Wings (7)	and Toronto Maple Leafs (11)	18
February 20, 1977	Chicago Black Hawks (8)	and Toronto Maple Leafs (10)	18
February 22, 1981	Quebec Nordiques (11)	and Washington Capitals (7)	18
March 19, 1981	Buffalo Sabres (14)	and Toronto Maple Leafs (4)	18
October 15, 1983	Chicago Black Hawks (8)	and Toronto Maple Leafs (10)	18

Most Assists (both clubs)

February 18, 1936	Montreal Maroons (16) and	New York Americans (20)	36
February 22, 1981	Quebec Nordiques (22) and	Washington Capitals (13)	35
October 7, 1983	Minnesota North Stars (17) and	Vancouver Canucks (16)	33
January 4, 1984	Edmonton Oilers (20) and	Minnesota North Stars (13)	33
October 14, 1978	New York Islanders (14) and	Toronto Maple Leafs (18)	32
February 25, 1978	Buffalo Sabres (24) and	Cleveland Browns (6)	30
October 29, 1981	Calgary Flames (8) and	Detroit Red Wings (22)	30
October 15, 1983	Chicago Black Hawks (15) and	Toronto Maple Leafs (15)	30
March 19, 1981	Buffalo Sabres (22) and	Toronto Maple Leafs (7)	29
October 10, 1981	Chicago Black Hawks (12) and	Toronto Maple Leafs (17)	29
December 15, 1981	New York Islanders (16) and	Quebec Nordiques (13)	29
October 19, 1983	Edmonton Oilers (16) and	Vancouver Canucks (13)	29
November 5, 1942	Detroit Red Wings (21) and	New York Rangers (7)	28
November 21, 1943	Boston Bruins (6) and	Montreal Canadiens (22	28
March 8, 1971	California Golden Seals (8) and	Vancouver Canucks (20)	28
December 21, 1975	Buffalo Sabres (26) and	Washington Capitals (2)	28
November 11, 1981	Minnesota North Stars (24) and	Winnipeg Jets (4)	28
January 11, 1938	Montreal Canadiens (10) and	Montreal Maroons (17)	27
March 4, 1944	Boston Bruins (15) and	New York Rangers (12)	27
October 16, 1968	Chicago Black Hawks (20) and	Minnesota North Stars (7)	27
January 18, 1973	Boston Bruins (13) and	New York Islanders (14)	27
February 20, 1977	Chicago Black Hawks (12) and	Toronto Maple Leafs (15)	27
February 19, 1980	Colorado Rockies (15) and	Philadelphia Flyers (12)	27

Most Goals (one club)

March 3, 1920 at Quebec City	Montreal Canadiens	16
January 23, 1944 at Detroit	Detroit Red Wings	15
November, 11, 1981 at Bloomington, Minnesota	Minnesota North Stars	15
January 10, 1920 at Montreal	Montreal Canadiens	14
January 21, 1945 at Boston	Boston Bruins	14
March 16, 1957 at Toronto	Toronto Maple Leafs	14
December 21, 1975 at Buffalo	Buffalo Sabres	14
March 19, 1981 at Buffalo	Buffalo Sabres	14
January 11, 1919 at Montreal	Montreal Canadiens	13
February 26, 1921 at Montreal	Montreal Canadiens	13
November 21, 1943 at Montreal	Montreal Canadiens	13
January 2, 1944 at New York	Boston Bruins	13
January 2, 1971 at Toronto	Toronto Maple Leafs	13
February 25, 1978 at Richfield, Ohio	Buffalo Sabres	13
November 19, 1983 at Edmonton	Edmonton Oilers	13

Most Assists (one club)

December 21, 1975 at Buffalo	Buffalo Sabres	26
February 25, 1978 at Richfield, Ohio	Buffalo Sabres	24
November 11, 1981 at Bloomington, Minnesota	Minnesota North Stars	24
March 16, 1957 at Toronto	Toronto Maple Leafs	23
November 21, 1971 at New York	New York Rangers	23
November 21, 1943 at Montreal	Montreal Canadiens	22
January 23, 1944 at Detroit	Detroit Red Wings	22
January 2, 1971 at Toronto	Toronto Maple Leafs	22
February 2, 1974 at Philadelphia	Philadelphia Flyers	22
February 22, 1981 at Landover, Maryland	Quebec Nordiques	22
March 10, 1981 at Calgary	Calgary Flames	22
March 19, 1981 at Buffalo	Buffalo Sabres	22
October 29, 1981 at Detroit	Detroit Red Wings	22
November 5, 1942 at Detroit	Detroit Red Wings	21
March 18, 1944 at Montreal	Montreal Canadiens	21
March 15, 1967 at Montreal	Montreal Canadiens	21
December 14, 1974 at Boston	Boston Bruins	21
February 18, 1976 at New York	New York Rangers	21
February 22, 1979 at Montreal	Montreal Canadiens	21

Most Points (both clubs)

February 22, 1981	Quebec Nordiques (33) and	Washington Capitals (20)	53
January 4, 1984	Edmonton Oilers (32) and	Minnesota North Stars (21)	53
February 18, 1936	Montreal Maroons (24) and	New York Americans (28)	52
October , 1983	Minnesota North Stars (26) and	Vancouver Canucks (26)	52
October 14, 1978	New York Islanders (21) and	Toronto Maple Leafs (28)	49
October, 15, 1983	Chicago Black Hawks (23) and	Toronto Maple Leafs (25)	48
March 19, 1981	Buffalo Sabres (36) and	Toronto Maple Leafs (11)	47
March 4, 1944	Boston Bruins (25) and	New York Rangers (21)	46
February 25, 1978	Buffalo Sabres (37) and	Cleveland Barons (9)	46
October 10, 1981	Chicago Black Hawks (20) and	Toronto Maple Leafs (26)	46
October 29, 1981	Calgary Flames (12) and	Detroit Red Wings (34)	46
December 15, 1981	New York Islanders (26) and	Quebec Nordiques (20)	46
October 19, 1983	Edmonton Oilers (26) and	Vancouver Canucks (20)	46
January 11, 1938	Montreal Canadiens (17) and	Montreal Maroons (28)	45
November 5, 1942	Detroit Red Wings (33) and	New York Rangers (12)	45
November 21, 1943	Boston Bruins (10) and	Montreal Canadiens (35)	45
February 20, 1977	Chicago Black Hawks (20) and	Toronto Maple Leafs (25)	45
November 11, 1981	Minnesota North Stars (39) and	Winnipeg Jets (6)	45
March 28, 1971	California Golden Seals (13) and	Vancouver Canucks (31)	44
December 21, 1975	Buffalo Sabres (40) and	Washington Capitals (4)	44
January 18, 1973	Boston Bruins (20) and	New York Islanders (23)	43
November 19, 1983	Edmonton Oilers (33) and	New Jersey Devils (10)	43
March 17, 1946	Detroit Red Wings (16) and	Toronto Maple Leafs (26)	42
March 16, 1947	Chicago Black Hawks (17) and	Detroit Red Wings (25)	42

Most Points (one club)

December 21, 1975	Buffalo Sabres	(14 goals, 26 assists)	40
November 11, 1981	Minnesota North Stars	(15 goals, 24 assists)	39
January 23, 1944	Detroit Red Wings	(15 goals, 22 assists)	37
March 16, 1957	Toronto Maple Leafs	(14 goals, 23 assists)	37
February 25, 1958	Buffalo Sabres	(13 goals, 24 assists)	37
March 19, 1981	Buffalo Sabres	(14 goals, 22 assists)	36
November 21, 1943	Montreal Canadiens	(13 goals, 22 assists)	35
January 2, 1971	Toronto Maple Leafs	(13 goals, 22 assists)	35
November 21, 1971	New York Rangers	(12 goals, 23 assists)	35
February 2, 1974	Philadelphia Flyers	(12 goals, 22 assists)	34
October 29, 1981	Detroit Red Wings	(12 goals, 22 assists)	34
November 5, 1942	Detroit Red Wings	(12 goals, 21 assists)	33
December 14, 1974	Boston Bruins	(12 goals, 21 assists)	33
February 22, 1979	Montreal Canadiens	(12 goals, 21 assists)	33
February 22, 1981	Quebec Nordiques	(11 goals, 22 assists)	33
March 10, 1981	Calgary Flames	(11 goals, 22 assists)	33
November 19, 1983	Edmonton Oilers	(13 goals, 20 assists)	33
March 18, 1944	Montreal Canadiens	(11 goals, 21 assists)	32
January 9, 1954	Montreal Canadiens	(12 goals, 20 assists)	32
March 15, 1967	Montreal Canadiens	(11 goals, 21 assists)	32
February 18, 1976	New York Rangers	(11 goals, 21 assists)	32
January 4, 1984	Edmonton Oilers	(12 goals, 20 assists)	32

Most Penalties (one club)

February 26, 1981	at Boston	Boston Bruins	42
February 26, 1981	at Boston	Minnesota North Stars	42
February 22, 1980	at Vancouver	Philadelphia Flyers	38
January 3, 1981	at Denver, Colorado	Boston Bruins	33
October 25, 1974	at Oakland, California	Philadelphia Flyers	30
March 11, 1979	at Philadelphia	Philadelphia Flyers	29
October 14, 1982	at Uniondale, New York	Pittsburgh Penguins	29
January 19, 1980	at Pittsburgh	Pittsburgh Penguins	27
January 3, 1981	at Denver, Colorado	Colorado Rockies	27
December 5, 1981	at Toronto	Toronto Maple Leafs	27
December 14, 1974	at St. Louis	St. Louis Blues	25
October 25, 1975	at Montreal	Boston Bruins	25
March 31, 1976	at Detroit	Detroit Red Wings	25
November 2, 1977	at Detroit	Detroit Red Wings	25
March 11, 1979	at Philadelphia	Los Angeles Kings	25
February 22, 1980	at Vancouver	Vancouver Canucks	25
March 21, 1983	at Bloomington, Minnesota	Minnesota North Stars	25
October 10, 1976	at Philadelphia	Philadelphia Flyers	24
December 5, 1981	at Toronto	Washington Capitals	24

Most Penalties (both clubs)

February 26, 1981	Boston Bruins (42) and	Minnesota North Stars(42)	84
February 22, 1980	Philadelphia Flyers (38) and	Vancouver Canucks (25)	63
January 3, 1981	Boston Bruins (33) and	Colorado Rockies (27)	60
March 11, 1979	Los Angeles Kings (25) and	Philadelphia Flyers (29)	54
December 5, 1981	Toronto Maple Leafs (27) and	Washington Capitals (24)	51
October 14, 1982	New York Rangers (22) and	Pittsburgh Penguins (29)	51
January 19, 1980	Edmonton Oilers (23) and	Pittsburgh Penguins (27)	50
March 31, 1976	Detroit Red Wings (25) and	Toronto Maple Leafs (23)	48
March 21, 1983	Chicago Black Hawks (23) and	Minnesota North Stars (25)	48
December 14, 1974	New York Rangers (22) and	St. Louis Blues (25)	47
November 2, 1977	Detroit Red Wings (25) and	Pittsburgh Penguins (22)	47
October 25, 1974	California Golden Seals (14) and	Philadelphia Flyers (30)	44
October 10, 1976	Los Angeles Kings (19) and	Philadelphia Flyers (24)	43
October 29, 1981	Philadelphia Flyers (22) and	Pittsburgh Penguins (21)	43

Most Penalties in Minutes (both clubs)

February 26, 1981	Boston Bruins (195)'	and	Minnesota North Stars (211)	406
March 11, 1979	Los Angeles Kings (186)	and	Philadelphia Flyers (194)	380
February 22, 1980	Philadelphia Flyers (189)	and	Vancouver Canucks (155)	344
January 3, 1981	Boston Bruins (159)	and	Colorado Rockies (120)	279
December 5, 1981	Toronto Maple Leafs (128)	and	Washington Capitals (133)	261
December 14, 1974	New York Rangers (113)	and	St. Louis Blues (143)	256
January 19, 1980	Edmonton Oilers (121)	and	Pittsburgh Penguins (134)	255
March 27, 1982	Philadelphia Flyers (123)	and	Washington Capitals (117)	240
October 14, 1982	New York Islanders (108)	and	Pittsburgh Penguins (132)	240
October 25, 1974	California Golden Seals (88)	and	Philadelphia Flyers (144)	232
March 21, 1983	Chicago Black Hawks (115)	and	Minnesota North Stars (108)	223
January 11, 1982	Hartford Whalers (115)	and	Quebec Nordiques (107)	222
October 29, 1981	Philadelphia Flyers (107)	and	Pittsburgh Penguins (105)	212

Most Penalties in Minutes (one club)

February 26, 1981	Minnesota North Stars	(11 misconduct, 13 major, 18 minor) 211
February 26, 1981	Boston Bruins	(9 misconduct, 13 major, 20 minor) 195
March 11, 1979	Philadelphia Flyers	(14 misconduct, 8 major, 7 minor) 194
February 22, 1981	Philadelphia Flyers	(10 misconduct, 11 major, 17 minor) 189
March 11, 1979	Los Angeles Kings	(14 misconduct, 8 major, 3 minor) 186
January 3, 1981	Boston Bruins	(9 misconduct, 7 major, 17 minor) 159
February 22, 1980	Vancouver Canucks	(9 misconduct, 11 major, 5 minor) 155
October 25, 1974	Philadelphia Flyers	(9 misconduct, 4 major, 17 minor) 144
December 14, 1974	St. Louis Blues	(9 misconduct, 7 major, 9 minor) 143
January 19, 1980	Pittsburgh Penguins	(7 misconduct, 8 major, 12 minor) 134
December 5, 1981	Washington Capitals	(,8 misconduct, 7 major, 9 minor) 133
October 14, 1982	Pittsburgh Penguins	(7 misconduct, 6 major, 16 minor) 132
December 5, 1981	Toronto Maple Leafs	(7 misconduct, 6 major, 14 minor) 128
March 27, 1982	Philadelphia Flyers	(9 misconduct, 3 major, 9 minor) 123
January 19, 1980	Edmonton Oilers	(6 misconduct, 9 major, 8 minor) 121
January 3, 1981	Colorado Rockies	(6 misconduct, 6 major, 15 minor) 120
March 27, 1982	Washington Capitals	(9 misconduct, 3 major, 6 minor) 117
January 11, 1982	Hartford Whalers	(8 misconduct, 5 major, 5 minor) 115
March 21, 1983	Chicago Black Hawks	(6 misconduct, 7 major, 10 minor) 115
December 14, 1974	New York Rangers	(6 misconduct, 7 major, 9 minor) 113
October 25, 1975	Boston Bruins	(6 misconduct, 4 major, 15 minor) 110
October 14, 1982	New York Islanders	(5 misconduct, 8 major, 9 minor) 108 ·
March 21, 1983	Minnesota North Stars	(5 misconduct, 6 major, 14 minor) 108

Most Shots on Net

March 4, 1941	at Boston	Boston Bruins	83
December 26, 1925	at New York	New York Americans	73
December 10, 1970	at Boston	Boston Bruins	72
December 26, 1925	at New York	Pittsburgh Pirates	68
March 24, 1981	at Bloomington, Minnesota	Minnesota North Stars	68
February 7, 1971	at Boston	Boston Bruins	67
April 5, 1970	at New York	New York Rangers	65
March 15, 1975	at Pittsburgh	Pittsburgh Penguins	65
March 25, 1980	at Bloomington, Minnesota	Minnesota North Stars	64
January 29, 1935	at New York	Toronto Maple Leafs	63
February 23, 1941	at Boston	Boston Bruins	63
November 10, 1969	at Boston	Boston Bruins	63
December 14, 1930	at New York	Detroit Falcons	62
April 1, 1976	at Philadelphia	Philadelphia Flyers	62
November 22, 1972	at Philadelphia	Philadelphia Flyers	60
February 21, 1976	at Pittsburgh	Pittsburgh Penguins	60

PERIOD

Most Goals (both clubs)

March 19, 1981	Buffalo Sabres (9) and Toronto Maple Leafs (3)	Second period	12
March 16, 1939	New York Americans (3) and New York Rangers (7)	Third period	10
January 8, 1976	Buffalo Sabres (6) and Vancouver Canucks (4)	Third period	10
December 7, 1982	Boston Bruins (4) and Quebec Nordiques (6)	Second period	10
October 26, 1982	Buffalo Sabres (5) and Montreal Canadiens (5)	First period	10

Most Goals (one club)

March 19, 1981	at Buffalo	Buffalo Sabres	Second period	9
January 23, 1944	at Detroit	Detroit Red Wings	Third period	8
March 16, 1969	at Boston	Boston Bruins	Second period	8
November 21, 1971	at New York	New York Rangers	Third period	8
March 31, 1973	at Philadelphia	Philadelphia Flyers	Second period	8
December 21, 1975	at Buffalo	Buffalo Sabres	Third period	8
November 11, 1981	at Bloomington, Minnesota	Minnesota North Stars	Second period	8

Most Assists (both clubs)

March 19, 1981	Buffalo Sabres (14) and Toronto Maple Leafs (5)	Second period	19
February 18, 1936	Montreal Maroons (6) and New York Americans (11)	Second period	17
March 30, 1969	Chicago Black Hawks (12) and Detroit Red Wings (5)	Second period	17
December 7, 1982	Boston Bruins (7) and Quebec Nordiques (10)	Second period	17
March 16, 1939	New York Americans (6) and New York Rangers (10)	Third period	16
January 21, 1943	New York Rangers (7) and Toronto Maple Leafs (9)	Third period	16
March 16, 1969	Boston Bruins (14) and Toronto Maple Leafs (2)	Second period	16
November 18, 1974	Minnesota North Stars (6) and Montreal Canadiens (10)	Second period	16
December 8, 1977	New York Rangers (4) and Philadelphia Flyers (12)	Third period	16
March 4, 1979	Boston Bruins (10) and Detroit Red Wings (6)	First period	16
February 19, 1980	Colorado Rockies (8) and Philadelphia Flyers (8)	Second period	16
March 12, 1980	Chicago Black Hawks (8) and Philadelphia Flyers (8)	Third period	16
November 11, 1981	Minnesota North Stars (14) and Winnipeg Jets (2)	Second period	16

Most Assists (one club)

November 21, 1971	at New York	New York Rangers	Third period	15
December 21, 1975	at Buffalo	Buffalo Sabres	Third period	15
January 23, 1944	at Detroit	Detroit Red Wings	Third period	14
March 16, 1969	at Boston	Boston Bruins	Second period	14
March 19, 1981	at Buffalo	Buffalo Sabres	Second period	14
November 11, 1981	at Bloomington, Minnesota	Minnesota North Stars	Second period	14
November 29, 1972	at Chicago	Chicago Black Hawks	Third period	12
December 23, 1978	at Uniondale, New York	New York Islanders	Second period	12
January 28, 1943	at Chicago	Chicago Black Hawks	Third period	12
March 18, 1944	at Montreal	Montreal Canadiens	Third period	12
March 30, 1969	at Chicago	Chicago Black Hawks	Second period	12
November 7, 1970	at Montreal	Montreal Canadiens	Second period	12
October 21, 1973	at Detroit	Detroit Red Wings	Third period	12
February 15, 1975	at Montreal	Montreal Canadiens	Third period	12
December 8, 1977	at Philadelphia	Philadelphia Flyers	Third period	12
October 24, 1979	at New york	New York Rangers	First period	12
December 6, 1979	at Philadelphia	Philadelphia Flyers	Second period	12
January 17, 1980	at Boston	Boston Bruins	Second period	12
April 4, 1980	at Hartford	Hartford Whalers	Second period	12

Most Points (both clubs)

March 19, 1981	Buffalo Sabres (23) and Toronto Maple Leafs (8)	Second period	31
December 7, 1982	Boston Bruins (11) and Quebec Nordiques	Second period	27
March 6, 1939	New York Americans (9) and New York Rangers (17)	Third period	26
March 30, 1969	Chicago Black Hawks (18) and Detroit Red Wings (8)	Second period	26
January 21, 1943	New York Rangers (11) and Toronto Maple Leafs (14)	Third period	25
March 16, 1969	Boston Bruins (22) and Toronto Maple Leafs (39	Second period	25
January 8, 1976	Buffalo Sabres (14) and Vancouver Cancuks (11)	Third period	25
March 4, 1979	Boston Bruins (15) and Detroit Red Wings (10)	First period	25
November 11, 1981	Minnesota North Stars (22) and Winnipeg Jets (3)	Second period	25
October 26, 1982	Buffalo Sabres (12) and Montreal Canadiens (13)	First period	25

Most Points (one club)

November 21, 1971	New York Rangers	Third period	(8 goals, 15 assists)	23
December 21, 1975	Buffalo Sabres	Third period	(8 goals, 15 assists)	23
March 19, 1981	Buffalo Sabres	Second period	(9 goals, 14 assists)	23
January 23, 1944	New York Rangers	Third period	(8 goals, 14 assists)	22
March 16, 1969	Boston Bruins	Second period	(8 goals, 14 assists)	22
November 11, 1981	Minnesota North Stars	Second period	(8 goals, 14 assists)	22
November 29, 1972	Chicago Black Hawks	Third period	(7 goals, 13 assists)	20
December 23, 1978	New York Islanders	Second period	(7 goals, 13 assists)	20
January 28, 1943	Chicago Black Hawks	Third period	(7 goals, 12 assists)	19
November 7, 1970	Montreal Canadiens	Second period	(7 goals, 12 assists)	19
March 31, 1973	Philadelphia Flyers	Second period	(7 goals, 12 assists)	19
January 17, 1980	Boston Bruins	Second period	(7 goals, 12 assists)	19
April 4, 1980	Hartford Whalers	Second period	(7 goals, 12 assists)	19

Most Penalties (both clubs)

February 26, 1981	Boston Bruins (33) and	Minnesota North Stars (34)	First period	67
February 22, 1980	Philadelphia Flyers (30) and	Vancouver Canucks (21)	Third period	51
March 11, 1979	Los Angeles kings (24) and	Philadelphia Flyers (26)	First period	50
January 9, 1980	Edmonton Oilers (18) and	Pittsburgh Penguins (23)	Second period	41
March 21, 1983	Chicago Black Hawks (17) and	Minnesota North Stars (20)	Third period	37
January 3, 1981	Boston Bruins (19) and	Colorado Rockies (17)	Third period	36

Most Penalties (one club)

February 26, 1981	at Boston	Minnesota North Stars	First period	34
February 26, 1981	at Boston	Boston Bruins	First period	33
February 22, 1980	at Vancouver	Philadelphia Flyers	Third period	30
March 11, 1979	at Philadelphia	Philadelphia Flyers	First period	26
March 11, 1979	at Philadelphia	Los Angeles Kings	First period	24
January 19, 1980	at Pittsburgh	Pittsburgh Penguins	Second period	23
February 22, 1980	at Vancouver	Vancouver Canucks	Third period	21
March 21, 1983	at Bloomington, Minnesota	Minnesota North Stars	Third period	20
January 3, 1981	at Denver, Colorado	Pittsburgh Penguins	Third period	19
October 14, 1982	at Uniondale, New York	Boston Bruins	Third period	19
October 25, 1974	at Oakland, California	Edmonton Oilers	Third period	18
January 19, 1980	at Pittsburgh	Colorado Rockies	Second period	18
January 3, 1981	at Denver, Colorado	Chicago Black Hawks	Third period	17
March 21, 1983	at Bloomington, Minnesota	St. Louis Blues	Third period	17
December 14, 1974	at St. Louis	Pittsburgh Penguins	Third period	16
November 2, 1977	at Detroit	New York Islanders	First period	16
January 6, 1979	at Uniondale, New York	Vancouver Canucks	Third period	16

Most Penalties in Minutes (both clubs)

March 11, 1979	Los Angeles Kings (184) and	Philadelphia Flyers (188)	First period	372
February 26, 1981	Boston Bruins (162) and	Minnesota North Stars (180)	First period	342
February 22, 1980	Philadelphia Flyers (164) and	Vancouver Canucks (138)	Third period	302
January 19, 1980	Edmonton Oilers (108) and	Pittsburgh Penguins (123)	Second period	231
March 27, 1982	Philadelphia Flyers (111) and	Washington Capitals (111)	Second period	222
January 3, 1981	Boston Bruins (106) and	Colorado Rockies (94)	Third period	200
December 14, 1974	New York Rangers (93) and	St. Louis Blues (103)	Third period	196
January 1, 1982	Hartford Whalers (102) and	Quebec Nordiques (94)	Third period	196
March 21, 1983	Chicago Black Hawks (100) and	Minnesota North Stars (95)	Third period	195

Most Penalties in Minutes (one club)

March 11, 1979	Philadelphia Flyers	First period	(14 misconduct, 8, major, 4 minor)	188
March 11, 1979	Los Angeles kings	First period	(14 misconduct, 7, major, 2 minor)	184
February 26, 1981	Minnesota North Stars	First period	(11 misconduct, 8, major, 15 minor)	180
February 22, 1980	Philadelphia Flyers	Third period	(10 misconduct, 8, major, 12 minor)	164
February 26, 1981	Boston Bruins	First period	(9 misconduct, 8, major, 16 minor)	162
February 22, 1980	Vancouver Canucks	Third period	(9 misconduct, 8, major, 4 minor)	138
January 19, 1980	Pittsburgh Penguins	Second period	(7 misconduct, 7, major, 9 minor)	123
October 25, 1974	Philadelphia Flyers	Third period	(9 misconduct, 2, major, 7 minor)	114
March 27, 1982	Philadelphia Flyers	Second period	(9 misconduct, 3, major, 3 minor)	111
March 27, 1982	Washington Capitals	Second period	(9 misconduct, 3, major, 3 minor)	111
January 9, 1980	Edmonton Oilers	Second period	(6 misconduct, 8, major, 4 minor)	108
January 3, 1981	Boston Bruins	Third period	(7 misconduct, 8, major, 8 minor)	106

CONSECUTIVE GAMES

Won

January 21, 1982 through	February 20, 1928	New York Islanders	15
December 3, 1929 through	January 9, 1930	Boston Bruins	14
February 23, 1971 through	March 20, 1971	Boston Bruins	13
January 6, 1968 through	February 3, 1968	Montreal Canadiens	12
February 24, 1927 through	March 24, 1927	Montreal Canadiens	11
February 4, 1930 through	March 11, 1930	Boston Bruins	11
April 1, 1975 through	October 26, 1975	Buffalo Sabres	11
January 21, 1982 through	February 13, 1982	Montreal Canadiens	11
December 19, 1939 through	January 13, 1940	New York Rangers	10
February 17, 1944 through	March 11, 1944	Montreal Canadiens	10
December 5, 1970 through	December 25, 1970	Boston Bruins	10
January 19, 1973 through	February 10, 1973	New York Rangers	10
March 9, 1973 through	March 28, 1973	Boston Bruins	10
October 14, 1978 through	November 3, 1978	Atlanta Flames	10
December 22, 1982 through	January 13, 1983	Philadelphia Flyers	10

Most Consecutive Games won or tied, Philadelphia Flyers

Won or Tied

October 14, 1979 through	January 6, 1980	Philadelphia Flyers	(won 25, tied 10) 35
December 14, 1977 through	February 23, 1978	Montreal Canadiens	(won 23, tied 5) 28
December 22, 1940 through	February 23, 1941	Boston Bruins	(won 15, tied 8) 23
January 29, 1976 through	March 18, 1976	Philadelphia Flyers	(won 17, tied 6) 23
October 27, 1974 through	January 15, 1975	Montreal Canadiens	(won 15, tied 6) 21
January 18, 1977 through	March 5, 1977	Montreal Canadiens	(won 17, tied 4) 21
February 21, 1980 through	April 6, 1980	Montreal Canadiens	(won 15, tied 6) 21
March 4, 1943 through	December 4, 1943	Montreal Canadiens	(won 13, tied 7) 20
March 9, 1975 through	October 19, 1975	Philadelphia Flyers	(won 17, tied 3) 20
November 16, 1976 through	January 1, 1977	Philadelphia Flyers	(won 15, tied 5) 20
March 9, 1977 through	October 26, 1977	Montreal Canadiens	(won 16, tied 4) 20
November 23, 1939 through	January 13, 1940	New York Rangers	(won 14, tied 5) 19
November 30, 1927 through	January 17, 1928	Montreal Canadiens	(won 15, tied 3) 18
January 6, 1945 through	February 25, 1945	Montreal Canadiens	(won 16, tied 2) 18
October 18, 1959 through	November 29, 1959	Montreal Canadiens	(won 15, tied 3) 18
December 28, 1968 through	February 5, 1969	Boston Bruins	(won 13, tied 5) 18
March 11, 1980 through	October 19, 1980	New York Islanders	(won 11, tied 7) 18

Lost

February 18, 1975 through	March 26, 1975	Washington Capitals	17
November 29, 1930 through	January 08, 1931	Philadelphia Quakers	15
December 30, 1975 through	January 29, 1976	Kansas City Scouts	14
February 24, 1982 through	March 25, 1982	Detroit Red Wings	14
March 16, 1943 through	November 37, 1943	New York Rangers	13
October 11, 1981 through	November 11, 1981	Washington Capitals	13
February 13, 1926 through	March 13, 1926	Montreal Canadiens	12
January 4, 1951 through	January 28, 1951	Chicago Black Hawks	12
December 27, 1972 through	January 16, 1973	New York Islanders	12
December 29, 1975 through	January 21, 1976	Washington Capitals	12
December 3, 1924 through	January 5, 1925	Boston Bruins	11
March 15, 1977 through	April 3, 1977	New York Rangers	11
January 22, 1983 through	February 10, 1983	Pittsburgh Penguins	11

Lost or Tied

October 19, 1980 through	December 20, 1980	Winnipeg Jets	(lost 23, tied 7) 30
February 12, 1976 through	April 4, 1976	Kansas City Scouts	(lost 21, tied 6) 27
January 23, 1944 through	November 9, 1944	New York Rangers	(lost 21, tied 4) 25
November 29, 1975 through	February 21, 1976	Washington Capitals	(lost 22, tied 3) 25
February 26, 1977 through	October 20, 1977	Detroit Red Wings ♦	(lost 20, tied 3) 23
December 17, 1950 through	January 28, 1951	Chicago Black Hawks	(lost 18, tied 3) 21
January 28, 1962 through	March 11, 1962	Boston Bruins	(lost 16, tied 4) 20
January 15, 1970 through	February 28, 1970	Minnesota North Stars	(lost 15, tied 5) 20
October 28, 1977 through	December 6, 1977	Washington Capitals	(lost 15, tied 5) 20
December 31, 1942 through	February 20, 1943	New York Rangers	(lost 14, tied 5) 19
February 22, 1977 through	March 31, 1977	Colorado Rockies	(lost 14, tied 4) 18
October 20, 1982 through	November 26, 1982	New Jersey Devils	(lost 14, tied 4) 18
January 2, 1983 through	February 10, 1983	Pittsburgh Penguins	(lost 17, tied 1)18
January 29, 1970 through	March 5, 1970	Los Angeles Kings	(lost 13, tied 4) 17
December 17, 1974 through	January 25, 1975	Washington Capitals	(lost 16, tied 1) 17

Shut-outs

February 7, 1929 through	February 28, 1929	Chicago Black Hawks	8
February 7, 1928 through	February 19, 1928	New York Rangers	4
February 14, 1928 through	February 26, 1928	Montreal Canadiens	4
December 6, 1928 through	December 18, 1928	Pittsburgh Pirates	4
December 27, 1967 through	January 03, 1968	Oakland Seals	4

Not Shut-out

February 10, 1980 through	January 12, 1983	Quebec Nordiques	230
March 14, 1970 through	February 21, 1973	Chicago Black Hawks	228
October 29, 1977 through	February 16, 1980	Boston Bruins	209
October 21, 1977 through	December 22, 1979	New York Islanders	187
March 6, 1971 through	November 8, 1973	Montreal Canadiens	185
March 15, 1981 through	*1982-83	Edmonton Oilers	172
November 4, 1974 through	November 15, 1976	Montreal Canadiens	168
March 4, 1980 through	March 10, 1982	New York Islanders	165
October 11, 1979 through	March 28, 1981	Montreal Canadiens	156
November 3, 1979 through	October 7, 1981	Buffalo Sabres	150
December 5, 1974 through	October 19, 1976	New York Islanders	142
March 31, 1981 through	March 17, 1983	Montreal Canadiens	142
February 7, 1980 through	December 18, 1981	Vancouver Canucks	141

Longest record of games not shut out, Quebec Nordiques

PLAYER RECORDS— CAREER

Most Seasons

Gordon Howe	26
Myles Horton	24
Alexander Delveccio	24
John Bucyk	23
Dean Prentice	22
Douglas Mohns	22
Stanley Mikita	22
Allan Stanley	21
George Armstrong	21
Eric Nesterenko	21
Henry Howell	21
Ronald Stewart	21
J. G. Y. Jean Ratelle	21
Aubrey Clapper	20
William Gadsby	20
Leonard Kelly	20
J. R. Marcel Pronovost	20
Jean Beliveau	20
J. Henri Richard	20
Norman Ullman	20
Douglas Harvey	19
Leo Boivin	19
Donald Marshall	19
Lawrence Hillman	19
Terrance Harper	19
J. H. Maurice Richard	18
R. Ronald Murphy	18
T. Richard Murphy	18
T. Richard Duff	18
Francis Mahovlich	18
Rodrigue Gilbert	18
V. Edwin Westfall	18
Philip Esposito	18
David Keon	18

Most Assists

Gordon Howe	1049
Stanley Mikita	926
Philip Esposito	873
Alexander Delveccio	825
John Buyck	813
Robert Clarke	809
J. G. Y. Jean Ratelle	776
Marcel Dionne	743
Norman Ullman	739
Jean Beliveau	712

J. Henri Richard	688
Guy Lafleur	685
Gilbert Perreault	656
Robert Orr	645
Andrew Bathgate	624
Rodrigue Gilbert	615
D. Bradford Park	600
David Keon	590
Darryl Sittler	585
Francis Mahovlich	570
Robert Hull	560
Leonard Kelly	542
Bryan Trottier	537
Denis Potvin	528
Wayne Cashman	516
Peter Mahovlich	486
Hubert Martin	485
A. Borje Salming	477
R. B. Theodore Lindsay	472
Kenneth Hodge	472
Thomas Lysiak	472
Dean Prentice	469
Jacques Lemaire	469

Most Games

Gordon Howe	1767
Alexander Delvecchio	1549
John Bucyk	1540
Myles Horton	1446
Henry Howell	1411
Norman Ullman	1410
Stanley Mikita	1394
Douglas Mohns	1390
Dean Prentice	1378
Ronald Stewart	1353
Leonard Kelly	1316
David Keon	1296
Philip Esposito	1282
J. G. Y. Jean Ratelle	1281
J. Henri Richard	1258
William Gadsby	1248
Allan Stanley	1244
V. Edwin Westfall	1227
Eric Nesterenko	1219

J. R. Marcel Pronovost	1206
George Armstrong	1188
Francis Mahovlich	1181
Donald Marshall	1176
Leo Boivin	1150
Robert Nevin	1128
Murray Oliver	1127
Jean Beliveau	1125
Douglas Harvey	1113
Garry Unger	1105
Hubert Martin	1101

Most Goals

Gordon Howe	801
Philip Esposito	717
Robert Hull	610
John Bucyk	556
J. H. Maurice Richard	544
Marcel Dionne	544
Stanley Mikita	541
Francis Mahovlich	533
Jean Beliveau	507
J. G. Y. Jean Ratelle	491
Norman Ullman	490
Guy Lafleur	486
Alexander Delvecchio	456
Darryl Sittler	446
Yvan Cournoyer	428
Gilbert Perreault	421
Garry Unger	413
Rodrigue Gilbert	406
William Barber	398
David Keon	396
J. A. Bernard Geof- frion	393
Stephen Shutt	392
Dean Prentice	391
J. Jean Pronovost	391
Lanny McDonald	385
Richard Martin	384
Reginald Leach	381
R. B. Theodore Lindsay	379
Jacques Lemaire	366
Michael Bossy	365
J. Henri Richard	358
Rick Kehoe	353
Andrew Bathgate	349

Gordon Howe, holder of career records for most games, most goals, most assists, and most points

Wayne Gretzky, holder of season records for most goals, most assists, and most points

Most Points

Gordon Howe	(801 goals, 1049 assists)	1850
Philip Esposito	(717 goals, 873 assists)	1590
Stanley Mikita	(541 goals, 926 assists)	1467
John Bucyk	(556 goals, 813 assists)	1369
Marcel Dionne	(544 goals, 743 assists)	1287
Alexander Delvecchio	(456 goals, 825 assists)	1281
J. G. Y. Jean Ratelle	(491 goals, 776 assists)	1267
Norman Ullman	(490 goals, 739 assists)	1229
Jean Beliveau	(507 goals, 712 assists)	1219
Guy Lafleur	(486 goals, 685 assists)	1171
Robert Hull	(610 goals, 560 assists)	1170
Robert Clarke	(341 goals, 809 assists)	1150
Francis Mahovlich	(533 goals, 570 assists)	1103
Gilbert Perreault	(421 goals, 656 assists)	1077
J. Henri Richard	(358 goals, 688 assists)	1046
Darryl Sittler	(446 goals, 585 assists)	1031
Rodrigue Gilbert	(406 goals, 615 assists)	1021
David Keon	(396 goals, 590 assists)	986
Andrew Bathgate	(349 goals, 624 assists)	973
J. H. Maurice Richard	(544 goals, 421 assists)	965
Robert Orr	(270 goals, 645 assists)	915
Yvan Cournoyer	(428 goals, 435 assists)	863
Dean Prentice	(391 goals, 469 assists)	860
R. B. Theodore Lindsay	(379 goals, 472 assists)	851

Most Penalties in Minutes

David Williams	2700
David Schultz	2294
Bryan Watson	2212
Andre Dupont	1986
Garry Howatt	1822
Carol Vadnais	1813
R. B. Theodore Lindsay	1808
J. J. Terrence O'Reilly	1803
Phillip Russell	1757
Gordon Howe	1685
Myles Horton	1611
William Gadsby	1539
Gerald Korab	1518
Paul Holmgren	1495
Robert Baun	1493
Daniel Maloney	1489
Reginald Fleming	1468
Robert Kelly	1454
Keith Magnuson	1442
Edward Shack	1437
Willi Plett	1435
David Hutchison	1413
Dennis Hextall	1398
Robert Clarke	1383
J. Angus Mortson	1370
Ferdinand Flaman	1370
S. Randall Holt	1364
Terrance Harper	1362
Henry Howell	1298
Gerhardt Dornhoefer	1291
D. Bradford Park	1291
J. H. Maurice Richard	1285

Season

Most Goals

1981-82	Wayne Gretzky	Edmonton Oilers	92
1970-71	Philip Esposito	Boston Bruins	76
1982-83	Wayne Gretzky	Edmonton Oilers	71
1978-79	Michael Bossy	New York Islanders	69
1973-74	Philip Esposito	Boston Bruins	68
1980-81	Michael Bossy	New York Islanders	68
1971-72	Philip Esposito	Boston Bruins	66
1982-83	Lanny McDonald	Calgary Flames	66
1981-82	Michael Bossy	New York Islanders	64
1974-75	Philip Esposito	Boston Bruins	61
1975-76	Reginald Leach	Philadelphia Flyers	61
1976-77	Stephen Shutt	Montreal Canadiens	60
1977-78	Guy Lafleur	Montreal Canadiens	60
1981-82	Dennis Maruk	Washington Capitals	60
1982-83	Michael Bossy	New York Islanders	60
1978-79	Marcel Dionne	Los Angeles Kings	59
1968-69	Robert Hull	Chicago Black Hawks	58
1980-81	Marcel Dionne	Los Angeles Kings	58
1982-83	Michel Goulet	Quebec Nordiques	57
1975-76	Guy Lafleur	Montreal Canadiens	56
1976-77	Guy Lafleur	Montreal Canadiens	56
1979-80	Daniel Gare	Buffalo Sabres	56
1979-80	Charles Simmer	Los Angeles Kings	56
1979-80	Blaine Stoughton	Hartford Whalers	56
1980-81	Charles Simmer	Los Angeles Kings	56
1982-83	Marcel Dionne	Los Angeles Kings	56

Most Assists

1982-83	Wayne Gretzky	Edmonton Oilers	125
1981-82	Wayne Gretzky	Edmonton Oilers	120
1980-81	Wayne Gretzky	Edmonton Oilers	109
1970-71	Robert Orr	Boston Bruins	102
1981-82	Peter Stastny	Quebec Nordiques	93
1973-74	Robert Orr	Boston Bruins	90
1974-75	Robert Orr	Boston Bruins	89
1974-75	Robert Clarke	Philadelphia Flyers	89
1975-76	Robert Clarke	Philadelphia Flyers	89
1969-70	Robert Orr	Boston Bruins	87
1978-79	Bryan Trottier	New York Islanders	87
1981-82	Denis Savard	Chicago Black Hawks	87
1979-80	Wayne Gretzky	Edmonton Oilers	86
1982-83	Denis Savard	Edmonton Oilers	86
1979-80	Marcel Dionne	Los Angeles Kings	84
1981-82	Michael Bossy	New York Islanders	83
1974-75	Peter Mahovlich	Montreal Canadiens	82
1980-81	Kent Nilsson	Calgary Flames	82
1971-72	Robert Orr	Boston Bruins	80
1976-77	Guy Lafleur	Montreal Canadiens	80
1981-82	Bryan Trottier	New York Islanders	79
1968-69	Philip Esposito	Boston Bruins	77
1973-74	Philip Esposito	Boston Bruins	77
1977-78	Bryan Trottier	New York Islanders	77
1978-79	Guy Lafleur	Montreal Canadiens	77
1980-81	Marcel Dionne	Los Angeles Kings	77
1982-83	Peter Stastny	Quebec Nordiques	77

Most Points

1981-82 Wayne Gretzky	Edmonton Oilers	(92 goals, 120 assists) 212
1982-83 Wayne Gretzky	Edmonton Oilers	(71 goals, 125 assists) 196
1980-81 Wayne Gretzky	Edmonton Oilers	(55 goals, 109 assists) 164
1970-71 Philip Esposito	Boston Bruins	(76 goals, 76 assists) 152
1981-82 Michael Bossy	New York Islanders	(64 goals, 83 assists) 147
1973-74 Philip Esposito	Boston Bruins	(68 goals, 77 assists) 145
1970-71 Robert Orr	Boston Bruins	(37 goals, 102 assists) 139
1981-82 Peter Stastny	Quebec Nordiques	(46 goals, 93 assists) 139
1979-80 Marcel Dionne	Los Angeles Kings	(53 goals, 84 assists) 137
1979-80 Wayne Gretzky	Edmonton Oilers	(51 goals, 86 assists) 137
1976-77 Guy Lafleur	Montreal Canadiens	(56 goals, 80 assists) 136
1981-82 Dennis Maruk	Washington Capitals	(60 goals, 76 assists) 136
1974-75 Robert Orr	Boston Bruins	(48 goals, 89 assists) 135
1980-81 Marcel Dionne	Los Angeles Kings	(58 goals, 77 assists) 135
1978-79 Bryan Trottler	New York Islanders	(47 goals, 87 assists) 134
1971-72 Philip Esposito	Boston Bruins	(66 goals, 67 assists) 133
1977-78 Guy Lafleur	Montreal Canadiens	(60 goals, 72 assists) 132
1980-81 Kent Nilsson	Calgary Flames	(49 goals, 82 assists) 131
1972-73 Philip Esposito	Boston Bruins	(55 goals, 75 assists) 130
1978-79 Marcel Dionne	Los Angeles Kings	(59 goals, 71 assists) 130

Most Penalties in Minutes

1974-75 David Schultz	Philadelphia Flyers	472
1981-82 Paul Baxter	Pittsburgh Penguins	409
1977-78 David Schultz	Los Angeles Kings, Pittsburgh Penguins	405
1975-76 H. Steven Durbano	Pittsburgh Penguins, Kansas City Scouts	370
1977-78 David Williams	Toronto Maple Leafs	351
1973-74 David Schultz	Philadelphia Flyers	348
1980-81 David Williams	Vancouver Canucks	343
1981-82 David Williams	Vancouver Canucks	341
1976-77 David Williams	Toronto Maple Leafs	338
1981-82 Glen Cochrane	Philadelphia Flyers	329
1975-76 Bryan Watson	Detorit Red Wings	322
1981-82 S. Patrick Price	Pittsburgh Penguins	322
1975-76 David Schultz	Philadephia Flyers	307
1975-76 Robert Gassoff	St. Louis Blues	306
1980-81 Paul Holmgren	Philadelphia Flyers	306
1981-82 Alan Secord	Chicago Black Hawks	303
1975-76 Dennis Polonich	Detroit Red Wings	302
1975-76 David Williams	Toronto Maple Leafs	299
1978-79 David Williams	Toronto Maple Leafs	298
1970-71 Keith Magnuson	Chicago Black hawks	291
1981-82 Willi Plett	Calgary Flames	288
1979-80 James Mann	Winnipeg Jets	287
1973-74 H. Steven Durbano	St. Louis Blues, Pittsburgh Penguins	284
1979-80 David Williams	Toronto Maple Leafs, Vancouver Canucks	278
1974-75 Andre Dupont	Philadelphia Flyers	276
1981-82 Ken Linseman	Philadelphia Flyers	275
1982-83 S. Randall Holt	Washington Capitals	275

Syl Apps, Jr.,

Jim Dorey scored 9 penalties on October 16, 1968

Game

Most Goals

January 31, 1920	M. Joseph Malone	Quebec Bulldogs	7
January 10, 1920	Edouard Lalonde	Montreal Canadiens	6
March 10, 1920	M. Joseph Malone	Quebec Bulldogs	6
January 26, 1921	Corbett Denneny	Toronto St. Patricks	6
March 7, 1921	Cyril Denneny	Ottawa Senators	6
February 3, 1944	Sydney Howe	Detroit Red Wings	6
November 7, 1968	Gordon Berenson	St. Louis Blues	6
February 7, 1976	Darryl Sittler	Toronto Maple Leafs	6

Most Assists

March 16, 1947	William J. Taylor	Detroit Red Wings	7
February 15, 1980	Wayne Gretzky	Edmonton Oilers	7
February 16, 1943	Elmer Lach	Montreal Canadiens	6
January 8, 1944	Walter Pratt	Toronto Maple Leafs	6
February 3, 1944	Donald Grosso	Detroit Red Wings	6
March 30, 1969	Patrick Stapleton	Chicago Black hawks	6
February 9, 1971	Kenneth Hodge	Boston Bruins	6
January 1, 1973	Robert Orr	Boston Bruins	6
March 8, 1975	Ronald Stackhouse	Pittsburgh Penguins	6
November 28, 1979	W. Gregory Malone	Pittsburgh Penguins	6
January 6, 1981	Michael Bossy	New York Islanders	6
February 25, 1981	Guy Chouinard	Calgary Flames	6
January 4, 1984	Mark Messier	Edmonton Oilers	6

Most Points

February 7, 1976	Darryl Sittler	Toronto Maple Leafs	(6 goals, 4 assists) 10
December 28, 1944	J. H. Maurice Richard	Montreal Canadiens	(5 goals, 3 assists) 8
January 9, 1954	M. Bert Olmstead	Montreal Canadiens	(4 goals, 4 assists) 8
December 11, 1977	Thomas Bladon	Philadelphia Flyers	(4 goals, 4 assists) 8
December 23, 1978	Bryan Trottier	New York Islanders	(5 goals, 3 assists) 8
February 22, 1981	Anton Stastny	Quebec Nordiques	(3 goals, 5 assists) 8
February 22, 1981	Peter Stastny	Quebec Nordiques	(4 goals, 4 assists) 8
November 19, 1983	Wayne Gretzky	Edmonton Oilers	(3 goals, 5 assists) 8
January 4, 1984	Wayne Gertzky	Edmonton Oilers	(4 goals, 4 assists) 8

Most Penalties

October 16, 1968	R. James Dorey	Toronto Maple Leafs	(3 misconduct, 2 major, 4 minor) 9
April 6, 1978	David Schultz	Pittsburgh Penguins	(2 misconduct, 2 major, 5 minor) 9
March 11, 1979	R. Randall Holt	Los Angeles Kings	(5 misconduct, 3 major, 1 minor) 9
March 8, 1981	Kimbel Clackson	Quebec Nordiques	(2 misconduct, 3 major 4 minor) 9
December 13, 1972	James Schoenfeld	Buffalo Sabres	(1 misconduct, 3 major, 4 minor) 8
February 25, 1976	David Maloney	New York Rangers	(1 misconduct, 3 major, 4 minor) 8
March 24, 1976	Dennis Polonich	Detroit Red Wings	(1 misconduct, 7 minor) 8
March 26, 1977	Phillip Russell	Chicago Black Hawks	(2 misconduct, 6 minor) 8
January 19, 1980	Russell Anderson	Pittsburgh Penguins	(2 misconduct, 3 major, 3 minor) 8
January 19, 1980	Orest Kindrachuk	Pittsburgh Penguins	(2 misconduct, 1 major, 5 minor) 8
February 26, 1981	Keith Crowder	Boston Bruins	(3 misconduct, 1 major, 4 minor) 8

Most Penalties in Minutes

March 11, 1979	S. Randall Holt	Los Angeles Kings	(5 misconduct, 3 major, 1 minor) 67
March 11, 1979	Francis Bathe	Philadelphia Flyers	(4 misconduct, 3 major)55
October 16, 1968	R. James Dorey	Toronto Maple Leafs	(3 misconduct, 2 major, 4 minor) 45
February 21, 1979	H. Steven Durbano	St. Louis Blues	(4 misconduct, 1 major)45
February 26, 1981	Keith Crowder	Boston Bruins	(3 misconduct, 1 major, 4 minor) 43
March 8, 1981	Kimbel Clackson	Quebec Nordiques	(2 misconduct, 3 major, 4 minor) 43
March 13, 1982	David Semenko	Edmonton Oilers	(3 misconduct, 2 major, 1 minor) 42
March 25, 1977	Leonard Frig	Cleveland Barons	(3 misconduct, 1 major, 3 minor) 41
January 19, 1980	Russell Anderson	Pittsburgh Penguins	(2 misconduct, 3 major, 3 minor) 41
April 6, 1978	David Schultz	Pittsburgh Penguins	(2 misconduct, 2 major, 5 minor) 40
October 18, 1970	Reginald Fleming	Buffalo Sabres	(3 misconduct, 1 major, 2 minor) 39
March 7, 1977	Paul Holmgren	Philadelphia Flyers	(3 misconduct, 1 major, 2 minor) 39
February 4, 1981	Christopher Nilan	Montreal Canadiens	(3 misconduct, 1 major, 2 minor) 39
October 19, 1960	Reginald Fleming	Chicago Black Hawks	(2 misconduct, 3 major, 1 minor) 37
December 3, 1967	Donald Awrey	Boston Bruins	(2 misconduct, 3 major, 1 minor) 37
December 21, 1975	Robert Gassoff	St. Louis Blues	(3 misconduct, 1 major, 1 minor) 37
March 11, 1979	Paul Holmgren	Philadelphia Flyers	(3 misconduct, 1 major, 1 minor) 37

Triple-Major Penalties

October 23, 1979	David Semenko	Edmonton Oilers
March 8, 1981	Kimbel Clackson	Quebec Nordiques

Triple-Minor Penalties

March 24, 1962	Reginald Fleming	Chicago Black Hawks
March 16, 1966	Reginald Fleming	New York Rangers
December 7, 1967	John Ferguson	Montreal Canadiens
October 17, 1970	Earl Heiskala	Philadelphia Flyers
March 10, 1971	John Ferguson	Montreal Canadiens
November 6, 1971	Keith Magnuson	Chicago Black Hawks
December 17, 1972	Bryan L. Hextall	Pittsburgh Penguins
March 28, 1973	Andre Dupont	Philadelphia Flyers
October 23, 1973	Robert Lalonde	Vancouver Canucks
February 12, 1975	Guy Lapointe	Montreal Canadiens
March 7, 1975	Chicago Black Hawks (bench)	
March 31, 1976	Jean Hamel	Detroit Red Wings
March 31, 1976	David Williams	Toronto Maple Leafs
April 4, 1976	Stanley Gilbertson	Pittsburgh Penguins
October 5, 1976	David Williams	Toronto Maple Leafs
October 24, 1976	Paul Holmgren	Philadelphia Flyers
November 20, 1976	J. Alexander Pirus	Minnesota North Stars
November 27, 1976	John Lynch	Washington Capitals
December 27, 1976	Neil Komadoski	Los Angeles Kings
February 23, 1977	Wayne Cashman	Boston Bruins
March 27, 1977	J. William Riley	Washington Capitals
January 21, 1978	David Schultz	Pittsburgh Penguins
March 11, 1978	James Pettie (goaltender)	Boston Bruins
March 24, 1978	Gordon Lane	Washington Capitals
January 6, 1980	Terry Ruskowski	Chicago Black Hawks
February 26, 1981	Keith Crowder	Boston Bruins
March 8, 1981	Kimbel Clackson	Quebec Nordiques
March 17, 1982	Dino Ciccarelli	Minnesota North Stars
March 8, 1982	Timothy Trimper	Winnipeg Jets
October 9, 1982	Paul Higgins	Toronto Maple Leafs

PERIOD
Most Goals

December 14, 1929	Alfred Lepine	Montreal Canadiens	Second period	4
November 20, 1934	Harvey Jackson	Toronto Maple Leafs	Third period	4
January 28, 1943	Maxwell Bentley	Chicago Black Hawks	Third period	4
March 4, 1945	Clinton Smith	Chicago Black Hawks	Third period	4
November 7, 1968	Gordon Berenson	St. Louis Blues	Second period	4
February 18, 1981	Wayne Gretzky	Edmonton Oilers	Third period	4
February 3, 1982	Grant Mulvey	Chicago Black Hawks	First period	4
February 13, 1982	Bryan Trottier	New York Rangers	Second period	4

Most Assists

November 8, 1942	Herbert O'Connor	Montreal Canadiens	4
January 28, 1943	Douglas Bentley	Chicago Black Hawks	4
January 23, 1944	Joseph Carveth	Detroit Red Wings	4
March 18, 1944	Phillipe Watson	Montreal Canadiens	4
March 4, 1945	William Mosienko	Chicago Black Hawks	4
December 29, 1962	Jean-Claude Tremblay	Montreal Canadiens	4
October 20, 1963	J. G. Philippe Goyette	New York Rangers	4
November 9, 1969	James Wiste	Chicago Black Hawks	4
December 16, 1970	Clifford Koroll	Chicago Black Hawks	4
March 24, 1971	Sylvanus M. Apps	Pittsburgh Penguins	4
February 15, 1972	Robert Orr	Boston Bruins	4
March 24, 1973	James Pappin	Chicago Black Hawks	4
March 8, 1975	Ronald Stackhouse	Pittsburgh Penguins	4
March 6, 1976	Charles Lefley	St. Louis Blues	4
December 23, 1978	Clark Gillies	New York Islanders	4
March 17, 1979	D. Bradford Park	Boston Bruins	4
January 30, 1980	Mark Howe	Hartford Whalers	4
March 5, 1980	Paul Mulvey	Washington Capitals	4
January 16, 1981	Richard W. Wilson	St. Louis Blues	4
February 13, 1982	Michael Bossy	New York Islanders	4
February 4, 1983	Wayne Gretzky	Edmonton Oilers	4
January 4, 1984	Mark Messier	Edmonton Oilers	4

Most Points

December 23, 1978	Bryan Trottier	New York Islanders	Second period (3 goals, 3 assists) 6
March 12, 1933	William Cook	New York Rangers	Third period (3 goals, 2 assists) 5
January 28, 1940	Leslie Cunningham	Chicago Black Hawks	Third period (2 goals, 3 assists) 5
January 28, 1943	Maxwell Bentley	Chicago Black Hawks	Third period (4 goals, 1 assist) 5
November 28, 1954	Leo LaBine	Boston Bruins	Second period (3 goals, 2 assists) 5
February 7, 1976	Darryl Sittler	Toronto Maple Leafs	Second period (3 goals, 2 assists)5

Most Penalties

March 11, 1979	S. Randall Holt	Los Angeles Kings	First period (5 misconduct, 3 major, 1 minor) 9
February 26, 1981	Keith Crowder	Boston Bruins	First period (3 misconduct, 1 major, 4 minor) 8
March 8, 1981	Kimbel Clackson	Quebec Nordiques	Second period (2 misconduct, 3 major, 3 minor) 8
October 16, 1968	R. James Dorey	Toronto Maple Leafs	Second period (3 misconduct, 2 major, 2 minor) 7
March 11, 1979	Francis Bathe	Philadelphia Flyers	First period (4 misconduct, 3 major)
January 19, 1980	Russell Anderson	Pittsburgh Penguins	Second period (2 misconduct, 2 major, 2 minor) 7
October 18, 1970	Reginald Fleming	Buffalo Sabres	First period (3 misconduct, 1 major, 2 minor) 6
December 13, 1975	Dennis Polonich	Detroit Red Wings	Third period (1 misconduct, 1 major, 4 minor) 6
October 10, 1976	David Hutchison	Los Angeles Kings	First period (1 misconduct, 2 major, 3 minor) 6
March 5, 1977	Andre Dupont	Philadelphia Flyers	First period (1 misconduct, 1 major, 4 minor) 6
March 5, 1977	Dennis Polonich	Detroit Red Wings	First period (1 misconduct, 1 major, 4 minor) 6
March 7, 1977	Paul Holmgren	Philadelphia Flyers	Second period (3 misconduct, 1 major, 2 minor) 6
March 11, 1979	Behn Wilson	Philadelphia Flyers	First period (2 misconduct, 2 major, 2 minor) 6
January 19, 1980	David Lumley	Edmonton Oilers	Second period (2 misconduct, 2 major, 2 minor) 6
February 14, 1981	Christopher Nilan	Montreal Canadiens	Third period (3 misconduct, 3 major, 1 minor) 6
March 21, 1983	Dino Ciccarelli	Minnesota North Stars	Third period (1 misconduct, 1 major, 4 minor) 6

Most Penalties in Minutes

March 11, 1979	S. Randall Holt	Los Angeles Kings	First period (5 misconduct, 3 major, 1 minor) 67
March 11, 1979	Francis Bathe	Philadelphia Flyers	First period (4 misconduct, 3 minor)
October 16, 1968	R. James Dorey	Toronto Maple Leafs	Second period (3 misconduct, 2 major, 2 minor) 44
February 26, 1981	Keith Crowder	Boston Bruins	First period (3 misconduct, 1 major, 4 minor) 43
March 8, 1981	Kimbel Clackson	Quebec Nordiques	Second period (2 misconduct, 3 major, 3 minor) 41
February 21, 1979	H. Steven Durbano	St. Louis Blues	Third period (4 misconduct)
October 18, 1970	Reginald Fleming	Buffalo Sabres	First period (3 misconduct, 1 major, 2 minor) 39
March 7, 1977	Paul Holmgren	Philadelphia Flyers	Second period (3 misconduct, 1 major, 2 minor) 39
February 14, 1981	Christopher Nilan	Montreal Canadiens	Third period (3 misconduct, 1 major, 2 minor) 39
December 21, 1975	Robert Gassoff	St. Louis Blues	First period (3 misconduct, 1 major, 1 minor) 37
March 11, 1979	Paul Holmgren	Philadelphia Flyers	First period (3 misconduct, 1 major, 1 minor) 37
January 19, 1980	Russell Anderson	Pittsburgh Penguins	Second period (2 misconduct, 2 major, 3 minor) 36
April 3, 1974	Ernest Deadmarsh	Atlanta Flames	Second period (3 misconduct, 1 major)
March 11, 1979	Melvin Bridgman	Philadelphia Flyers	First period (3 misconduct, 1 major)
March 11, 1979	Steven Jensen	Los Angeles Kings	First period (3 misconduct, 1 major)
November 1, 1969	Thomas Polanic	Minnesota North Stars	Second period (2 misconduct,
March 11, 1979	Behn Wilson	Philadelphia Flyers	First period (2 misconduct, 2 major, 2 minor) 34
January 19, 1980	David Lumley	Edmonton Oilers	Second period (2 misconduct, 2 major, 2 minor) 34

CONSECUTIVE GAMES
Played

February 24, 1968 *		Garry Unger	914
March 27, 1973	through December 21, 1979	Craig Ramsay	776
October 8, 1975	through February 10, 1983	Douglas Jarvis	640
October 7, 1955	through 1982-83	Andrew Hebenton	630
February 10, 1952	through March 22, 1964	John Wilson	580
October 7, 1972	through March 20, 1960	William Harris	576
December 4, 1968	through November 28, 1979	Daniel Grant	555
December 13, 1956	through December 19, 1975	Alexander Delvecchio	548
February 16, 1972	through November 11, 1964	Jean-Paul Parise	512
October 27, 1973	through November 30, 1979	John Marks	509
November 16, 1926	through March 21, 1937	J. Murray Murdoch	508
	hasn't ended		

Gary Unger played 914 consecutive games

Scored Goal

1921-22	Harry Broadbent	Ottawa Senators	16
1917-18	M. Joseph Malone	Montreal Canadiens	14
1920-21	Edouard Lalonde	Montreal Canadiens	13
1979-80	Charles Simmer	Los Angeles Kings	13
1917-18	Cyril Denneny	Ottawa Senators	12
1981-82	David Lumley	Edmonton Oilers	12
1920-21	Cecil Dye	Hamilton Tigers—Toronto St. Patricks	11
1921-22	Cecil Dye	Toronto St. Patricks	11
1982-83	Marcel Dionne	Los Angeles Kings	11
1962-63	Andrew Bathgate	New York Rangers	10
1968-69	Robert Hull	Chicago Black Hawks	10
1978-79	Michael Bossy	New York Islanders	10
1944-45	J. H. Maurice Richard	Montreal Canadiens	9
1960-61	J. A. Bernard Geoffrion	Montreal Canadiens	9
1961-62	Robert Hull	Chicago Black Hawks	9
1970-71	Philip Esposito	Boston Bruins	9
1977-78	Darryl Sittler	Toronto Maple Leafs	9

GOALTENDERS
CAREER

Most Seasons

Terrance Sawchuk	21
Lorne Worsley	21
Glenn Hall	18
J. Jacques Plante	18
Harry Lumley	16
Edward Johnston	16
Rogatien Vachon	16
John Bower	15
Cesare Maniago	15
Anthony Esposito	14
John Ross Roach	14
Walter Broda	14
Roger Crozier	14
Gary Smith	14
Gilles Gilbert	14
L. Philippe Myre	14
Clinton Benedict	13
Vernon Forbes	13
Charles Hodge	13
Edward Giacomin	13
Bernard Parent	13
Gerald Cheevers	13
Gary Edwards	13
Gilles Meloche	13
James Rutherford	13
Alexander Connell	12
Roy Worters	12
Cecil Thomson	12
Douglas Favell	12
William Smith	12

Most Games

John Bower	953½ (971)
Daniel Bouchard	891⅖ (906)
Francis Brimsek	858⅕ (868)
Gary Smith	837 (861)
John Ross Roach	826⅙ (837)
Roy Worters	801⅔ (804)
Roger Crozier	771⅔ (795)
George Hainsworth	627⅖ (629)
William Smith	595 (610)
James Rutherford	585½ (607)
David Kerr	583 (600)
Elwin Rollins	570 (592)
Claude Rayner	551⅔ (553)
L. Philippe Myre	543 (568)
Terrance Sawchuk	533⅔ (551)
Glenn Hall	518½ (537)
Anthony Esposito	514
Lorne Worsley	493½ (532)
J. Jacques Plante	490⅙482⅔
Harry Lumley	(484)
Rogatien Vachon	476⅙ (515)
Walter Broda	465
Edward Giacomin	444 (465)
Bernard Parent	431⅔ (457)
Gilles Meloche	429⅔ (431)
Edward Johnston	428⅗ (430)
Cecil Thomson	422½ (424)
Cesare Maniago	420⅔ (439)

Numbers in parentheses
indicate games played in.

Most Shut-outs

Terrance Sawchuk	103
George Hainsworth	94
Glenn Hall 84	84
J. Jacques Plante	82
Alexander Connell	81
Cecil Thompson	81
Anthony Esposito	75
Lorne Chabot	72
Harry Lumley	71
Roy Worters	67
Walter Broda	61
John Ross Roach	58
Clinton Benedict	57
Edward Giacomin	54
Bernard Parent	54
David Kerr 51	51
Rogatien Vachon	51
Kenneth Dryden	46
Lorne Worsley	43
Charles Gardiner	42
Francis Brimsek	40

Average (200 or More Games)

Alexander Connell	2.00
George Hainsworth	2.02
Lorne Chabot	2.11
Charles Gardiner	2.12
Cecil Thompson	2.14
David Kerr	2.23
William Durnan	2.36
Gerard McNeil	2.36
Roy Worters	2.37
J. Jacques Plante	2.39
Clinton Benedict	2.40
Terrance Sawchuk	2.52
Glenn Hall	2.52
John Ross Roach	2.54
John Bower	2.54
Walter Broda	2.56

Michael Palmateer, goaltender with most assists

Most Assists

Michael Palmateer	23
Daniel Bouchard	23
Anthony Esposito	22
Kenneth Dryden	19
Gilles Meloche	19
Michel Larocque	18
James Rutherford	15
Bernard Parent	12
Gerald Cheevers	11
Edward Johnston	10
Rogatien Vachon	10
L. Philippe Myre	10
Glenn Hall	9
Edward Giacomin	9
Edward Staniowski	9
Gilles Gilbert	9
Edward Mio	9
J. Jacques Plante	8
Gary Smith	8
Douglas Favell	8
Terrance Sawchuk	7
Allan Smith	7
Gary Edwards	7
Robert Sauve	7
Rejean Lemelin	7

Most Penalties in Minutes

William Smith	327
Terrance Sawchuk	229
Gerald Cheevers	214
Gary Smith	197
Daniel Bouchard	194
Douglas Favell	152
Allan Smith	152
Lorne Worsley	145
Bernard Parent	112
Gilles Gilbert	110
Glen Hanlon	109
L. Philippe Myre	101
Harry Lumley	95
Peter Peeters	94
J. Jacques Plante	92
Glenn Hall	88
Gilles Meloche	85

SEASON

Most Shut-outs

1928-29	George Hainsworth	Montreal Canadiens	22
1925-26	Alexander Connell	Ottawa Senators	15
1927-28	Alexander Connell	Ottawa Senators	15
1927-28	Harold Winkler	Boston Bruins	15
1969-70	Anthony Esposito	Chicago Black Hawks	15
1926-27	George Hainsworth	Montreal Canadiens	14
1926-27	Clinton Benedict	Montreal Maroons	13
1926-27	Alexander Connell	Ottawa Senators	13
1927-28	George Hainsworth	Montreal Canadiens	13
1928-29	John Ross Roach	New York Rangers	13
1928-29	Roy Worters	New York Americans	13
1953-54	Harry Lumley	Toronto Maple Leafs	13

Average (35 or more games)

1928-29	George Hainsworth	Montreal Canadiens	0.98
1927-28	George Hainsworth	Montreal Canadiens	1.09
1925-26	Alexander Connell	Ottawa Senators	1.17
1928-29	Cecil Thompson	Boston Bruins	1.18
1928-29	Roy Worters	New York Americans	1.21
1927-28	Alexander Connell	Ottawa Senators	1.30
1928-29	Clarence Dolson	Detroit Cougars	1.43
1928-29	John Ross Roach	New York Rangers	1.48
1926-27	Clinton Benedict	Montreal Maroons	1.51
1926-27	George Hainsworth	Montreal Canadiens	1.52
1928-29	Alexander Connell	Ottawa Senators	1.52
1928-29	Clinton Benedcit	Montreal Maroons	1.54

1980-81	Michael Palmateer	Washington Capitals	8
1974-75	Gilles Meloche	California Golden Seals	6
1981-82	Grant Fuhr	Edmonton Oilers	6
1978-79	Michael Palmateer	Toronto Maple Leafs	5
1980-81	Edward Mio	Edmonton Oilers	5
1981-82	Patrick Riggin	Calgary Flames	5
1981-82	Edward Staniowski	Winnipeg Jets	5
1982-83	Rejean Lemelin	Calgary Flames	5
1971-72	Edward Johnston	Boston Bruins	4
1971-72	Allan Smith	Detroit Red Wings	4
1972-73	Kenneth Dryden	Montreal Canadiens	4
1973-74	James Rutherford	Pittsburgh, Detroit	4
1974-75	James Rutherford	Detroit Red Wings	4
1976-77	Gerald Cheevers	Boston Bruins	4
1977-78	Anthony Esposito	Chicago Black Hawks	4
1977-78	Michel Larocque	Montreal Canadiens	4
1979-80	Robert Sauve	Buffalo Sabres	4
1980-81	Daniel Bouchard	Calgary Flames	4
1982-83.	Daniel Bouchard	Quebec Nordiques	4
1982-83	Per-Erik Lindbergh	Philadelphia Flyers	4
1982-83	D. Andrew Moog	Edmonton Oilers	4

Most Penalties in Minutes

1979-80	Gerald Cheevers	Boston Bruins	62
1973-74	Andrew Brown	Pittsburgh Penguins	60
1978-79	William Smith	New York Islanders	54
1980-81	Allan Smith	Colorado Rockies	51
1973-74	Gary Smith	Vancouver Canucks	47
1976-77	Gerald Cheevers	Boston Bruins	46
1979-80	Glen Hanlon	Vancouver Canucks	43
1972-73	William Smith	New York Islanders	42
1974-75	Daniel Bouchard	Atlanta Flames	42
1970-71	Allan Smith	Pittsburgh Penguins	41
1982-83	William Smith	New York Islanders	41
1957-58	Terrance Sawchuk	Detroit Red Wings	39
1979-80	William Smith	New York Islanders	39
1967-68	Douglas Favell	Philadelphia Flyers	37
1979-80	L. Philippe Myre	Philadelphia Flyers	37
1981-82	Daniel Bouchard	Quebec Nordiques	36
1977-78	William Smith	New York Islanders	35
1981-82	Marco Baron	Boston Bruins	35
1982-83	Gregory Stefan	Detroit Red Wings	35
1979-80	Daniel Bouchard	Atlanta Flames	34
1974-75	Gary Smith	Vancouver Canucks	33
1980-81	William Smith	New York Islanders	33
1982-83	Peter Peeters	Boston Bruins	33
1971-72	Douglas Favell	Philadelphia Flyers	32
1953-54	Terrance Sawchuk	Detroit Red Wings	31
1978-79	Glen Hanlon	Vancouver Canucks	30
1980-81	Richard Sevigny	Montreal Canadiens	30

GAME

Most Assists

March 19, 1972	Edward Giacomin	New York Rangers	2
January 17, 1975	Gilles Meloche	California Golden Seals	2
December 11, 1977	Daniel Bouchard	Atlanta Flames	2
December 11, 1977	Anthony Esposito	Chicago Black Hawks	2
January 28, 1978	Michel Larocque	Montreal Canadiens	2

Most Goaltenders

There are several instances in which each club used 2.
There are three instances in which each club used 3.

April 3, 1966   Toronto Maple Leafs

John Bower played first period
Terrance Sawchuk played second period
Bruce Gamble played third period

November 13, 1968   St. Louis Blues

Glenn Hall played first 2 minutes of game
Robert Irons played next 3 minutes of game
J. Jacques Plante played rest of game

December 11, 1968   St. Louis Blues

J. Jacques Plante played to 16:11 of first period
Gary Edwards played rest of first period
Glenn Hall played second and third periods

Most Shots Stopped

March 4, 1941 Samuel LoPresti Chicago Black Hawks 80
(Boston Bruins shot 83 times, defeated Chicago 3-2)

CONSECUTIVE GAMES

Played

October 6, 1955 through November 7, 1962 Glenn Hall 503

Shut-outs

1927-28	Alexander Connell	Ottawa Senators	(463 minutes, 29 seconds) 6
1928-29	George Hainsworth	Montreal Canadiens	(343 minutes, 5 seconds) 4
1930-31	Roy Worters	New York Americans	(324 minutes, 40 seconds) 4
1948-49	William Durnan	Montreal Canadiens	(309 minutes, 21 seconds) 4
1927-28	Lorne Chabot	New York Rangers	(297 minutes, 42 seconds) 4
1930-31	Charles Gardiner	Chicago Black Hawks	(290 minutes, 12 seconds) 4

Stan Mikita won scoring title four times.

NATIONAL HOCKEY LEAGUE
SCORING CHAMPIONS

Season	Player and Club	Games Played	Goals	Assists	Points
1982-83	Wayne Gretzky Edmonton	80	71	125	196
1981-82	Wayne Gretzky Edmonton	80	92	120	212
1980-81	Wayne Gretzky Edmonton	80	55	109	164
1979-80	Marcel Dionne Los Angeles	80	53	84	137
	Wayne Gretzky Edmonton	79	51	86	137
1978-79	Bryan Trottier New York Islanders ..	76	47	87	134
1977-78	Guy Lafleur Montreal	78	60	72	132
1976-77	Guy Lafleur Montreal	80	56	80	136
1975-76	Guy Lafleur Montreal	80	56	69	125
1974-75	Robert Orr Boston	80	46	89	135
1973-74	Philip Esposito Boston	78	68	77	145
1972-73	Phil Esposito, Boston	78	55	75	130
1971-72	Phil Esposito, Boston	76	66	67	133
1970-71	Phil Esposito, Boston	78	76	76	152
1969-70	Bobby Orr, Boston	76	33	87	120
1968-69	Phil Esposito, Boston	74	49	77	126
1967-68	Stan Mikita, Chicago	72	40	47	87
1966-67	Stan Mikita, Chicago	70	35	62	97
1965-66	Bobby Hull, Chicago	65	54	43	97
1964-65	Stan Mikita, Chicago	70	28	59	87
1963-64	Stan Mikita, Chicago	70	39	50	89
1962-63	Gordie Howe, Detroit	70	38	48	86
1961-62	Bobby Hull, Chicago	70	50	34	84
1960-61	Bernie Geoffrion, Montreal	64	50	45	95
1959-60	Bobby Hull, Chicago	70	39	42	81
1958-59	Dickie Moore, Montreal	70	41	55	96
1957-58	Dickie Moore, Montreal	70	36	48	84
1956-57	Gordie Howe, Detroit	70	44	45	89
1955-56	Jean Beliveau, Montreal	70	47	41	88
1954-55	Bernie Geoffrion, Montreal	70	38	37	75
1953-54	Gordie Howe, Detroit	70	33	48	81
1952-53	Gordie Howe, Detroit	70	49	46	95
1951-52	Gordie Howe, Detroit	70	47	39	86
1950-51	Gordie Howe, Detroit	70	43	43	86
1949-50	Ted Lindsay, Detroit	69	23	55	78
1948-49	Roy Conacher, Chicago	60	26	42	68
1947-48	Elmer Lach, Montreal	60	30	31	61
1946-47	Max Bentley, Chicago	60	29	43	72
1945-46	Max Bentley, Chicago	47	31	30	61
1944-45	Elmer Lach, Montreal	50	26	54	80
1943-44	Herbie Cain, Boston	48	36	46	82
1942-43	Doug Bentley, Chicago	50	33	40	73
1941-42	Bryan Hextall, New York	48	24	32	56
1940-41	Bill Cowley, Boston	46	17	45	62
1939-40	Milt Schmidt, Boston	48	22	30	52
1938-39	Toe Blake, Montreal	48	24	23	47
1937-38	Gordie Drillon, Toronto	48	26	26	52
1936-37	Dave Schriner, New York Americans	48	21	25	46
1935-36	Dave Schriner, New York Americans	48	19	26	45
1934-35	Charlie Conacher, Toronto	48	36	21	57
1933-34	Charlie Conacher, Toronto	42	32	20	52
1932-33	Bill Cook, New York Rangers	48	28	22	50

1931-32	Harvey Jackson, Toronto	48	28	25	53
1930-31	Howie Morenz, Montreal Canadiens	39	28	23	51
1929-30	Cooney Weiland, Boston	44	43	30	73
1928-29	Ace Bailey, Toronto	44	22	10	32
1927-28	Howie Morenz, Montreal Canadiens	43	33	18	51
1926-27	Bill Cook, New York	44	33	4	37
1925-26	Nels Stewart, Montreal Maroons	36	34	8	42
1924-25	Babe Dye, Toronto	29	38	6	44
1923-24	Cy Denneny, Ottawa	21	22	1	23
1922-23	Babe Dye, Toronto	22	26	11	37
1921-22	Punch Broadbent, Ottawa	24	32	14	46
1920-21	Newsy Lalonde, Montreal	24	33	8	41
1919-20	Joe Malone, Quebec	24	39	6	45
1918-19	Newsy Lalonde, Montreal	17	23	9	32
1917-18	Joe Malone, Montreal	20	44	* *	44

* *Number of assists not recorded

NATIONAL HOCKEY LEAGUE LEADING GOAL SCORERS

Season	Player and Club	Games Played	Goals
1982-83	Wayne Gretzky Edmonton	80	71
1981-82	Wayne Gretzky Edmonton	80	92
1980-81	Michael Bossy New York Islanders	79	68
1979-80	Daniel Gare Buffalo	76	56
	Charles Simmer Los Angeles	64	56
	Blaine Stoughton Hartford	80	56
1978-79	Michael Bossy New York Islanders	80	69
1977-78	Guy Lafleur Montreal	78	60
1976-77	Stephen Shutt Montreal	80	60
1975-76	Reginald Leach Philadelphia	80	61
1974-75	Philip Esposito Boston	79	61
1973-74	Philip Esposito Boston	78	68
1972-73	Phil Esposito, Boston	78	55
1971-72	Phil Esposito, Boston	76	66
1970-71	Phil Esposito, Boston	78	76
1969-70	Phil Esposito, Boston	76	43
1968-69	Bobby Hull, Chicago	74	58
1967-68	Bobby Hull, Chicago	71	44
1966-67	Bobby Hull, Chicago	66	52
1965-66	Bobby Hull, Chicago	65	54
1964-65	Norm Ullman, Detroit	70	42
1963-64	Bobby Hull, Chicago	70	43
1962-63	Gordie Howe, Detroit	70	38
1961-62	Bobby Hull, Chicago	70	50
1960-61	Bernie Geoffrion, Montreal	64	50
1959-60	Bobby Hull, Chicago	70	39
	Bronco Horvath, Boston	68	39
1958-59	Jean Beliveau, Montreal	64	45
1957-58	Dickie Moore, Montreal	70	36
1956-57	Gordie Howe, Detroit	70	44
1955-56	Jean Beliveau, Montreal	70	47
1954-55	Bernie Geoffrion, Montreal	70	38
	Maurice Richard, Montreal	67	38

Bobby Hull—seven times league goal-scoring leader.

1953-54	Maurice Richard, Montreal	70	37
1952-53	Gordie Howe, Detroit	70	49
1951-52	Gordie Howe, Detroit	70	47
1950-51	Gordie Howe, Detroit	70	43
1949-50	Maurice Richard, Montreal	70	43
1948-49	Sid Abel, Detroit	69	28
1947-48	Ted Lindsay, Detroit	60	33
1946-47	Maurice Richard, Montreal	60	45
1945-46	Gaye Stewart, Toronto	50	37
1944-45	Maurice Richard, Montreal	50	50
1943-44	Doug Bentley, Chicago	50	38
1942-43	Doug Bentley, Chicago	50	33
1941-42	Lynn Patrick, New York Rangers	47	32
1940-41	Bryan Hextall, New York Rangers	48	26
1939-40	Bryan Hextall, New York Rangers	48	24
1938-39	Roy Conacher, Boston	47	26
1937-38	Gordon Drillon, Toronto	48	26
1936-37	Larry Aurie, Detroit	45	23
	Nels Stewart, Boston, New York Americans	43	23
1935-36	Bill Thoms, Toronto	48	23
	Charlie Conacher, Toronto	44	23
1934-35	Charlie Conacher, Toronto	48	36
1933-34	Charlie Conacher, Toronto	42	32
1932-33	Bill Cook, New York Rangers	48	28
1931-32	Charlie Conacher, Toronto	45	34
1930-31	Charlie Conacher, Toronto	40	31
1929-30	Cooney Weiland, Boston	44	43
1928-29	Ace Bailey, Toronto	44	22
1927-28	Howie Morenz, Montreal Canadiens	43	33
1926-27	Bill Cook, New York Rangers	44	33

NHL STANDINGS

1926-27

Canadian Division

	W	L	T	PTS
Ottawa	30	10	4	64
Montreal Canadiens	28	14	2	58
Montreal Maroons	20	20	4	44
New York Americans	17	25	2	36
Toronto	15	24	5	35

American Division

	W	L	T	PTS
New York Rangers	25	13	6	56
Boston	21	20	3	45
Chicago	19	22	3	41
Pittsburgh	15	26	3	33
Detroit	12	28	4	28

1927-28

Canadian Division

	W	L	T	PTS
Montreal Canadiens	26	11	7	59
Montreal Maroons	24	14	6	54
Ottawa	20	14	10	50
Toronto	18	18	8	44
New York Americans	11	27	6	28

American Division

	W	L	T	PTS
Boston	20	13	11	51
New York Rangers	19	16	9	47
Pittsburgh	19	17	8	46
Detroit	19	19	6	44
Chicago	7	34	3	17

1928-29

Canadian Division

	W	L	T	PTS
Montreal Canadiens	22	7	15	59
New York Americans	19	13	12	50
Toronto	21	18	5	47
Ottawa	14	17	13	41
Montreal Maroons	15	20	9	39

American Division

	W	L	T	PTS
Boston	26	13	5	57
New York Rangers	21	13	10	52
Detroit	19	16	9	47
Pittsburgh	9	27	8	26
Chicago	7	29	8	22

1929-30

Canadian Division

	W	L	T	PTS
Montreal Maroons	23	16	5	51
Montreal Canadiens	21	14	9	51
Ottawa	21	15	8	50
Toronto	17	21	6	40
New York Americans	14	25	5	33

American Division

	W	L	T	PTS
Boston	38	5	1	77
Chicago	21	18	5	47
New York Rangers	17	17	10	44
Detroit	14	24	6	34
Pittsburgh	5	36	3	13

1930-31

Canadian Division

	W	L	T	PTS
Montreal Canadiens	26	10	8	60
Toronto	22	13	9	53
Montreal Maroons	20	18	6	46
New York Americans	18	16	10	46
Ottawa	10	30	4	24

American Division

	W	L	T	PTS
Boston	28	10	6	62
Chicago	24	17	3	51
New York Rangers	19	16	9	47
Detroit	16	21	7	39
Philadelphia	4	36	4	12

1931-32

Canadian Division

	W	L	T	PTS
Montreal Canadiens	25	16	7	57
Toronto	23	18	7	53
Montreal Maroons	19	22	7	45
New York Americans	16	24	8	40

American Division

	W	L	T	PTS
New York Rangers	23	17	8	54
Chicago	18	19	11	47
Detroit	18	20	10	46
Boston	15	21	12	42

1932-33

Canadian Division	W	L	T	PTS	American Division	W	L	T	PTS
Toronto	24	18	6	54	Boston	25	15	8	58
Montreal Maroons	22	20	6	50	Detroit	25	15	8	58
Montreal Canadiens	18	25	5	41	New York Rangers	23	17	8	54
New York Americans	15	22	11	41	Chicago	16	20	12	44
Ottawa	11	27	10	32					

1933-34

Canadian Division	W	L	T	PTS	American Division	W	L	T	PTS
Toronto	26	13	9	61	Detroit	24	14	10	58
Montreal Canadiens	22	20	6	50	Chicago	20	17	11	51
Montreal Maroons	19	18	11	49	New York Rangers	21	19	8	50
New York Americans	15	23	10	40	Boston	18	25	5	41
Ottawa	13	29	6	32					

1934-35

Canadian Division	W	L	T	PTS	American Division	W	L	T	PTS
Toronto	30	14	4	64	Boston	26	16	6	58
Montreal Maroons	24	19	5	53	Chicago	26	17	5	57
Montreal Canadiens	19	23	6	44	New York Rangers	22	20	6	50
New York Americans	12	27	9	33	Detroit	19	22	7	45
St. Louis	11	31	6	28					

1935-36

Canadian Division	W	L	T	PTS	American Division	W	L	T	PTS
Montreal Maroons	22	16	10	54	Detroit	24	16	8	56
Toronto	23	19	6	52	Boston	22	20	6	50
New York Americans	16	25	7	39	Chicago	21	19	8	50
Montreal Canadiens	11	26	11	33	New York Rangers	19	17	12	50

1936-37

Canadian Division	W	L	T	PTS	American Division	W	L	T	PTS
Montreal Canadiens	24	18	6	54	Detroit	25	14	9	59
Montreal Maroons	22	17	9	53	Boston	23	18	7	53
Toronto	22	21	5	49	New York Rangers	19	20	9	47
New York Americans	15	29	4	34	Chicago	14	27	7	35

1937-38

Canadian Division	W	L	T	PTS	American Division	W	L	T	PTS
Toronto	24	15	9	57	Boston	30	11	7	67
New York Americans	19	18	11	49	New York Rangers	27	15	6	60
Montreal Canadiens	18	17	13	49	Chicago	14	25	9	37
Montreal Maroons	12	30	6	30	Detroit	12	25	11	35

1938-39	W	L	T	PTS
Boston	36	10	2	74
New York Rangers	26	16	6	58
Toronto	19	20	9	47
New York Americans	17	21	10	44
Detroit	18	24	6	42
Montreal	15	24	9	39
Chicago	12	28	8	32

1939-40	W	L	T	PTS
Boston	31	12	5	67
New York Rangers	27	11	10	64
Toronto	25	17	6	56
Chicago	23	19	6	52
Detroit	16	26	6	38
New York Americans	15	29	4	34
Montreal	10	33	5	25

1940-41	W	L	T	PTS
Boston	27	8	13	67
Toronto	28	14	6	62
Detroit	21	16	11	53
New York Rangers	21	19	8	50
Chicago	16	25	7	39
Montreal	16	26	6	38
New York Americans	8	29	11	27

1941-42	W	L	T	PTS
New York	29	17	2	60
Toronto	27	18	3	57
Boston	25	17	6	56
Chicago	22	23	3	47
Detroit	19	25	4	42
Montreal	18	27	3	39
Brooklyn	16	29	3	35

1942-43	W	L	T	PTS
Detroit	25	14	11	61
Boston	24	17	9	57
Toronto	22	19	9	53
Montreal	19	19	12	50
Chicago	17	18	15	49
New York	11	31	8	30

1943-44	W	L	T	PTS
Montreal	38	5	7	83
Detroit	26	18	6	58
Toronto	23	23	4	50
Chicago	22	23	5	49
Boston	19	26	5	43
New York	6	39	5	17

1944-45	W	L	T	PTS
Montreal	38	8	4	80
Detroit	31	14	5	67
Toronto	24	22	4	52
Boston	16	30	4	36
Chicago	13	30	7	33
New York	11	29	10	32

1945-46	W	L	T	PTS
Montreal	28	17	5	61
Boston	24	18	8	56
Chicago	23	20	7	53
Detroit	20	20	10	50
Toronto	19	24	7	45
New York	13	28	9	35

1946-47	W	L	T	PTS
Montreal	34	16	10	78
Toronto	31	19	10	72
Boston	26	23	11	63
Detroit	22	27	11	55
New York	22	32	6	50
Chicago	19	37	4	42

1947-48	W	L	T	PTS
Toronto	32	15	13	77
Detroit	30	18	12	72
Boston	23	24	13	59
New York	21	26	13	55
Montreal	20	29	11	51
Chicago	20	34	6	46

1948-49	W	L	T	PTS
Detroit	34	19	7	75
Boston	29	23	8	66
Montreal	28	23	9	65
Toronto	22	25	13	57
Chicago	21	31	8	50
New York	18	31	11	47

1949-50	W	L	T	PTS
Detroit	37	19	14	88
Montreal	29	22	19	77
Toronto	31	27	12	74
New York	28	31	11	67
Boston	22	32	16	60
Chicago	22	38	10	54

1950-51	W	L	T	PTS
Detroit	44	13	13	101
Toronto	41	16	13	95
Montreal	25	30	15	65
Boston	22	30	18	62
New York	20	29	21	61
Chicago	13	47	10	36

1951-52

	W	L	T	PTS
Detroit	44	14	12	100
Montreal	34	26	10	78
Toronto	29	25	16	74
Boston	25	29	16	66
New York	23	34	13	59
Chicago	17	44	9	43

1952-53

	W	L	T	PTS
Detroit	36	16	18	90
Montreal	28	23	19	75
Boston	28	29	13	69
Chicago	27	28	15	69
Toronto	27	30	13	67
New York	17	37	16	50

1953-54

	W	L	T	PTS
Detroit	37	19	14	88
Montreal	35	24	11	81
Toronto	32	24	14	78
Boston	32	28	10	74
New York	29	31	10	68
Chicago	12	51	7	31

1954-55

	W	L	T	PTS
Detroit	42	17	11	95
Montreal	41	18	11	93
Toronto	24	24	22	70
Boston	23	26	21	67
New York	17	35	18	52
Chicago	13	40	17	43

1955-56

	W	L	T	PTS
Montreal	45	15	10	100
Detroit	30	24	16	76
New York	32	28	10	74
Toronto	24	33	13	61
Boston	23	34	13	59
Chicago	19	39	12	50

1956-57

	W	L	T	PTS
Detroit	38	20	12	88
Montreal	35	23	12	82
Boston	34	24	12	80
New York	26	30	14	66
Toronto	21	34	15	57
Chicago	16	39	15	47

1957-58

	W	L	T	PTS
Montreal	43	17	10	96
New York	32	25	13	77
Detroit	29	29	12	70
Boston	27	28	15	69
Chicago	24	39	7	55
Toronto	21	38	11	53

1958-59

	W	L	T	PTS
Montreal	39	18	13	91
Boston	32	29	9	73
Chicago	28	29	13	69
Toronto	27	32	11	65
New York	26	32	12	64
Detroit	25	37	8	58

1959-60

	W	L	T	PTS
Montreal	40	18	12	92
Toronto	35	26	9	79
Chicago	28	29	13	69
Detroit	26	29	15	67
Boston	28	34	8	64
New York	17	38	15	49

1960-61

	W	L	T	PTS
Montreal	41	19	10	92
Toronto	39	19	12	90
Chicago	29	24	17	75
Detroit	25	29	16	66
New York	22	38	10	54
Boston	15	42	13	43

1961-62

	W	L	T	PTS
Montreal	42	14	14	98
Toronto	37	22	11	85
Chicago	31	26	13	75
New York	26	32	12	64
Detroit	23	33	14	60
Boston	15	47	8	38

1962-63

	W	L	T	PTS
Toronto	35	23	12	82
Chicago	32	21	17	81
Montreal	28	19	23	79
Detroit	32	25	13	77
New York	22	36	12	56
Boston	14	39	17	45

1963-64

	W	L	T	PTS
Montreal	36	21	13	85
Chicago	36	22	12	84
Toronto	33	25	12	78
Detroit	30	29	11	71
New York	22	38	10	54
Boston	18	40	12	48

1964-65

	W	L	T	PTS
Detroit	40	23	7	87
Montreal	36	23	11	83
Chicago	34	28	8	76
Toronto	30	26	14	74
New York	20	38	12	52
Boston	21	43	6	48

1965-66					1966-67			
	W	**L**	**T**	**PTS**		**W**	**L**	**T**	**PTS**
Montreal 41		21	8	90	Chicago 41		17	12	94
Chicago 37		25	8	82	Montreal 32		25	13	77
Toronto 34		25	11	79	Toronto 32		27	11	75
Detroit 31		27	12	74	New York 30		28	12	72
Boston 21		43	6	48	Detroit 27		39	4	58
New York 18		41	11	47	Boston 17		43	10	44

Chicago led the West Division in 1966-67 with 94 points.

393

1967-68

East Division	W	L	T	PTS	West Division	W	L	T	PTS
Montreal	42	22	10	94	Philadelphia	31	32	11	73
New York	39	23	12	90	Los Angeles	31	33	10	72
Boston	37	27	10	84	St. Louis	27	31	16	70
Chicago	32	26	16	80	Minnesota	27	32	15	69
Toronto	33	31	10	76	Pittsburgh	27	34	13	67
Detroit	27	35	12	66	Oakland	15	42	17	47

1968-69

East Division	W	L	T	PTS	West Division	W	L	T	PTS
Montreal	46	19	11	103	St. Louis	37	25	14	88
Boston	42	18	16	100	Oakland	29	36	11	69
New York	41	26	9	91	Philadelphia	20	35	21	61
Toronto	35	26	15	85	Los Angeles	24	42	10	58
Detroit	33	31	12	78	Pittsburgh	20	45	11	51
Chicago	34	33	9	77	Minnesota	18	43	15	51

1969-70

East Division	W	L	T	PTS	West Division	W	L	T	PTS
Chicago	45	22	9	99	St. Louis	37	27	12	86
Boston	40	17	19	99	Pittsburgh	26	38	12	64
Detroit	40	21	15	95	Minnesota	19	35	22	60
New York	38	22	16	92	Oakland	22	40	14	58
Montreal	38	22	16	92	Philadelphia	17	35	24	58
Toronto	29	34	13	71	Los Angeles	14	52	10	38

1970-71

East Division	W	L	T	PTS	West Division	W	L	T	PTS
Boston	57	14	7	121	Chicago	49	20	9	107
New York	49	18	11	109	St. Louis	34	25	19	87
Montreal	42	23	13	97	Philadelphia	28	33	17	73
Toronto	37	33	8	82	Minnesota	28	34	16	72
Buffalo	24	39	15	63	Los Angeles	25	40	13	63
Vancouver	24	46	8	56	Pittsburgh	21	37	20	62
Detroit	22	45	11	55	California	20	53	5	45

1971-72

East Division	W	L	T	PTS	West Division	W	L	T	PTS
Boston	54	13	11	119	Chicago	46	17	15	107
New York	48	17	13	109	Minnesota	37	29	12	86
Montreal	46	16	16	108	St. Louis	28	39	11	67
Toronto	33	31	14	80	Pittsburgh	26	38	14	66
Detroit	33	35	10	76	Philadelphia	26	38	14	66
Buffalo	16	43	19	51	California	21	39	18	60
Vancouver	20	50	8	48	Los Angeles	20	49	9	49

1972-73

East Division	W	L	T	PTS
Montreal	52	10	16	120
Boston	51	22	5	107
New York Rangers	47	23	8	102
Buffalo	37	27	14	88
Detroit	37	29	12	86
Toronto	27	41	10	64
Vancouver	22	47	9	53
New York Islanders	12	60	6	30

West Division	W	L	T	PTS
Chicago	42	27	9	93
Philadelphia	37	30	11	85
Minnesota	37	30	11	85
St. Louis	32	34	12	76
Pittsburgh	32	37	9	73
Los Angeles	31	36	11	73
Atlanta	25	38	15	65
California	16	46	16	48

Montreal took 1972-73 honors in East with 120 points.

395

1973–1974

East Division

	W	L	T	PTS
Boston	52	17	9	113
Montreal	45	24	9	99
New York Rangers	40	24	14	94
Toronto	35	27	16	86
Buffalo	32	34	12	76
Detroit	29	30	10	68
Vancouver	24	43	11	59
New York Islanders	19	41	18	56

West Division

	W	L	T	PTS
Philadelphia	50	16	12	112
Chicago	41	14	23	105
Los Angeles	33	33	12	78
Atlanta	30	34	14	74
Pittsburgh	28	41	9	65
St. Louis	26	40	12	64
Minnesota	23	38	17	63
California	13	55	10	36

1974-1975

Clarence S. Campbell Conference

Lester Patrick Division

	W	L	T	PTS
Philadelphia	51	18	11	113
New York Rangers	37	29	14	88
New York Islanders	33	25	22	88
Atlanta	34	31	15	83

Conn Smythe Division

	W	L	T	PTS
Vancouver	38	32	10	86
St. Louis	35	31	14	84
Chicago	37	35	8	82
Minnesota	23	50	7	53
Kansas City	15	54	11	41

Prince of Wales Conference

James Norris Division

	W	L	T	PTS
Montreal	47	14	19	113
Los Angeles	42	17	21	105
Pittsburgh	37	28	15	89
Detroit	23	45	12	58
Washington	8	67	5	21

Charles F. Adams Division

	W	L	T	PTS
Buffalo	49	16	15	113
Boston	40	26	14	94
Toronto	31	33	16	78
California	19	48	13	51

1975–1976

Clarence S. Campbell Conference

Lester Patrick Division

	W	L	T	PTS
Philadelphia	51	13	16	118
New York Islanders	42	21	17	101
Atlanta	35	33	12	82
New York Rangers	29	42	9	67

Conn Smythe Division

	W	L	T	PTS
Chicago	32	30	18	82
Vancouver	33	32	15	81
St. Louis	29	37	14	72
Minnesota	20	53	7	47
Kansas City	12	56	12	36

Prince of Wales Conference

James Norris Division

	W	L	T	PTS
Montreal	58	11	11	127
Los Angeles	38	33	9	85
Pittsburgh	35	33	12	82
Detroit	26	44	10	62
Washington	11	59	10	32

Charles F. Adams Division

	W	L	T	PTS
Boston	48	15	17	113
Buffalo	46	21	13	105
Toronto	34	31	15	83
California	27	42	11	65

1976–1977

Clarence S. Campbell Conference

Lester Patrick Division

	W	L	T	PTS
Philadelphia	48	16	16	112
New York Islanders	47	21	12	106
Atlanta	34	34	12	80
New York Rangers	29	37	14	72

Conn Smythe Division

	W	L	T	PTS
St. Louis	32	39	9	73
Minnesota	23	39	18	64
Chicago	26	43	11	63
Vancouver	25	42	13	63
Colorado	20	46	14	54

Prince of Wales Conference

James Norris Division

	W	L	T	PTS
Montreal	60	8	12	132
Los Angeles	34	31	15	83
Pittsburgh	34	33	13	81
Washington	24	42	14	62
Detroit	16	55	9	41

Charles F. Adams Division

	W	L	T	PTS
Boston	49	23	8	106
Buffalo	48	24	8	104
Toronto	33	32	15	81
Cleveland	25	42	13	63

1977–1978

Clarence S. Campbell Conference

Lester Patrick Division

	W	L	T	PTS
New York Islanders	48	17	15	111
Philadelphia	45	20	15	105
Atlanta	34	27	19	87
New York Rangers	30	37	13	73

Conn Smythe Division

	W	L	T	PTS
Chicago	32	29	19	83
Colorado	19	40	21	59
Vancouver	20	43	17	57
St. Louis	20	47	13	53
Minnesota	18	53	9	45

Prince of Wales Conference

James Norris Division

	W	L	T	PTS
Montreal	50	10	11	129
Detroit	32	34	14	78
Los Angeles	31	34	15	77
Pittsburgh	25	37	18	68
Washington	17	49	14	48

Charles F. Adams Division

	W	L	T	PTS
Boston	51	18	11	113
Buffalo	44	19	17	105
Toronto	41	29	10	92
Cleveland	22	45	13	57

1978–1979

Clarence S. Campbell Conference

Lester Patrick Division

	W	L	T	PTS
New York Islanders	51	15	14	116
Philadelphia	40	25	15	95
New York Rangers	40	29	11	91
Atlanta	41	31	8	90

Conn Smythe Division

	W	L	T	PTS
Chicago	29	36	15	73
Vancouver	25	42	13	63
St. Louis	18	50	12	48
Colorado	15	53	12	42

Prince of Wales Conference

James Norris Division

	W	L	T	PTS
Montreal	52	17	11	115
Pittsburgh	36	31	13	85
Los Angeles	34	34	12	80
Washington	24	41	15	63
Detroit	23	41	16	62

Charles F. Adams Division

	W	L	T	PTS
Boston	43	23	14	100
Buffalo	36	28	16	88
Toronto	34	33	13	81
Minnesota	28	40	12	68

1979–1980

Clarence S. Campbell Conference

Lester Patrick Division	W	L	T	PTS
Philadelphia	48	12	20	116
New York Islanders	39	28	13	91
New York Rangers	38	32	10	86
Atlanta	35	32	13	83
Washington	27	40	13	67

Conn Smythe Division	W	L	T	PTS
Chicago	34	27	19	87
St. Louis	34	34	12	80
Vancouver	27	37	16	70
Edmonton	28	39	13	69
Winnipeg	20	49	11	51
Colorado	19	48	13	51

Prince of Wales Conference

James Norris Division	W	L	T	PTS
Montreal	47	20	13	107
Los Angeles	30	36	14	74
Pittsburgh	30	37	13	73
Hartford	27	34	19	73
Detroit	26	43	11	63

Charles F. Adams Divsion	W	L	T	PTS
Buffalo	47	17	16	110
Boston	46	21	13	105
Minnesota	36	28	16	88
Toronto	35	40	5	75
Quebec				

1980–1981

Clarence S. Campbell Conference

Lester Patrick Division	W	L	T	PTS
New York Islanders	48	18	14	110
Philadelphia	41	24	15	97
Calgary	39	27	14	92
New York Rangers	30	36	14	74
Washington	26	36	18	70

Conn Smythe Division	W	L	T	PTS
St. Louis	43	18	17	107
Chicago	31	33	16	78
Vancouver	28	32	16	74
Edmonton	22	45	13	57
Colorado	9	57	14	32
Winnipeg				

Prince of Wales Conference

James Norris Division	W	L	T	PTS
Montreal	45	22	13	103
Los Angeles	43	24	13	99
Pittsburgh	30	37	13	73
Hartford	21	41	18	60
Detroit	19	43	18	56

Charles F. Adams Divsion	W	L	T	PTS
Buffalo	39	20	21	99
Boston	37	30	13	87
Minnesota	35	28	17	87
Quebec	30	32	18	78
Toronto	28	37	15	71

1981–1982

Clarence S. Campbell Conference

James Norris Division	W	L	T	PTS
Minnesota	37	23	0	94
Winnipeg	33	33	14	80
St. Louis	32	40	8	72
Chicago	30	38	12	72
Toronto	20	44	16	56
Detroit	21	47	12	54

Conn Smythe Division	W	L	T	PTS
Edmonton	48	17	15	111
Vancouver	30	33	17	77
Calgary	29	34	17	75
Los Angeles	24	41	15	63
Colorado	18	49	13	49

Prince of Wales Conference

Lester Patrick Division	W	L	T	PTS
New York Islanders	54	16	10	118
New York Rangers	39	27	14	92
Philadelphia	38	31	11	87
Pittsburgh	31	36	13	75
Washington	26	41	13	65

Charles F. Adams Divsion	W	L	T	PTS
Montreal	46	17	17	109
Boston	43	27	10	96
Buffalo	39	26	15	93
Quebec	33	31	16	82
Hartford	21	41	18	60

1982-1983

Clarence S. Campbell Conference

James Norris Division	W	L	T	PTS
Chicago	47	23	10	104
Minnesota	40	24	16	96
Toronto	28	40	12	68
St. Louis	25	40	15	65
Detroit	21	44	15	57

Conn Smythe Division	W	L	T	PTS
Edmonton	47	21	12	106
Calgary	32	34	14	78
Vancouver	30	35	15	75
Winnipeg	33	39	8	74
Los Angeles	27	41	12	66

Prince of Wales Conference

Lester Patrick Division	W	L	T	PTS
Philadelphia	49	23	8	106
New York Islanders	42	26	12	96
Washington	39	25	16	94
New York Rangers	35	35	10	80
New Jersey	17	49	14	48
Pittsburgh	18	53	9	45

Charles F. Adams Divsion	W	L	T	PTS
Boston	50	20	10	110
Montreal	42	24	14	98
Buffalo	38	29	13	89
Quebec	34	34	12	80
Hartford	19	54	7	45